Japan and American Children's Books

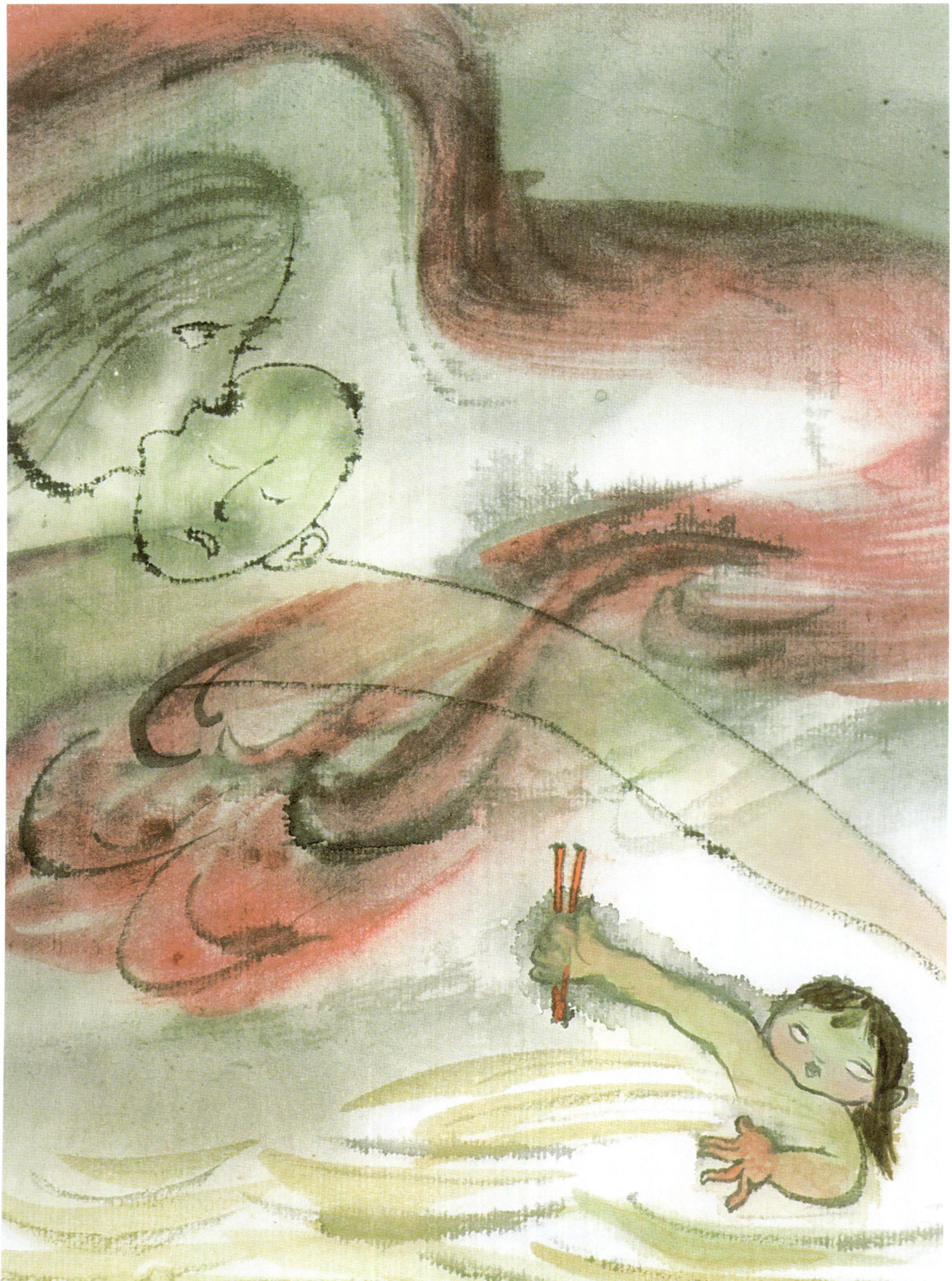

Japan and American Children's Books

A JOURNEY

Sybille A. Jagusch

FOREWORD BY *Carla D. Hayden*
INTRODUCTION BY *J. Thomas Rimer*

OPPOSITE
(Detail) *Hiroshima no Pika*, written and illustrated by Toshi Maruki. New York: Lothrop, Lee & Shepard, 1980, page 14.

Rutgers University Press in association with the Library of Congress
NEW BRUNSWICK, CAMDEN, AND NEWARK, NJ, AND LONDON • WASHINGTON, DC

RUTGERS UNIVERSITY PRESS

LIBRARY LIBRARY OF CONGRESS

Published by Rutgers University Press in association with the Library of Congress

Library of Congress Cataloging-in-Publication Data

Names: Jagusch, Sybille A., author.
Title: Japan and American children's books : a journey / Sybille A. Jagusch.
Description: New Brunswick, New Jersey : Rutgers University Press in association with the Library of Congress, [2021] | Includes bibliographical references and index.
Identifiers: LCCN 2020027545 | ISBN 9781978822627 (paperback ; alk. paper) | ISBN 9781978822870 (cloth ; alk. paper) | ISBN 9781978822634 (epub) | ISBN 9781978822641 (mobi) | ISBN 9781978822658 (pdf)
Subjects: LCSH: Children's literature, American—History and criticism. | Japan—In literature. | Japanese in literature. | Japan—Relations—United States. | United States—Relations—Japan.
Classification: LCC PS159.J3 J34 2021 | DDC 810.9/9282—dc23
LC record available at https://lccn.loc.gov/2020027545

A British Cataloging-in-Publication record for this book is available from the British Library.

∞ The paper used in this publication meets the requirements of the American National Standard for Information Sciences—Permanence of Paper for Printed Library Materials, ANSI Z39.48-1992.

www.rutgersuniversitypress.org

Manufactured in the United States of America

Cover: *The Children in Japan*, by Grace Bartruse, illustrated by Willy Pogány. New York: McBride Nast, 1915.

Book design by Lisa Tremaine. Typeset in Adobe Garamond Pro by Integrated Books International.

This Journey is dedicated to Hidekazu Sato

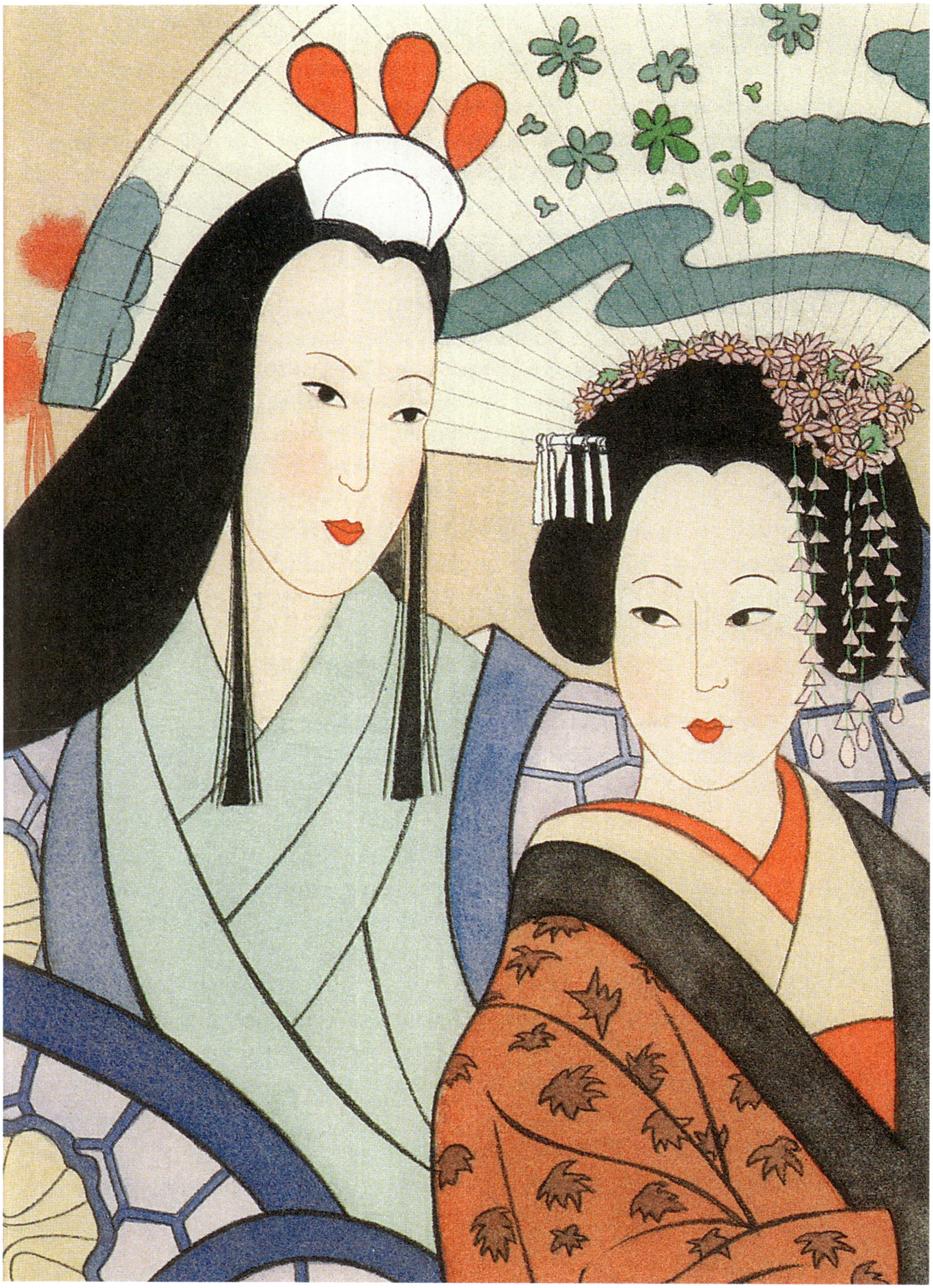

CONTENTS

OPPOSITE
(Detail) Lady Murasaki Shikibu and Sei Shōnagon in *Japanese Portraits*, by Dorothy and Thomas Hoobler, illustrated by Victoria Bruck. Austin, TX: Raintree Steck-Vaughn, 1994, page 13.

FOREWORD

As a longtime children's librarian, I have observed that books for young people can be deceptively simple, often tricking readers into assuming that their messages are small or unimportant. But that perception belies a powerful experience: making connections between words, pictures, and stories opens up the world for young readers.

In this volume, Sybille A. Jagusch examines the way children's books opened up the unknown world of Japan to Western audiences. In doing so, she has authored the first book to examine the history of Japanese–American relations through the representations of Japan in American children's literature.

This book also takes on the enormous task of documenting the evolution and development of children's book publishing in the United States. I especially appreciate that Jagusch highlights the contributions of individual editors and librarians. Children's librarians can have a powerful impact on young people at a pivotal stage in their lives, and I am proud to see the careers of several paid tribute here.

No one is better suited to write this book than Dr. Jagusch, whose love of children's literature is equaled only by her love of Japan. Dr. Jagusch is one of the Library's greatest treasures. She was appointed chief of the Children's Literature Center in 1983, and over the ensuing years she has devoted her expertise, energy, and imagination to what she describes as a "children's book life," expanding the Library's extensive collections of rare and remarkable children's literature and organizing numerous lectures, exhibitions, and symposia that bring together members of the national and international children's book community.

The Library of Congress holds more than 600,000 children's books, periodicals, maps, and other media. Founded in 1963, the Children's Literature Center assists users in gaining access to all children's materials dispersed throughout the Library. I invite you to explore these delightful collections in person or online at www.loc.gov.

—Carla D. Hayden
Librarian of Congress

JAPON — JAPAN.

ASIE. — Du 31° au 54° lat. N. & du 128° au 150° long. E. — From the 31° to the 54° lat. N. and from the 130° to the 152° long. E. — V. PITT. No 12.

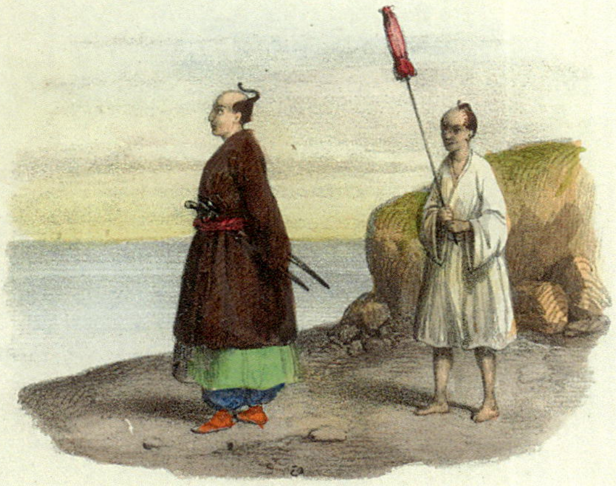

Seigneur japonais. – A japanese of high rank.

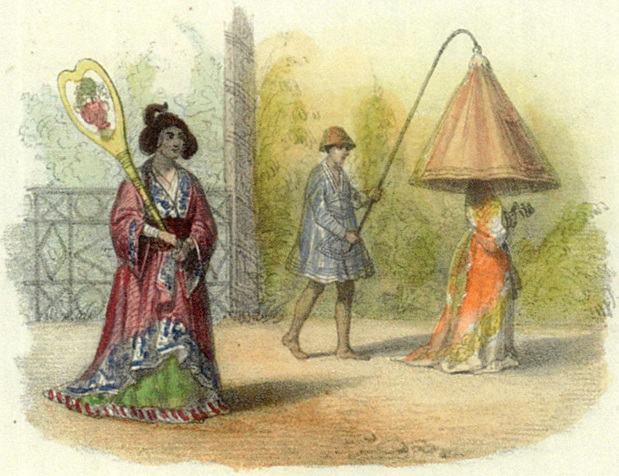

Dames japonaises. – Japanese ladies.

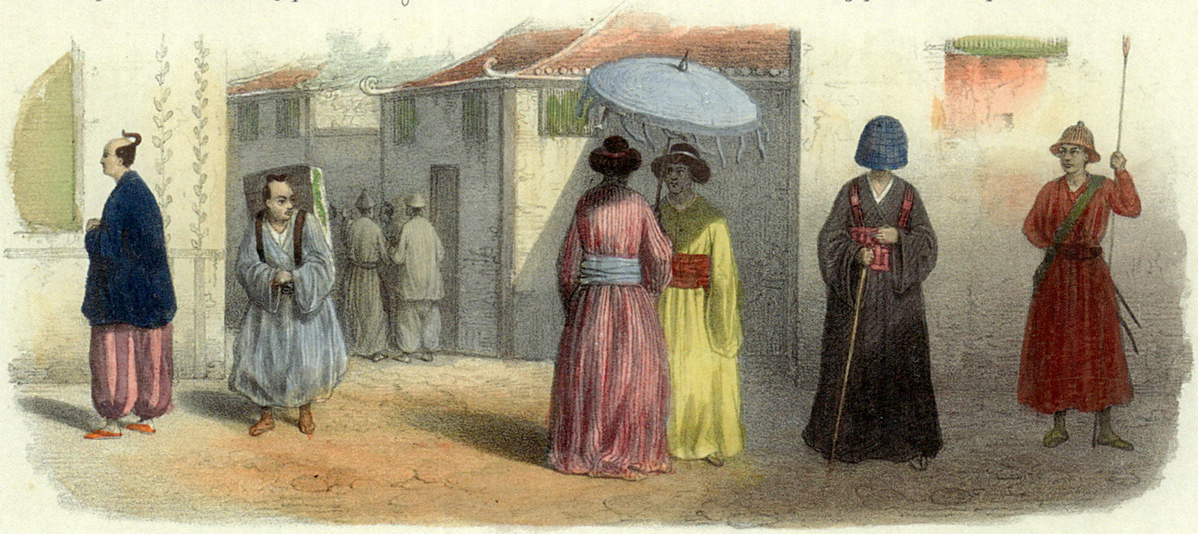

Habitans de Nangasaki. – Inhabitants of Nangasaki.

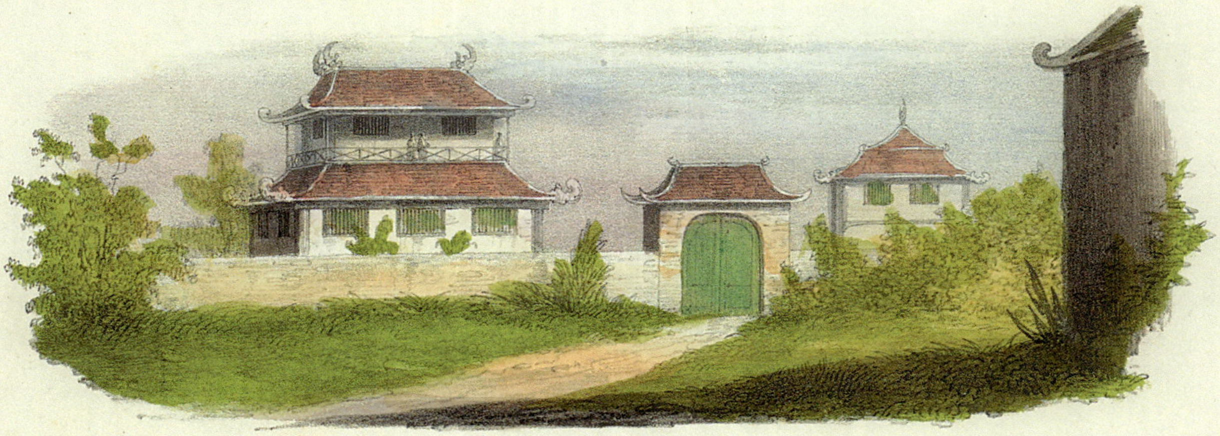

Habitations au Japon. — Habitations of the Japanese.

INTRODUCTION

The span of this remarkable illustrated "Journey," assembled with such scrupulous taste and understanding by Sybille A. Jagusch, provides a fascinating account of how two disparate societies and cultures, their images reflected in a kind of double mirror, have gradually come closer to each other as their mutual contacts have continued to increase. It is, indeed, the shifting parameters of this continuing mutual fascination between these cultures, with all its vicissitudes, that drive this compelling narrative along. There are multiple "journeys" to be experienced in this study.

First, the reader can witness the shifting images of Japan as perceived in the West, itself caught up in vast changes. Early on there is only a dim, telescopic view of Japan, a distant, virtually mythological land. By the end of the twentieth century, the view of Japan presented in Western children's literature, mirroring the growth of Western adult understanding, has become quite nuanced and accurate, with close-ups of the details of Japanese social and interior life presented in a fashion that today's children can easily appreciate and understand.

Second, this volume serves, to a surprising degree, as a social history of a modernizing and Westernizing Japan, first as observed from the outside, and then, particularly after World War II, from the inside as well, as Japanese authors and illustrators begin to participate in the dialogue. The books described here also embrace larger social and political issues, from the challenges of the Russo-Japanese War (1904–1905) to a number of distressing episodes during World War II, culminating in the dropping of the atomic bomb—although these often painful incidents are glimpsed through the eyes of children (or rather, selected for them to view through the eyes of adult writers, who tend to sanitize them). Nevertheless, as Dr. Jagusch points out, most of the children's books discussed here avoid overt political and social commentary. For example, the drab grimness of the aftermath of war, so eloquently revealed in her citation by William J. Sebald, describing the devastation of Tokyo and Yokohama in 1945, seems to have found relatively little reflection in the children's literature written at the time.

OPPOSITE
"Japon – Japan," in *Récréations instructives: Voyage pittoresque à travers le monde*, by Félix Achille Saint-Aulaire. Paris: Aubert, 1840.

In this context, still another story is told here, this one concerning the Japanese diaspora, and in particular, the lives of those Japanese who came to live in the United States beginning in the late nineteenth century. The accounts of Japanese American citizens who were imprisoned in U.S. camps during World War II, as presented in a milder form in children's literature, are particularly poignant; and even though some of these stories contain more or less happy memories, a sense of the somber remains.

A third "journey" examines how the work of scholars and writers on Japan has been adapted, or simplified, by the authors who set out to address children and young people. Again, as the decades progressed, information on Japan gathered by scholars, missionaries, travelers, and diplomats grew ever more precise and nuanced. From the reader's point of view today, watching how the authors of these books and stories for children select from among the ever-increasing amount of disparate material available to them provides a commentary on certain problems which inevitably arise through the limitations of second-hand observation. Based on accounts that were roughly contemporary, the writers of children's books at the end of the nineteenth century, at their best, were able to create a reasonably accurate picture of contemporary life in Japan. Yet by the 1920s and later, these same earlier sources were all too often still being put to use. The result was the creation of a certain number of children's texts that, in hindsight, now seem increasingly out of touch with the shifting political and cultural realities of the time. Indeed, the quaint and the nostalgic do not vanish altogether until the coming of war.

In the course of her study, Dr. Jagusch has provided glimpses of a number of writings based on first-hand observations of Japan, often from unexpected sources, that even now strike us as particularly fresh and revealing. Among the most arresting to me are the extracts from the diary of William Speiden, who at the age of seventeen found himself on Commodore Matthew Perry's ship as he made his visit to Edo (later Tokyo) in 1853. Mr. Speiden's acute eye and sense of wonder, as well as his common sense, make vivid all over again the remarkable nature of these first encounters between the Japanese and the Americans.

Dr. Jagusch has provided her readers with a virtual parade of noted authors who wrote on Japan, ranging from Marco Polo to such historically important visitors to Tokugawa Japan as Engelbert Kaempfer (1651–1701), the German naturalist and physician, and Philipp Franz von Siebold (1796–1866), the celebrated physician, botanist, and traveler. After Meiji, her field of vision expands to include, among others, a redoubtable amateur explorer, the British Isabella Bird (1831–1904), and the novelist and naval officer Pierre Loti (1850–1923). Here,

Dr. Jagusch provides some fascinating extended excerpts from Loti's 1893 love story, *Madame Chrysanthème,* which, soon after its publication, was to become the inspiration for the play by David Belasco that led in turn to Puccini's 1904 opera *Madama Butterfly.*

A fourth "journey," and a particularly delightful one, reveals the successive developments in the art of book illustration, both in terms of shifting visual styles and in the accuracy of their depiction of Japan. Early illustrations, created before the opening of Japan in 1868, often look vaguely oriental but lack many specific characteristics of Japanese dress or scenery. Even after the opening of the country, illustrations tended, perhaps not surprisingly, to stress the picturesque. It would appear, based on the colorful examples provided here, that a rendering of the look of ordinary Japanese children (and adults) would have to wait until the appearance of Japanese and Japanese American artists who themselves came to create the more accurate and effective images found in many postwar books. In this regard, the odyssey of Taro Yashima and his children's books is as remarkable and touching a spiritual and artistic journey as any I know.

Finally, the book provides an excellent account of the history of publishing of children's books and magazines that relate to Japan. This rich material might have provided the basis for a whole book in itself.

For the adult reader, such as myself, one particularly fascinating aspect of this volume is to observe, as one decade succeeds another, the ways in which the authors of these various books made their tacit decisions as to what material might be considered effective or appropriate for children. The move from the exotic to the familiar says a good deal both about the authors (a small but increasing number of whom began to travel to Japan in order to make their observations at first hand) and the expanding parameters of etiquette concerning the kinds of material felt to be suitable and appropriate. The atomic bomb and the camps for Japanese Americans are at one extreme, of course, but the shift away from the exotic towards the familiar and down-to-earth is obvious, and mirrors in turn the level of increased familiarity between the two cultures. More and more can now be assumed, on both sides of the Pacific.

There are some surprises as well. For example, some Japanese children's stories are mentioned or retold, but relatively few in comparison with what one might be expected to find in, say, American children's books dealing with Europe during the same period. There one might easily find any number of children's versions of such literary landmarks as such French tales by Charles Perrault, or German ones by the brothers Grimm. In this context it should be noted, however, that while translations of French and German texts of all kinds have circulated in America since its inception, translations from Japanese literature into English are basically a postwar phenomenon. As Dr. Jagusch notes, Dorothy and Thomas Hoobler in their *Japanese Portraits* do mention such renowned Japanese classics as *The Tale of Genji* and *The Pillow Book* of Sei Shōnagon (both of which have been adapted for children in Japan), but their own book was published relatively recently, in 1994. These sorts of literary connections, so familiar between America and Europe, have only more recently begun to come into their own in the case of Japan.

This volume of multiple journeys has the capacity to fascinate and instruct Western readers, whatever the nature of their interests. It should also fascinate many Japanese readers, who will surely be intrigued to witness, as chronicled in these sometimes charming and always revealing examples, the ways in which their country has been perceived through these often tumultuous centuries.

—J. Thomas Rimer
Professor Emeritus, Department of East Asian Languages & Literatures, University of Pittsburgh

NOTE TO THE READER

Dear Reader,

My childhood world could not have been farther away from anything Japanese. As a young child I loved the Grimm Brothers' enchanted princes and princesses, dwarfs and witches. When I got older there were the solemn hymns of Luther and Bach and stories of the Prussian kings. Not a glimpse of Japan anywhere. There were, however, a few hints of Asia in my family's background. My paternal great grandmother owned a silk company; another relative brought home a Siamese princess. The rest lived in great splendor, in Berlin, apparently favoring Chinese furniture.

On January 24, 1945, a particularly snowy East Prussian day, my family became refugees, fleeing to what would become the Russian Zone. Harsh years followed. (Only years later would my father reveal that he carried the dead bodies of two of his children in a box to a cemetery, asking strangers to bury them with their loved ones.) Eventually, fleeing once again, we crossed the border into the British Zone which would become part of West Germany. My favorite children's book from my young adolescent years was *Andshana* by Käthe von Roeder-Gnadeberg (1951), about a young girl from India who was sent to a place that felt cold and dark to her—my own country. It was the closest I came to Asia in those days.

In the early 1960s, I sailed for New York. Years later I would learn that daughters of the samurai don't cry. Apparently, daughters of Prussia were brought up the same way. After having said good bye to family and friends—some of whom I would never see again—I cried only when their faces had become a blur as the ship was slowly leaving the harbor.

By the 1970s I had become a children's librarian. Japan surfaced poignantly in one of the first American children's books I read. *Journey to Topaz* by Yoshiko Uchida (1971) told the shocking story of eleven-year-old Yuki, whose family is sent to an American internment camp.

In 1983, I began a new chapter in what was turning out to become a children's book life. The Library of Congress asked me to become the chief of its Children's

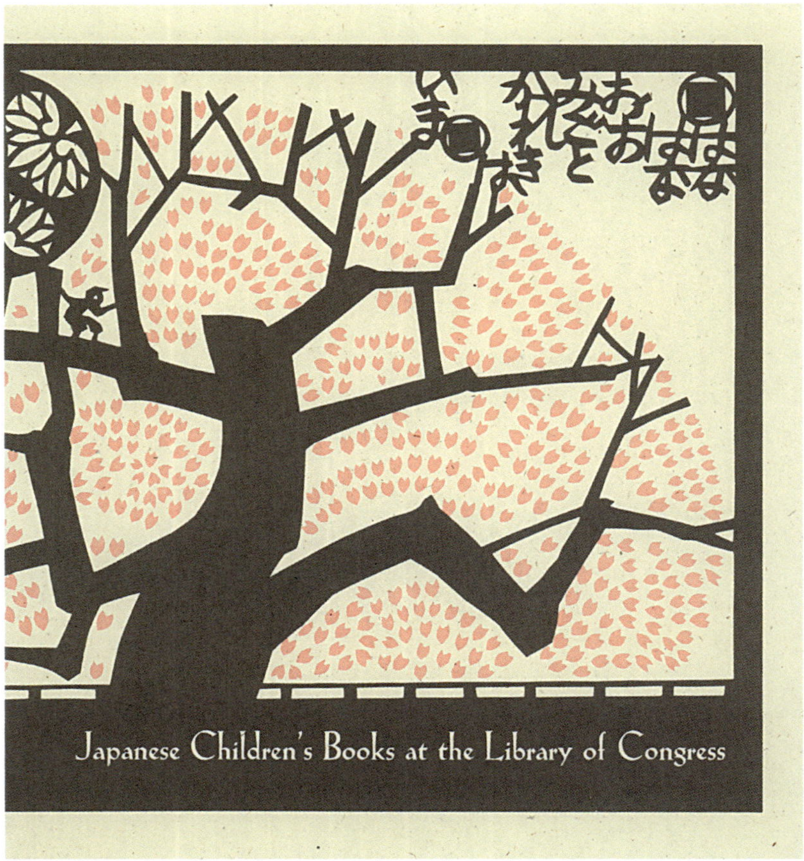

FIGURE N.1
Japanese Children's Books at the Library of Congress: A Bibliography of Books from the Postwar Years, 1946–1985, compiled by Tayo Shima and edited by Sybille A. Jagusch. Washington, DC: Library of Congress, 1987. Illustrations by Mitsumasa Anno, first published in *Momotaro* [Peach Boy] (Tokyo: Iwasaki Bijitsusha, 1973).

Literature Center. My predecessor, the indefatigable, internationally recognized Virginia Haviland, had already made it known throughout the children's book world. On a summer day a few years later, a cheerful young woman walked into my office. A Japanese children's book editor, charming and forceful, Tayo Shima became a volunteer right then and there. Within a few weeks, we began planning a major symposium which was documented in two Library of Congress publications: *Japanese Children's Books at the Library of Congress: A Bibliography of Books from the Postwar Years, 1946–1985* (1987) and *Window on Japan: Japanese Children's Books and Television Today* (1990). Both were decorated with illustrations by Japan's leading children's book illustrator, Mitsumasa Anno, one of the symposium's speakers.

Little did I know at the time that this program would be the beginning of a long and passionate journey that would include many visits to Japan and would culminate in the publication of the present volume.

In 1994, Emperor Akihito and Empress Michiko paid a visit to the Library of Congress. I was asked to entertain the Empress with a selection of children's books. We have been friends since then.

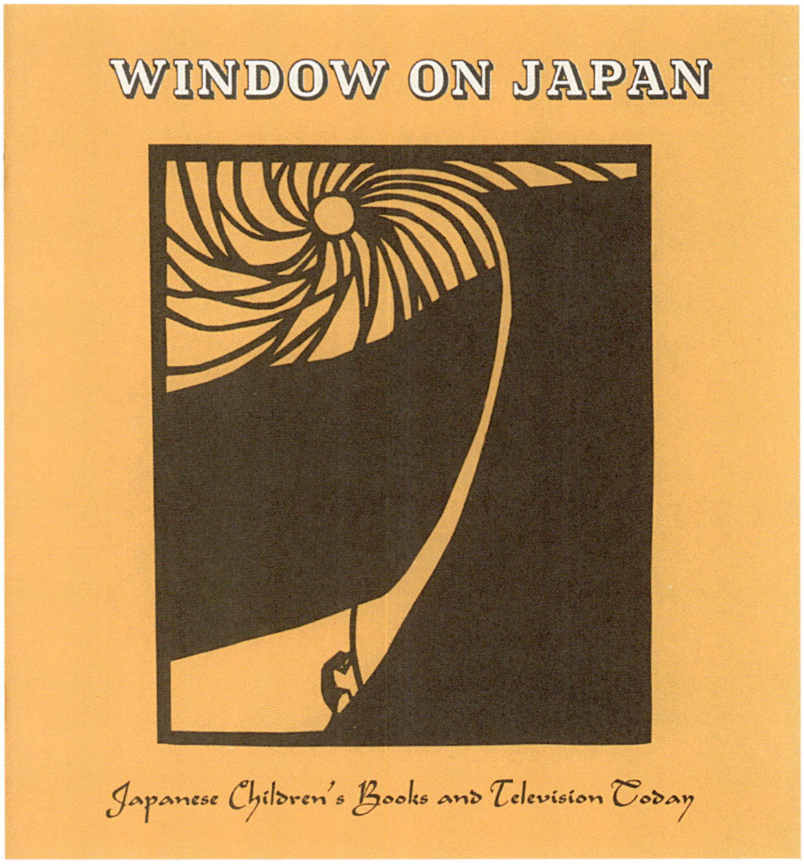

FIGURE N.2
Window on Japan: Japanese Children's Books and Television Today, edited by Sybille A. Jagusch. Washington, DC: Library of Congress, 1990. Illustrations by Mitsumasa Anno, first published in *Kirigami no irasutorēshon* (Tokyo: Iwasaki Bijitsusha, 1976).

A number of years later, the elegant international children's book editor Ann Beneduce called. I showed her some notes for a proposal (that had been rejected) for a Library of Congress exhibition featuring American children's books about Japan.

Had I thought of writing a book about this topic? She asked. No, not at all. She offered to become my editor. Wonderful years followed when we worked together on the first draft of this book.

In the meantime, I had become a collector of adult, and then children's books about Japan. Early acquisitions include Commodore Perry's official report of his journey to Japan in 1853, and the first German edition of Engelbert Kaempfer's *Geschichte und Beschreibung von Japan* (The History and Description of Japan, 1777). Among my children's book treasures were *The Best of Old Japan,* with its moving black-and-white photographs by Francis Haar (1951); *The Cheerful Heart* by Elizabeth Gray Vining (1959), which reminded me of my own refugee childhood; and the moving story *My Brother, My Sister, and I* by Yoko Kawashima Watkins (1994).

However, most of the information about their remarkable country came from my Japanese friends who were determined to teach me the way of Japan.

They arranged a visit to the Katsura Imperial Villa, where I learnt about Prince Genji and moon viewing; they took me to experience *yabusame,* the colorful re-enactment of Heian-period equestrian archery. They introduced me to a nō player who taught me how to slide around on the wooden floor wearing a mask. I saw performances of Kabuki, sumo, the solemn Nō and Bunraku, Japan's classical puppets. I slept in an eerie monastery on Mount Koya; watched the Wajima lacquerware craftsmen; glanced in awe at the Ise Grand Shrine, the holy Shinto site devoted to Amaterasu, the sun goddess; and spent days on Nagasaki's Deshima, where Kaempfer, who had lived not far away from where I went to school in northern Germany, began to write the first Western history of Japan.

Here then, in this coming together of two of my life's great loves, are essays featuring children's books about Japan. From the beginning I decided not to critique individual books for their artistic or literary style, their accuracy, or their relevance. Rather, the books chosen aim to provide an overview of how, as a group, American children's books of the last two centuries have portrayed Japan.

Included are books by prominent as well as by obscure or long-forgotten writers. Some of the books might have been popular with children while others seem to have never been opened. I have chosen factual as well as fictional accounts, including travelogues, histories and geographies, diaries, novels, folk and fairy tales, as well as picture books for the youngest readers. The idea has been to let the books speak for themselves. Therefore, lengthy excerpts have been selected when possible.[1]

These children's books with their special point of view and purpose reveal the evolving relationship between Japan and America. They also provide a glimpse of a traveler between these two places.

—Sybille A. Jagusch
October 2020

Japan and American Children's Books

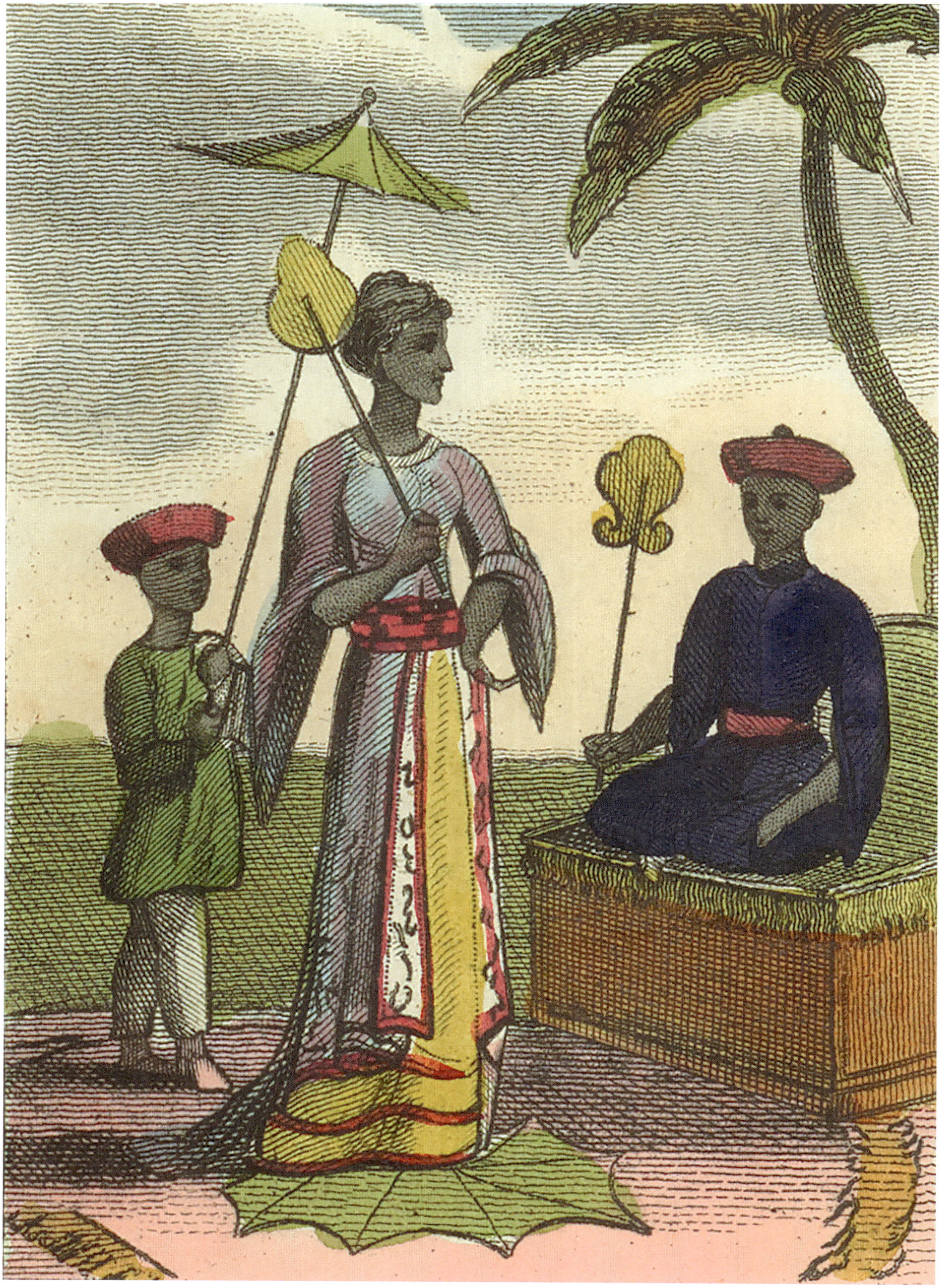

Prologue

Japan in Early Books for Children
From Comenius to Commodore Perry

Descriptions of Japan appeared in European children's books long before the United States sent Commodore Perry to Japan in 1853, and before Americans began to produce, around the time of that historic visit, what could be defined as its own children's literature. Heavily religious and didactic texts were distributed to the young since colonial days, however. Stories and information came from European, and especially British, children's books. Brought home by travelers like Benjamin Franklin, they were sometimes adapted to the American market, but most were sold as is. Thus, descriptions of Japan in early European children's books slowly found their way into books for young Americans.

Japan in Early European Children's Books

In 1658, near Nuremberg, Germany, Jan Amos Komensky (Latinized as Johann Amos Comenius), published what is regarded as the first book specifically written for children. A clergyman and a pedagogue originally from Bohemia, near the Hungarian border, Comenius had already written many books advocating a new and universal education system that emphasized schooling for both boys and girls, physical education, the learning of crafts, and the use of child-centered school books. The book for which he would be most remembered, *Orbis sensualium pictus* (The Visible World in Pictures, fig. P.1), included text in both German and Latin as well as quaint illustrations, which some say Comenius created himself. *Orbis pictus*, as the little picture primer came to be called, created an immediate sensation. Within a year it was published in England, and within a decade it had appeared in ten new editions. Translated, copied, adapted, revised, and supplied with new illustrations, it became the most used school book in Europe for the next century.[1]

In this hallmark work Comenius writes of God, the heavens, the earth, and the elements; of trees, fruit, flowers, birds, and insects; of animals, fish, and human activities. He describes trades such as beekeeping, blacksmithing, and stone masonry; children's games and sports; and the arts of writing, papermaking, and

OPPOSITE
(Detail) "Man and Woman of Japan," in *A Geographical Present: Being Descriptions of Principal Countries of the World*, by Mary Anne Venning. London: Darton, Harvey, and Darton, 1818, 2nd edition, opposite page 83.

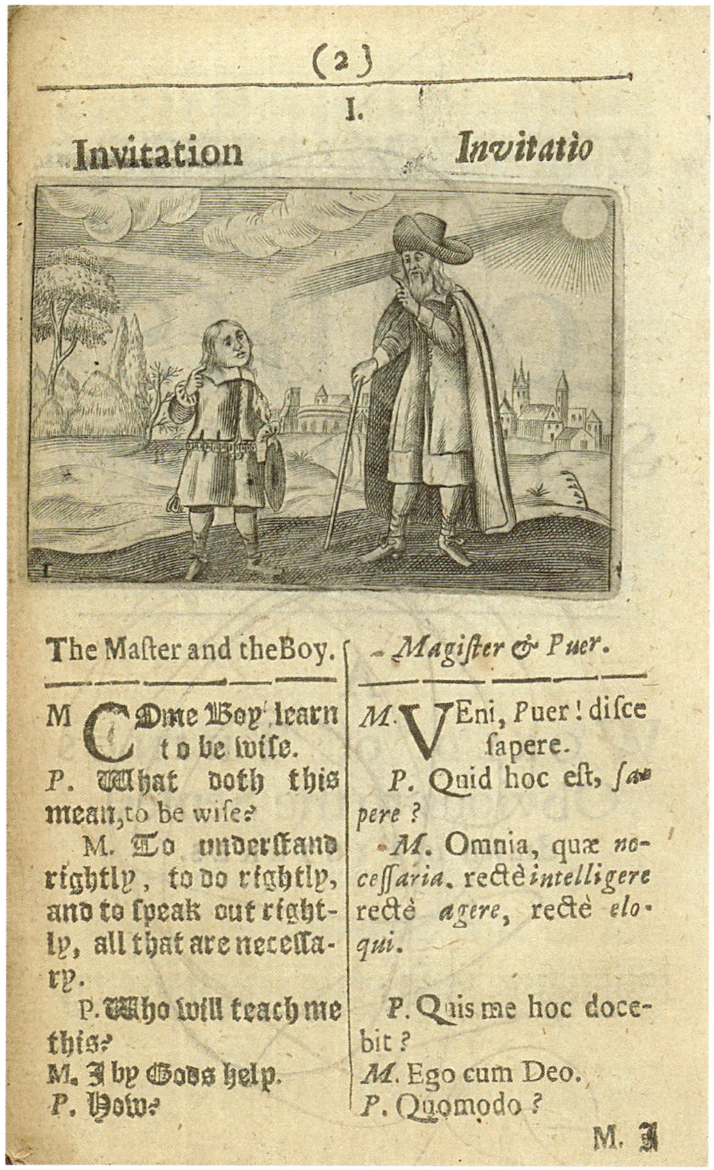
(2)

I.

Invitation — Invitatio

The Maſter and the Boy.	Magiſter & Puer.
M. Come Boy, learn to be wiſe.	M. Veni, Puer! diſce ſapere.
P. What doth this mean, to be wiſe?	P. Quid hoc eſt, ſapere?
M. To underſtand rightly, to do rightly, and to ſpeak out rightly, all that are neceſſary.	M. Omnia, quæ neceſſaria, rectè intelligere rectè agere, rectè eloqui.
P. Who will teach me this?	P. Quis me hoc docebit?
M. I by Gods help.	M. Ego cum Deo.
P. How?	P. Quomodo?

M. I

FIGURE P.1
"Invitation," The Master and the Boy, in *Orbis sensualium pictus*, by Johann Amos Comenius. London: J. Kirton, 1664, page 2.

printing. Comenius also introduces the continent of Asia, next to Europe, Africa, and America. China is mentioned in the text of this early work,[2] but Japan appears only as a tiny lozenge-shaped body on the *Orbis pictus* map of the terrestrial sphere.

Some seventy-five years later, in 1736, a brief description of Japan appeared in what is believed to have been the first geography text expressly made for children, *Géographie des enfan[t]s, ou méthode abrégée de la géographie: Divisée par leçons, avec la liste des cartes nécessaires aux enfan[t]s* by Nicolas Lenglet du Fresnoy, who was known throughout Europe for his theological, historical, and geographical works. A year after its publication in France, a translation appeared in England, where it became so popular that, by 1744, *The Geography for Children* was already in its third edition; by 1816, it was in its twenty-sixth.[3]

Fresnoy used the question-and-answer-style borrowed from the catechism, a style that would later be used in many informational texts for children:

> Q. What are the parts of the surface of the earth?
> A. Six: Europe, Asia, Africa, America, the unknown land under the North Pole, and that under the South Pole, besides the islands belonging to each part. . . .
>
> Q. How do you call America?
> A. 'Tis called the New World, because lately discover'd. 'Tis also named the West Indies, to distinguish it from the East Indies.
>
> Q. Which is at this day the most renowned part of the world?
> A. Europe; by the politeness of its manners, the policy of its government, and the wisdom of its various laws.
>
> Q. Are those advantages to be found in the other parts of the world?
> A. The farthermost parts of Asia are better governed than the western parts of it; most states of Africa are still barbarous; and, except what the Europeans possess in America, the rest is still savage and unpolished: The other parts are little known. . . .[4]
>
> Q. Are not the islands of Japan amongst those of Asia?
> A. They are very considerable by their riches and trade; the largest is Niphon, the capital of which and of all Japan is Yedo: Meaco, a rich and trading town, was heretofore the capital: Ximo, and Cikoko, are two other islands of Japan with some lesser.[5]

A few decades later, German educational reformer Johann Bernhard Basedow made brief note of Japan in the *Elementarwerk* (1774), a comprehensive compendium of elementary knowledge influenced by *Orbis pictus*. Aimed at students, teachers, and parents, *Elementarwerk* included engravings by Daniel Chodowiecki (illustrator of works by Rousseau, Shakespeare, and Voltaire, among others). The book's text and illustrations deal with logic, religion, history, plants and animals, machines and trades, practices of war, and historical personages and events. *Elementarwerk* also featured maps and geographical information about the known areas of the globe, including Europe, Africa, and America. The author placed the following countries in Asia:

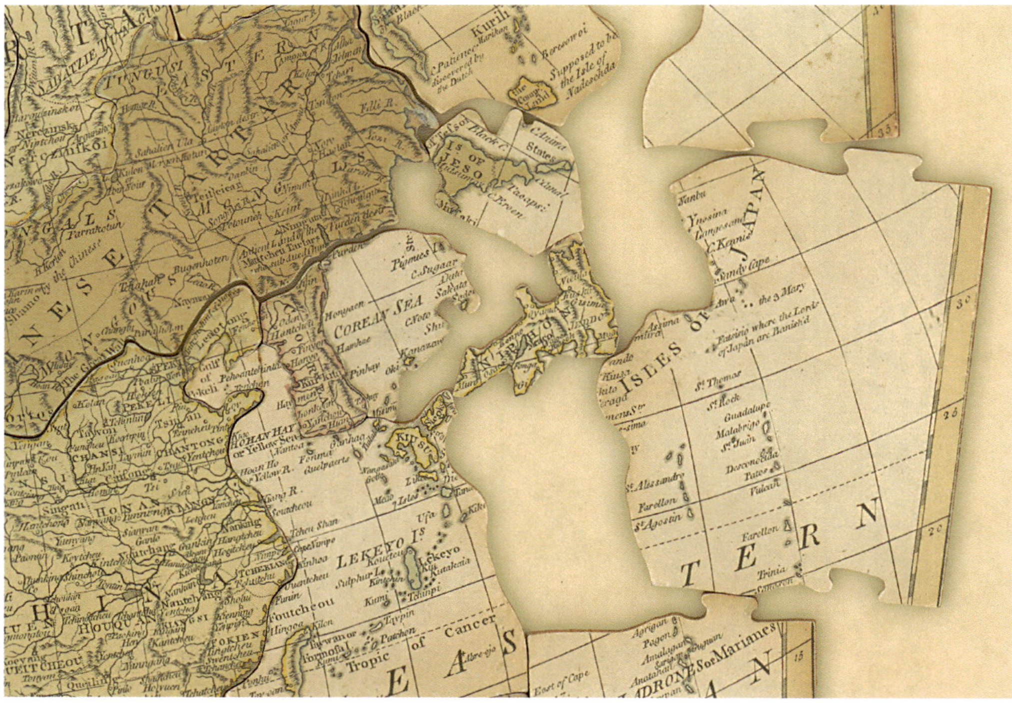

FIGURE P.2
(Detail) *Asia, Divided into its Empires, Kingdoms and States, with Their General Subdivisions*, by T. Woodman & H. Mutlow, 1772.

> Asian Turkey . . . Arabia . . . Persia . . . India . . . China. . . . In the north-east of China lies a large and populated Island, Japan, and north of it, the country of Jeddo. . . .
>
> The Asian islands, which excepting the European colonies, are all Mohammedan or pagan, contain many peoples and rulers, for example Japan with the capital of Jeddo.[6]

About thirty years before *Elementarwerk* appeared in Germany, John Newbery left his hometown of Redding, England, where he had learned the business of printing, to start afresh in London. There he opened a shop selling medicines and books and became a publisher. Although his stock consisted mostly of adult books, Newbery also became so well known for his children's books that America's highest honor for children's literature is the John Newbery Medal.[7] An "author of considerable ingenuity and wit,"[8] Newbery surrounded himself with fine writers who created children's texts for him, sometimes anonymously. Newbery's successful children's books included *Little Pretty Pocket Book, Intended for the Instruction and Amusement of Little Master Tommy and Pretty Miss Polly* (1744), and such informational works as *Geography Made Familiar and Easy to Young Gentlemen and Ladies* (1748), which included the following information about Japan:

> The Isles of Japan . . . are under several petty Kings, but all together form a large Empire subject to one absolute Sovereign. The chief of them is *Niphon*, (usually call'd *Japan*) about 700 Miles of Length, wherein is YENDO or YEDO, a vast, rich, and populous City, the Capital of the Empire, as *Meaco* was formerly. The

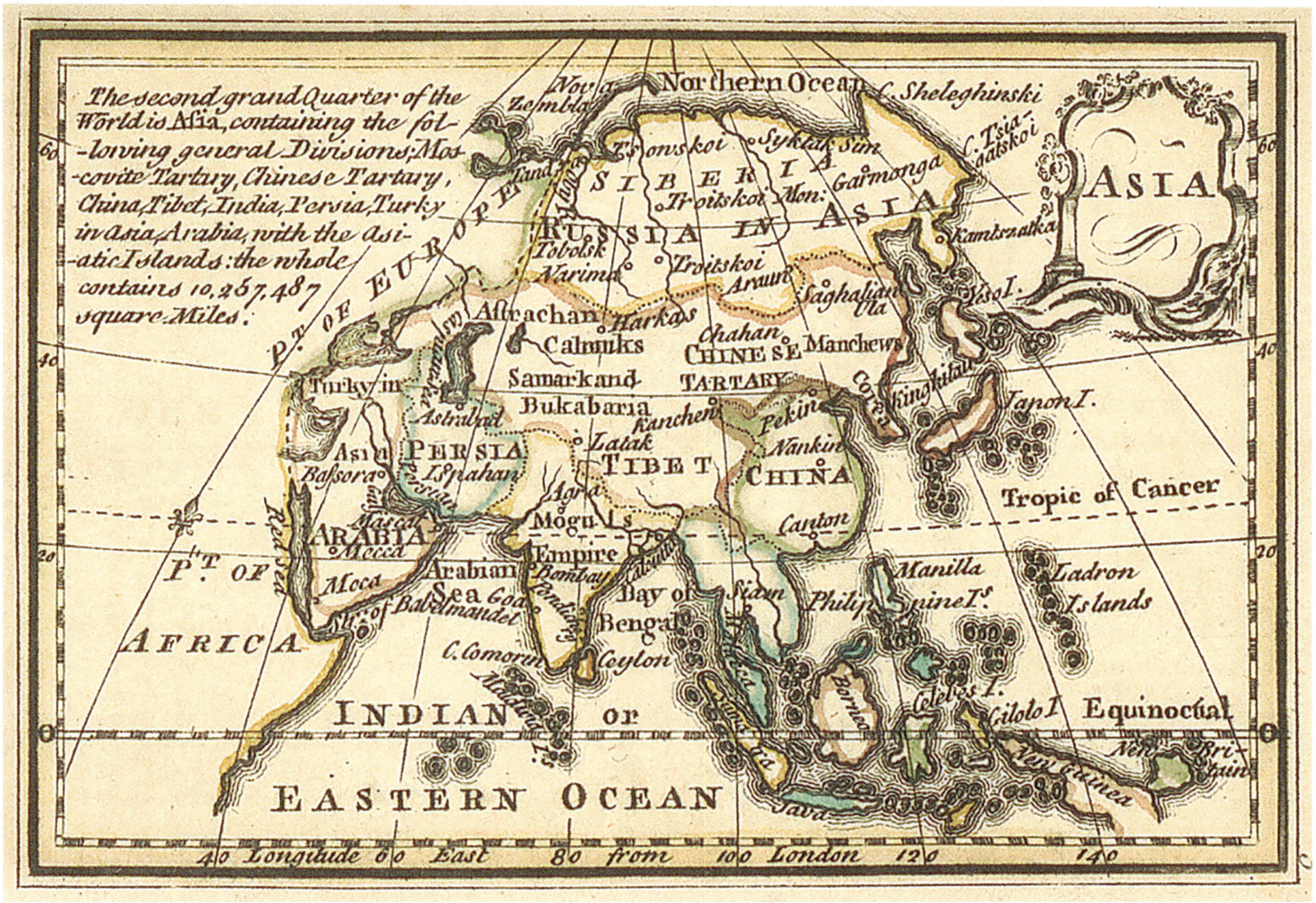

FIGURE P.3
Atlas Minimus, or A New Set of Pocket Maps of the Several Empires, Kingdoms and States of the Known World, with Historical Extracts Relative to Each, engraved by John Gibson. London, J. Newbery, 1758.

rest of the Japan Islands are of little Note, except *Ximo* and *Xicoco.* These Islands are much overspread with Woods and Mountains, but the Soil is good, producing Plenty of Corn, Fruits, and Pasture. Their Air is somewhat cold, but very wholesome. The Inhabitants are Idolaters, and at present will permit no Christian to set foot in the Country, or trade with them, except the *Dutch,* who bring them thence Gold, Silver, Copper, fine Cabinets, and other curious *Japan* and lacquer'd Ware.[9]

Newbery also published the handsome *Atlas Minimus, or A New Set of Pocket Maps of the Several Empires, Kingdoms, and States of the Known World* (1758, fig. P.3). With an emphasis on European countries, this small volume presented maps and descriptions of countries from America to Brazil, China, Hungary, Peru, and Switzerland. Though the introduction states that the "greatest care and attention" was paid "to modern Discoveries,"[10] Japan was not among the many countries mentioned in the text; it only appears on the world map. There is only a brief reference to Japan in Newbery's *The Newtonian System of Philosophy Adapted to the Capacities of Young Gentlemen and Ladies . . . by Tom Telescope* (1761), and it makes only a cameo appearance in *A Museum for Young Gentlemen and Ladies, or A Private Tutor for Little Masters and Misses* (1790).

It is possible that some of these early works were available in America, either imported from Europe for resale in the New World or in pirated editions. It appears that no original American works for children of this period contained information about Japan.

After John Newbery's death in 1767, his widow made John Harris, an experienced bookman, manager of the Newbery firm. Gradually developing his own style, Harris published children's books—including nursery stories and rhymes, tongue twisters and nonsense rhymes, fairy tales, and the first known limerick—that were both elegant and playful and included sparkling hand-colored illustrations.

Harris's extraordinarily successful list included his books of instruction, among them the imaginatively illustrated *The Costume, Manners, and Peculiarities of Different Inhabitants of the Globe: Calculated to Instruct and Amuse the Little Folks of all Countries* (1821), which did not include Japan. The Japanese were featured in *The Traveller, or An Entertaining Journey round the Habitable Globe* (1820), which stated that the author would introduce his "juvenile companions to . . . nearly all nations and tribes of the world."[11]

The greater part of the book is devoted to Britain, which, the book declared, "has long been the most important nation in the world." Yet the author does assess the people of other nations, informing his readers, for example, that "The Dutch are cold, sober, calculating, and eager in the pursuit of gain; the Belgians are lively, gay, and more given to expense than their neighbors"; and Germans are "frank, sensible, laborious, and brave in war."[12]

After many pages about China and the Chinese, who "consider themselves the most enlightened people in the world,"[13] the author includes, in this description of Japan, details that had not appeared in earlier children's books:

> The Japanese, in many respects, resemble their neighbors the Chinese; but they pretend to be their superiors in civilization, and mental cultivation in general; they even appear to be more advanced in the arts and sciences. They have printing-presses, universities, and academies. The Japanese have carried out agriculture of silk and cotton; their porcelain is highly esteemed, as are also their iron, brass, gold, and silver works.
>
> The three principal islands are Niphon, Ximo, and Xicoco. The Japanese empire is governed despotically by a secular sovereign, called Kuba-Sama, and by an ecclesiastical chief, called Dairo-Sama.[14]

Harris also published *Cosmorama; A View of the Costumes and Peculiarities of All Nations* (1827) by the cartographer Jehoshaphat Aspin. After inviting his young readers on an armchair trip, Aspin provides a broad description of the Japanese:

> The Japanese are described as a nervous vigorous people, whose bodily and mental powers assimilate much nearer to those of Europe than is attributed to Asiatics in general. Their features are masculine; and the small lengthened Tatar eye, which almost universally prevails, is the only feature of resemblance between them and the Chinese. . . . The common color of their eyes is dark brown, or blue, with the lids forming a deep furrow, and the eyebrows higher than with most other nations. In their persons, the Japanese are of the middle stature, and seldom corpulent; their heads are commonly large, necks short, and noses, though not flat, rather broad and short. . . .
>
> The extravagance of the Japanese character lies in a fondness for magnificence and show, when they appear abroad; and few nobles have less than fifty or sixty attendants, richly clad and armed, some on foot, but most of them on horseback. These people are described as intelligent, prudent, frank, obedient, polite, good-natured, industrious, economical, sober, hardy, cleanly, upright, faithful, brave, and invincible; yet, with all their virtues, they are accused of being suspicious, superstitious, haughty, and vindictive. . . .[15]

Among Harris's most popular authors was Isaac Taylor. In addition to his work as an engraver and water colorist, Isaac Taylor was the pastor of the church in Ongar (in Essex), founded a Sunday school, lectured widely, and fathered eleven children. Taylor wrote and illustrated numerous books and took the geographical travel book to another level. He became best known for his *Scenes* book series.[16] In *Scenes in Asia: For the Amusement and Instruction of Little Tarry-at-Home Travellers* (1819, fig. P.4), he includes some less-than-complimentary assessments, telling his young readers, for example, that the "Turks ruin everything wherever they come, by their superstition, their ignorance, and their want of taste," the Circassians sell

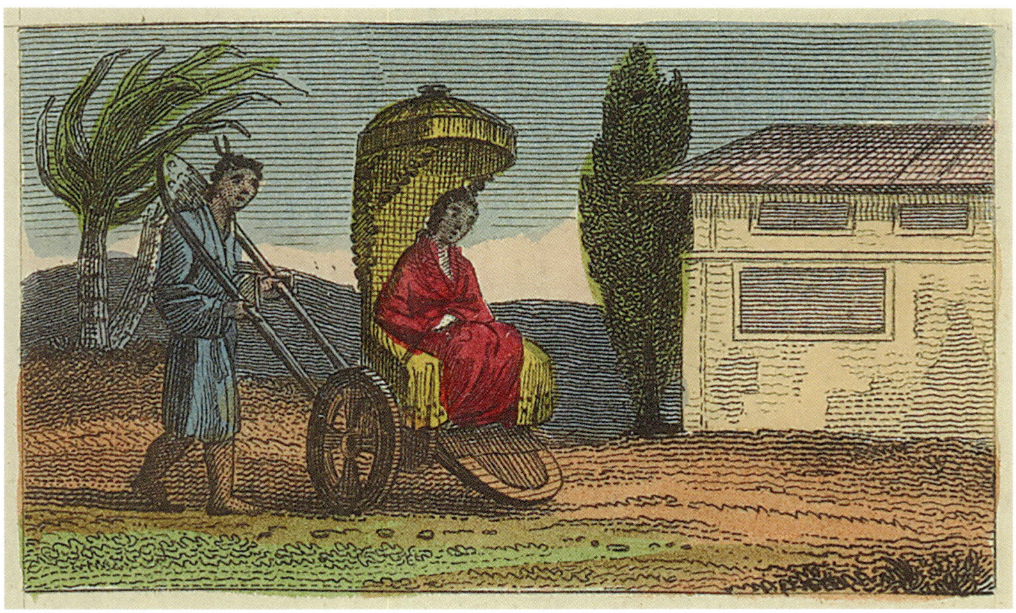

FIGURE P.4
"Japan Isles," in *Scenes in Asia: For the Amusement and Instruction of Little Tarry-at-Home Travellers*, by Isaac Taylor. London: Harris and Son, 1819, opposite page 30.

their daughters "as with so many head of cattle," the Tibetans "believe that the deity actually lives among them," a "stupidity [that] is spread half over Asia," while "almost all the people of India are desperately addicted to gaming."[17] About Japan and the Japanese, Taylor wrote:

> Their dress is one or two more loose gowns, tied round the waist with a sash; and such it has been without alteration for more than two thousand years. Men and women wear the same, only the women wear more in number at a time, and have them longer. The difference of rank only appears in the rich having their gowns of silk, and the poorer sort of cotton. . . .[18]
>
> The Japanese are a very jealous nation, extremely bigoted to their own superstitions, and fond of their ugly idols. It seems that, years ago, when the Portuguese had some establishment in the islands, they took great pains to make proselytes to Christianity, at least to popery. Their success herein, and especially some of the means they made use of to obtain converts, gave great offense to the Japanese; who drove them out, and began a grievous persecution against all the natives, who had been induced to profess the name of Christ. Their hatred to Christ and his gospel continues still; and one method by which they show it, and endeavor to discover if any remnants of this religion can yet be found, is by an annual ceremony, which takes place soon after their new year begins. They have crosses, and crucifixes, and images of the Virgin Mary, which they know are held, by papists at least, in high veneration. These are regularly carried into every house, and every person, young or old, is obliged to come forward and trample upon them; even babes are trained to it, their feet are placed upon them, to instill into them, early and constantly, a contempt and hatred of the Christian religion.[19]

Japan Becomes More Visible

While Japan is curiously absent from a number of books published in the early nineteenth century, it is represented with handsome illustrations in *Geography Embellished with a Variety of Views from Nature for the Bookcase of Instruction and Delight* (1802), in the illustrated album *La géographie en estampes, ou Mœurs et costumes des différens peuples de la terre* (between 1815 and 1821, fig. P.5), and in *Voyage pittoresque à travers le monde—Picturesque Voyage round the World* (ca. 1845). *The World in Miniature, or Panorama of the Costumes, Manners, & Customs of all Nations* (1825) includes this passage about the people of Japan:

> [The Japanese] are highly civilized, and display a great diversity of character; but the virtues far predominate over the vices; and even their pride is useful as it prevents them from stooping to the mean vices of the maritime Chinese, who cheat whenever they can take the advantage. They have none of the vanity, so common among Asiatics and the Africans of adorning themselves with shells, glass beads, and polished metal plates; neither are they fond of the useless European ornaments of gold and

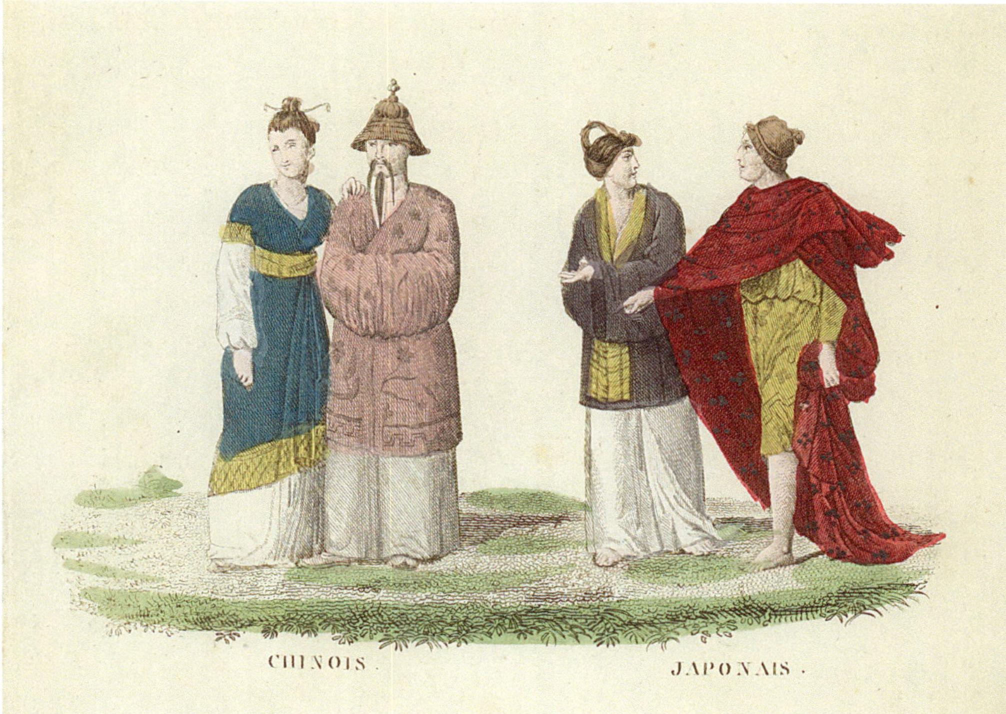

FIGURE P.5
La géographie en estampes, ou Mœurs et costumes des différens peuples de la terre. Paris: Chez Lecerf, graveur, et á la Librarie d'Éducation de Pierre Blanchard, 1819, 2nd edition, opposite page 85.

> silver. . . . The Japanese sit always on their hams. Before dinner begins, they make a profound bow, and drink to the health of their guests. The females eat by themselves. Both men and women are fond of tobacco, which is smoked continually.[20]

Mary Anne Venning contributed this early nineteenth-century view of the Japanese in *A Geographical Present: Being Descriptions of the Principal Countries of the World* (1818, fig. P.6):

> The Japanese are active, but do not equal more northern nations in bodily strength. The colour of the face is commonly yellow: their narrow eyes and high eye-brows resemble the Chinese. . . .
>
> Economy is a virtue practiced from the emperor's palace to the meanest cottage. It renders the poor contented, and prevents excess among the rich. Hence, scarcity is rarely known in Japan, though the state is populous. . . . Their curiosity is excessive: nothing imported by the Europeans can escape it.
>
> The religion of Japan is Pagan, divided into sects, who live amicably among themselves.[21]

London-born Frederick Shoberl, a well-known author, translated the work of Isaac Titsingh, who sailed for Japan in 1779 to assume the post of *opperhooft*, or chief of the Dutch trading post in Nagasaki. Eager to surpass the narratives of the early travelers to Japan, Titsingh wanted to produce a work about Japan based on Japanese sources. While he never achieved his ambitious goal (apparently, he did not gain sufficient mastery of the Japanese language), his collection of incomplete papers was published after his death as *Mémoires et anecdotes sur la dynastie*

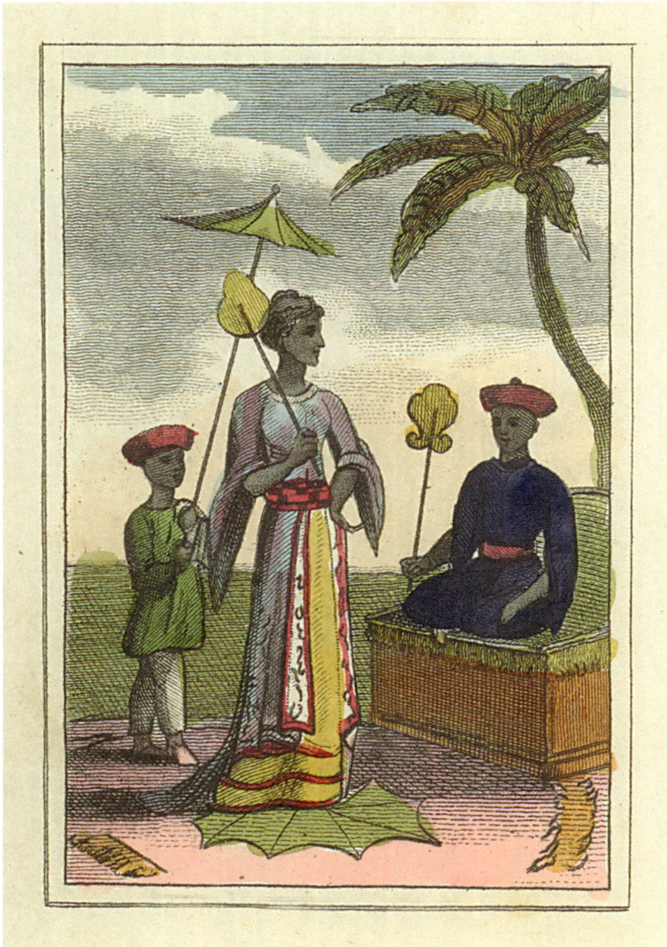

FIGURE P.6
"Man and Woman of Japan," in *A Geographical Present: Being Descriptions of Principal Countries of the World*, by Mary Anne Venning. London: Darton, Harvey, and Darton, 1818, 2nd edition, opposite page 83.

régnante des djogouns (Memoirs and Anecdotes of the Reigning Dynasty of the Shoguns, 1820). The edition of one thousand copies sold out immediately.[22]

Shoberl translated the book into English, learning a great deal about Japan in the process. He named the translation *Illustrations of Japan: Private Memoirs and Anecdotes of the Reigning Dynasty of the Djogouns, or Sovereigns of Japan* (1822). Only a year later, the London publisher Rudolph Ackermann released Shoberl's own book, *Japan* (1823, figs. P.7–8). This elegant tome was part of Ackermann's impressive forty-three-volume series *The World in Miniature*, which aimed "to increase the store of knowledge concerning the various branches of the great family of Man, not only for adults, but also keeping in view the instruction and amusement of the juvenile student."[23] *Japan* was illustrated by numerous engravings, some of which had appeared in a similar work, the four-volume *Le Japon ou mœurs, usages et costumes des habitants de cet empire* by Jean Baptiste Joseph Breton (1818). Throughout the book, Shoberl acknowledges the works of the early Japan travelers, including Engelbert Kaempfer, Carl Peter Thunberg, Pierre Francois Xavier de Charlevoix, Georg Heinrich von Langsdorff, Adam Johann von Krusenstern, Captain Vasily Golownin, and Isaac Titsingh.[24]

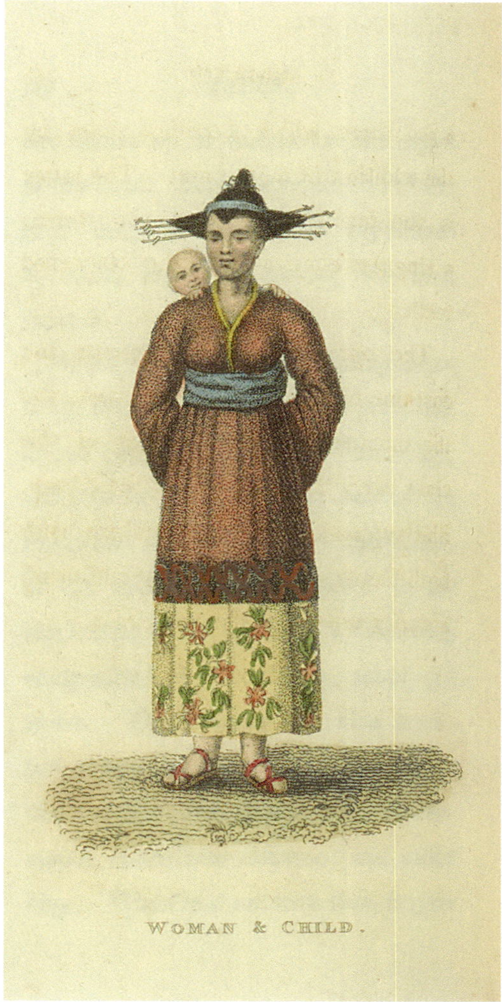

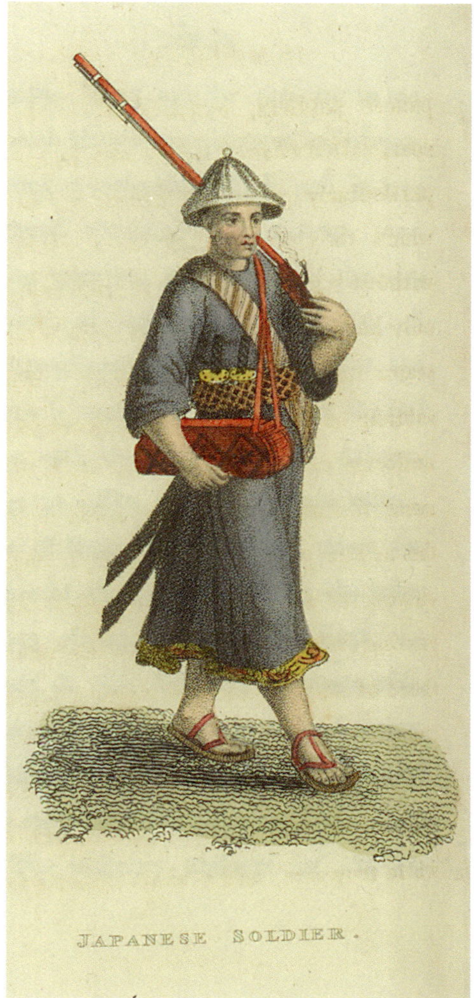

FIGURES P.7 AND P.8 "Woman and Child" and "Japanese Soldier," in *The World in Miniature: Japan*, edited by Frederic Shoberl. London: R. Ackermann Repository of Arts, 1823, pages 141 and 59.

Shoberl compressed the great amount of information he had collected into a small encyclopedic work. He wrote about the Japanese character, Japanese government and religion, dress and language, houses, festivals, marriage and funeral customs, and other topics. He provided, by far, the most detailed information on Japan to be found in European sources for young readers up to that time:

> Upon the whole, the Japanese cannot be regarded as handsome or well-shaped, though to this observation most of the grandees form exceptions. Their countenances express frankness and good nature, but according to our European notions of beauty, they appear at first sight to be somewhat repulsive. The Japanese are superior to the Chinese, not merely in a physical, but also in a moral point of view. Thunberg characterizes them as intelligent, prudent, inquisitive, industrious, ingenious, sober and temperate, cleanly, sincere, just, honorable, suspicious, superstitious, proud, revengeful, brave, nay invincible. Writers who are much less disposed to draw a favorable picture of these people cannot deny them many of these valuable qualities . . . which, indeed, are but too frequently accompanied by

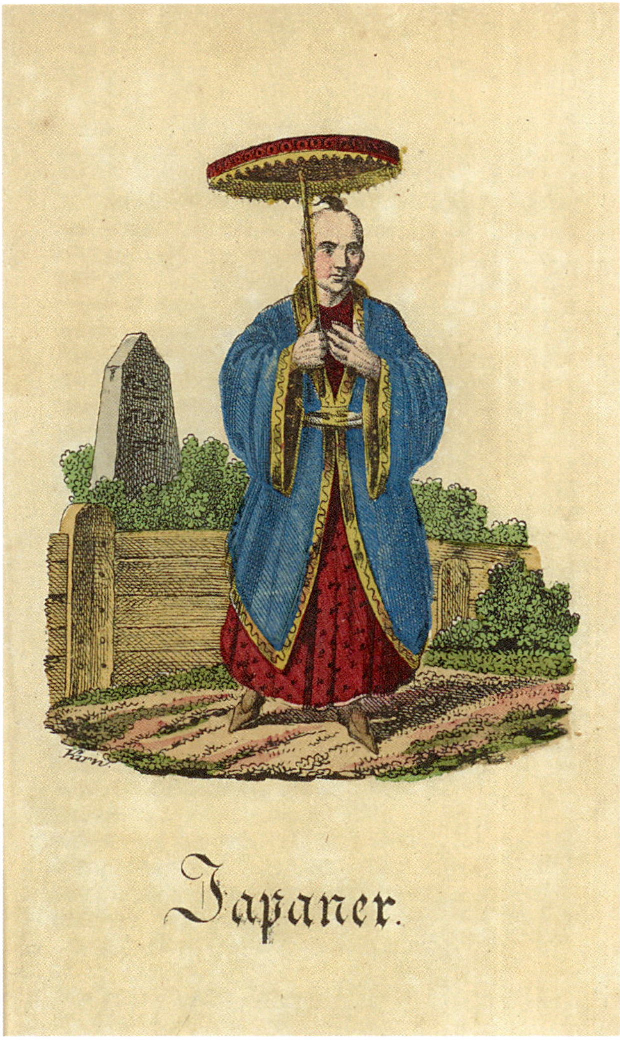

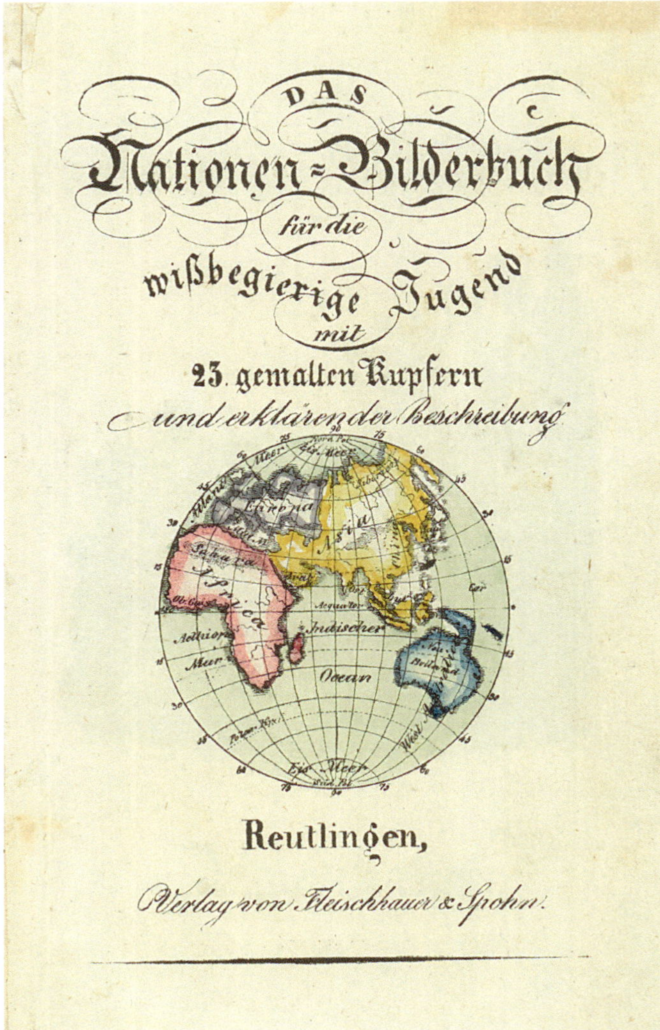

FIGURES P.9 AND P.10
"Japaner," and title page, in *Das Nationen-Bilderbuch für die wissbegierige Jugend*. Reutlingen: Verlag von Fleischhauer & Spohn, n.d. "Japaner" opposite page 16.

pride. It has been moreover admitted for centuries, that the Japanese is brave, even to the sacrifice of his own life, and that for this reason the country has never yet been subdued by a foreign power. . . .[25]

Though the Japanese sedulously avoid all foreign intercourse, yet it is a fact, attested by the older voyagers, that every possible facility has for ages been given to internal communications. Even at the commencement of the last century their roads were described as excellent, and their inns numerous, where refreshments, as well as shelter, were to be had in abundance. The arrangements of their roads seems to have been most systematic: the provinces being separated by broad roads serving as boundaries, while each smaller division was bounded by a narrower road; and the former were so wide that the most numerous trains of princes and great lords, amounting sometimes to twenty thousand in each, could pass one another without confusion or delay, adopting the plan pursued on our roads, those proceeding to the capital taking one side, and those going from it the other. These roads are planted like avenues, with fountains at intervals; and they are kept dry and clean by drains and ditches, which are also rendered subservient to the draining or irrigation of the neighboring fields.[26]

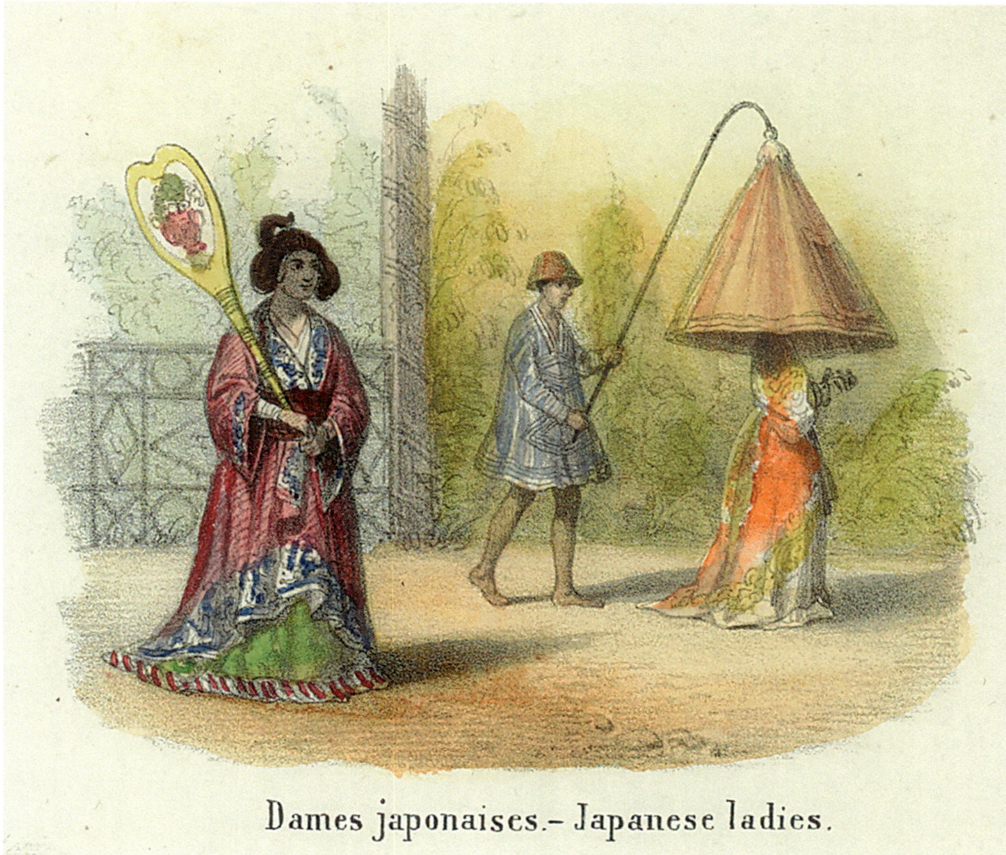

FIGURE P.11
"Dames japonaises – Japanese ladies," in *Récréations instructives: Voyage pittoresque à travers le monde*, by Félix Achille Saint-Aulaire. Paris: Aubert, 1840.

Another volume from this time, *Das Nationen-Bilderbuch für die wissbegierige Jugend* (Nations' Picture Book for Youth Eager to Learn, 1835, figs. P.9–10), introduces peoples from Africa, Europe, Asia, and Australia. The descriptive texts are accompanied by full-color illustrations depicting twenty-three men in their native costumes. The author's description of the Japanese includes these observations:

> The Japanese have brown-yellow skin, black hair, and are of medium height. Their heads are big, their eyes small, the eyebrows ample. The women remove them, while the men shave off their beards. Their noses are pressed down, their cheeks are shallow, their legs are crooked.
>
> They take care of their fields with a great deal of competence, produce fine materials from cotton and silk, and superb metal works . . . They have higher and lower schools, and even print shops, and are more educated than the Chinese. . . . [Their] houses are made from wood. Instead of windows, there are frames covered with paper. There are no chairs or tables. Bathrooms are common. The military roads are flanked by trees. There are inns everywhere.[27]

Japan in Early American Books for Children

During the final decades of the eighteenth century and into the nineteenth, few American children were privileged enough to have any books at all. Those lucky few might receive a book published in England and brought home by a well-to-do father, or the rare children's book imported, pirated, adapted, and printed by an American bookseller.[28] Consisting mostly of hornbooks, primers, spellers, and cheaply produced chapbooks, children's books were didactic and pious. The morose title of one of the most widely read children's books in Britain, published by James Janeway in 1671, provides a taste of its content: *A Token for Children: Being an Exact Account of the Conversion, Holy and Exemplary Lives and Joyful Deaths of Several Young Children*. The book was adapted by the Reverend Cotton Mather for American children in 1771.

Few children's books imparted information about other people and places. Gradually however, Americans began to publish their own informational children's books, some of which included information about other countries, including Japan. Generally written by clergymen, who were among the best-educated people in the country, geography texts also included history, civics, and moral lessons. Combining fact and fiction, they described the world's peoples and their activities.[29]

Often presented in catechismal style, these geography texts were either without maps or illustrations or had very few.[30] They were generally products of the author's imagination, coupled with information the author freely copied from earlier books and newspapers, almost always leaving their sources unnamed.

Many of these early American texts—including Robert Davidson's *Geography Epitomized, or A Tour Round the World: Being a Short but Comprehensive Description of the Terraqueous Globe* (1784) and *Elements of Geography* (1790) by Benjamin Workman—barely mentioned Japan. *Geography Made Easy* (1784), by the New Haven clergyman and Yale graduate Jedediah Morse, went through numerous editions and remained for years the most popular geographical textbook of its day.[31] It features a map of Japan's two major islands, "Jedo" and "Niphon," and the following text:

> The Japanese islands, forming an empire, governed by a despotick king, lie about 150 miles east of China. The soil and production of these islands are much the same as those of China. The Japanese are the grossest idolators, and irreconcilable to Christianity. They are of a yellow complexion, narrow eyes, short noses, black hair. A sameness of dress prevails through the whole empire, from the emperor to the peasant. The first compliment offered to a stranger in their houses is a dish of tea, a pipe of tobacco. Obedience to parents, respect to superiors, characterize the nation. Their penal laws are very severe, but punishment is seldom inflicted. The inhabitants have made great progress in commerce and agriculture.[32]

A Short but Comprehensive System of the Geography of the World: By Way of Question and Answer (1795)[33] by the New England physician and educator Nathaniel Dwight contains some information about the Japanese, including the following lines:

> Q. What do you say of their disposition?
> A. They are jealous, but courteous to strangers. They are idolators, and very superstitious. They hate the Christians, and hold no intercourse with any Europeans, beside the Dutch. They are obedient to parents and to government. . . .[34]
>
> Q. What state of improvement are they in?
> A. They are more improved than the Hindoos, but not so much so as the Chinese. Learning is hardly known by name among them, but in their manufactures they are proficient, and greatly excel in their Japan ware.[35]

In the 1810 edition of *A New System of Modern Geography* by Elijah Parish, young Americans learn that "the forests [of Japan] abound with all sorts of wild beasts, from the furs of which and from elephants' teeth they make considerable traffic. The elephant is not only found in the great plenty in their woods, but is bred up in their towns and cities."[36] (Elephants are not native to Japan but were brought in for entertainment.) The author adds:

> The Japanese are generally very acute, of a quick comprehension, good understanding, modest, patient, and courteous, excelling all the Orientals in docility. They are so just in their dealings, that one may absolutely depend on their word; and contrary to the Chinese, they disdain to take advantage of those with whom they deal. . . . In their temples they have a large mirror, to remind the worshippers that as their personal blemishes are visible in the glass, so their secret sins are visible to God. They are careful in the education of their children, using nothing but praise and rewards to incite them to duty. Parents and masters are answerable for the crimes of those whom they ought to have better instructed.[37]

Jesse Olney, author of *A Practical System of Modern Geography, or A View of the Present State of the World* (1830), declares, in his brief text about Japan, that the Japanese "are the most civilized people of Eastern Asia" and notes their remarkable "industry and ingenuity" and their careful attention to education.[38]

Between 1827 and 1850, Samuel Griswold Goodrich, whom his readers knew as Peter Parley,[39] produced 175 books and sold more than seven million copies.[40] His works went through numerous editions and were pirated, imitated, and translated into other languages, including Turkish, Persian, and Japanese.[41] They were so popular that a contemporary complained that the whole "country was swarmed and sickened of the very name of Parley."[42] Goodrich produced books of morals and manners, biographies, dictionaries, short stories, travelogues, and histories.[43]

Part schoolbook, part adventure story, travel report, and moral lesson, Goodrich's *The Tales of Peter Parley about Asia* (1830) was filled with characterizations of the various Asian people, including those of Afghanistan, who "are fond of poetry and fine horses"; the Tartars, who are "bold and daring robbers"; and Arabians, who are a "wandering race, living in tents, and subsisting chiefly by means of their flocks."[44] About the Japanese and their islands Goodrich writes:

> The whole of these islands are in extent about three times as large as New England, yet they have a population about double that of the whole of the United States! . . . Japan is very subject to earthquakes. The people are obliged to build their houses low, to prevent their being shaken down by these dreadful convulsions of nature. The thunder and lightning are terrible in this country, during the summer. . . .
>
> Formerly Europeans were admitted into Japan, and the Christian religion was propagated, to a considerable extent, by Portuguese missionaries. But the government of Japan grew jealous, and at length banished all Europeans from the kingdom. A dreadful persecution then commenced, against those Japanese who had embraced Christianity.
>
> The most cruel tortures were inflicted on them. Roasting alive was one of the most merciful punishments granted to those sufferers. Forty thousand people perished in this horrible persecution. Europeans are still excluded from Japan; and a rock, about sixty rods in length, occupied by the Dutch for the purposes of trade, is the only spot in the whole empire where foreigners are permitted to live.[45]

Goodrich's *Manners and Customs of the Principal Nations of the Globe* (1845), a collection of articles about some fifty countries, regions, and peoples of the world, also included material on the Japanese, noting how they differ from the Chinese:

> The people differ most especially from the Chinese, their nearest neighbors, notwithstanding the resemblances in form and lineaments. Instead of that tame, quiet, orderly, servile disposition, which makes them the prepared and ready subjects of despotism, the Japanese have a character marked by energy, independence, and a lofty sense of honor. Although they are said to make good subjects, even to the severe government under which they live, they yet retain an impatience of control, and a force of public opinion, which render it impossible for any ruler wantonly to tyrannize over them. Instead of that mean, artful, truckling disposition so general among Asiatics, their manners are distinguished by a manly frankness, and all their proceedings by honor and good faith. They are habitually kind and good

> humored when nothing occurs to rouse their hostile passion, and they carry the ties of friendship even to a romantic height. To defend and serve a friend in every peril, and to meet torture and death rather than betray him, are considered duties which nothing can abolish. . . . Their greatest defect seems to be a haughty pride, which runs through all classes, rising to the highest pitch among the great, and leading them to display an extravagant pomp in their retinue and establishments.[46]

In 1855, Charles H. Davis of Philadelphia published a quaint little book called *Stories of Asia* by Alice Hawthorne. Describing the lives and lore of many ethnic and national groups, Hawthorne tells her young readers that the [Syrian] Druze are open, sincere, and display an "engaging manner,"[47] that Greeks are numerous and intelligent, Bedouins "ignorant and superstitious,"[48] Calmuck Tatars "athletic and revolting,"[49] and Nepaulese [*sic*] "not remarkably moral."[50] Imagining the people of Japan, the author incorporated, verbatim, lines from Goodrich's *Manners and Customs of the Principal Nations of the Globe*:

> The Japanese, seem, in personal appearance, to be a somewhat altered and improved variety of the Monguls and Chinese. Their eyes are, even in a greater degree, small, pointed, oblong, sunk in the head, with a deep furrow made by the eyelids; they have almost the appearance of being pink-eyed. Their heads are in general large, and their necks short; their hair is black, thick, and shining from the use of oil. They are, however, robust, well-made, active, and easy in their motions.

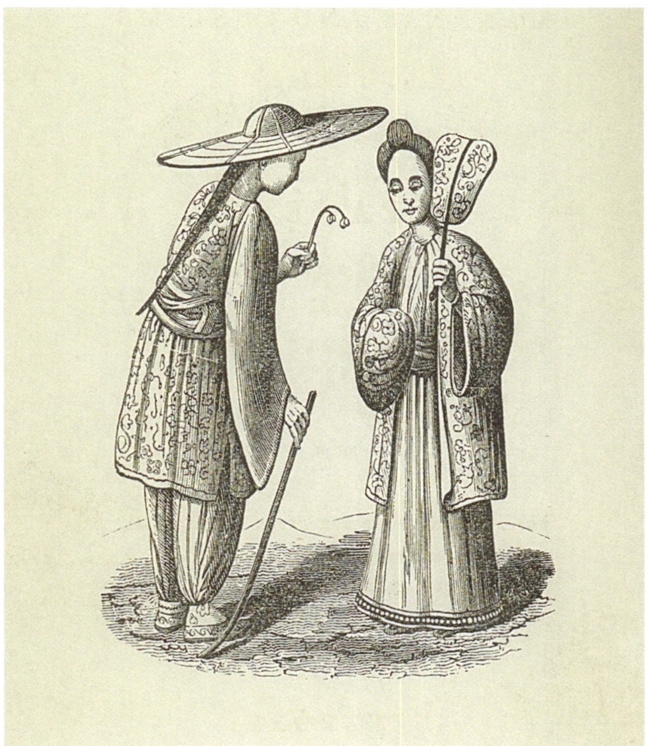

FIGURE P.12
"Japanese," in *Manners and Customs of the Japanese*. New York: Harper & Brothers, 1841, frontispiece. (This image also appears opposite page 127 in *Stories of Asia* by Alice Hawthorne. Philadelphia: Charles H. Davis, 1855.)

> Their complexion, yellow and passing into brown, appears to be entirely produced by the climate; since ladies who are constantly protected from the heat of the sun are as white as any in Europe.
>
> The national character is strikingly marked, and strongly contrasted with that which generally prevails throughout Asia.[51]

By 1860, descriptions of Commodore Perry's expeditions to Japan seven years earlier began to appear in some publications for young American readers. This note was posted in *Merry's Museum and Parley's Magazine*:

> Until very recently, but little has been known of Japan, except its place upon the map. When I was a boy, I used to think it was too far off to be reached by Americans, and too insignificant to be cared for if it could be reached. But our field of view and of action is constantly widening. Having extended our domain to the Pacific, and planted States on its shores, we begin to look eagerly across it, for whatever may be found there, to satisfy our roving and adventurous commerce. Following the footsteps of England, we have established an open intercourse with China and her hundreds of millions; and now England may, if she chooses, follow us into the door we opened into the hitherto un-approachable wall of Japan.
>
> So wholly unknown, so strange, so curious, Japan seems like a new world, and her inhabitants like a new race of beings. It will be a long time before we shall become fully acquainted with them.[52]

A new era had begun.

PART I

From Early Children's Books to the End of the Nineteenth Century

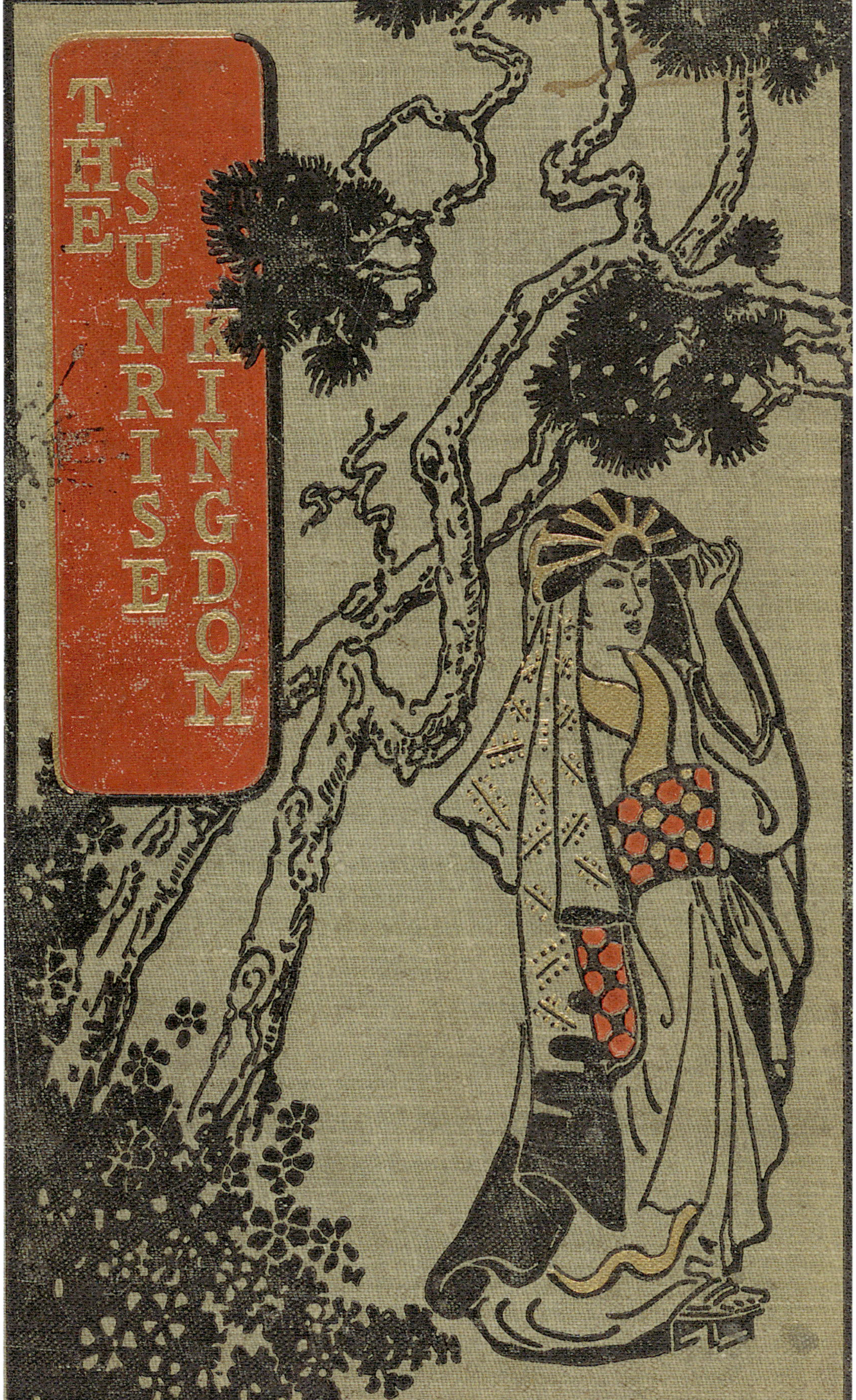
THE
SUNRISE
KINGDOM

I

They Went to Japan

The Post-Perry Travelers and Their Stories for the Young

On July 8, 1853, Commodore Matthew Calbraith Perry sailed with his squadron of four ships through the Uraga Channel and into Edo (now Tokyo) Bay. He carried a letter from President Millard Fillmore asking the Japanese for friendly relations and trade with the United States. Despite his forceful approach, Perry did not expect to negotiate an agreement with the Japanese during this first visit.

He returned on February 13, 1854. On March 31, after lengthy negotiations, Perry signed the first treaty with Japan, which would open the ports of Shimoda and Hakodate to trade. (A later treaty was negotiated in 1858 by Townsend Harris, the first American envoy.) In 1856, the official three-volume *Narrative of the Expedition of an American Squadron to the China Seas and Japan, Performed in the Years 1852, 1853, and 1854* provided thorough documentation of these historic visits.[1] Perhaps more intriguing than the richly illustrated official *Narrative*

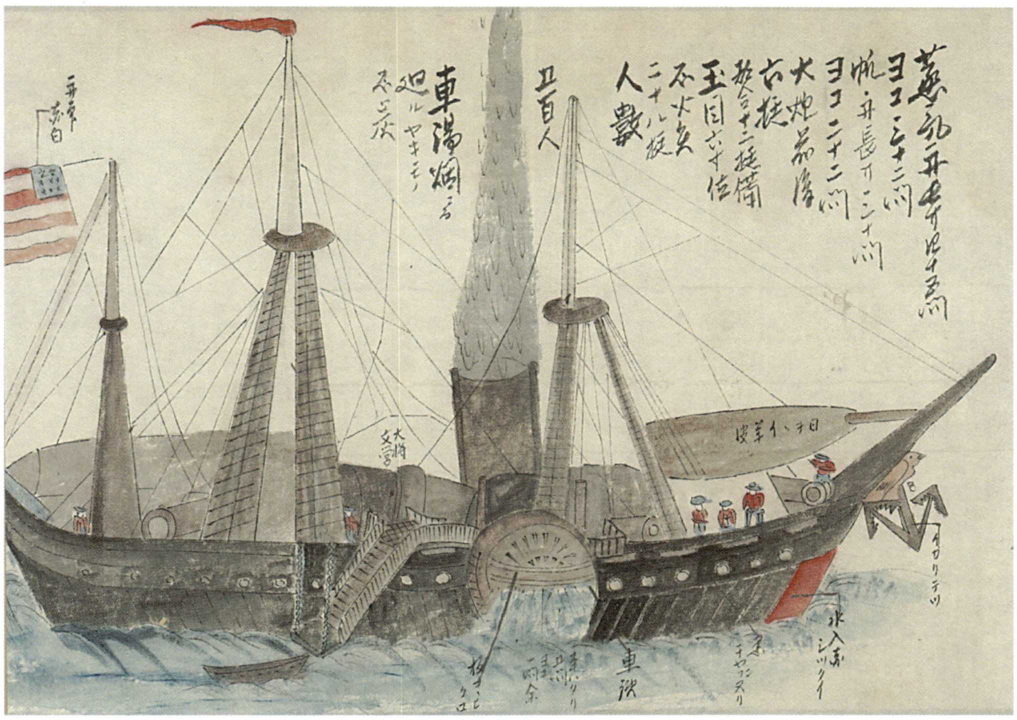

FIGURE I.1
Steamboat, possibly the U.S.S. *Susquehanna*, shown during Commodore Matthew C. Perry's first landing at Kurihama, Japan, July 8, 1853. Artist unknown.

OPPOSITE
The Sunrise Kingdom, or Life and Scenes in Japan and Woman's Work for Woman There, by Julia D. Carrothers. Philadelphia: Presbyterian Board of Publication, 1879.

was the eyewitness account of an inconsequential traveler who served as purser's clerk on the Perry expedition. Little is known of sixteen-year-old William Speiden of Washington, DC, whose father was Perry's purser. Yet Speiden's youthful excitement at participating in this great adventure is amply evident in the three-hundred-page diary that he kept from March 1852 to February 1855. Now held in the Library of Congress Manuscript Division, this extraordinary record includes the following excerpts.

William Speiden's Narrative

Journal of a Cruise in the U.S. Steam Frigate Mississippi
The first journey

Oposite [*sic*] the Town of "Oragawa"
Bay of Jedo Near "Jedo."
Friday, July 8th, 1853

As soon as we anchored a number of Japanese Boats came alongside . . . and endeavoring without success to put on board of us the usual implications to Foreigners to depart, left us and went toward the shore, w[h]ere they must certainly have all come to the opinion that we were a queer sort of people. From our ship was discovered that a large number of these Boats gathered around the Susquehanna [Commodore Perry's flagship]. And of these Boats containing some high functionaries, and perhaps a little more bold, went alongside, and were received at the gang way by Capt. Buchanan and some of his officers. Several questions were put to these Japanese Mandarins, by Mr. Portman, . . . who acted as Interpreter. . . . they were asked what the distance was to Yedo, they said it was eighteen miles or so, and also, whether the water was deep all the way, they said it was nearly all the way. The Japanese then inquired how many ships, guns, and Men we had, they were told that we had not asked them such a question as this, so that we could not answer it, and they soon left. Before leaving, however, ten Boats surrounded the "Susquehanna" . . . the Commodore . . . told Lieut. C. to say to them that . . . if all the Boats were not away in fifteen minutes, we would not be responsible for the consequences. They took the hint and soon vamo[o]sed . . . shortly after six o'clock, another boat . . . carrying the Governor of "Oragawa," went alongside the "Susquehanna," and he . . . being told the object of our visit and that we wished to have some one of high rank to whom to deliver the Letter so that it would reach the Emperor, replied that he was the highest person of authority at this place, and that it would be sure death to him if he delivered the letter, but if the Commodore wished he would dispatch a messenger to Jedo to inform the Emperor of the cause of our visit, that it would take two days for the message to go and the same time to come besides the detention while at Jedo. He was told that the Commodore would wait three days for a proper person to come and convey the letter, and if no one arrived in that time, he would go to Jedo, land men and deliver the letter himself.

"Oragawa," Japan. Monday, July 11th, 1853

> At nine o'clock this morning . . . hove up the anchor and stood up the Bay of Yedo, with four Boats (one from each ship) ahead sounding . . . All the way up the Bay, about one hundred Japanese Boats kept compassing with us . . . one of the Japanese [in the nearest boat] spoke out in good English and said "Do you go back," and then tried to throw us a line, by which we might tow him, this we did not do . . . Also while going up the Steam Whistle was got into operation, and blew several times, this seemed to terrify these People exceedingly, they stopped sculling, stood up in their boats, and looked with amazement, and seemed to say, "What on earth would we do next."

The following day, July 12, after much consulting among themselves, the Japanese agreed to "receive the Commodore and the President's letter on shore the day after tomorrow, as then there would be a proper person from Jedo, appointed by the Emperor to negotiate with us."

Jedo Bay, July 14th, 1853

> . . . At half past nine all the Boats stood off from the Flag Ship and went ashore, where we were drawn up in line to receive the Commodore. When we landed the Japanese to the number of six thousand were drawn up in line, along the borders of the Bay, their front files extended over a mile, and with their Banners innumerable and blue and scarlet pennants, presented a most beautiful . . . appearance. . . . The Commodore stood off from the Susquehanna at ten minutes before ten, and was saluted by them with 13 Guns. . . . Presently a White Boat with broad pennant painted on each bow, or otherwise called the Commodore's barge was seen to near the shore, and in a few moments of ten or at ten o'clock precisely, three long and loud rolls of some half dozen drums, proclaimed . . . that the Great Mogul had landed, and immediately the two Bands struck up Hail Columbia. Really, it made the blood thrill in my veins, to behold such an imposing and beautiful sight. . . . after showing the respect due to our Superior, we fell in, dividing the files of the Marines & Men, marched then all of us off to . . . the House built for our reception. . . . the officers went in, but the Marines were drawn up in front to prevent an attack although nothing of this sort was expected . . . The first room we entered was about 20 feet square, on each side there were paintings on oil of Birds, and other things very roughly done, around this Room on mats, with their hats in their laps sat a dozen or so of old Men but still of some account, with their heads hung down, looked as if their last day had come . . . On one side were four large Chairs intended for the Commodore and staff who on entering took seats in them, on the other side, were three chairs, one was occupied by the Prince of Edzu, First Counsellor [sic] of the Emperor, he was appointed by the Emperor to negotiate with us and I have heard that he ranks the same as our Secretary of State. This person's appearance was very gloomy and downcast, and his expression seemed to say that this was great fun for us but, it was anything else for him. . . .

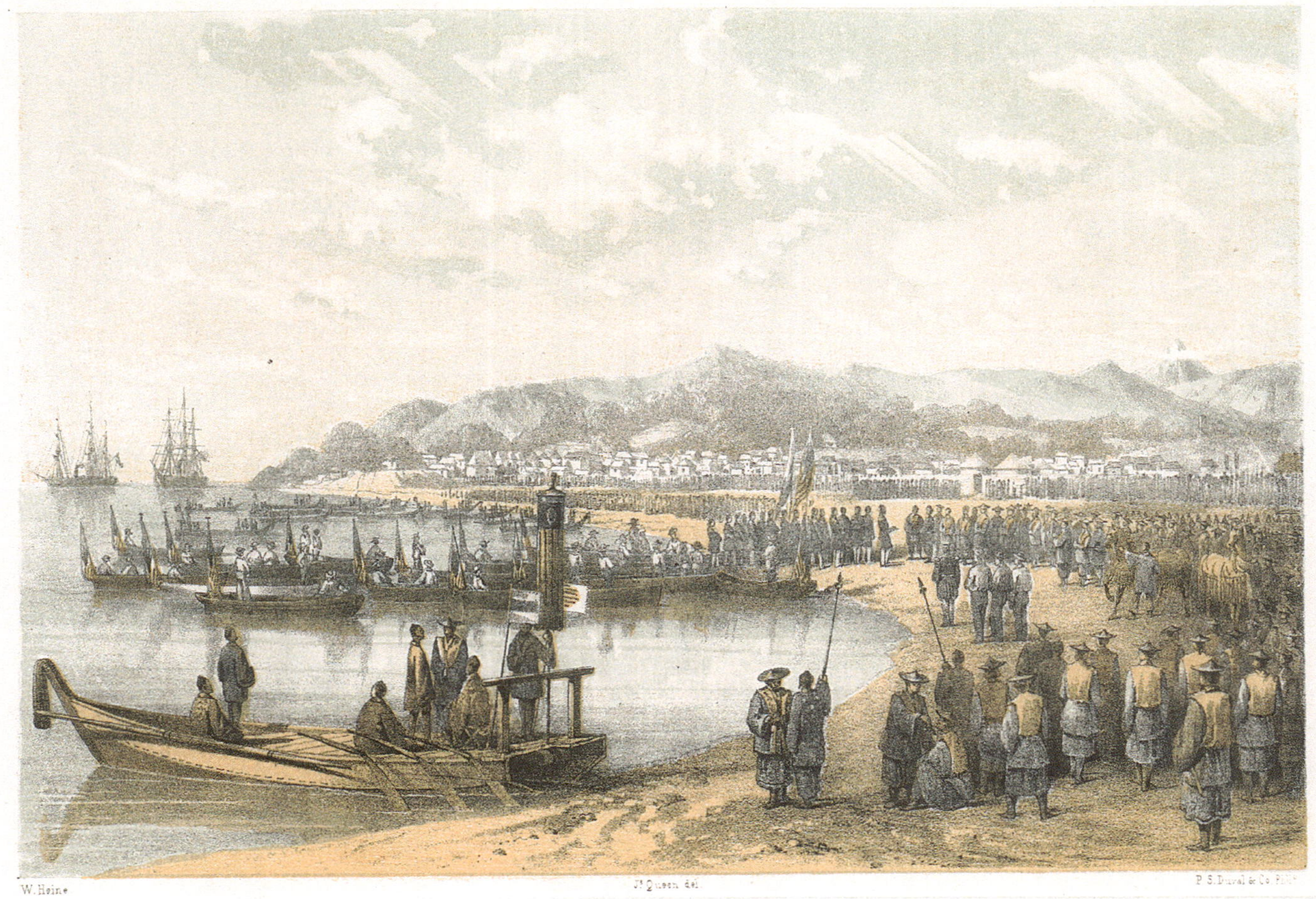

FIGURE 1.2
"First Landing at Gorahama," by Wilhelm Heine, lithograph by P. S. Duval & Co. Published in Matthew C. Perry, *Narrative of the Expedition of an American Squadron to the China Seas and Japan, Performed in the Years 1852, 1853, and 1854* (Washington, DC: Nicholson, 1856).

> The Commodore then told the Prince through Mr. Portman, our Interpreter who [relayed it through a Japanese interpreter, who spoke with the prince] . . . "That as he supposed it would take some time to give an answer to the Letter, he would return again next Spring to receive it, and that while we remained here he should survey the Bay and endeavour [*sic*] to find a safe and commodious anchorage for his Ships as he would bring a good many more with him." The Prince did not like this much but nodded in assent.

As the American squadron arrived a second time in Japanese home waters on February 13, 1854, Speiden described in his diary his view of Mount Fuji and surrounding mountains all covered in snow. Over the next few days, men of the squadron went ashore to make observations, "not disturbed in the least by the Natives, the few they met were sociable & friendly." On February 18, the Japanese visited Perry's flagship, the *Powhatan*, and engaged the Americans in an exchange of presents, mainly foodstuffs; Speiden noting in his diary that the Americans received much more than they gave. Then, on March 8, in an entry written at "Yokohama, Jedo Bay," Speiden described the second formal arrival ceremony, using information provided by the ship's chaplain, since Speiden, himself, was unable to attend:

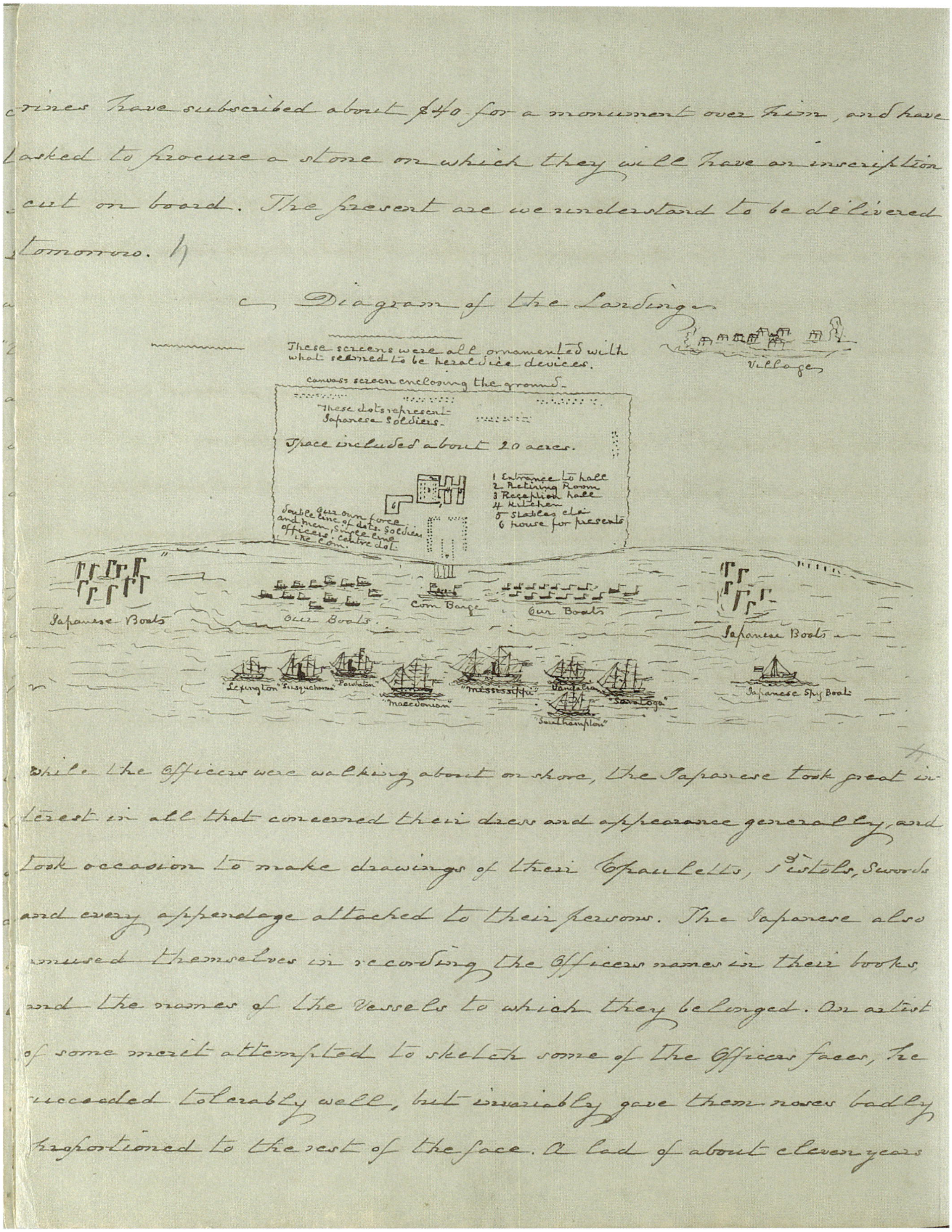

-rines have subscribed about $40 for a monument over him, and have asked to procure a stone on which they will have an inscription cut on board. The present are we understand to be delivered tomorrow.

Diagram of the Landing

While the Officers were walking about on shore, the Japanese took great interest in all that concerned their dress and appearance generally, and took occasion to make drawings of their Epaulets, Pistols, Swords and every appendage attached to their persons. The Japanese also amused themselves in recording the Officers names in their books, and the names of the vessels to which they belonged. An artist of some merit attempted to sketch some of the Officers faces, he succeeded tolerably well, but invariably gave them noses badly proportioned to the rest of the face. A lad of about eleven years

FIGURE 1.3
Sketch diagram of the second landing of Americans in Japan by William Speiden, Jr. Speiden Journal, vol. 1, ca. March 1854.

> Our own force comprised altogether about 500 persons. It consisted of the Commodore, his escort of 4 or 5 officers from each ship. 160 Marines with their officers. 240 Sailors armed with muskets, pistols and cutlasses with officers to regulate them. Three bands of music, etc. . . .
>
> The Commodore, as Ambassador was received on this Landing with the usual flourishes of drums, arms, etc., his escort forming a line with uncovered heads, as he passed up also uncovered, the officers closed into line behind him and were then conducted up to the reception room. (As they entered the hall the Japanese flag was hoisted in one of our boats, and the field pieces saluted it with 21 guns, and when the Japanese Commissioner was introduced he was saluted with 27 guns). . . .
>
> We then went over to their soldiers and still against their will, but without any rising of subsequent ill feeling, we inspected their arms which consisted of bows and arrows or matchlock guns or spears, the official having two swords, one a long and the other a short one, both very sharp. Except their swords, which seem to be more for show than use, their arms are of the most primitive kind, very neatly and handsomely got up, but again behind the times and of little comparative use in modern warfare . . .

On March 19, 1854, the U.S. ship *Supply* arrived from Shanghai with mail for the members of Perry's expedition. "Here we are in Japan," wrote Speiden, "the most distant [frontier] of the world from home . . . still we can hear from our friends in a little over three months." Five days later Commodore Perry went ashore "to receive the Presents of the Japanese in return for those sent out by our Government and delivered last Monday."

> The Commodore and his escort of officers and marines . . . were received by the Japanese Commissioners. The Presents, which were seven large [?] loads of Rice together with several large boxes containing lacquered ware etc., were delivered by the Commissioners and received by the Commodore who ordered the Rice to be sent on board the "Supply" and the other articles to the "Powhatan" . . . the Commodore and Officers were [then] led out into an open space by the side of the Reception House, where some fifty or sixty giantlike men were assembled and who performed some wonderful feats of strength, fighting, wrestling etc.
>
> March 27th, 1854
>
> [Reporting on a banquet Commodore Perry hosted for the Japanese Commissioners, which left Speiden hoping that "the Americans and Japanese will soon be on lasting terms of friendship":] After sitting at table about an hour and a half, the Commodore came up from below with the Commissioners and proposed that they should all go forward and hear the "Japanese old Minstrels" (a band of Ethiopians on board the "Powhatan") who by their comical acts while playing and afterwards dancing, afforded immense amusement for the Japanese, who kept in one [?] roar of laughter, being all a little tinged from the effects of "Old Tom," alias [*sic*]. Cherry Cordial

> and Champagne etc, I noticed one of the Commissioners who had taken over his allowance, threw one of his arms around the Commodore's neck, rest his head on his epaulette, and laugh and chat at a great rate. Really it was an amusing sight.

On March 31, Speiden recorded:

> I on this occasion was one of the few who landed, and who accompanied Commodore Perry to the 'House of Reception.' [Perry] and staff, went into the Audience Chamber for an interview with the Japanese Commissioners . . . the rest of the officers remained in the Banquet Hall [where] a feast was . . . set before us . . . After the Commodore and the Commissioners had been in private contact for some time . . . the long desired Treaty . . . of "Amity and Intercourse" was signed. Two ports are to [be] opened to us . . . [and] the Commodore [will] decide which ones we will take, it is believed that he wishes "Shamodi" [*sic*] for a coal Depot, and "Chak-a-date" [*sic*] for a resort for our whalers . . . While on shore, I saw for the first time, the little locomotive, car & tender, which was sent out by our government as a present to the Emperor of Japan, it is a beautiful thing.[2]

While young Speiden left us his lively first-person account of Perry's historic expeditions to Japan, surprisingly few American children's books describe these dramatic journeys and the events leading up to them. Some sixty years afterwards, Ruth Gaines did include a fairy-tale interpretation in her book *Treasure Flower: A Child of Japan* (1916), in which she compared the history of Japan to the story of Sleeping Beauty, "who dreamed away a hundred years . . . and was kissed awake one happy morning by the prince." Japan, before it received its first Western visitors, was, Gaines wrote, "a princess among nations" with "courteous and beauty-loving people," who welcomed visitors from Asia—and, at first, visitors from Portugal and Holland. Yet some of the early European missionaries engaged in practices that the Japanese found offensive:

> So the Princess Japan, pricked by the Christian spindle which she did not know how to use—unable to see that danger lay, not in the Christian religion itself, the gospel of love and self-sacrifice, but in the narrow-minded and grasping men who misunderstood the teaching of their Master, Christ—shut her bright eyes and fell into an enchanted sleep that lasted more than two hundred years. . . . The people lived as their ancestors had lived, bound by immemorial custom. . . . Yet even in sleep we do grow, else we die. And Princess Japan was not dead when the Prince came sailing over the Pacific Ocean and gave her the rousing smack which opened her eyes to the outside world once more.[3]

By the mid-nineteenth century, Gaines continued, many Western vessels were sailing in Pacific waters, and the United States, whose whaling ships and merchant vessels were among them, was offended by Japan's failure "to give

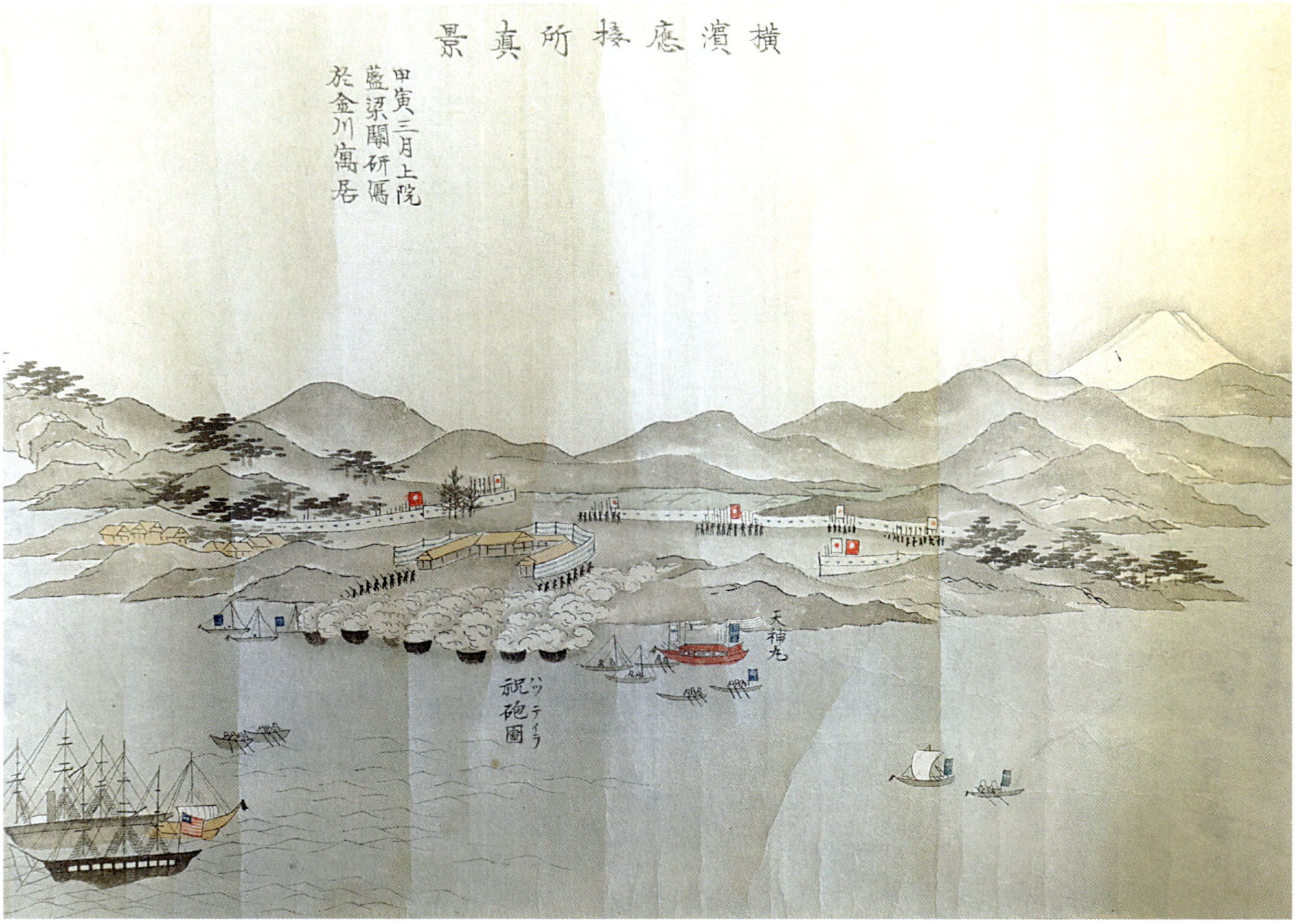

FIGURE 1.4
Kinkai kikan [Strange View of the Coast of Kanagawa] by Ōtsuki Bankei, 1854. U.S. Navy boats firing a cannon salute, depicted as clouds of smoke.

help to ships wrecked in her waters" and its cruel treatment of "the sailors who were sometimes cast away on her shores." This led, in July 1853, to the arrival of Commodore Perry and his armed squadron. "What do you suppose the sleeping princess thought when she saw those strange magic ships, sailing against the wind, without sails? There were no ships run by steam in the old days before Japan curled up for her long nap," Gaines wrote of the 1854 agreement to open two ports to American vessels for the protection of ship-wrecked sailors and the provisioning of ships. "And in August, 1856, our first American Consul General to Japan, Mr. Townsend Harris, arrived in Shimoda."[4]

After Perry Opened Japan

By the 1870s, Japan had become a great lure. "It is unquestionably the unique nation of the globe—the land of dream and enchantment," American missionary Arthur May Knapp wrote in 1897, "the land which could hardly differ more from our own were it located on another planet, its people not of this world."[5] In addition to the "blasé" tourists, the travelers to Japan included art aficionados, the *oyatoi gaikokujin* (foreign experts invited by the Japanese government), diplomats, journalists and writers, linguists, physicians, artists, teachers, and missionaries. Many wrote about their experiences and impressions, creating works for both adults and children.

Algernon Mitford, who has been called "the standard-bearer of Japanese studies,"[6] was an unlikely man to become associated with children's books. After graduating from Eton and Oxford University, Mitford joined the Foreign Office and served in St. Petersburg and Peking before being sent to Japan in 1859 as a member of the British Legation.[7] A man who boasted that his "life had been largely spent amongst men who in many lands made the history of their time,"[8] Mitford counted among his acquaintances Queen Victoria, Lord Randolph Churchill, James McNeill Whistler, and Oscar Wilde. Mitford traveled in Europe and the United States, returning to Japan in both 1873 and 1906. During the latter trip, Mitford, by then Lord Redesdale, accompanied Prince Arthur of Connaught and his delegation on their mission to confer the Order of the Garter on Emperor Meiji, an event to which Mitford proudly devoted a whole book (*The Garter Mission to Japan*, 1906).[9] A memoirist and "an uncannily brilliant linguist"[10] (he had learned Chinese while posted in Peking), Mitford immersed himself in the study of Japanese and was soon able to collect "from native sources," as he noted in 1871, "a quantity of legends of Old Japan which throw an entirely new light upon the manners and customs which have astonished travelers so much and of which they have made such an egregious mess in their books."[11]

The result of his research, the two-volume *Tales of Old Japan*, contains the classic "The Forty-Seven Rônins" and a broad selection of information about Japanese customs and traditions. He included facts about the rites and ceremonies (as well as tales) of the art of the sword (fig 1.5), wrestling (fig. 1.6), and seppuku (hara-kiri), which he was one of the first Western visitors to witness; the Yoshiwara (the pleasure quarters), marriage customs, and child rearing; and superstitions relating to

FIGURES 1.5 AND 1.6 "Forging the Sword" and "A Wrestling Match," in *Tales of Old Japan*, by A. B. Mitford, with illustrations "drawn and cut on wood by Japanese artists." Vol. 1. London, Macmillan, 1871, pages 71 and 204.

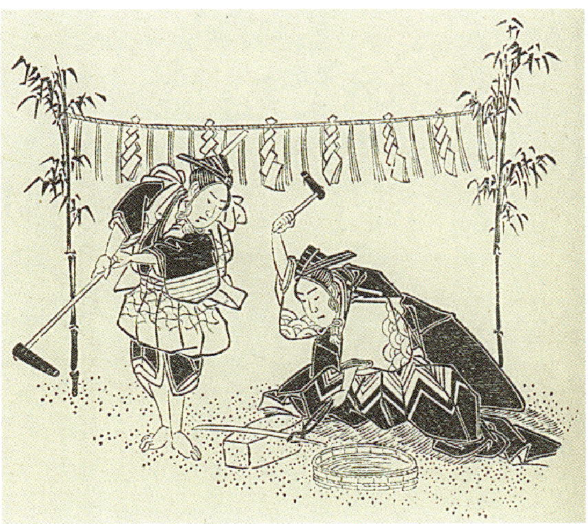

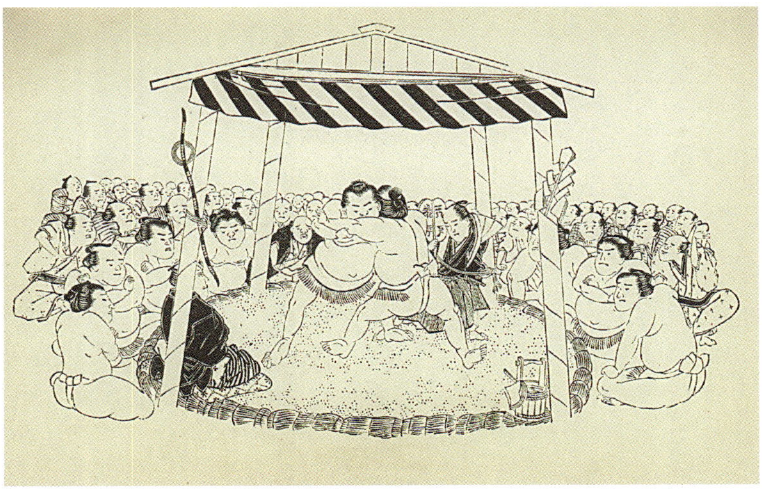

cats, foxes, and badgers—which in Japanese folklore can attain human form and bewitch human beings. He also included stories for children that are thought to be the first Japanese fairy tales to appear in a Western language:

> With the exception of that of the "Elves and the Envious Neighbor," which comes out of a curious book on etymology and proverbial lore, called the *Kotowazagusa*, these stories are found printed in little separate pamphlets, with illustrations, the stereotype blocks of which have become so worn that the print is hardly legible. These are the first tales which are put into a Japanese child's hands; and it is with these, and such as these, that the Japanese mother hushes her little ones to sleep. . . . those which I give here are the only ones which I could find in print; and if I asked the Japanese to tell me others, they only thought I was laughing at them, and changed the subject. The stories of the "Tongue-cut Sparrow," and the "Old Couple and their Dog," have been paraphrased in other works upon Japan; but I am not aware of their having been literally translated before.[12]

Mitford's wide-ranging *Tales* included "The Accomplished and Lucky Tea-Kettle," which miraculously transforms itself into a badger; "The Crackling Mountain," about a cruel badger who is justly punished; and "The Story of the Old Man Who Made Withered Trees to Blossom," which begins with the man's dog finding a pot of gold. His book immediately became a standard reference work,[13] appeared on lists of noted books about Japan,[14] and was deemed by one reviewer "one of the truest, appreciative, and artistic portraits of life and conditions in the Land of the Rising Sun that [had] ever been seen in print."[15]

While Mitford had a fine ear for language, American Helen Hyde saw Japan mostly through her artist's eye. Born in San Francisco, she attended art schools in New York, Berlin, and Paris. Félix Régamey, her art teacher in France, where he also headed the Museum of Japanese Art in Paris, "thrilled me with his descriptions of the loveliness of things Japanese," she once said, "and, as he had been to Japan many times and had lived there for long periods, he knew his topic thoroughly." While studying with Régamey, she "fully made up [her] mind to become a professional illustrator, and bent all [her] energies, for a while, in this direction."[16]

In 1899, Hyde sailed for Japan, where she stayed for more than twelve years. After living in Tsukiji, the foreign enclave, she moved to the Akasaka area of Tokyo, building there a fine Japanese house equipped with Western comforts and Japanese servants. To Hyde,

> Japan was . . . a new world filled with art possibilities beyond one's dreams . . . The difficulty lay in approaching my favorite subjects, the children. The little ones were shy of the "strange eyes of the foreigner," and the mothers really palpitated with fear at the consequences which might overtake their precious infants if I magically put them on sheets of paper. I literally had to secure a working vocabulary of the

> language, so that I could talk directly to the mothers, before I could get models for my paintings, and I had to enter, more or less intimately, into the daily domestic life of the womankind before I could secure anything like confidence. Those were days filled with delight and disappointments—delight when, in odd moments, I had been able to snatch from Japan some little darling in a brilliant-colored kimono and to transfer it at last successfully to paper; disappointments when, for love or money, I could find no one willing to rent me a Japanese house, because foreigners "were such dirty people, with their shoes and fires and things." Not that they, with their exalted forms of politeness, ever said so directly to me at the time, but I know now how they feel about their toy and immaculately clean little dove-cotes.[17]

Hyde became a commercial success,[18] but she had her detractors. After praising her oil paintings, color prints, and water colors "of Oriental provenances," a reviewer added:

> One hesitates to welcome [these pictures] as cordially as perhaps may be their due, because an artist who is not born an Oriental seems to be wasting time and energy while engaged in such work . . . for no matter how long one lives among them one can never become an Oriental. And then one runs the risk of losing grasp on Occidental ideas, people, and methods without becoming thoroughly anything else than an exiled Occidental. Such considerations, however, rarely influence artists, who follow the line of least resistance and very naturally continue to paint such pictures as find favor and sell.[19]

In 1901, Hyde published *Jingles from Japan as Set Forth by the Ghinks* (fig. 1.7). A reviewer who described the book as "quaint and good to look at" [20] echoed perhaps Hyde's own realization that her "baby books[21] and jingles [had] met with [only] fair success, [and that they] did not seem [her] forte."[22] String-stitched and illustrated in Japanese ink-painting style, *Jingles from Japan* featured roly-poly children, plum blossoms and bamboo, kites and coolies, farmers, geisha, and Mount Fuji. Hyde's sister Mabel (who visited her in Japan) concocted the light verses—which might have been the reason for the handsome album's limited appeal:[23]

> "Would you?"
>
> If all your doors were paper,
> And your windows too,
> And you nearly froze when the wind arose,
> What do you think you'd do?
>
> If your house had solid shutters,
> Which were put up in the rain,
> And with a knot hole's spark you sat in the dark,
> Do you think you would complain?

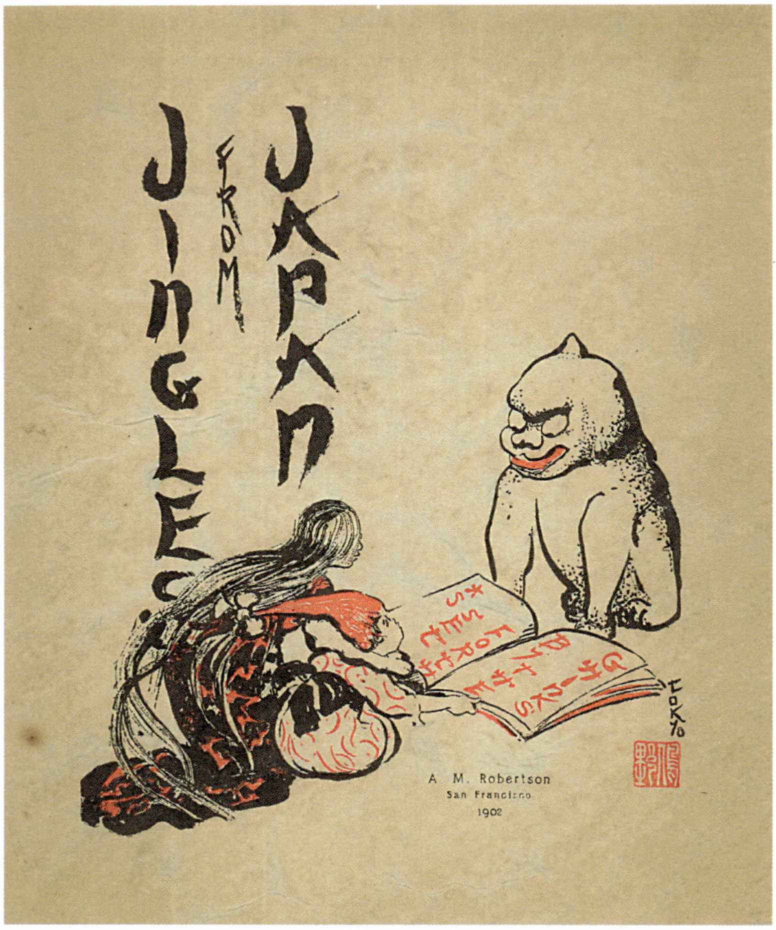

FIGURE 1.7
Jingles from Japan as Set Forth by the Ghinks, by Mabel Hyde, illustrated by Helen Hyde. San Francisco: A. M. Robertson, 1901.

> But when vicious little earthquakes
> Shake you to and fro,
> With sulky growl, and typhoons howl,
> It's time to pack and go![24]

What the two sisters meant by the book's subtitle "*set forth by the Ghinks*" is unknown. Are the "ghinks" the two impish Western girls featured at the beginning of the book? Was the term meant as another slight toward the Japanese, whom Hyde once described as "a people so lacking in physical beauty themselves that, like some of the ugly women we occasionally meet, they have cultivated a charm to compensate for their deficiencies . . . that . . . amply compensates for the niggardliness of fate."[25]

Although Helen Hyde's creations are held by the Library of Congress and the Smithsonian American Art Museum in Washington, DC, her name has faded. Not so that of the late-nineteenth-century Japan-traveler Lafcadio Hearn. Born in 1850 on the Greek island of Lefkada, Hearn grew up in Ireland and was sent to the United States at nineteen. He went to New Orleans in 1877 and worked there as a journalist. In 1890, *Harper's* magazine, which published his successful first novel *Chita* (1889), sent him to Japan. By the early twentieth century the books he had written for adult readers included *Glimpses of Unfamiliar Japan* (1894), *Out of the East: Reveries and Studies in New Japan* (1895), and *Japan: An Attempt at Interpretation* (1904).

Attracted to the exotic and occult, Hearn set out to retell the old Japanese tales which were, as Japanese writer Kiyoshi K. Kawakami explained in 1911, much different from Western fairy tales, as they rarely included fairy-like beings. Instead "[t]hey tell of weird doings of ghosts and spirits, grotesque performances of goblins and devils, and the witchery and mischief of badgers, foxes, cats, and dogs."[26]

Hearn's retellings of the tales—which may have been transcribed by his Japanese wife from oral sources[27]—include "The Boy who Drew Cats" and "The Goblin Spider," both eerie tales of monsters and goblins appearing in haunted temples; "The Old Woman who Lost her Dumpling," who outsmarted the wicked *oni* (monsters) and got away with their magic rice paddle; and the legend of Hamaguchi Gohei, the rice farmer who saved the people of his village:

> Hamaguchi's big thatched farmhouse stood at the verge of a small plateau overlooking a bay. . . . From its outer verge the land sloped down in a huge green concavity . . . to the edge of the water; and the whole of this slope, some three quarters of a mile long, was so terraced as to look, when viewed from the open sea, like an enormous flight of green steps, divided in the centre by a narrow white zigzag,—a streak of mountain road.

One autumn evening, as people in the village below were preparing for the harvest festival, an earthquake struck. "It was not strong enough to frighten anybody; but Hamaguchi, who had felt hundreds of shocks in his time, thought it was queer,—a long, slow, spongy motion . . . The house crackled and rocked gently several times; then all became still again." Hamaguchi watched the sea:

> It had darkened . . . and it was acting strangely. It seemed to be moving against the wind. *It was running away from the land.*
>
> Within a very little time the whole village had noticed the phenomenon . . . They were running to the beach . . . to watch it. . . .
>
> Hamaguchi Gohei himself had never seen such a thing before; but he remembered things told him in his childhood by his father's father, and he knew all the traditions of the coast. He understood what the sea was going to do. . . .
>
> [He told his little grandson to light a torch] . . . and the old man hurried with it to the fields, where hundreds of rice-stacks, representing most of his invested capital, stood awaiting transportation. . . . he began to apply the torch to them,—hurrying from one to another as quickly as his aged limbs could carry him. The sun-dried

stalks caught like tinder; the strengthening sea-breeze blew the blaze landward; and presently, rank behind rank, the stacks burst into flame, sending skyward columns of smoke that met and mingled into one enormous cloudy whirl.

To the villagers, the huge blaze outweighed the importance of the strangely behaving sea. All came running up the hill toward Hamaguchi's farm to help fight the fire. After a while, they looked toward the sea and saw something amazing and terrible approaching. . . .

"*Tsunami!*" shrieked the people; and then all shrieks and all sounds and all power to hear sounds were annihilated by a nameless shock heavier than any thunder, as the colossal swell smote the shore with a weight that sent a shudder through the hills, and with a foam-burst like a blaze of sheet-lightning. Then for an instant nothing was visible but a storm of spray rushing up the slope like a cloud; and the people scattered back in panic from the mere menace of it. When they looked again, they saw a white horror of sea raving over the place of their homes . . . tearing out the bowels of the land as it went. Twice, thrice, five times the sea struck and ebbed, but each time with lesser surges: then it returned to its ancient bed and stayed,—still raging, as after a typhoon.

On the plateau for a time there was no word spoken. All stared speechlessly at the desolation beneath . . . The village was not; the greater part of the fields were not; even the terraces had ceased to exist; and of all the homes that had been about the bay there remained nothing recognizable except two straw roofs tossing madly in the offing. The after-terror of the death escaped and the stupefaction of the general loss kept all lips dumb, until the voice of Hamaguchi was heard again, observing gently,—"*That was why I set fire to the rice.*"[28]

Like Lafcadio Hearn, Englishman Basil Hall Chamberlain published extensively on Japan. In 1873, the twenty-year-old adventurer arrived in the country where he would remain for more than three decades. A scholar who was "fond of learning new languages,"[29] he taught English at the Tsukiji Naval Academy before becoming, in 1886, professor of Japanese and Philology at the Imperial University of Tokyo. One of his students, Yuzo Ota, later described Chamberlain's amazing ability to "speak in Japanese of each [historical] period perfectly fluently, beginning with Japanese of the most ancient period"—and, in each case, "correctly . . . Even the great authorities of Japanese studies in our country cannot help being stupefied with sheer admiration."[30]

After publishing *The Classical Poetry of the Japanese* (1880), Chamberlain became the first to translate into a European language *Kojiki* and *Nihonshoki*, the ancient Japanese chronicles.[31] His other books included *A Simplified Grammar of the Japanese Language* (1886), the accompanying *A Romanized Japanese Reader, Handbook of Colloquial Japanese* (1887), and the widely cited, encyclopedic *Things*

Japanese (1890). Chamberlain retold or translated a number of stories for children, including *The Fisher-Boy Urashima* (1886), who, after descending into the kingdom under the sea, returns to earth to learn that everyone he had known had vanished a long time before; *The Serpent with Eight Heads* (1886), in which the otherworldly Susa kills the eight-headed monster; and *The Birds' Party* (1887), a tale of the Ainu (the indigenous people of northern Japan) in which a party is spoiled because Mr. and Mrs. Pigeon failed to invite Crow. (Chamberlain's works are discussed in detail in chapter 5.)

A frequently cited children's book of the time was written by Matilda Chaplin Ayrton, a British physician, who arrived in Tokyo in 1873 with her husband, William E. Ayrton, a professor at the Imperial College of Engineering. Upon her return home after a five-year stay, Ayrton wrote *Child-Life in Japan and Japanese Child-Stories* (1879), a lovingly painted picture of Japanese childhood. Written for her daughter, who was born in Tokyo, it was dedicated to her child's nurse. In her introduction, Ayrton wrote of all the things she had loved in Japan, especially,

> the babies, brown and half naked, scrambling about so happily; for, what has a baby to be miserable about in a land where it is scarcely ever slapped, where its clothing, always loose, is yet warm in winter, where it basks freely in air and sunshine, and lives in a house, that from its thick grass mats, its absence of furniture, and therefore of commands not to touch, is the very beau-ideal of an infant's playground.[32]

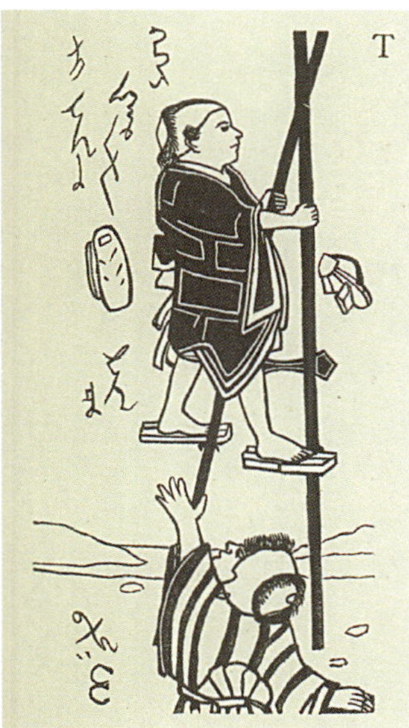

FIGURE 1.8
[Boy on Stilts] in *Child-Life in Japan and Japanese Child Stories*, by Matilda Chaplin Ayrton, illustrations "drawn and engraved by Japanese artists." London: Griffith, Farran, Okeden & Welsh, 1888, page 81.

Ayrton began her book with "Seven Scenes of Child-Life in Japan." Here, boys (girls are not mentioned) play in the snow, perform on their bamboo flute and drum, spin tops, romp with their puppies and pet turtles, and walk on stilts (figs. 1.8–10).[33]

The section of folktales (a number of which she received from Basil Chamberlain) includes the story of two girls who sacrifice their lives to keep their father from hunting; the tale of a Chinese mother who thrusts her son into the ocean hoping he would join his father in Japan; and the story of the young girl who, gazing into her mirror, believed the image to be that of her deceased mother. "The Games and Sports of Japanese Children," added as an appendix and compiled by William E. Griffis, highlights festivals—including Girl's Day and Boy's Day—and such children's games as battledore and shuttlecock, *go* and *sho-gi*, both popular Japanese board games.

Handsomely illustrated by Japanese artists, *Child-Life in Japan* was reissued in 1888 (Ayrton died in 1883). In 1901, an abridged edition, edited by William E. Griffis, was published for American readers.

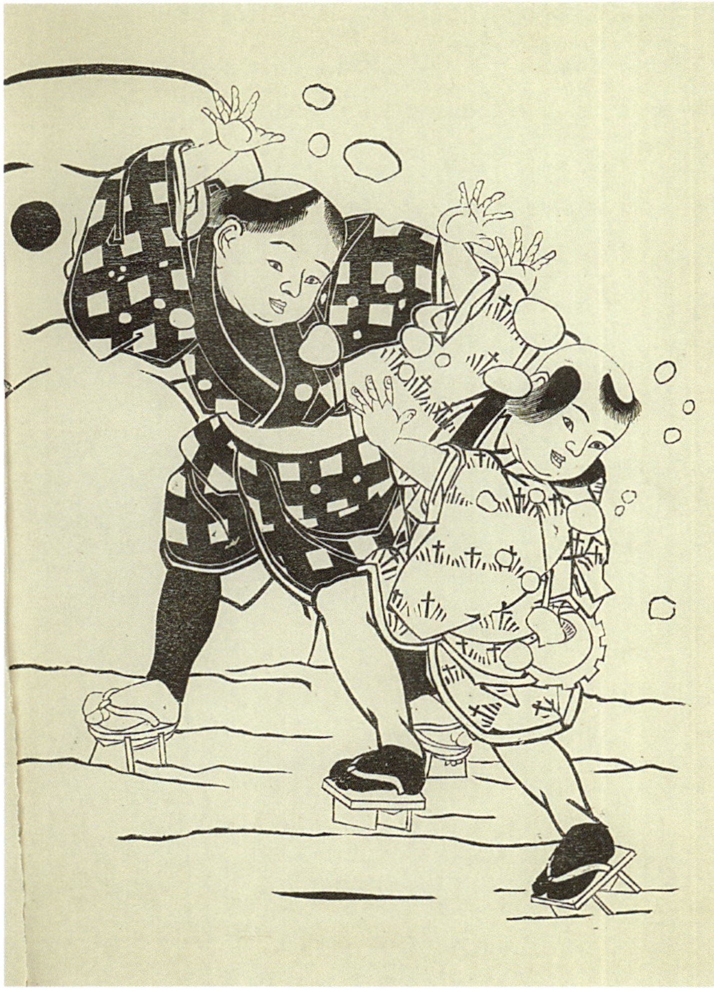

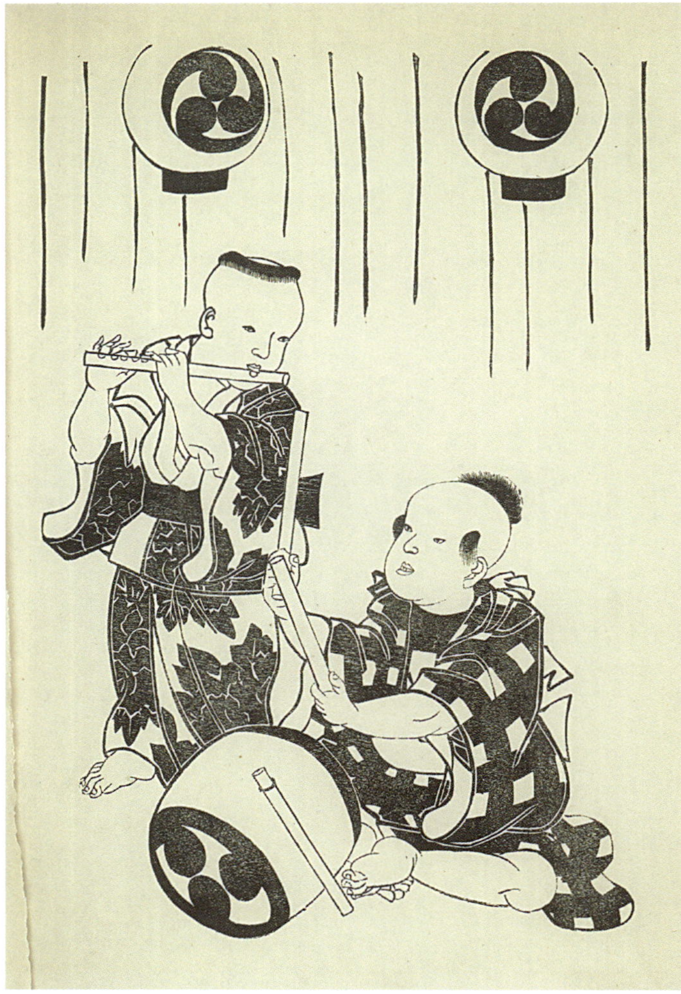

FIGURES 1.9 AND 1.10
"Snowballing" and "Musical Boys" in *Child-Life in Japan and Japanese Child Stories*, by Matilda Chaplin Ayrton, pages 4 and 6.

The Missionaries and Teachers

The greatest contribution to American children's books about Japan at the turn of the twentieth century was made by teachers and missionaries.

In her *All about Japan: Stories of Sunrise Land Told for Little Folks* (1905), American Belle M. Brain tells of the "great rejoicing . . . when the news reached America that Commodore Perry had opened Japan,"[34] and Christian people at once began to talk about sending missionaries. Among the earliest to arrive after Japan's ports opened to the United States were Dr. and Mrs. Hepburn of the American Presbyterian Church, who landed at Kanagawa in October that year. Brain writes of the "hard times" the missionaries faced:

> The common people were friendly enough, but the upper classes hated foreigners with a bitter hatred, missionaries and merchants alike, and they were in constant danger.
>
> "The foreigners have no right to come here and live on our sacred soil," declared the proud *samurai*, with their hands on their two sharp swords. "Let us drive them out of our land."
>
> Every day the missionaries expected their lives to be taken, or their houses to be burned down over their heads. Between the years 1861 and 1864 there was so much trouble that several foreigners connected with the legations were assassinated, and some new buildings of the British legation were blown to atoms.[35]

The official anti-Christian edict was not rescinded until 1873. "So for a long time," wrote Brain, "the missionaries could do nothing but learn the language and translate a few tracts and parts of the Bible into Japanese." But even learning the language was difficult, for few Japanese were willing to help them—and many of those who did turned out to be spies for the Japanese government. One even confessed to Dr. Hepburn, "When I came to your house to teach you Japanese, I did it because I thought it would give me a good chance to kill you."[36] Brain continued:

> But the missionaries were so kind and so patient that by and by the Japanese found out that they were not enemies, but friends. Dr. Hepburn was what we call a medical missionary [and] . . . was able to win many hearts by his skill in curing diseases and healing wounds.
>
> After a while the missionaries found another way to reach the people. The young Japanese were so eager to learn English that they were willing to come to foreigners to be taught. So some of the missionaries took private pupils in their homes, and others accepted positions in the government schools.
>
> Of course, they were not allowed to teach Christianity, but their influence was so strong that in after [*sic*] years many of their pupils became Christians.[37]

The American missionaries Julia D. and Christopher Carrothers lived in Tsukiji from 1869 to 1877. Julia Carrothers founded *Rokuban Gakkō* (later, *Joshi Gakuin*), a private mission school for girls, while her husband founded *Tsukiji Daigaku*, a men's college. After returning to America, Carrothers wrote *The Sunrise Kingdom, or Life and Scenes in Japan and Woman's Work for Woman There* (1879, fig. 1.11), in which she described a unique Japanese method of storytelling:

> One of the most singular amusements for children is called *h'yaku mo-no ga-ta-ri* ("the one hundred things"). A hundred tapers are put into a large saucer of oil and lighted. The children sit quietly down in a dark corner of the room, at some

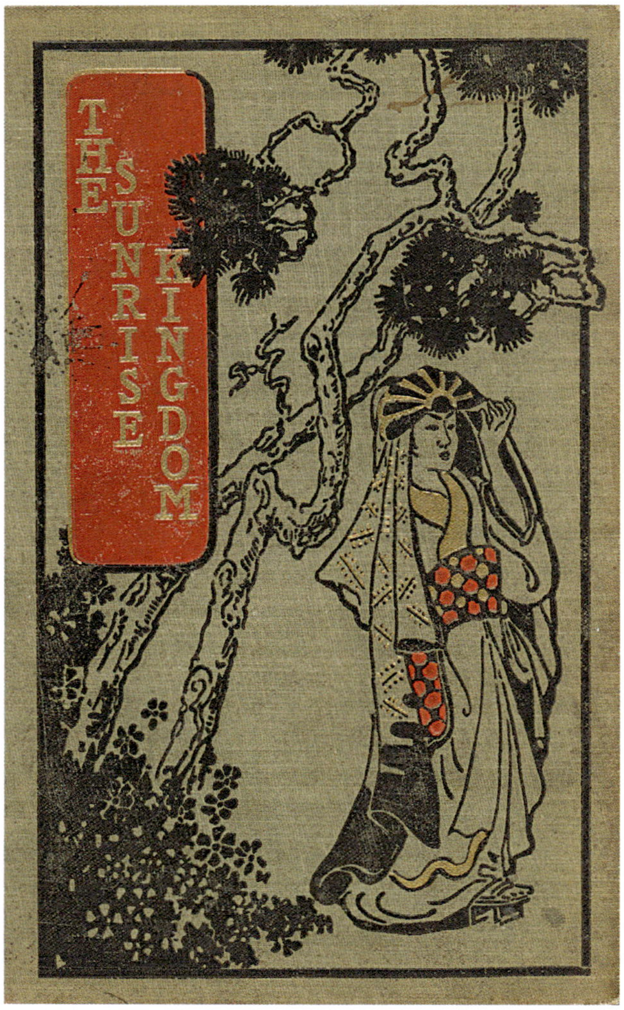

FIGURE I.11
The Sunrise Kingdom, or Life and Scenes in Japan and Woman's Work for Woman There, by Julia D. Carrothers. Philadelphia: Presbyterian Board of Publication, 1879.

> distance from the lights, and begin to tell ghost-stories, with which Japanese literature abounds. Then one child is sent to extinguish a light. When this is done, the story-telling again begins, when another child is sent to put out another light. The stories become more and more frightful in their character; the room becomes darker and darker as light after light is extinguished; the imagination of the children becomes more excited, until the room seems to them filled with hobgoblins and demons; and at last the screaming little ones rush from the house, and the game is over.[38]

Carrothers's long and detailed children's book, *Kesa and Saijiro, or Lights and Shades of Life in Japan* (1888), evolves around the story of Japanese children wanting to become Christians. It centers on Saijiro, son of a Confucian scholar and teacher and "the pet and pride of the villagers, who prophesied that he would be a scholar and fill his father's place in the school."[39]

When Saijiro becomes an orphan, he and other children are sent to school in the foreign concession at Tsukiji, where they are taught by American missionaries. Thereafter, the various characters wrestle with abandoning their "idols," secretly or openly confess to the religion of the missionaries, and come to question the old Japanese traditions and beliefs. Saijiro's studious roommate, Harukichi, who tells Saijiro that he wishes "to study and be a teacher of the Christian doctrine,"[40] even defies his parents. After praying that Jesus would give him strength, Harukichi feels his prayer is answered as he enters his home and bows before his father and mother: "I have been baptized as a Christian . . . and am going . . . to study to be a teacher of Christianity to my people. . . . O honorable parents, . . . receive me as your son." Carrothers continued the narrative:

> Then came angry expostulations and rebukes on the part of the father and bitter weeping from the mother. . . ."I hate the Christians," she said; "they teach children to disobey their parents. Oh, my son, I fear the wraths of the gods. And will you no more worship at the ancestral tablets, no more go up with me to the holy shrine, no more read with me the holy doctrines of Buddha?" . . . The poor woman rocked to and fro in her agony.
>
> "See," said the father, "you are crushing your mother with sorrow."
>
> Harukichi had risen and stood upright. "Honorable father," he said, "one of the chief commandments of the Christian religion is, 'Honor thy father and thy mother.' But when the commands of God are different from those of our earthly parents, we are to obey God. It grieves my heart to see my mother's tears, but, honorable, beloved parents, my resolution is taken; I am a Christian and shall remain one."
>
> Then said the father, "You know my will. Go out from my house and come back no more, nor expect anything from me, until you repent of your evil and return to the faith of your ancestors."[41]

In Carrothers's telling, Christian love overcomes all obstacles as the Japanese parents forgive and allow their children to follow their hearts.[42]

By far the most comprehensive contribution to books for young readers about Japan by a missionary-teacher was made by William E. Griffis, who felt that his calling to work in Japan was predestined. He noted near the end of his life:

> Providence so ordered that I should see, when almost a baby, the launching, in 1850, of Commodore Perry's (sometime) flagship, the frigate *Susquehanna*; that I should have as a classmate the son of our American Minister, Pryn, who had been to Japan; that I should during my four years at Rutgers College . . . teach the first Japanese students in America; that I should spend another four years in educational work in the interior and capital of Dai Nippon; that my sister Margaret Clark Griffis, should be principal of the first government school for girls; and that I should remain on constant terms of intimacy with Nippon's sons and daughters ever since meeting them at my home, at the Asiatic society, and in a hundred ways.[43]

After graduating from Rutgers in 1869, where he studied physics, chemistry, and mathematics, Griffis began to fulfill his destiny. Guido Verbeck, Dutch-American missionary in Japan and a member of the Dutch Reformed church—which had close ties to Rutgers College—was asked by Lord Matsudaira Shungaku of Echizen to recommend an American who could "establish a scientific school on the American principle and teach the natural sciences" in Fukui, Echizen.[44] Griffis arrived in Japan in December 1870, began studying Japanese (which he never mastered), gathered information for his future publications, and, through his host Guido Verbeck, met "several of the great daimios [lords] and many officers and Samurai who had been active in the Restoration [of the monarchy in 1868]." At that time, Griffis later wrote,

> it was uncertain . . . what kind of country New Japan was going to be. Everything seemed to me as strange as moon-land or the under-sea world. The Samurai all wore swords and top-knots, and many of them scowled at the American; the processions of the daimios were gay and full of fuss and show; the *kugé* [court nobles] had black teeth, spotted foreheads, and brick-shaped hats; the Eta, or pariah, were still treated as beasts in human form; and everything was strange, lovely, or horrible. It was Old Japan almost unchanged.[45]

Soon Griffis was sent to teach science in Western Honshu, traveling by "*kago*, jinrikisha, horse, steamer, and on foot . . . on sea, river, lake, and land, by way of Kobe and Osaka" until he reached Fukui, a "daimio's castle town," where he was "entirely alone, and hundreds of miles away from a white person."[46]

His initial reaction to Fukui was shock, and, unlike most of the early Western travelers in Japan, he frankly noted "the utter poverty of the people, the contemptible houses, and the tumble-down look of the city, as compared with the trim dwellings of an American town . . . I realized what a Japanese—an Asiatic city—was [and] I was disgusted."[47]

These first impressions were soon revised as Griffis was overwhelmed by Japanese hospitality. He wrote to his sister Maggie that his hosts "acted so generously *above* their contract, that it . . . move[d] me almost to tears."[48] Their generosity included providing him with a beautiful mansion "once belonging to an ancient Japanese family, and still bearing the crest of the Tokugawa family on the lofty painted gable."[49] Griffis vowed "to make Fukui College the best in Japan . . . to make a national textbook on Chemistry, to advocate the education of women, to abolish the drinking of sake, the wearing of swords," and also "the promiscuous bathing of the sexes."[50]

After returning to the United States in 1874, Griffis wrote some twenty books about Japan[51] as well as hundreds of magazine and newspaper articles, and he lectured widely about his experiences.[52] Among his best-known works are *The Mikado's Empire* (1876), which by 1913 had gone through twelve editions and was "the most popular early book on Japan."[53] He wrote books about major figures of his day, including *Matthew Calbraith Perry: A Typical American Naval Officer* (1887), *Townsend Harris: First American Envoy in Japan* (1895), and *Hepburn of Japan and His Wife and Helpmates* (1913).

For young readers, Griffis wrote histories, stories, and a historical novel. He collected and retold Japanese folktales. His articles about Japan appeared in the young people's publication *St. Nicholas* magazine as early as 1875. He even acquired Japanese children's books for his personal Japonica collection of bibles, Edo-period fiction, maps, religious texts, history, geography, games and songs.[54]

He also wrote texts for Japanese students of English, after a representative of the H. H. Bancroft publishing company asked him to produce "a primer, a speller, two readers, all filled with original matter suited specially for the Japanese," in addition to textbooks in geography, chemistry and physics.[55] With the help of his sister, who had joined him in Tokyo, Griffis produced, among others, *The New Japan Primer* (1872), *The New Japan Spelling Book* (1872, fig. 1.12), and *The First Reader of the New Japan Series* (1873).

Griffis's long and didactic *Honda the Samurai, A Story of Modern Japan* (1890) tells of a young man, Honda Jiro, who attempts to assassinate Commodore Perry but gradually comes around to his elders' views. Instead of killing the foreigners, Griffis's story advises, the Japanese need to adopt "their learning, weapons, and moral principles."[56] At first Honda Jiro is repulsed by the foreigners:

> The hairiness of their faces, the ugliness of many of them, and their curious dress and manners impressed him at first with intense dislike.
>
> When, however, he reflected on the substantial nature of their ships, stores, houses, and public buildings; as he occasionally saw a golden-haired child, or beautiful young girl; noticed the freedom of all, as shown in riding on horseback and in vehicles; and as he considered the mighty change that had passed over Yokohama, order came out of the chaos of his feeling and calm from the storm of his impressions. He went back to his inn with a determination stronger than ever to know the secrets of their thought and life; for beneath these leaves, he thought, must be strong, deep roots.[57]

After observing the work of American medical missionaries, young Honda becomes a Christian teacher, travels around the world studying education, and sends his son to an American school, while believing "in holding fast to what is best and truest in [the Japanese] national character."[58]

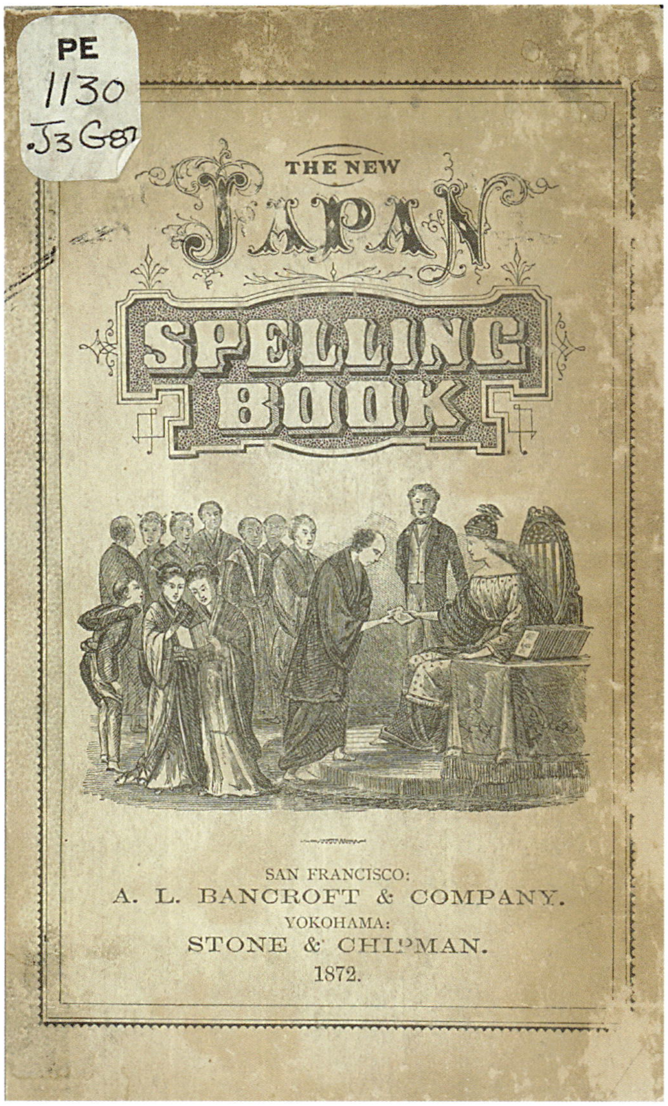

FIGURE 1.12
The New Japan Spelling Book, by William Elliot Griffis. San Francisco, A. L. Bancroft, 1872.

Griffis's *Japan in History, Folklore and Art* (1892), part of the *Riverside Library for Young Readers*, appears to be the first monographic history of Japan for young readers. Gleaning much of the information from his own *The Mikado's Empire*, it weaves myths, religion, folklore, art, and customs into a chronological tale of Japan's long history. About the momentous historical events that he had witnessed himself, Griffis wrote:

> The chief events since 1874 have been those leading to the promulgation of the written constitution of February 11, 1889, under which Japan is now governed. New orders of nobility were created. . . . The Samurai, now called *shizoku*, gave up wearing swords, and relinquished their hereditary incomes, paying taxes like the common people; the latter being admitted to the privileges, under restrictions, of voting for and in the local and national assemblies, and also of serving in the army and navy. The various classes below the *shizoku* were made one, the *hei-min*, or people. The land-tax was first equalized and then reduced. Local government was

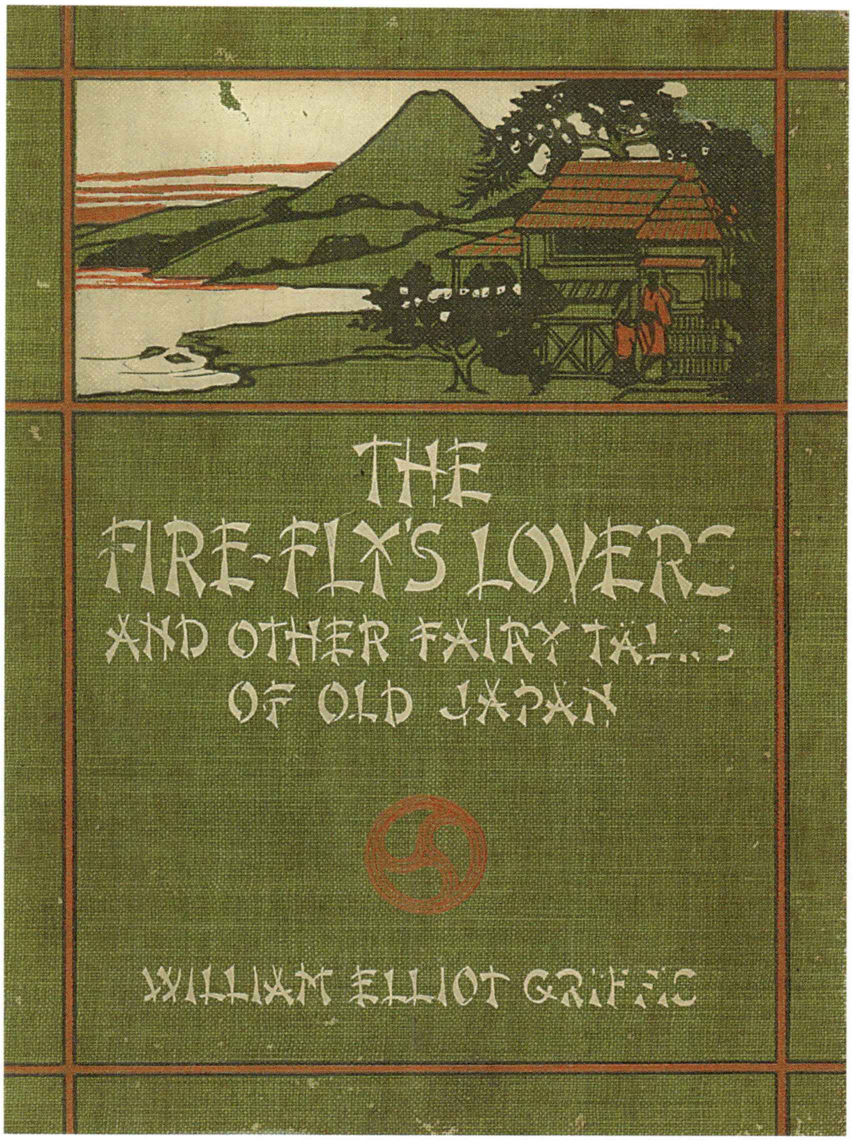

FIGURE 1.13
The Fire-fly's Lovers and Other Fairy Tales of Old Japan, by William Elliot Griffis. New York: T. Y. Crowell, 1908.

> introduced into all the *ken*, or prefectures, the Christian missionaries and native churches doing very much for the education of the people . . . The number of public officers and underlings was greatly diminished. In a word, government became national and uniform. . . .
>
> With her . . . hearty acceptance of modern principles of law and justice, with her railways, telegraphs, lighthouses, schools, colleges, postal and money systems, Japan now asks to be acknowledged and received by the treaty powers as an equal among the civilized nations. With her constitution, granting liberty of conscience to all subjects of the Emperor, and with her increasing Christian population, the day cannot be distant when tardy justice will be meted to her. . . . Japan [is] now one of the great Powers of the world.[59]

Griffis also published collections of folk and fairy tales, among them *Japanese Fairy World: Stories from the Wonder-lore of Japan* (1880, fig. 1.14). Perhaps his most notable contribution to children's literature, it became a standard reference work and helped to make Japanese fairy tales known throughout the West.[60] Among the thirty-four stories were the well-known "The Tongue-cut Sparrow," about the cruel and greedy wife who gets her just reward from the sparrow she injured; "Benkei and the Bell," about the stolen bell that Benkei the warrior monk has to return to its monastery; and the creation myth "How the Sun Goddess was Enticed Out of her Cave," the tale of Amaterasu who, after a fight, hid and deprived the world of light. About his passion for these children's tales, Griffis wrote:

> During a residence of nearly four years among the people, my eyes were opened to behold the wondrous fertility of invention, the wealth of literary, historic, and classic allusion, of pun, myth, and riddle, of heroic wonder, and legendary lore in Japanese art, I at once set myself to find the source of the ideas expressed in bronze and porcelain, on lacquered cabinets, fans, and even crape [*sic*] paper napkins and tidies. Sometimes I discovered the originals of the artist's fancy in books, sometimes only in the mouths of the people and professional story-tellers. Some of the stories I first read on the tattooed limbs and bodies of the native foot runners, others I first saw in flower-tableaux at the street floral shows of Tokyo. Some of the stories have appeared in English before, but most of them are printed for the first time.[61]

In 1926, when he was eighty-three, the indefatigable Griffis visited Japan one more time. "The only living American who saw the Japanese feudal system in operation, and witnessed its overthrow and extinction,"[62] and who had "resolved to be the interpreter of Japan in America, to make the man of the Orient and the man of the Occident understand each other better,"[63] he

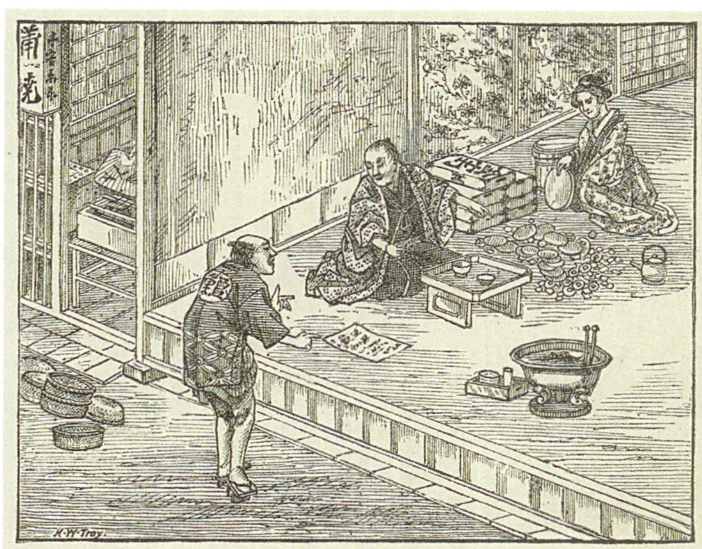

FIGURE 1.14
"A Jingle for a Sniff," in *Japanese Fairy World*, by William Elliott Griffis. Schenectady, NY: James H. Barhyte, 1880, page 206.

was lavishly welcomed and honored and thanked his hosts by giving "some 250 addresses."[64] A month before his death in 1928, he presented the Japanese ambassador with the manuscript of "Reminiscences of the Meiji Tenno,"[65] his final work about Japan.

More than half a century earlier, in 1871, E. Warren Clark had written to Griffis, his friend and former Rutgers classmate, about their dreamland, which "lit up our imaginations . . . [caused] our dreams to run wild in fairy land, [and sent] our poetic fancies . . . soar[ing] to marvelous heights."[66] With Griffis's help, Clark went to Japan as a science teacher and stayed from 1871 to 1875. A deeply committed Christian who had studied theology at the École de Théologie in Geneva, he refused to sign his government contract, which forbade any Christian teaching. However, the Japanese officials were so impressed by his steadfastness (or perhaps his sense of humor), that they not only withdrew the clause but turned a blind eye to his Bible classes.

Clark's *Life and Adventure in Japan* (1878), written for young readers, tells of his teaching at the Scientific School of Shizuoka, "the hot-bed of the 'Jo-ii' or anti-foreign party,"[67] where an attempt on his life failed, and at Kai-sei Gakko college in Tokyo. Although the Japanese paid him well and built him a fine, Western-style house, he explained that his sojourn in Japan was not "easy and dreamy" but filled with the hard work of supervising students and assistants, organizing classes "in various scientific departments, both theoretical and practical," and giving lectures "through the threefold medium of English, French, and Japanese."[68]

There are many lighthearted details in this lively view of early Meiji Japan (Clark even names one of his chapters "comical experiences"). One tells of his inviting the "ex-tycoon" for tea. The shōgun (Tokugawa Yoshinobu, the last of the dynasty) declined politely (on an elegant, perfumed note), sending, instead, an immense china bowl. It was so large that Clark could not resist climbing into it to have his picture taken. This gave one of his Japanese servants, the legendary Sam Patch, the idea to try it as a bathtub. Unfortunately, after he had poured several gallons of hot water into it, the exquisite present exploded with a terrific noise.

On a number of occasions, Clark performed scientific experiments which were "a constant source of delight to the Japanese."[69] On one such occasion, Clark reported,

> a number of Samurai gentry [were] on the back seats, who do not like foreigners very well, but who looked on very wisely, as though they understood every thing

> that was going on. As they declined to come up to the table like the other people, or to touch any of the instruments, I thought I would close the entertainment by sending them a few electrical compliments.
>
> At my request they all joined hands with great glee, thinking they were too far away to get hurt. I then connected my large Ruhmkorff's coil, which is a very powerful machine, with a battery hidden in the closet, and took the long wires to the Samurai gentlemen at either end of the line. They innocently took the wires, and the next moment I touched the key of the coil, and sent them an electric shock which tumbled the whole of them over among the benches![70]

The canny Clark also told of his ultimate and amusing "experiment": a picture show produced with his stereopticon, which took him to the innermost sanctum of Japan—the imperial palace.

> The empress and ladies of the imperial court were exceedingly desirous of seeing the beautiful pictures of western countries. But of course the ladies could not leave the palace; so I sent word politely to the lord chamberlain . . . that I would come to the palace and give the empress an entertainment, and that the Mikado might come to the exhibition if he saw fit.
>
> The offer was a novel one, as no foreigner had ever been admitted to the palace in such a way before; but my proposition was gladly accepted. . . . Accordingly, about eight o'clock on Tuesday evening I had my instruments set up in the palace, and the large curtain suspended from the top of the partition of the apartment. Two large screens were arranged around the instruments; where the officers at first fixed them so as to shut off the seats intended for the emperor and his household from all the rest of us in the room. But as soon as they had retired to give notice that all was ready, I made a slight and quick change, and pulled the screens backward, so as to make way clear for a larger picture on the curtain. I placed the Mikado's elegant chair in the little alcove, formed at the end of the zigzag screen, just to the left of my stereopticon, where he would have the finest possible view in the room. . . .
>
> I had requested Mr. Katz, of the Naval Department, to lend one of the marine bands to give music for the occasion. On riding up to the gate of the palace that evening I met *two* bands . . . marching up the hill; they formed in line in two companies, inside the gate, numbering sixty men in all . . . I placed the musicians in a side room to play the pieces appropriate to the foreign countries, the pictures of which would be shown in geographical order. . . .
>
> The emperor and empress were ushered into the room, followed by an impressive retinue, consisting chiefly of young ladies dressed in white, with their long, dark hair streaming behind, and broad red sashes encircling their waists; the effect was very pretty, and quite unique, as this charming procession of fair ones entered, and quietly seated themselves behind his majesty, while the band struck up the "Mikado's Hymn," and the word "Welcome," with the wreath of flowers, was thrown by the brilliant light upon the curtain.

Clark showed views of English and Scottish places of interest, many scenes of American cities and natural wonders, and scenes from European capitals—while a Japanese diplomat explained to the Mikado, who seemed "exceedingly interested" in what he was seeing. When the exhibition ended, Clark hoped to catch a good glimpse of the Japanese ruler, but preparations seemed under way to spirit the Mikado and his court away before he could get a good look at them.

> Science came to my assistance . . . The punctilious lord chamberlain knew not the marvelous potency of the magnesium light. No sooner had the fair retinue risen from their seats than I raised the magic clock-lamp from one of the instruments, and shot a broad beam of white light, dazzling as the sun, down the long corridor through which the procession must pass. In an instant the Japanese lanterns glimmered like fireflies, and the darkness of the corridor changed to daylight. The Mikado and empress passed out first, followed by the ladies of the court, who walked quietly, two by two, and hand in hand. . . . The fair young faces turned one by one toward the brilliant light, which their curiosity led them to look at, and I noticed the little dots placed upon their foreheads, which designated the highest rank of nobility. Some of the ladies were very pretty; they wore their hair in thick tresses down the back, which style is only allowable for ladies of the court. Their eyes were slightly oblique.
>
> The Mikado is a little taller than the average Japanese, with an open, fair countenance, having no decided expression except that of serenity. His profile is not very pleasing, but his forehead is high, and his eyes are manly and expressive. His dark hair curls a little at the temples. He steps with ease and carries his figure erect. On the whole, the Mikado is a sensible man and a good emperor, but as "god" he is fast becoming a failure.[71]

In 1875, after four years in Japan, Clark decided to leave, saying sayonara to a country that had affected him deeply:

> As I reached the steamer, all was quiet on board, and the rain-drops were pattering on the slippery deck. The night was dark, and the wind whistled mournfully through the rigging as I went below. At early dawn the steamer was sailing down the harbor, bound for Shanghai, China. The Japanese sun-flag floated at the stern, for the vessel belonged to the new Japanese line of the "Mitsu-Bishi" Company. I looked out of the cabin window at the murky waters of the Yellow Sea, and realized at last that I was face to face with all the dread uncertainties of a long and lonely journey around the world.[72]

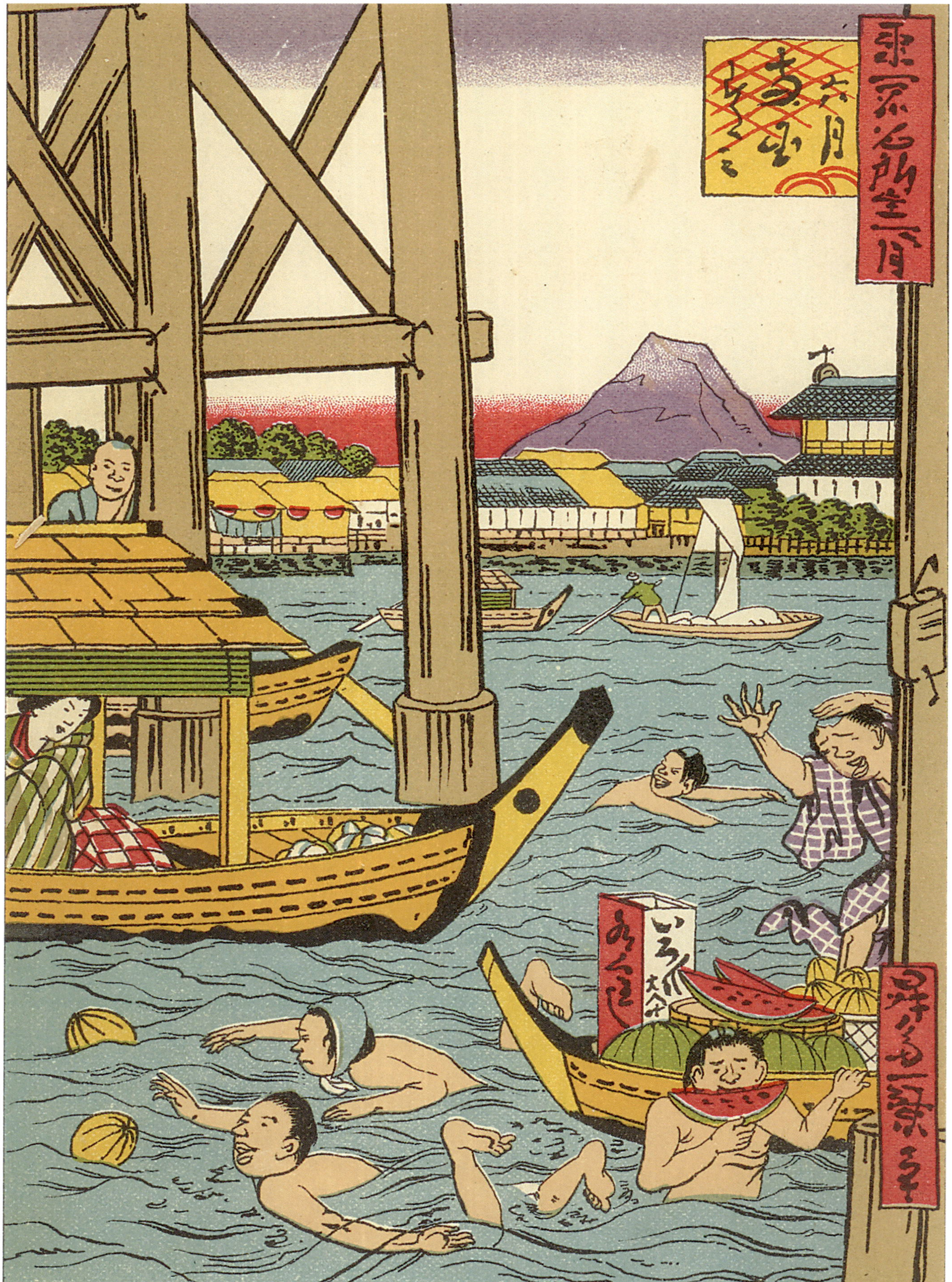

2

Fact and Fiction

Travelogues and Adventure Tales about Japan to the Turn of the Twentieth Century

By the 1880s, American children's books were coming into their own. A writer in the literary magazine *The Dial* noted:

> So much of the time and talent of authors and artists, and so much of the enterprise of publishers, are concentrated upon the production of juvenile literature nowadays, that grown folks may be pardoned if some sparks of envy are enkindled in their breasts. To think of the dearth of children's books when we, but one or two generations back, were young! How should we have stared to see the piles upon piles of beautiful volumes to-day heaped upon the shelves and counters of book dealers, resplendent in gilded covers and crowded with exquisite engravings, plain and colored, in illustrations of the most captivating stories, sketches, and poems, and all for the delectation of readers ranging from the one and two year old toddling in the nursery up to the boy and girl of sixteen![1]

While all of the children's books published in the United States during the first half of the nineteenth century would have filled no more than a small bookcase, children's books now appeared in publishers' catalogs[2] and were reviewed in newspapers and magazines.[3] American books such as Louisa May Alcott's *Little Women* (1868), Mark Twain's *Tom Sawyer* (1876), and L. Frank Baum's *The Wonderful Wizard of Oz* (1900) were becoming as popular as imported classics, including Lewis Carroll's *Alice's Adventures in Wonderland* (1866), Robert Louis Stevenson's *Treasure Island* (1883), and the Grimm Brothers' *Household Tales* (1861). At the same time, American children's books also began dealing with people and places far beyond the nation's borders. An article aimed at young audiences, printed in the *Los Angeles Times* in 1892, reflected that mood. While walking through the hustle and bustle of "passing teams, and the hurry and rush of the street cars" in Los Angeles, the writer decided to take his readers on an imaginary journey to Tokyo, in the "far-off island Kingdom of Japan":

OPPOSITE
Adventures of Two Youths in a Journey to Japan and China, by Thomas W. Knox. New York: Harper & Brothers, 1880, frontispiece.

> I wonder—thought I, how it would seem to live in a big city where there were neither horses nor street cars, and where all people, even invalids and little children,

> could move about at their leisure without danger of accident . . . where everybody rides in the queer little two-wheeled carriages, called jinrikishas, which are pushed along by steeds that never shy or break their harness and run away . . . I hope that you will read some of the many books written about this wonderful island-kingdom of Japan and learn much more of its interesting people.[4]

Among the books about Japan which were part of this children's book blossoming were autobiographical narratives, boys' adventure books, sweet stories for girls, and a new genre, the travelogue. Combining fact and fiction, travelogues attempted mostly to use stories to instruct. Even Mary Mapes Dodge, author of the popular *Hans Brinker, or The Silver Skates* (1865, fig. 2.1), admitted that her true motive for writing the story had been pedagogical, "to give my young readers a just idea of Holland and its resources, . . . present true pictures of its inhabitants and their everyday life . . . [and] free them of certain current prejudices concerning that noble and enterprising people."[5]

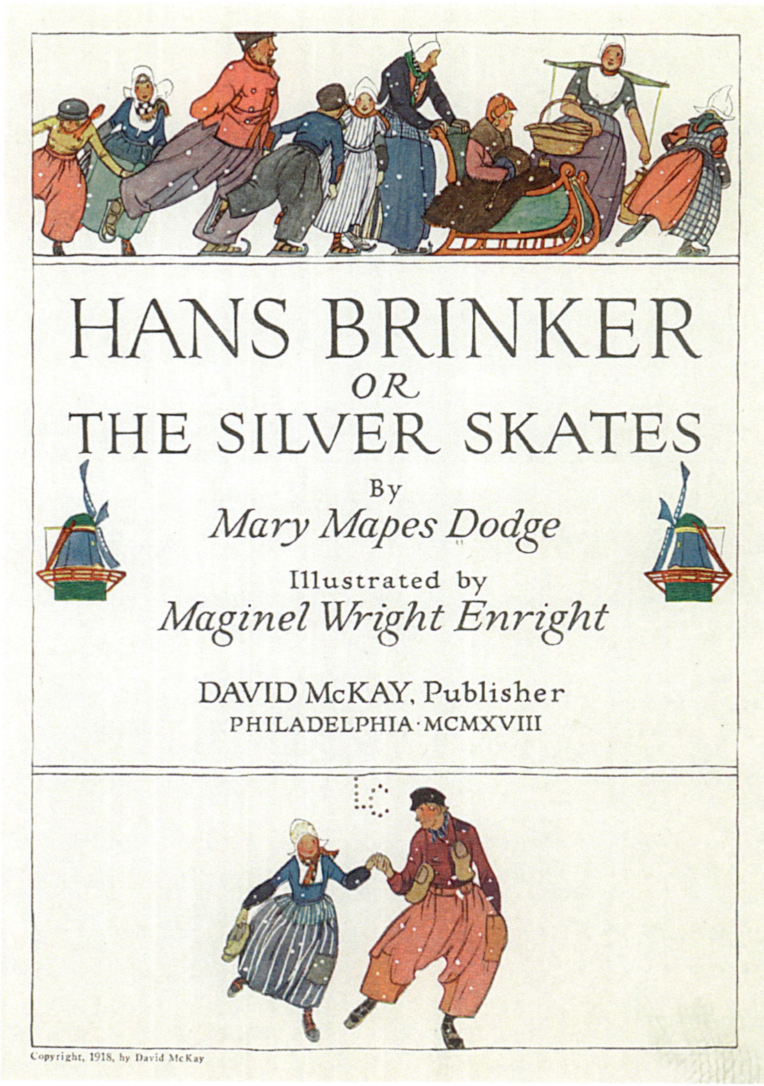

HANS BRINKER
OR
THE SILVER SKATES
By
Mary Mapes Dodge
Illustrated by
Maginel Wright Enright
DAVID McKAY, Publisher
PHILADELPHIA·MCMXVIII

Copyright, 1918, by David McKay

FIGURE 2.1
Hans Brinker, or The Silver Skates, by Mary Mapes Dodge. Philadelphia: David McKay, 1918.

However, few writers possessed Dodge's skill at weaving information unobtrusively into a good story. Generally, travelogue authors used the clumsy device of a teacher or guardian who accompanied young travelers on their journeys and who took every opportunity to inundate them with lengthy and didactic lectures. Tudor Jenks's *The Century World's Fair Book for Boys and Girls: Being the Adventures of Harry and Philip with Their Tutor, Mr. Douglass, at the World's Columbian Exposition* (1893) and Edward A. Rand's *All Aboard for Sunrise Lands: A Trip through California across the Pacific to Japan, China and Australia* (1883) are typical examples. Yet, despite these shortcomings, travelogues, which were often handsomely produced, were so popular that publishers happily gave in to the demand for more.

One of the most prolific travel writers for young people, Hezekiah Butterworth, was so successful at producing these travel stories that he is said to have become a "literary millionaire."[6] An assistant editor of the *Youth's Companion* from 1870 to 1894 and a contributor to the *Atlantic Monthly*, *St. Nicholas* magazine, and *Wide Awake*, Butterworth also wrote and edited a number of histories and biographies, including *Young Folks' History of America* (1881), *In the Boyhood of Lincoln* (1892), and *In the Days of Jefferson* (1900).

Butterworth began his series, *Zigzag Journeys*, with *Zigzag Journeys in Europe* (1880),[7] which he wrote before ever setting foot on the continent. Sixteen more volumes followed, among them *Zigzag Stories in the Occident* (1883), *Zigzag Stories in India* (1887), and *Zigzag Journeys around the World* (1895).[8] Eventually Butterworth did visit Europe, Canada, Cuba, and South America, yet he also continued to write books about countries he never saw, including India, the British Isles, and Japan.

In the deluxe edition of *Zigzag Journeys around the World* (1895, fig. 2.2), the last book in the series, which featured a splendid cover with gold-embossed lettering and images of Mount Fuji and flying cranes, Butterworth wrote:

> Japan has gone to the front of the Asiatic world. India is enslaved; China, with her long history and teeming millions of population, stands on the defensive with an unheroic record. . . . Japan has caught the spirit of the Western World. She has been studying all the arts of progress. . . . The secret of her sudden rise and progress is education.[9]

Aside from introducing the Japanese land and people, whom he describes as "honest, clean, and frugal, with a high sense of honor,"[10] Butterworth highlights customs that the early travelers found especially exotic, including:

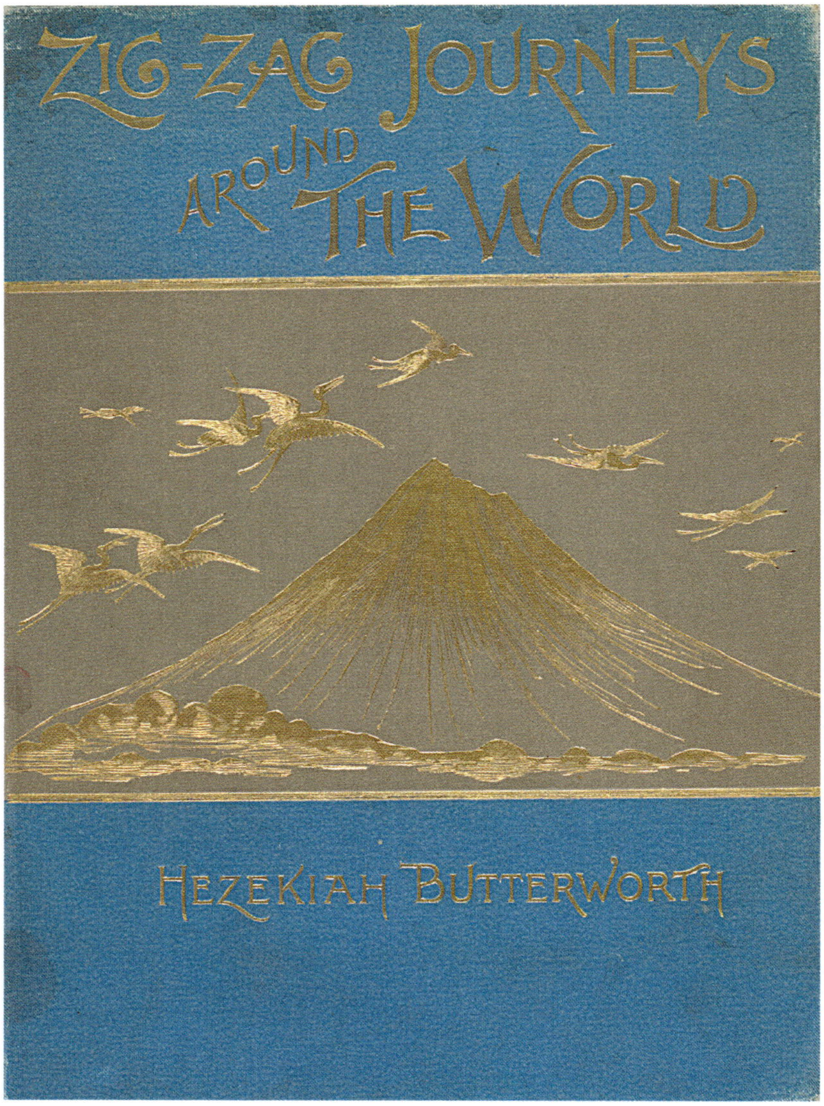

FIGURE 2.2
Zigzag Journeys around the World, by Hezekiah Butterworth. Boston: Estes and Lauriat, 1895.

> hara-kiri, or the committing of suicide by two cross-cuts on the abdomen by a short-pointed knife. When a maiden marries, her teeth are blackened, her eyebrows plucked out, and she makes herself as *ugly* as possible.[11]

Important Writers of the Late Nineteenth Century

If Hezekiah Butterworth's Japan report was secondhand, two other writers more than made up for his shortcomings. Not only had Thomas Knox and Edward Greey traveled to Japan, their travelogues provided the most extensive and substantial information about Japan in any books for young American readers at the time. Knox, like Butterworth, became a literary phenomenon. He and his travel books were so popular among young men about to reach voting age, one article declared, "that, if nominated for President of the United States a few years hence, he would stand a good chance of election."[12]

Born in New Hampshire, Thomas Wallace Knox left school at age ten, then worked as a farmhand, a teacher, and as headmaster of a school he founded in Kingston, New Hampshire. A voracious reader, he was inspired by *Robinson Crusoe* and the Peter Parley books and, even as a child, dreamed of exotic travel. After working as a reporter for the *Denver Daily News* and serving a brief stint in the army during the Civil War, he became a correspondent for the *New York Herald*, a job that sent him on his first journey around the world. Three years later, Knox went on an extensive trip to Siberia, Mongolia, China, western Russia, and France. His articles for the *New York Herald* were published as *Overland through Asia* (1870).

An enterprising man and an inventor as well, Knox became the first representative of the Western Associated Press in New York and in 1873 reported on the Vienna International Exposition—the first international exposition in which the Japanese government officially participated. After touring the Middle East, he went on yet another round-the-world trip in 1877, this time stopping in China, Siam, and Japan.[13]

In *Adventures of Two Youths in a Journey to Japan and China* (1879, figs. 2.3–4), which Knox believed was the first volume of its kind for young readers, the author noted that, while the characters in the book were fictitious,

> The routes they traveled, the cities they visited, the excursions they made, the observations they recorded—in fact, nearly all that goes to make up this volume—were the actual experiences of the author at a very recent date. In a few instances I have used information obtained from others, but only after careful investigation has convinced me of its entire correctness. I have aimed to give a faithful picture of Japan and China as they appear to-day.[14]

A Dr. Bronson—who had traveled twice around the world and who spoke several languages—is cast as the tutor of Frank Bassett and his cousin Fred. When the three travelers arrive in Yokohama, Japan, Bronson's job begins in earnest. After their first excursion and their observation of the "dignified natives," he begins his encyclopedic tutorials, which cover topics from fire ladders to festivals, from *kosatsu* (government sign-boards) to teeth blackening.

Knox's characters admired the Japanese. "The more I see of the Japanese, the more I like them," one of the boys says, "and think them a kind-hearted and happy people."[15] Knox also takes sides when he comments on Japan's seclusion policy:

> The Japanese had been exclusive for a long time, and wished to continue so. They had had an experience of foreign relations two hundred years ago . . . It was

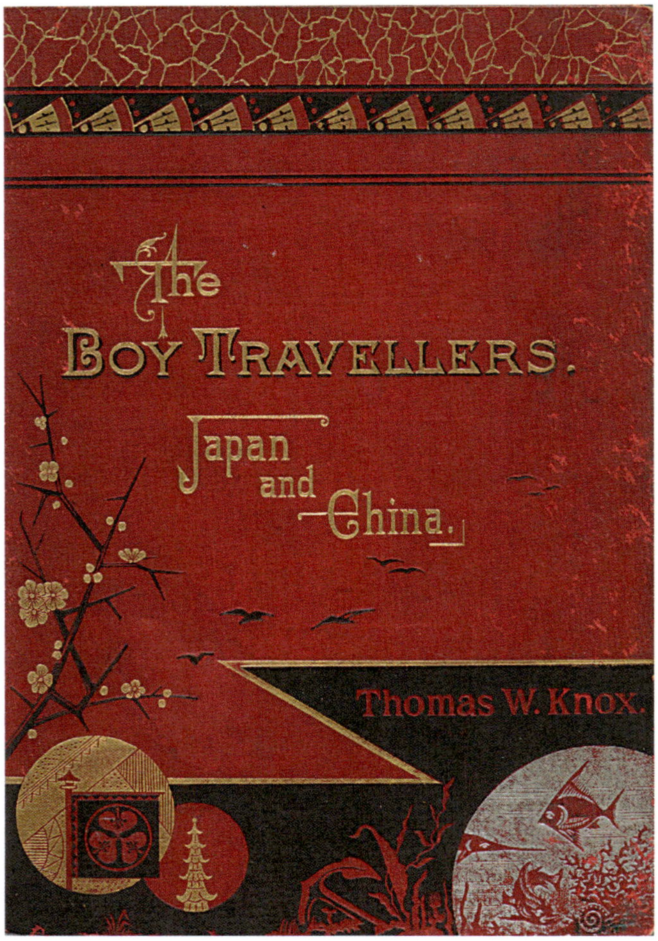

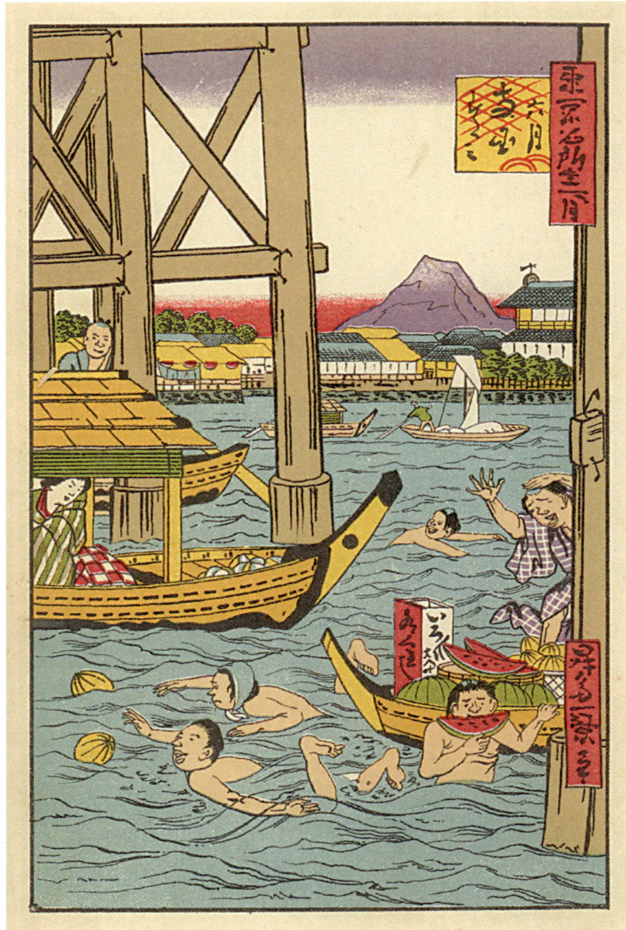

FIGURES 2.3 AND 2.4
Adventures of Two Youths in a Journey to Japan and China, by Thomas W. Knox. New York: Harper & Brothers, 1880, cover and frontispiece.

unsatisfactory, and they chose to shut themselves up and live alone. If we wanted to shut up the United States, and admit no foreigners among us, we should consider it a matter of great rudeness if they forced themselves in, and threatened to bombard us when we refused them admittance. We were the first to poke our noses into Japan, when we sent Commodore Perry here with a fleet. The Japanese tried their best to induce us to go away and let them alone, but we wouldn't go. We stood there with a copy of the treaty in one hand, and had the other resting on a cannon charged to the muzzle and ready to fire. We said, "Take the one or the other; sign a treaty of peace and good-will and accept the blessings of civilization, or we will blow you so high in the air that the pieces won't come down for a week."[16]

While Knox was compiling his encyclopedic work, Edward Greey was doing much the same thing. A poet, writer, translator, would-be playwright, and art connoisseur,[17] Greey was born in Sandwich, England and, after a military education, became, in 1860, a captain in the British Army. He was sent to China, then to Japan, where he became an attaché of the British Legation.[18]

Greey wrote and translated a number of plays and books, among them *A Captive of Love* (1886), a retelling of one of the dramatic and popular *yomi hon*

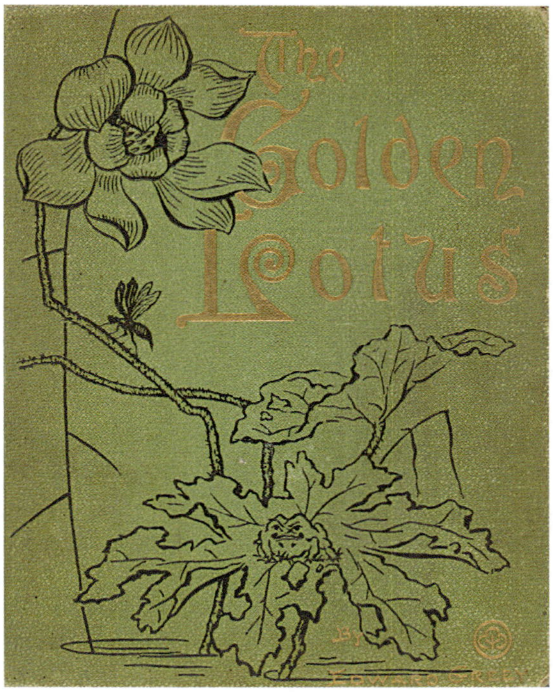

FIGURE 2.5
The Golden Lotus and Other Legends of Japan, by Edward Greey. Boston: Lothrop, Lee & Shepard, 1905.

(books for reading) by Takizawa Bakin, and Tamenaga Shunsui's *The Loyal Ronins: A Historical Romance* (1884), the classic story of the forty-seven rōnins, which he translated with Shiuichiro Saito. In *The Golden Lotus and Other Legends of Japan* (1883, fig. 2.5), a handsome volume for which he also drew the cover design, Greey assembled bits of Japanese tales. He interspersed these with his own impressions of Japan, which he had also included in several previously published articles on such topics as Japanese theater,[19] street performers,[20] and food.[21] Greey's description of the *moji-yaki*, the street vendor who cooked sweets on his portable griddle,[22] a scene described in many an American children's book, is but one example of the writing that earned him well-deserved praise in the *New York Times*, which called his descriptions of Japanese scenes "so novel and crisp, so light-hearted and good-humored, that it makes the reader long for a ticket from San Francisco to Yokohama."[23]

Greey was the first writer of books for young Americans who had lived in Japan for an extended period. In addition to speaking Japanese, he could also read it—a much more difficult achievement. His travelogues, *Young Americans in Japan; or, The Adventures of the Jewett Family and Their Friend Oto Nambo* (fig. 2.6) and its sequels *The Wonderful City of Tokio; or, Further Adventures of the Jewett Family and Their Friend Oto Nambo,* and *The Bear-Worshippers of Yezo and the Island of Karafuto (Saghalin),*[24] were published in the early 1880s to great reviews and became the most cited works about Japan for juveniles for years to come. In the preface to the first volume of the trilogy he wrote:

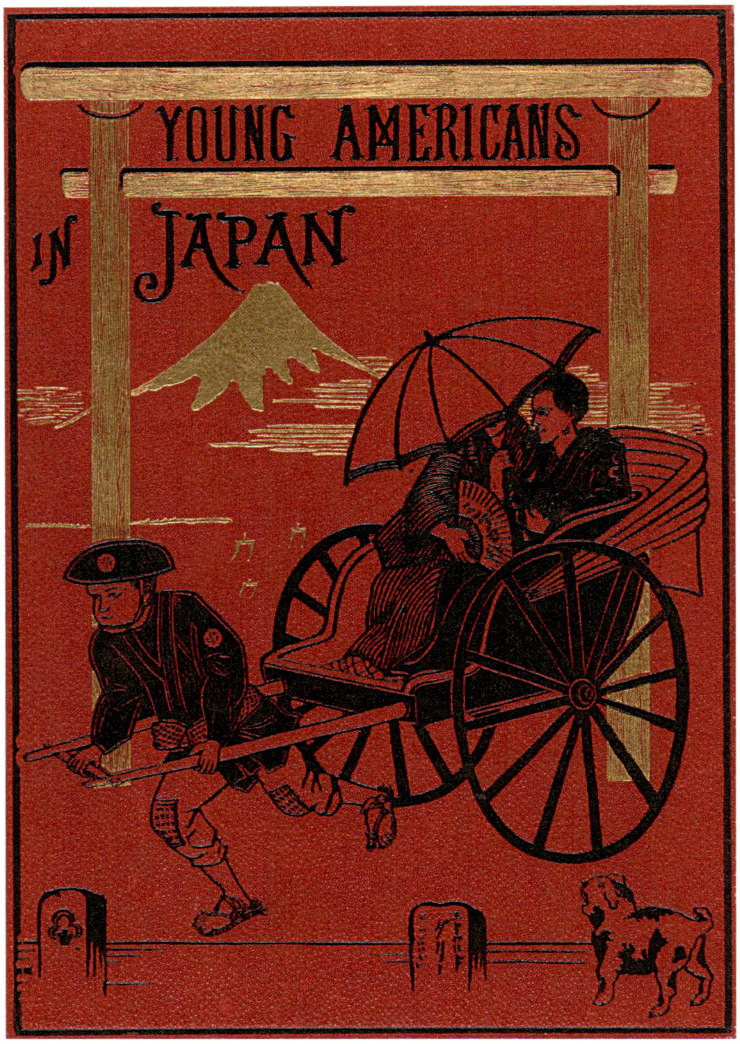

FIGURE 2.6
Young Americans in Japan; or, The Adventures of the Jewett Family and Their Friend Oto Nambo, by Edward Greey. Boston: Lee and Shepard, 1882.

> When I first landed in Japan, the feudal system was in full force; the Mikado (Emperor) was virtually a prisoner in Kioto, and none of his subjects were allowed to leave the country. Today the Mikado rules the land, moves among his subjects like a Western monarch, and is seeking, by every means, to elevate the condition of his people. Japanese merchants are doing business in the principal cities of the world, her earnest students are to be found in our great colleges, and her art illuminates our homes, and has won the admiration of all nations.[25]

Greey explained the intention behind writing about an American family and a young Japanese man educated in the United States:

> In Johnnie, Fitz, and Sallie Jewett I have endeavored to depict the keen intelligence of our rising generation; in Oto Nambo, the modern Japanese, who, in adopting Western civilization, has abandoned the traditions of his forefathers; in Mr. and Mrs. Nambo and their friends, the old conservatives who consider the telegraph an invention of demons. The story, though essentially a work of fiction, is founded

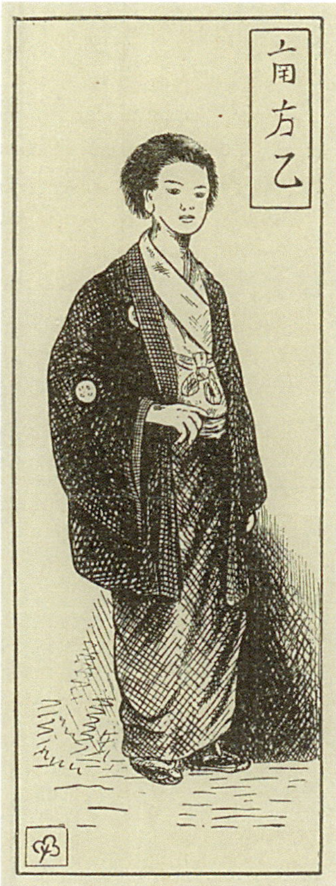

FIGURE 2.7
"Oto Nambo," in *Young Americans in Japan*, by Edward Greey, page 3.

> on facts that have come under my personal observation, and is intended to make young Americans better acquainted with their good neighbors who inhabit the "Land of the Rising Sun."[26]

The linear and fact-filled *Young Americans in Japan* begins in a walled garden in the United States, where "two boys and a little girl were earnestly engaged in . . . putting the finishing touches to a strange-looking instrument"—a small "cannon" designed to fire cucumbers at unwanted intruders. Yet the cannon's first cucumber-splattered target, caught just as he opens the garden door, turns out to be a Japanese man.[27]

> "Hello—are you a tramp?" cried Fitz, gaping at their victim. "Goodness!" gasped Johnnie. "It's—a—lady!"
>
> The cause of their amazement was a pale-faced, gentle-looking individual, dressed in a white robe, dark petticoat, and wide-sleeved over-garment of silk, who regarded them for an instant, then said, in very excellent English:
>
> "A thousand pardons. Can you inform me where the Professor Jewett lives? . . ."
>
> "Yes, Miss; that is the Professor's house, and we are his children."
>
> The stranger gravely brushed off some seeds that had fallen upon his bushy, black hair, and smiling he said: "I am not a young lady, I am a boy; my name is Oto Nambo."
>
> "Are you a Chinese?" bluntly inquired Fitz. "No," proudly answered the lad, "I am a Japanese. . . ."
>
> "How come you entered by the garden door?"
>
> The young Japanese told them that he been so directed by a woman whom he had met on the street, adding, merrily: "She evidently took me for a Chinese, and thought I was in the laundry business."[28]

The young man had come with a letter of recommendation from Dr. Jewett's brother, asking Dr. Jewett to take in the "truly noble, gentle, honorable boy" as a student and member of his household.[29]

Oto Nambo, son of a *daimio's* chief councilor, who displays "gentleness of manner, decision of character, nobility of nature and general amiability,"[30] becomes a brother to the Jewett children, who are delighted at their parents' decision to take Oto in. "Won't it be jolly?" cried Fitz. "You can teach us Japanese, and we'll instruct you in baseball and lots of things. Say, why do you not wear American clothes?"[31]

Five years later the young Japanese-American team—Johnnie, now sixteen, Fitz, thirteen, Oto, nineteen, and fourteen-year-old Sallie—prepares to go on an extended trip to Japan:

> The boys . . . were all strong, active, and intelligent, and could speak, read, and write Japanese as well as they could English and French.
>
> Sallie . . . like her brothers, was well versed in Japanese, in addition to which she could play on a *samisen* (Japanese guitar), which Oto had imported for her.[32]

Greey's description of the Jewetts' six-month journey is filled with information about everyday life in Japan, including local characters like the night watchmen, acrobats, and fortune tellers, the pipe maker and tobacconist, the rice farmer, charcoal vendor, wood-cutter, and the *obi* dyer; historic incidents and personages; old trades, such as pottery mending; popular entertainment, including cards, shadow play, marionettes, and peep-shows; arts and crafts; music and medicine; customs; religious traditions and superstitions; and all kinds of "legends and bric-a-brac lore."[33] Greey also scatters Japanese words and their translations throughout the text, including kimono (long robe), *hashi* (chopsticks), *matsuri* (festival), *kago* (litter), *norimono* (enclosed litter), and *kakemono* (wall scroll).

The two American boys react honestly and, at times, brashly and irreverently to their many new experiences (which include a Japanese massage, a wedding and a funeral, hunting, and a sick man being treated with "deer-horn powder, with a pinch of toad-dust").[34] Oto, their gracious host and tour guide, patiently explains the traditions of his country. Yet it is clear that his stay in America has led him to challenge some of those same traditions; he tells his parents, for example, that he can no longer practice Buddhism.

Oto accepts the Americans' teasing with humor but more than holds his own. When the Americans are served raw fish (which they don't like), listen to Japanese music (which they like even less), or see a group of drunken men (which they find disgraceful), Fitz remarks: "You Japanese are a strange people." With a smile, Oto replies, "So are you Americans."[35] Many of the experiences of the "honorable little-gentlemen-from-afar,"[36] as the young Americans are charmingly called by an old Japanese woman, show the differences and similarities between Japan and the United States, even as Japan is shown to leave behind some of its traditional ways. The story ends after a grand New Year's celebration in Tokyo when the Jewetts learn that their father has received an appointment at the Imperial College and that the family will stay in Japan for another three years.

The Wonderful City of Tokio (fig. 2.8) was published a year after *Young Americans in Japan*. The Jewetts now live in a former *yashiki* (the residence of a lord) and explore their environment as actively as they did in the first volume (figs. 2.9–10). Once again Greey introduces an abundance of information, especially about Japanese arts, crafts, and old trades, including the *ha-go–ita-uri* (the battledore seller), the *uyekiya* (flower seller), the *mushi-uri* (insect peddler), and

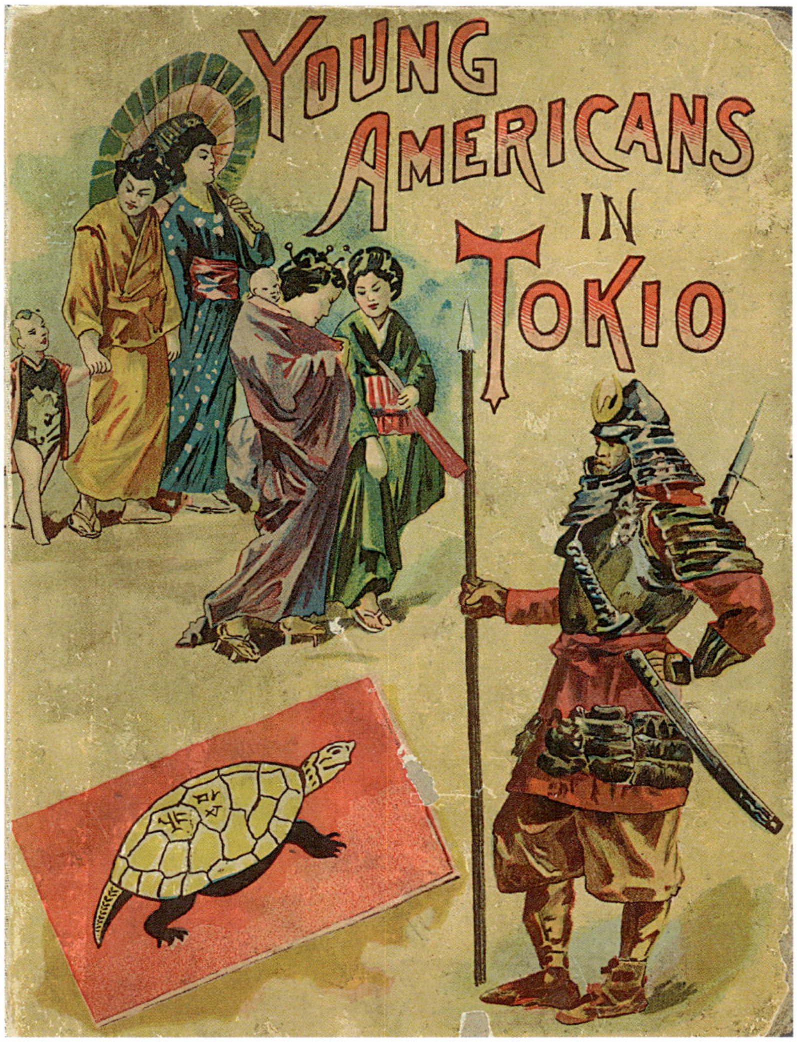

FIGURE 2.8
Young Americans in Tokio, by Edward Greey. Boston: Charles E. Brown, 1892. A mass-market edition of Greey's *The Wonderful City of Tokio* (1883).

the *hon-ya* (book seller). Fact-filled lectures prepare the young Americans for their new experiences, which include watching a sumo wrestling match, a visit to a pottery, and travel to the ancient sites of Kyoto, Nara, and Ise.

Their friend Oto, now a physician, is their host and tour guide once more. The American boys again pepper him with questions and both sides continue their good-natured but pointed banter. At a restaurant recommended by Oto, for example, Fitz says,

> "How rank the candles smell. You have gas in the streets, so why do you not introduce it in your restaurants?"
>
> "Because our people dislike the odor," quietly answered Oto. "You enjoy the smell of gas; we prefer that of our *ro-soku.*"

A few minutes later when some geishas began to play and sing, two of them keeping time by knocking wooden blocks together, the hungry and petulant Johnnie says,

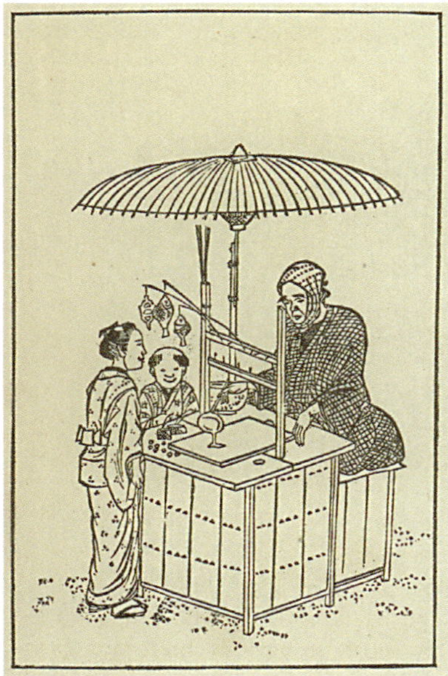

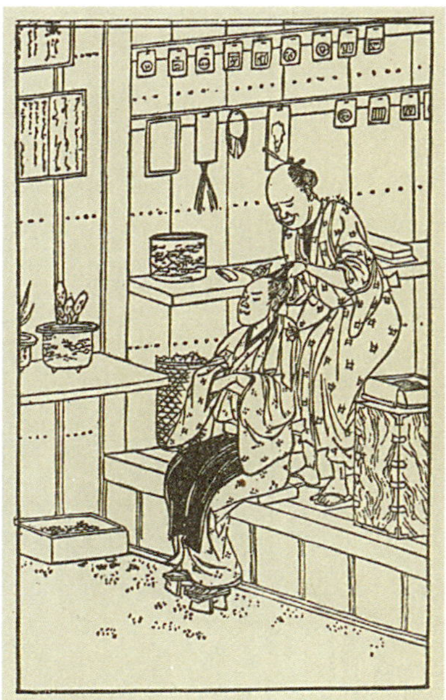

FIGURES 2.9 AND 2.10
"Candy-Maker" and "Hair Dresser at Work," in *The Wonderful City of Tokio; or, Further Adventures of the Jewett Family and Their Friend Oto Nambo*, by Edward Greey. Boston: Lee and Shepard, 1883, pages 228 and 233.

> "Do you call that noise music? . . . I think it is a dreadful racket."
>
> "When I was in America," quietly remarked Oto, "I went with you to a minstrel show. One of the performers played upon the bones and gave me a very bad headache, but I did not make unkind remarks about him."[37]

The last book of the series, *The Bear-Worshippers of Yezo* (fig. 2.11), is devoted to the Ainu of northern Japan and Karafuto (Saghalin) [*sic*] which, when Greey traveled there, still belonged to the Empire of Japan.[38]

Though in the first volume of the Americans' tour, a Japanese person describes the Ainu as "mere animals,"[39] Greey introduces them here as "a quaint people that are almost unknown to my countrymen, and who, like our Indians, are rapidly disappearing from the face of the earth."[40] Once again, Greey provides an overwhelming amount of information about the habitat, customs, and mores of the "savages." The young Americans watch them fishing, become familiar with their language (Greey provides a mini lexicon), observe the *Iyomante* (killing and worshipping the bear), and observe the "Hinzinzo Dance" (fig. 2.12). Next, the visitors sail from northern Japan to Saghalin with a Russian guide, who, like the Ainu guide, conveniently speaks fluent English.

Throughout the story, Professor Jewett, who is studying the conditions of the Ainu, provides didactic explanations and moral admonitions (when offered some vodka, he explains that his family "has been raised upon strict temperance principles").[41] Mrs. Jewett, meanwhile, poses naïve questions, as when she asks a tattooed Ainu woman, "What is the matter with your mouth?" The interaction continues:

> "How is it [the tattooing] done?" inquired Sally, regarding her pityingly.
>
> "My mother scratched the lines round my mouth with a knife, and rubbed soot into them: then the marks were washed with an infusion of the bark of a tree, which made them blue. My hands are ornamented in the same way."
>
> "Did it hurt you?" inquired the young lady. "Not much," she replied, drawing up the sleeve of her kimono, and exhibiting her arm: "my decoration is not all finished. Every Aino woman has this adornment." "Well," murmured Fitz, speaking in English, and critically inspecting the lines, "I should call it a disfigurement."[42]

At the end of their journey, Professor Jewett decides against accepting the Japanese government's offer of further employment. "Your mother has had enough of traveling," he says, "and I want you, boys, to go to college."[43]

Many journals reviewed *The Bear-Worshippers* because of the popularity of the first two volumes and the Western fascination with the Ainu:

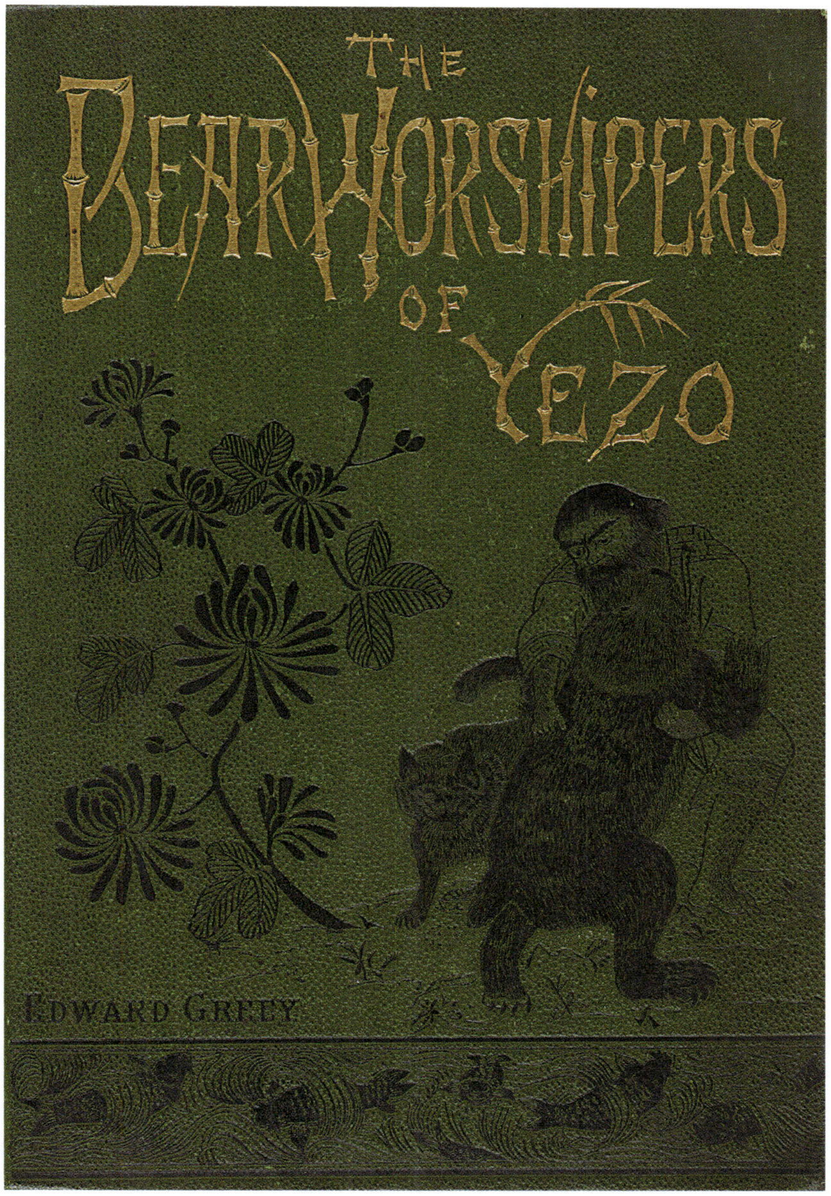

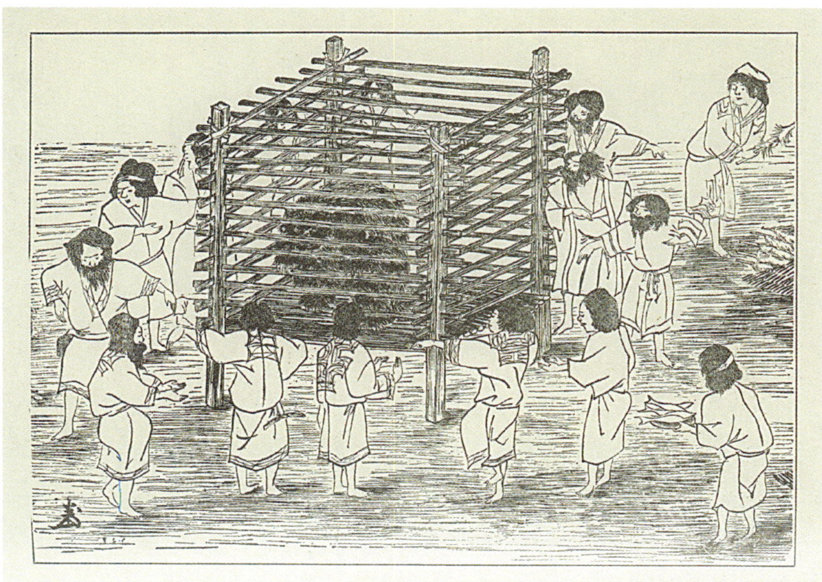

FIGURES 2.11 AND 2.12
Cover and "Hinzinzo Dance," in *The Bear-Worshippers of Yezo and the Island of Karafuto (Saghalin)*, by Edward Greey, illustrated by Rinzo and Ichiske Hamada. Cover by Edward Greey. Boston: Lee and Shephard, 1884. "Hinzinzo Dance," page 136.

> What [Mr. Greey] saw with his own eyes, together with what he has read and borrowed from Japanese books, he has digested into a story of travel. He looks at these curious people not with prejudice, but with real interest, albeit his sleeve is often near his mouth, to hold the laughs that frequently fall into the proverbial receptacle. The ways of these primitive peoples in the cold land are funny enough. The lack of soap and water as a detergent suggests the need of missionary work; but then to civilize them would spoil the point of much of Mr. Greey's lively and fascinating book. Evidently his own supply of insect-powder must have been large to have accomplished so much visiting in Aino and Santan huts, but his narrative is irreproachable, as well as informing and amusing.[44]

A few years after Greey completed his trilogy, Shiukichi Shigemi published his memoir, *A Japanese Boy, By Himself* (1889), which provides firsthand information illuminating the life of a young man like the Jewett's friend Oto. The book describes in detail his childhood and early youth in the small seaport town of Imabari, on the western coast of Shikoku, the smallest of Japan's four major islands. The author, who came to the United States to study at Yale University, modestly confesses that he tried to "prudently suppress everything personal and brought forward only those experiences that the generality of Japanese boys are destined to undergo."[45] Luckily for the reader, Shigemi does, at times, tell about his personal family life, lifting the book from a mere informational catalog about Japan to a genuine picture of Japanese home life during the early Meiji era (1868–1912). He tells about many experiences from his school days, such as learning the cumbersome writing system, going to the public bath, attending festivals, flying kites, and enjoying home entertainments. "In Japan," he notes intriguingly at one point, "we have more social freedom than people are apt to think."[46]

Japan in Adventure Stories for Boys

The earnest travelogues by Knox and Greey were challenged by newer and much more entertaining adventure stories with foreign sights and settings by such authors as Willis Boyd Allen, Herbert Strang, Kirk Munroe, and Edward Stratemeyer.

Inspired by Horatio Alger's rags-to-riches stories, the young Stratemeyer decided that he, too, would be a writer. He became much more than that, eventually producing over thirteen hundred books that were translated into more than a dozen languages and inspired "movies, television series, cartoon shows, comic books, [and] coloring books."[47] In 1893, he became editor of *Good News,* a magazine for boys; he also edited *Young People of America* and established his own magazine, *Bright Days*, in 1896.

Stratemeyer's breakthrough came in 1898 with his seventeenth book, *Under Dewey at Manila; or, The War Fortunes of a Castaway*, which was published immediately after Admiral George Dewey's victory at the battle of Manila Bay during the Spanish-American War.[48] The story introduced the young protagonist Larry Russell and his chums, who would reappear in a number of subsequent books, those about Japan among them. Some reviewers were generous, one praising *Under Dewey at Manila* as "a narrative of experiences and adventure . . . wholesome in spirit and full of excitement" and comparing it favorably with other "graphic stories of peril and adventure suggested by the late war."[49] Others were less enthusiastic, one, for example, giving him credit for having "taken pains to verify all the facts and incidents of the wonderful battle," but also stating that "as a story the book ha[d] little merit."[50] Whether or not his work had merit, Stratemeyer became so successful that, in 1906, he embarked on a far-reaching business venture by founding the Stratemeyer Literary Syndicate. Under his name, hundreds of ghost writers would flesh out stories he conceived and outlined.

Stratemeyer's action-filled adventure stories, many of which contained a mystery, were created to "entertain and instruct"[51] and stressed courage, kindness, and bravery. Good deeds and sense of duty were rewarded; crime was punished.

A master not only of mass production but also of communication and marketing, Stratemeyer addressed his young readers directly, either in the foreword or in the text of a story, introducing the characters, noting previous books, and providing historical context, including places, battles, and military commanders. Yet, as Stratemeyer's fame and fortune advanced, and his factory-like production of juvenile books grew, some critics began to call his books "exploitation of juvenile taste" and a "danger to character development."[52]

Three of the four titles in Stratemeyer's *Soldiers of Fortune* series deal with the Russo-Japanese war and were published as that conflict was still raging (1904–1905). The protagonist, Gilbert Pennington, who had already served in Cuba with the Rough Riders, in the Philippines under General MacArthur, and then in China during the Boxer Rebellion, "had drifted into the army more because of his intense patriotism than for any desire to become a fighter of men."[53] His friend Ben Russell and his brother Larry later joined him. They and their friend Luke Striker are the leading characters throughout the series.

In *Under the Mikado's Flag; or, Young Soldiers of Fortune* (1904), Pennington is a selling agent for the Richmond Importing Company and is pursuing Ivan Snokoff, a Russian businessman who has cheated Gilbert's company. Gilbert's adventures begin in Port Arthur and end, after he reunites with his pals, with his joining the Japanese navy. As the mystery and adventures unfold, Stratemeyer reveals which side he favors. "The resources of Russia are tremendous," he writes, "but that nation has many troubles at home. On the other hand, the sturdy

Japanese are fighting with wonderful bravery—thinking nothing of facing death at every turn—and with a strategy which is as successful as it is astonishing."[54]

In the next title in the *Soldiers of Fortune* series, *At the Fall of Port Arthur; or, A Young American in the Japanese Navy* (1905), Stratemeyer concentrates on the adventures of Larry Russell and Luke Striker, who are on the American ship *Columbia* on their way from Manila to Nagasaki, carrying cargo for the Richmond Importing Company destined for the Japanese government. Also on board is the Russian Ostag Semmel, who starts a mutiny, holding Captain Ponsberry, Larry, and Luke hostage. After a great deal of suspenseful action, Larry and Luke are saved by the Japanese. It is clear in this book as well that Stratemeyer leans toward a Japanese victory over the Russians. In an exchange between Larry and Captain Ponsberry, the captain notes that, while both nations have powerful navies, the Japanese ships "are of the up-to-date types." Furthermore, "the Japanese guns are of the latest pattern—just as they are on our new [U.S.] warships."[55] Elsewhere in the story, after witnessing a drill aboard the Japanese ship, an enthusiastic Larry tells Luke, "this beats the Russians all hollow. I never saw anything so well done!" Luke agrees—in fact Larry quickly guesses that Luke "would like to join the Japanese navy, just to have a mix-up or two with the Russians."[56]

The final book, *Under Togo for Japan; or, Three Young Americans on Land and Sea* (1906, fig. 2.13) again follows the four young Americans featured in the previous titles. Gilbert and Ben have now joined the Japanese Army, while Larry and Luke serve in the Japanese Navy. The war between Russia and Japan once again provides the historical background. Yet what drives the busy plot is Gilbert and Ben's search for the wealthy Nathan Chase of the Anglo-Chinese Trading Company—father of the beautiful Grace—whom two Russians have kidnapped.

One reviewer called *Under Togo for Japan* an "unusually interesting and attractive book for boys"[57]; two others were less complimentary. "Mr. Stratemeyer in his latest boys' story takes some of his former characters to the Far East and places them, without much regard for probability, in the forefront of the Battle of the Sea of Japan," one wrote, "so that the reader at times wonders whether Admiral Togo [commander in chief of the Japanese navy] or Larry Stryker [*sic*] was the real hero on that occasion."[58] While Stratemeyer was "an ingenious artificer," another wrote, he "will give his boy readers, we fear, the false impressions that Americans had a large share in the Japanese triumphs. It is a story for unjaded appetites to devour—and forget."[59]

It was true that Stratemeyer's books lacked literary polish and were filled with incidents of tenuous logic. Yet, *Under the Mikado's Flag*, *At the Fall of Port Arthur*, and *Under Togo for Japan* all conveyed a positive image of a nation about which the average young American reader knew little. The young Americans who joined the

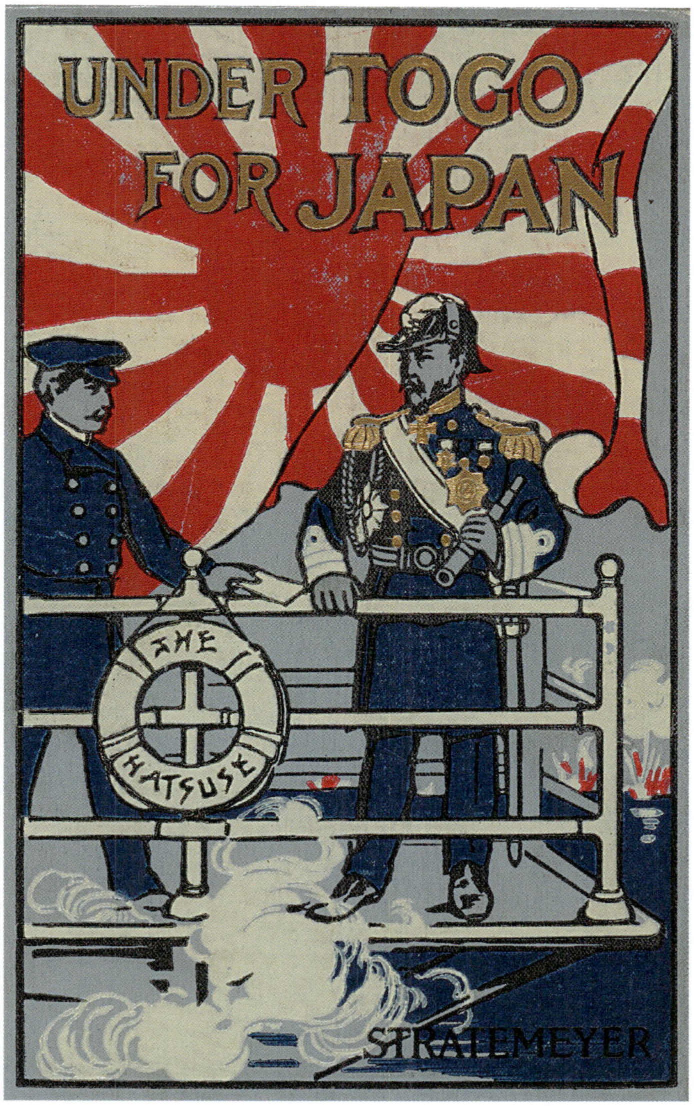

FIGURE 2.13
Under Togo for Japan; or, Three Young Americans on Land and Sea, by Edward Stratemeyer, illustrated by A. B. Shute. Boston: Lothrop, Lee & Shepard, 1906.

Japanese army and navy on a lark and fought in the Russo-Japanese war admired the Japanese and observed that they fought like "regular tigers"[60] and ran their army "like clockwork."[61] Stratemeyer's books, less expensive and simpler in style and design than the hefty Greey and Knox books, reached by far the largest audience of young American readers of any children's books about Japan at that time.

Willis Boyd Allen, whose own story has disappeared, also chose to write about the Far Eastern conflict. In *The North Pacific: A Story of the Russo-Japanese War* (1905), Allen entertains the reader with the adventures of American journalist Fred Larkin, who travels to Port Arthur in search of war stories from both sides of the conflict.[62] In contrast to the energetic Americans and the Russians, whom he portrays as weak and tragic, Allen describes the "Japs" as "small brown men," "diminutive assailants," and "eager brown hordes,"[63] while portraying them also as disciplined, intelligent, well-trained, and heroic. Two suspicious Japanese men who appear as cabin stewards on the American ship *Osprey* in the very beginning of the book reflect Allen's image of the Japanese:

> Although their dress was that of the American gentlemen, a very slight accent in their speech, their jet-black hair, and a trifling obliquity in their eyes would have at once betrayed their nationality to a careful observer. He would have known that they were of a people famous for their shrewdness, their gentle manners, their bravery, their quick perceptions, and their profound patience and tireless resolution in accomplishing their ends—the "Yankees of the Orient"—the Japanese.[64]

Allen provides many details that reveal his thorough research for this long book, as in this description of Japanese soldiers engaged in peaceful pursuits while in camp:

> With the army go camp-followers who are allowed to sell fans, handkerchiefs, cigarettes, tea, soaps, tooth-brushes, and writing paper. For the officers are carried great iron kettles in nets, two on a pony; these are used in heating water for baths, as well as to cook the company mess of rice. A few squares of straw matting make a bath-house, and a big stone jar is the tub of comfort for the almond-eyed campaigner. Much time is also spent in correspondence. The field post carried an immense amount of mail every day between Antung and the front. Around the camp of Oshima's regiment could be seen, in the quieter hours of the day, hundreds of soldiers sitting cross-legged under the trees, painting artistic epistles to their dear ones at home with brushes on rolls of thin paper.[65]

After much gruesome fighting on both sides, a unit commanded by Captain Oshima prepares to join an assault on Port Arthur, which the Japanese hope to take the following day, October 29, the emperor's birthday. "Until late at night his men were busy cleaning themselves as best as they could, and changing their linen," Allen writes. "They were preparing for death. The Japanese must die spotless in body as well as soul, to inherit eternal happiness."[66]

Herbert Strang, whose name appeared on other adventure stories set at the time of the Russo-Japanese war, was a pseudonym used by two different men employed by Oxford University Press.[67] Together they produced over fifty stories that would "please boy readers," including *Kobo, A Story of the Russo-Japanese War* (1905).[68] While this book includes war action, most of its 367 densely printed pages are devoted to the adventures of Bob Fawcett, a British engineer in service to the Japanese. During his many exploits he saves the life of Lieutenant Yamaguchi, kills a tiger and a bear, is captured by the Russians and, after an especially daring excursion, does away with Chang-Wo, a Chinese villain and archenemy of the noble Japanese Rokuro Kobo. (While in Korea, Bob also saves the lives of Mrs. Pottle, an American, and her beautiful niece, who are "doing Asia"—and he wins the hand of the beautiful niece as well.)

While Strang describes the Chinese as grim characters and the Koreans as a "soft, inert, unwarlike race,"[69] he presents the Japanese as a people of "perfect courtesy and smiling hospitality," "self-restraint" and "extraordinary military promise."[70] His protagonist, Bob, describes elegantly served Japanese food—dishes of fine "prawns in batter, fish cakes, rice in bowls of gold lacquer"—and is most impressed by his host's elegant house, the samurai ideals of the soldiers, and the general population. On a long train trip to the Japanese city of Sasebo, he observes, at one station, a train carrying soldiers off to war:

> He was struck by the air of joyous confidence that marked their [the soldiers'] bearing, and the look of pride with which the women and children on the platforms bade them farewell. There was none of the frenzied enthusiasm and the bitter grief which he had noticed in the crowds that sped the British soldiers on their way to South Africa five years before; there was no kissing or hand-shaking, no hanging on the necks of the departing warriors, no impeding of their movements as they entrained, no tearful last words. A few shouts of "Banzai! Banzai!" as the train moved off, and then the throng dispersed in perfect order and decorum, to hide their sorrow, perhaps, in the seclusion of their own homes . . . it was like the departure of a band of Crusaders in the great days of old.[71]

Kirk Munroe was among the other writers who chose the Russo-Japanese conflict as a background for their stories. Born in a one-room log cabin on the Wisconsin bank of the Mississippi river, Munroe began a life of adventure at sixteen when he spent a summer in Kansas City (then still considered the Wild West) and went on a surveying trip to Colorado, Arizona, New Mexico, and Southern California. He endured physical hardship and deprivation, but relished the danger and excitement. Instead of going to Harvard as he had planned, he took another surveying job on the Northern Pacific Railroad. Later, he worked as a special correspondent for the *New York Sun*, an assistant editor for the *New York Times*, and then as editor of the newly founded *Harper's Young People.* In 1883, he settled down in Florida to begin a prolific writing career.[72]

In 1903 Munroe went on a world tour, which included China, Korea, and Japan. Many of his travel and adventure experiences at home and abroad were later woven into his stories. *The Flamingo Feather* (1887), a historical novel of a French boy living among the Indians of Florida, for example, drew on his life among the Seminole Indians. He released a new book nearly every year, including *The Golden Days of '49: A Tale of the California Diggings* (1889) and *The Coral Ship: A Story of the Florida Reefs* (1893). Reviewers praised Munroe's books and, during the 1893 Chicago World's Fair, ten thousand children voted for him as their favorite author.

Munroe's *For the Mikado, or A Japanese Middy in Action* (1905, fig. 2.14), which reflects his ardent admiration of Japan, was based on his own experiences in Port Arthur, where he happened to be at the outbreak of the Russo-Japanese war. It is the story of Takahaki Matsu who, after winning a national scholarship competition, enters the United States Naval Academy in Annapolis, Maryland, as a protégé of the Emperor. When war breaks out Takahaki is recalled to Japan. He is promoted to commander of a submarine torpedo boat and is aided through life-threatening adventures by his friend Dunster Brown, his Annapolis roommate. Takahaki is killed in action during the moving conclusion of the story.

Munroe casts the Russians as the villains. Despite his use of an awkward, stereotypical dialect, the author imbues his young Japanese protagonist with unfailing courage and a sense of honor:

> "Do you know," remarked Dunster "that you are the very first Jap I ever met, and—"
>
> "I beg your pardon," interrupted Takahaki stopping short and drawing himself up very stiffly, "but it is that I ask of you to no more name a man of the Mikado as a 'Jap.'"

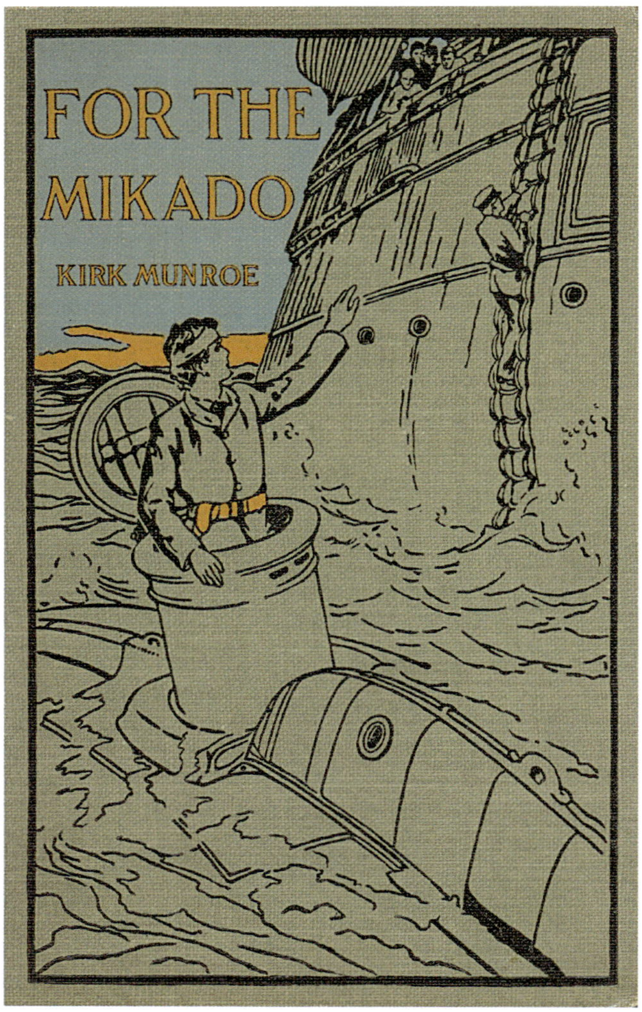

FIGURE 2.14
For the Mikado, or A Japanese Middy in Action, by Kirk Munroe. New York: Harper and Brothers, 1905.

> "Not to call you a 'Jap,'" retorted Dunster, with a puzzled air— "but you are one, aren't you? What else could I call you?"
>
> "The men of the Mikado, in Engrish, are 'Japanese,' and one must die before he submit to be said a 'Jap.' . . .
>
> "Do you mean that it is considered an insult?" asked Dunster.
>
> "Hei, hei, yes, that is it! The insurt!" declared Takahaki, vehemently. . . . "So I ask of you, please, if you be so kind, never more to say to me that bad word 'Jap.'"
>
> "Of course not," replied Dunster . . . "That is, I'll try to remember, and I promise to apologize each time that I forget and make a slip. But you mustn't take it too much to heart if some of the other fellows call you 'Jap.' Some of them may do so just to tease you, but they won't mean anything by it."
>
> "If *one* time, some man say to me 'Jap,' I speak to him. He excuse, I excuse. If *two* time, I no excuse. It is insurt, and for honor of my Mikado I must teach him some better. . . .
>
> "He may say to me 'pig,' 'foolo,' what he like, I not care. It mean me, Takahaki; but if he say 'Jap,' then he mean every Nippon man. He mean my Mikado."[73]

In *A Son of Satsuma, or With Perry in Japan* (1901, fig. 2.15), another suspenseful story of friendship between an American and a Japanese youth, Munroe again combines fact and fiction as he relates the adventures of Robert (Bob) Whiting, a stowaway on the *Friendship,* which is on its way to the Far East. During his long journey, which occurs before Commodore Perry's expeditions, he saves the life of Shimadzu Katto, who, Bob soon learns, is a "deft-handed, capable, and always cheerful son of old Japan." The young man learns English quickly, then explains to Bob why he does not want to return to Japan. "Do you mean to say," asks Bob, "that if a poor chap gets blown to sea from your country, the same way as you did, but finally gets picked up and carried back again, he would be killed for what he couldn't help?" "Yep. Head off, quick," Katto warns. "Everybody, —Chinese, Engris, Meric, Dutch, Spaniard, everybody. No can hab in Dai Nippon."[74]

Katto tells Bob about the early Spanish and Portuguese missionaries who forced their way into Japan, and who were eventually expelled. This caused the government to initiate its isolation policy, closing the country to all foreigners and to its own people, even those who were washed away from her shores. Bob thought that,

> under the circumstances, he didn't blame the Japs for hating foreigners and keeping their country to themselves. At the same time he imagined that, just because it had been shut up for so long, it must be the most interesting land in all the world to visit, and wished more than ever that he might some time have the chance. From that moment he became an ardent student of the Japanese language with the ever-patient Katto as teacher.[75]

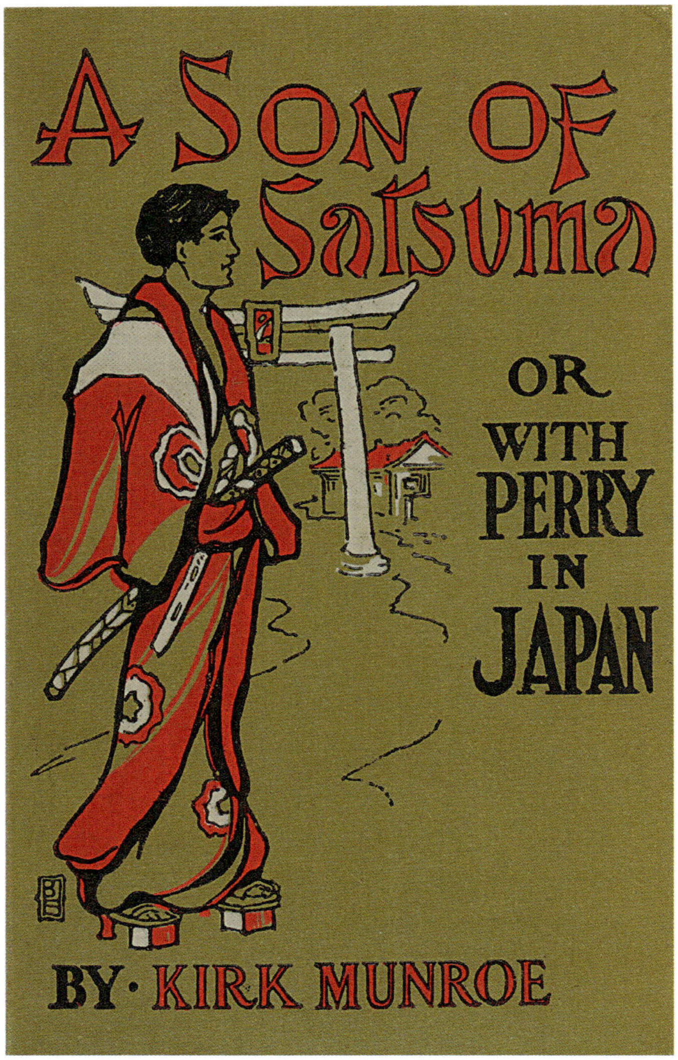

FIGURE 2.15
A Son of Satsuma, or With Perry in Japan, by Kirk Munroe. New York, C. Scribner's Sons, 1901.

After a journey filled with dramatic adventures and coincidence—including Katto's daring rescue of Bob, who is kidnapped and condemned to slave work—the two youths finally manage to land in Japan. There they are saved by Katto's father, who turns out to be none other than the mighty *daimio* of Satsuma. Bob is officially adopted into his clan. He teaches the Japanese English while they, in turn, teach him Japanese ways, including the samurai's way of the sword:

> They taught him sword play, and impressed upon him the various nice points of sword etiquette. They warned him never to withdraw a sword from its sheath in presence of a friend except upon special request, or in an emergency; as to exhibit a drawn sword was the equivalent to a threat. . . . They posted him as to how he might take a most cruel and satisfactory revenge upon an enemy by simply ripping open his own bowels, which act they called hara-kiri, or happy despatch [*sic*]. They even taught him how to cut off his own head, which, they said, was a thing he would naturally desire to do if defeated in battle.[76]

The adventures of Bob and Katto end on a high, if improbable, note. They travel to Uraga arriving just in time to watch Commodore Perry's squadron sail into the bay. They tender their services as interpreters.

A reviewer of *A Son of Satsuma* noted "the abundant supply of adventures, hair-breadth escapes and exciting situations," the "crisp and entertaining" style, and the book's "sure-fire appeal to all boys who love the sea," but did not acknowledge just how sensitive and positive a book about Japan it was.[77]

Japan in Books for Girls

In 1905, a reviewer commented on the "great change in books for girls" that had been occurring during the previous twenty years. Most of the older books were of "the goody-goody order, with little sense of character, and inordinately dull." But as girls' "lives [had] broadened with school and college life," new writers had emerged who gave girls "books of their own."[78]

However, early twentieth-century American books about Japan generally described American girls as self-confidant and assertive, while their Japanese counterparts were presented as quite the opposite. The main Japanese characters in some of these stories, like O-Heart-San in *O-Heart-San: The Story of a Japanese Girl* (1908, fig. 2.16) by Helen Eggleston Haskell,[79] are beautiful but meek and frail.

Reviewers of *O-Heart-San* called it a "dainty little tale" and suggested that American girls would read it "with pleasure."[80] The sweet concoction of incongruous happenings and images in "the story of O-Heart-San, the beautiful, and of Haru, the young Prince Imperial of Japan" presents Japan as a fairy-tale country and describes the heroine as "small and slender" with "deep and soft" black eyes that are "so sad that they seemed just ready to overflow with tears." Though the daughter of a humble wood carver, O-Heart-San was famous throughout Tokyo for her beauty and gentleness.[81]

One night, O-Heart-San has a dream that her father, a collector of dreams, deems especially exquisite. Even the Prince wants to buy it and promptly arrives. He invites O-Heart-San to the Imperial Palace where she meets Maid Margery, daughter of an American diplomat. Margery visits O-Heart-San's house, finding it "cunning" and like a "magnified Japanese lantern."[82] She finds her new Japanese friend's life less charming, especially when she learns that O-Heart-San's father has arranged for her betrothal to Yori-Sada, a wealthy silk merchant. Though O-Heart-San's "heart grew heavy with despair" thinking of becoming the slave of the ugly fat Yori-Sada, she "merely prostrated herself reverently at her mother's feet and murmured: "It shall be as you say, O honorable mother."[83]

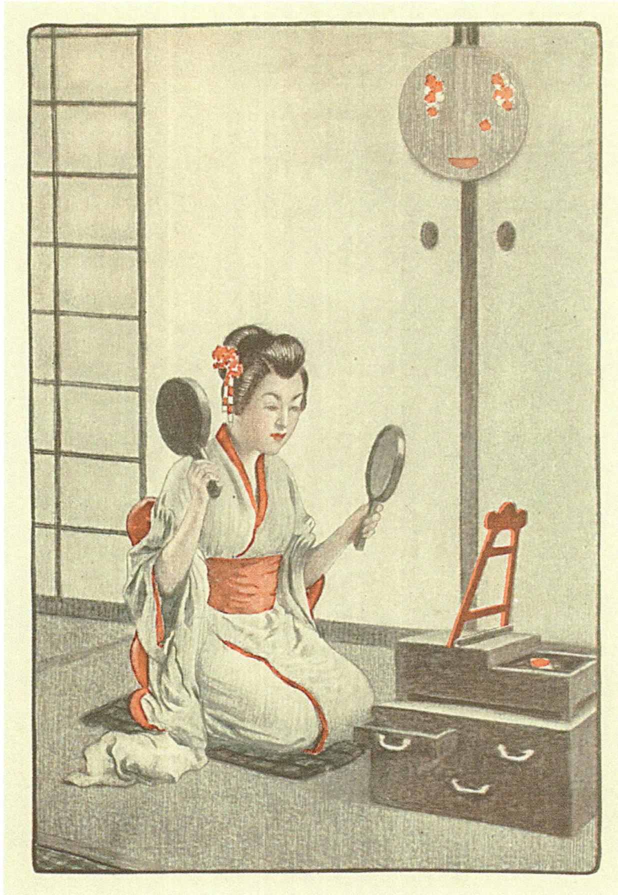

FIGURE 2.16
"Dropped gently to her knees before a tiny chest of drawers," in *O-Heart-San: The Story of a Japanese Girl*, by Helen Eggleston Haskell, illustrated by Frank P. Fairbanks. Boston, L. C. Page, 1908, opposite page 12.

Margery tells O-Heart-San how happy she is to be an American, that she will go to school for many years and eventually select her own husband. She is also determined to save O-Heart-San from her fate. Though her first attempt fails, a greater opportunity soon arrives. After Prince Haru's guest, the cesarevitch visiting from Moscow, is attacked by a Japanese man, O-Heart-San tries to take her life to atone for the insult. Her American friend knows just what to do. Margery rushes to the Imperial Palace and summons the Prince, who swiftly arrives in his glass coach. He arranges for the annulment of O-Heart-San's betrothal, pays her parents a pension and sends O-Heart-San to school so she can become a nurse.

The stories by "Frances Little" (Fannie Caldwell Macaulay), who left Kentucky to work for four years as a kindergarten teacher in Hiroshima, continue in the O-Heart-San mode.[84] Macaulay published *The Lady of the Decoration* (1906), *The Lady and Sada San* (1912), and *Jack and I in Lotus Land* (1922), and the handsomely designed *Little Sister Snow* (1909, fig. 2.17), which were all set in Japan. *Little Sister Snow* tells a sentimental story, perpetuating the image of the meek and beautiful Japanese woman who has few rights, hides her emotions, and is expected to devote her life to her husband and family.

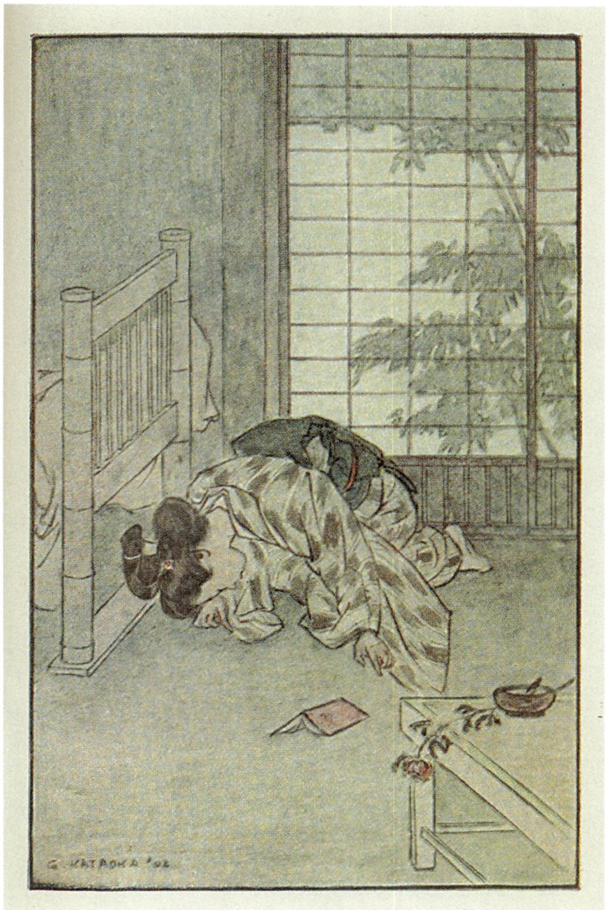

FIGURE 2.17
"Very helpless and lonesome," in *Little Sister Snow,* by Frances Little, illustrated by Genjiro Kataoka. New York: Century, 1909, opposite page 120.

Yuki, the much beloved, beautiful daughter of an impoverished family of high rank, has been prepared for her future life with the best education her parents can afford. One day she is told that, after careful consideration, her father has selected a husband for her, "Saito San, a wealthy officer in the Emperor's household." For this, Yuki gives thanks to the gods, for even though Saito San was "a far-away, shadowy being," her marriage to such a prominent figure meant that "her father and mother would live in luxury for the rest of their lives."[85]

Then, out of the blue a letter arrives. It is from Richard Melton Merrit, an American whom Yuki had met many years before. Now Merrit, who has been sent back to Japan by his government, is looking for a place to stay for a few months. Her father's house had been suggested because of Yuki's knowledge of English. During Merrit's stay, Yuki falls in love with him. The story begins to take on a Madame-Butterfly feeling when Merrit has to return to America. After he has left, Yuki finds a blank diary in his room and confides her feelings to her secret new friend:

> I tell my troublesome [*sic*] to this little book what spells "Diary" in golden letters on back. . . .

> Japanese girl very naughty if she love man. She made for the take care of man's mother, man's house. Very bad for Japanese girl to say love when she marry with man. Merrit San say 'Merican girl speak love with eyes when lips are shame. Japanese girl cover the eye with little curtain when man comes. She no must peep out one little corner. No must see, no must hear, no must speak the love.[86]

Later she writes:

> What shall I do to less my anxious? To-day at temple I ask Buddha. He never speak. He always look far away at big sea. He no care, though tears of the heart make damp the kimono sleeve. The Christians' God I no can see. But Merrit San say he is everywhere and listens for voice of troublesome. I no can make him hear, though I say the loud prayer. . . . I believe Christians' God more better than Buddha, because Merrit San say he make everything truly. He make me, he make Merrit San, he make the beautiful love. Maybe some day that big God hear about Japanese girl's heart of trouble and speak the peace.[87]

Finally, there is *Treasure Flower: A Child of Japan* (1916, fig. 2.18) by Ruth Gaines, which begins on a stormy night when a mysterious infant girl is left with a priest and his wife. Treasure Flower, as they name her, turns out to be the highborn Princess Plum Blossom, and as she gets older, she befriends Lynette Bowne:

> [Lynette's] hair hung in curls that even in the dawn light showed a rich red gold. Her brown eyes just matched her short, brown frock; she wore, instead of *geta* [wooden clogs], white stockings and low, buttoned shoes. In short, she was a little American girl, one whom Treasure Flower would impolitely have called a "hairy barbarian." Not that she had ever seen one before; but Uncle Cedar-mount had told her about them. It was all on account of them, so he said, that Lord Fuwa had been murdered in Yedo, and the castle had become an ownerless ruin and the Temple of Benten so poor.
>
> For had these red-headed *oni* [monsters] not come, only three decades ago, with fire-eating ships such as were never before seen in Yedo Bay, and demanded of the Government the right to settle and to trade; a right strictly denied all foreigners except the Dutch for two hundred and fifty years? Why! at the very cross road to the Castle by which both children had come that morning, still stood the edicts promulgated so long ago, forbidding any Christian to enter and any Japanese to leave the realm on pain of death. Nevertheless, the foreigners had effected an entrance, bringing in their train a bitter civil war.[88]

When Treasure Flower is stricken by cholera, as are many others in the village, her uncle, a priest, is at first reluctant to ask the foreign doctor (Lynnette's father) for help. But a friend urges her uncle to reconsider:

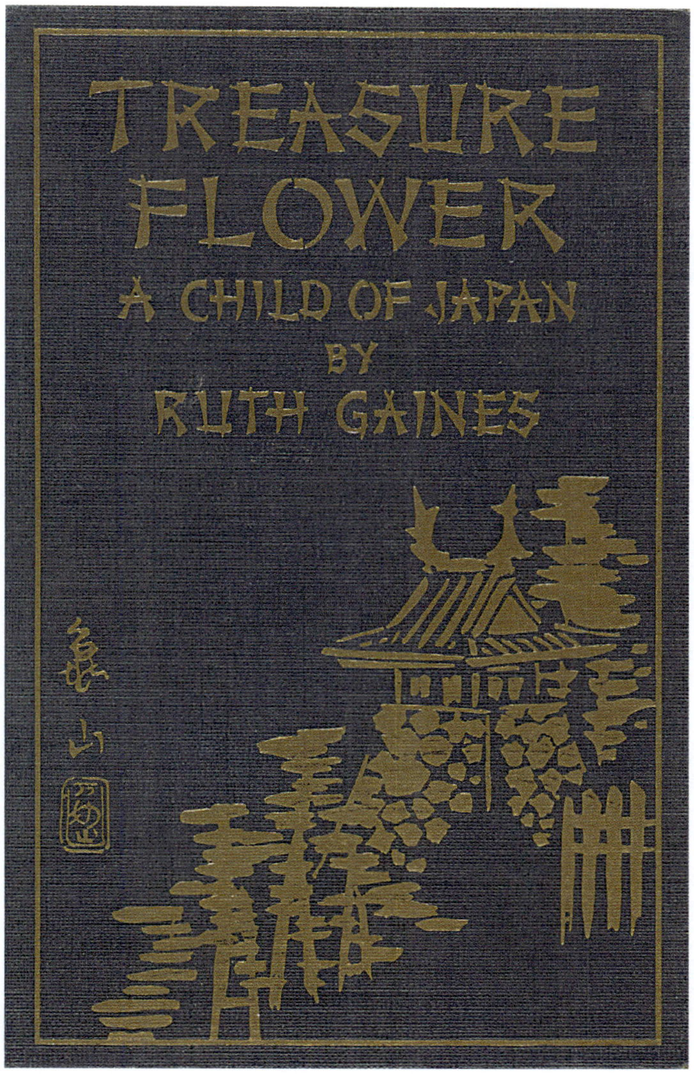

FIGURE 2.18
Treasure Flower: A Child of Japan, by Ruth Louise Gaines. New York: E. P. Dutton, 1916.

> "Now you know," he [the friend] continued, at the look of alarm on Uncle Cedar-mount's face, "I am not much in favor of these foreigners, with their strange religion and their overbearing ways. But some things they do know more about than we do; and this man certainly knows medicine. My wife is so much better today that I came here to offer my thanks."[89]

Treasure Flower survives. And as the doctor leaves, Uncle Cedar-mount's thoughts turn to the goddess Benten, one of the Seven Lucky Gods that dispense good fortune from their treasure ships:

> That evening, in the Temple of *Benten*, a silent prayer went up to the goddess; a prayer of thanksgiving for the black ships and the hairy foreigners. And as he prayed, a daring thought came into the good Priest's mind. *What if the Black Ships of the foreigners were after all the Treasure Ships of Benten in disguise?*"[90]

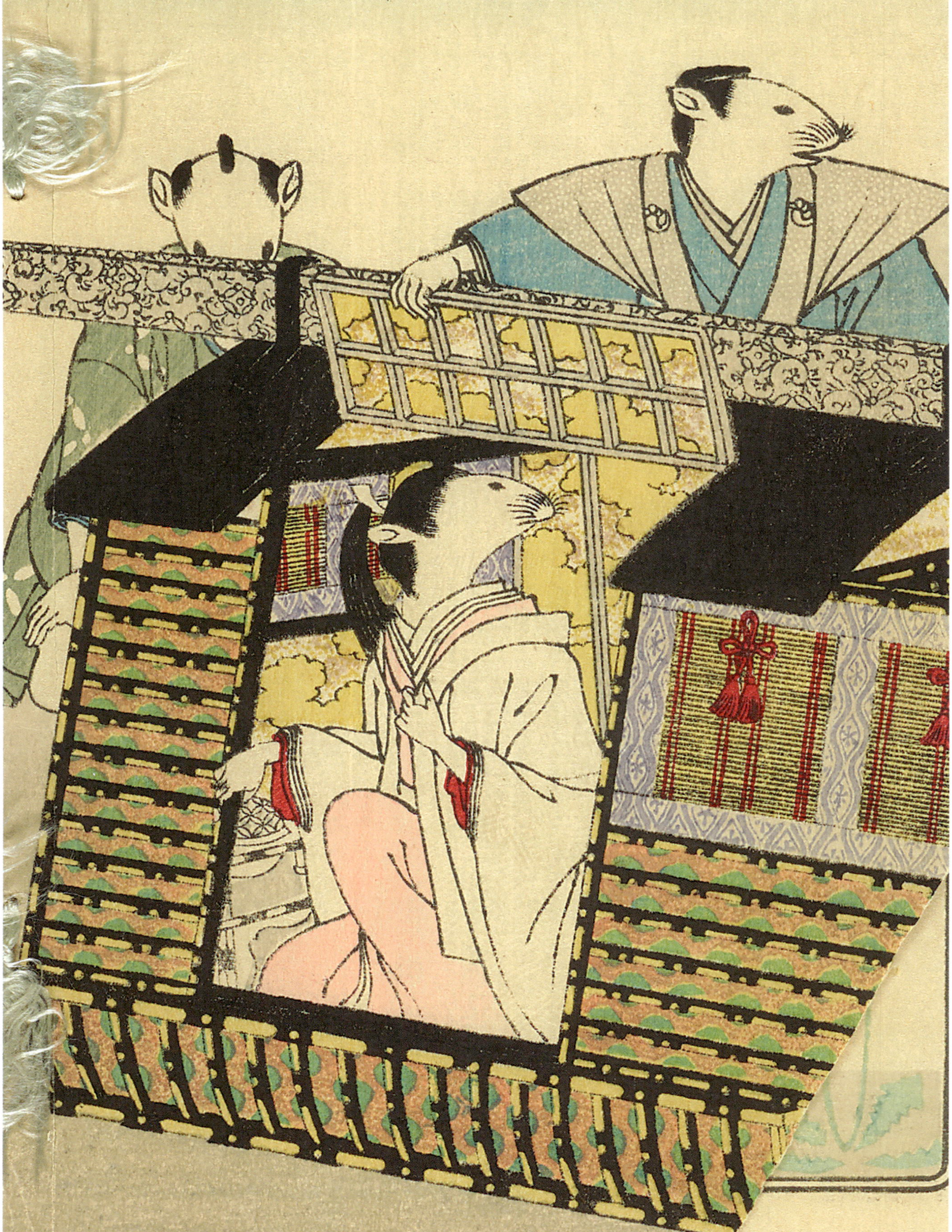

3

Takejiro Hasegawa

The Foreigners' Publisher

Takejiro Hasegawa grew up in Kyobashi. However, it was in the nearby foreign settlement of Tsukiji, the "place of bright missionary and educational undertakings,"[1] where he became exposed to Western ideas, made his contacts, and where he would find the authors and illustrators of his children's books. The son of a prosperous merchant family, Hasegawa took Bible and English lessons from Julia Carrothers (who became his friend and mentor), worked as a tour guide and English tutor, and became a student at the Short-Term Commercial Training Institute.[2] Next, Hasegawa set up his own business, distributing mineral water, cosmetics, picture frames, and French wine. He also began to import textbooks from England and America.[3] In 1884, he established his own publishing firm and became "Meiji Japan's preeminent publisher of wood-block-illustrated crepe paper books."[4] Hasegawa brought together talented writers and artists to translate and illustrate Japanese tales, making Japanese culture accessible to Western audiences.

Tsukiji, the Foreign Settlement

Tsukiji, today best known for its fish market, played a fascinating role not only in the life of the enterprising Hasegawa but also in the development of Tokyo. Ieyasu (1543–1616), the first Tokugawa shogun, chose for his capital, Edo, a town claimed from a swampy area known as *musashi no hara* (the Musashi moor).[5] Tsukiji, located near Edo Bay, rose from reclaimed land when "the bounds of the sea were pushed back, after the Great Fire of 1658."[6] The area became home of temples and fine *yashiki* (mansions) of the *daimio*, notable among them Lord Nakatsu of the Okudaira clan, whose Tsukiji residence became a center of *rangaku* (Dutch, or Western learning).[7] Thus, in the early days, Tsukiji became known as a place of "moral and intellectual advancement of the people of the Empire," radiating "an uplifting influence that [was] felt afar."[8]

In 1867, fourteen years after Commodore Perry sailed into Edo Bay, Tsukiji was declared a foreign settlement, and by 1874 some 250 foreigners lived there,

OPPOSITE
(Detail) *Nedzumi no yome-iri* [The Mouse's Wedding], translated by David Thompson, illustrated by Sensei Eitaku. Tōkyo: Kōbunsha, 1885.

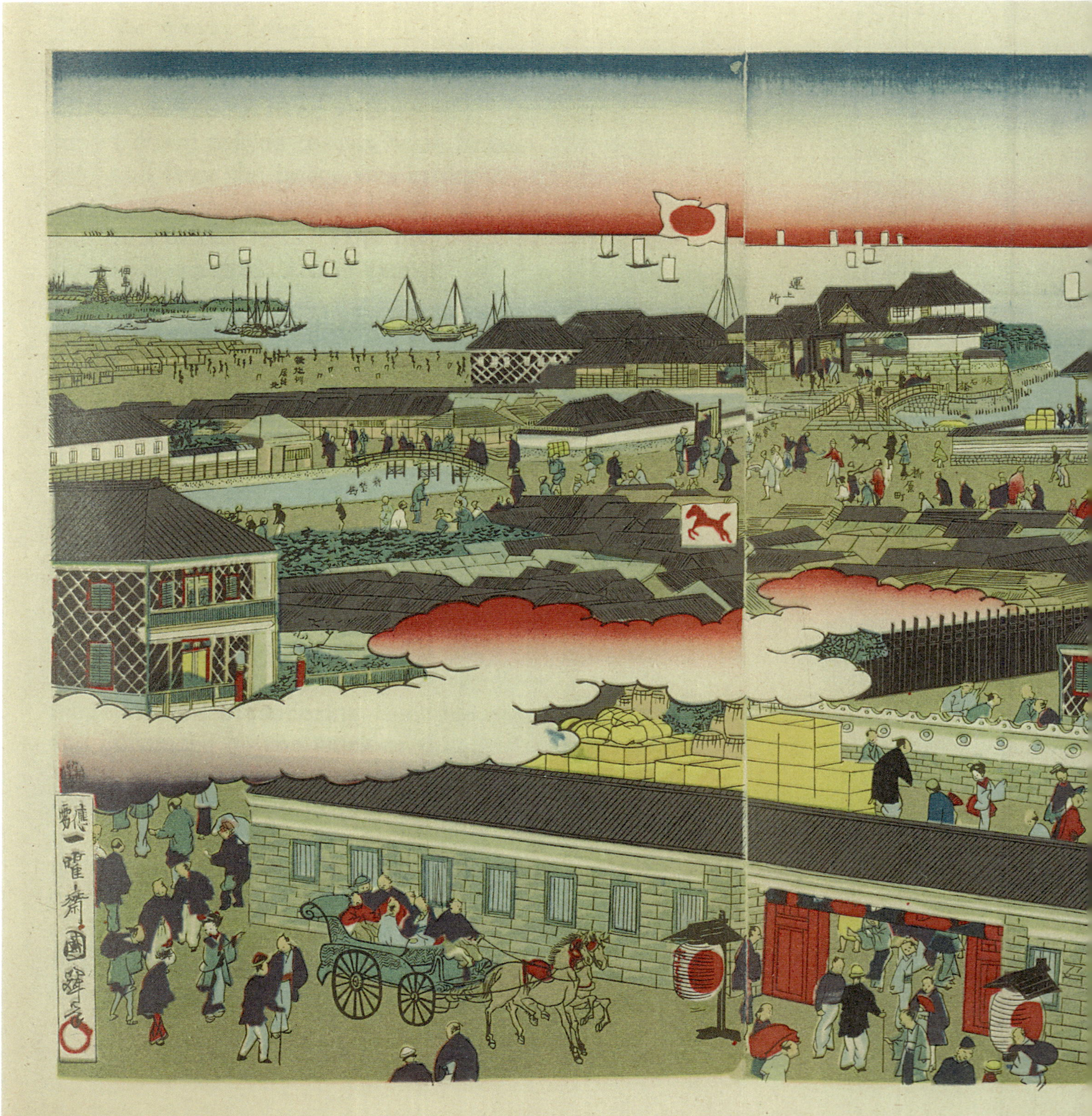

FIGURE 3.1

Tokyo Tsukiji Hoterukan [Tokyo Tsukiji Hotel], by Kuniteru Ichiyōsai (1830–1874). Published by Kichibei Kagaya, Tokyo, late 19th century. Reproduced in *Tell Me about Tokyo* by George Caiger. Tokyo: Hokuseido Press, 1939, opposite page 64.

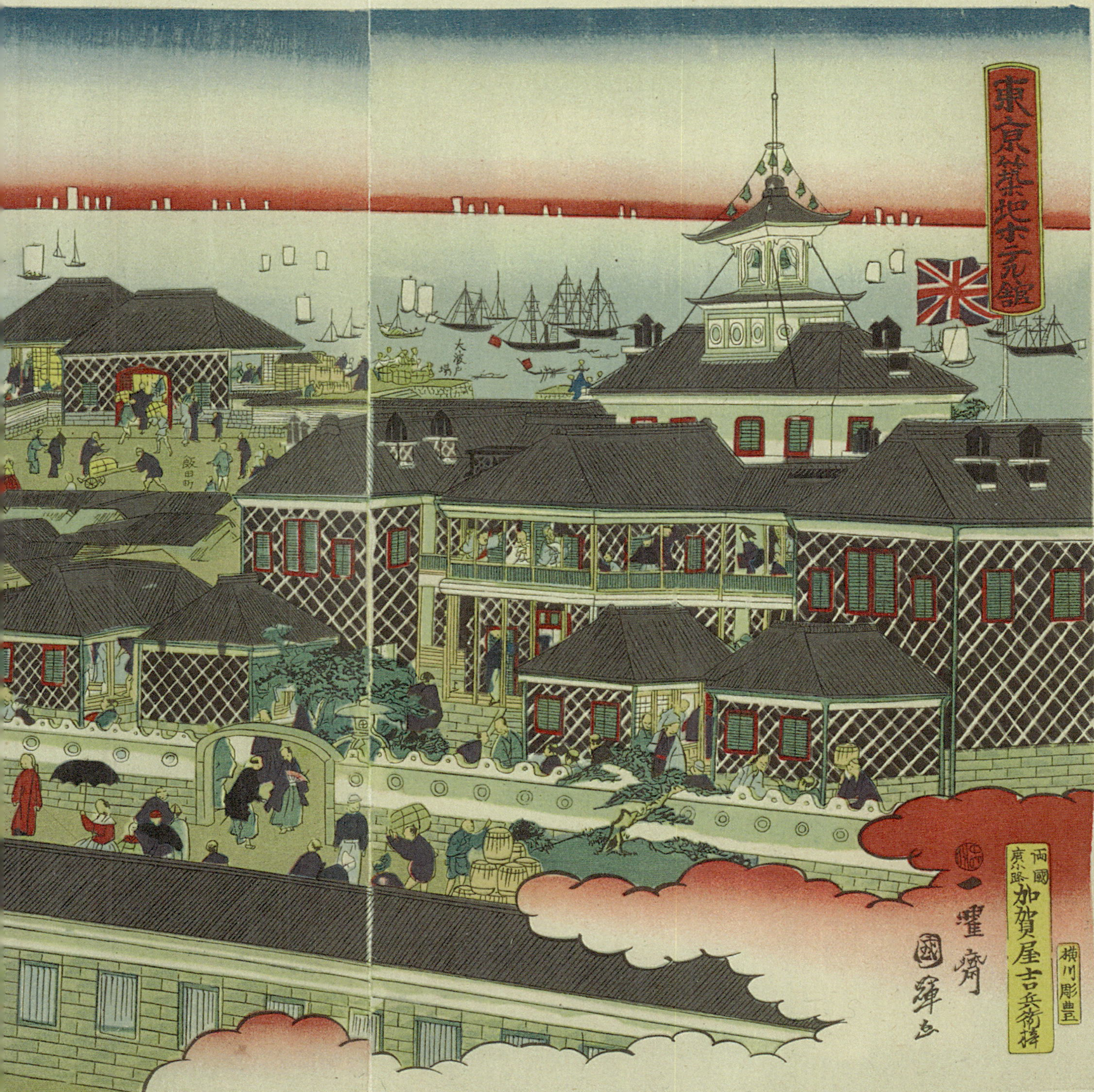
東京築地ホテル館
両國
原小路
加賀屋吉兵衛梓
横川彫豊
一曜斎
國輝画

most of them British or American.[9] At that time, when Japanese authorities still strove to temper foreign influence, "no foreigners [were] allowed to live in Tokio outside of Tsukiji, unless in Government or Japanese employ."[10] When the foreigners arrived in Tsukiji, which lay between Edo Castle, the Sumida River, and the bay, it had become part of the "low city," home of artisans and shopkeepers.[11] It was close to Nihonbashi (the bridge of Japan)—built by Ieyasu in 1603—where Japan's five major highways began. (One of them, the *Tōkaidō* or Eastern Sea Road, was immortalized by nineteenth-century Ukiyo-e artist Utagawa Hiroshige's *Fifty-three Stations of the Tōkaidō*.) Tsukiji, with its entrance gate and its night watchmen patrolling the streets, was "small, tight, and cozy," a place for country "bumpkin[s]."[12] Mary Fraser, the American wife of a British diplomat, who lived there in the late nineteenth century, described it as,

> close to the sea, and . . . cooler in these hot days than our own house farther inland. When I drive down there, it always delights me to watch the junks, with their huge sails, white or saffron, moving along the wide canal on the incoming tide, to watch the woodmen piling timber in the yards along the banks, to see the crowded ferry boats carrying the people from shore to shore.[13]

In 1872, William Griffis, who had just returned from his teaching position in Echizen (now Fukui), described changes he discovered in Tokyo and Tsukiji:

> Landing at Tsŭkiji, I finish my winter journey of three hundred and thirty miles. At the French hotel, a good square meal seems such a triumph of civilization . . . Tōkiō is so modernized that I scarcely recognize it. No beggars, no guard-houses, no sentinels at Tsŭkiji, or the castle-gates; city ward-barriers gone; no swords worn. . . . The age of pantaloons has come. Thousands wearing hat[s], boots, coats; carriages numerous; jin-riki-shas countless . . . New bridges span the canals . . . Hospitals, schools, and colleges; girls' seminaries numerous. Railway nearly finished . . . Three hundred foreigners reside in Tōkiō. An air of bustle, activity, and energy prevails. . . . Old Yedo has passed away forever.[14]

The American and British legations and those of some ten other countries were now located in Tsukiji, and several hotels had also opened there, including Thompson's hotel and the Seiyōken hotel. The Tsukiji Hoterukan, the first Western-style hotel, touted its bay view, more than one hundred rooms, a billiard room, and other Western amenities.[15] The Naval Training Center had moved from Nagasaki to Tsukiji, which was by then the site of a number of new schools.[16] In the 1870s some eighty-seven missionaries were stationed in Tokyo,[17] representing a variety of denominations, including American Presbyterian, Methodist, Baptist, and American Episcopal.[18] After 1873, when the law prohibiting Christianity was rescinded, numerous churches were built in Tsukiji, including the international, interdenominational Tokyo Union Church,[19] the Trinity Cathedral, the Tsukiji Mission Church, a Roman Catholic Church, and the Methodist Episcopal Church.

To its great advantage, Tsukiji was close to the Ginza, "the busiest, noisiest, unhandsomest, and most flamboyant of the metropolitan streets . . . best known of all to foreigners, by whom it [was] often called the Broadway of Tokyo."[20] Tsukiji was also close to the Tokyo business district of Nihonbashi and its many bookstores, including the Suharaya, Maruzen, and Hakubunkan.[21] It had its own hospital (St. Luke's), its own dairy shop (cows had to be imported to Japan),[22] and the Shintomiza Kabuki theater. Among the important businesses established was the Tokyo Tsukiji Type Foundry, which introduced moveable English-language type[23] and which became one of Hasegawa's printers.

In 1872, four Westerners founded the Asiatic Society of Japan, which, by the following year numbered 186 members. In November of 1881, the Society, which published the scholarly journal *Transactions of the Asiatic Society of Japan*, moved from Yokohama to Tsukiji. By 1900, the Society boasted 229 members,[24] including British diplomat Sir Rutherford Alcock, physicist and electrical engineer W. E. Ayrton, editor and scholar Captain Francis Brinkley, and Japanologist Basil Hall Chamberlain.[25] American physician and translator James Curtis Hepburn, author William Eliot Griffis, and diplomat and scholar Sir Ernest Satow were also members.[26]

All about Japan (1905), a children's book by Belle M. Brain, records some of the momentous changes that happened in Japan after the Meiji restoration in 1868:

> When the great revolution was over, and the emperor took his place at the head of the nation, Japan "put on her seven-league boots," and began to make giant strides in civilization. While her gates were shut, during those two long centuries, she had fallen behind Western nations in every way. They had great armies and navies, and railroads and telegraph lines and steam engines, and newspapers and schools and colleges, and she had not.
>
> As soon as she found out how far ahead of her they were, she made up her mind to catch up with them. So instead of driving foreigners out, she invited them to come and teach her Western ways.
>
> Very soon the most wonderful changes took place. Under the direction of wise and skillful men from Europe and America, the armies of Japan were drilled, great ships were built, mines were opened, new industries were started, and schools established all over the empire. At Tokyo a great university was opened. . . .
>
> Then one day in 1872—June 12th, I believe it was—a great crowd gathered to see the first railway train start on its eighteen-mile journey from Tokyo to Yokohama.
>
> And before long the people were busy sending telegrams and writing letters, for telegraph lines were put up all over Japan, and a fine postal system [was]

introduced by an American who had been in the Post Office Department at Washington.

In the old days letters were sent by special messengers and it cost so much that only the rich could afford it. Now they are delivered anywhere in the empire for two cents, and more than three hundred million are sent every year, besides eighty million papers and magazines. The neat little Japanese postmen, with their blue suits, wide butter-bowl hats, straw sandals and mail-bags under their arms or in little two-wheeled cars, carry the mail all over Japan, excepting where there are steam cars. They travel from station to station on a swift run, mile after mile, uphill and down, never stopping till they reach the place where another postman is waiting to take the mail and run on his turn.

One of the greatest changes took place on New Year's Day, 1873, when they began to use the same calendar that we use, instead of the one the Chinese use, which follows the moon in its changes. Since that time they have dated the days and months as we do, but not the years. Instead of counting the years from the birth of the Lord Jesus, they count them from the reign of the first Mikado, and also from the new period, Meiji, or "Enlightened Rule," which began with the reign of the Emperor Mutsu Hito in 1868. Thus 1873 was the year 2,533 of the empire and the 6th year of Meiji.[27]

Gradually, Tsukiji embraced these changes. The 1906 children's book *When I Was a Boy in Japan* (fig. 3.2) by Sakae Shioya provides a glimpse of how different and perhaps enchanting Tsukiji's foreign ambiance appeared to a Japanese boy:

One day, with a curious mind, I started for the place where the foreigners lived together, about a mile from my home. As I neared the settlement I made several discoveries. First, the houses looked very prim and square, straight up and down, painted white, or in some light color. When viewed from a distance they looked as if they were so many gravestones in a temple yard. Unfortunately, it was the only comparison that occurred to a country boy. As I looked again, I found out another fact. That was, that while Japanese houses were nestling under the trees, foreign houses were above them. In fact, there was nothing more than low bushes around the houses. So my conclusion was that foreigners lived in grave-stone-like houses, and did not like tall trees, being tall themselves, perhaps. As I entered a street I found everything just contrary to my expectations. Streets were deserted instead of being thronged; only one or two people and a dog were seen crossing. I went on, when, as luck would have it, I neared a Catholic temple from which two men, or women,—I could not distinguish which,—dressed in black, with hoods of the same color, came! How dismal, I thought, and immediately took [to] my heels till I came to another part of the street where the houses faced the sea. I wanted to see a boy or a girl, anyway, if I could not find a crowd. As I looked I saw something white at one of the gates, and what was my delight when I found it to be a little girl! I approached her, but not very near, as we could not talk to each other. I just kept at an admiring distance. I stood there, one eye on her and the other on the sea, lest I should drive her in by looking at her with both my eyes, and began to examine her.

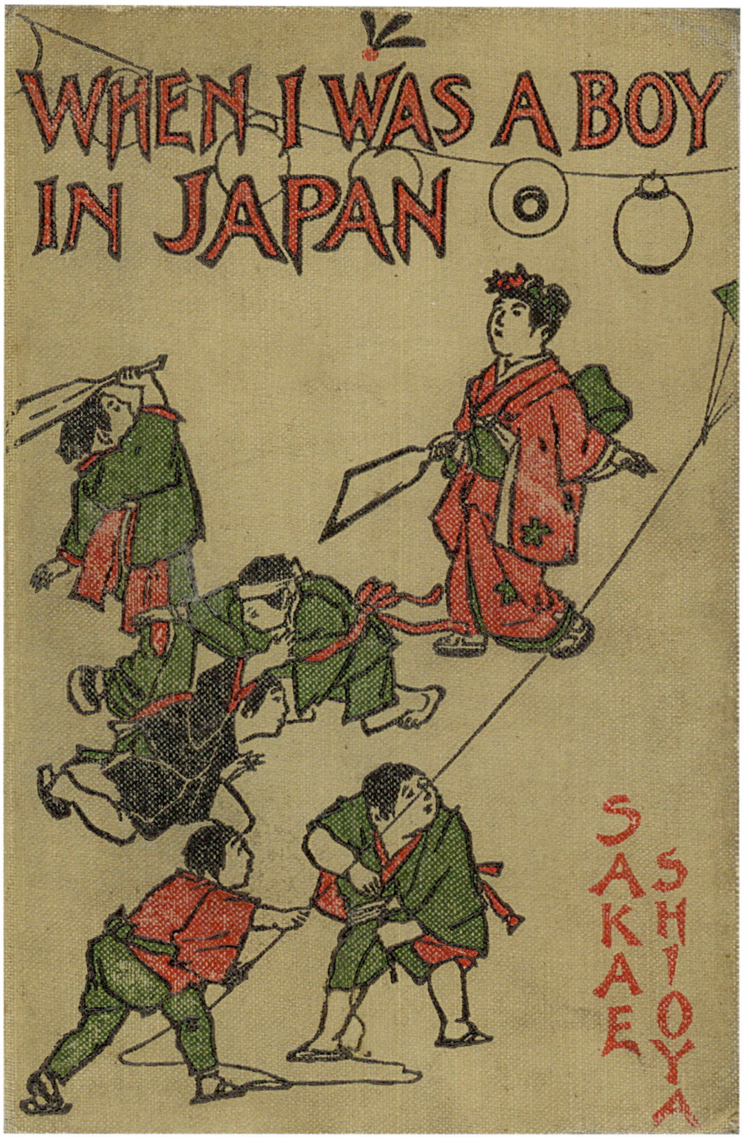

FIGURE 3.2
When I Was a Boy in Japan, by Sakae Shioya. Boston: Lothrop, Lee & Shepard, 1906.

> What a pretty creature she was! With her face white as a lily and her cheeks pink as a cherry flower, she stood there watching me. Her light hair was parted, a blue ribbon being tied on one side like a butterfly. She had on a white muslin dress with a belt to match the ribbon, but what was my astonishment to find that I could not see any dress beyond her knees! I could not believe it at first, but the dress stopped short there, and the slender legs, covered with something black,—I did not care what,—were shooting out. Might not some malicious person have cut it so? "Oh, please, for mercy's sake, cover them," was my thought. "I don't care if you have a long dress, the skirt trailing on the ground." But was I mistaken in my standard of criticism? I looked at myself, and, sure enough, my kimono reached down to my feet![28]

Takejiro Hasegawa's Crepe Paper Books

It was in this rich milieu that Takejiro Hasegawa found the inspiration and resources for his publishing enterprise. He began by seeking Japanese customers, for many Japanese people were eager to learn English. However, his books were also popular among the Western residents. Combining Western and Japanese styles of bookmaking, Hasegawa began to produce black-and-white and full-color books on plain and crepe paper.[29]

Although crepe paper was produced as early as, or perhaps even earlier than, the *Bunka Bunsei* era (1804–1829),[30] the creping process was a jealously guarded secret (perhaps an unnecessary precaution, as the process was so laborious it discouraged wide use). It was the German geographer Johann Justus Rein who employed his "scientific eye" to unveil the mystery[31] while he was on an official mission to collect information about the industries and commerce of Japan. He actually discovered copies of the *momi dai* (*momu* means to rub or soften; *dai* means table)[32]— the crepe paper press—that Hasegawa would later use. In an 1886 book, he described in great detail how the *momi dai*, in combination with processes like moistening the material, produced a paper as soft and pliable as a chamois (fig. 3.3).[33]

Hasegawa aggressively expanded his business beyond Tsukiji. He exhibited at the major trade fairs: the Third National Industrial Exhibition in 1890 in Ueno Park in Tokyo, the Universal Exposition held in Paris in 1893, and the 1893 World's Columbian Exposition in Chicago.[34] He also exhibited at fairs in Osaka (1903), Portland, Oregon (1905), Liege, Belgium (1905), and London (1910). His books ranged from a crepe-paper edition of *Karma* produced for the Open Court Publishing Company in Chicago and *A Story of Early Buddhism* (1894) by Paul Carus, to *L'École de Village*, one act from the Kabuki play *Sugawara Denju Tenarai Kagami* (1899) by Takeda Izumo (translated by Karl Florenz), a publication

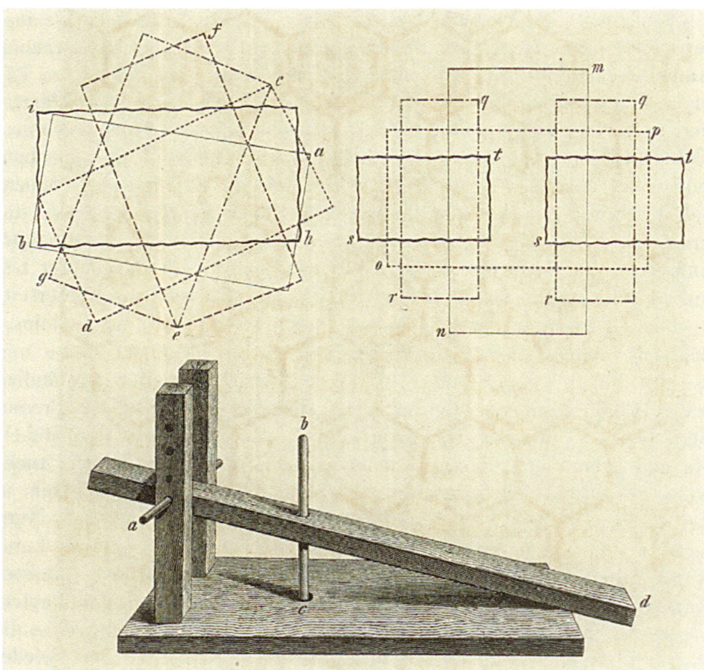

FIGURE 3.3
"Vorrichtung zur Darstellung von Krepppapier" [Device for crepe paper making], in *Japan nach Reisen und Studien im Auftrage der Königlich Preussischen Regierung*, by Johann Justus Rein. Vol. 2. Leipzig: Verlag von Wilhelm Engelmann, 1886, page 487.

displayed at the 1900 Universal Exposition in Paris. Other notable books he published included *Favorite Flowers of Japan* (1901), an exquisite advertising catalog with text by American Mary E. Unger who, with her husband Alfred Unger, owned a nursery in Yokohama; and Julia Carrothers's *Japan's Year* (1905), an elegantly decorated album about Japan's culture based on the calendar year.

Hasegawa's Children's Books and Their Creators

Not only was crepe paper handsome and appealing to Western buyers for its exotic quality, it was a practical and durable medium for children's books. As one of Hasegawa's authors, the British-born Mrs. W. H. Smith, wrote in the introduction to *The Children's Japan* (fig. 3.4):

> This little work, printed on Hasegawa's untearable crêpe, will it is hoped be welcomed for the fact that it can be placed in the hands of very young as well as older children without fear of torn leaves and dislocated covers. These books can be subjected to an amount of rough usage which no other books can stand.[35]

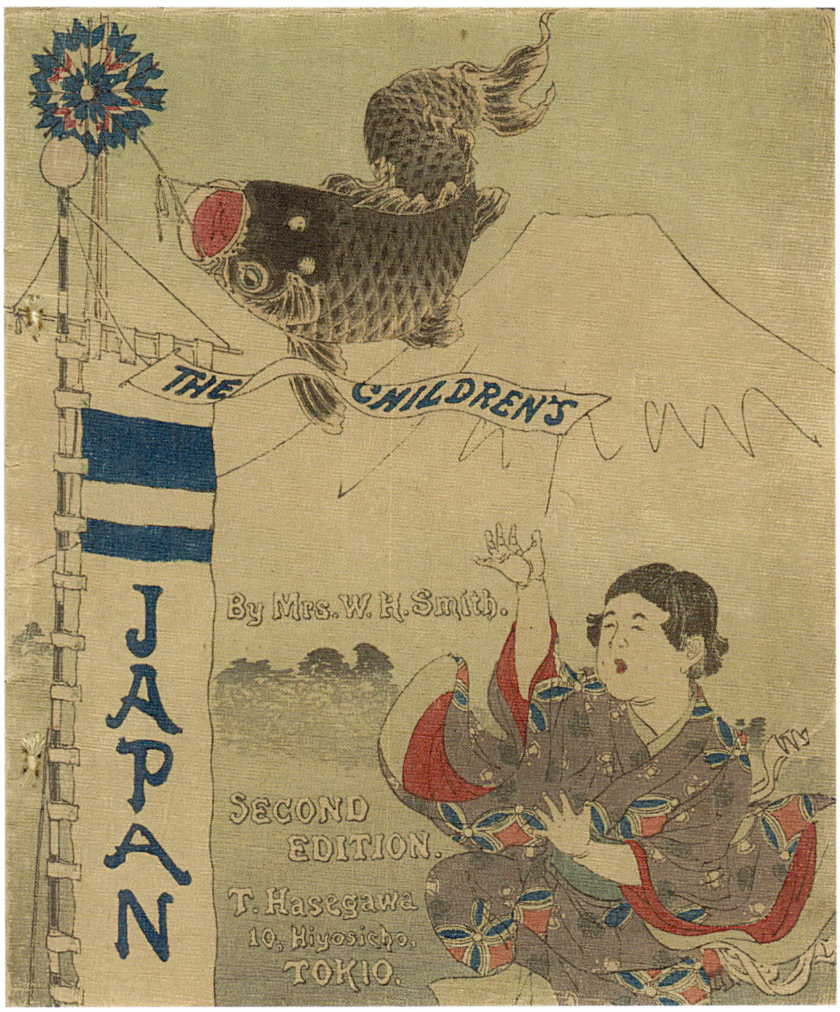

FIGURE 3.4
The Children's Japan, by Mrs. W. H. Smith, illustrated by Shōsō Mishima. Tokyo: T. Hasegawa, 1892.

In her book, handsomely illustrated by Shōsō Mishima, Smith introduced young Western readers to "Japanese Houses," "Japanese Babies" and "Older Babies," "A Japanese Holiday," "Japanese Music," and other aspects of Japanese life:

> A Japanese house has no bricks, no walls, no chimnies [*sic*] and no windows. This sounds very funny, and so it is, yet a Japanese house is both pretty and comfortable. . . .[36]
>
> The Japanese though the most artistic people in the world are also the most simple in their daily lives. Their furniture consists of two or three heavy quilts called *futons* for each person, and which serves for both bed and bed-clothes. Some small, flat cushions on which they sit; very small tables about 6 inches high, several *hibachis* or fire boxes, and some lamps, cups, bowls, wooden tubs, and saucepans. These things, with of course clothes, which are kept in a sort of chest-of-drawers, and a beautifully painted silken scroll which answers to our pictures, are the principal belongings of a Japanese family. Chairs are not used, neither are knives, forks, nor spoons, everything for which we require the latter articles being done by two dainty little sticks called "chopsticks" which the Japanese use very cleverly. These people rise early; are nearly always cheerful, and very polite to each other and strangers. They laugh and chatter at their work, but are not of course so busy as Europeans in their houses as they have so little to dust and keep tidy and clean.[37]

Hasegawa also produced *A Day with Mitsu* (1894, fig. 3.5) by the missionary Mary G. Kimura. This beautifully illustrated book described the activities and pastimes of the young boy Mitsu, including his morning toilette (cleaning his teeth with a dash of salt), flying his kite, going to school, and practicing reading and writing:

> In Tokyo, one of the largest cities in the world, in Red Hill Ward, on Spirit South Hill Street, in one of the highest parts of the city, among many girls and boys dwells one by the name of Mitsu.
>
> In large families in Japan, children are often numbered. This little boy, being the third son in his home, was named Mitsu, the Japanese word for three. His parents having too many children, he was adopted into a family where there were none. . . . Mitsu, usually rises with the sun and his elders. His dress for every day is a long, loose, narrow garment tied around the waist with a white sash, and on holidays he wears silk garments and crêpe sashes, but he always has immense, long, broad sleeves, which also serve as pockets. How a Yankee boy would envy these store-house pockets, especially in winter, when Mitsu wears several kimono's [*sic*] all having the same kind of sleeves . . . In them are kept paper handkerchiefs, kite strings, tops, boats, bean bags, popped rice, toasted *mocha* [*sic*, rice balls], peanuts, and in winter time a small tin box, filled with powdered charcoal, lighted with a match, and tightly closed, which keeps Mitsu warm for a whole half day.[38]

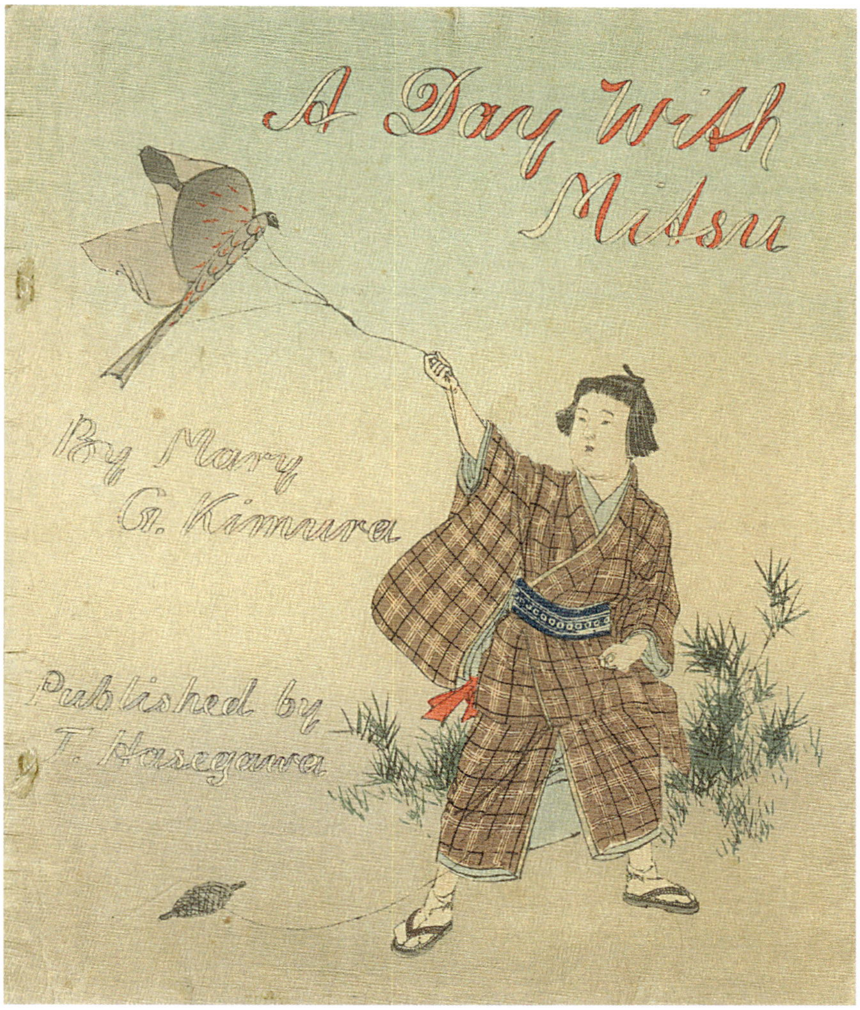

FIGURE 3.5
A Day with Mitsu, by Mary G. Kimura, illustrated by Yoshimune. Kyōbashi-ku [Tokyo]: hanken shoyū Hasegawa Takejiro, 1894.

Japan-admirer Mae St. John Bramhall, an American journalist who arrived in Yokohama with her husband in 1890, also contributed to Hasegawa's list of publications, though in a minor way. Bramhall had spent two years traveling through Japan, which she described as an "aesthetic abode of the bamboo and aromatic crib of the lotus,"[39] enjoying art treasures in private and public collections. During a "five-weeks' dilly-dally in Kioto," she experienced an "ecstatic eight hours . . . of uninterrupted beauty-feast," as she was shown an heirloom of fifteenth-century *katana* (swords), *tsuba* (sword-guards) and armor; tea-ceremony utensils, *netsuke* (carved ornaments), formal kimono and *obi*, and pottery—which for centuries had been kept in a "go-down," one of those "great fire-proof, treasure-filled store-houses of Japan."[40] (Bramhall's ecstasy over all these treasures did not prevent her from referring to her Japanese host as "the little Jap.")[41]

Summing up her observations of Japanese children, Bramhall wrote in her oft-cited *The Wee Ones of Japan*, published by Harper & Brothers in 1894 (fig. 3.6):

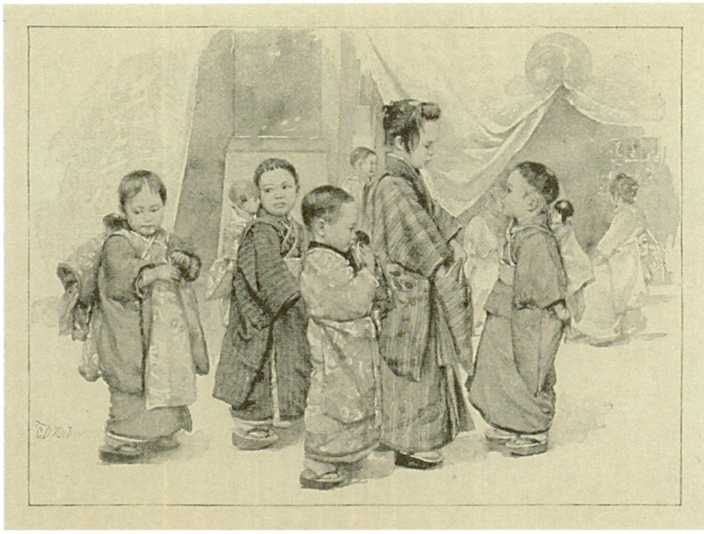

FIGURE 3.6
"A Flock of Gayly Attired Little Maidens Going Out to Tableau," in *The Wee Ones of Japan*, by Mae St. John Bramhall, illustrated by C. D. Weldon. New York: Harper and Brothers, 1894, page 108.

> After weeks and months of almost constant study of [Japanese children] . . . [one] can but regard these youngsters of Nippon as the most amusing uncommon children in the world and—with apologies to my little American friends—[they are] the very best-disciplined darlings to be found upon the ample bosom of Mother Earth.[42]

Bramhall had indeed seen many children, as she had just returned from a "leisurely jaunt round the world."[43] Yet while she describes Japanese children as "the most universally lovable, Wee Ones on earth,"[44] she also refers to them as the "little brown people," the "diminutive Nipponites," and the "*café au lait* elves" whose skin is "hardly as fine and never so fair as that of our own housed-up pink-and-white babies" and whose "black hair sometimes sets one sighing for the rings of twisted sunbeams composing so many American tresses."[45]

For Hasegawa, Bramhall produced *Japanese Jingles* (1891), which had been published previously in the *Japan Gazette*, Yokohama's first daily English-language newspaper.[46] The twenty-three long and wordy poems—some of which were translations from the Japanese—tell of butterflies and spiders, sunsets and Japanese lanterns, lovely maidens and tea by the fire. Handsomely illustrated by Kason Suzuki with designs of flowers and birds, old farmhouses nestled in the landscapes, and other iconic Japanese images, the thick crepe-paper book was in such demand that Hasegawa published a second edition and showed it at the 1893 World's Columbian Exposition in Chicago.

The book included Bramhall's poem "Little Nurse Fire-Fly," which was devoted to the "Little People of Japan":

> Are you sweet, fair children in bed and asleep?
> The Night-Wind said, with a tip-toed peep
> Over the brim of the garden wall—

> . . .
> The garden was dewy, and dim, and damp;
> And the Fire-Fly-Nurse with her wee, night-lamp,
> Flew here, and flew there, in her soft, still round,
> To see that the flowers were all sleeping sound . . .[47]

Hasegawa also produced illustrated calendars, including *The Months of Japanese Children, 1902*, which showed full-color scenes of roly-poly children playing on New Year's Day, gathering shellfish in April, watching fireworks in June, and engaging in other activities then common in Japanese life.

However, Hasegawa had his greatest success publishing the crepe-books of fairy tales for which he is known today. Published in many languages, including English, German, Dutch, Japanese, Spanish, and Portuguese, they became the staple of his publishing venture. Julia Carrothers, his teacher, encouraged him in this enterprise, lauding his books as welcome additions to what was available for Japanese children at the time, literature whose flaws she described in her 1879 publication, *The Sunrise Kingdom*:

> What has our little O I-ne san to read? Hundreds of small books with bright pictures, the chief peculiarity of which is that the story is written, not under the pictures, but on their face. We have some before us—gay little specimens of infant literature, and filled with intensely glaring illustrations of men and animals in every grotesque form and dress. In each picture are scattered columns of curious characters, to us incomprehensible, but containing to them the story designed to be illustrated. . . .[48]
>
> Most of [Japan's] children's story-books are filled with tales of ghosts and hobgoblins and embellished with most frightful pictures, so that their imaginations are constantly tortured with the horrible visions thus called up.[49]

Hasegawa's large group of friends and acquaintances, a number of whom already had a deep interest in Japanese fairy tales, provided a rich pool of writers, translators, and illustrators for his books. His circle included a number of the most respected artists of his generation, many of whom went on to help create paintings and prints that began to successfully incorporate elements from Western art new to Japan. These included Eitaku Kobayashi, who illustrated the largest number of the fairy tales; Kason Suzuki, who had been a student of the celebrated Tokugawa painter Yōsai Kikuchi and whose work had appeared in newspapers and magazines; Shōsō Mishima, also a student of Yōsai; Arai Yoshimune, an experimental printmaker; and Gyokushō Kawabata, one of the most respected and admired painters of the period. They contributed substantially to the quality of Hasegawa's books and to his success and helped as well to inadvertently expose readers to the work of some of the finest Japanese artists active at the time.[50]

Prominent among the translators in Hasegawa's group was David Thompson, who had come to Japan as early as 1863. Mastering Japanese quickly, Thompson taught English at Tsukiji Daigaku [University], established a church in Tsukiji, was an interpreter at the American legation, and became an active member of the Asiatic Society. Thompson retold the first six fairy tales Hasegawa published, beginning with *Momotaro; or, Little Peachling* (1885), perhaps the most famous Japanese fairy tale:

> A long time ago there lived an old man and an old woman. One day the old man went to the mountains to cut grass; and the old woman went to the river to wash clothes. While she was washing a great big thing came tumbling and splashing down the stream. When the old woman saw it she was very glad, and pulled it to her with a piece of bamboo that lay near by. When she took it up . . . and looked at it she saw that it was a very large peach. She then quickly finished her washing and returned home intending to give the old man the peach to eat. When she cut the peach in two, out came a child from the very large kernel. Seeing this the old couple rejoiced and named the child Momotaro or Little Peachling because he came out of a peach.[51]

Thompson also retold *The Tongue-Cut Sparrow* (1885, fig. 3.7), in which a greedy wife is punished for her cruel deed; *The Battle of the Monkey and the Crab* (1885), wherein a monkey murders his friend, a crab, who is avenged by his companions; *The Old Man Who Made the Dead Trees Blossom* (1885), the tale of a kindly old man whose love for his dog leads to great riches and blossoming trees; and *Kachi-Kachi Mountain* (1885), in which a rabbit avenges an old woman's death by killing a deceitful badger. On the more cheerful side, *Nedzumi no yome-iri* [*sic*], or *The Mouse's Wedding* (1885, fig. 3.8), tells the story of a distinguished, beautifully and formally dressed family of anthropomorphized mice whose only son, Fukutara, of a "gentle disposition" like his father Tawara no Kanemochi, is now old enough to take a wife. What lends this dainty little album of late Edo period wedding customs its dry wit are the mice's demeanor and facial expressions and inside comments—printed in smaller type—such as "The bridegroom is fine looking," "Black teeth become you," "Women should not show the white of their teeth," "Has the silk-stuff come from the dyer?" and "Look here! Musculus! Can't we have a drink?"[52]

For a retelling of the tale *Nayotake no Kaguya-hime* (Princess Splendor of the Feathery Bamboo, fig. 3.9), Hasegawa turned to Edward Rothesay Miller, a

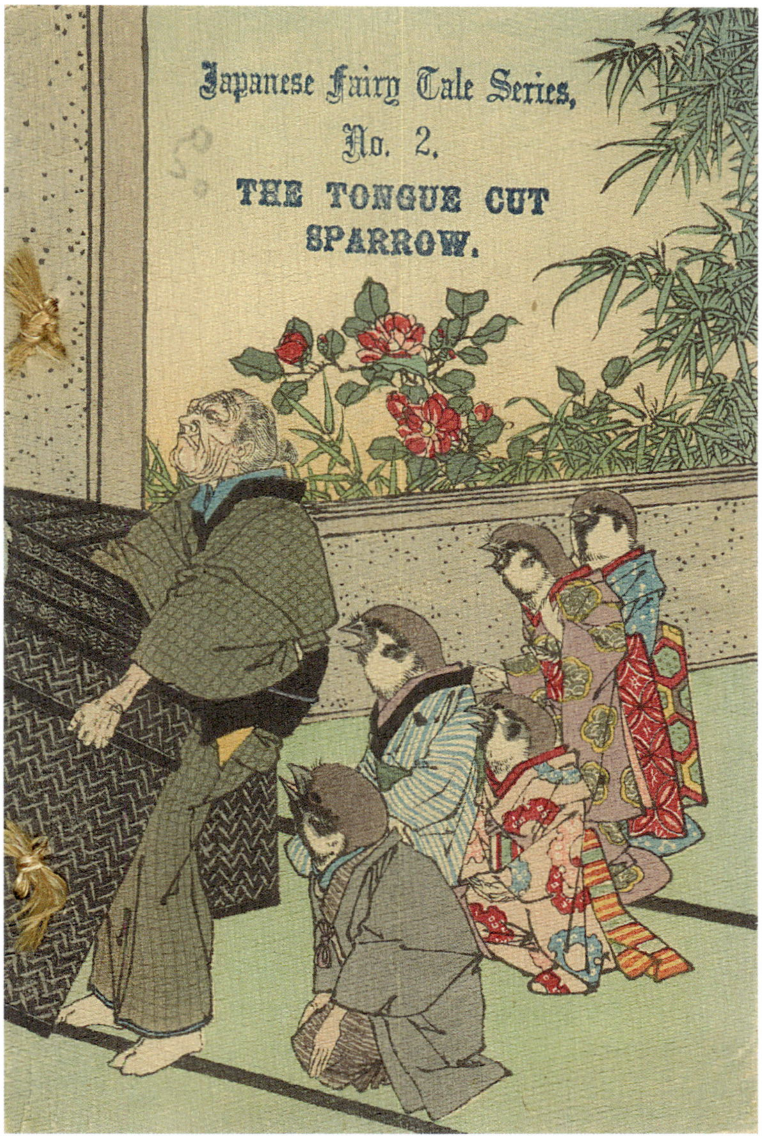

FIGURE 3.7
The Tongue-Cut Sparrow, by David Thompson, illustrated by Sensei Eitaku. Tōkyō: Hasegawa Takejirō, 1885.

missionary fluent in Japanese. The tale had appeared in many literary works as long ago as the eleventh century. It was retold in a number of anthologies and adaptations, such as *Myths and Legends of Japan*[53] and *The Tale of the Shining Princess*.[54] The tragic story tells of an otherworldly princess who is found by an old bamboo cutter and who must eventually return to her heavenly realm.

Basil Hall Chamberlain was another prominent member of the Tsukiji community and a Hasegawa contributor. In Chamberlain's retelling of *Urashima* (1886), the classic myth of Taro, a fisherman travels to the bottom of the sea and discovers upon his return that three hundred years have passed. Chamberlain also wrote *The Serpent with Eight Heads* (1886), a version of the creation myth of Amaterasu, the sun goddess; *The Silly Jelly Fish* (1887), which explains why this fish does not have any bones; *My Lord Bag-o'-Rice* (1887), whose title refers to the hero's magic rice bag; and *The Princes Fire-Flash and Fire-Fade* (1887), in which

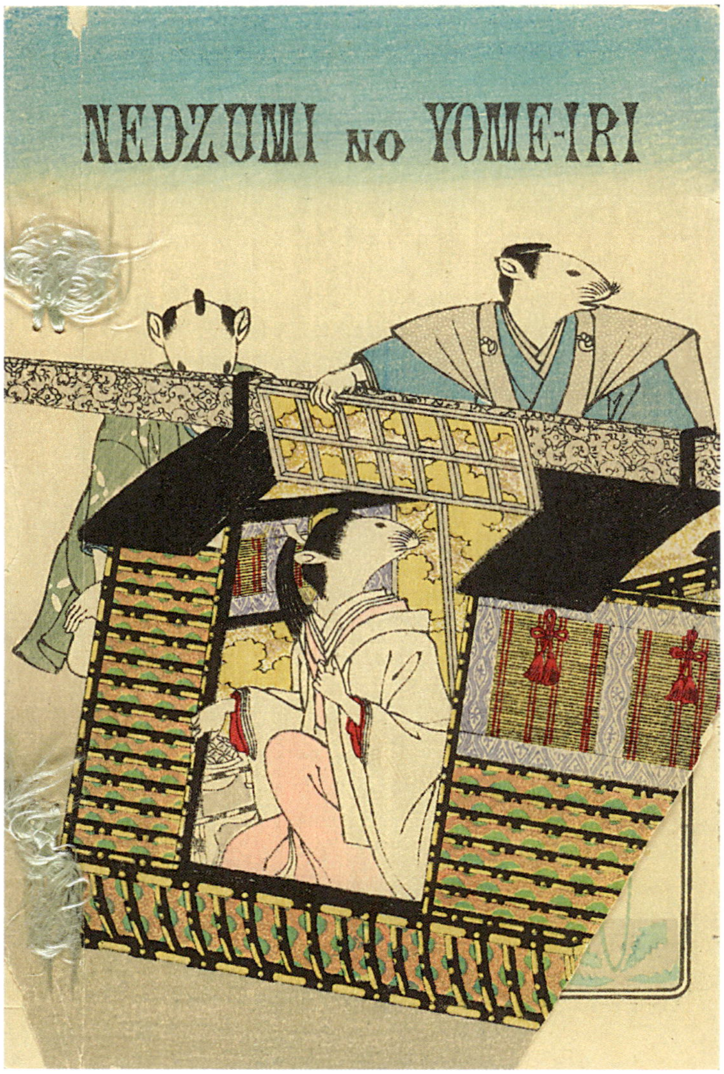

FIGURE 3.8
Nedzumi no yome-iri [The Mouse's Wedding], translated by David Thompson, illustrated by Sensei Eitaku. Tōkyō: Kōbunsha, 1885.

the Sea-King helps Prince Fire-Fade to overcome his mean-spirited brother. Chamberlain's most original contribution, however, was his retelling of Ainu tales, which he gleaned "from the dictation of native informants"[55] and which had never been published before.

Chamberlain wrote in the preface to his study and collection of Ainu tales:

> I visited the island of Yezo for the third time in the summer of 1886, in order to study the Aino language,[56] with a view to elucidate by its means the obscure problem of the geographical nomenclature of Japan. But, as is apt to happen on such occasions, the chief object of my visit soon ceased to be the only object. He who would learn a language must try to lisp in it, and more especially must he try to induce the natives to chatter in it in his presence. Now in Yezo, subjects of discourse are few. The Ainos stand too low in the scale of humanity to have any notion of the civilized art of "making conversation." When, therefore, the fishing and the weather are exhausted, the European sojourner in one of their dreary, filthy . . . hamlets will find himself,—at least I found myself,—sadly at a loss for

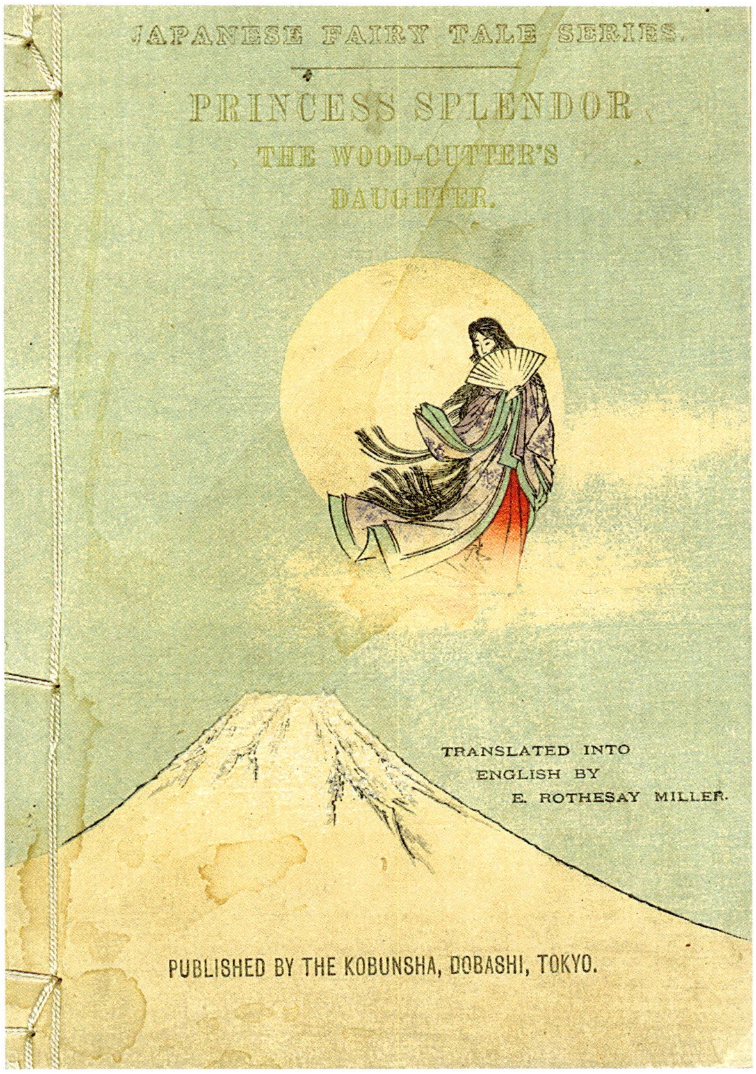

FIGURE 3.9
Princess Splendor, the Wood-cutter's Daughter, translated by E. Rothesay Miller, illustrated by Kobayashi Eitaku. Tokyo: Kobunsha, 1889.

any further means of setting his native companions' tongues in motion. It is then that fairy-tales come to the rescue. Simply to repeat something which they have known by heart ever since the days of their childhood is not such an effort to their easily-tired brains as is the keeping up of a conversation with one who speaks the language imperfectly. Their tongues are at once loosened.

In my own case, I found myself, after a short time, listening to the stories for their own sake,—not merely as linguistic exercises; and I ventured to include a few of them in the "Memoir of the Ainos" which was published a few months ago by the Imperial University of Japan. . . . I have, therefore, now collected and classified all the tales that were communicated to me by Ainos, in Aino, during my last stay in the island, and more latterly in Tokyo, when . . . by the kind assistance of the President of the University, Mr. H. Watanabe, an exceptionally intelligent Aino was procured from the North, and spent a month in my house. . . .

[T]he general tenor and tendency of the tales and traditions of the Ainos wear a widely different aspect from that which characterizes the folk-lore of Japan. The

> Ainos, in their humble way, are addicted to moralizing and to speculating on the origin of things. A perusal of the . . . tales will show that a surprisingly large number of them are attempts to explain some natural phenomenon, or to exemplify some simple precept. . . . [The Aino] does not "make believe" like the European nurse, even like the European child, who has always, in some nook or corner of his mind, a presentiment of the skepticism of his later years . . . Nine of [these tales] have already been printed . . . at the end of Mr. Batchelor's grammar included in the same "Memoir." All the others are now given to the world for the first time, never having yet appeared in any language, not even in Japanese.[57]

For his young audiences, Chamberlain explained in his book *The Hunter in Fairy-Land* (fig. 3.10):

> The Ainos are people who live in an island called Yezo. The men all have long black beards, and they spend their time in hunting and fishing. They are very poor

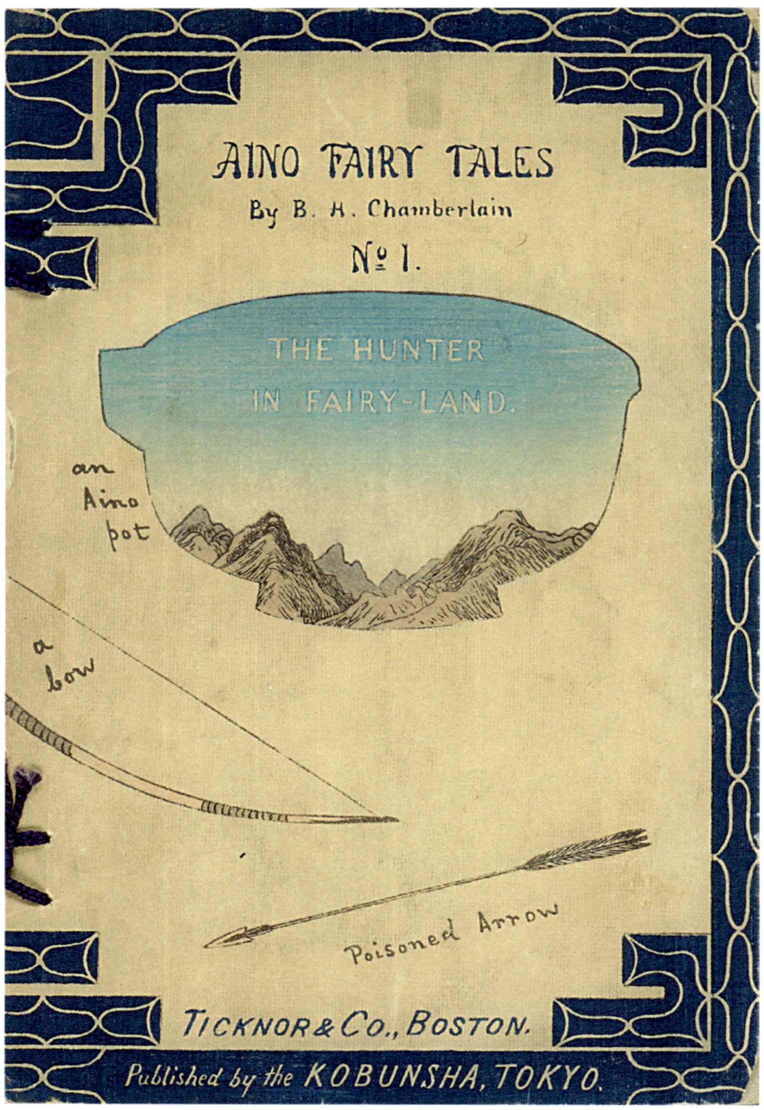

FIGURE 3.10
The Hunter in Fairy-Land, by Basil Hall Chamberlain, illustrated by Sensei Eitaku. Tokyo: Kobunsha, 1887.

> and very ignorant, yet even these poor people love their children. Often of an evening when they all sit round the fire together before going to bed, the mothers tell their little ones pretty fairy-tales and fables. I have listened to some of these, and am now going to tell them to you in English, because they are new stories, which you have never heard before.[58]

Hasegawa published three Ainu tales translated by Chamberlain. Their covers are embellished by the distinct design motifs appliquéd or embroidered on Ainu robes. They include *The Hunter in Fairy-Land* (1887), a quintessential Ainu story, as it highlights a bear, the central animal of the Ainu's physical and spiritual life[59]; *The Birds' Party* (1887), whose kimono-clad hosts, Mr. and Mrs. Pigeon, asked the hawk, the stork, the eagle, and many others to come to a fête but forgot to invite the crow[60]; and *The Man Who Lost His Wife* (1889), about a faithful husband who rescues his wife from a wicked goblin.

Scottish-born Kate James came to Japan with her husband, who taught at the Tsukiji Naval Academy. James retold for Hasegawa a number of fairy tales that she had translated from the Japanese for her own children. Among them are *Schippeitaro* (1888), *The Ogre's Arm* (1889), and *The Ogres of Oyeyama* (1891), all three about ogres and monsters. She also retold *The Wooden Bowl* (1887), about a young girl who hides her beauty under a bowl, and *The Matsuyama Mirror* (1886, fig. 3.11), a moving story of a young girl who believes that the image in her mirror is that of her late mother.

Hasegawa's star contributor, Lafcadio Hearn, praised James in a letter to a friend:

> I'm trying to write an essay—no, a fantastic-philosophical sketch—about Mirrors and Souls. Especially Souls. Which causes me to think about Mrs. James's version of the "Matsuyama Kagami [Mirror]."
>
> Who is Mrs. James? I have read her version about fifteen times, and every time I read it, it affects me more. And I can't help thinking that the woman who could thus make the vague Japanese incident so beautiful must have a tender and beautiful soul,—whoever she is,—whether missionary or not.[61]

Hearn arrived in Japan in 1890, after establishing his reputation as a journalist and writer. Still the best known of the Western storytellers of Japan, he became a close friend of Basil Hall Chamberlain, who helped him acquire teaching positions in Matsue and, later, at the Imperial University in Tokyo.[62]

Hasegawa was eager to meet this new arrival, hoping to take advantage of "Hearn's international reputation."[63] Chamberlain sent Hearn the following advice:

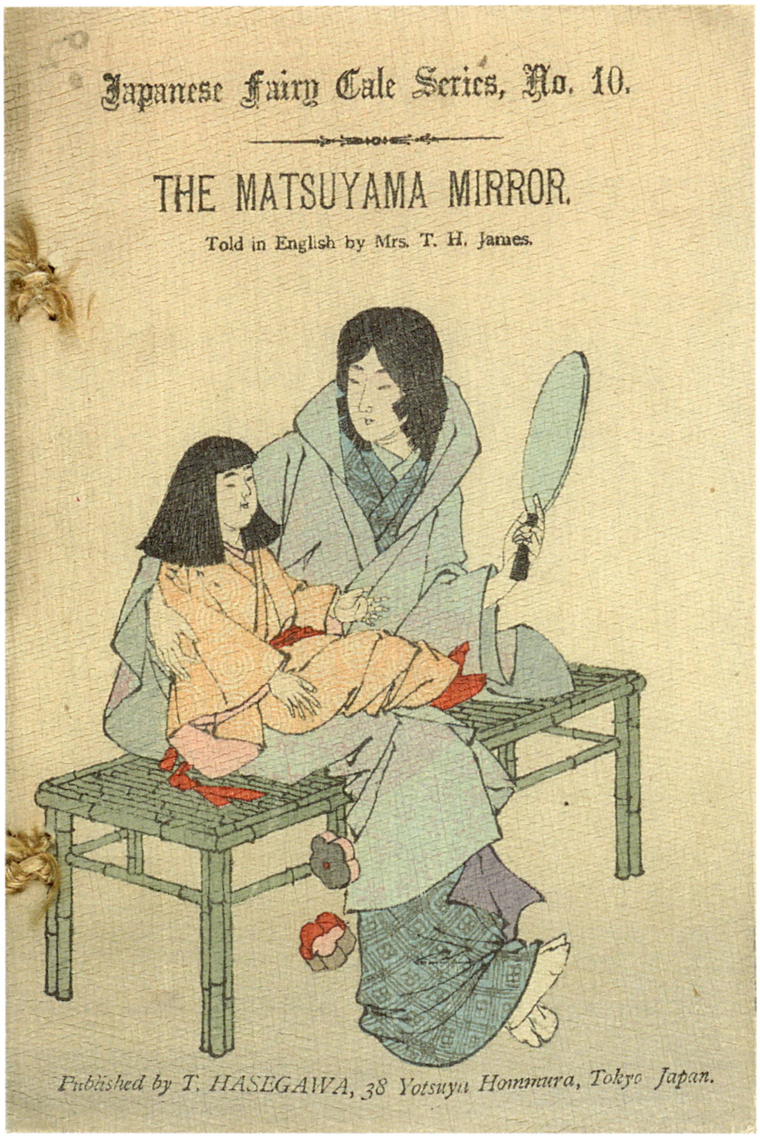

FIGURE 3.11
The Matsuyama Mirror, told in English by Mrs. T. H. [Kate] James, illustrated by Sensei Eitaku. Tokyo: T. Hasegawa, 1886.

> One thing to be remembered is that [Hasegawa] is not omnivorous. Only a single tale at a time is his view of things, each taking long to illustrate, and various other circumstances, as I know from experience, causing delay.[64]

Hearn's *The Goblin Spider* (1899, fig. 3.12) tells of what happens when a samurai tries to kill a fearsome goblin that can change its shape, appearing as half a body with only one eye and, finally, as a monstrous hairy spider. Other tales retold by Hearn and published by Hasegawa included *Chin chin kobakama* (1903), a moral tale of a beautiful and rich girl who is punished for her laziness; and the light-hearted *The Old Woman Who Lost Her Dumpling* (1902):

> Long, long ago there was a funny old woman, who liked to laugh and to make dumplings of rice-flour. One day, while she was preparing some dumplings for dinner, she let one fall; and it rolled into a hole in the earthen floor of her little

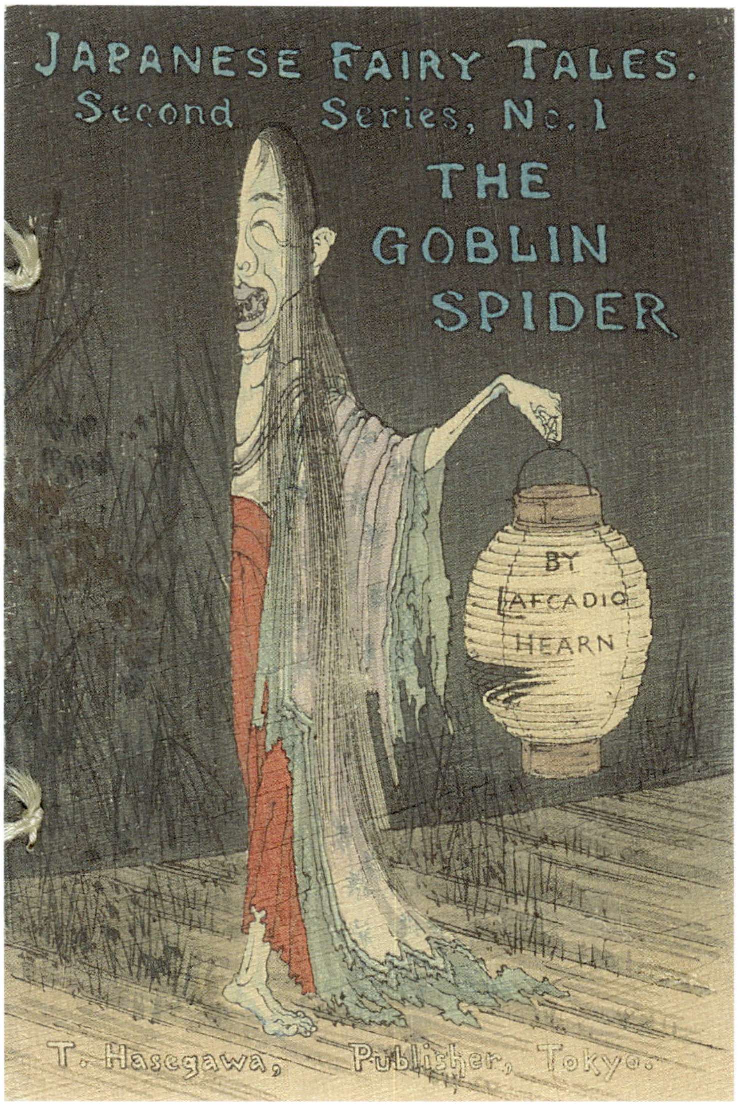

FIGURE 3.12
The Goblin Spider, rendered into English by Lafcadio Hearn, illustrated by Kason Suzuki. Tōkyō: Hasegawa Takejirō, 1899.

> kitchen and disappeared. The old woman tried to reach it by putting her hand down the hole, and all at once the earth gave way, and the old woman fell in.[65]

In the alien world in which she lands, the fearless little woman encounters and defies the man-eating *oni* and then escapes with their magic rice paddle. The story's quaintness was captured seventy years later by Arlene Mosel and Blair Lent in their Caldecott-award winning *The Funny Little Woman* (1972).

Hearn's eerie *The Boy Who Drew Cats* (1898, fig. 3.13) was destined to become a classic. Illustrated by Kason Suzuki, the story was apparently based on the life of the fifteenth-century painter Tōyō Sesshū, one of Japan's great Zen priest-painters, revered for his Chinese-style, black-ink landscape paintings.[66] *The Boy Who Drew Cats* tells the haunting tale of the young, clever boy whose father, concerned that the boy was weak and small and thus unable to help on the farm, sent him to a temple to become a priest. Hearn wrote:

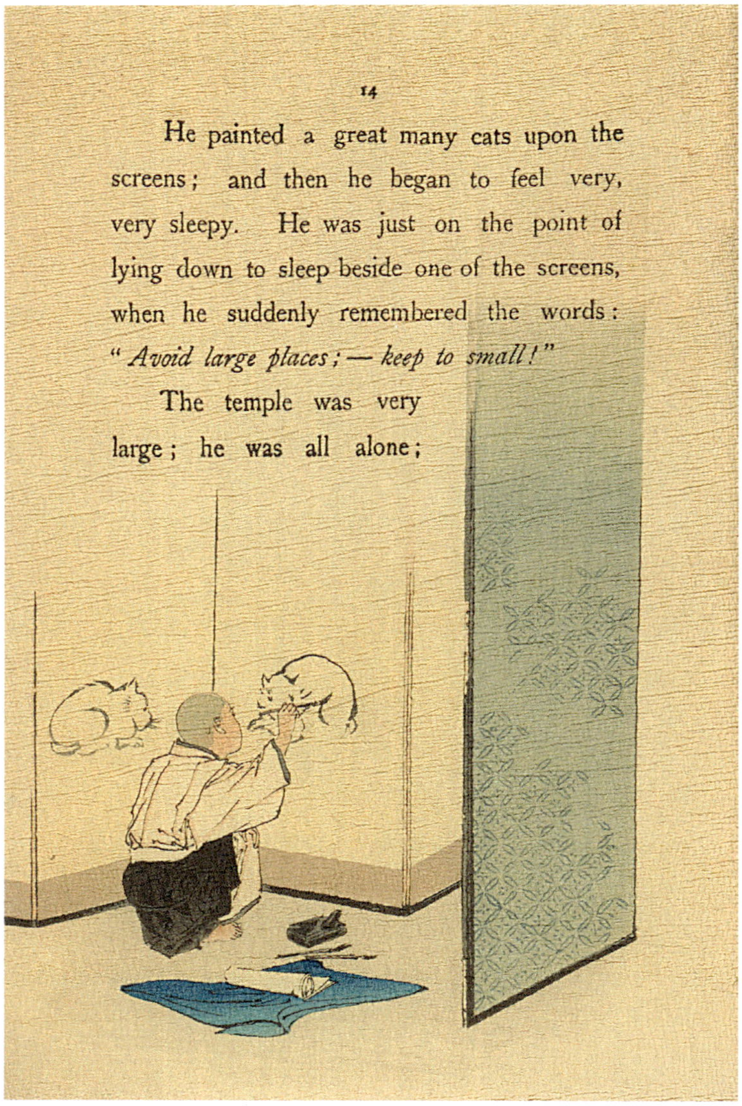

FIGURE 3.13
The Boy Who Drew Cats, rendered into English by Lafcadio Hearn, illustrated by Kason Suzuki. Tokyo: Hasegawa Takejirō, 1898.

The boy learned quickly what the old priest taught him, and was very obedient in most things. But he had one fault. He liked to draw cats during study-hours, and to draw cats even where cats ought not to have been drawn at all. Whenever he found himself alone, he drew cats. He drew them on the margins of the priest's books, and on all the screens of the temple, and on the walls, and on the pillars. Several times the priest told him this was not right; but he did not stop drawing them because he could not really help it. . . . [Finally the priest sent him away.]

The boy left the temple very sorrowfully . . . He remembered a large temple in the next village. . . .

Now that big temple was closed up but the boy did not know this fact. The reason it had been closed up was that a goblin had frightened the priests away, and had taken possession of the place. Some brave warriors had afterward gone to the temple at night to kill the goblin; but they had never been seen alive again. Nobody had ever told these things to the boy;—so he walked all the way to the village hoping to be kindly treated by the priests. . . .

> The boy went at once to the temple, and knocked. There was no sound inside. He knocked and knocked again; but still nobody came. At last he pushed gently at the door, and was quite glad to find that it had not been fastened. So he went in, and saw a lamp burning,—but no priest. . . .
>
> Then he noticed that everything in the temple was grey with dust, and thickly spun over with cobwebs. So he thought to himself that the priests would certainly like to have an acolyte, to keep the place clean. . . . What most pleased him, however, were some big white screens, good to paint cats upon. Though he was tired, he looked at once for a writing-box, and found one, and ground some ink, and began to paint cats.
>
> He painted a great many cats upon the screens; and then he began to feel very, very sleepy. . . .
>
> He found a little cabinet, with a sliding door, and went into it, and shut himself up. Then he lay down and fell fast asleep.
>
> Very late in the night he was awakened by a most terrible noise—a noise of fighting and screaming. It was so dreadful that he was afraid even to look through a chink of the little cabinet: he lay very still, holding his breath for fright.
>
> The light that had been in the temple went out; but the awful sounds continued, and became more awful, and all the temple shook.
>
> [Finally] . . . he got out of his hiding-place very cautiously, and looked about. The first thing he saw was that all the floor of the temple was covered with blood. And then he saw, lying dead in the middle of it, an enormous, monstrous rat,—a goblin-rat,—bigger than a cow!
>
> But who or what could have killed it? . . . Suddenly the boy observed that the mouths of all the cats he had drawn the night before were red and wet with blood. Then he knew that the goblin had been killed by the cats which he had drawn. . . .[67]

Enterprising and creative, Takejiro Hasegawa lived and worked at the right time and place. He seems to have fit perfectly into a world where East and West met and flourished. By seeking out skilled writers and artists and by publishing translations of Japanese tales in beautiful and durable editions, he helped to build a bridge between Japan and the Western world. Hasegawa died on July 19, 1938, at the age of eighty-five. His workshop still greets passersby in Negishi, Taito-ku in northeastern Tokyo. His crepe paper fairy-tale books—preserved in private and institutional collections—are pleasing reminders of his creative bookmaking, which combined the best of Japanese and foreign traditions.

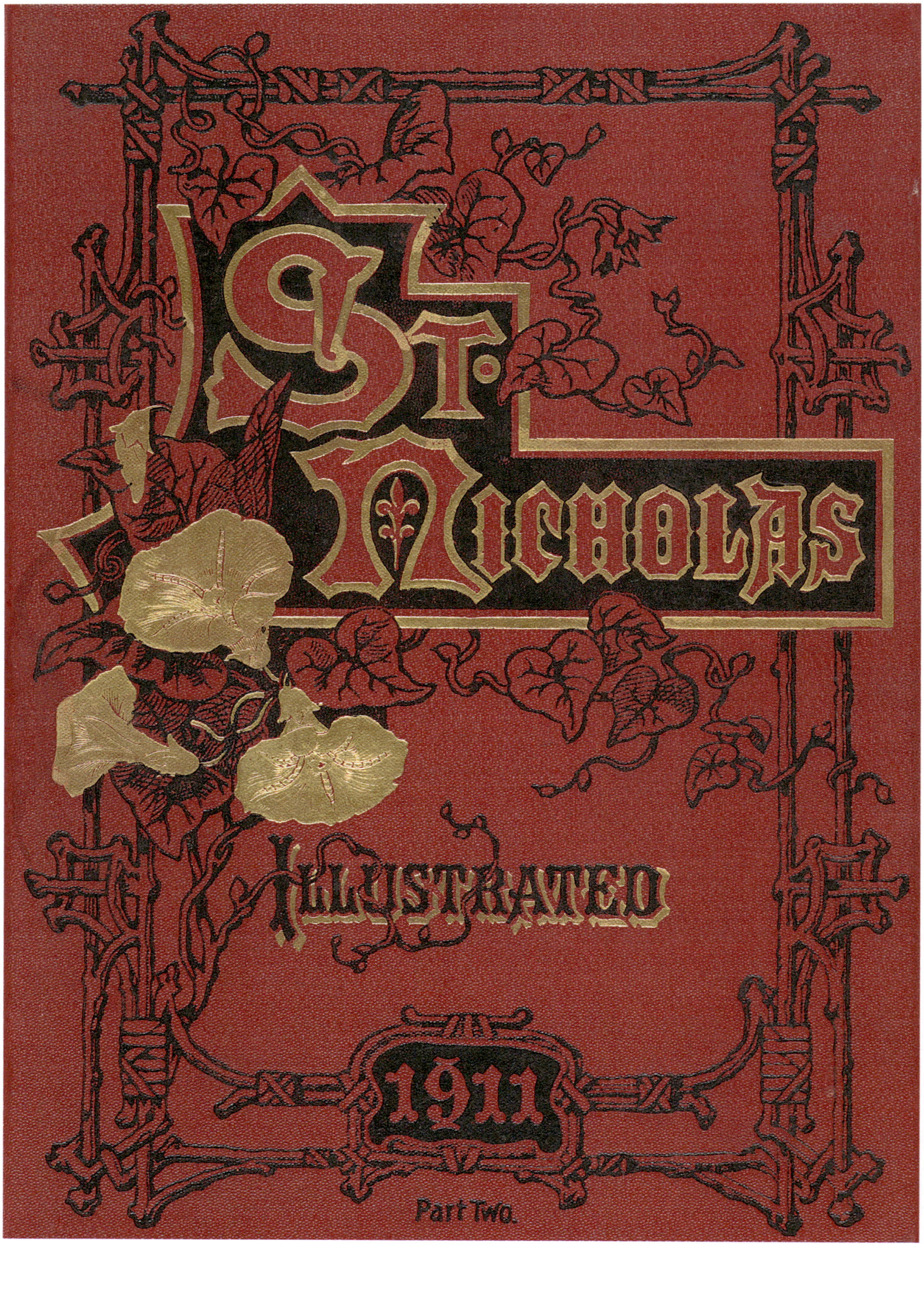
St. Nicholas
Illustrated
1911
Part Two.

4

Japan in *St. Nicholas* Magazine

Among children's magazines established during the final decades of the nineteenth century—including *Wide Awake, The Riverside Magazine for Young People, Our Young Folks,* and *Harper's Young People*—*St. Nicholas: Scribner's Illustrated Magazine for Girls and Boys* made the most lasting contribution to American children's literature. As Alice M. Jordan, Boston Public Library's leading children's book specialist wrote, "within [the] red covers [of *St. Nicholas*] lies the very kernel of American books for children."[1]

In *St. Nicholas* magazine young American readers first read and saw the works of distinguished writers and illustrators such as Louisa May Alcott, Samuel Langhorne Clemens (Mark Twain), and N. C. Wyeth. Contributors who wrote about Japan included Hezekiah Butterworth, Jack London, Bayard Taylor, Kirk Munroe, and Lucy Fitch Perkins.[2]

At a time when few children's libraries existed, when most children's books were didactic and moralistic, and when illustrations were largely unimaginative, *St. Nicholas* carried its engaging stories and pictures "to every corner of the country."[3] It was embraced and loved, anticipated and shared. May Lamberton Becker, a *St. Nicholas* reader who later became an editor, wrote:

> *St. Nicholas* came to us like anything in nature, like the seasons, like the weather. In summer we knew it would bring us outdoor reading, in September *St. Nicholas* knew we were back in school; when winter's cold had firmly settled in, Thanksgiving stories and directions for homemade presents announced the approach of that great annual event, the Special Christmas Number, a real "visit of St. Nicholas" coming early enough for us to rehearse its entertainments for parlor performance or memorize its verses for the Sunday School tree. . . . Each of us on our block read every word of it. Those who did not subscribe borrowed it from their best friends, and those who did, kept track of each copy lest it should be too often borrowed away and lost.[4]

FIGURE 4.1 (OPPOSITE)
St. Nicholas, cover for bound volume of 1911 issues.

Well before becoming a noted advertising executive, Earnest Elmo Calkins was the very first reader of *St. Nicholas.* In 1931, he wrote of the day in November 1873

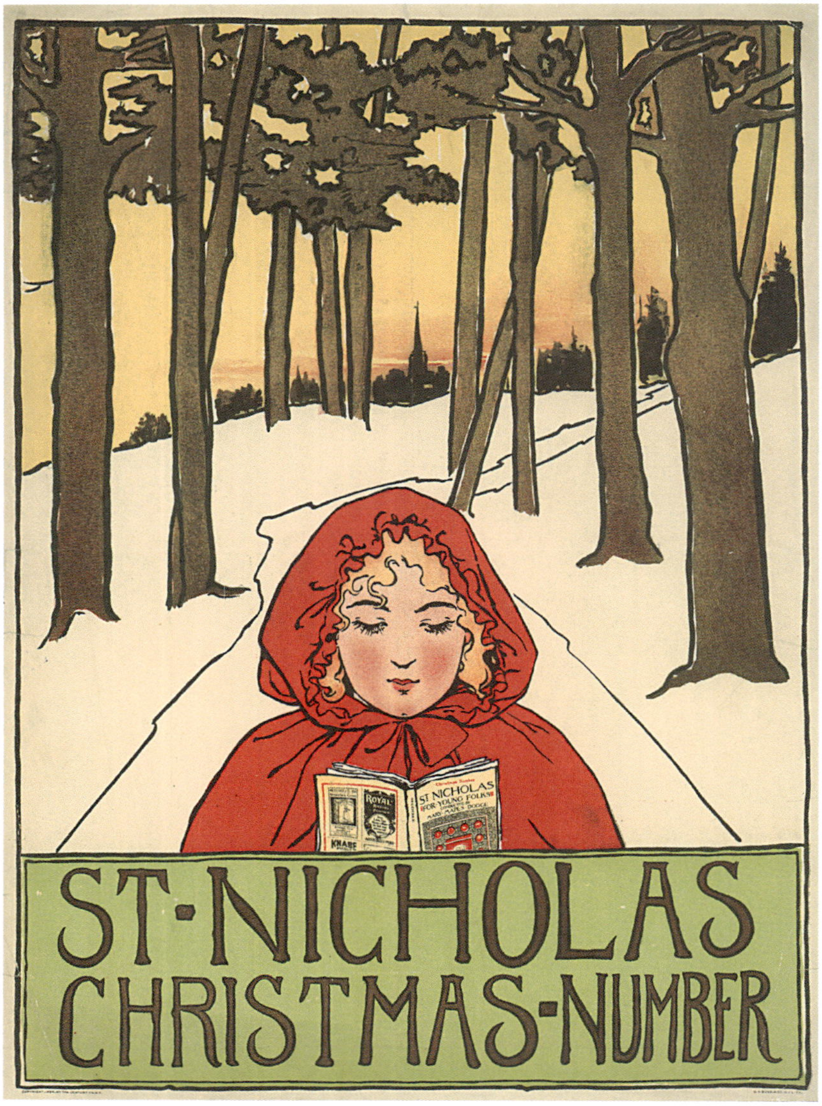

FIGURE 4.2
"St. Nicholas Christmas Number," illustration by Frank Berkeley Smith. *St. Nicholas* vol. 24, no. 2 (December 1896).

that his father came home with the first issue, "gay with red-and-black cover," and that his exposure to *St Nicholas* that year,

> was the opening of a door into a new world. . . . No boy or girl in these days of abundant reading-matter can possibly know how eagerly we who were little folks fifty years ago longed for something to read—something of our own kind, about boys and girls, instead of grown-up books.[5]

The woman who brought about this children's reading tour-de-force was Mary Mapes Dodge, daughter of the prominent New York editor and scientist James Jay Mapes, who made certain that Mary and her four brothers and sisters had fine tutors and governesses and were surrounded by ideas and books. In 1851, Mary wed William Dodge, with whom she had two children before his untimely death in 1858.

Thereafter, and upon her father's urging, Dodge began editing *Working Farmer* and *United States Journal*, two magazines he owned, and in 1863 she began contributing her own stories to *Harper's New Monthly Magazine.*

In 1872, Roswell Smith, one of the founders of *Scribner's Monthly* (highly regarded as a proponent of "the highest aesthetic and moral ideals")[6] suggested to Dodge the creation of a new monthly periodical for young readers. The following year, Dodge outlined the mission and spirit of what was to become her magazine:

> The child's magazine needs to be stronger, truer, bolder, more uncompromising than [an adult periodical]. . . . A magazine for children must also be didactic, conveying a system of ideals and values . . . by hints dropped incidentally here and there; by a few brisk, hearty statements of the difference between right and wrong; a sharp, clean thrust at falsehood, a sunny recognition of truth, a gracious application of politeness, an unwilling glimpse of the odious doings of the uncharitable and base. . . . Harsh, cruel facts—if they must come, and sometimes it is important that they should—must march forward boldly, say what they have to say, and go.[7]

In the first issue of *St. Nicholas*,[8] "the cheeriest, prettiest, jolliest, welcomest magazine that boys and girls, or their parents either, had ever beheld,"[9] the frontispiece illustration, depicting a boy stretched out in a meadow playing his flute for a duckling family, broadcast the carefree spirit and joy of the new adventure (fig. 4.3). *St. Nicholas*, which flourished under Dodge's leadership for thirty-two years, soon increased its pages from forty-eight to ninety-six, nearly doubled its circulation (from 40,000 to approximately 70,000),[10] and absorbed several other juvenile periodicals along the way.

In addition to several "departments" that appeared in every issue, *St. Nicholas* addressed an amazing array of subjects, from "adjutant birds" and "biceps" to Jane Addams and Hull House; from the "Negro dialect" to the Crystal Palace in London. Nonfiction included American history, science and technology, natural science, and crafts, teaching young readers about practical matters of their world. Fiction included stories with historical, domestic, or fantastical settings; mysteries and adventures; and stories specifically aimed at boys or girls.

The magazine also featured editorials, reprints of notable works, poems and amusing vignettes, games, rebuses, musical scores, riddles, and readers' letters. Young subscribers were encouraged to send in their translations of *St. Nicholas* stories published in French and German; or, as members of the St. Nicholas League (begun in 1899), to contribute stories, poems, drawings and even photographs. (The League became a Who's Who of American letters. Stephen Vincent Benét, F. Scott Fitzgerald, Norman Rockwell, and many others were *St. Nicholas* readers in their youth.)

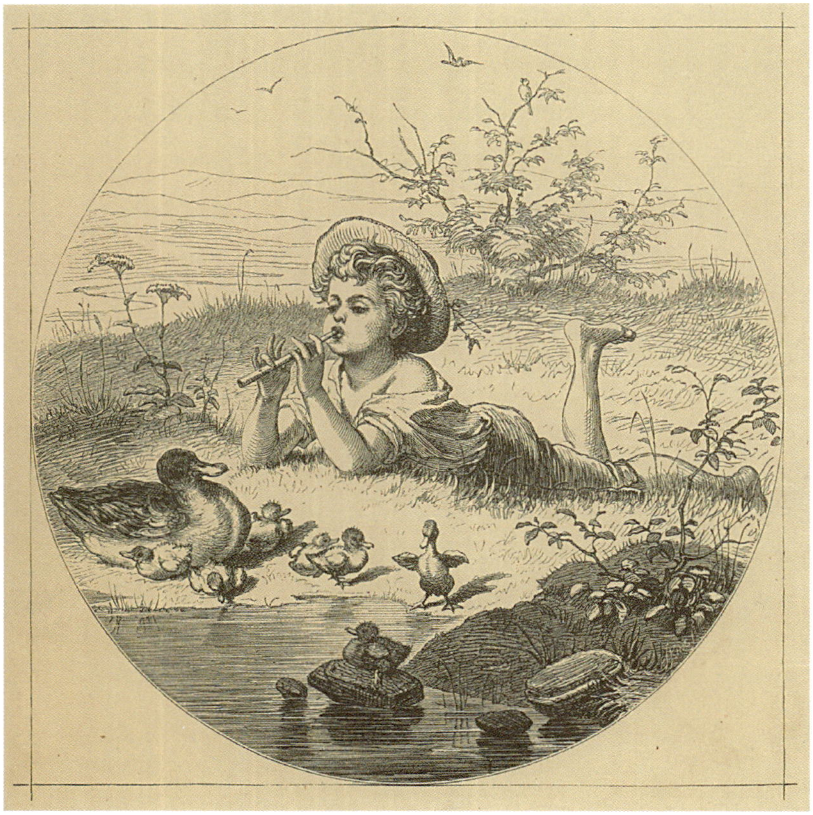

FIGURE 4.3
Frontispiece from *St. Nicholas* vol. 4, no. 1 (November 1873).

The articles in *St. Nicholas* were written on a high, almost adult reading level. (Several of the *St. Nicholas* Japan articles were reprinted in the *Washington Post.*) Its many illustrations, a mixture of black-and-white drawings and photographs, were informative and entertaining. The magazine's mood was that of adventure and fun, of learning and mind-stretching.

Writers Who Brought Japan to *St. Nicholas*

From the beginning, *St. Nicholas* had an international outlook. Many of its informational articles dealt with travel to foreign places, Japan being prominent among them. With access to authors and illustrators who worked for *Scribner's Monthly* (*St. Nicholas*'s parent magazine), Dodge was able to engage well-informed Japan travelers, such as William Elliot Griffis, who published in *St. Nicholas* a biographical piece about the artist Hokusai (March 1883) and an article filled with technical information about Japanese whale hunting (December 1882). His playful information-story about Harukichi, "Blossom Boy of Tokio," published in July 1879, described the quintessential Japanese child (in Griffis's words) who "was carried on his nurse's back, or on his mother's or sister's"; whose "silk robe was embroidered with the designs of the pine-tree, stork, and tortoise"; whose "skin was as soft as a peach, and of a color like *café-au-lait*"; whose "cheeks were as rosy as a plum blossom," and whose clothes "were just made to play in. Not a button or strap anywhere about them, nor a pin to stick him."[11] In March 1877, Griffis published an article about kite flying (fig. 4.4), a traditional Japanese pastime:

> Of all the sports at which the boys in Japan amuse themselves, kite-flying seems to afford the most fun and enjoyment. Japanese kites are not plain coffin-shaped bits of tissue-paper, such as American boys fly. They are made of tough paper stretched on light frames of bamboo, and of all shapes,—square, oblong, or oval. They are also made to imitate animals. I have often, in my walks in Japan, seen a whole paper menagerie in the air. There were crying babies, boys with arms spread out, horses, fishes, bats, hawks, crows, monkeys, snakes, dragons, besides ships, carts, and houses. Across and behind the top of the kite, a thin strip of whalebone is stretched, which hums, buzzes, or sings high in air like a hurdy-gurdy or a swarm of beetles. When the boys of a whole city are out in kite-time, there is more music in the air than is delightful. The real hawks and crows, and other birds, give these buzzing counterfeits of themselves a wide berth. In my walks, I often was deceived when looking up, unable to tell at first whether the moving black spots in the air were paper, or a real, living creature, with beak, claws, and feathers. . . .
>
> On the faces of the square Japanese kites you can see a whole picture-gallery of the national heroes. Brave boys, great men, warriors in helmet and armor, hunters with bows and arrows, and all the famous children and funny folks in the Japanese fairy tales, are painted on them in gay colors, besides leaping dragons, snow-storms, pretty girls dancing, and great many other designs.[12]

American writer and photographer Eliza Ruhamah Scidmore traveled to China, Thailand, India, and Ceylon and lived in Japan for several years, contributing

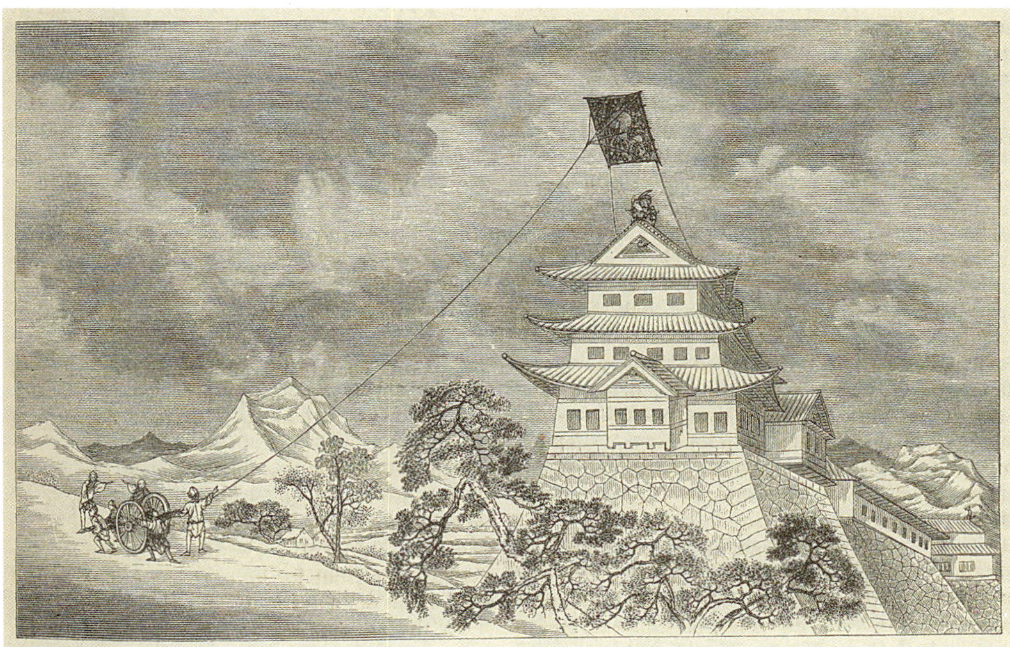

FIGURE 4.4
"Attempting to Rob the Golden Fish," in "The Golden Fish of Owari Castle," by William E. Griffis. *St. Nicholas* vol. 4, no. 5 (March 1877): 325. Illustration "drawn by a Japanese artist."

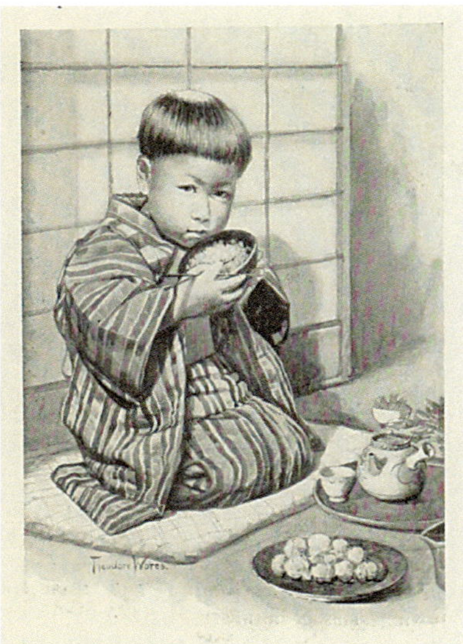

FIGURE 4.5
"Master Kumataro Eating with Chopsticks" in "Glimpses of Child Life in Japan," written and illustrated by Theodore Wores. *St. Nicholas* vol. 28, no. 9 (July 1901): 806.

articles to *National Geographic Magazine* (on whose Board of Managers she served), *Harper's Bazaar, Century*, and *Asia*. In them she described *cha no yu*, Japan's exalted form of tea drinking, refined over centuries by scholars and poets, shōguns and emperors; imperial receptions given by Emperor Meiji and his consort, the Empress Haru (Scidmore lamented the fact that court dress was giving way to European attire); Japanese silk culture; fish markets; the Japanese exhibits at the 1893 World's Fair in Chicago, and other aspects of Japanese culture. For *St. Nicholas* Scidmore wrote "How to Use a Pair of Chopsticks" (April 1890) and "Yoshi Hito, Haru no Miya, the Child of Modern Japan" (July 1889), an article about the boy who would reign from 1912 to 1926 as Japan's 123rd emperor, known as the Emperor Taisho.

In her 385-page, information-packed 1891 book *Jinrikisha Days in Japan*, Scidmore revealed the deep love of Japan that also infused her articles for young *St. Nicholas* readers. Japan, she wrote, was a "dream of Paradise, beautiful from the first green island off the coast to the last picturesque hill-top," and its people were "the fine flower of the Orient, the most polite, refined, and aesthetic of races, happy, light-hearted, friendly and attractive."[13] This affection was reciprocal. So greatly did the Japanese esteem her work as a goodwill ambassador between the United States and Japan—she played an important role in bringing the cherry trees to Washington, DC—that at the request of the Japanese government, her ashes were interred in Yokohama.

American novelist and poet Mary Fenollosa was the wife of Ernest F. Fenollosa, who was an early Western advocate for the preservation of Japanese art, a founder of the Tokyo School of Fine Arts, and a curator at the Museum of Fine Arts, Boston. She wrote extensively about Japan. Her most endearing book is the handsomely illustrated *Blossoms from a Japanese Garden: A Book of Child-Verses* (1913, fig. 4.6), a Japan-adoring collection of her own and others' poems (with color plates by an anonymous Japanese artist). Highlighting the usual themes of Boys' Day, cherry blossom viewing, kite flying, and the deer that roam freely around the temples of Nara, the volume includes as well verses about a typhoon, about Take who skips school, naughty children who call the foreigners names, and a young girl child lamenting having to carry her baby sister on her back:

> To-day I'm four years old! To-day
> My cruel mother tied
> The baby sister on my back
> Although I kicked and cried:
> And in the garden, there I saw—
> (I wish that I were dead!)

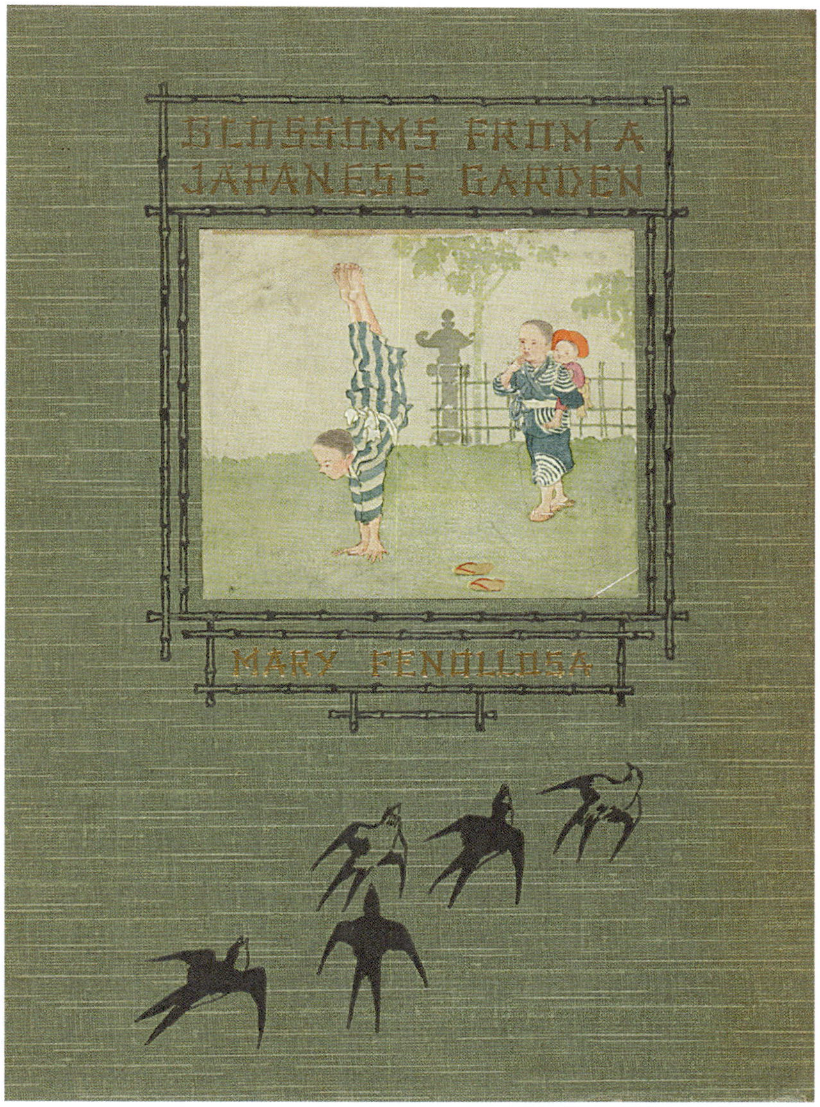

FIGURE 4.6
Blossoms from a Japanese Garden: A Book of Child-Verses, by Mary McNeil Fenollosa. New York: Frederick A. Stokes, 1913.

My brother turning somersaults
And standing on his head![14]

Fenollosa contributed the poem "The Fifth of May in Japan" to the May 1901 issue of *St. Nicholas*:

The year has many a holiday:
But brightest is the Fifth of May,
When drums and guns and warlike toys
Bring ecstasy to little boys.

Above the houses, far and near,
The paper fishes then appear;
From bamboo poles they wheel and play,
As though about to dart away.

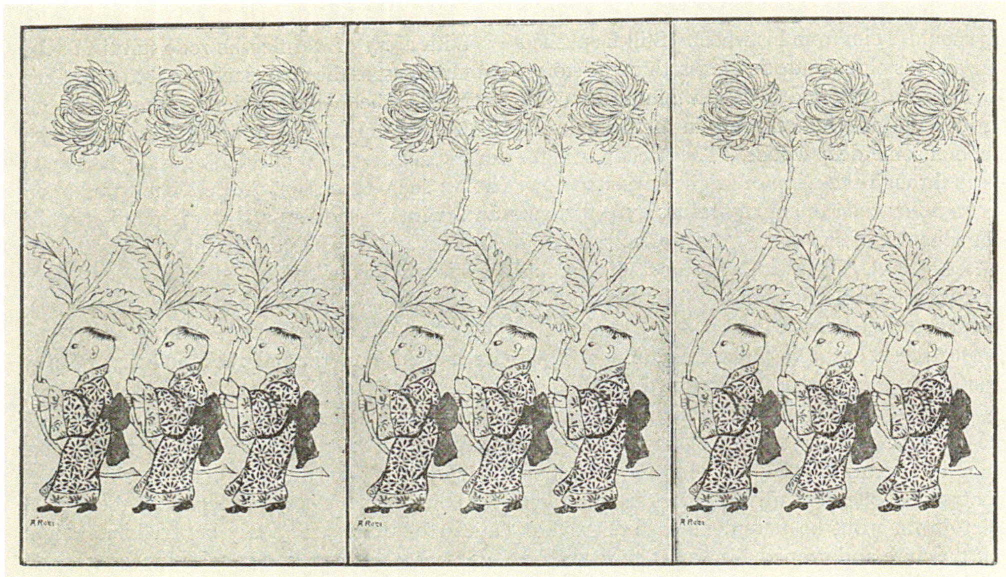

FIGURE 4.7
Illustration for "The Little Japanese at Home," by Ida Tigner Hodnett. *St. Nicholas* vol. 25, no. 6 (April 1898): 486.

The sky is like a globe o'erhead;
The roofs like purple pebbles spread;
And all the world has now become
One jolly big aquarium.[15]

Other well-known contributors about Japan included Mae St. John Bramhall and Jack London. Dodge also engaged many writers who are now much lesser-known, including Ida Tigner Hodnett, T. Yamagata, N. A. Smith, J. W. Tomkins, M. L. Todd, Mrs. W. D. Tisdale, Arthur L. Shumway, M. Johnson, T. Wores, A. N. Benjamin, Bertha Runkle, Isabel E. MacKay, H. Irving Hancock, Anna Rogers, and E. S. Yule. Their articles about Japan were positive and informative.

St. Nicholas's View of Japan

Griffis, Scidmore, Fenollosa, and the other Americans who wrote about Japan helped make *St. Nicholas*'s coverage of that faraway country truly remarkable. The magazine's third issue included an article about Japanese games by "a Japanese Boy."[16] The May 1874 edition featured a version of the Japanese legend of Momotaro, the peach boy, one of Japan's most beloved child heroes, who arrived, magically, at the home of an old childless couple in a large peach, left them briefly on a successful quest to defeat an army of demons, and returned triumphant.[17] Between 1873 and 1918, Japan was second only to England in the number of articles *St. Nicholas* published about foreign lands.

St. Nicholas readers learned about Japanese social life and customs. They read biographical sketches of Japanese people as well as Japanese folktales, poems, and historical fiction featuring Japan. They learned about Japanese top-spinning, received lessons in basic linguistics (e.g. *Harukichi* derives from *haru*, or spring); glimpsed Japanese students in a *sho gakko* (primary school) and other common Japanese sights (jinrikishas, festivals, games, the fish market). They discovered what little girls wore under their kimonos ("no other under-clothing is worn except a short skirt wrapped around her waist")[18]; how to eat with chopsticks; and that the emperor "grew up in the palace, never being allowed to see a foreigner until he was nineteen years of age."[19] Even a bit of holiday poetic humor came with a Japanese twist (and a drawing of a fan illustrated with jolly Santa Claus in kimono):

> "O Santa San"
>
> What if he strayed to far Japan,—
> The dear old Saint,—and there began
> For all their girls and boys to plan,
>   Without a pause?
>
> For, drive his reindeer low or high,
> No open chimney could he spy,
> No empty stockings hanging nigh!
> He would grow homesick by and by,
>   With ample cause.
>
> For should they catch that puzzled man,
> They'd surely paint him on a fan
> And label it "O Santa San—
>   *Our* Santa Claus!"[20]

The November 1888 edition included a lengthy article about the Shōgun and the Emperor that included the following passage:

> The feudal system had a very minute code of honor, and there grew out of it a most exalted sense of loyalty and devotion. History is full of the stories of men who sacrificed their lives for their lords; but the rule did not work both ways—the lord did not lay down his life for his vassal.
>
> The farmers and other classes in the province of the daimio put themselves under his protection, and paid him tribute. These taxes were enormous, for upon them depended the support of the unproductive class, the two-sworded gentry called Samurai, or warriors. So all revenue came into the hands of the military class, and the Kugé, or court nobles, became very poor in this world's goods, but not poor in spirit. The lowest Kugé was superior in rank to the Shogun.

> Besides the Emperor's family there were set apart four families of imperial descent, from whom the Emperor might choose an heir for the throne in case there was no heir in his own family. The throne did not always descend to the eldest son, but the father might choose as heir the son who seemed to him most suitable. The Emperor's daughters sometimes married nobles, and sometimes married into the royal families belonging to the dynasty.
>
> Under this double system of government, the Mikado and the Shogun, the outside world supposed there were two emperors, one spiritual, the other a temporal emperor. This "temporal Emperor" was merely the Mikado's general. The Mikado, the "son of heaven," lived in Kioto, a city beautifully situated, in a palace much like a temple in outward appearance, but with little of the splendor of a European palace. Magnificence of display might do very well for upstart generals, but was unseemly for the semi-divinity of royalty. The Shogun lived at Yeddo, which was thus the real seat of government.[21]

The January 1904 article "Japanese Athletics for American Boys" gave young readers a short history of samurai and the martial art of jiu-jitsu:

> More than twenty-five hundred years ago there sprang into existence, in Japan, an order of knights, who were known as *samurai.* To them was imparted all the learning, the polite breeding, and the forms of superiority that mark the gentlemen. They were skilled in arms and versed in the arts of war, for they were the emperor's fighting-men, and none but they were allowed to bear arms.
>
> As there could not always be war on hand, and as it was considered beneath the dignity of the samurai to go into any ordinary callings, it came about naturally that these little knights found much idle time on their hands. Being men of war, they turned their attention to athletic feats. One among the samurai conceived the idea of learning, by practice, the location of every sensitive nerve and muscle in the body. After that he discovered all the joints of the bones that could be seized in such a way as to give momentary power over the muscles of an adversary. He practiced with his fellow samurai, and thus by degrees was developed the most wonderful system of athletics known in the world. The Japanese call this work *jiu-jitsu.* The deft pressures applied in the practice of jiu-jitsu produce only momentary pain but do not really injure the muscles or nerves. In all other things the Japanese are the most polite people in the world; so it follows that even in their fighting they have developed a humane yet effective method of self-defense. They do not strike out with the clenched fist, and seek to bruise as do the Anglo-Saxons in their boxing contests.[22]

The Lives of Japanese Children

The magazine also celebrated the lives and experiences of Japanese children, the darlings of Western visitors and writers. With their straight black hair bobbed appealingly they looked like dolls, enthused one writer, who added that in their "pretty dress . . . and courteous manner" Japanese kindergarten children were the "most picturesque in the world."[23] Even their names were adorable, the author noted. There was Miss Perfume, Miss Silk Umbrella, Miss Arrow Island, In the Bamboo, High Tree, Mountain, Long-tail Tiger, Middle-of-the-field, Before the River, and Three Valleys. Wrote another Western traveler: "If the children are too much looked after in China, and not enough in Korea, the place where child life seems an all-the-year-round picnic is Japan."[24] Describing the home and community of his little Japanese neighbor, another writer thought Japan deserved to be called a children's paradise. Not only were Japanese children the happiest he had ever seen, they also displayed the greatest respect for their parents and elders, who, in return, bestowed their "unfailing love and attention . . . upon the little ones of the 'Sunrise Kingdom.'"[25]

St. Nicholas writers described Japanese children as quick learners who were industrious and polite. They never pout, answer back or say *naze* (why?).[26] They overcome their fears, like young Jiro, who kills a snake. They always thank their parents politely, as Jiro did, making a low bow, after his parents surprised him with a set of miniature weapons on Boys' Day.[27] Most of the Japanese children featured in *St. Nicholas* stories grow up in well-to-do families with their own nurses and servants; they live in large houses with a *kura* (storage house), wear silk (not cotton) kimonos, and are surrounded by loving parents. One such domestic setting is described—from an American point of view—in a story about a day set aside especially for Japanese girls, the Feast of Dolls. In the story, young sisters Lugi and Komme go to bed early after returning from school,

> for their mother wanted plenty of time to arrange the dolls and toys on tables, and to do this requires as much time as Santa Claus requires to fill stockings or to trim Christmas-trees. . . .

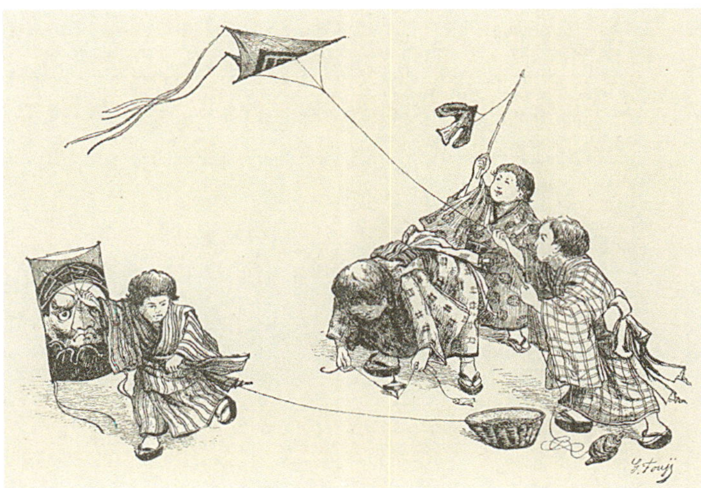

FIGURE 4.8
"Little Japanese Boys with Kites and a Top," by G. Fouji, for "The Little Japanese at Home" by Ida Tigner Hodnett, page 492.

> Nearly every large house in Japan has a smaller house beside or near it, which is fire-proof. In this storehouse the valuable things are kept. The servants went to this house and brought a great many boxes into the largest room of the dwelling. Then Komme and Lugi's mamma and papa opened the boxes and arranged the tables. Everything in the boxes was wrapped in silk. . . .
>
> The little girls rose earlier than usual the next morning. They quickly dressed, putting on their best robes of red crepe and curiously-figured silk, and went first to their parents, as Japanese children always do, and wished them "good morning." They did not eat much breakfast, as they were too eager to see their dolls. . . . you would hardly believe it, but they had over a hundred dolls. Japan is, above all others, the land for dolls. Some of them were two hundred years old. Think of that! They had belonged to Komme's great-grandmother's great-grandmother. . . .
>
> There were Mikados and Mikados' wives, and Tycoons and Tycoonesses, and ladies and gentlemen of the Court, boy-babies and girl-babies, and young Japanese ladies and young Japanese gentlemen. All were dressed in a manner entirely different from any American dolls. The Mikado's wife and ladies of the Court wear their hair far down their backs, and have on a kind of loose pantaloons of cherry-red silk. The Tycoon had on a very high black cap perched on the front part of his head, and he and his officers and men always wore swords in their silk girdles.[28]

The tale of "Saigo's Picnic" tells American readers about the discipline expected of upper-class Japanese boys (fig. 4.9). The Story children, whose father is the U.S. consul-general in Yokohama, are invited to a picnic and cherry blossom viewing by Saigo, youngest son of Count Minamoto:

> Count Minamoto was one of those obstinate old-fashioned nobles who lay like boulders in the path of new Japan. Not an inch would he yield in politics,

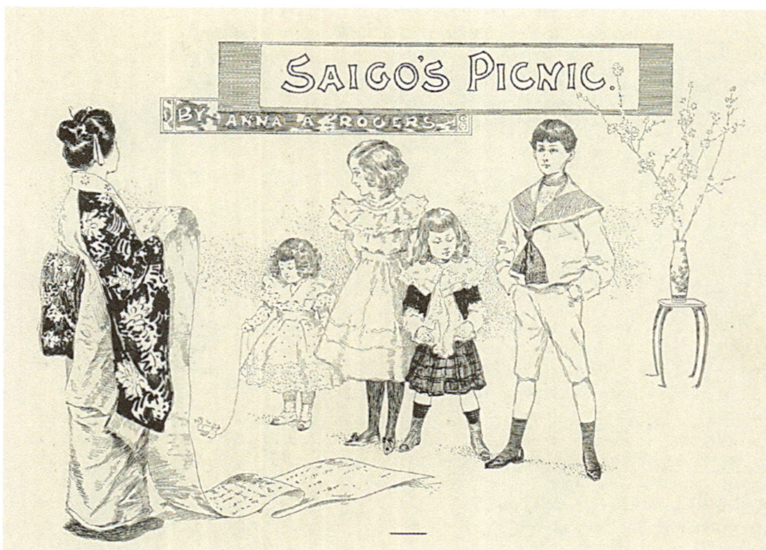

FIGURE 4.9
"Saigo's Picnic," by Anna A. Rogers, illustrated by Charles M. Relyea. *St. Nicholas* vol. 26, no. 7 (May 1899): 533.

> costume, or manner of living to the pressure of his government toward European ideas, at that time all-prevailing. His sons were taught English and several other languages simply that they might be prepared later on to thwart the endless tricks of wicked foreigners, who, the count considered, were fast ruining his beloved country. Saigo's acquaintance with the Storys was encouraged solely on that account; and then, the count thought, the Americans were too young and primitive a people to have lost all their virtues![29]

Saigo meets the Story children, "a riotous lot,"[30] at the Shimbashi station in Tokyo:

> He [Saigo] was about Lee's [the oldest Story boy] age, but half a head shorter,—a straight, lithe, dark little fellow, with a fine, delicate-featured face, splendid white teeth, and a smile "you could eat with a spoon," as Lee expressed it. Saigo was dressed entirely in the old-style native costume of his class: a short, square-sleeved, stiff coat, and very wide trousers (called *hakama*), all of rich, dull-colored silk; his hair in a queue on the top of his head, with temples smooth-shaven,—a tiny copy of his old-fashioned father. He bowed slowly and, of course, without shaking hands, to each of his guests in turn, drawing in his breath in the most approved style. Two men-servants stood behind him, and bowed each time their little master did. They wore dark-blue costumes, with the Minamoto crest stamped in white on their dark "mushroom" hats and loose cloaks.[31]

Accustomed to American ways, the Story children endured many small trials throughout the picnic. They were particularly uncomfortable sitting on *tatami* (mats) in the native style:

> The Storys got pains in their legs and agonies in their backs, and they twisted and turned and wound and unwound themselves, to the vast astonishment of the Minamotos, who, of course sat perfectly still on their heels, serene and comfortable through it all.[32]

The difference between the youngest members of each party becomes "extremely painful"[33] when little Julie suddenly announces that she would prefer "a sam handwich, big and fick, and with lots of musted."[34] But worse was still to come. Julie, tired of the elaborate Japanese lunch procedure, creates an "excessively shocking scene" when she rolls over on the blanket and lands in the middle of the feast. After lunch the Japanese host invites his American friends to compose poems, a situation which once more highlights the awkwardness of his guests. The arrival of a troupe of street performers finally puts the Americans at ease as they "fairly rolled on the ground with laughter . . . while the Japanese

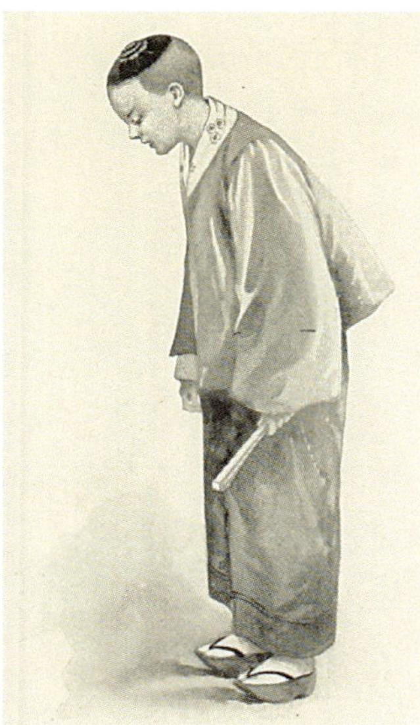

FIGURE 4.10
"Saigo Bowed Slowly to Each of the Guests in Turn" by Charles M. Relyea, for "Saigo's Picnic," by Anna A. Rogers, page 534.

children never for an instant lost their quiet, smiling, dignified air of condescending amusement."[35]

Bidding farewell to his American visitors, their young host once again demonstrates samurai upbringing. Thrown from his horse, he hides his painful injury and continues to smile until his guests leave:

> The whistle of the locomotive sounded, the native guard blew his toy trumpet, and the train moved slowly off. A little cloud of Story handkerchiefs waved frantically from the car window; and then, when it was all over, the smile died suddenly out of Saigo's face, and he fell back unconscious into the arms of the *betto* [servant].[36]

Some *St. Nicholas* articles portray young Americans visiting Japan as spunky and self-assured. The budding American writer Jack London went to Japan at seventeen and was a newspaper correspondent during the 1904–1905 Russo-Japanese war. In his short story, "In Yeddo Bay," London wrote of the pluck and ingenuity of Alf Davis, a sixteen-year-old sailor on the *Annie Mine*, an American sailing-schooner anchored at Yokohama. Alf, who had spent the day ashore and lost his purse, is taunted by the restaurant owner to pay his twenty-five *sen*. Returning to his ship at eleven o'clock at night becomes a big problem because none of the native boatmen is willing to take him to his ship before he has paid. Worse, they band together and threaten him, and the harbor police refuse to come to his aid. London wrote:

> Then it was that all of Alf's American independence flamed up in his breast. He had a born dislike of being imposed upon . . . Down went Alf's cap on the office floor. Right and left he kicked off his low-cut shoes. Trousers and shirt followed. "Remember," he said in ringing tones, "I, as a citizen of the United States, shall hold you, the city of Yokohama, and the government of Japan responsible for those clothes. Good night."[37]

Alf then plunged into the sea and swam to his boat. He had won the admiration of the Japanese boatmen, who were in such awe of his pluck that they gave him the freedom of the harbor. As long as the *Annie Mine* remained in port, they took Alf wherever he needed to go without requiring payment.[38]

Changing Views of the Japanese

Most *St. Nicholas* writers displayed a positive, even admiring attitude towards the Japanese though at times they seemed condescending, as in the poem, "The Jingle of the Little Jap" by Isabel MacKay, which *St. Nicholas* published in 1907 (fig. 4.11):

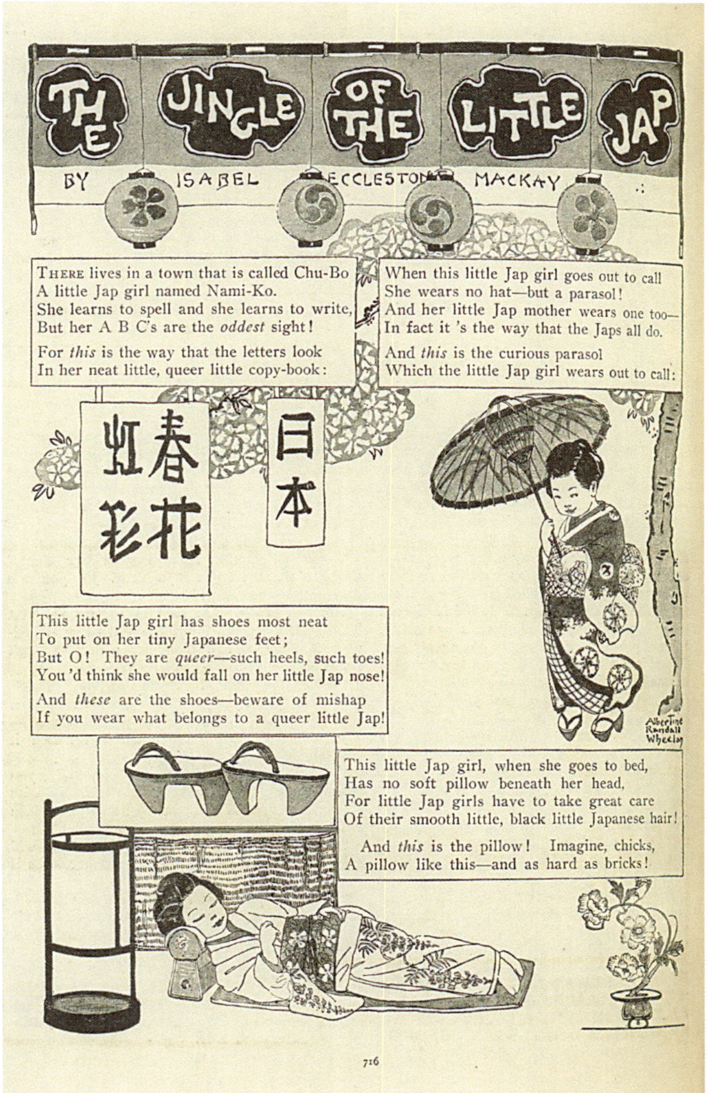

FIGURE 4.11
"The Jingle of the Little Jap," by Isabel Eccleston MacKay, illustrated by Albertine Randall Wheelan. *St. Nicholas* vol. 34, no. 8 (June 1907): 716.

There lives in a town that is called Chu-Bo
A little Jap girl named Nami-ko.
She learns to spell and she learns to write,
But her ABC's are the *oddest* sight!

For *this* is the way that the letters look
In her neat little, queer little copy-book:

This little Jap girl has shoes most neat
To put on her tiny Japanese feet:
But O! They are *queer*—such heels, such toes!
You'd think she would fall on her little Jap nose!
. . . .
This little Jap girl, when she goes to bed,
Has no soft pillow beneath her head,

> For little Jap girls have to take great care
> Of their smooth little, black little Japanese hair!
>
> And *this* is the pillow! Imagine, chicks,
> A pillow like this—and as hard as bricks![39]

Other coverage, however, was friendly and fair, as in a detailed report on the relationship between the United States and Japan that the magazine published in 1888:

> We, the people of the United States, were the first among nations to knock at Japan's door and ask to be on visiting terms with our far-off neighbor, who for about two hundred and fifty years had lived like a hermit. That knock hastened the Japanese revolution, and this revolution overthrew their double system of government and restored the Mikado to his proper place as the real ruler of the country.
>
> This "land of dainty decoration" is destined to stand high among the world's nations. The strides it has made in civilization since that revolution of twenty years ago remind us of the boy who stole the giant's seven-league boots, in the fairy tale.
>
> Although they are studying us, as well as our sciences, our religion, and our civilization, they have no intention of adopting all our customs. On the contrary, they are examining our ways carefully, in order that they may adopt the good, and reject the bad or whatever is unsuited to their conditions of life.[40]

By the end of the nineteenth century, *St. Nicholas* had presented the most comprehensive information about Japan for juvenile readers to be found anywhere in American children's literature. However, after the Sino-Japanese war of 1894–1895 and the Russo–Japanese War a decade later—and after the 1905 death of Mary Mapes Dodge and her replacement as editor by William Fayal Clarke— the magazine began to reflect changing American attitudes toward Japan. No longer were the Japanese seen as the charming little people from the isle of paper-walled houses. There were fewer articles about Japanese history and culture and fewer stories about Japan as the children's paradise; more articles were military and patriotic in nature. Teiichi Yamagata's 1904 article, "A Japanese 'Middy,'" for example, is the detailed, first-person narrative of a young Japanese who serves as an interpreter on the Chinese warship *Yu-yen*, graduates from the Naval College in 1884 as a *hanbun* (a midshipman), takes part in several battles, resigns from the Imperial Japanese navy, then goes to the United States for further study.[41]

Ten years after Yamagata's article appeared, World War I (1914–1918) engulfed the world. Although the war was an important topic in *St. Nicholas,*[42] the magazine gradually de-emphasized its coverage of Japan. The September 1918 issue featured one more story about Japan written in the style of earlier times. In line with the need for cooperation among the wartime Allies, "From the Cradle of True Politeness" emphasized tolerance and international understanding:

> Far, far away from here, so far away that you must travel twenty whole days and twenty whole nights to reach it, there is a strange country that is an island . . . those who live there name it Nippon—the Land of the Rising Sun. Wise men have called it "The Cradle of True Politeness" . . . From this place to America, when he was very young, came Yoshio. His skin was yellow, like that of all his people, and his eyes were slanting, but his heart beat with love and hatred and fear like yours and mine. . . . Yoshio's uncle took him to the school which was to make an

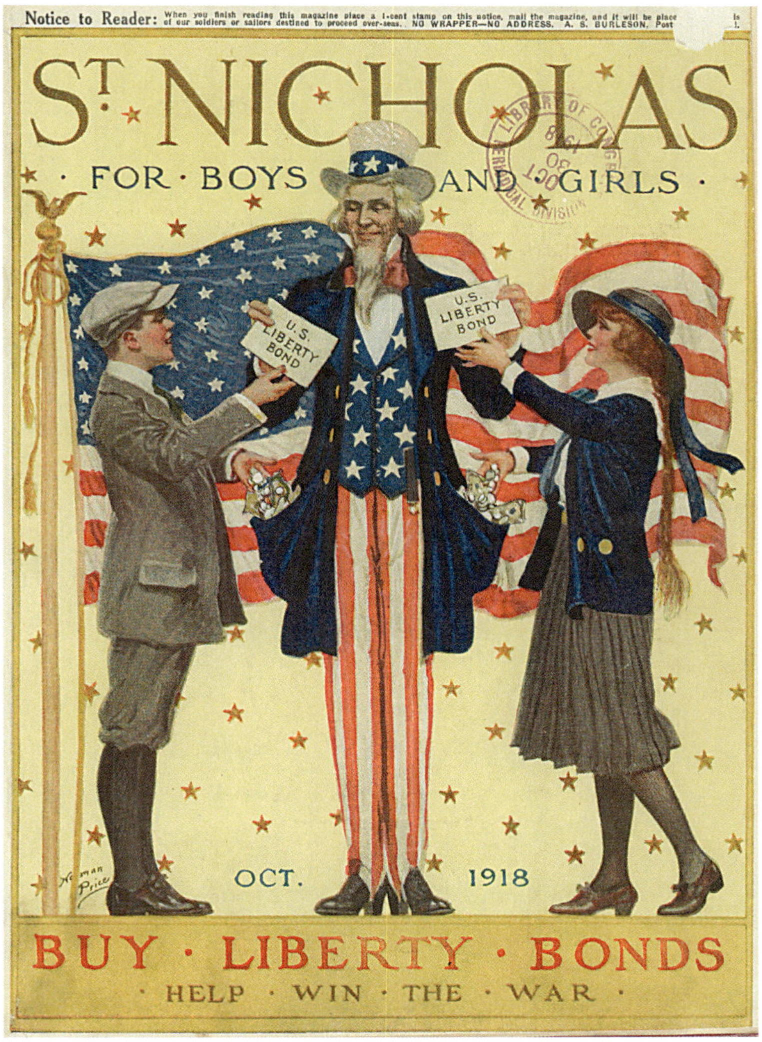

FIGURE 4.12
"Buy Liberty Bonds, Help Win the War," illustrated by Norman Price. *St. Nicholas* vol. 45, no. 12 (October 1918).

> American of the boy from the East. In amazement the lad gazed at the noisy children and marveled at the strange games they played. He was eager to join them in their play, but when his uncle left him alone he could only stand and watch. Long he waited expectantly for the American children to welcome him as a playmate, as he would have welcomed them had they been strangers in Japan, but they paid no attention to the boy other than to stare rudely at him until he blushed under his yellow skin and turned his slanting eyes on the ground. . . .
>
> When they refused to let him join in their games he [Yoshio] would go off, sad-eyed, by himself and wonder why they shunned him . . . He would have cried, only he remembered that his father had told him that the sons of Samurai never cry.[43]

Then, one day, a little girl appears lonely like Yoshio.

No more was Yoshio sad. His heart leaped and his "slanting eyes" danced with joy as he said in the flowery language of their far-away land:

> "Fair maid of the land of Nippon, flower of heaven, breath of my father's home, these children of the curly yellow hair and the laughing blue eyes have hearts of stone beneath their smiling faces. Let us play together, little maid from the Land of the Rising Sun."[44]

The two Japanese children play their Japanese games which, of course, were "gentler than those enjoyed by the American school-children. They did not run and jump and yell, because that was not part of the games they had learnt at home."[45] Eventually, however,

> the children of America and the boy and girl from Japan came to forget the difference in the color of their skins and the shape of their eyes. Then they were all happy, just as all people who think of others' comfort before their own always are.[46]

The Watch Tower

In the September 1915 issue *St. Nicholas* initiated "The Watch Tower: A Department of Current History." S. E. Forman, the Watch Tower's initial editor, explained that Watch Tower articles would be about events "that are truly great, the things that are making important changes in the affairs of the world."[47]

After 1915, most articles about Japan appeared in the Watch Tower, and the tone of Japan-based articles gradually began to change, turning away from travel stories, stories of young samurai, and romantic pieces about the strange and magical land far away on the other side of the Pacific. An idyllic illustration accompanies the rare poem, "Little People of Japan," which appeared outside the Watch Tower, as did a few other lighthearted articles—including one about the young Crown Prince Hirohito and his three brothers, and the story of Genichiro Yamada, a young Japanese boy who donated his annual allowance to the American Red Cross to help those who suffered in the Santa Barbara earthquake, in gratitude for American assistance to the victims of the Kanto earthquake of September 1923.[48] Even during World War I, however, when America and Japan were allies, most of the articles in *St. Nicholas*, while remaining positive in tone, were beginning to express concern about the growing tensions between the United States and Japan. For example, a September 1917 article stated:

> For several years past, many of our citizens have been regarding Japan as an enemy of the United States, and we have heard a great deal about the trouble the Japanese are preparing for us. Men on the floor of Congress have prophesied that Japan would certainly make war upon us . . . Orators on many a platform in fervid language have told their audiences how the Japanese will land upon the Pacific coast and take possession of California and other Pacific States. A great many Americans have not been at all alarmed by predictions of this kind, for it has seemed to them that Japan would not wish to wage war upon her best customer, and the United States is her best customer. . . .
>
> Still, in the minds of many thoughtful Americans, there have been misgivings about Japan. We have discriminated against the Japanese in our immigration policy and we have refused to give the full privileges of American citizenship to Japanese aliens. This treatment has no doubt caused some resentment in the Japanese mind. Then, since we took possession of the Philippine Islands [1898] our influence in the Far East has been a matter of concern to Japan. She has felt that the Americans will every year become more and more dangerous as rivals in trade. So there has been some reason why the United States and Japan have not been as friendly as two nations ought to be. But recent events have gone far toward doing away with this distrust and jealousy and have tended to draw the two nations together in bonds of friendship. Americans and Japanese are now fighting side by side in the war against Germany, and every day Japan is coming to see more and more clearly that she has less to fear from American influence in the Orient than she would have from the German influence if it were strongly established there.[49]

In March 1924, as Congress was considering restrictive immigration legislation, the Watch Tower described limitations the federal and California state governments had already placed on Japanese immigrants and Japanese Americans—and a likely retaliatory Japanese measure:

> Japanese are not eligible to citizenship in the United States. Aliens not eligible to citizenship are forbidden by the laws of California to own land in that State. Those laws were recently declared constitutional by the Supreme Court of the United States. And in January it was said that the Government of Japan would probably pass a law making it impossible for citizens of California to own land in Japan.[50]

In June, after the United States enacted the Immigration Act of 1924, effectively prohibiting Japanese immigration, the editor wrote:

> On April 12, Ambassador Hanihara of Japan presented to our Government a formal note of protest from his Government against exclusion of Japanese immigrants as provided for in a bill then under debate in Congress [the bill became law in May]. The note asserted that the good faith of America was involved, and that "grave consequences" might be expected if the bill became law. In the language of diplomacy, "grave consequences" generally means something like war; but it was shown by the context to imply in this instance nothing more definite than an end to Japan's friendly feeling for this nation which, of course, would be sufficiently serious and deplorable. . . .
>
> Japan is a proud nation, zealous for its rights. So is the United States. Japan does not want to be an object of unfair discrimination. The United States is not willing to have its affairs regulated by others. And the people of California and the Pacific Coast are bitter because they say the Japanese settlers destroy American standards of labor and living and remain subjects of Japan, giving no loyalty to America. Our laws forbid them to become naturalized citizens. . . .
>
> But the Japanese question is different from those in which our relations with European Governments are involved. . . . To the Watch Tower man, in April, it looked as though the right thing to do would be to pass the immigration bill without Japanese exclusion, and then to have a talk with the Japanese Government—a frank and earnest talk, aiming at a settlement that would be satisfactory to both sides.[51]

In August, as tensions continued, the editor wrote:

> When Japan was stricken by the great earthquake [September 1, 1923] America was quick to send help, in goods, services, and money. At that time it seemed as though nothing could ever set America and Japan against each other in war-like hostility. America contributed millions of dollars to Japanese relief. . . .
>
> Will not that [hospital in Japan built with American funds] be a splendid memorial to the friendship of the earthquake time? And does it seem possible that with such an institution in existence, the two countries can manage to work themselves into a war fever? It *is* possible, but it would be a foolish and wicked thing, and we can't believe it will happen.[52]

In 1927, the Watch Tower commented on Emperor Yoshihito's death; featured a photo of the *torii* (gate) to the Yasukuni shrine, where Japanese troops prayed for heroes of many Japanese wars who are interred there; and noted how wariness of Japan's growing power was used to affect domestic events. The Watch Tower editor continued to argue for peaceful relations between Japan and the United States:

> But even if resentment still lives in Japanese minds, there is this fact to be considered, that Japan could not send a fleet and an army across the Pacific to invade this continent-wide republic. Japan had a terrible "set-back" in the earthquake that shook Tokio. Japan needs to build up her trade, and Japan could not afford a war with America, even if she were foolish enough to want to fight us. So it is silly to talk about Japan and the United States as though they were "natural" enemies; and harmful, because seeds of hate, once sown in international fields, are apt sometime to bring forth a deadly harvest.
>
> There is room for the United States on this side of the Pacific, and for Japan on the other—and plenty of reasons for the two countries to cherish friendly relations and develop a commerce that will be profitable to both. We of The Watch Tower do not want to travel through life with our eyes shut; we do not want to dodge the truth; we are brave and wise to the facts, even when they are not pleasant—especially then, for that is the time of danger. But we do not see any reason why Americans should distrust the Japanese or hate them or fear them. They have our friendship—and our wish that America may never give them cause for suspicion or fear of this nation.[53]

Four years later, in November 1931, the Watch Tower editor highlighted Japan's recent occupation of Manchuria:

> Manchuria is a vast prairie land larger than Texas, nominally a part of China, but for thirty years past the arena of a three-cornered struggle for control between China, Russia and Japan. The Russo-Japanese war of 1904 left Japan master of Korea and South Manchuria. . . . Japan, with 60,000,000 people on her overcrowded islands, wants and must have room to expand and to sell her manufactured goods. In Manchuria she has pursued a policy of "peaceful penetration" . . . In the last year or two there have been constant clashes between the [Japanese and the Chinese]. A Japanese army captain was executed as a spy recently, and Japan flamed with anger. Then a bridge was blown up on the South Manchurian Railway, operated by Japan, and the Japanese blamed it on the Chinese.
>
> Japan is torn between a strong military party and a peaceful one. The latter happens to be in power just now, with Baron Wakatsuki as Premier and Baron Shidehara as Foreign Minister. But the army in Manchuria took matters into their own hands, and in short order seized every city in South Manchuria, including

Mukden, the capital. . . . Nanking sent a note to the League of Nations begging protection . . . Japan said it had no intension of conquering Manchuria, and would withdraw its troops, but whether the government at Tokyo can control the hot-headed militarists is another question . . . only a little match [is needed] to touch off the Manchurian tinder-box.[54]

In April 1932, using a political cartoon (fig. 4.13) showing a Japanese attempting "Hara-Kiri" with a huge hatchet titled "War Madness" facing a military leader with a toothy grimace who was clad in traditional Japanese armor, the Watch Tower editor wrote this introduction to a detailed article describing the military actions in the region:

Japan and China are at war—a war more serious than any fight that has occurred since Armistice Day, 1918, and yet neither side has declared war. Last September, as all the world knows, Japan embarked on a military occupation of Manchuria. Within four months she had completely overrun that province as far north as the Chinese Eastern Railroad, seized its chief cities, cleared it of bandits, installed

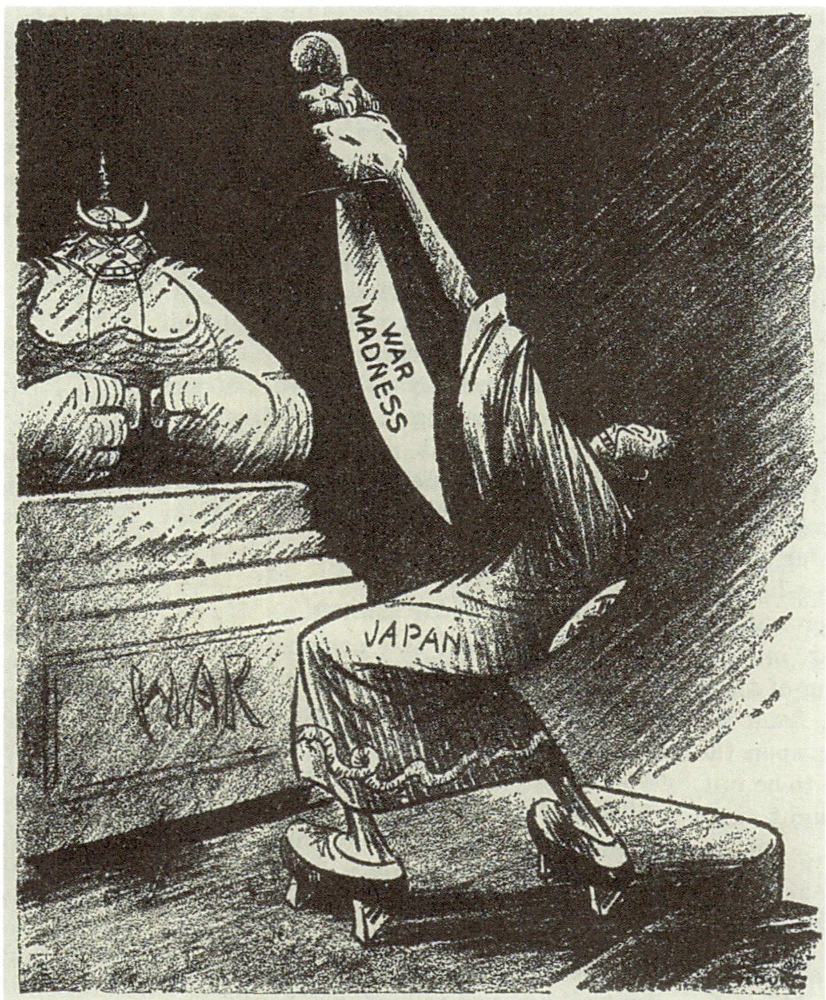

FIGURE 4.13
"Hara-Kiri," by H. M. Talburt in the *New York World-Telegram*, reprinted in "The Watch Tower, a Review of Current Events: War in the Far East," by Kenneth Miller Gould. *St. Nicholas* vol. 59, no. 6 (April 1932): 324.

> Japanese in control of all railroads, banks, and industries, and encouraged the setting up of an independent state . . . [55]

In the main body of the magazine from 1930 onward, there are only occasional items of international interest, though the Watch Tower continued to track Japan's conflict in Manchuria. In December 1931, the Watch Tower editor wrote:

> The most threatening conflict in the world today, that between Japan and China in Manchuria, continued to cause sleepless nights for international statesmen. The League of Nations became the chief actor in the drama when its Council invited the United States [not officially a member of the League], over the determined protest of Japan, to send a representative to sit with it in its discussions of the Manchurian squabble . . . Japan resented this action and intimated that she might withdraw from the League.[56]

The Watch Tower of January 1932 devoted a lengthy article to "The Manchurian War." It reported on the League of Nations warning Japan to withdraw from Manchuria, and ended by saying:

> The outstanding fact just now is that the Japanese military forces in the field have taken the bit in their teeth and that the civil government at Tokyo, which has peaceful intentions, has little or no control over the army.[57]

* * *

St. Nicholas was changing. In 1931, it was sold to the American Education Press. Increasingly the covers took on a mass-market look, and its articles, too, aimed more at popular appeal than education, concentrating on fashion, parties, movie stars, and how to decorate your room. In the spring of 1932, *St. Nicholas* abolished the Watch Tower while continuing its main features, including fiction, articles, poetry, and its miscellaneous departments. There were a few pieces here and there about foreign countries, among them one more story about Japan. Published in April 1935, it tells the story of Suki, who lives with her grandmother in a traditional Japanese house. When Miss Pearson, a friend from America, announces her visit, Suki rents Western furniture to prepare their house for the guest. As it turns out, Miss Pearson much prefers to sip her tea while sitting on the *tatami* in grandmother's quaint room. "You see, Suki, I don't want to feel at home [she said]. I came to Japan because I love Japanese things so much and wanted to get into the spirit of the country."[58]

Five years later, in February 1940, *St. Nicholas* ceased publication.

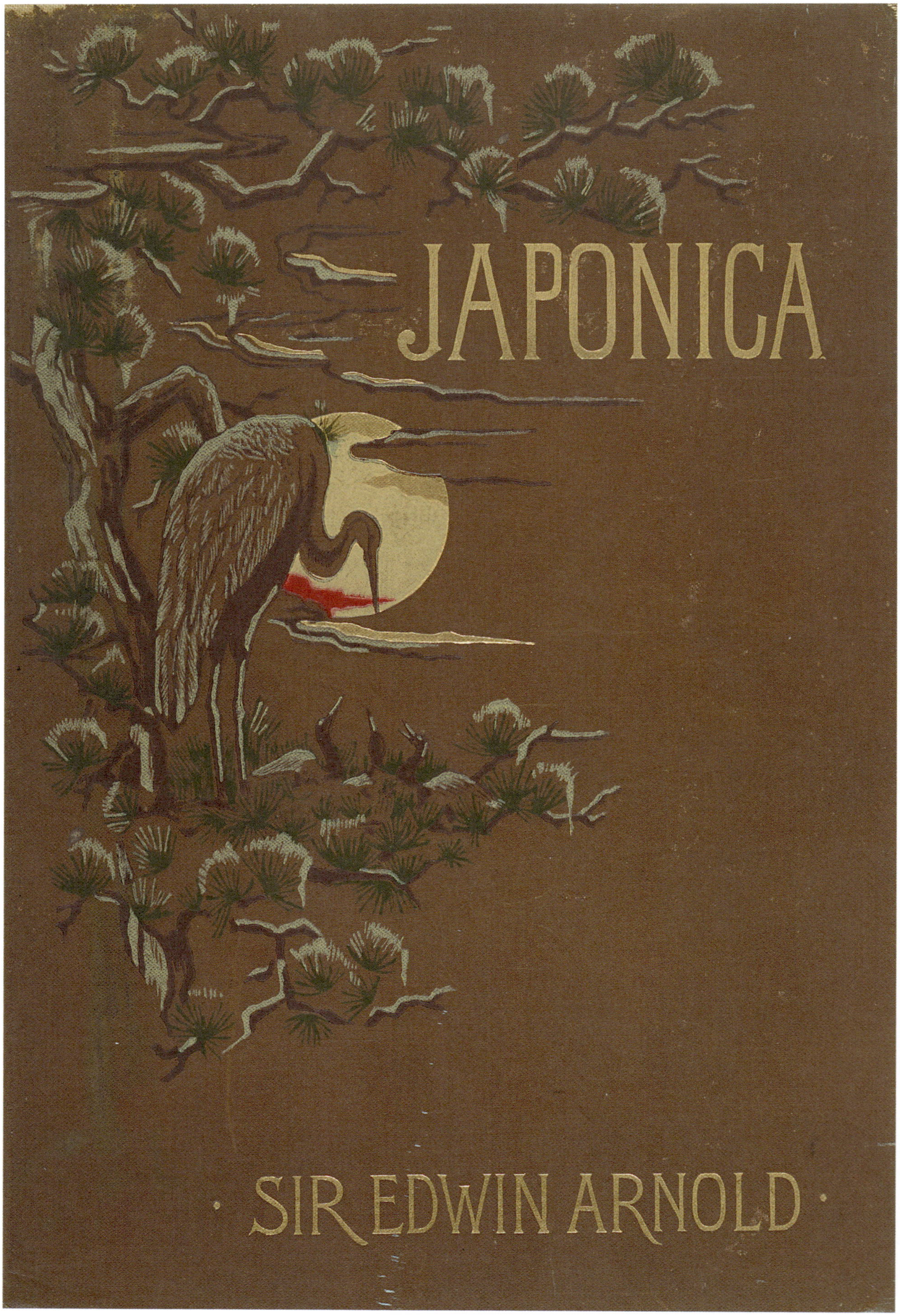
JAPONICA
SIR EDWIN ARNOLD

5

The Children's Book Writers and Their Information Sources

From Marco Polo to Madame Chrysanthème

Late nineteenth-century writers telling the story of Japan for young readers could choose their facts and fancies from a wealth of diverse interpretations. Early sources include Marco Polo's fairy-tale description, Engelbert Kaempfer's fastidious research, Isabella Bird's travelogue, William Griffis's prolific oeuvre, and a Frenchman's romantic novel of his liaison with a Japanese girl he named Chrysanthème.

A number of the children's books, such as Helen Ainslie Smith's *History of Japan in Words of One Syllable* (1887, fig. 5.2), gave no hint of their sources,

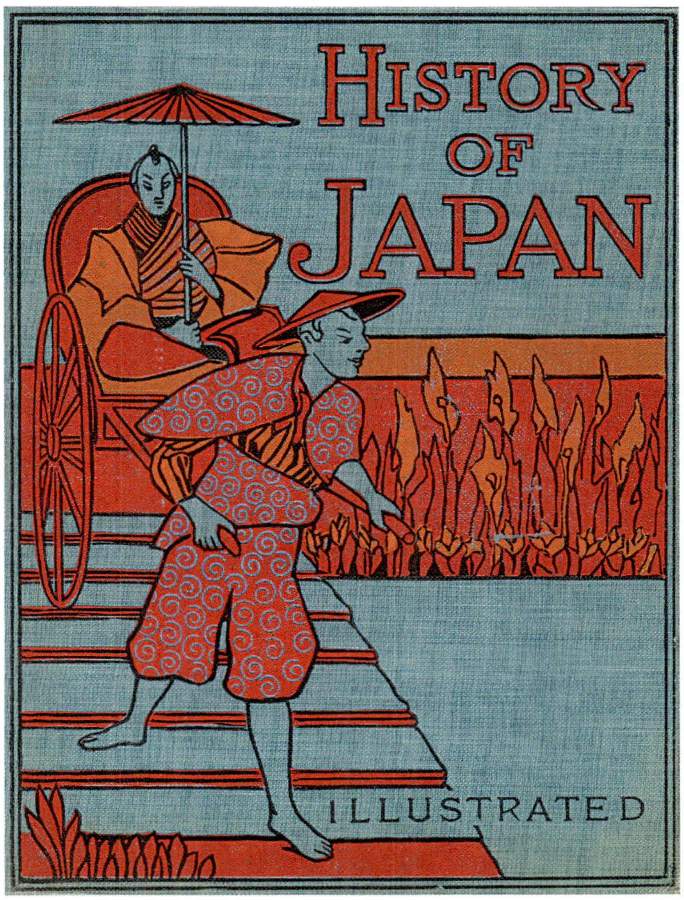

FIGURE 5.1 (OPPOSITE) *Japonica*, by Sir Edwin Arnold, illustrated by Robert Blum. New York: C. Scribner's Sons, 1891.

FIGURE 5.2 *History of Japan in Words of One Syllable*, by Helen Ainslie Smith. New York: G. Routledge, 1887.

while others remained vague. In the introduction to *Zigzag Journeys around the World* (1895), Hezekiah Butterworth wrote that he had received help from "several travelers."[1] William Dalton, the author of *The English Boy in Japan*, wrote that he had gathered his information "from the latest as well as the earliest authorities."[2] Unlike Edward Greey, who wrote *Young Americans in Japan* (1882), few authors could state that their facts derived from "personal observation."[3] "No writer on Japan can fail to acknowledge deep obligations to that noble band of English students, Messrs. [Ernest Mason] Satow, [William George] Aston, and [Basil Hall] Chamberlain," wrote William Griffis,[4] while Edward A. Rand, author of *All Aboard for Sunrise Lands* (1891, fig. 5.3) acknowledged assistance from the Rev. D. Crosby Greene, D.D., of the Japan Mission of the American Board.[5] In the preface to *Japan: The Eastern Wonderland* (ca. 1885), D. C. Angus, who expressed concern that he might not give accurate information about a Japan that had undergone "extraordinary change . . . within the last thirty years,"[6] included Griffis's *The Mikado's Empire*; A. Humbert's *Le Japon Illustré*; *Life and Adventure in Japan* by E. Warren Clark; Eugene

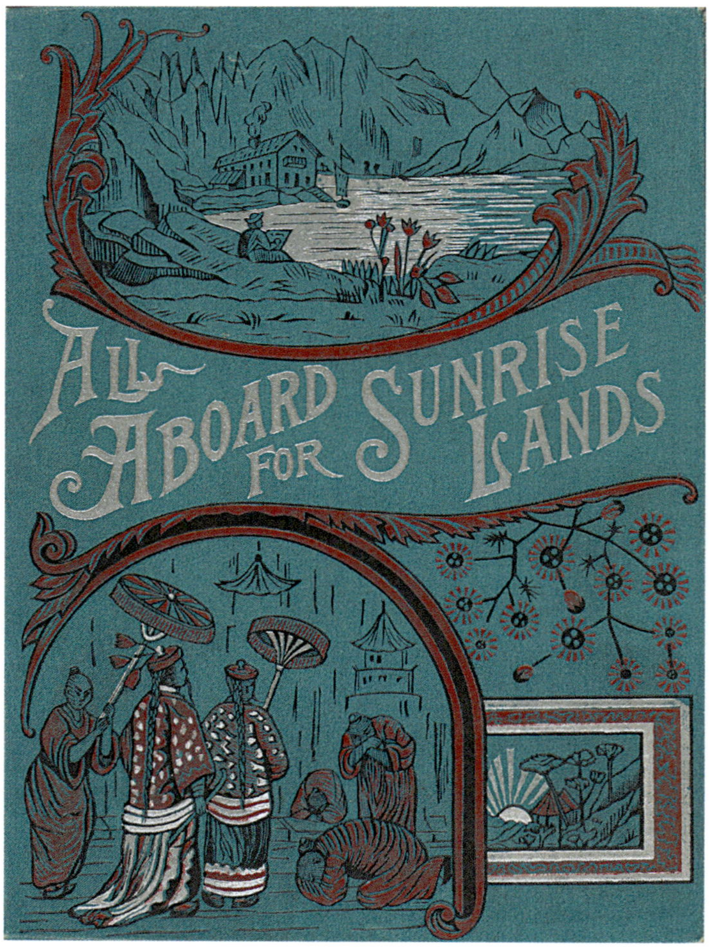

FIGURE 5.3
All Aboard for Sunrise Lands: A Trip through California across the Pacific to Japan, China and Australia, by Edward A. Rand. New York: Fairbanks, Palmer, 1883.

Stock's *Japan*; and works by Sir Rutherford Alcock, Sir Edward Reed,[7] and Isabella Bird on his list of sources.

In the preface to her small book for children, *Stories about Japan*, first published by the Religious Tract Society in 1870, Annie R. Butler notes that the information included is "a mosaic from many sources." Along with Reed, Bird, Stock, Warren, and Griffis, she credited J. J. Rein's "learned work," *Japan*, Henry James Coleridge's *Life and Letters of Xavier*, and American periodicals *Missionary Link* and *Children's Work for Children* (fig. 5.4).

In addition to thanking various friends who had been to Japan as well as several American missionary societies for providing their publications, Butler acknowledged the help she received with illustrations from London publisher John Murray and Eugene Stock of the Church Missionary Society, who allowed her to use images from the Japanese edition of *Pilgrim's Progress*.[8]

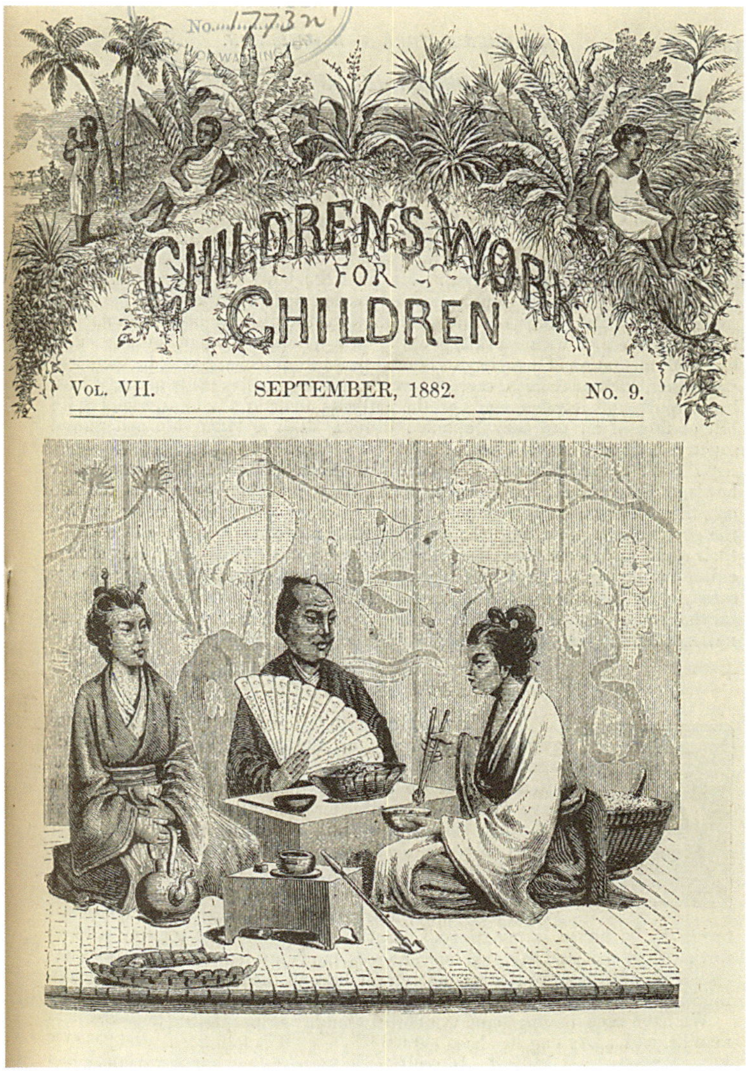

FIGURE 5.4
"A Dinner in Japan," in *Children's Work for Children* vol. 7, no. 9 (September 1882).

The Earliest Information Source: Marco Polo's Japan

Thomas W. Knox stands out for providing unusually extensive information about the source he used for *The Travels of Marco Polo for Boys and Girls* (1885, fig. 5.5). After stating that he "ha[d] followed as closely as possible the original text . . . by the famous Venetian . . . who dictate[d] his story to his Fellow Captive in the gloomy Prison of Venice," he gave "especial acknowledgement . . . to Colonel Henry Yule, whose admirable edition of 'The Book of Ser Marco Polo' [1871] has been made the basis of the present volume." Knox pronounced Yule's work "the best of all the many editions of Marco Polo's Travels." [9]

Then Knox cites Marco Polo's colorful, hearsay description—the earliest-known Western source—which was to define the image of Japan throughout the Middle Ages. (Polo, who is said to have traveled as far as the fabled court of the Kublai Khan in China, never reached Japan.)[10]

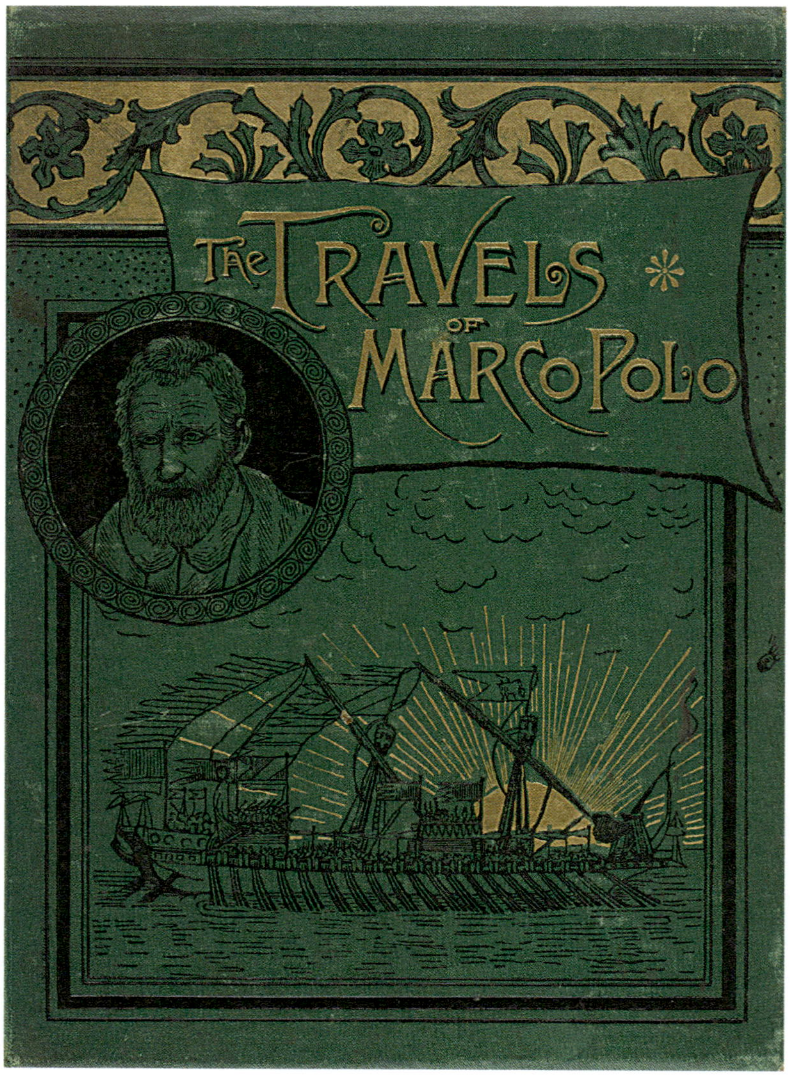

FIGURE 5.5
The Travels of Marco Polo for Boys and Girls with Explanatory Notes and Comments, by Thomas W. Knox. New York: G.P. Putnam's Sons, 1885.

> Chipangu [Japan] is an Island towards the east in the high seas, 1500 miles distant from the Continent; and a very great Island it is. The people are white, civilized, and well-favoured. They are Idolaters, and are dependent on nobody. And I can tell you the quantity of gold they have is endless; for they find it in their own Islands, and the King does not allow it to be exported. Moreover few merchants visit the country because it is so far from the main land, and thus it comes to pass that their gold is abundant beyond all measure. . . . the Lord of that Island . . . hath a great Palace which is entirely roofed with fine gold . . . Moreover, all the pavement of the Palace, and the floors of its chambers, are entirely of gold . . . and the windows also are of gold, so that altogether the richness of this Palace is past all bounds and all belief. . . .
>
> They have also pearls in abundance . . . In this Island some of the dead are buried, and others are burnt. When a body is burnt, they put one of these pearls in the mouth . . . They have also quantities of other precious stones.[11]

Lest his young readers accept Marco Polo's description of Japan as fact, Knox added that the story of "the palace with a golden roof . . . [was] an interesting fable, [and that Japanese palaces were] noted for their inexpensive character . . . [and] of modest exterior and no architectural beauty."[12]

Not citing any sources, Belle M. Brain, author of *All about Japan: Stories of Sunrise Land Told for Little Folks* (1905) continued Japan's early story by telling her readers that "Zipangu" was discovered "quite by accident" in 1542, when "Mendez Pinto, a Portuguese navigator [and his companions] who had been sailing about in the Eastern seas, took passage on a Chinese junk bound for China." As it turned out the "the commander of the junk was a pirate . . . the pilot was killed and a terrible storm drove them far out to sea." But at last, as Brain reports:

> When they had about given up hope, there was a glad cry of 'Land! Land!' . . . It proved to be Tane-ga-shima, one of the islands of Japan, lying just south of Kyushu. At last the long-searched-for Zipangu was found. . . .
>
> Never before had men like these been seen in Japan. Like the sailors of Europe in the early days, the Japanese were afraid to sail very far out into the ocean. Their junks were small and frail, and they too, had strange stories of the sea that filled their hearts with fear. . . . So, while they knew all about China and Korea, and some of the islands near by, they had no idea there were any other countries in the world. And now these strange-looking men had come, with their white faces, and heavy beards, and curious weapons, the like of which had never before been seen in Japan. Who could they be?
>
> "They must be nobles of high rank like our *samurai*," the people decided when they saw that the strangers wore swords. So they received them kindly and treated them with great respect.[13]

The "Peephole" of Dejima

Incorporating information from J. J. Rein, Sir Edward Reed and Isabella Bird, Annie R. Butler, the author of *Stories about Japan*, describes the turbulent relationship between the Japanese and the Christians and what happened after the departure of Francis Xavier, the first Western missionary in Japan:

> But the Jesuit priests who succeeded Xavier were not of his spirit. They did not, as he had done, occupy themselves solely with religion, but they began to interfere with the politics of the country in which they were working—which a missionary should never do.
>
> And the consequences were what they might have foreseen. Their converts were persecuted and massacred; they themselves were driven out of the country, and Christianity was strictly prohibited. And now a notice . . . was posted up in the streets—a notice which remained there for 230 years:
>
> > So long as the sun shall warm the earth, let no Christian be so bold as to come to Japan; and let all know that the King of Spain himself, or the Christian's God, or the great God of all, if He violate this command shall pay for it with His head.
>
> And now the land of the sun goddess had gone fast asleep again, and round it there grew up once more the hedge of mystery and silence—a hedge through which none but the Dutch were allowed even to peep. The Dutch, you must know, had once told tales to the Japanese Government about some Jesuit plot, and were, on that account, allowed to remain in a remote corner of the kingdom when every other European had been driven away.[14]

"The remote corner" was explained by Brain in *All about Japan,* providing no sources:

> This was at Deshima, an odd fan-shaped island in the harbor of Nagasaki . . . where the Dutch merchants were allowed to have a station for trade. You remember that when the foreigners were banished from Japan, the Chinese and the Dutch were allowed to stay. This was because the Chinese were heathen like themselves, and the Dutch were Protestants, not Roman Catholics like the Spaniards and Portuguese. Then, too, I am sorry to say, the Dutch were not brave enough to acknowledge to the Japanese that they were Christians at all . . . [when asked, one Dutchman declared] "I am not a Christian, I am a Dutchman."
>
> The little island was connected with the mainland by a stone bridge . . . No one could cross the bridge without permission, and boats were not allowed to pass under it.

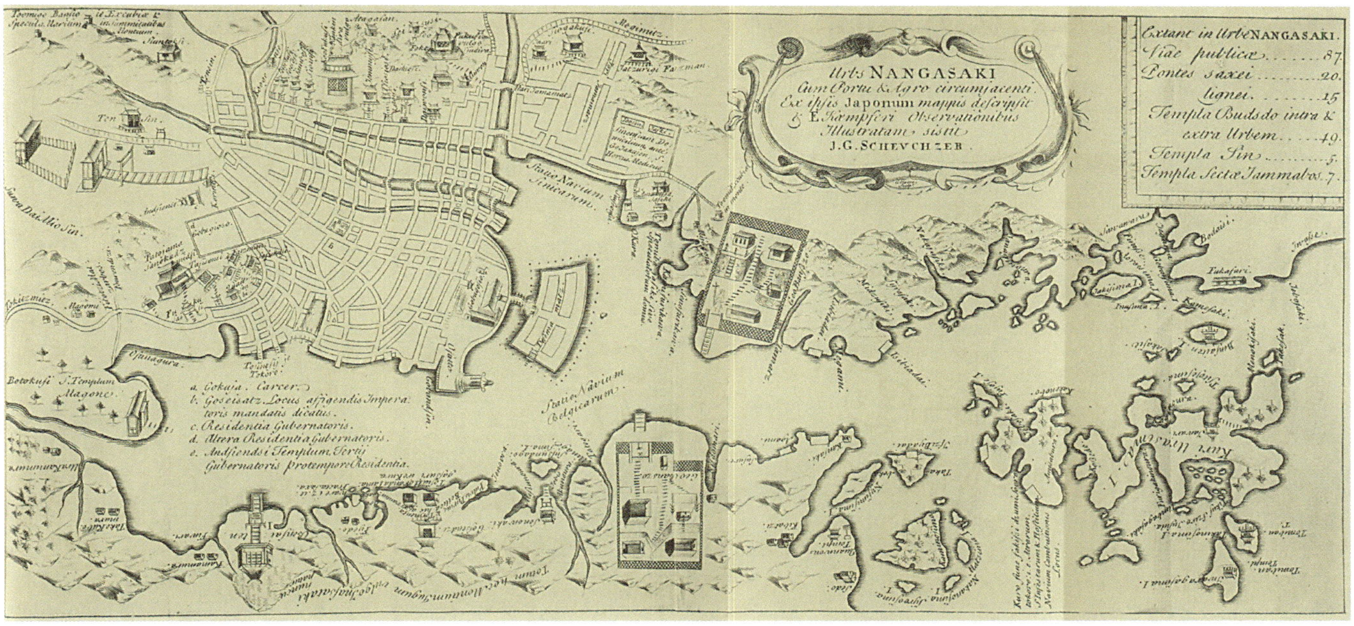

FIGURE 5.6
"A map of the city of Nagasaki . . ." featuring Dejima, in *The History of Japan, Together with a Description of the Kingdom of Siam, 1690–92*, by Engelbert Kaempfer, translated by J. G. Scheuchzer. Vol. 2. Glasgow: J. MacLehose and Sons, 1906, opposite page 80.

"We have to put up with many insulting regulations at the hands of these proud heathens," one of the Dutchmen wrote home. "We may not keep Sundays nor feast-days, nor allow our spiritual songs or hymns to be heard; never mention the name of Christ; nor carry with us any form of the cross, or any sign of Christianity."

Once or twice a year ships came from Holland bringing things from Europe to exchange for the gold, silver, camphor and beautiful porcelains, bronzes and silks of Japan.

It must have been an exciting time for the little colony when the great water gates of the harbor were opened and the big ship sailed in bringing news from home.[15]

William Dalton, writer and sometime editor of the *London Daily Telegraph*, most likely never traveled to any Asian country. Yet a number of his books are set in Asia, including *Will Adams, the First Englishman in Japan: A Romantic Biography* (1861) and another book based on an actual person, *The English Boy in Japan; or, The Perils and Adventures of Mark Raffles among Princes, Priests, and People of That Singular Empire* (1858). In the introduction to *The English Boy* Dalton provides no specific reference, yet he seems concerned about his sources, stating that "the manners, customs, and legends, which his tale is intended to illustrate, have been gathered from the latest as well as the earliest authorities." And furthermore, he even explains that his "study of a highly interesting, but at present somewhat over-rated people" had already been sent to press "before the news of the treaty signed with Japan reached European ears."[16]

The Englishman John Raffles rises to the position of secretary of the Dutch trading post at Dejima. After three years, he returns to Batavia on the island of Java, where he is reunited with his wife and young son Mark. He brings with him his Japanese protégé, the noble Toda Sofats, the son of Governor Yammasiro [*sic*] of Nagasaki, who had become a friend and confidant of Mark's father. Sofats had left Japan as a stowaway—a feat punishable by death.

Throughout the numerous cliffhanging adventures that follow, the author relishes the opportunity to tell his readers all about Japan, from men's dress, sandals, and hats, festivals and food, priests and religious rites, to forms of punishment, and much, much more—all told in great and convincing detail, gleaned, so it seems, from a source the author simply identifies as "an old Dutch author."[17]

About Dejima, Dalton writes:

> When the Hollanders first made their appearance in Japan, they found, as was the case all throughout the East, the Portuguese not only established as merchants, but as successful religious propagandists; for a large portion of even the princes and great lords had submitted to the supremacy of the Pope of Rome; and there can be little doubt but by this time Popery would have been the established faith of Japan, had not the insolence of the priests and the treachery of the Portuguese Government, which sought to subdue the empire, caused the Emperor to order all professing Christianity, whether Portuguese propagandists or Japanese converts, to be destroyed. The Dutch managed to save themselves by helping the Emperor, with artillery and sword, to destroy their European brethren. They were, however, properly punished for their mean and selfish wickedness; for although, by way of reward for their services, the Zigoon, as the natives designate one of their two Emperors, permitted them to remain in Japan, that prince felt so much contempt for a people who could assist in destroying their brother Europeans, that he made them exchange their comfortable Factory at Firando for the small artificial island of Desima [*sic*], wherein he commanded that they should for ever confine themselves. . . .
>
> Built in the shape of a fan, some 600 feet in length, by 240 across, this miserable town stands out like a pier of breakwater from the city of Nagasaki . . .
>
> For greater security and the prevention of egress and ingress, the island is surrounded with a high fence surmounted by iron spikes. The sea-gates are always shut, except at the entrance and exit of the Dutch vessels. In the harbour, upon thirteen high posts, is written the governmental order, that no boats or persons are to come within the ports or to approach the Dutch quarter, under very severe penalties. The Dutch are not allowed to build houses of stone, but simply huts of fir-wood. Moreover, every Japanese who is permitted to enter their service, as clerk, interpreter, or porter, is a Government spy, and bound two or three times a year to take a solemn oath, signed with his own blood, of hatred to the Christian religion, and that he will contract no friendship with his Dutch employers, nor afford them

> any information respecting the language, laws, manners, religion, or history of the country . . . the number of Dutchmen is limited to eleven, namely, a president, secretary, physician, and eight clerks, all of whom are so rigorously under the surveillance of keepers, that on their periodical visits to the Zigoon, to make presents and do homage, they are not allowed to speak, without permission, even to the servants of the inns at which they lodge . . .[18]

Engelbert Kaempfer and Other Pre-Perry Sources

Not only considered the "the finest work on Japan of his age,"[19] Engelbert Kaempfer's *The History of Japan* (1727) remained the most authoritative work about Japan up to the mid-nineteenth century. A physician and natural scientist; an omnivorous student of history and philosophy, and of ancient and modern languages; a man of patience and x-ray-like observation,[20] Kaempfer's work lent itself well as a resource, allowing his readers "to enter the world of late seventeenth-century Japan and see, smell, and hear what he did on the small island in the harbor of Nagasaki and on his travels to Edo."[21]

Born in 1651 in the Westphalian merchant town of Lemgo, Kaempfer attended the local Latin schools and studied at several universities, including those at Danzig, Warsaw, and Königsberg.[22] Between 1674 and 1694, his *Familenstammbuch*—a sort of family register—had signatures in Latin, Dutch, French, English, Russian, and German in addition to Armenian, Georgian, Persian, Turkish, Arabic, Siamese, Chinese and Japanese.[23]

In 1681, Kaempfer accepted the position of secretary on King Karl XI of Sweden's expedition to Persia, during which he avidly made notes in his diary, sketched, and drew maps. Almost a decade later, on September 25, 1690, Kaempfer arrived in Nagasaki, employed by the *Vereenigde Nederlandse Oost Indische Compagnie* (Dutch East India Company) as the physician of the Dutch factory on Dejima. Despite the prison-like setting and the fact that the Japanese "had to swear by their blood that they would neither disclose to us anything about local conditions nor enter into a friendly relationship with us,"[24] Kaempfer's interpreter (to whom he first taught Dutch) supplied him with books, manuscripts, maps, and information provided by other Japanese informers.

Kaempfer's reporting of his two court journeys (he traveled different routes in 1691 and 1692) is the most fascinating of his Dejima work, especially for young readers (fig. 5.7). With his camouflaged compass Kaempfer was able to devise cartographic descriptions of rivers, bridges, and roads; of islands, mountains and valleys, harbors and castles. He made sketches, noted directions and distances, and compiled the most accurate details of Japan by a Western traveler until that time.[25]

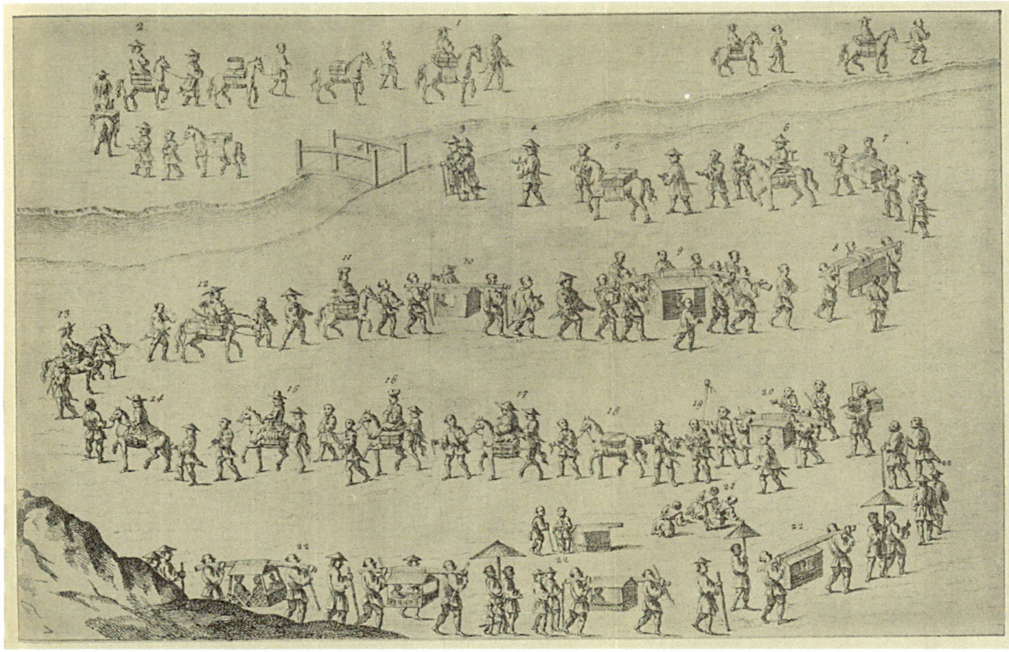

FIGURE 5.7
"The Retinue of the Dutch Ambassadors in their Journey to Court," in *The History of Japan*, by Engelbert Kaempfer, opposite page 368.

Kaempfer's notes included information about travel on the *Saikaido*, one of the major highways, which was "diligently maintained" and, "like the floor of a farmhouse . . . cleaned and swept daily."[26] He noted the cost of renting a horse, buying meals, and securing accommodations at the official post stations.[27] There were numerous descriptions of modes of travel, such as the *norimono*, in which important travelers were carried on the long journey, that would find their way into future children's books.

The highlight of Kaempfer's journey was the audience with the shōgun (fig. 5.8). After describing the audience hall, he writes:

> The shogun had first been seated next to the women at some distance in front of us, but now he moved to the side, as close to us as he could behind the blind. He

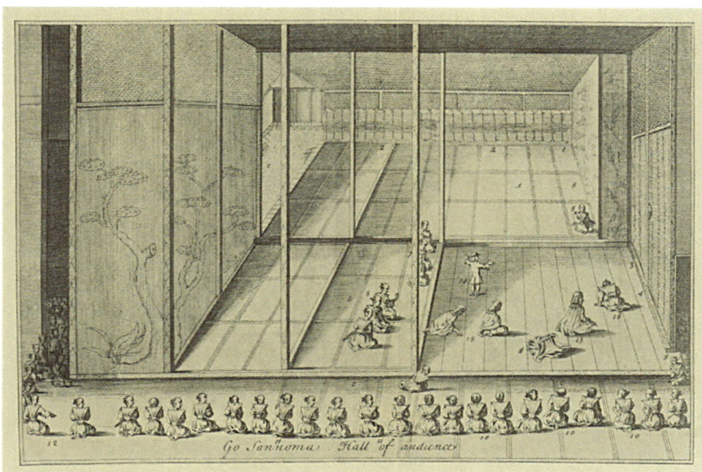

FIGURE 5.8
"Hall of Audience," in *The History of Japan*, by Engelbert Kaempfer, opposite page 96.

> had us take off our *cappa*, or ceremonial robes, and sit upright so that he could inspect us; has us now stand up and walk, now pay compliments to each other, then again dance, jump, pretend to be drunk, speak Japanese, read Dutch, draw, sing, put on our coats, then take them off again. . . . At the demand of the shogun we had to put up with providing such amusements and perform innumerable other monkey tricks. . . .
>
> After we had been drilled for two hours—albeit always after courteous requests—tonsured servants served each of us with small Japanese dishes on separate little tables; instead of knives we were given two small sticks.[28]

In *All about Japan*, Belle M. Brain included this description of Kaempfer's performance:

> When they entered the "Hall of a Hundred Mats" where the shogun sat behind a curtain, they were required to crawl on their hands and knees and bow again and again to the floor. When they went out they had to go backwards, "crawling exactly like a crab," so they said. This ceremony over, they were expected to go through a great many ridiculous performances for entertainment of the lords and ladies of the court.
>
> "We had to rise and walk to and fro," says one of them who wrote a famous book; "to exchange compliments with each other, then to dance, jump, represent a drunken man, speak broken Japanese, paint, read Dutch, and German, sing, put on our cloaks and throw them off again."
>
> We can hardly understand how these staid and dignified old Hollanders could have been willing to do such absurd and foolish things. But they did it, as they themselves confess, "for the love of gain."[29]

Philipp Franz von Siebold was another author-traveler whose work writers would later consult for their children's books. After studying medicine, zoology, botany, geography, and ethnology in his native Würzburg, Siebold arrived in Dejima in 1823. His success in inoculating Japanese against smallpox and performing cataract surgery drew physicians from all over Japan who wanted to study under him. The authorities even gave him permission to open a school.

Like Kaempfer before him, Siebold went to Edo for an audience with the shōgun, collecting specimens and making observations along the way. Meeting with Japanese physicians and scholars of Dutch studies, Siebold hoped for a prolonged stay in Edo or even into Japan's north. But he had to be satisfied with a rich bounty of "animals, plants, minerals and other items from the world of nature, extending to materials such as maps, books, and pictures, and even further to items used in everyday Japanese life, products of trade from various parts of the country, and survey data of various geographical features."[30]

Using Kaempfer and Siebold as sources, Robert Van Bergen describes a remarkable connection between the two men in his children's book, *The Story of Japan* (1897). He relates that Siebold came across "a camphor tree that had been mentioned by another traveler from Deshima in 1691 [no other than Kaempfer himself]. He measured it and found it about fifty feet in circumference. It was still standing in 1826, and was green and healthy."[31]

In Van Bergen's description of the court journey, he tells how the Dutch were entertained by various *daimio*, that they had guidebooks that helped them gauge distances and costs, and he states that "roads in Japan are uniformly good, and are kept scrupulously clean." Van Bergen notes a unique way the Japanese measured the length of their journey:

> One of the sights which struck the travelers was the number of stalls where straw shoes for horses and oxen are sold. The people counted the distances by the number of horseshoes that were required.[32]

Van Bergen also notes:

> These journeys were always begun in February, that month with March, April, and May being the most pleasant for traveling. It took a long time to make the necessary preparations, for the Japanese are very fond of ceremonies, and the omission of even one would have been deemed a serious insult.
>
> The party of Hollanders going to the capital usually consisted of the general agent, his secretary, and the physician, together with a large number of native officials and servants. Most of the journey was made on land, and each of the Hollanders, as well as each of the native officials, was carried in a norimono (noh-ree'-moh-noh), a sort of sedan chair, with windows closed with bamboo curtains and a roof like that of a house. All these norimono required bearers. Besides these there were the carriers of the presents, the boxes containing clothing, cooking apparatus, chairs, etc., and the numerous cooks and body servants of the Dutch and the officials. Altogether there were not less than two hundred persons, and although they were frequently entertained by the daimio through whose territories they passed, the expense connected with such a trip was very heavy.[33]

Carl Peter Thunberg

The Swedish physician and botanist Carl Peter Thunberg arrived in Nagasaki in 1775. Considered the founder of Japanese botany and author of, among many other works, *Flora Japonica* (1784), Thunberg includes this description in his *Travels in Japan* (1801):

> The Japanese are well made, active, easy in their motion, and stout limbed, though of inferior strength to the northern inhabitants of Europe. The men are of middling size, and not much inclined to corpulency. Their skin is of a yellowish color, sometimes bordering on brown, and sometimes on white, according to their exposure to the affects [*sic*] of the sun. Ladies of distinction, who seldom go abroad without being covered from the sun and air, are perfectly white. The distinguishing characteristic is their oblong, small, sunk eyes, in which respect they resemble the Chinese. Their eye brows are also placed pretty high, and the eyelids form, in the great angle, a deep furrow. Their heads are generally large; their necks short; their hair black, thick and glossy; and their noses though not flat, are rather short and thick.[34]

Some fifty years later, this paragraph, drawn from Thunberg's description, appears without attribution in the children's book *Stories of Asia* by Alice Hawthorne:

> The Japanese, seem, in personal appearance, to be a somewhat altered and improved variety of the Monguls and Chinese. Their eyes are, even in a greater degree, small, pointed, oblong, sunk in the head, with a deep furrow made by the eyelids; they have almost the appearance of being pink-eyed. Their heads are in general large, and their necks short; their hair is black, thick, and shining from the use of oil. They are, however, robust, well-made, active, and easy in their motions.[35]

From Commodore Perry to the End of the Nineteenth Century

Three years after the publication of Commodore Perry's *Narrative of the Expedition of an American Squadron to the China Seas and Japan Performed in the Years 1852, 1853, and 1854* (1856), which was, surprisingly, rarely cited as a resource by children's book writers, a French publisher issued a bibliography listing no fewer than seven hundred books about Japan.[36] By the 1890s, wrote Basil Hall Chamberlain, that number had increased seventy-fold. Each separate aspect of Japanese culture as well as the physical characteristics of the country itself "has a little library to itself," Chamberlain wrote.[37]

In *Things Japanese*, one of the books most often cited by those writing about Japan, Chamberlain presented his own list of best books about Japan. (William E. Griffis's list showed many of the same titles.)[38] Chamberlain's top-ten choices were:

1. *Japan: Travels and Researches Undertaken at the Cost of the Prussian Government* (1884) and its sequel *The Industries of Japan, Together with an*

Account of its Agriculture, Forestry, Arts and Commerce (1889), by Dr. Johannes Justus Rein;

2. *The Mikado's Empire* by William E. Griffis (1876);
3. Murray's *Handbook for Central and Northern Japan* by Ernest Satow and A. G. S. Hawes (1884);
4. *The Transactions of the Asiatic Society of Japan* (published annually since 1874);
5. *Japan as It Was and Is* by Richard Hildreth (1855);
6. *Young Japan, Yokohama and Yedo: A Narrative of the Settlement and the City from the Signing of the Treaties in 1858, to the Close of the Year 1879, With a Glance at the Progress of Japan During a Period of Twenty-One Years* by John R. Black (1880);
7. *The Capital of the Tycoon: A Narrative of a Three Years' Residence in Japan* by Sir Rutherford Alcock (1863);
8. *Descriptive and Historical Catalogue of Japanese and Chinese Paintings in the British Museum* by Dr. William Anderson (1886);
9. *Tales of Old Japan* by A. B. Mitford (1871);
10. *Unbeaten Tracks in Japan* by Isabella Bird (1881).

Many of these works became the sources of children's book writers.

Japan nach Reisen und Studien im Autrage der Königlich Preussischen Regierung (1881), published in a revised edition as *Japan: Travels and Researches Undertaken at the Cost of the Prussian Government* (1884) and *The Industries of Japan* (1889), were written by Johann Justus Rein,[39] a member of the 1860 Prussian Japan expedition. They topped Chamberlain's list. Chamberlain writes, "No person wishing to study Japan seriously can dispense with these admirable volumes," adding:

> Of the two, that on the "Industries" is better:—agriculture, cattle-raising, forestry, mines, lacquer-work, metal-work, commerce, etc.,—everything, in fact, has been studied with a truly German patience, and is set forth with a truly German thoroughness. The other volume is occupied with the physiography of the country, that is, its geography, fauna, flora, etc., and with an account of the people both historical and ethnographical, and with the topography of the various provinces.[40]

Annie R. Butler was among the children's book writers who acknowledged Rein's influence, placing his "learned work about *Japan*" first on her list of acknowledged sources in the preface to *Stories about Japan* (1888, fig. 5.9).[41]

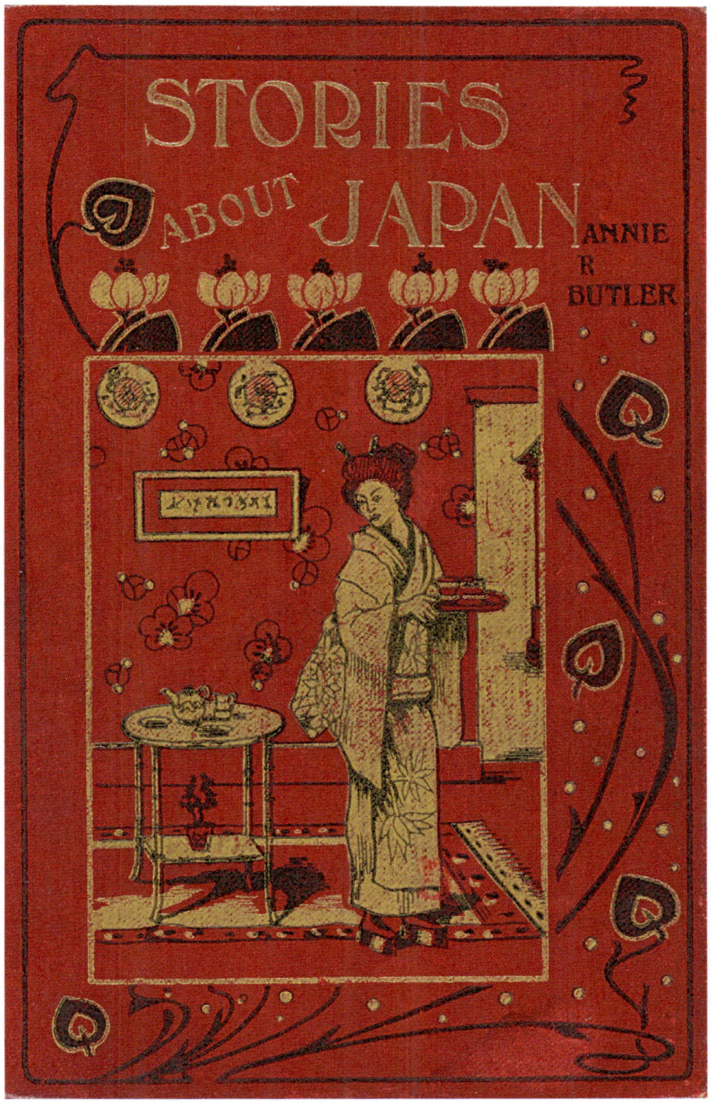

FIGURE 5.9
Stories about Japan, by Annie R. Butler. London: The Religious Tract Society, 1888.

Isabella Bird: *Unbeaten Tracks in Japan*

Isabella Bird was forty-seven when she decided to go to Japan. Her doctor recommended a change of scenery. Though a seasoned traveler (she had already explored Hawaii and the Rocky Mountains), Bird was anxious about her Japan adventure and would have liked to have given up the whole idea had she not felt "ashamed of [her own] cowardice."[42] Instead, she planned an itinerary that would take her to Aomori, Hakodate, and Yezo—the northernmost island of Japan. She hired a servant, got herself a horse, and collected her travel gear (an air pillow, an India-rubber bathtub, Liebig's extract of meat, raisins, brandy, copies of the *Transactions of the Asiatic Society of Japan,* and Ernest Satow's Anglo-Japanese dictionary).[43] Bird endured torrential rains, mudslides, and collapsing roads and bridges; she fell off her horse time and again. Whether riding or walking, the pace was slow. Her back often hurt. She was stung by hornets, bitten by mosquitoes and fleas. Most accommodations were primitive, food sparse. On some days the humidity was so high that the mildew had to be wiped off the leather gear every couple of hours.

Wherever Bird appeared, she became an attraction. Even at night she was the object of the "concentrated stare" of many dark eyes that watched her through holes poked in the shoji screens. Yet, Bird took it all in stride—even rejoiced in the freedom of being a lone woman where few Western men had ever been—and described her experiences in Japan in long, candid letters to her sister back home. She wrote of festivals, a wedding, and a funeral, which she attended in disguise. She found the country beautiful; some places like "paradise." She loved the children, admiring their parents' care. When she stayed in a private mansion, enjoying the elegance of its simple design, she also observed the grinding poverty and diseases of the rural population whose kindness she accepted with gratitude. Her most rewarding experience came when she met the aborigines of Yezo. "I am in the lonely Aino land," she wrote, "living for three days and two nights in an Aino hut, and seeing and sharing the daily life of complete savages, who go on with their ordinary occupations just as if I were not among them . . . All but two or three . . . are the most ferocious-looking of savages . . . but as soon as they speak the countenance brightens into a smile as gentle as that of a woman, something which can never be forgotten."[44]

Thomas W. Knox, the author of *The Travels of Marco Polo for Boys and Girls* (1885) was among the many writers of children's books who acknowledged Bird. Annie R. Butler, author of *Stories about Japan*, also adopted information from Bird:

> I know that once, when a lady called Miss Bird was traveling through Japan, the children ran away in terror, because they thought she was—what do you think? A big ape! . . . The Japanese are, as a nation, extremely courteous, industrious, quick at learning, independent, and neat. Miss Bird, of whom I told you just now, says that during a journey of 1,200 miles, or so, no one ever tried to cheat her, and that only one was at all impolite. That one was a child, and it was severely scolded for its rudeness.[45]

As to her own information sources, Bird acknowledged the assistance of Ernest Satow, Secretary of the British Legation (and author of an Anglo-Japanese dictionary she consulted), who arranged for her passport to areas off-limits to ordinary Westerners. She also consulted native guides, maps, and the *Transactions of the Asiatic Society of Japan* and read books by Austrian diplomat Baron Joseph Alexander von Hübner, Philipp Franz von Siebold, Basil Hall Chamberlain, and William E. Griffis, as well as A. B. Mitford.

William Griffis: *The Mikado's Empire*

William Elliot Griffis, whose *The Mikado's Empire* (1876, fig. 5.10) has been described as "the best single interpretation of Japan by an American,"[46] acknowledged the help of many friends, including Ernest Satow, A. B. Mitford, American missionary and translator James Curtis Hepburn, German diplomat and East Asia expert Max von Brandt, and British diplomat Sir Harry Parkes, the editor of the *Japan Mail*; as well as the papers of the Asiatic Society of Japan, the *Japan Herald*, and the *Japan Gazette*.[47] Griffis apparently also relied on information collected from his Japanese students, who supplied information on their "native cities and towns, the geography of their provinces, games played by Japanese children, Japanese money, signs and theaters, burial customs, their first impression of foreigners, etc."[48]

An intricately detailed history of Japan, *The Mikado's Empire* provides information about many aspects of everyday Japanese life, including fan makers, festivals, the tattooed *bettō* (runner), and the *kotatsu*:

> In the very centre of the room lift up that square foot of matting, and you will find a stone-lined bowl, a few inches deep. In this the fat and red-cheeked chambermaid puts a shovelful of live coals. Over it she sets a wooden frame, a foot high, called a *yagura,* after the castle tower it imitates. Over this she spreads a huge quilt. It is an extemporary oven, in which you can bake yourself by drawing the quilt about you, and find a little heaven of heat, exchanging shivers for glow. A *kotatsu* may be safely warranted to change a grumbler, who believes Japan to be a wretched hole of a barbarian country, into a rhapsodist who is ready to swear that the same country is a paradise, within ten minutes.[49]

Of special interest to children's book writers was the information Griffis provides on children's games and amusements. He describes storytellers, dancers,

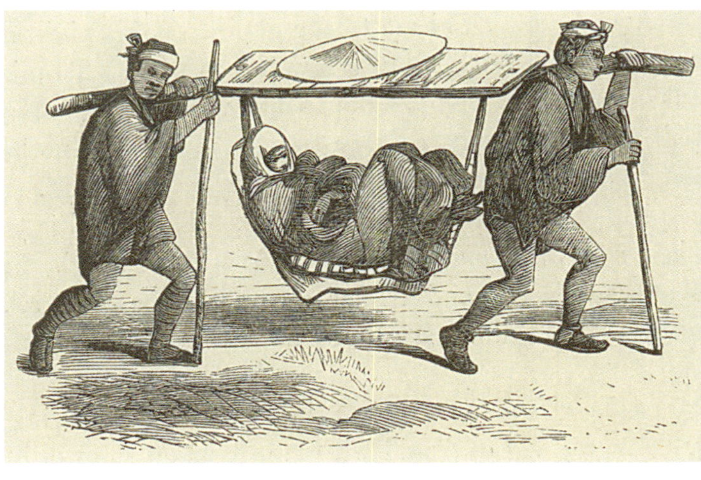

FIGURE 5.10
"How We Rode to Odani," in *The Mikado's Empire*, by William Elliot Griffis. New York: Harper and Brothers, 1890, page 544. Originally printed in *The Capital of the Tycoon* by Sir Rutherford Alcock (1863).

actors, magicians, flute players, singers, and itinerant sellers of candy, griddle cakes, and sweetened beans; games of battledore and shuttlecock and card games of many varieties; puzzles, the strategy board game *go*, kites, tops, finger games, riddles and puns, mythological creatures, proverbs and folktales. Though, as Sir Edward J. Reed noted, "more than one reader of cultivated taste" complained about Griffis's tendency to "gush," the "occasional tawdriness of his style," and his citing information without proper acknowledgment.[50] One example of what Basil Hall Chamberlain deemed the "genuine value of [his] book"[51] was Griffis's poignant eyewitness account of the falling of feudalism:

> July 18th, 1871. . . .
>
> The thunderbolt has fallen! The political earthquake has shaken Japan to its centre. . . . An imperial proclamation just received orders that the hereditary incomes of the samurai be reduced, all sinecure offices abolished, and the salaries thereto attached turned over to the imperial treasury. The number of officials is to be reduced to the lowest minimum. The property of the *han* [domain or estate of a warrior] is to become that of the Imperial Government. The Fukui *han* is to be converted into a *ken,* or prefecture, of the Central Government.[52]
>
> October 1st, 1871
>
> From an early hour this morning, the samurai in *kamishimo* (ceremonial dress) have been preparing for the farewell, and have been assembling in the castle. . . . Arranged in the order of their rank, each in his starched robes of ceremony, with shaven-crown, and gun-hammer top-knot, with hands clasped on the hilt of his sword resting upright before him as he sat on his knees, were the three thousand samurai of the Fukui clan. . . .
>
> Matsudaira Mochiaké, late Lord of Echizen, and feudal head of the Fukui clan, who was tomorrow to be a private nobleman, now advanced down the wide corridor to the main hall. He was a stern-visaged man of perhaps thirty-five years of age. He was dressed in purple satin hakama, with inner robe of white satin, and outer coat of silk crepe of a dark slate hue, embroidered on sleeve, back, and breast with the Tokugawa crest. In his girdle was thrust the usual side-arm, or *wakizashi,* or dirk, the hilt of which was a carved and frosted mass of solid gold. . . . As he passed, every head was bowed, every sword laid prone to the right, and Matsudaira, with deep but unexpressed emotion, advanced amidst the ranks of his followers to the centre of the main hall. There, in a brief and noble address, read by his chief minister, the history of the clan and of their relations as lord and vassals, the causes which had led to the revolution of 1868, the results of which had restored the imperial house to power, and the Mikado's reasons for ordering the territorial princes to restore their fiefs, were tersely and eloquently recounted. In conclusion, he adjured all his followers to transfer their allegiance wholly to the Mikado and the imperial house. Then, wishing them all success and prosperity in

> their new relations, and in their persons, their families, and their estates, in chaste and fitting language he bid his followers solemn farewell.[53]

> December 1st, 1871
>
> The outer wall of the castle has been leveled, and the moat filled up. The gates have been sold for their stone, wood, and copper. Many old yashikis [mansions] of ancient and once wealthy families have been torn down and converted into shops. The towns-people and shop-keepers are jubilant at getting a foot-hold on the sites hitherto reserved for the samurai. Old armor, arrows, spears, flags, saddlery, dresses, norimonos, and all the paraphernalia of the old feudal days can now be bought dirt cheap.[54]

> January 26th, 1872
>
> We are now on the Tōkaidō. . . . Over this road tramped the armies of Iyéyasŭ . . . moved the processions of the daimiōs, advanced the loyal legions from Fushimi to Hakodaté. Today a different sight makes my heart beat and my eyes kindle . . . here, in the heart of Japan, I see before me telegraph-poles; their bare, grim, silent majesty is as eloquent as pulses of light. The electric wires will soon connect the sacred city of the Sun Land with the girdle that clasps the globe.[55]

Richard Hildreth, an American journalist and author of many books, including the six-volume *History of the United States* (1856–1860), never visited Japan. Yet one modern reviewer has called his *Japan as It Was and Is* "still by far the best of the early treatises on Japan."[56] First published in 1855, this influential work appeared in limited editions in Japan in 1902 and 1905 and was reissued, in a revised edition with an introduction by William Elliot Griffis, in 1906. Drawing from numerous sources, Hildreth excerpted an amazing amount of background information and telling details: comparing Kaempfer's Dejima with that of Thunberg's time, for example, he found that nothing much had changed, except that the "paper windows of the Japanese" had been replaced by glass.[57] As he notes in the introduction to the book,

> From Kaempfer [*History of Japan*], whose name has become so identified with Japan, but into whose folios few have the opportunity or courage to look, I have made very liberal extracts. Few travelers have equaled him in picturesque power. . . .[58]

Aimé Humbert's *Japan and the Japanese*

Japan and the Japanese (1874, fig. 5.11) by Swiss politician, educator, and traveler Aimé Humbert was originally published in France as *Le Japon Illustré* (1869). This handsome book provides a wealth of details about Japan's history, social conditions and customs, religion, and arts. Representing the Swiss Republic as Minister Plenipotentiary in Japan from 1863 to 1864, Humbert was able to travel outside the limits of the foreign settlement of Yokohama. The unsigned preface of *Japan and the Japanese* provides a snapshot of Humbert's research methods:

> [Humbert and his assistant] studied the country and the people, visiting the neighboring towns, and rambling at all seasons over the pleasant country around the Bay of Yeddo. Armed with their sketching implements and a note-book, they jotted down their observations; sometimes seated at the foot of an ancient cedar; sometimes squatted on the threshold of a rustic tavern; or again, more slyly, intrenched [*sic*] in the back shop of some friendly tradesman, who good-naturedly aided them in their inquiries. A large number of photographs were taken, under M. Humbert's own eye; and he speaks of the treasures, in the way of engravings, Indian-ink sketches, and coloured pictures, all valuable illustrations of the hidden scenes of Japanese political life and history, which he obtained by frequent visits to the print-shops of Yeddo.[59]

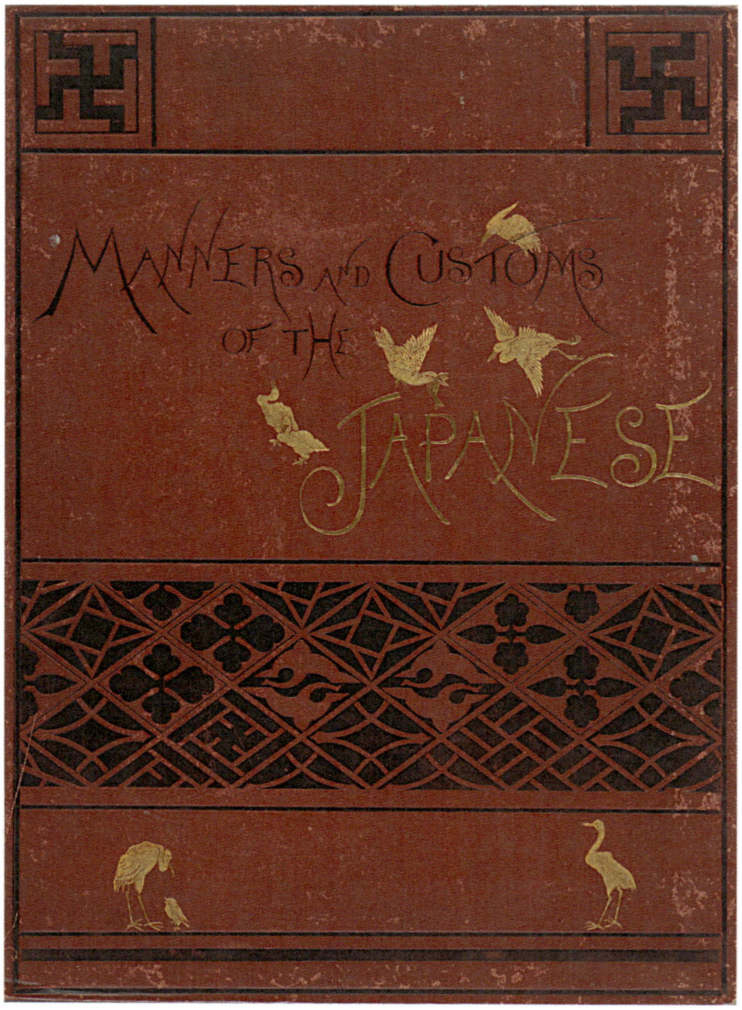

FIGURE 5.11
Manners and Customs of the Japanese, by Aimé Humbert. London: R. Bentley & Son, 1874. The title page reads "Japan and the Japanese."

Though the emphasis is on the history of Japan—citing information from Engelbert Kaempfer, Philipp Franz von Siebold, Carl Peter Thunberg, and Sir Rutherford Alcock—Humbert interspersed his text with his personal observations, including those regarding Japan's "luxuriant spring vegetation":

> All along the hedges, in the orchards, and about the villages, tufts of flowers and foliage of dazzling hue stand out against the dark tints of a background of pines, firs, cedars, cypress, laurels, green oak, and bamboos. . . .
>
> The bamboo, much employed in the capacity of a support for these trees, frequently lends his elegant foliage to the branches of young fruit trees which have no other adornment than their bunches of flowers. But I love the bamboo most when it grows in solitary groups, like a tuft of gigantic reeds. There is nothing more picturesque in the whole landscape than these tall green polished stems, with their golden streaks and their tufted tops, and all around the chiefs the young slender offshoots with their feathered heads, and a multitude of long leaves streaming in the wind like thousands of fluttering pennons.[60]

Illustrations from *Japan and the Japanese* (e.g. "Children's Games," "Winter Dress of the Fishermen and Peasants," and "Sleeping Mousnees" [*sic*]) were reproduced in numerous children's books. *A Queer People,* by "L. R. L." (late 1870s, fig. 5.12), tries to explain just how "queer" or odd everything is about the Japanese, including their dress, their "ABC," their religion and so on. Edward Greey's *The Wonderful City of Tokio* (1883) and Edward A. Rand's *All Aboard for Sunrise Lands* (1891) also reproduced illustrations, though the source was rarely acknowledged.

Another title on Basil Hall Chamberlain's list of noteworthy sources about Japan, the fact-filled *The Capital of the Tycoon: A Narrative of a Three Years' Residence in Japan* (1863, fig. 5.13), by her "Majesty's envoy extraordinary and minister plenipotentiary in Japan," Sir Rutherford Alcock, had, according to one contemporary magazine reviewer, only one fault, its "intolerable verbosity." Alcock, the reviewer continues,

> probably knows both the country and its capital better than any living European, and has poured out his stores of knowledge with unreserved profusion . . . native feudalism and European discomforts, the tricks of the Tycoon's Government and the drift of English diplomacy, Japanese women's immodesty and European merchants' aggressiveness, the system of agriculture and Japanese toilettes, the policy of the oligarchy and native caricature all are described with a fullness which leaves on the reader's mind the impression of acquiring exhaustive knowledge. The author's style is clear and simple, his mind has few prejudices . . . His book will be read with almost excited interest by all men who have time, and they will concur

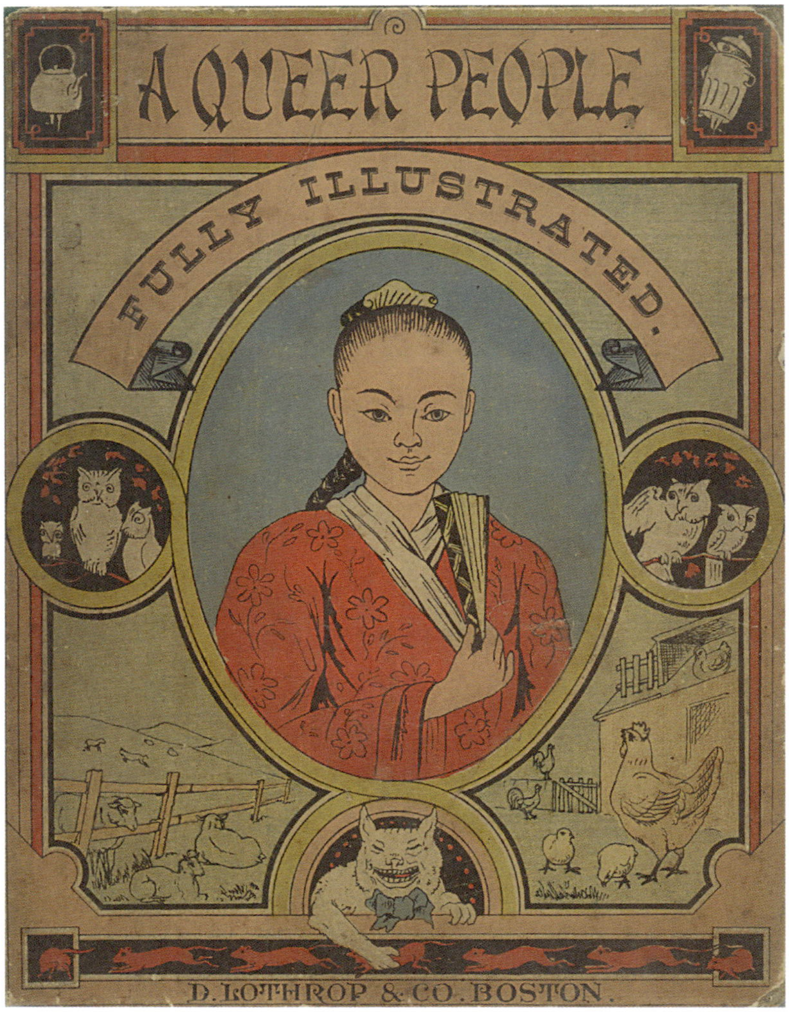

FIGURE 5.12
A Queer People, by L.R.L. [Fanny Roper Feudge] Boston: D. Lothrop, ca. 1878.

> with us in annoyance at the diffusive garrulity by which its permanent value has been so greatly reduced.[61]

Chamberlain said of his own work, *Things Japanese: Being Notes on Various Subjects Connected with Japan* (1890), that he intended to address questions about Japan he was "perpetually being asked." He put those answers "into the shape of a dictionary, not of words but of things,—or shall we rather say a guidebook, less to place than to subjects? . . . In order to enable the reader to supply deficiencies and to form his own opinions," he added, "we have, at the end of almost every article, indicated the names of trustworthy works bearing on the subject treated in the article."[62]

The book includes more than a hundred articles on topics ranging from the abacus and the Asiatic Society of Japan to writing, the island of Yezo, and the status of women. The entry on "topsy-turvydom" dealt with a topic favored by authors of both adult and children's books about Japan. "It has often been

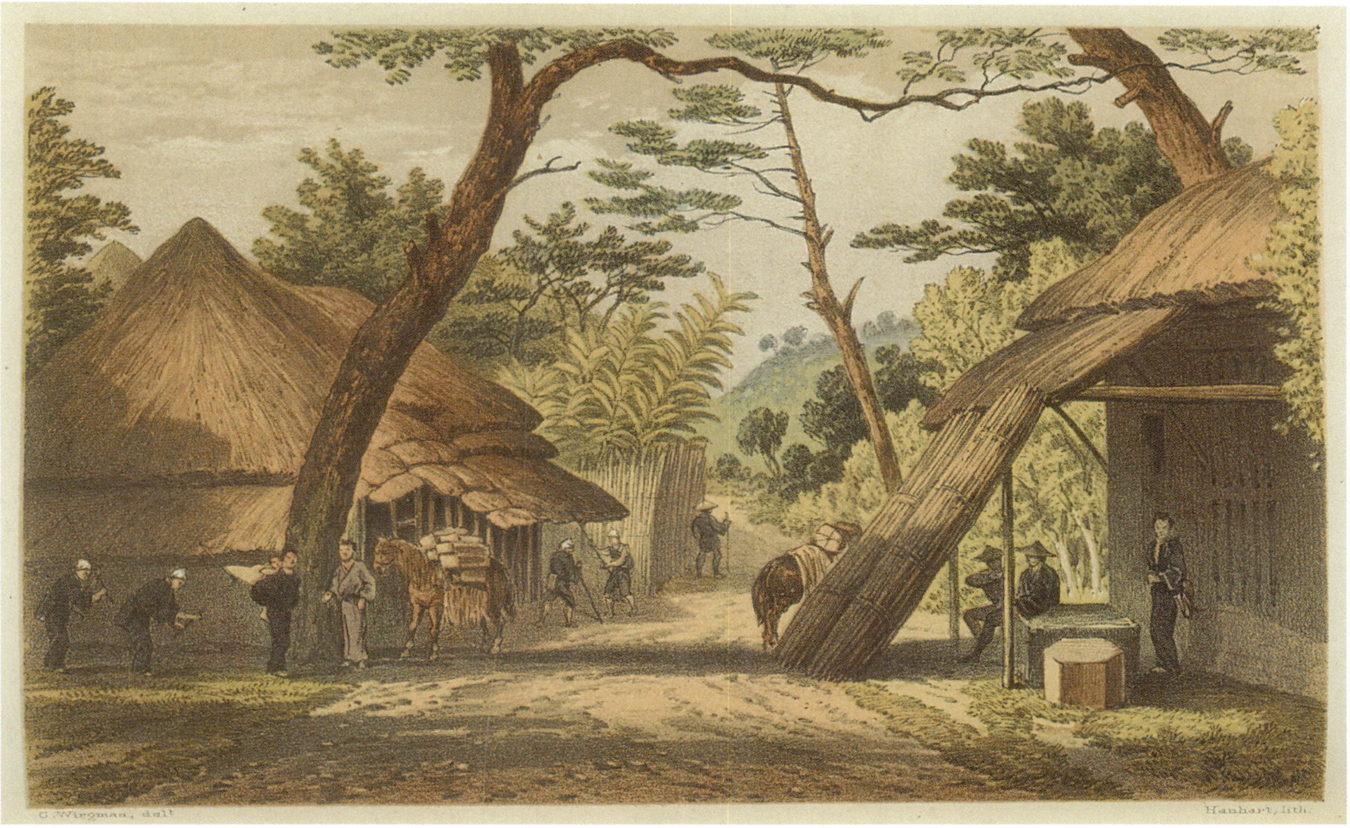

FIGURE 5.13
The Capital of the Tycoon: A Narrative of a Three Years' Residence in Japan, by Sir Rutherford Alcock. Vol. 2. London: Longman, Green, Longman, Roberts, and Green, 1863, opposite page 83.

remarked that the Japanese do many things in a way that runs directly counter to European ideas of what is natural and proper," Chamberlain wrote, adding that "a Tokyo lady" had recently asked him "why foreigners did so many things topsy-turvy, instead of doing them naturally, after the manner of her own country-people."[63]

The 1905 edition of her *Stories about Japan*, Annie R. Butler provides several examples of what Western children would consider Japan's topsy-turvydom:

> Here the cats have no tails, and the bells have no tongues (they are struck from the outside). The birds sing but little, and our mode of kissing is an art unknown. The horse stands with his head from the stall; and when the rider mounts, it is from the right, not the left . . . The teeth of the saw and the thread of the screw run in the opposite direction of ours. The tailor sews from, and the carpenter planes towards him . . . Everything pretty is put at the back, instead of the front, of a building . . . If you went into a school, you would find the children reading down instead of across the page, and from the end instead of from the beginning of the book.[64]

Of course, children's authors also consulted works not on Chamberlain's list. A favorite seems to have been British poet and journalist Edwin Arnold's book of essays, *Japonica* (1891, fig. 5.1), with romantic illustrations by Robert Blum.

Pierre Loti's *Madame Chrysanthème*

Toward the end of the century, an influential information source appeared that was not written by an explorer, diplomat, teacher, or missionary. The author of this fictional work was Pierre Loti (nom de plume of French naval officer Louis-Marie-Julien Viaud), whom Lafcadio Hearn considered his "chosen literary master."[65] Regarded by some as the "first literary observer of talent" to come to Japan,[66] Loti was already famous when in 1885 he arrived in Nagasaki, the setting of his *Madame Chrysanthème* (1887).[67]

Driven by a "lifelong hunger for '*ailleurs*'" (elsewhere),[68] Loti joined the French Navy in 1863. To support his impoverished family, he began writing and illustrating magazine articles about his travels to Turkey, Tahiti, Senegal, Algiers, Morocco, India, and Japan. These exotic places became settings for his romantic, semi-autobiographical novels, which were quickly translated into numerous languages. *Aziyade* (1879), his first book, the tale of his passionate love for a Turkish harem girl, made him famous overnight. Though inducted into the Académie Française, which "enjoyed an almost mythical prestige, election to its ranks being considered the apotheosis of glory,"[69] Loti always remained an outsider in French society—an outsider with dramatic flair. A handsome man, he hid his diminutive stature behind elaborate costumes and, forever play-acting, treated his friends to lavish theatrical fêtes.

Madame Chrysanthème was one of Basil Hall Chamberlain's recommended books about Japan, though a contemporary reviewer called the novel "a crude and vulgar episode"[70]—and Chamberlain, himself, noted that "the volume [was] in nowise to be recommended either to misses or missionaries."[71]

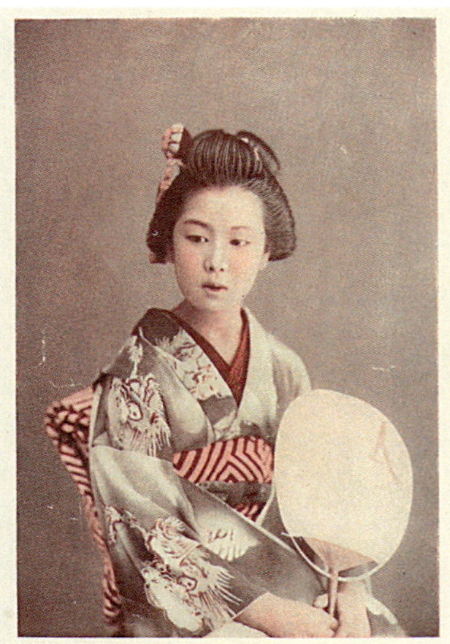

FIGURE 5.14
[Young Girl in Kimono] in *Japan (Madame Chrysanthème)*, by Pierre Loti, illustrated by Rossi and Myrbach. London: T. W. Laurie, 1915, page 102.

The reason for Chamberlain's wariness about the story of the French sailor who comes to Nagasaki becomes clear as the story unfolds. As his ship drifts into the beautiful Nagasaki harbor under a starry sky, the sailor (a fictionalized version of Loti) imagines his new and enchanted life. "I shall at once marry," he tells his fellow sailor.

> Yes—I shall choose a little yellow-skinned woman with black hair and cat's eyes. She must be pretty. Not much bigger than a doll. . . . [we will have a] little paper house, in the middle of green gardens, prettily shaded. We shall live among flowers, everything around us shall blossom, and each morning our dwelling shall be filled with nosegays, nosegays such as you have never dreamt of.[72]

Soon after the ship is in port, M. Kangourou, the go-between, arrives with a girl. Her name is Jasmin, and the sailor looks her over:

> Why, I know her already! Long before setting foot in Japan, I had met with her, on every fan, on every tea-cup with her silly air, her puffy little visage, her tiny eyes, mere gimlet-holes above those expanses of impossible pink and white which are her cheeks.
>
> She is young, that is all I can say in her favor; she is even so young that I should almost scruple to accept her. The wish to laugh quits me suddenly, and instead, a profound chill fastens on my heart. What! Share an hour of my life even with that little doll? Never! The next question is, how to get out of it?[73]

But he does not get out of it. Soon, the go-between makes the necessary arrangements. The sailor can have her for twenty dollars a month and "little by little," he becomes "accustomed to my Japanese household, to the strangeness of the language, costumes, faces."[74] The sailor continues:

> The house is just as I fancied it should be in the many dreams of Japan I had made before my arrival, during my long night watches: perched on high, in a peaceful suburb, in the midst of green gardens;—made up of paper panels, and taken to pieces according to one's fancy, like a child's toy . . . From our verandah, we have a bewildering bird's-eye view of Nagasaki, of its streets, its junks and its great pagodas, which, at certain hours, is lit up at our feet like some fairy-like scene. . . .[75]
>
> Through the transparent blue gauze appeared my little Japanese, as she lay in her sombre night-dress with all the fantastic grace of her country, the nape of her neck resting on its wooden block, and her hair arranged in large shiny bows. Her amber-colored arms, pretty and delicate, emerged, bare up to the shoulders, from her wide sleeves.[76]

Yet, all too soon, the ship is preparing to leave for China. The temporary wife is easily cast aside.

> At the outer gate I stop for the last adieu . . . Well, little mousmé, let us part good friends; one last kiss even, if you like. I took you to amuse me; you have not perhaps succeeded very well, but after all you have done what you could: given me your little face, your little curtseys, your little music; in short, you have been pleasant enough in your Japanese way. And who knows, perchance I may yet think of you sometimes when I recall this glorious summer.[77]

In 1898, American lawyer John Luther Long retold Loti's *Madame Chrysanthème* in his story *Madame Butterfly*, which also included details from a similar story that his sister, Jennie Correll, brought back from Japan.[78]

In this tale, U.S. Navy lieutenant B. F. Pinkerton, stationed in Nagasaki, acquires as his wife seventeen-year-old Cho-Cho-San, or Madame Butterfly

(Cho-cho is the Japanese word for butterfly). Soon Pinkerton returns to America, leaving behind Cho-Cho-San and the child he has fathered.

Cho-Cho-San, disowned by her family, waits for Pinkerton's return. Finally, Mr. Sharpless, the sympathetic American consul, reports that Pinkerton's ship will soon arrive in Nagasaki.

Cho-Cho-San and Suzuki, her maid, see him standing on the deck next to a blonde woman, as the ship sails into the harbor.

In the consul's office, Cho-Cho-San learns that the blonde woman is Pinkerton's American wife. She claims Cho-Cho-San's "lovely" baby, then she turns to Cho-Cho-San, calling her "charming, lovely," and a "pretty *plaything*" and asking for a kiss:

> Cho-Cho-San stared at her with round eyes—as children do when afraid. Then her nostrils quivered and her lids slowly closed. "No," she said, very softly. "Ah, well," laughed the other, "I don't blame you. They say you don't do that sort of thing—to women, at any rate. I quite forgive our men for falling in love with you."[79]

Cho-Cho San's apparent attempt to kill herself, as described at the end of Long's story, was presented much more darkly in the final scene of Giacomo Puccini's opera adaptation *Madama Butterfly* which premiered in 1904. By performing a sort of ritual seppuku—with the short sword her father had left her—Cho-Cho San's death created a tragic heroine whose story became immortal and widely known.[80]

It seems certain that Frances Little, author of the children's book *Little Sister Snow* (1909; see chapter 2) knew of the tragic Japanese story when she wrote about Yuki, a young Japanese girl who falls in love with Richard Merrit, an American. (He had met Yuki's family during an earlier visit). This time he comes to board with them while on business in Japan. (As in Cho-Cho-San's story there is a wealthy suitor. Arrangements for Yuki's marriage to Saito San, "a[n] . . . officer in the Emperor's household" have already been made.)[81]

After much anticipation, Merrit arrives. He greets Yuki with outstretched hands, while she glanced at him briefly and "touched her head to the floor in gracious courtesy."[82]

Yuki and her family watch Merrit, even when he unpacks his suitcase. He shows Yuki a photo of his fiancée. Little writes:

> That night Yuki San lay once more on her soft *futon* and watched the shadow on the night-lamp play upon the screens. . . . "Dat most nice girl in picture," she said

> to herself. "Him make marry with dat girl, he say." Then she added inconsequently, with a sigh, "I much hope Saito San go to war for long, long time."[83]

Enchanted by Merrit, Yuki acts as his tour guide and interpreter, each day succumbing more and more to his charm:

> For two halcyon months Yuki San lived in a dream . . . they went on jolly excursions, visited ancient temples, and picnicked under the shadow of the *torii.* The father and mother always trotted close behind, and Yuki San . . . gaily translated the speeches from one to another. She talked incessantly, laughing over her own mistakes, and growing prettier and more winsome every day.[84]

Too soon it is time for Merrit to leave, and time for Yuki to leave her home and join the household of the man to whom she has been betrothed. She writes a final entry in the blank diary Merrit had left for her:

> Ah, little book, to-night I make big fire in my heart and burn all my wickeds in it. Next day I make more fire and burn you. To other house I must go all white and purely as Merrit San say . . . To-day I go temple, and I make promise I no more speak of Merrit San's name; no more the think of his face in my heart.[85]

After she had burnt the little book in the brass vessel at the entrance to the shrine, Yuki prayed. The she turned to go home.

> She paused by the clump of bamboo where so short a time before she had gleefully tied together two boughs in the name of Merrit and herself. Tiptoing to reach the high boughs which Merrit had held for her to tie, she drew them downward to slip the thong that bound them. After holding them to her soft cheek a moment, she let them fly apart, while she closed her eyes and whispered softly: "Good-by, beautiful love, good-by."[86]

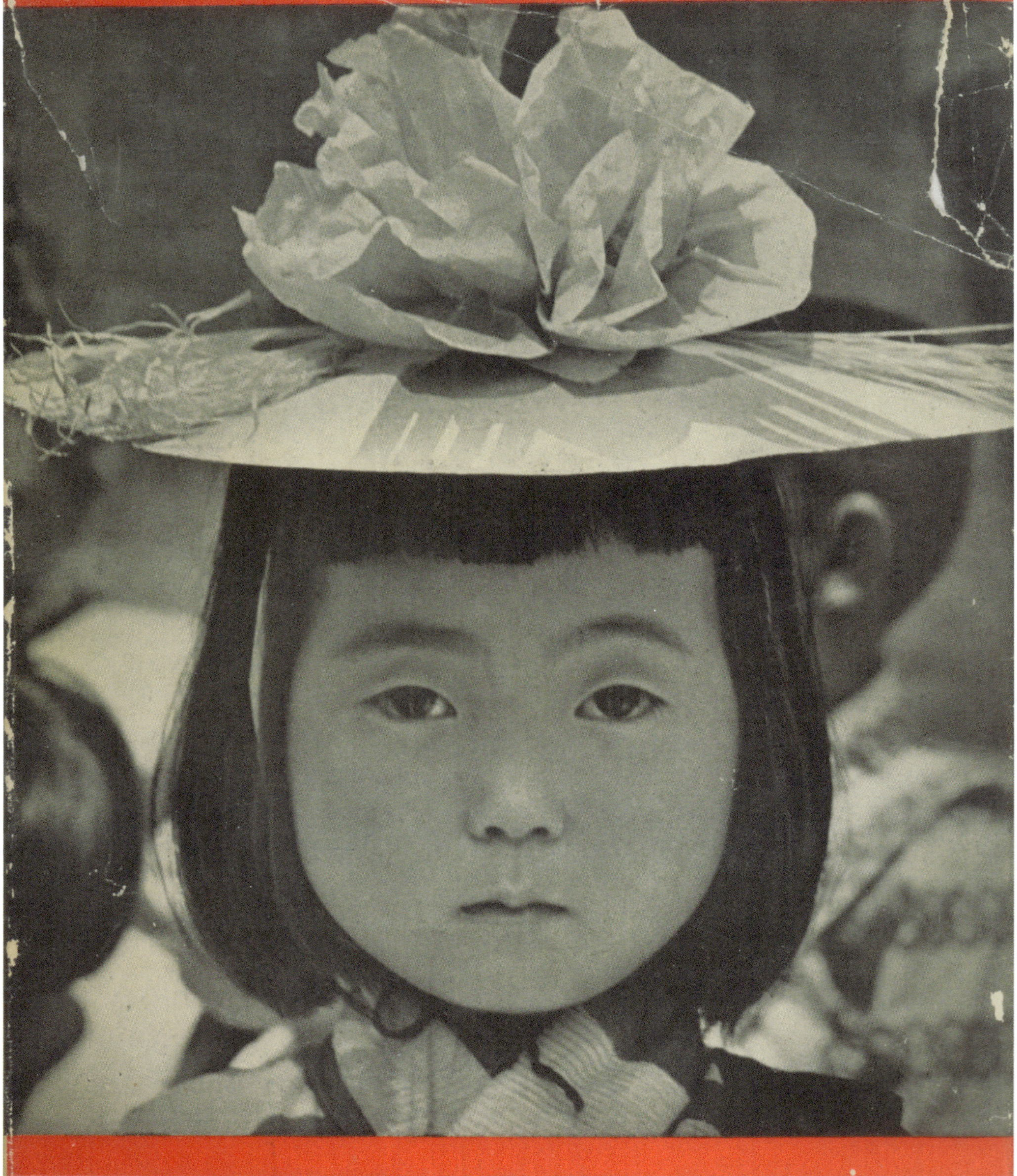

THE BEST OF OLD JAPAN

FRANCIS HAAR

PART II

The Twentieth Century

OPPOSITE
The Best of Old Japan, by
Francis Haar. Rutland, VT:
Charles E. Tuttle, 1951.

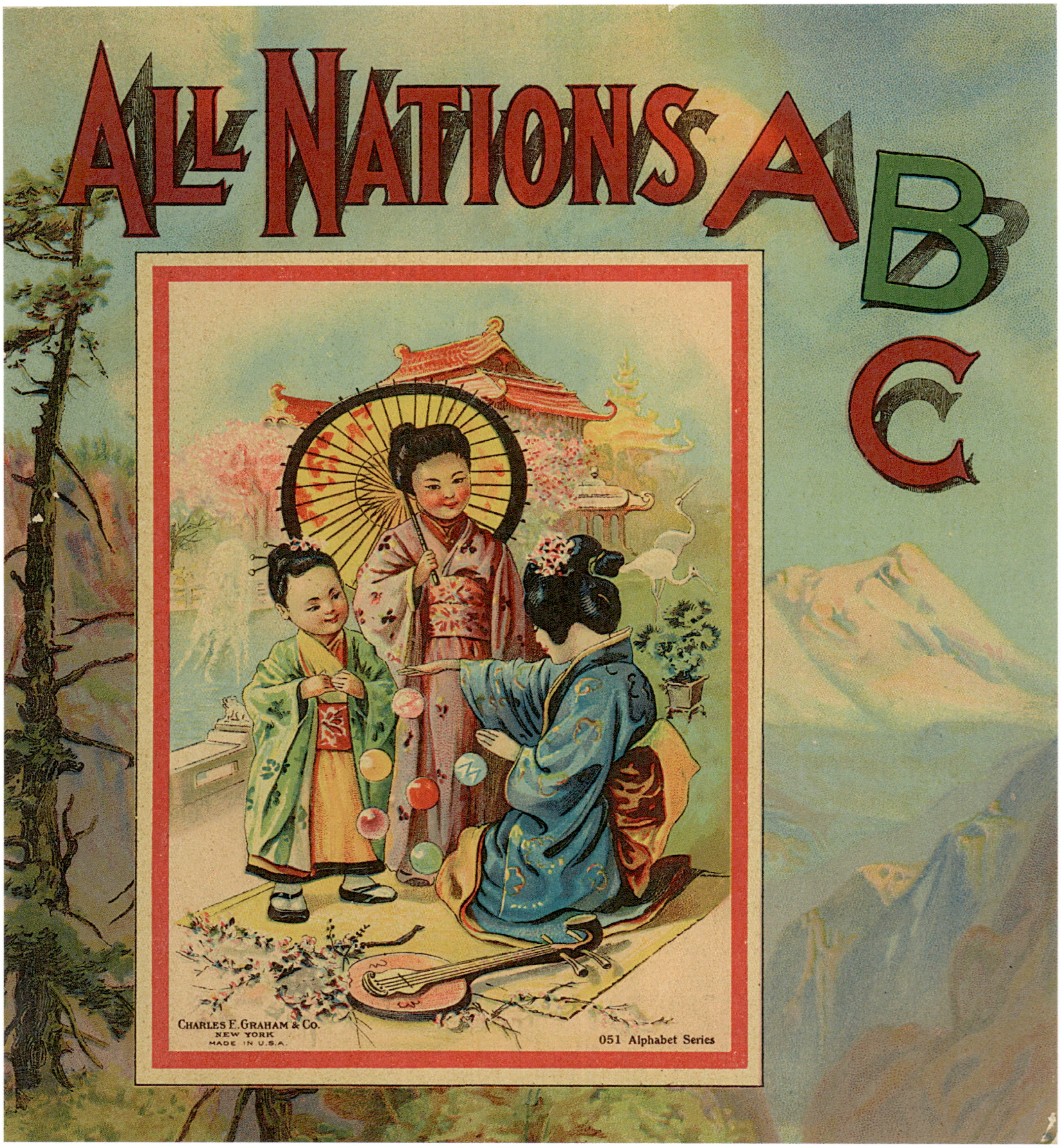
ALL NATIONS ABC
CHARLES E. GRAHAM & CO.
NEW YORK
MADE IN U.S.A.
051 Alphabet Series

6

Globetrotting in Children's Books

From 1900 to World War II

> From the days of Peter Parley, we have been taking "peeps," "glimpses," "zigzag journeys," and "excursions" to various countries at an educational trot. Peter Parley and Jacob Abbott [best known for his *Rollo* travel books] did some traveling, to be sure, but they . . . dwelt chiefly on the peculiarities and differences of the people they met and the places they visited. Neither they nor any of their long train of successors have given a sense of what it is like to live in another country and know the people as "real folks."[1]

Anne Carroll Moore, guardian of American children's literature, leveled that valid criticism in 1920. Nearly a century had passed since Peter Parley's travels, but children's books about foreign countries were still didactic and stuffed with repetitive detail. Around the turn of the century, a new crop of such books had begun to sprout. With more illustrations (increasingly in color), bound in smaller volumes, and written in less formal style, the new globetrotting series such as *Peeps for Little Children*, *Little People of Other Lands*, *The Little Cousin Series*, *Twin Travelers*, and *Christmas in . . .* , which devoted a chapter or a whole book to a particular country, were still similar to their nineteenth-century predecessors, except that they were intended for a much younger audience.

While many of these "geograph[ies] trying to be a story" (as one young reader aptly described them)[2] concentrated on Europe, others like *The Brownies around the World* (1892) by Palmer Cox, *All Nations ABC* (ca. 1890, fig. 6.1), and *Kids of Many Colors* (1901) by Grace Duffie Boylan, branched out to other countries. Holland was among the most popular—perhaps due to the popularity of *Hans Brinker, or The Silver Skates* (1865). Increasingly, Japan was featured as well.

FIGURE 6.1 (OPPOSITE) *All Nations ABC*. New York: Charles F. Graham, ca. 1890.

Ume San in Japan (1909) by Etta Blaisdell McDonald and Julia Dalrymple, one volume in McDonald's *Little People Everywhere* series, is a typical example of these books. Highlighted were special celebrations (the doll festival, New Year's Day), living in a Japanese-style house (sleeping on *tatami* mats with a wooden

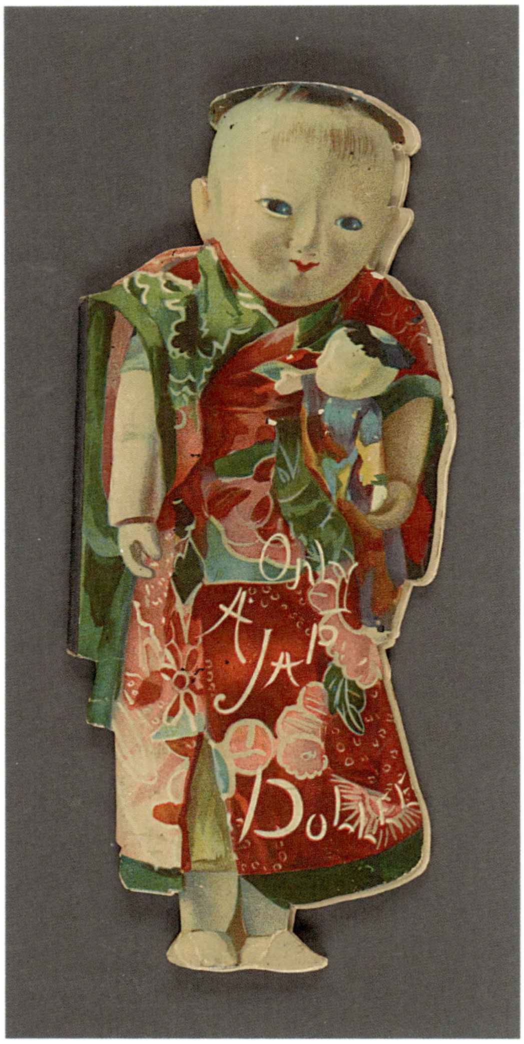

FIGURE 6.2
Only a Jap Dollee, by Helen Marion Burnside, illustrated by E. A. Cook. London: Raphael, Tuck & Sons, ca. 1900.

pillow, taking a bath), visiting a temple, riding in a jinrikisha, watching street entertainers, and playing games.[3] From *Child Life in All Nations; or, The Earlingtons' Trip around the World* (1901) by Amelia Howard Botsford, young readers learned that the Japanese are a "gentle and kind-hearted people,"[4] who are "spotlessly neat and clean," and live in "great big doll's houses."[5] Botsford describes Japanese girls as especially sweet:

> Of all the girls I have seen I think a little Japanese would make the sweetest little sister. They are such dear, smiling little creatures and pretty, too, I think, in spite of their slanted eyes. Japan is such a pleasant country and the boys and girls so charming that I am almost sorry to leave this land and go to China.[6]

Our Little Japanese Cousin (1901, fig. 6.3) by Mary Hazelton Wade presents a similarly pleasant picture. The author describes young Lotus Blossom as "always happy" because "Papa and Mama are always kind and ready to play with her."

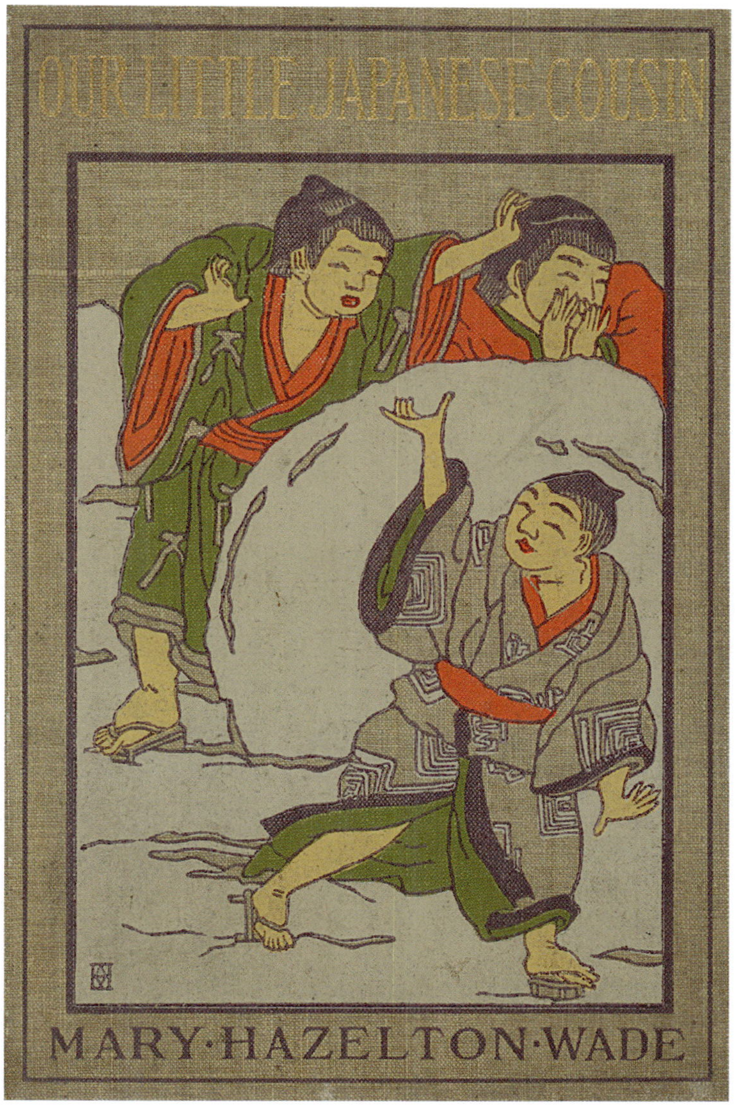

FIGURE 6.3
Our Little Japanese Cousin, by Mary Hazelton Wade, illustrated by L. J. Bridgman. Boston, L. C. Page, 1901.

Even her home is "a sort of playhouse," always tidy because there are "no chairs in the way, no table-scarfs to pull down, no ink-wells to tip over. . . ."[7]

And Lotus Blossom is not alone in her contentment:

> Such happy, childlike people are the Japanese! They are ready to enjoy everything. Even the funerals are cheerful, and have nothing sad and dreary about them. Why should they, when the people believe that they always will live, and that they will come back to earth again to enjoy the beautiful fields and flowers and sunshine in new bodies? . . .
>
> Among all the festivals of the year, I must not forget to tell you of the plum-viewing. . . . When the spring days arrive and the blossoms begin to appear, the child people are very happy. If they are happy, of course they must show it. . . . The children watch for the great day's arrival when the flowers will be in full bloom . . . As they near the plum-orchard they find the road lined with stands, which have been put up for the day. It seems as though everything one could

desire were on sale: cakes, tea, fruit, fans, sweets of all kinds, toys, etc. . . . But the orchard! Was there ever a lovelier sight? Hundreds of trees loaded with fragrant pink blossoms!

The people write poems about them, and pin them on the branches, to show how much they appreciate the beautiful sight which Nature has given them. . . .

And now, children, we must bid these dear cousins good-bye for a little while. Although they worship in strange ways, and read their books upside down, besides doing many other things in a manner that seems strange to us, yet we can learn much from their simple, childlike natures.[8]

The theme of Japan as a children's paradise is repeated time and again. In the preface to *Ume San in Japan*, for example, the authors write:

Japan is a paradise of flowers and of treasure-flowers, as the Japanese mothers call their babies. In no other country in the world do they both form so large a part of the daily life of the people. From the first white plum blossom to the last gorgeous chrysanthemum the path of the days is strewn with beautiful blossoms; and from the time of the Dolls' Festival to the New Year's Celebration there is a constant round of simple pleasures for the children.

Happy children! who are always laughing and never crying; who are taught filial respect, reverence, and unquestioning obedience, but are surrounded in their homes with an atmosphere of kindness, cheerfulness and loving care.[9]

Even Japanese dolls are forever happy. In the book *Dolls of Many Lands* (1913, fig. 6.4) one of them says:

My eyes are black and slant just a little, like the real Japanese, and my face is creamy yellow, with tints of roses in the cheeks. . . . Of course, I can't cry, as white children's dolls sometimes do, but why should I? My mistress never cries; nor does her baby sister. They are always happy, and their parents are most kind and tender. Never is a cross word spoken in the home.[10]

Lindley Smyth also writes about the happiness of the Japanese in *True Stories about Children of All Nations* (1906):

In this island country the boys and girls know how to make themselves happy at all seasons of the year, and this is no wonder, for, as we shall see presently, they have no end of toys, and amusements; and one thing that would, no doubt, make them happier than anything else is that they are most loving and obedient children to very fond parents who never punish them.

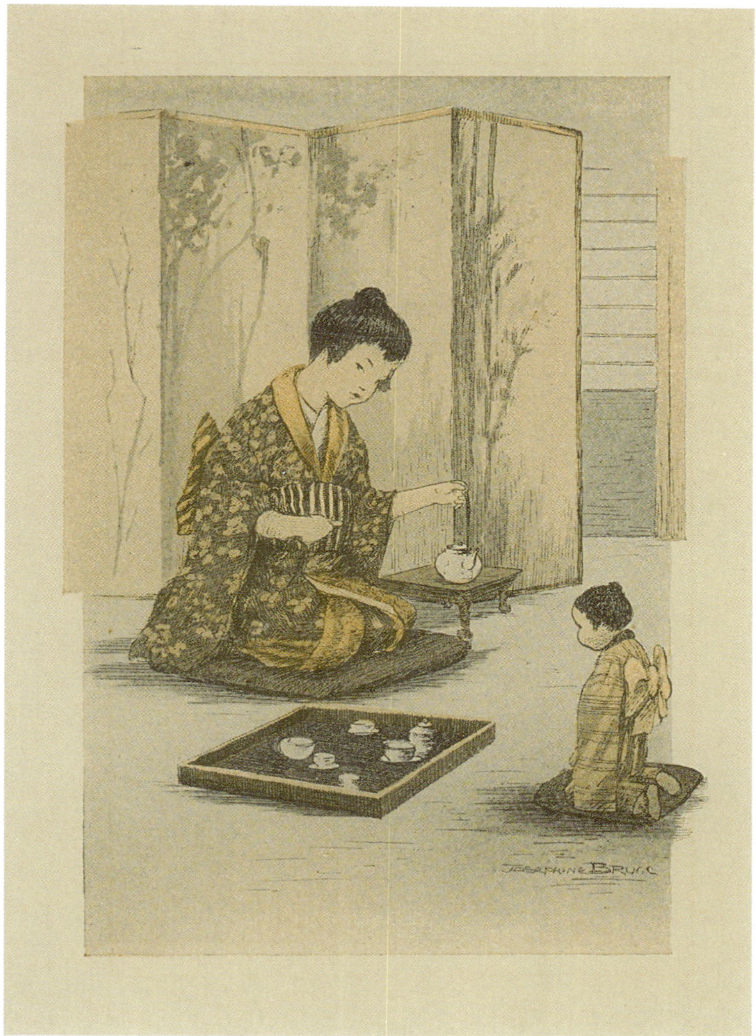

FIGURE 6.4
Dolls of Many Lands, by Mary Hazelton Wade, illustrated by Josephine Bruce. Boston: W. A. Wilde, 1913.

> The people of Japan are very eager to gain knowledge; and to see the little black eyes of the brown-face babies roaming about as if seeking something, at two or three weeks of age, one would fancy that they had inherited a thirst for knowledge. . . .
>
> Education is a great thing in Japan, and schools may be seen on all sides. Both boys and girls of all ranks and classes are expected, not only to learn to read and write, but to know something about the written history of their own country . . . Most Japanese children are therefore sent to school, and may be seen on their way thither learning their lessons out loud.
>
> The Japanese are a reading people, and a great many book-stalls are to be found in their streets, and on these may be found many picture-books for the little ones. In the same way that children learn their lessons out loud, their elders have a habit of reading aloud to themselves.[11]

In his introduction to *Around the World with the Children* (1917), Frank George Carpenter, a journalist and international traveler, adds another dimension. Observing a group of Japanese children, he writes:

> See how the children have gathered around us! They are bending almost to the ground and bowing in Japanese fashion, as they say, "Ohayo" (o-hi'o), which means, "Good morning." All are polite and good-natured except one bad boy at the back of the crowd, who cries out: "See the furry-headed foreigners; they have white skin and eyes like a cat's." We look more closely at the Japanese children, and we do not wonder that we seem strange to them. They have light yellow skin, and their eyes are a trifle aslant and do not open as wide as ours do. The Japanese think that their slant eyes and yellow skin are just right, and that our straight eyes and white skin are ugly.[12]

In *Little People of Japan* (1902), author Lenore E. Mulets describes how Kaga, a typically happy baby, learns to sit in the Japanese fashion:

> After the bath was over, the baby's father set him down on the mat where all the children might watch him. Then he crossed the baby's little legs under him, for that is the way the Japanese sit instead of sitting upon chairs as we do. We should have thought this a queer way to make the baby sit, for he looked like one of those little idols which the Japanese worship in their homes and temples.
>
> There was a reason why the baby's father set him in this position on his first birthday. It was because he wished the baby's muscles and bones to get used to this position so that his legs would shorten as he grew up . . . Short legs are the fashion in Japan, just as crippled feet are the fashion with ladies in China; and, of course, a beautiful child, born on New Year's Day, must not be neglected and allowed to grow up with straight legs. . . .[13]
>
> [E]very day Kaga grew fatter and stronger and more beautiful. He liked to clutch at the neck of his sister's kimono with his little brown hands and spread his little legs so that his feet twined into the obi at her waist. He looked like a laughing monkey, with his head bobbing this way and that as he played at peek-a-boo with the other children from behind his sister's neck.[14]

Lois Swinehart, a missionary and author of *Jane in the Orient* (1924) made perhaps the oddest claims about the Japanese. Describing Japan as a fairyland, and calling Japanese trains "Toy Limited" or "Lilliputian Limited," [15] she also found the food less than palatable:

> After we had sampled each of the queer-looking articles in the *bendos* [*sic*], we looked at each other squarely in the face. Silently we collected those attractive boxes, and solemnly we pitched them out of the [train] window. Let him who will, eat Japanese food. A people that eats seaweed salad, preserved beans and raw fish must have national peculiarities in other ways.[16]

Swinehart described other "queer" ways of the Japanese:

> Japanese think differently than we do. They are very self-conscious and sensitive, and I know the reason why, now. It's their shoes. The Japanese shoe is an unyielding platform of wood, supported beneath by two piers. Threaded into this platform is a "V" shaped thong. This strap holds foot and board together, by twining over the great toe—separating it from the other toes, and securely binding the ball of the foot to the shoe. I can remember how dreadfully nervous it always made me as a child to get anything between my toes when I went barefoot,—and think and pity these people of the Orient who have something between their toes all the time, and I'm sure this accounts for a lot of their queer ways. No wonder they remove their shoes when entering their homes.[17]

Japan in Full Color

Most of the books about Japan for younger children were unremarkable in text and illustrations. Some, however, were presented in larger format with the type of colorful illustrations that characterize the modern picture book. A notable example is Bertha Upton's bold, bright, and dramatic *The Golliwogg's Bicycle Club* (1896, fig. 6.5), one of thirteen titles in the *Golliwogg* series. It showed Japan with

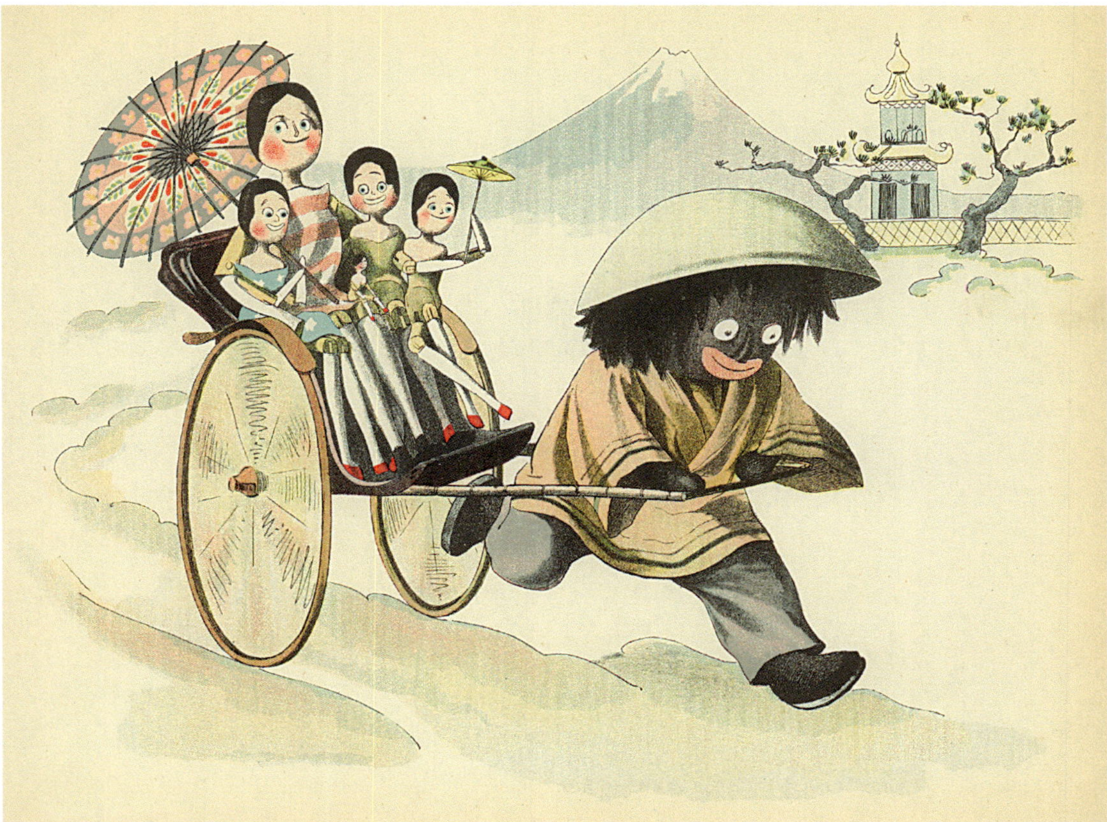

FIGURE 6.5
The Golliwogg's Bicycle Club, by Bertha Upton, illustrated by Florence K. Upton. London: Longmans, Green, 1896, page 33.

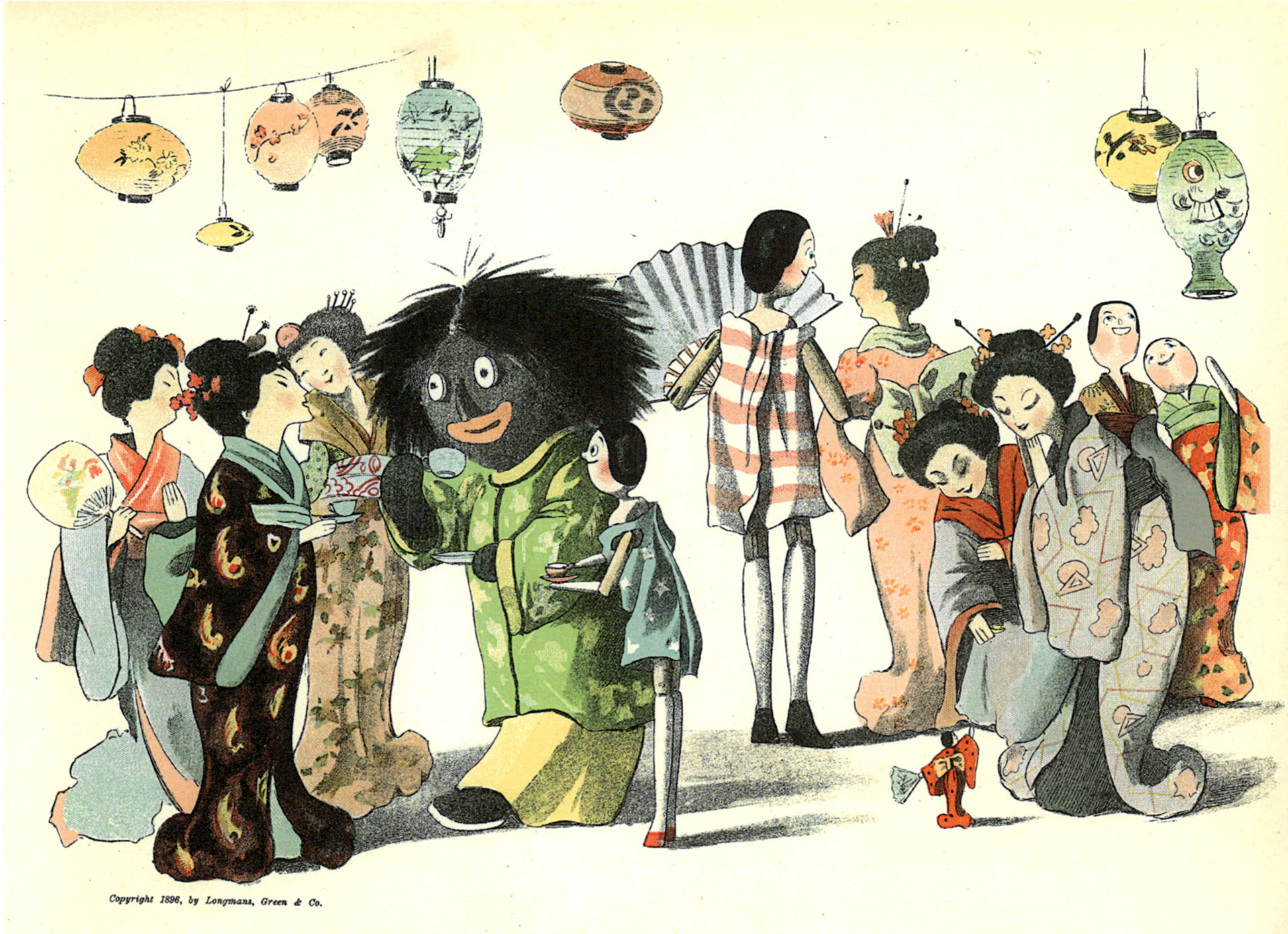

FIGURE 6.6
The Golliwogg's Bicycle Club, by Bertha Upton, page 37.

a whimsical charm as it had never been shown before. The rhymed "adventure" story introduces the oddly matched group of five dainty girl peg dolls and their gallant leader, the Golliwog, an oversized rag doll. Bushy-haired, with big eyes and lips, menacing in some images, warm and soft in others (when he gets sea sick), he takes his friends on a world tour. In Japan, he changes into a kuli's coat and gives the girls a jinrikisha ride. At a party, dressed in a kimono, he is fêted by a group of kimonoed beauties who admire him "rapturously" (fig. 6.6). Whatever white audiences might have thought of a "blackface" character in a picture book for children, today the Golliwogg's racist image is understandably controversial.[18]

Another example is Henry Mayer's *The Adventures of a Japanese Doll* (1901, fig. 6.7). "Showy [and] oblong"[19] and obviously influenced by the Golliwoggs, the book tells of Ting-a-ling, a Japanese doll on a full-color fantasy-voyage to Germany, Egypt, Africa, America, Switzerland, Holland, and other places, and home to Japan.

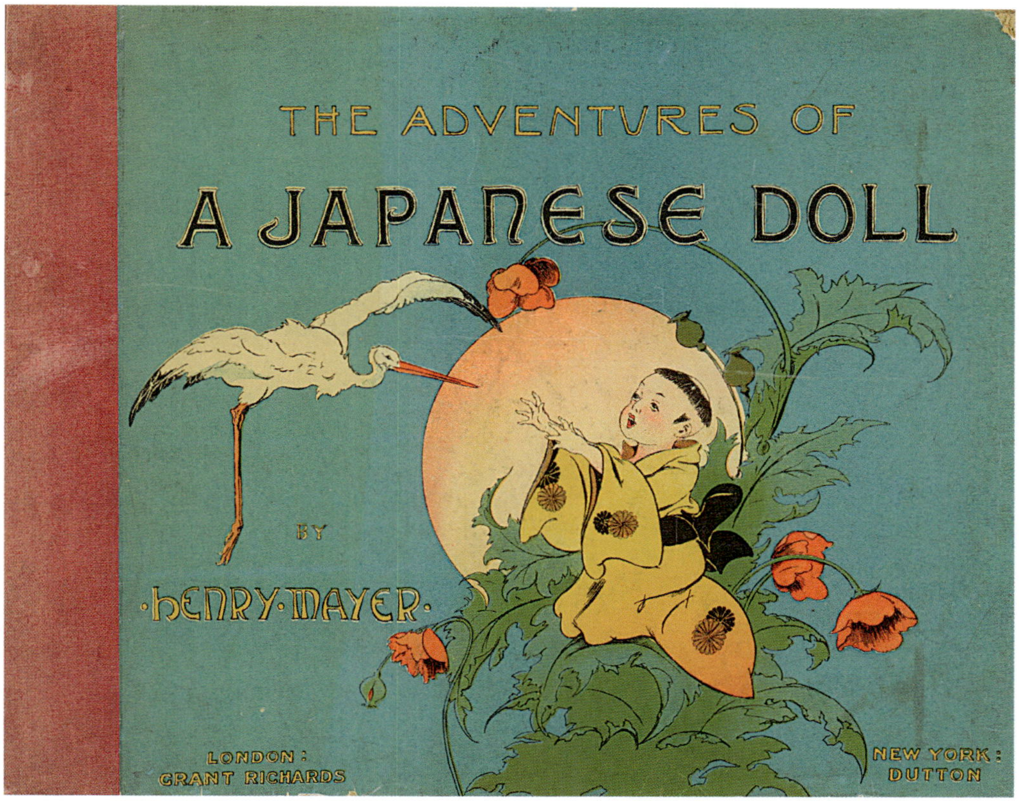

FIGURE 6.7
The Adventures of a Japanese Doll, by Henry Mayer. New York: E. P. Dutton, 1901.

Handsome as the new picture books could be, the authors and illustrators did not always find the right tone or match the text with pictures. Old clichés were now wrapped in decorative packages. Hungarian-born William Andrew Pogány, who was, among other things, a set designer for the Metropolitan Opera, makes the pages of *The Children in Japan* (1911, fig. 6.8) into a pastel-colored stage filled with kimono-clad women, thatched houses, pagodas, geisha and samurai, acrobats and sumo wrestlers. The book's author, Grace Bartruse, who declares that Japanese "gods are as kind and mild as the simple folk themselves,"[20] writes:

> The children take a Rickshaw now,
> And as they run Jack sees
> A lot of people in the fields
> At work like busy bees.
> . . .
> The Japs, they find, work very hard
> To cultivate the soil,
> And splendid crops of maize and rice
> Reward their humble toil.[21]

The art nouveau-style jacket design of Helen L. Campbell's *Story of Little Metzu: The Japanese Boy*, first published in 1905, which features a boy in a formal

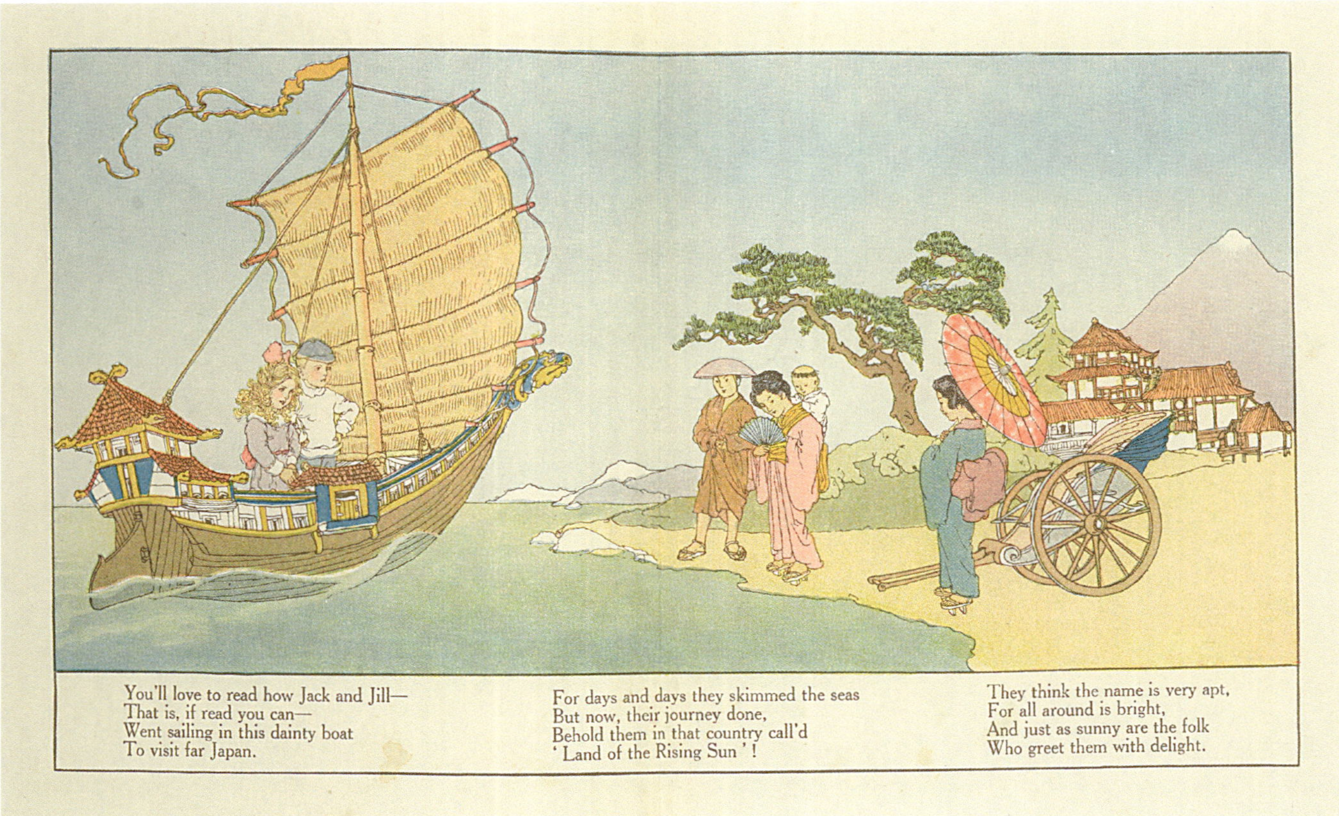

FIGURE 6.8
The Children in Japan, by Grace Bartruse, illustrated by Willy Pogány. New York: McBride Nast, 1915.

kimono standing near an imaginative red *torii* (gateway to a Shinto shrine), with the snow-capped Mount Fuji in the background (fig. 6.9), seems to promise a book revealing new attitudes. Yet Japan is described as "a strange, beautiful country," while the Japanese are a "strange little people," who live in a "strange little island kingdom" and have "strange customs." They have "strange toys," "queer birds," "strange dancing," and "very queer looking boats."[22]

Gustine Weaver, the author of *The House That a Jap Built* (1909), which was bound and lettered in imitation Japanese style, lived and studied in Japan. She liked the title because "the dear old jingle [This is the house that Jack built] . . . smack[ed] of childhood days."[23] The word "Jap" seems to have been used as a derogatory term from the days of Commodore Perry's landing and came into common usage by Westerners, even in children's books. The word is also used in the title of *Little Japs at Home* (1905, fig. 6.10) by Alice Calhoun Haines, an album of didactic text accompanied by romantic portraits of little Japanese girls in glowing color by Alice Mar (the same portraits appeared, with three additional images, in the companion volume, *Japanese Child Life*, published the same year, fig. 6.11).[24] Bound in faux wood, the little volume *O'Kissme San, A Doll from Japan* (1908) by Harvey Gaskell tells of a "Jap" doll much loved by her Western mistress, while the stories and illustrations in Helen Marion Burnside's *Only a Jap Dollee*, die-cut in

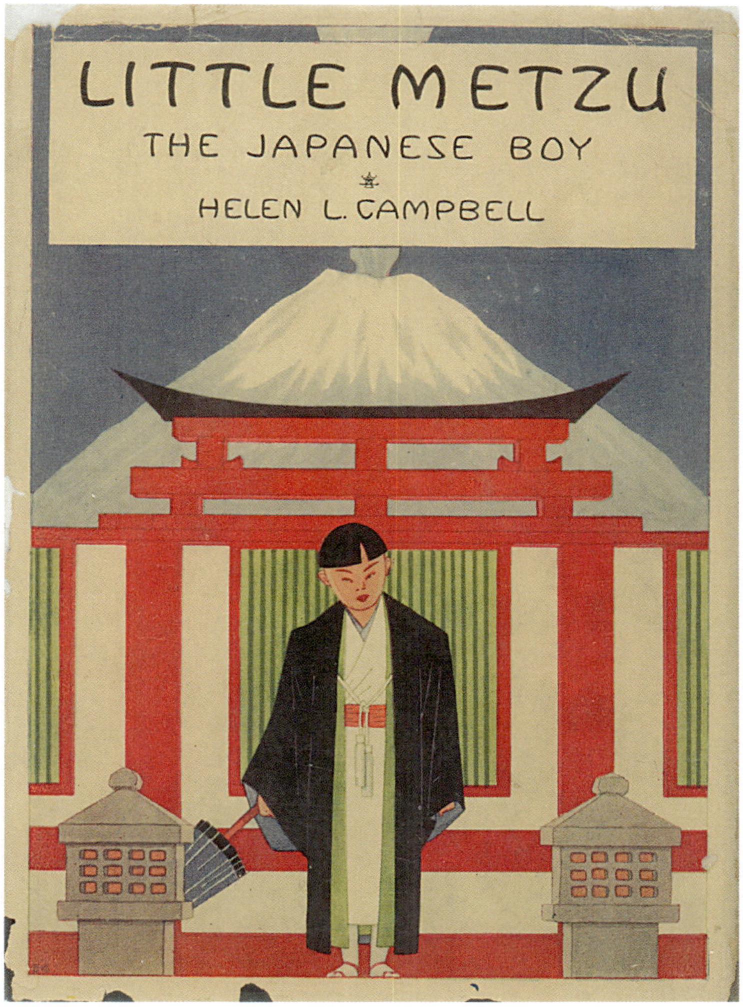

FIGURE 6.9
Story of Little Metzu: The Japanese Boy, by Helen L. Campbell. Boston: Educational Publishing Company, 1905.

the shape of a doll, mixes, or rather confuses Japanese and Chinese images.[25] A unique early-twentieth-century series, the *Stump Books*, included one title about Japan—closed with Japanese-style clasps—*Ten Little Jappy Chaps*, by G. E. Farrow. The "chaps" disappear one after the other in an oft-used chanting style:

> Ten little Jappy chaps
> Hoped it would be fine,
> The rain it pelted,
> one was melted,
> then there were but nine.
> . . . .
> Two little Jappy chaps
> a-fooling with a gun,
> The gun was loaded
> and exploded—
> then
> there was but one.[26]

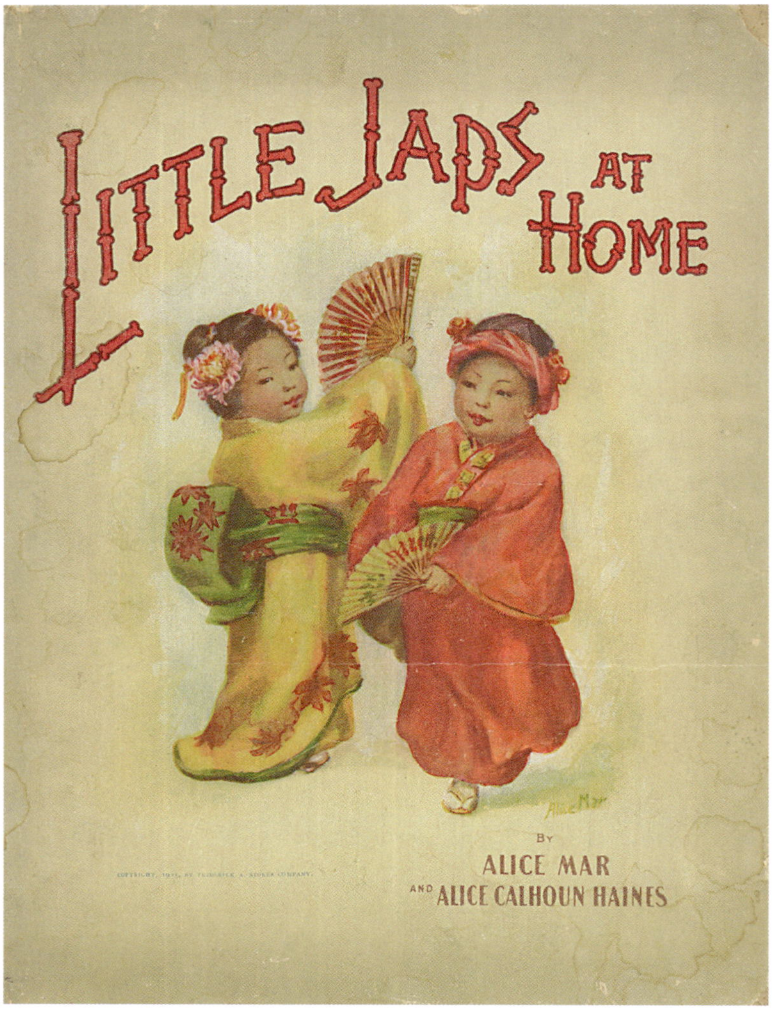

FIGURE 6.10
Little Japs at Home, by Alice Calhoun Haines, illustrated by Alice Mar. New York: Frederick A. Stokes, 1905.

A "Jap" and a blond Western doll are main characters in Clara Bell Thurston's story *The Jingle of a Jap* (1906, fig. 6.12), which had a kimonoed doll attached to its Japanese-motif cover. The sweet illustrations in Thurston's book belie the harsher text:

A little heathen Japanese,
Afflicted in that part,
Upon a lovely big wax doll,
Completely lost his heart.

Her eyes were of the brightest blue,
her hair the fairest flax,
her gowns were of the latest cut,
her cheeks the pinkest wax.

He told her that he loved her;
then he offered heart and hand;
she shook her curls and said,
"Dear Jap, I cannot understand.

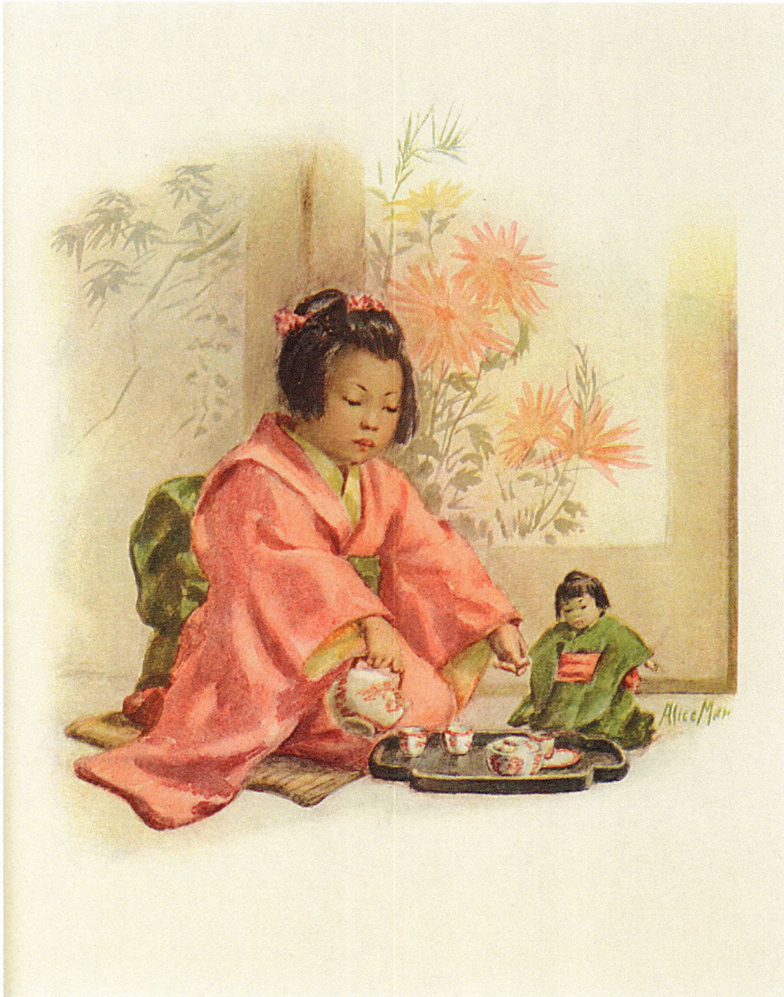

FIGURE 6.11
Japanese Child Life, by Alice Calhoun Haines, illustrated by Alice Mar. New York: Frederick A. Stokes, 1905, opposite page 4.

You talk in such a funny way—
Like no one else I know;
I hope you won't be angry,
'cause I have to tell you so!"

The Jap doll sadly turned away,
And sat him down to think—
While all that night, and all the next,
He never slept a wink. . . .

While he, poor Jap, had dresses on,
Exactly like a girl,
His eyes were small, and oh—his hair
Had not the slightest curl!

Poor little ugly Japanese,
his heart was nearly broken;
he turned and sadly walked away,
all filled with grief unspoken.

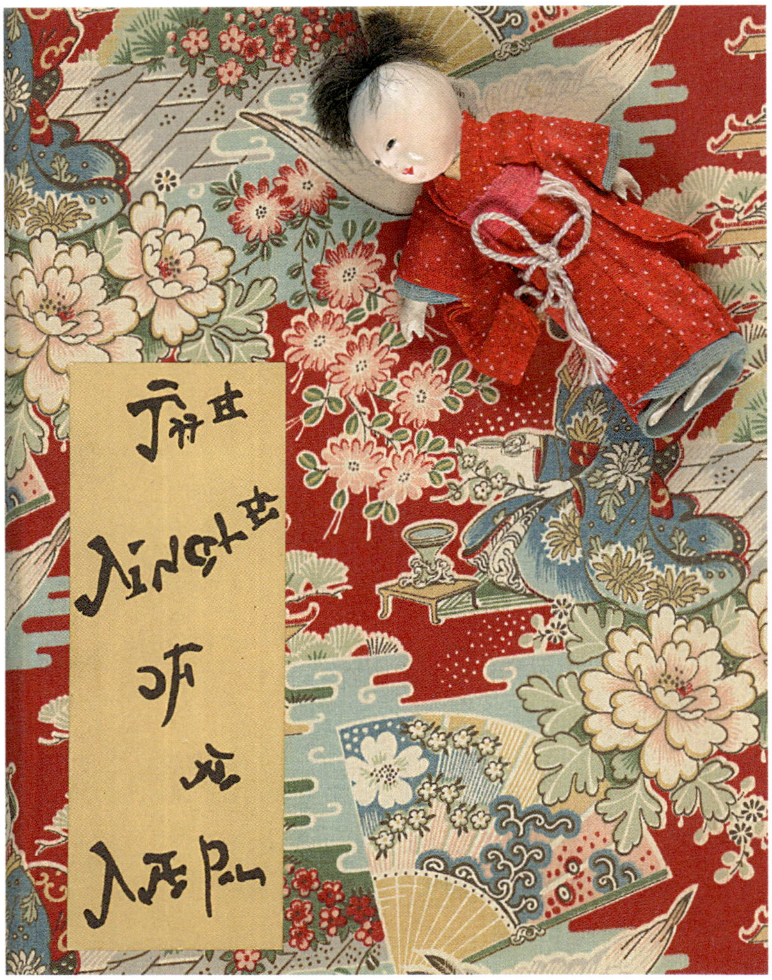

FIGURE 6.12
The Jingle of a Jap, by Clara Bell Thurston. Boston: H. M. Caldwell, 1906.

He sat beside the Noah's ark,
While tears began to rise;
Was he so ugly after all?
Had he such squinty eyes?

They never told him so at home,
Nor laughed at him at all,
There he was quite—yes, just as good
As any other doll.[27]

Finally, in 1912, a book was published that made Japan look real. Although the main character still lives in an idealized world and is still "only" a girl, Take, in Lucy Fitch Perkins's *The Japanese Twins* (fig. 6.13), is bright and loving, and gently questions her role as a daughter, future mother, and mother-in-law. Though it still describes Japan as an ideal land of happiness, the story makes the reader think of Take as a human being first, before thinking of her as a girl who lives somewhere else.

Perkins began her career writing and illustrating books for adults, including *A Book of Joys: The Story of a New England Summer* (1907), her own first-person rambling about the glory of nature. Edith Harrison's *The Moon Princess: A Fairy*

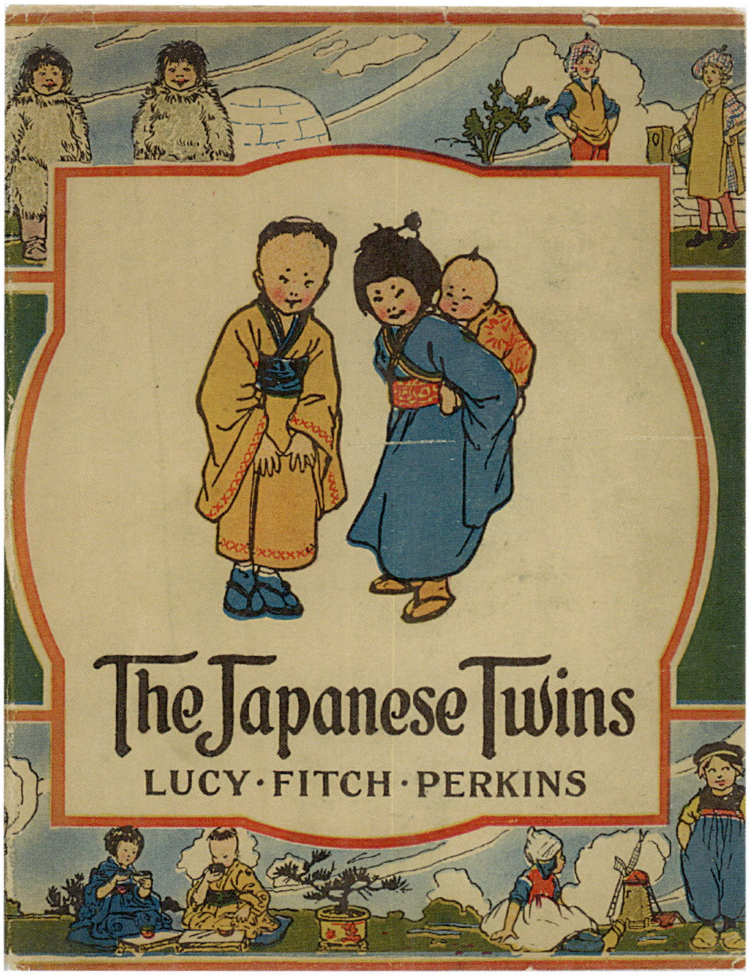

FIGURE 6.13
The Japanese Twins, written and illustrated by Lucy Fitch Perkins. Boston: Houghton Mifflin, 1912.

Tale (1905), and Nathaniel Hawthorne's *A Wonder Book* (1908) were among the books she illustrated. A new direction for Perkins came about fortuitously when Edwin O. Grover, a publishing friend, saw sketches of Dutch children she had drawn for her four-year-old son. Grover suggested she write a story to accompany them. The result was *The Dutch Twins* (1911). Living at a time of unprecedented immigration, Perkins had been thinking about writing stories that would embrace "the necessity for mutual respect and understanding between people of different nationalities." She felt that such a theme would have to be presented in "a way that holds [children's] interest and engages their sympathies" and that it would have to be "personalized—made vivid through its effect upon the lives of individuals."[28] A visit to Ellis Island and to a Chicago school that was trying to cope with students of many nationalities further helped Perkins find her own voice.

Perkins wrote twenty-six titles for her *Twins of the World* series, including *The Irish Twins* (1913), *The Eskimo Twins* (1914), *The French Twins* (1918), and *The Italian Twins* (1920). Unlike most of the children's novels of the past, which were written for older children, her books were written for a much younger audience. The children she describes reveal their own feelings and thoughts, and become closer to the reader. In their unpretentious format, the books look playful and inviting with their large typeface, simple black-and-white illustrations, uncluttered layout, and colorful jackets.[29]

Perkins begins *The Japanese Twins* by setting the stage for her image of a Meiji-era Japanese family:

> Away, away, ever so far away, near the western shores of the Pacific Ocean, lie the Happy Islands, the Paradise of children. Some people call this ocean the "Pacific" and they call the Happy Islands "Japan", but the meaning is just the same. Those are only their grown-up names, that you find them by on the map . . . They are truly Happy Islands, for the sun shines there so brightly that all the people go about with pleasant, smiling faces, and the children play out of doors the whole year through without ever quarreling. And they are never, never spanked! Of course, the reason for that is that they are so good they never, never need it! . . .
>
> Now, can you think of anything nicer in this world than being Twins, and living with a Mother and Father and Grandmother and a Baby Brother, in a dear little house, in a dear little garden, in a dear little, queer little town in the middle of the Happy Islands that lie in the Ocean of Peace?[30]

The two main characters, the boy Taro and his sister Take, let readers listen in as they discuss or experience, among other things, the arrival of their new baby brother, the features of their traditional house such as its *tokonoma* (display shelf). Readers see them observing the Japanese custom of taking off one's shoes when entering the house, celebrating holidays, visiting a temple, buying pancakes from a street vendor, and listening to stories around the *kotatsu* (a table heated from below).

As the story proceeds, Take begins to question her traditional role of submission and service. After all, *take*, which means bamboo in Japanese, symbolizes strength and the ability to bend, rather than break in the face of adversity. Little Take is learning to measure up to the meaning of her name, when, one day, after a visit to the family's *kura* (storehouse), her father displays the family's sword:

> "Father, am I not a child of the Samurai, too?"
>
> "Yes, my daughter," her Father answered, "but you are a girl. It is not your fault, little one," he added kindly. "We cannot all be boys, of course. But to the keeping of the Sons is given the honor of the Family. It is a great trust."
>
> "Don't I do anything at all for the honor of my Family?" asked Take.
>
> "When you are grown up you will marry and live with your husband's family and serve them in every way you can," her Father answered. "You will belong to them, you see. Now you must be a good girl and mind your Father and Grandmother, and Mother, and your brothers."
>
> "I am just as old as Taro," said little Take, "and I think I know just as much. Why can't he mind me some of the time? I think it would be fair to take turns!"
>
> "But Taro is a *boy*," said her Father. "That makes all the difference in the world. Japanese girls must always mind their brothers!"

"Must I mind Bōt'Chan [the new baby brother], too?" asked Take.
"Yes, Bōt'Chan, too."
"Won't anybody ever mind me at all?" asked Take.
"When you get to be a mother-in-law, then you can have your turn," said her Father, smiling. "Your son's wife will obey you."
"Will my son obey me, too?" asked Take.
"No, you must obey him if he is the head of the house," her father explained.
"It is a very long time to wait," sighed Take, "and nothing but a daughter-in-law to mind me at last."
Her under lip puckered a little and she frowned—a little frown—right in the middle of her forehead.
"Tut, tut," said her Father. "Girls and women should always be gentle and smiling. You must never frown."
He looked quite shocked at the very idea of such thing.[31]

Later in the story young Take again challenges her position. When her mother explains the meaning of "Paragons," Take asks for a story about women paragons, to which her mother responds with a story of a young girl who sacrifices herself for her father, who is attacked by a tiger.

"Did the tiger eat her up?" said Taro.
"I suppose he did," Mother answered.
"Was it noble of her to be eaten up so her father could get away?" Take asked.
"Oh, very noble!" said the Mother.
"Well, then," said Take, "was it very noble of the father to run away and let her stay and be eaten up?"
"The lives of women are not worth so much as those of men," Mother answered.[32]

Perkins illustrated *The Japanese Twins* with her own soft charcoal drawings (fig. 6.14). Unlike illustrations in most children's books published up to this time,

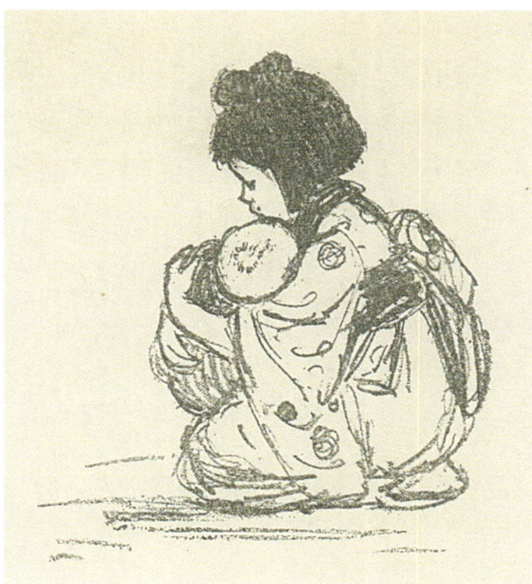

FIGURE 6.14
The Japanese Twins, by Lucy Fitch Perkins, page 61.

the drawings follow the text closely and extend the story. The author even uses the images to interact with young readers. ("Here is a picture of Take peeping into the kettle," Perkins writes.)[33] *The Japanese Twins* was widely read and remembered. Three of those who read the book as children—children's book author Beverly Cleary, editor Ann Beneduce, and children's librarian Margaret Coughlan—have said that it gave them their first and positive impression of Japan, an image that stayed with them always.[34]

A Remarkable Children's Book Addendum

A timely, yet unusual addendum to a children's book was written in 1916 by Florence Converse,[35] editor of *Little Schoolmates*, her series of books about children of other lands. Her long comment appeared in letter form as an introduction to *Treasure Flower: A Child of Japan* by Ruth Gaines, one title in the series. Calling it "A Letter to the One who reads this book" Converse begins:

> Dear Schoolmate:
>
> Do you remember the story of the Sleeping Beauty,—the little princess who dreamed away a hundred years in her drowsy castle in the forest, and was kissed awake one happy morning by the prince? . . .
>
> Do you remember?
>
> If you do, the story of Japan will seem almost like a twice-told tale. Listen![36]

Before forecasting the 1924 National Origins Act, which would end all immigration from Japan until 1965, Converse takes young readers through Japan's long history, from "once upon a time, in the beginning of things, long before America was discovered" to Commodore Perry's arrival and the issue of Japanese immigration to the United States:

> As early as 1869 there seem to have been Japanese silk growers in California; and a few Japanese sailors and students found their way to our shores from time to time, but not until 1885 did they begin to come in considerable numbers. . . .
>
> Mr. H. A. Millis, who has made a careful study of the Japanese in America, tells us that they are intelligent, studious, cleanly in their habits, generous, temperate, law-abiding, moral, industrious, [and] ambitious. That they are well educated and usually have had some schooling before they come to America, and that no adult immigrants, unless it be the Hebrews, show so great a desire to learn the English language, although they do not learn to speak it as well as some other races in the

> same length of time. They are quick to adopt our customs and dress and food, and they read newspapers and magazines and take an interest in what is happening in the United States.
>
> This is a long list of virtues and good qualities, and yet you may have heard, especially if you live in a western State, that the Japanese are not desirable immigrants, and that the United States would be better off without them. Why do some Americans wish to keep the Japanese out of the United States? . . .
>
> Many people feel that the United States ought to be a white country; they think that our forefathers really had white men in mind when they made the Constitution, and that our affairs would be much less complicated if the negroes had never been brought over from Africa. But it is not the negroes' fault that they are here, it is entirely the white men's fault, and now the negro has earned the right to share in the governing of the land which his labor has helped to prosper. It is his land as well as ours. But, to bring in another dark race to share the country and the government with white men only confuses things still more. The Japanese themselves can easily understand this point of view, for it was because they were determined to keep Japan for the Japanese, and to rule their islands without the interference of white foreigners, that they drove out the Christian missionaries in the seventeenth century. . . .
>
> So, it would seem that sooner or later the United States must make up its mind to one of two things: either the Japanese and other Asiatic peoples must be allowed to come in as freely as European immigrants come, to be citizens and to own land; or, we must confess frankly that we want to be a white country.[37]

Olive Beaupré Miller's Book House for Children

As she remembered watching the trains go by from her grandfather's house in Aurora, Illinois, Olive Beaupré Miller wrote:

> Then and there I vowed that some day I would go off on trains and ships and see the whole wide world. And I have pretty well lived up to that vow, except that I have gone by airplanes and automobiles, as well as by trains and ships. . . . The material I gathered on these trips I put into many books for children.[38]

Beaupré began writing and illustrating books when she was still a child, and continued through her high school and Smith College days. As a young mother she was so occupied with her writing that, one day, she forgot to feed her infant daughter,[39] for whom she would later write her first rhymes and stories published in *Sunny Rhymes for Happy Children* (1917), which by the 1980s was in its thirty-eighth printing.[40] *Come Play with Me* (1918) and *Whisk Away on a Sunbeam* (1919) followed. In 1919, Beaupré and her husband, Harry Miller, established their own publishing company, naming it The Book House for Children. Soon, Beaupré began work on *My Book House*, an illustrated six-volume anthology of works by nearly 200 authors. Proudly advertising it as "Your Child's Foundation in Culture and Character,"[41] Beaupré described her years of searching for the right material:

> Librarians in all parts of the country were consulted, libraries ransacked, hundreds of books read and re-read in the quest for all the stories and poems that children love and need. Authorities on children's books were interviewed, famous writers of children's stories contributed of their experience, copyright permissions were secured. All versions of the well known classics were critically compared.[42]

My Book House comprised *In the Nursery* (1920), *Up One Pair of Stairs* (1920), *Through Fairy Halls* (1920), *The Treasure Chest* (1920), *From the Tower Window* (1921), and *The Latch Key* (1921). Sold by subscription and door-to-door by an eager and well-trained group of saleswomen, the anthology was well received, as evidenced by this 1921 review in *The Dial*:

> My Book House . . . is a child's library of stories and poems drawing on all phases of the world's literature, from the Bible to Shakespeare, from ancient times to the present day. Although it is evident that the stories have been chosen with a purpose to make "right" attractive and "wrong" distasteful, they have nothing of the flavor of a Sunday-school paper. The high literary tone maintained throughout the six volumes allows a grown-up to read them to his children without contracting a bad headache. Excellent binding and illustrations combine with intelligent arrangement of the contents to make them one of the most attractive of juvenile libraries.[43]

Others approved as well. A teacher called the anthology "a goldmine of the literature"; a storyteller found it "absolutely invaluable"; a parent praised the "artistic make-up" and the "real joy" the books provided for the whole family.[44] By 1928, Book House for Children had branch offices in New York, Boston, Philadelphia, Houston, and Los Angeles.[45]

Little Pictures of Japan

In 1923, the Millers traveled to Europe to find stories and poems for their new series *My Travelship*. The result was *Nursery Friends from France* (1925), *Tales Told in Holland* (1926), and *Little Pictures of Japan* (1925). Mrs. Miller wanted American children to learn about other countries from each country's own literature, "not by something written about them."[46] In *Little Pictures of Japan* she introduced a hitherto little-mentioned subject: Japanese poetry.[47] After careful research, during which she consulted books on Japanese poetry by Basil Hall

Chamberlain, Lafcadio Hearn, Yone Noguchi, and such lesser-known writers as Curtis Page and Clara Walsh, Miller wrote:

> Now the Japanese people are never very tall. They live in little houses, and they like little things,—little, little, little things. They love to make tiny carvings and paintings so small that their figures can only be seen through a magnifying glass. They like to have the tiniest of wire cages in which they keep little singing insects instead of birds; and they can make a whole garden with growing trees and fish ponds wherein real, live fishes swim, all so small it could be set upon a tea tray! And so they make little poems too,—little, little, little poems,—hokku [haiku] poems with a whole world of meaning all shut up in seventeen syllables,—just the flash of a picture as if a window had been suddenly opened upon some beautiful scene, and then as suddenly closed again,—just a flash, and all the rest left for him who hears, to imagine and to feel.[48]

Miller filled her anthology with seasonal haiku, and those by long-ago emperors and venerable poets:

> "Autumn Winds"
>
> Though it does not show
> Plainly to my eyes as yet,
> Autumn's come, I know;
> I am alarmed because
> The wind is blowing so.[49]
> *Fujiwara no Toshiyuiki (d. 907)*
>
> "The Pine Tree"
>
> Lo!
> Fresh and green amid the snow,
> A pine-tree.[50]
> *Author unknown*
>
> The old pond,—aye!
> A frog leapt into it,—
> List, the water sound![51]
> *Matsuo Bashō (1644–94)*
>
> The mists of daybreak seem
> To paint as with a fairy brush
> A landscape in a dream.[52]
> *Yosa Buson (1716–84)*

She retold stories about Bashō and old legends, among them the love story of the Tanabata festival—still celebrated by the Japanese every summer:

> There dwelt of old in the skies an Emperor of Heaven who had a beautiful daughter named Tanabata. Now Tanabata lived in a little house of her own on a star, and passed all her days in weaving shining garments for her august father, the Emperor. For years and years the maiden loved her work and rejoiced in it, and found no greater pleasure than weaving the gleaming sky-yarn into gleaming sky-garments. But one day as she sat before her loom at the door of her starry dwelling, Tanabata saw a handsome peasant lad pass by, leading an ox. The peasant lad looked at Tanabata, and Tanabata looked at the peasant lad, and straightway they loved each other. Then the heart of Tanabata grew unquiet. No more was she so joyous in weaving. She was thinking ever of the young herdsman, passing from star to star with his ox. By and by, Tanabata's father, the Emperor, guessed her secret and said to her: "Daughter, since you think so much of that young lad, you shall have him for a husband."
>
> Tanabata bowed to the blue floor of Heaven in gratitude to her august father. Hikoboshi, the herd boy, was summoned at once to the star and given permission to wed the little weaver of the skies. Happy indeed were the two and joyous was her wedding.

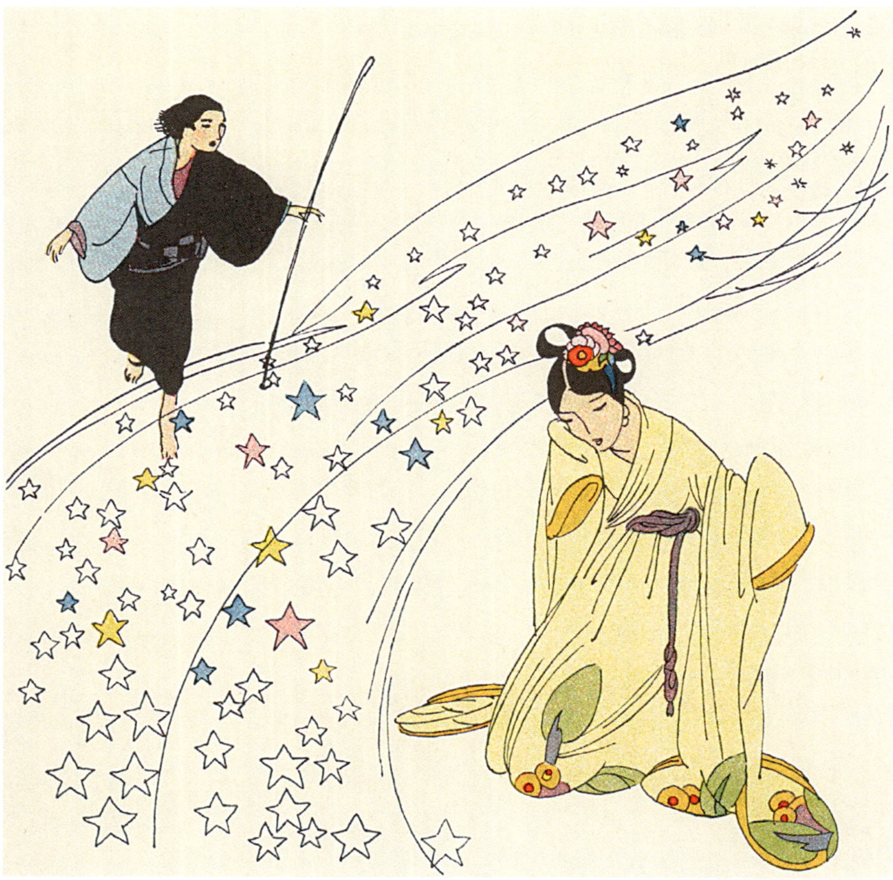

FIGURE 6.15
Little Pictures of Japan, edited by Olive Beaupré Miller, illustrated by Katherine Sturges. Chicago: The Book House for Children, 1925, page 184.

> As time went by they proved to be more and more completely devoted to one another. But alas! so devoted were they, that they began to think only of themselves, of being always together . . . And so they fell to neglecting their duties, to doing less and less work, until at last they were doing no work at all . . . Then was the Emperor of Heaven greatly displeased. He called the two before him and said:
>
> "You have neglected your duties through caring only for one another. In punishment you shall be separated and live apart, with the River of Heaven flowing between you. Once a year from this time forward, and once a year only, shall you see each other. That shall be on the seventh night of the seventh month."[53]

Miller commissioned Katherine Sturges to illustrate the volume and sent her to Japan to become acquainted with Japanese culture. Sturges had studied at the Art Institute of Chicago, drew fashion designs for *Harper's Bazaar* and other magazines, and was among a group of artists whose textile designs were exhibited at the Metropolitan Museum of Art.[54] *Little Pictures of Japan* gave Sturges a fine opportunity to draw highly decorative kimono designs, which appear on many pages of the profusely illustrated book. In 1925, the supervisor of the children's department of the Chicago Public Library commented on this Miller-Sturges collaboration to the *Chicago Tribune*:

> How lovely it would be if children could get their first idea of Japan from delightful pictures such as these.
>
> The poems, too, are pictures; little flashes of beauty.
>
> The people in Japan love poetry and everyone, young or old, rich or poor, writes poetry. No wonder the author has found such a wealth of charming verses, a whole year of them, beginning in the spring and giving us the most beautiful thoughts for each of the seasons. All nature is reflected in these little gems about the cuckoo and the nightingale, the snail and frog, the butterfly and firefly, wisteria and plum blossoms. . . . The illustrations are so lovely as to beggar description.[55]

Nine years later, a reviewer for the *Los Angeles Times* was equally complimentary:

> Dainty pictures etched in silver words. Color pictures, lively and simple, but suggestive of the dreams of lands far away. Together they have made a book that must greatly enrich the nursery of any child fortunate enough to possess so lovely an album of imaginative portraits. Some of these songs have been familiar to Japanese children for more than 1000 years, but neither time nor distance nor alien race can take from them their universal message nor rob them of the beauty in which they were conceived.[56]

In 1933, Miller finished her ambitious four-volume *My Book of History* (fig. 6.16), about which Dorothy Loring Taylor later wrote:

> The story is absolutely authentic but is so picturesquely told that people and events come to life and the reader feels as though he were reading a story book rather than a history.
>
> Instead of presenting scattered unconnected events, it presents one continuous flow of history, tracing that western culture which came down to us via Egypt, Crete, Greece and Rome, being spread by the Roman conquests to Western Europe.
>
> Then at the proper time the story travels with European explorers, like Marco Polo, to the east and we are introduced to those great eastern cultures which developed outside the stream of our western cultures. Thus we begin to understand better those peoples whose background and manner of thinking are quite different from our own and whom we so need to understand today—namely, the people of China, Japan, India, Persia and Russia which always faced east rather than west.[57]

Miller's decision to devote one of the four volumes to the history and culture of Asia was remarkable. In comparison, Donald Peattie's *A Child's Story of the World* (1937)[58] mentions Japan only in passing. The same is true of Jane Werner Watson's *The Golden History of the World* (1955).[59] Miller explores the age of shōguns and samurai, Buddhism, and Kublai Khan's thirteenth-century attempts to conquer Japan. *My Book of History* became immensely popular; by 1955 it was in its ninth printing.[60]

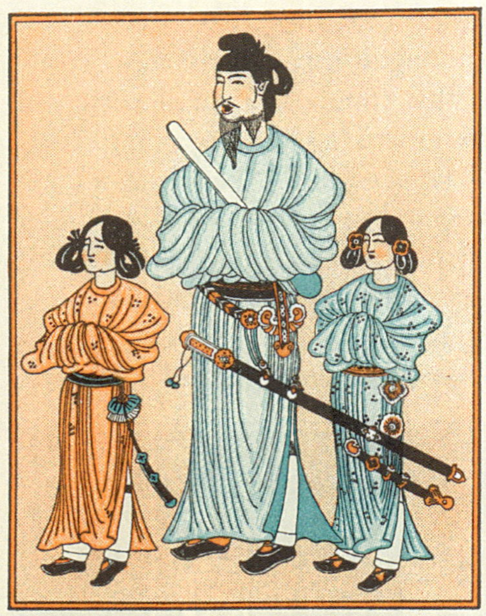

Prince Sho-ta-ke Tai-shi, head of the Soga family and guardian of Buddhism, the new religion of Japan. (A painting, Imperial Household.)

FIGURE 6.16
My Book of History: A Picturesque Tale of Progress, by Olive Beaupré Miller. Vol. 4, *Explorations*. Chicago: The Book House for Children, 1933, page 190.

Japan in Children's Books of the 1930s

Most children's books from the 1930s still described the old Japan. The author of *'Round the World with Esther Brann* (1935, fig. 6.17) wrote:

> How would you like to live in a paper house?
> In JAPAN there are lots of them.
>
> In JAPAN you can ride in a *Jin-rikisha*.
> That's a little carriage pulled by a man instead of a horse.[61]

Great Sweeping Day (1936) by Esther Wood tells the story of Taro Chan, another boy who "lived in a little paper house in Japan,"[62] whose adventures teach American children about house cleaning day, the umbrella and clog maker, rice planting, feeding the silk worms, a parade, and the Boy's Day festival. Mary Windsor's *Little Friends from Many Lands* taught young readers that "our little [Japanese] friends love colorful and gay and happy things. And that's the way they are themselves."[63] *Yasu-bo and Ishi-ko: A Boy and Girl of Japan* (1934) by Phyllis Ayer Sowers reiterated such often-mentioned details from old Japanese culture as teeth blackening and wooden pillows. However, a few 1930s books

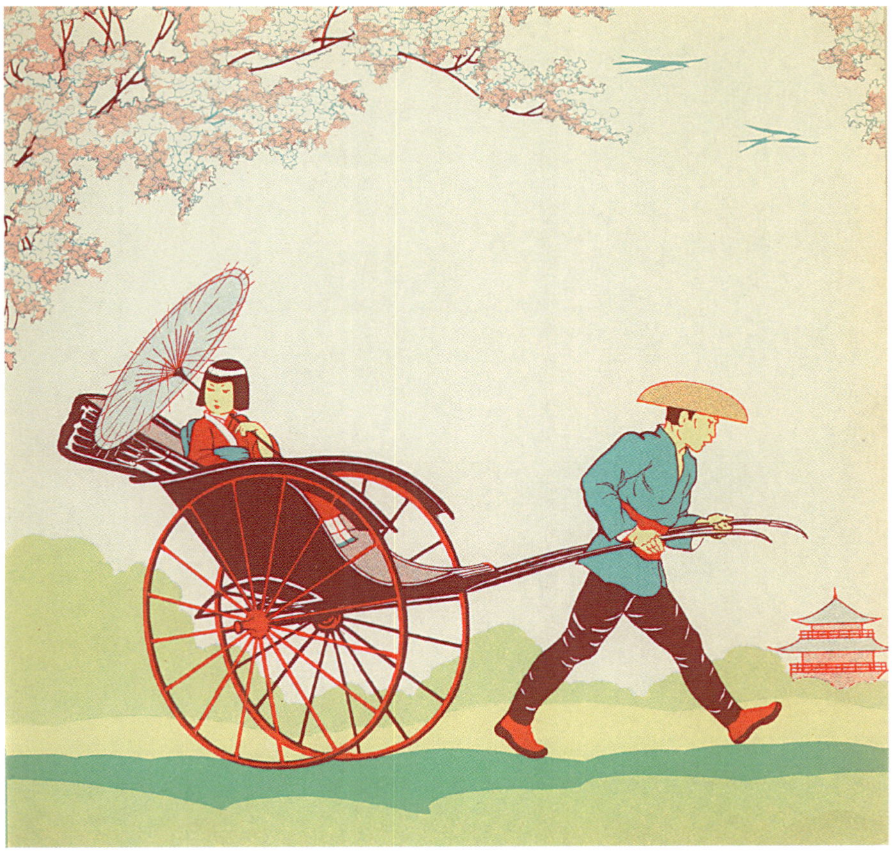

FIGURE 6.17
'Round the World with Esther Brann, by Esther Brann. New York, Macmillan, 1935.

began to address the changes occurring in the Japanese-American world. In *Haruko, Child of Japan* (1934), Eva D. Edwards tells of a young Japanese girl whose family goes to California to help her uncle on his flower farm. After three years the family returns to Japan:

> It hardly seemed possible to the little family that the long trip was over. They were really in the beautiful harbor of Yokohama again. . . . Mother was so happy that Haruko decided to be happy too, although she was not quite sure that she wanted the journey to end. But the "chug-chug" of the big engine had stopped . . ."Shall I be Japanese or American, Mother?'
>
> Haruko looked at the pretty little print dress and low heeled black slippers. They lay beside the blue kimono and the bright obi and the white wooden geta [sandals] . . . "Which do you wish, Little Flower?" [her mother] asked. Haruko was very still for a minute. She knew that she must choose. She remembered so many good times she had known when she had worn the little pink dress with its round neck and short sleeves. She liked the pink socks, too. How happy she had been when Uncle Tomi had brought them to her. The obi was lovely, but oh, so many times it had to be wound about a little girl's body. And the geta were so hard to keep on when one wanted to run! "I think I'll be American," she said, and pulled on the pretty socks.[64]

Stella Burke May, author of *Children of Japan* (1936), describes Japan as a quaint and beautiful fairyland of small people surrounded by dainty things. Yet she also informs her young readers that there were now "houses built like houses in the United States, schools with desks and chairs like those in American schools, and pupils wearing clothes of western style . . . [Japanese] hear American songs and see motion pictures from Hollywood," and "Japanese boys and girls live two kinds of lives. Part of the time they are Japanese children. The rest of the time they seem more like children of the western world."[65]

Elinor Hedrick and Kathryne Van Noy's *Kites and Kimonos* (1936, fig. 6.18) also considers the meeting of Japanese and Western life. It is the story of young

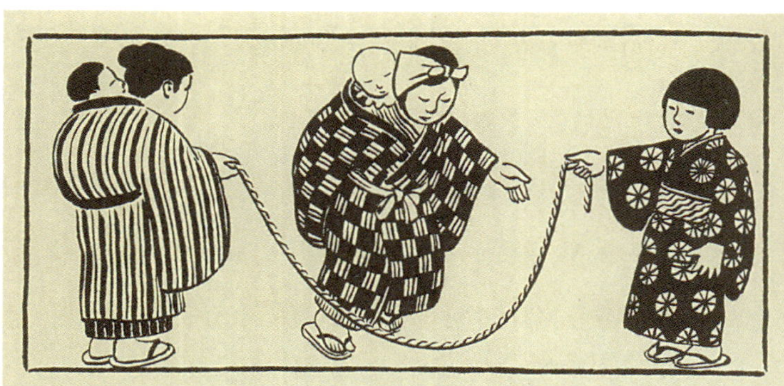

FIGURE 6.18
Kites and Kimonos, by Elinor Hedrick and Kathryne Van Noy, illustrated by Bunji Tagawa. New York: Macmillan, 1936, page 92.

Momo, her brother Takashi, their parents, grandmother, and two maids. Their father has just returned from America and has brought presents for the family (fig. 6.19):

> The children crowded around Mother. When she opened the package, they saw something blue. Mother took it out and held it up. "What a funny-looking kimono! Where are the sleeves?" asked Momo.
>
> "This is a dress like those American women wear. Here are the sleeves. They do not wear large sleeves as we do," explained Father.
>
> "I do not think it looks as if it would be very comfortable," Mother said.
>
> "But it is pretty, Mother," Momo said.
>
> "I should not like to wear it," said Grandmother as she looked at it carefully. . . .
>
> The next morning Father and the children took a motor bus to the street-car line. The bus was like those used in America. A man drove the bus. There was a girl who collected the fares. She was dressed in a short dark-blue skirt and a long white waist. Momo thought she looked very funny because she was not wearing a kimono. Father told her that many American girls dress like that.[66]

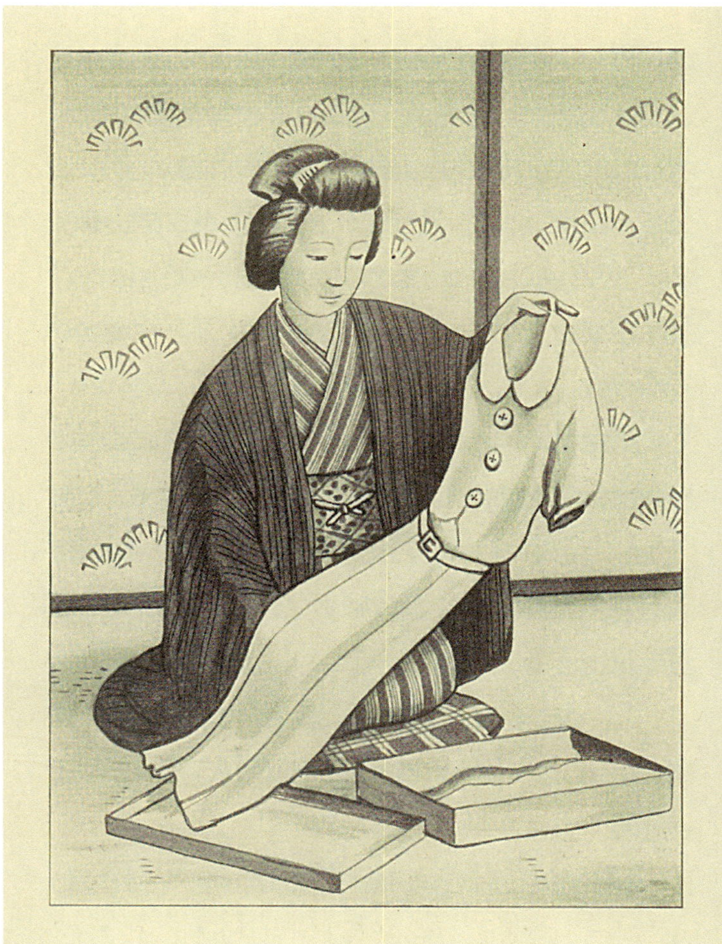

FIGURE 6.19
Kites and Kimonos, by Elinor Hedrick and Kathryne Van Noy, page 6.

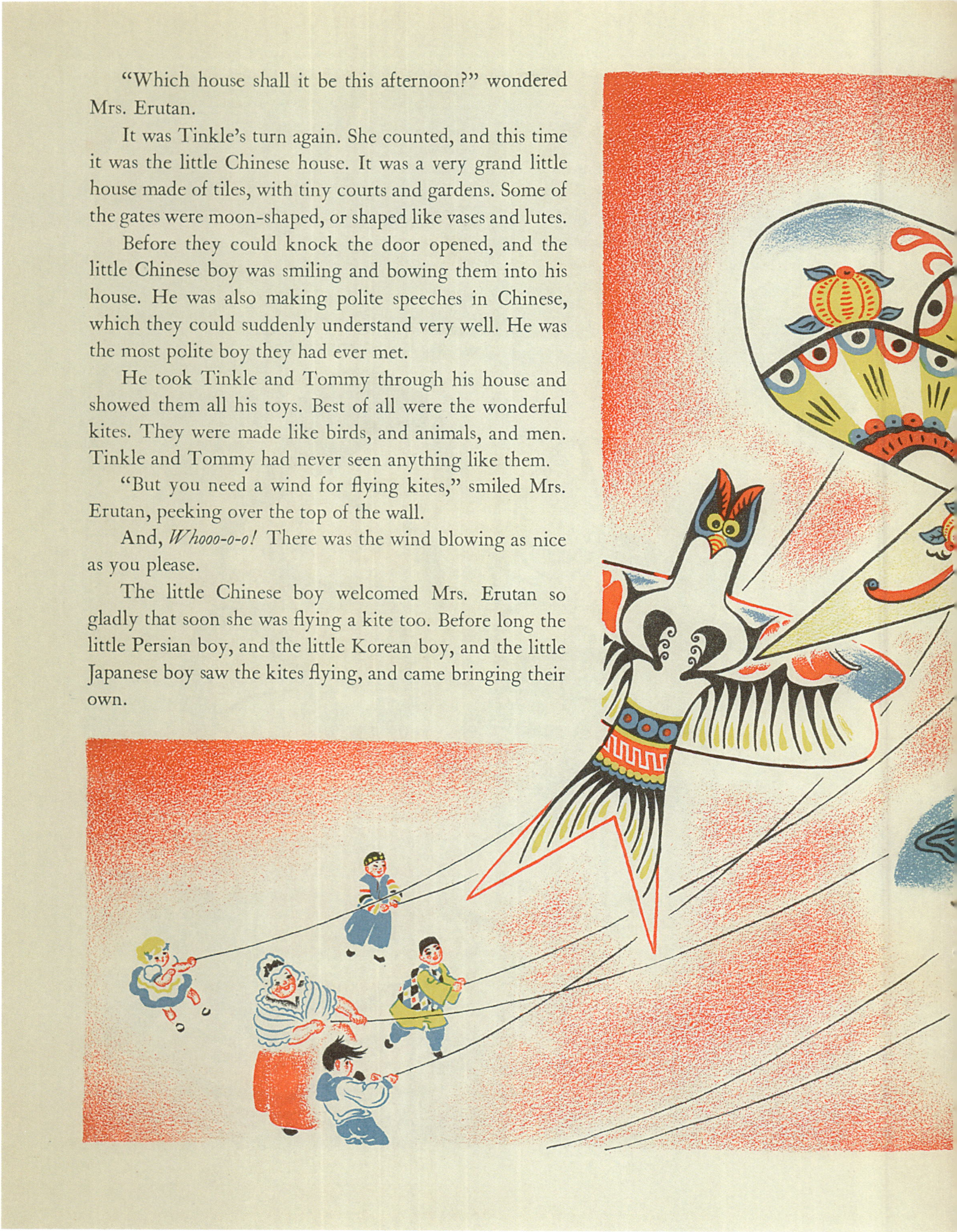

"Which house shall it be this afternoon?" wondered Mrs. Erutan.

It was Tinkle's turn again. She counted, and this time it was the little Chinese house. It was a very grand little house made of tiles, with tiny courts and gardens. Some of the gates were moon-shaped, or shaped like vases and lutes.

Before they could knock the door opened, and the little Chinese boy was smiling and bowing them into his house. He was also making polite speeches in Chinese, which they could suddenly understand very well. He was the most polite boy they had ever met.

He took Tinkle and Tommy through his house and showed them all his toys. Best of all were the wonderful kites. They were made like birds, and animals, and men. Tinkle and Tommy had never seen anything like them.

"But you need a wind for flying kites," smiled Mrs. Erutan, peeking over the top of the wall.

And, *Whooo-o-o!* There was the wind blowing as nice as you please.

The little Chinese boy welcomed Mrs. Erutan so gladly that soon she was flying a kite too. Before long the little Persian boy, and the little Korean boy, and the little Japanese boy saw the kites flying, and came bringing their own.

FIGURE 6.20

The Magic City of Children, by Peggie Porcher. New York: Lynn, 1936.

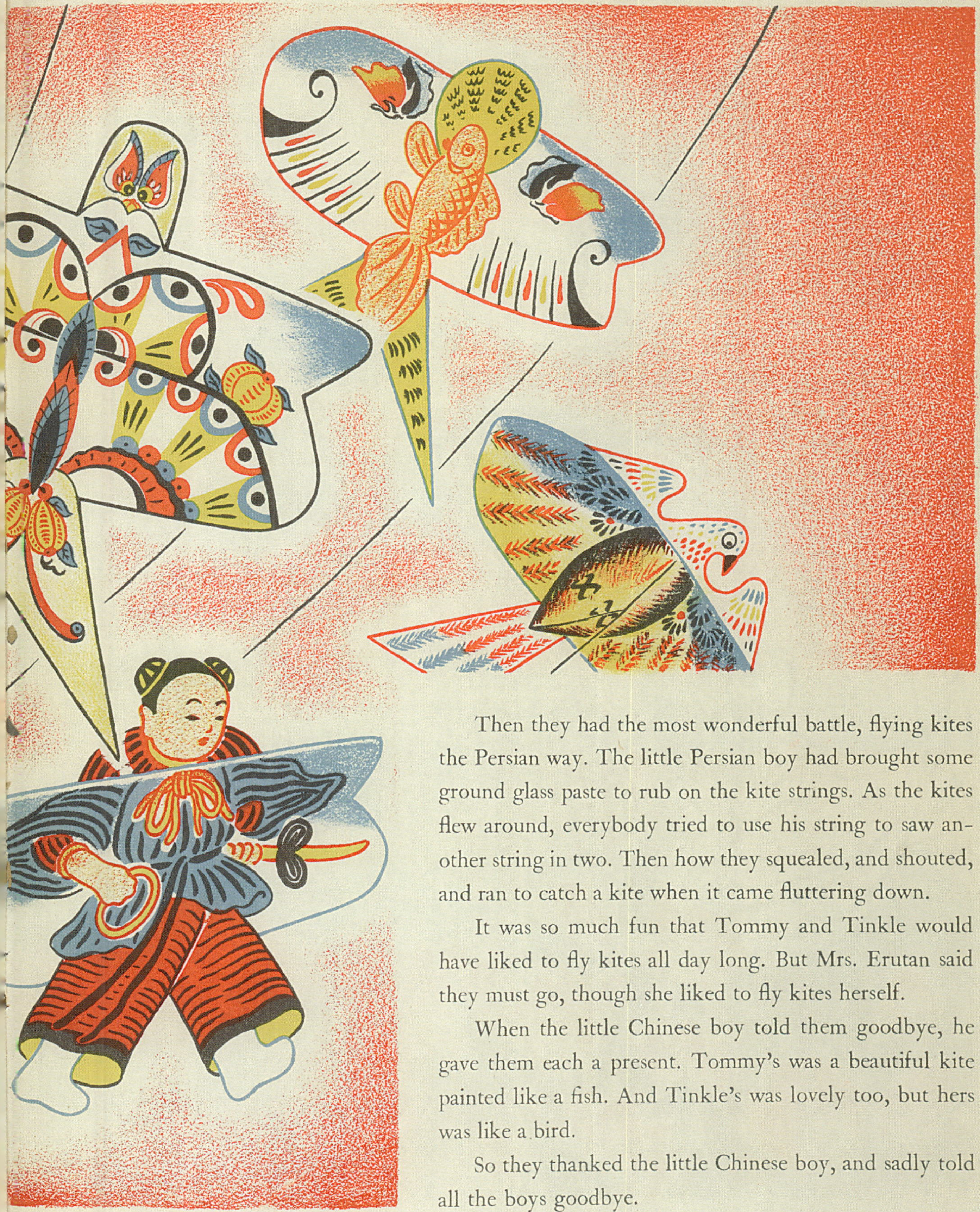

Then they had the most wonderful battle, flying kites the Persian way. The little Persian boy had brought some ground glass paste to rub on the kite strings. As the kites flew around, everybody tried to use his string to saw another string in two. Then how they squealed, and shouted, and ran to catch a kite when it came fluttering down.

It was so much fun that Tommy and Tinkle would have liked to fly kites all day long. But Mrs. Erutan said they must go, though she liked to fly kites herself.

When the little Chinese boy told them goodbye, he gave them each a present. Tommy's was a beautiful kite painted like a fish. And Tinkle's was lovely too, but hers was like a bird.

So they thanked the little Chinese boy, and sadly told all the boys goodbye.

In Holling C. Holling's *The Twins Who Flew around the World* (1931), which was inspired by Charles Lindbergh's historic transatlantic flight four years earlier, Japan is the first foreign destination of Bobby and Barbara's fanciful plane ride:

> It was with deep relief that [Barbara] spied something on the horizon. It loomed up across the line of sea and sky like a chocolate cream with a white frosting on top. And suddenly she knew what it was! "Bobby," she cried above the roar of the exhaust, "there's Fuji-yama, the sacred mountain of Japan! Just as it is in our geography!" . . .
>
> In another hour they had actually reached Japan! While smiling Japanese took care of the plane at the aerodrome the twins were escorted to the Imperial Hotel in Tokyo, where a Japanese dinner awaited them. The table was low, and they kneeled on cushions instead of sitting in chairs. A cheerful-faced lady in a beautiful kimono waited on them, and she seemed to know exactly what they wanted before they asked for it. There was a stove right on the table! But it didn't look like a stove. It was a brightly polished bronze bowl, and inside nestled a bed of red coals. The Japanese lady cooked their food over this in a bronze basin, and how good it did taste to the weary travelers. Its name was "sukiaki" and there was almost everything in it, from tender bamboo shoots, bean cakes and sliced onions to greens sprinkled with water chestnuts and bits of chicken, all of it simmered together in chicken broth. It tasted something like very best chop suey, but much better.[67]

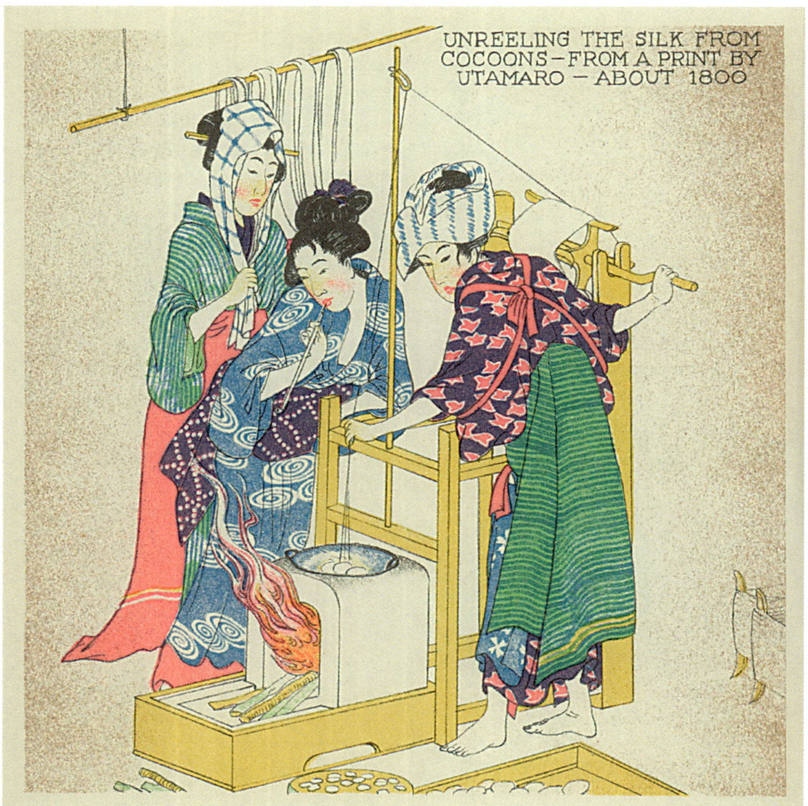

FIGURE 6.21
"Unreeling the Cocoon," in *The Story of Silk*, written and illustrated by Maud and Miska Petersham. Philadelphia: John C. Winston, 1939.

There were more literary trips around the world in which Japan was a featured stop, including *Peter and Peggy Go round the World* by Jane Harvey (1931), *Johnny round the World* (1933) by André and William La Varre, and V. R. Lowe's *Sammy Goes around the World* (1934). In *The Magic City of Children* (1936, fig. 6.20) by Peggie Porcher, Tinkle and Tommy and a friendly witch go on another imaginative tour around the world. They are flying on a leaf. The children only have to count "Eeny-meeny-miney-mo"[68] and off they go to see the Hungarian, Hawaiian, Mexican, Chinese, Dutch, and Eskimo homes and fly their kites with Chinese, Persian, Korean, and Japanese children.

Maud and Miska Petersham did not produce a travel book, but a handsome introduction to Japanese art with their *The Story Book of Silk* (1939, fig. 6.21) which featured several prints by Kitagawa Utamaro.[69]

On the Eve of World War II

Another look at different countries, published in 1939 as World War II began in Europe, mixed a small dose of fantasy with a large dose of reality and patriotism. In Enid La Monte Meadowcroft's *Aren't We Lucky!*, Christopher receives for his birthday a pair of magic glasses that allow him to look at all the places around the whole world. In England he sees "men, women, and children . . . trying on gas-masks, learning how to use them and how to find their way quickly to the nearest shelter in case of an air-raid." In Spain, then in a bitter civil war, "he saw men fighting, dying, lying wounded on the ground." In Italy he saw "that all the boys . . . even the six-year olds, were learning how to fight . . . for Italy is a country ruled by a dictator." As he continued looking through his binoculars, Christopher saw

> that most of the men of Germany seemed to be in the army. Or in factories making guns, tanks and airplanes. Many men, too, were in prisons or in concentration camps . . . And he saw the soldiers of Germany on the march—in trucks, in cars, on motor-cycles, and afoot . . . and watched them invade the little country of Czechoslovakia. . . . He discovered that Russia, a vast country rich in everything a country needs, was also a dictatorship, ruled by a powerful party. He saw that men who criticized the leader of the party were imprisoned or shot.[70]

Christopher saw horrible things in China:

> Whole cities of that peace-loving nation were lying in ruins. Many thousands of people lay dead and dying. Millions more were homeless. Some were living in the

> streets. Others were frantically fleeing from the cities, hurrying to get out of the way before the terrible Japanese soldiers should attack them. He saw the soldiers of Japan entering the cities and little villages, brutally killing women and children, robbing the people of their food and of their belongings.[71]

Then Christopher looked at Japan:

> He saw a group of school children pounding rice cakes to send to Japanese soldiers who were fighting in China. They laughed and sang as they worked, for they were too little to know the meaning of war, especially when that war was being fought in another land. He saw that in Japan, as in Italy and Russia and Germany, schoolboys were learning to be soldiers. Even the girls were being taught how to handle rifles and machine guns. And Japanese women were drilling, getting ready to fight when they should be needed.
>
> In one city Christopher saw crowds gathered to say good-by to the Japanese troops as they started off for the battle-fields in China. He watched the soldiers taking leave of their wives and children and wondered how many would come back.
>
> In another city he saw train-loads of soldiers returning from China. They were the wounded who could fight no longer. Crippled and blind, many of them would never again be able to live like other men. Christopher saw some of these soldiers who had been blinded, learning how to play on wooden flutes so that they might some day be able to earn their livings as musicians.
>
> He could see as he looked about that Japan is a small country and does not have all the things it needs for its people, but he wondered why the Japanese were not content to get those things by peaceful trading instead of by killing and stealing.[72]

Finally, Christopher looked at America. He saw great forests, coal mines, oilfields, gas wells, factories and cotton fields. He saw schools and churches and parks "where children of every race, nationality, and religious belief played happily together." He looked through his binoculars and saw "people . . . who live in terrible places. Why, some of them were even too poor to give their children shoes so that they could go to school." And how could he help, he asked his father.

> "You can grow up to be the kind of citizen this country needs. Stand up always for what you know to be right. Learn to think clearly. Don't agree thoughtlessly with everything you hear, for there are men paid to say certain things which they hope will bring about a different form of government in this country. . . .

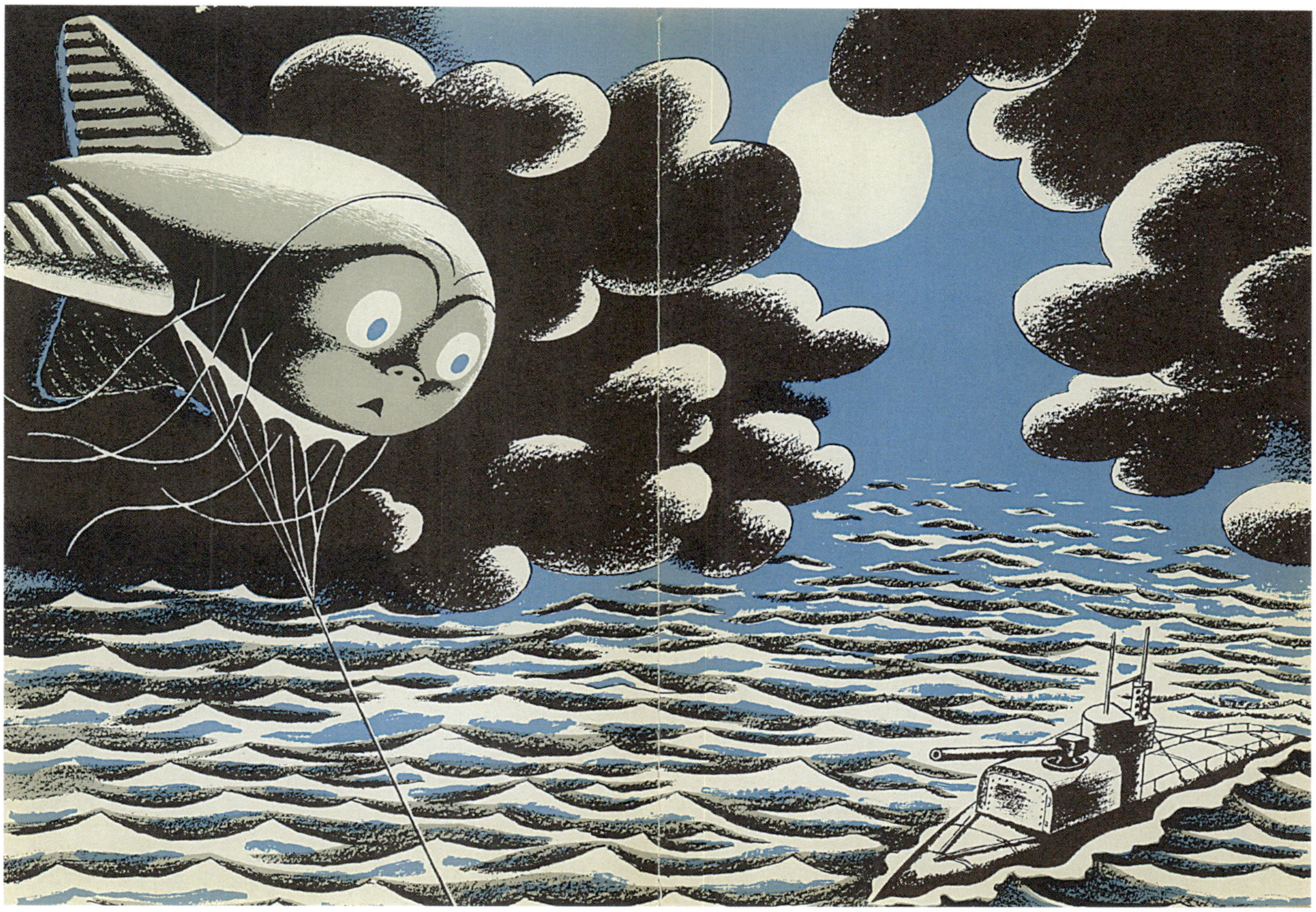

FIGURE 6.22
Bobo the Barrage Balloon, by Margaret A. McConnell, illustrated by Tibor Gergely. New York: Lothrop, Lee & Shepard, 1943, pages 19–20.

"You are sure to hear some one say some day, 'Oh, we need a dictator to make this country really prosperous.' Or, 'What we ought to do is to go over and clean up that European mess.' Or, 'We don't want people of that race and belief in our country.' It is talk of this kind that leads to war and dictatorship. And we don't want either in America."[73]

In 1943, an oddly playful picture book appeared. *Bobo the Barrage Balloon* by Margaret McConnell tells the story of an air defense balloon who bravely downs a Japanese reconnaissance plane (fig. 6.22). "Badly bruised and torn, and quite sick from all the salt water that had got into his secret construction,"[74] Bobo is saved and rushed to the Mending Hospital. In the end, he receives a citation for bravery from the president of the United States.

Only a year later, in 1944, Arensa Sondergaard wrote, in *My First Geography of the Pacific* (fig. 6.23):

The capital city, Honolulu, on the island of Oahu, is a busy place, with modern office buildings, private homes, schools, banks, churches, and shops. Newspapers

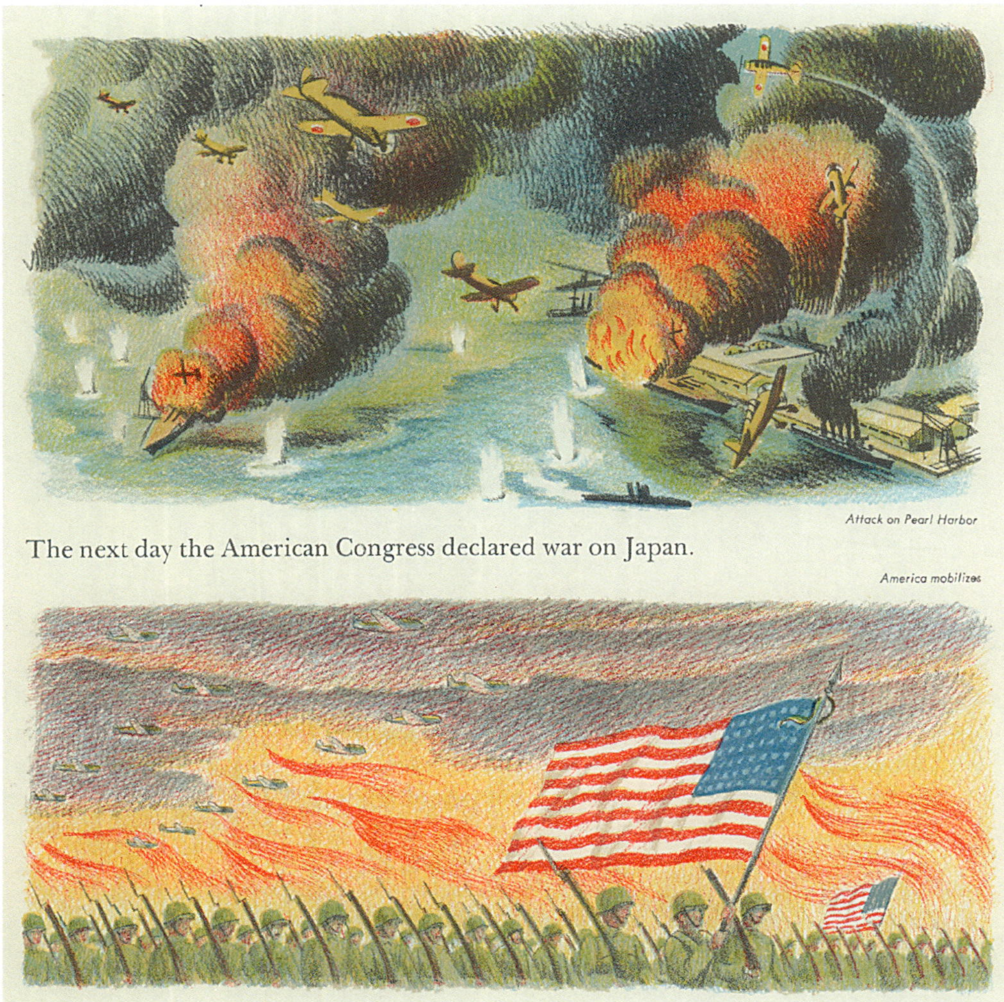

FIGURE 6.23
My First Geography of the Pacific, by Arensa Sondergaard, illustrated by Cornelis [pseud., Cornelius DeWitt]. Boston: Little, Brown, 1944, page 22.

> carry news from all over the world, and into the harbor come fast ocean liners and big freighters, providing a frequent link with the American mainland.
>
> Not far from Honolulu is the famous American naval base of Pearl Harbor. Here, on December 7, 1941, a peaceful Sunday was shattered by a treacherous Japanese air and naval attack. Severe damage was done to the base and to its warships and planes, and there were many casualties among American soldiers, sailors, and civilians. The next day the American Congress declared war on Japan.[75]

The same year Sondergaard's book appeared, the *New York Times*, in an article titled "Folk Rhymes for Children," reported about a professor at the English Department of State Teachers College in Frostburg, Maryland, who had been collecting children's rhymes and jingles for more than a decade. Dorothy G. Howard found the children's ditties uncannily tuned into the American political landscape, especially the 1944 presidential election campaign.[76]

Two examples from Howard's unpublished collection reflected the current dangerous state of world affairs:

A tisket, a tasket,
Ole Hitler's in the basket;
Eenie, meenie, Mussolini,
He will be there too.

and:

Eenie, meenie, minie mo
Catch a Jap by the toe
If he hollers make him say
I surrender to the U.S.A.[77]

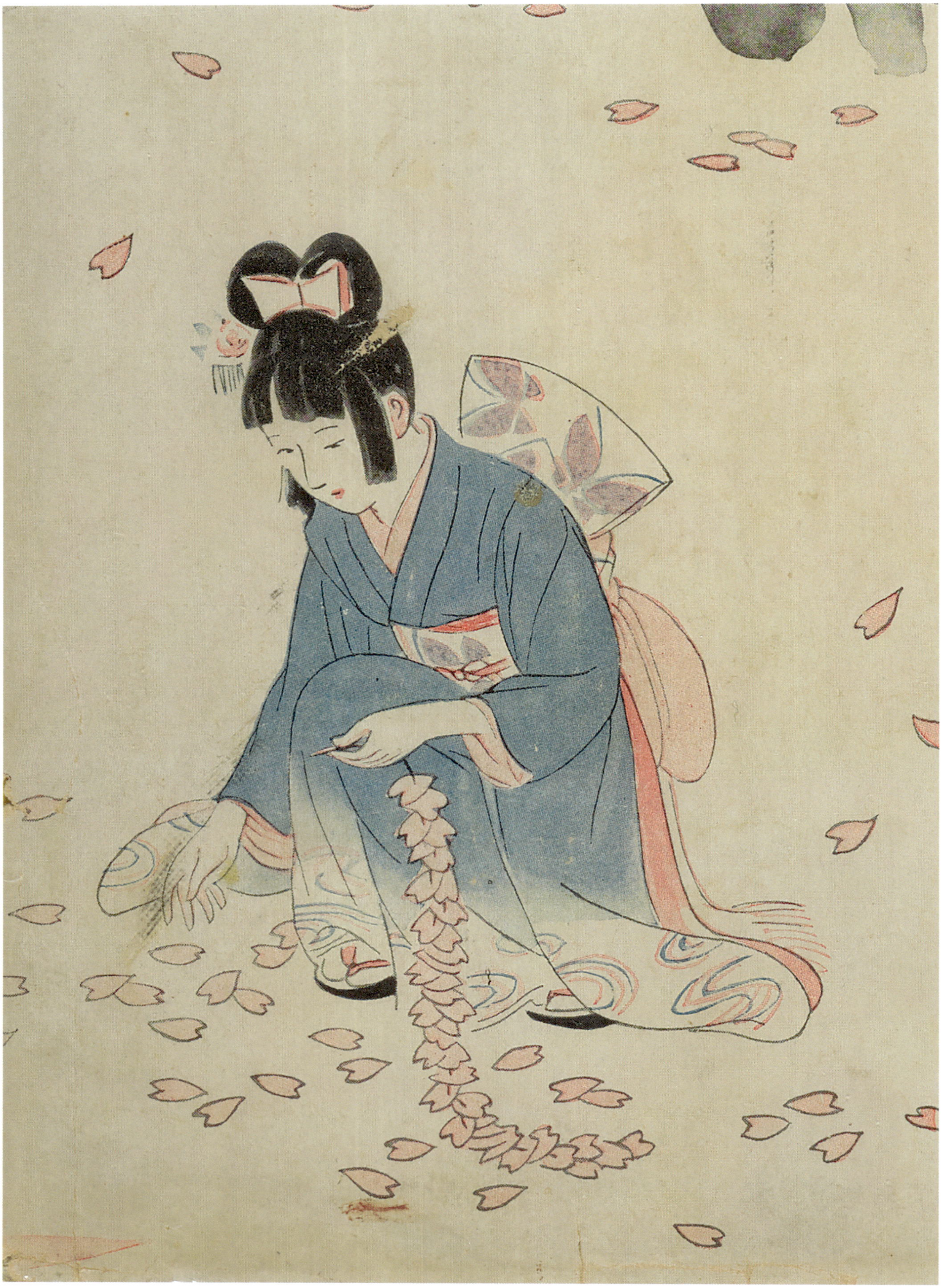

7

Louise Seaman Bechtel

America's First Children's Book Editor and Her Books about Japan

In 1918, George P. Brett, president of Macmillan publishers,[1] took a step that made publishing history:[2]

> The organization of so large a firm as The Macmillan Company necessitates the breaking up of different kinds of book-making into separate departments. For many years, children's books (as apart from school books) were handled as part of the regular "trade" books. It occurred to me that these books would benefit more than any others, perhaps, from separate editorial supervision. In 1918 I discovered, after some searching and experiment with young men and women editors, a college girl working in our advertising department. She had had several years of teaching. Her training at the house, in the educational, editorial, trade manuscript reading and advertising departments, had given her an idea of publishing routine. So Louise Seaman [Bechtel] was appointed head of the first Children's Book department.[3]

Bertha E. Mahony, editor of the influential journal the *Horn Book Magazine*, would later describe Bechtel as a "young woman of candor and charm . . . ideals, vision, [and] enthusiasm,"[4] while a British publicist commented: "Amazing, the way you Americans entrust such very important jobs to mere girls. Is Miss Seaman really the head of a Macmillan department?"[5]

And, indeed, she seemed to have been the right person at the right place and time. By 1934, the year she retired, the "pioneer with a pioneer's infectious vigor and high spirits . . . [who had the] gift of making writing exciting and rewarding in itself" had published more than six hundred books. Looking back to the beginning of her career, Bechtel wrote her impression of that time:

> The happiest years for children's bookmaking came after the First World War, with the influx of books and also of artists from Europe. Then bookmaking stepped away from its tradition. It was a time of sufficient prosperity for American publishers and public to support experimental bookmaking.[6]

OPPOSITE
(Detail) *A Daughter of the Samurai*, by Etsu Inagaki Sugimoto, illustrated by Tekisui Ishii. Garden City, NY: Doubleday, Page, 1925.

Anne Carroll Moore, dominant voice of American children's literature during the first four decades of the twentieth century, agreed. Moore maintained that the 1920s were as golden as the early years of *St. Nicholas* magazine and that American children's books of that decade displayed extraordinary vigor and variety in their writing, illustrations, and design.[7] At the same time, many children's books still reflected the simple moralities of the turn of the twentieth century—or even the late nineteenth[8]—and showed little awareness of contemporary currents of their own or other countries. In 1940, Bechtel herself would write that honest portraits of foreign lands were a rare phenomenon in 1920s American children's books.[9]

Bechtel was fortunate to begin her career under the tutelage of Brett. The father of three children, he "remembered a great deal about their reading tastes," a fact that must have influenced his belief that "children's books are perhaps more important than any other kind. Through these books one reaches young minds at the plastic age when moral character is being formed. Hence the importance of their selection and editing cannot be overestimated."[10] Describing Bechtel's job, he said:

> Miss Seaman's work, like that of any department manager, is that of directing the publication of her own books. This means manuscript reading, arranging author's and artist's contracts, planning the format of a book and its price, . . . writing her own advertising and doing publicity for her own books; making her own catalog and as much selling and sales suggesting as possible. I believe her experience handling the general house publicity for a year, and handling twenty city accounts for children's books for a year, contributed a great deal to her efficiency as a publisher.[11]

He understood his young editor's many challenges:

> [Seaman] inherited a list of several hundred famous children's books, from our English and American lists. Her first task was to know these books in relation to the general field of children's reading, to re-catalog them attractively and re-issue those that had been neglected. At the same time she was putting through the press new books by [the British illustrator Arthur] Rackham, . . . [American writer] Miss [Cornelia] Meigs [and others] . . . and learning to make books.[12]

And so, on one of her first days on the job, when Bechtel was told to read the catalog, she "was fascinated. Hundreds of pages of wonderful books, not only from Macmillan London, but from Cambridge University Press, A. & C. Black . . . etc."[13] Initially, the list Bechtel developed was "sternly literary"[14] as she sought "to keep to the high standards of publication" and "build solidly on the fine list of books for young people" that the Macmillan Company had long produced.[15] Her first catalog, published in 1920, contained over 250 titles, half of which were produced in England, half in the United States.[16] Within a decade the number of her inherited books would be much reduced and she had truly come into her own.

Bechtel's handsome 1930 catalog was a showcase of her imagination, her knowledge of children's books, and her sense of design. It introduced a remarkable variety of topics and genres and showed her sophistication and her ability to find creative new authors and illustrators. A benchmark, it was the culmination of her work and contained all her books to date, including the "Complete List of All Macmillan Books for Boys and Girls."[17] It was filled with thoughtful book descriptions, background notes and reviews, quotations, biographical sketches, photos, illustrations, and decorative vignettes.

Bechtel's books included such traditional folk and fairy tales and classics as *Memoirs of a London Doll* (1922) and *The White Cat and Other Old French Fairy Tales* (1928), as well as stories, nonfiction, and books from and about other countries. Her picture books were especially fine—answering Bertha Mahony's lament, in an August 1928 magazine article, about the paucity of American-made picture books.[18]

Bechtel published a number of translations (listed in her catalog as "Macmillan Books—Beautiful Printing from Europe), including *Spin, Top, Spin* (1929) with illustrations by Elsa Eisgruber and *Peregrin and the Goldfish* by Sigmund Freud's niece, Tom Seidmann-Freud (1929). Noteworthy American-made books with bold and individualistic designs included Elizabeth Coatsworth's *The Sun's Diary* (1929), and Boris Artzybasheff's iconic *The Fairy Shoemaker and Other Fairy Poems* (1928).[19]

Other headings in the 1930 catalog were "Macmillan Books—The Very Best Fairy Tales," "The Little Library," "New Animals Stories," and "Explorers, Young and Old." The catalog section titled "Macmillan Books—at only fifty cents" listed "Famous Tales," "Nursery Stories," and the small-format "The Happy Hours Books," which included *The ABC Nonsense Book* by Edward Lear and such classic nursery tales as *Goldilocks and the Three Bears*. George Brett seemed especially interested in these categories and suggested that Bechtel pay attention to books like "The Work and Play Books," or biographies for young readers such as Albert Bigelow Paine's *A Girl in White Armor: The True Story of Joan of Arc* (1927), and Ida M. Tarbell's *The Boy Scouts' Life of Lincoln* (1921).[20]

Bechtel's Books about Other Countries

Bechtel's deep interest in children's books about other countries is also evident in her 1930 catalog. It featured a number of translated books in addition to American books about other countries, which included China, Hungary, Italy, Mexico, and

Norway. The number of books about Japan was remarkable. The list contained *Japan* (1907, one of the *Peeps at Many Lands* series); *Green Willow and Other Japanese Fairy Tales* (1910); *Little Black Eyes* (1927); *The Picture Book of Travel* (1928); *The Begging Deer and Other Stories of Japanese Children* (1928); *When I Was a Girl: The Stories of Five Famous Women as Told by Themselves* (1930); *Prince Bantam: Being the Adventures of Yoshitsune the Brave and His Faithful Henchman Great Benkei of the Western Pagoda* (1929); and *The Cat Who Went to Heaven* (1930).[21]

Japan (1907) was Bechtel's oldest book in the group. Published by Adam and Charles Black in London, Bechtel sold it through her catalog as an imported title for $1.00. *Japan* was written by John Finnemore, a popular British writer of books for boys, whose life story has largely vanished.[22] Finnemore produced more than fifty books—many of which were published by Black—including the *Teddy Lester* and *Three School Chums* series. He also wrote adult fiction and compiled a number of volumes for young readers about other countries—none of which he probably ever visited—including America, France, and India and Japan.[23]

Most likely, Bechtel was aware that Finnemore's *Japan* had a British slant and that the British references would not be clear to her young American audience. However, that was only a minor flaw, for here was an author who had created a narrative filled with lively details and who must have done a great deal of research. *Japan* presents pleasing, at times fictionalized descriptions of an idyllic Japan, including the cheerful lives of the country's boys and girls enjoying such games as bouncing balls, hunting for grasshoppers, and playing in the river with toy waterwheels. Finnemore describes Japanese houses, their floors covered with "beautiful mats, as white as snow and as soft as a cushion,"[24] and freshly cut boughs of flowers in the *tokonoma*. He depicts perfectly behaved children, servants of fine breeding, farmers, *jinrickisha* pullers, and policemen, all of whom excel at what they were doing.[25] British artist Ella du Cane's romantic illustrations of roly-poly children spinning tops, playfully waving the Imperial Navy flag, or looking at the display in a doll shop add to the impression of Japan as an ideal country (figs. 7.1–2).[26]

Finnemore also tells about a more serious side of Japanese life. Describing the traditional Japanese house and how the "Japs," as he calls them, cope with disasters such as earthquakes, he writes:

> A Japanese house is one of the simplest buildings in the world. Its main features are the roof of tiles or thatch, and the posts which support the latter. By day the walls are of oiled paper; by night they are formed of wooden shutters, neither very thick nor very strong. As a rule, the house is of but one story, and its flimsiness comes from two reasons, both very good ones.

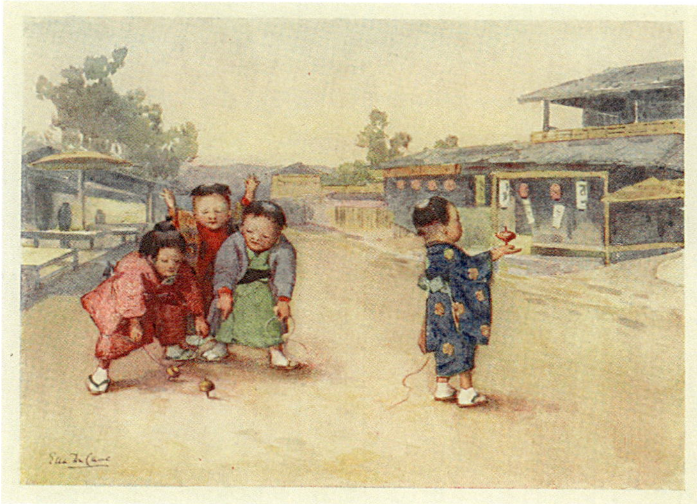

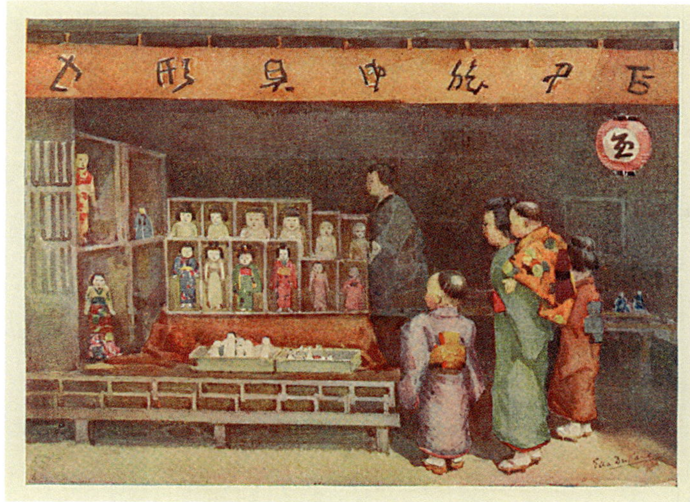

FIGURES 7.1 AND 7.2
"Fighting Tops" and "The Toy Shop," in *Peeps at Many Lands: Japan*, by John Finnemore, illustrated by Ella Du Cane. London: A. and C. Black, 1908, pages 40 and 48.

> The first is that Japan is a home of earthquakes, and when an earthquake starts to rock the land and topple the houses about the people's ears, then a tall, strong house of stone or brick would be both dangerous in its fall and very expensive to put up again. The second is that Japan is a land of fires. The people are very careless. They use cheap lamps and still cheaper petroleum. A lamp explodes or gets knocked over; the oiled paper walls burst into a blaze; the blaze spreads right and left, and sweeps away a few streets, or a suburb or a city, or a whole village. The Jap takes this very calmly. He gets a few posts, puts the same tiles up again for a roof, or makes a new thatch, and, with a few paper screens and shutters, there stands his house again.[27]

Among other things, Finnemore muses about Japan's "puzzling" writing system, "oddly" different from that used in the West (fig. 7.3):

> Their books are very odd-looking affairs to us. Not only are they printed in very large characters, but they seem quite upside down. To find the first page you turn

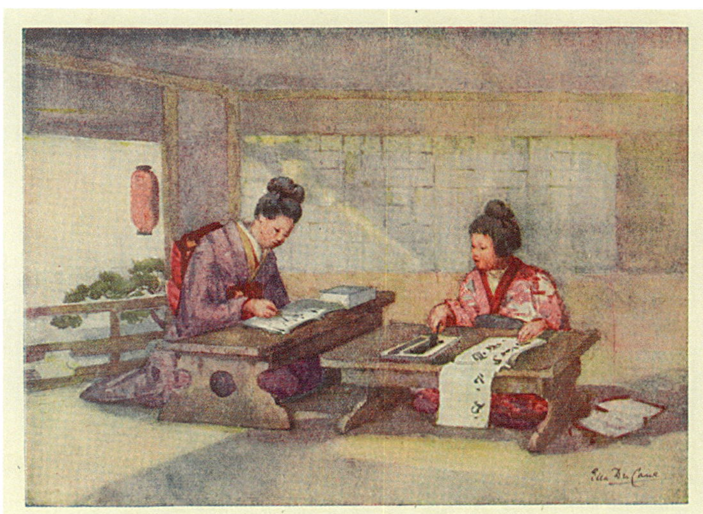

FIGURE 7.3
"The Writing Lesson," in *Peeps at Many Lands: Japan*, by John Finnemore, page 10.

> to the end of the book, and you read it backwards to the front page. Again, you do not read from left to right, as in our fashion, but from right to left. Nor is this all: for the lines do not run across the page, but up and down. Altogether, a Japanese book is at first a very puzzling affair. When the writing lesson comes, the children have no pens; they use brushes instead. They dip their brushes in the ink, and paint the words one under the other, beginning at the top right-hand corner and finishing at the bottom left-hand corner.[28]

About Japan's food, which he most likely never tasted, Finnemore writes:

> [At dinner], the unhappy foreigner tastes one dish after the other, finds each one worse than the last, and concludes to wait till the next course. This is composed of a very dainty, raw, live fish, which one dips in sauce before devouring. Then comes rice, and the chopsticks of the Japanese feasters do work in marvelous fashion. With their strips of wood or ivory they whip the rice grain into their mouths with wonderful speed and dexterity, but our unlucky foreigner gets one grain into his mouth with in five minutes, and is reduced to beg for a spoon.
>
> The next course is of fish soup and boiled fish, and potatoes appear with the fish; but, alas! The fish is most oddly flavoured and the potatoes are sweet; they have been beaten up with sugar into a sort of stiff syrup. Next comes seaweed soup and the coarse evil-smelling daikon radish, served with various pickles and sauces.[29]

Using the same title as he chose for the original volume, Finnemore produced a second book about Japan, in which he acknowledged his British sources, Basil Hall Chamberlain and Isabella Bird among them. *Japan* (1911, fig. 7.4), part of the *Peeps at History* series, was written for somewhat older children. In this remarkably detailed account of Japan's long history, Finnemore begins with Marco Polo, the Venetian, who tells of "Chipangue, an island towards the east, in the high seas." He compares Japan's invasion of Korea to the Norman invasion of England, which brought that country new ideas and new ways of life; likens the reign of the fourth-century emperor Nintoku to that of King Alfred; and tells of Japan's Middle Ages, from about 650 to 1050, when the powerful Fujiwara family ruled the country. He describes the rise of the military clans and the war between two of them, the Taira and the Minamoto, which led to the downfall of Japan's feudal system and the era of the samurai.

Finnemore also presents a quintessential Japanese subject rarely described with such thoughtfulness in American children's books:

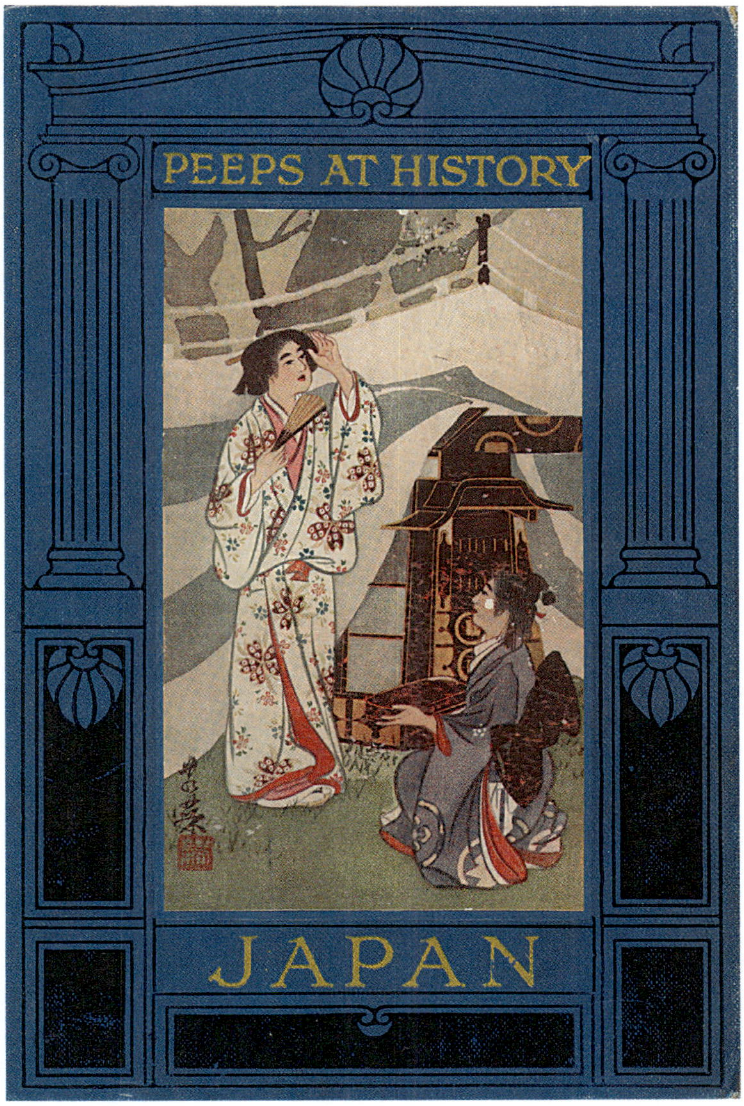

FIGURE 7.4
Peeps at History: Japan, by John Finnemore, illustrated by Wakana Utagawa. London: A. and C. Black, 1911.

What was a Samurai?

He was, first of all and last of all, a soldier—a man who had the right to bear two swords, to wield one in defence of his lord, to use the other to take his own life before he would suffer dishonour. . . .

The young Samurai was brought up in a school of the most severe discipline. He was made to endure hardship without complaint, to despise pleasure and gain, to practice self-denial without hope of praise, to fear nothing save dishonour. Above all, he was trained to give perfect obedience and perfect loyalty to his lord. His life was to be nothing to him if his lord required it, or if his honour would be stained by keeping it. One of the first things he was taught was the ceremony of *hara-kiri*, the manner in which his own life was to be taken if need should arise. . . .

The Samurai were a well-educated class. The school day of a young Samurai was divided into two parts. In the early portion of the day he worked under teachers who taught him to love the learning and literature of Japan, while the latter part

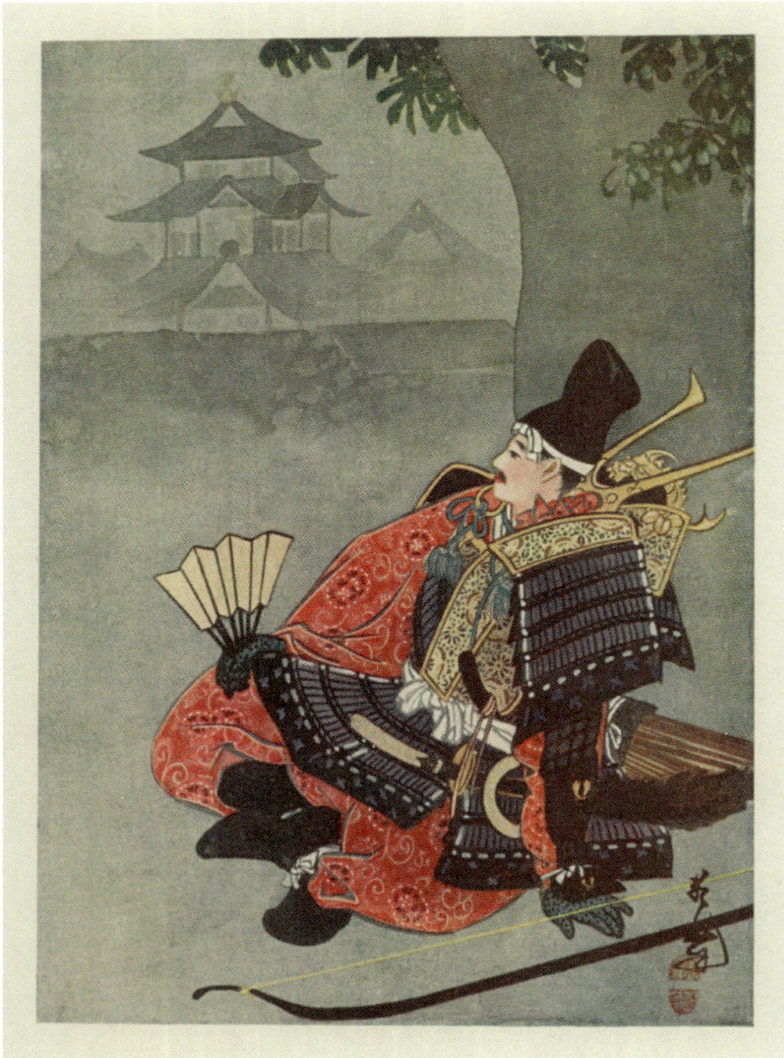

FIGURE 7.5
"Warrior of the Ashikaga Period," in *Peeps at History: Japan*, by John Finnemore, frontispiece.

> of the day was spent in training his body to the use of arms. He learned how to ride a horse, how to shoot with the bow, how to handle the spear, and, above all and beyond all, how to wield a sword. The sword of a Samurai was not only the emblem of his rank, but also the idol of his heart. It was the most precious thing he owned, and he took the greatest care of it; if it bore the name of a famous maker that was a matter for special pride. . . .
>
> For centuries, then, the people of Japan were ranged in these four classes—Samurai, farmers, craftsmen, and merchants—and the Samurai bore rule over the rest.[30]

Finnemore ends his long Japan story with the country's entry into the modern age, explaining that Japan's ambition had been to become the "Britain of the East, a great naval and trading power" (fig. 7.6).[31] The Battle of Port Arthur in 1905 demonstrated, Finnemore writes, that the "Yamato Damashii, the Spirit of Old Japan, still filled the heart of the nation and, though the Russians 'fought splendidly,' the heroic islanders were not to be denied."[32]

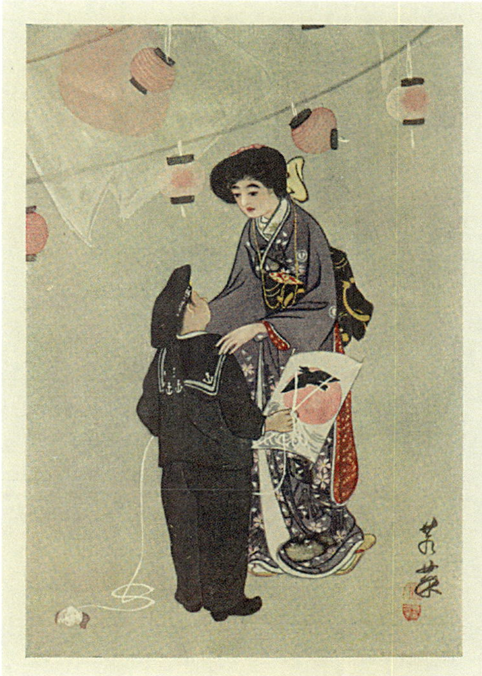

FIGURE 7.6
"Young Japan of To-day," in *Peeps at History: Japan*, by John Finnemore, page 73.

Green Willow and Other Japanese Fairy Tales (1910, fig. 7.7) by Grace James was also British in origin.[33] James was born in Tokyo, where her father, a naval officer, was a member of the British Naval Mission. Her parents came to Japan during the early days of the Meiji Restoration (1868), providing the background for her future storytelling:

> My parents came to Japan where men wore long hair and dressed it in the *chomagé*, where women blacked their teeth in token of conjugal fidelity, where people travelled by *kuruma* and by *kago*, where the *andon* burned dimly behind the *shoji*, and where the peerless sacred mountain brooded, enigmatic and apart, giving no prophecy of the momentous changes that should come.[34]

Green Willow was a fine addition to Bechtel's list. James selected the stories from the "the *Ko-ji-ki*, or *Record of Ancient Matters*," and other sources.[35] Her collection contains stories with universal folk motifs, such as the quest for immortality, the wicked stepmother, and the power of envy. Yet it also includes selections uniquely Japanese, including the story of the magic tea kettle that turns into a badger; the story of Tanabata, a young woman so deeply in love with her husband that she neglects her heavenly duties; and the creation myth of the sun goddess Amaterasu Omikami, who is tricked into emerging from her hiding place so that the world can see her divine countenance once again.

Having grown up in the old Japan, James felt at home with these immortal tales and employed a writing style in *Green Willow* that evoked their

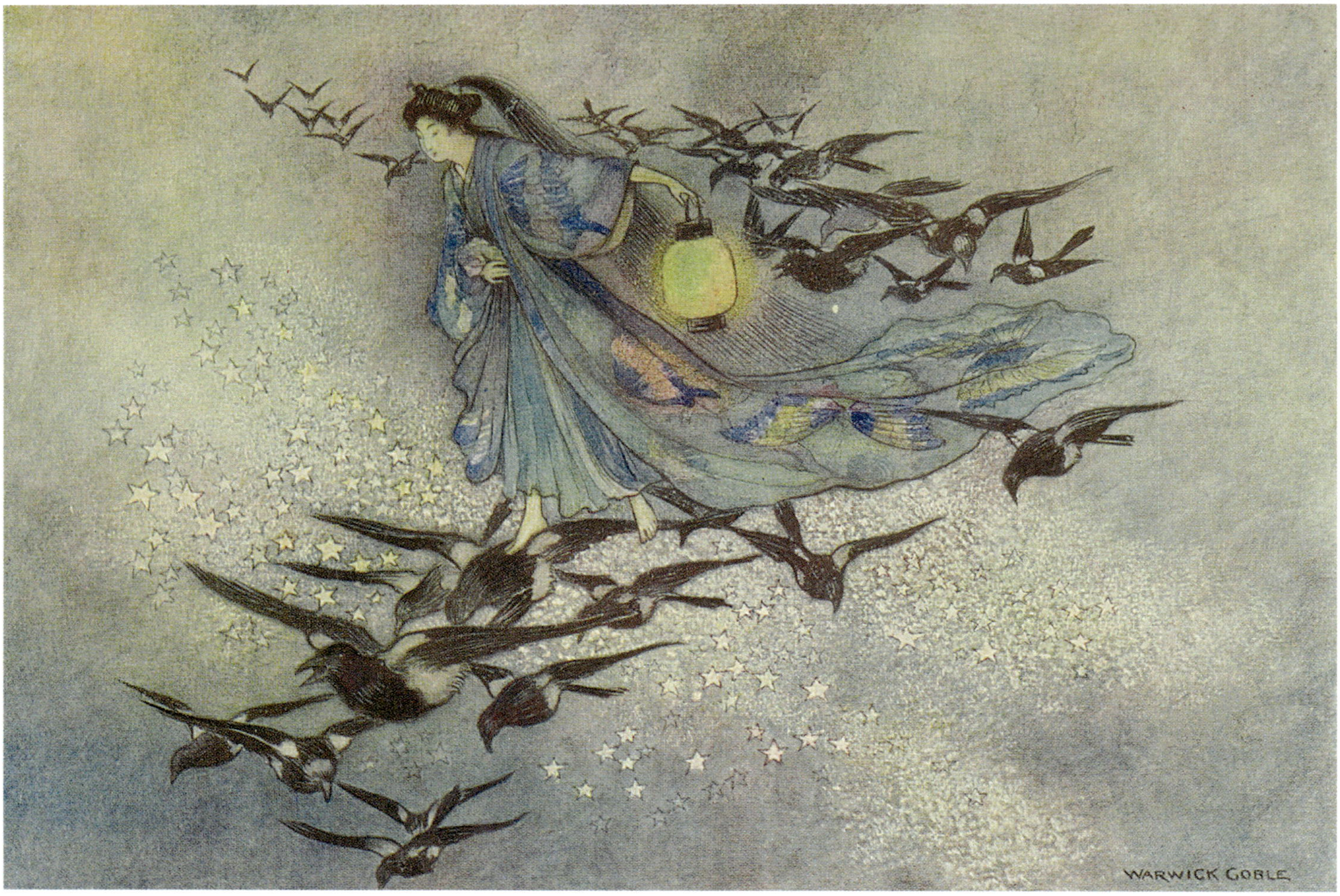

FIGURE 7.7
Green Willow and Other Japanese Fairy Tales, by Grace James, illustrated by Warwick Goble. London: Macmillan, 1910, page 65.

mythological setting. This is how she began "The Sea King and the Magic Jewels":

> This is a tale beloved by the children of Japan, and by the old folk—a tale of magical jewels and a visit to the Sea King's palace. . . .
>
> Howbeit, in the fullness of time, the lady, Blossoming-Brightly-as-the-Flowers-of-the-Trees, bore two men children, and called the elder Fire Flash and the younger Fire Fade.
>
> Prince Fire Flash was a fisherman, who got his luck upon the wide sea, and ran upon the shore with his august garments girded. And again, he tarried all the night in his boat, upon the high wave-crests. And he caught things broad of fin and things narrow of fin, and he was a deity of the water weeds and of the waters and of the fishes of the sea.
>
> But Prince Fire Fade was a hunter, who got his luck upon the mountains and in the forest, who bound sandals fast upon his feet, and bore a bow and heavenly-feathered arrows. And he caught things rough of hair and things soft of hair, and

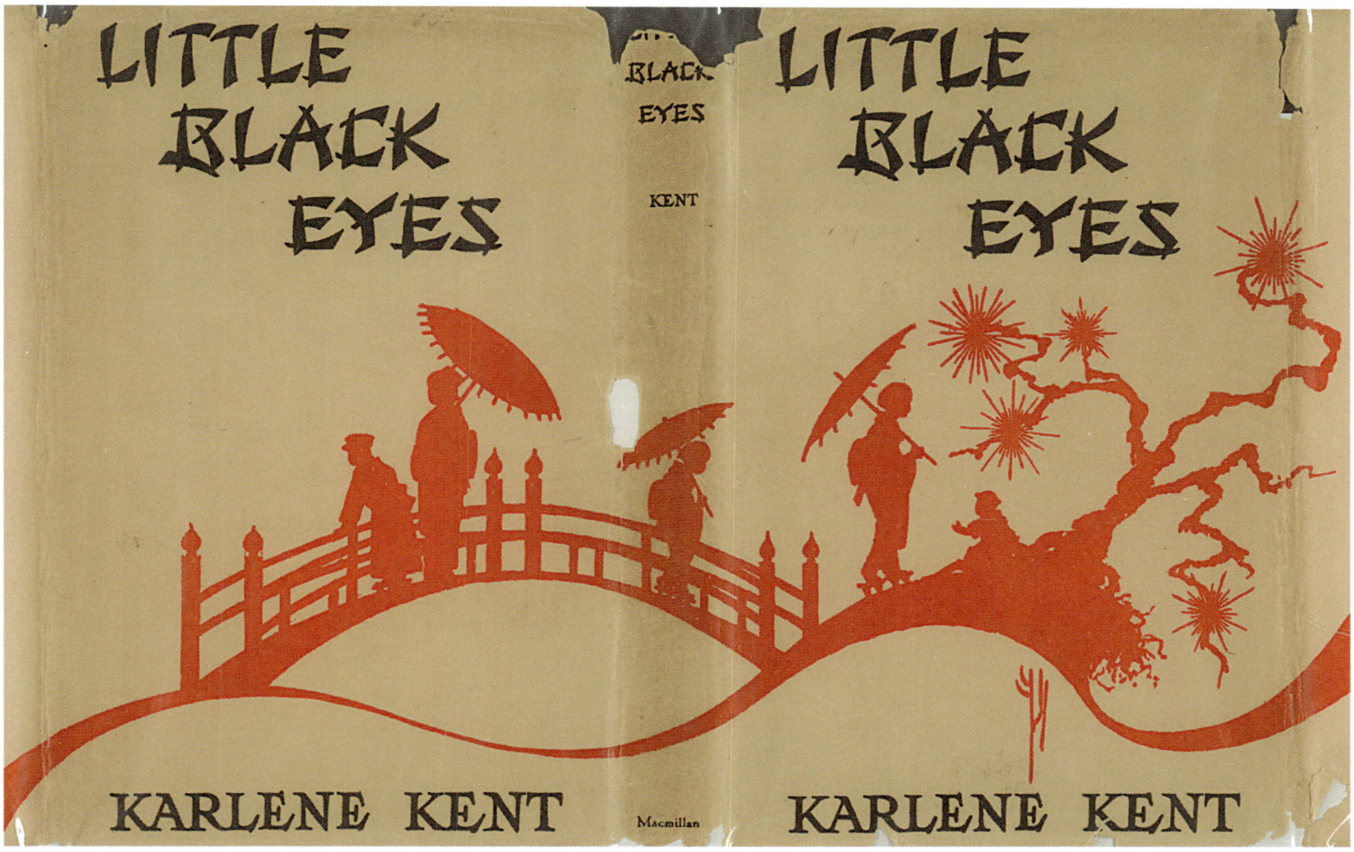

FIGURE 7.8
Little Black Eyes: The Story of a Little Girl in Japan, by Karlene Kent, illustrated by Carroll C. Snell. New York: Macmillan, 1927.

> he knew the trail of the badger and the wild cherry's time of flowering. For he was a deity of the woods.[36]

Green Willow was embellished with reproductions of muted watercolors showing languid maidens in flowing robes, the work of British artist Warwick Goble. Goble shared a passion with his more famous contemporary, Edmund Dulac, for exotic scenes of Arabia, India—and Japan.[37]

Little Black Eyes: The Story of a Little Girl in Japan[38] was among the American titles about Japan in Bechtel's 1930 catalog (fig. 7.8). Written by Karlene Kent, it tells the story of Chiyo, who is brought up to be an obedient and graceful girl who minds her manners and always behaves properly. Like young Take in Lucy Fitch Perkins's *The Japanese Twins* (see chapter 6), Chiyo quietly revolts against the rules, as when she boldly throws her leg over the bouncing ball, which her grandmother finds most unladylike. Chiyo desperately wants to join her brother in his for-boys-only games, and he finds a way to include her—almost:

> "Little Chiyo," he began, "of course, you know that girls never do the things boys do. It would not be virtuous. But as I am the grandson of a soldier and will be a big man some day, I have thought of a plan. A soldier should have someone to do

> things for him. So I thought I might take you along with me today grasshopper hunting and you could carry the lunch and serve it. Of course, being a girl, you couldn't carry the bamboo cage, but I am sure you wouldn't want to, for only boys do that."[39]

In this sunny and believable story, the author, who had lived in Japan for several years with her husband and young daughter, creates a vignette of Japanese family life during the late 1920s. Children celebrate the girls' day festival; visit the temple for the new baby's christening; jump rope and eat pancakes made by the street vendor; go to the Kabuki theatre; and bow to the Emperor's image in school. Yet the Western way of life is clearly intruding. On her christening day, the baby wears a kimono and a Western hat, a "funny little silk hat that wobbled about ridiculously on her head," according to Grandmother, who thought of it as an example of "shocking Western fashion."[40] When an American family comes to visit, young Chiyo asks her mother if foreigners are devils:

> When Chiyo wandered back into the house [from playing outside], she found her mother dressing.
>
> "Are you going out, honorable Mother?" she inquired. "No, Chiyo, but we have foreign company coming to call. Your father met a Western woman and she is bringing her little girl here to see you."
>
> "Oh, Mother, are they foreign devils?"
>
> "No, no, Chiyo, you mustn't believe such things. Long ago when we didn't know the foreigner, who came from way across the seas, we were naturally very much afraid of him, and some silly people said he was the foreign devil. But that is not true, and just because he dresses very differently from us and looks so pink and white we must not be unkind to him. Now, little Chiyo, you must be a good Japanese girl to-day and not laugh at the big foreigner and his queer ways."[41]

Chiyo has a new experience when she observes, with astonishment, the American girl who "jumped out [of the rickshaw] with a loud bang and nearly fell on her head," whose "bare legs [you could see] way up to the knee," who refused to drink tea and who, "had run right in [from outside] without taking her shoes off and, of course, tracked mud in from the garden."[42]

Little Black Eyes features black-and-white silhouettes by Carroll C. Snell, including depictions of women in kimono with paper umbrellas; a *torii*; and a mother and child walking on their high *geta*. Some of Snell's illustrations highlight the contrast between Eastern and Western ways touched upon in the story, as in the picture of the young Japanese girl bowing gently, hands turned down, toes turned in, looking modestly and ever so politely at the pretty, curly haired

American girl in her short-sleeved summer dress who is sitting down to put on her shoes while immodestly exposing her legs.[43]

Another book about Japan on Bechtel's 1930s list is *The Begging Deer and Other Stories of Japanese Children* (fig. 7.9),[44] a collection of stories by Dorothy Rowe, who had grown up in China and whose *The Rabbit Lantern and Other Stories of Chinese Children* (1925)—handsomely illustrated by Chinese artist Ling Jui Tang—*Horn Book Magazine* editor Bertha Mahony had called "one of the loveliest and most perfect books for small children."[45] Rowe's Japanese collection was not based on her own experience. Aware of this shortcoming, she asked a friend who had lived in Japan to vouch, in the introduction to *The Begging Deer*, for the stories' "entire accuracy" and "local color."[46]

The gently didactic stories—some of which had first appeared in the *Christian Science Monitor,* the *Child's Garden*, and *Child Life*—tell American youngsters of their obedient, patient, and polite Japanese counterparts. Unlike the

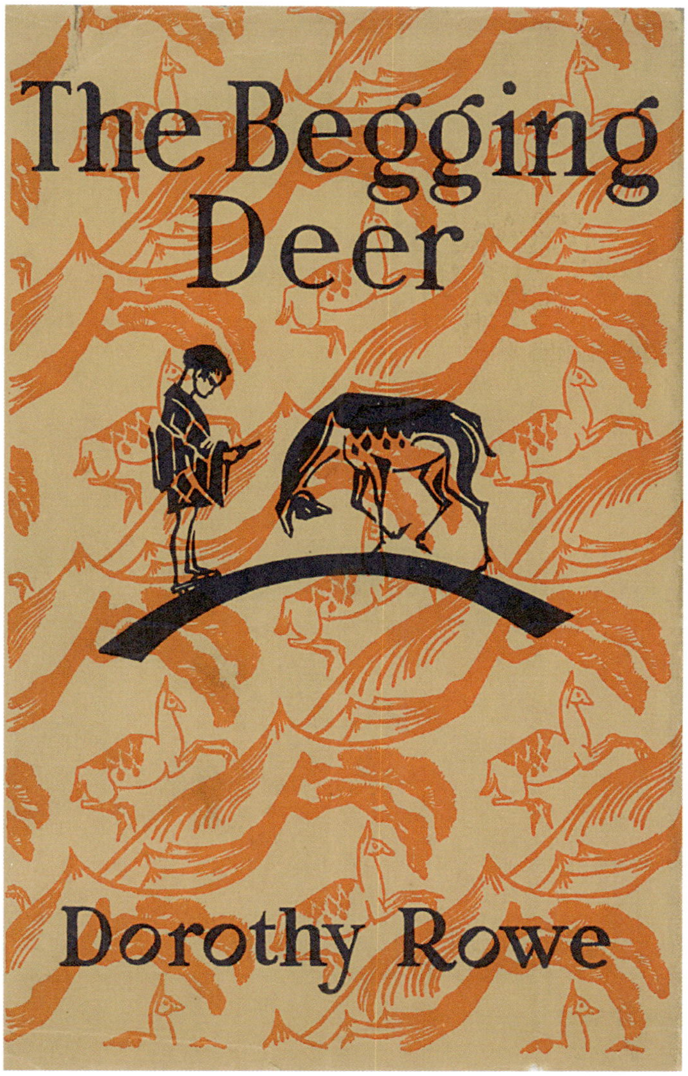

FIGURE 7.9
The Begging Deer and Other Stories of Japanese Children, by Dorothy Rowe, illustrated by Lynd Ward. New York, Macmillan, 1928.

Chinese children in the author's books about China, portrayed as important members of the family who are expected to help with chores, the Japanese children in *The Begging Deer* are described as living in a circumscribed and innocent world. The stories tell of Yozo, a young boy who overcomes his fear of animals when he encounters the deer in Nara; of Raiko, who goes on a school excursion to the temple of Chion, famous for its singing floorboards; of Hanako, who competes with her cousins for her grandmother's praise for her flower arrangement. Even Ukiko, a peasant girl, seems to live in an idyllic setting:

> Ukiko was only seven, and she had been happy all her life. She lived in the most beautiful place in all the world, a little toy-sized farmhouse in a tiny toy-sized farm by a pond no bigger than a doll's, and all in the small, lovely country of Japan. Of course, she was happy!
>
> In her home there was Mother who wore soft, colored kimonos and Father who wore short blue coats with big white letters on the back of them, and Big Brother who was the kindest brother in all the world.[47]

At least one of the stories features a Japanese child who displays some refreshing naughtiness. Frustrated by his new parrot's disinterest in learning to speak Japanese, Tetsuoto calls him *baga* (stupid). Delightfully, *baga* is the one word the parrot remembers, screeching it over and over when Tetsuoto's aunt comes to visit.[48]

Bechtel's Defining Books about Japan

When Bechtel began her job at Macmillan, Berta and Elmer Hader were still trying to make a living by creating illustrations for children's pages in women's magazines and newspapers. After they illustrated several nursery stories for Bechtel's "Happy Hour books," however, their careers took off—lasting into the 1960s and including a Caldecott medal for *The Big Snow* (1948). The informational *Picture Book of Travel*[49] was the first book the husband-and-wife team both wrote and illustrated (fig. 7.10). It had all the attributes Bechtel wanted: simplicity, strong design, and bold color. In her 1930 catalog, where it is listed under the category, "Macmillan Picture Books," she writes:

> The Macmillan Picture Books are a group planned to give information as youngsters want to have it, clear and direct, not embodied in stories or conversation, not "talked down" or "primerized." The three listed on this page [*The Picture Book of Ships, The Picture Book of Flying, The Picture Book of Travel*] are printed by offset

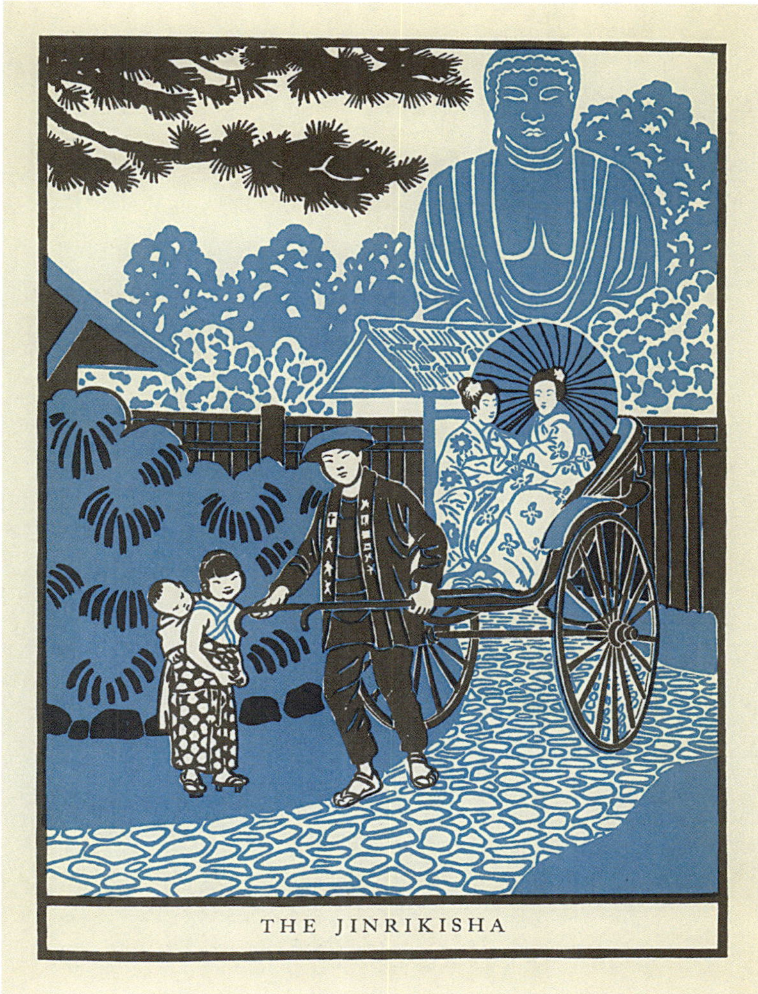

FIGURE 7.10
The Picture Book of Travel: The Story of Transportation, written and illustrated by Berta and Elmer Hader. New York, Macmillan, 1928, page 45.

> lithography, using flat color process, without any benday, which is very effective, brilliant, simple and interesting when employed by intelligent artists. It necessitates a strong basic pattern for each picture, therefore is easily "read" by young children. The books are "modern" in the sense that they are the first color books to combine modern artists' ideas of bookmaking, blocking out type, etc., with simple information for young people.[50]

The Haders' *Picture Book of Travel*, which illustrated travel modes through the ages, introduced such man-powered travel conveyances as the litter, the palanquin, and the sedan chair—but not the Japanese *kago*, a steady feature in nineteenth-century travel books. The Haders, however, did include in their depiction of Japanese life the *jinrikisha*—crediting the Japanese with its invention—in a tourist-style setting: a *jinrikisha* man in a coat decorated with faux Japanese lettering is hurrying over European-style cobblestones. The Haders also depicted two women in padded winter kimono and a little, bare-chested girl with a toddler tied to her back, roofs shown improbably close to the big statue of Buddha in Kamakura. Although Japan makes only a cameo appearance in the Haders' book, it does, at least, take its place next to other Western and Asian countries.

For older children Bechtel published *When I Was a Girl: The Stories of Five Famous Women as Told by Themselves* (1930).[51] It included autobiographical sketches of the German opera singer Ernestine Schumann-Heink, the American sculptor Janet Scudder, French scientist Marie Curie, American social work pioneer Jane Addams, and the Japanese writer Etsu Inagaki Sugimoto. Four of the stories had already appeared in print, including Sugimoto's *A Daughter of the Samurai*, which was originally published in 1925 (fig. 7.11).[52] The version in *When I Was a Girl* was abridged.

Etsu Inagaki Sugimoto had not been brought up to be a gentle butterfly.[53] Born in 1874, six years into Emperor Meiji's reign, in the castle town of Nagaoka in Echigo (today Niigata Prefecture) in the snow country of Japan, she was raised in the same manner Japanese boys generally were and was called Etsu-*bo*—an addition attached to a boy's name—and not as Etsu-*ko*, the ending given a girl's name.

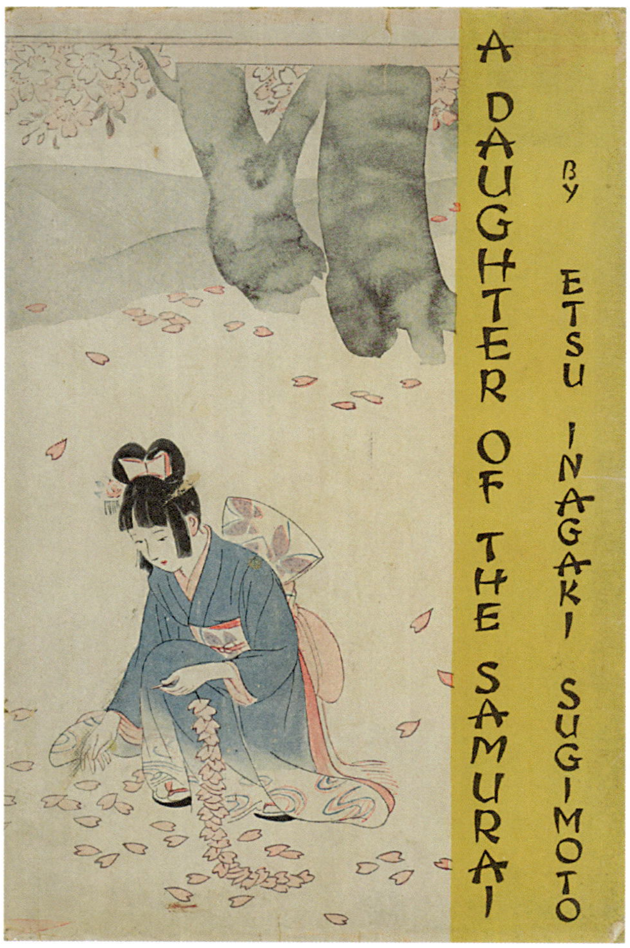

FIGURE 7.11
A Daughter of the Samurai, by Etsu Inagaki Sugimoto, illustrated by Tekisui Ishii. Garden City, NY: Doubleday, Page, 1925.

Although the Inagaki clan had been highly distinguished in feudal times (among the family's precious treasures were gifts by Tokugawa Ieyasu, the first Tokugawa shōgun),[54] its position became precarious after the Restoration. Writes Sugimoto:

> We lived just on the edge of town in a huge, rambling house that had been added to from time to time ever since I can remember. As a result, the heavy thatched roof sagged at the gable joinings, the plaster walls had numerous jogs and patches, and the many rooms of various sizes were connected by narrow, crooked halls that twisted about in a most unexpected manner. . . .
>
> That our home was such a makeshift was the result of one of the tragedies of the Restoration. Echigo Province was one of those that had believed in the dual government. To our people, the Mikado was too sacred to be in touch with war, or even annoying civil matters, and so they fought to uphold the shogun power to which, for generations, their ancestors had been loyal. . . .
>
> Because of certain unusual circumstances, my father was the only executive in power, and thus it was that during the wars of the Restoration he had the responsibility and the duties of the office of daimio.
>
> At the bitterest moment that Nagaoka knew, Echigo found herself on the defeated side. When my mother learned that her husband's cause was lost and he taken prisoner, she sent her household to a place of safety, and then, to prevent the mansion from falling into the hands of the enemy, she with her own hands set fire to it and from the mountain-side watched it burn to the ground.[55]

Once released from prison, Etsu's father built a house on the remains of his family estate. Because "it had always been considered a disgrace for [men of samurai rank] to handle money," he left business affairs to one of his trusted servants and "devoted his life to reading, to memories, and to introducing unwelcome ideas of progressive reform to his less advanced neighbors."[56] Though the family still observed the traditional customs and rituals, it also depended on the income derived from selling its priceless heirlooms to secondhand art dealers for pennies.

Her grandmother wanted free-spirited Etsu to be trained as a priestess, but Etsu's father, to whom she was very close, brought her up according to the teachings of Confucius and the way of the samurai, which stressed duty and courage, loyalty and self-discipline. All the details of young Etsu's life were measured against this code. The daughter of a samurai never cried; her curly hair was straightened in a painful process because "a samurai's daughter should not be willing to resemble a beast;"[57] she learned to sleep in a controlled position because the daughter of a samurai was always prepared; and she also learned to sit motionless during long lessons in an unheated room. At times her mother voiced concern that the harsh discipline might be too punishing for young Etsu. One day, when Etsu's hands were blue from cold, her father, resting his hand on Etsu's shoulder, said to her mother:

> "We must not forget . . . the teaching of a samurai home. The lioness pushes her young over the cliff and watches it climb slowly back from the valley without one sign of pity, though her heart aches for the little creature. So only can it gain strength for its life work."[58]

Yet Etsu's life comprised more than strict discipline. She romped through the fields with her dog (though her conservative grandmother frowned on such behavior); helped the servants take the family's heirlooms out of storage for a thorough airing; and listened to her grandmother tell old myths and legends. On special occasions the servants prepared beautiful and formal meals served on fine lacquered dishes; everyone dressed up in their silk kimono, and precious antique treasures were displayed. The family enjoyed important festivals, including the reenactment of a battle at a shrine dedicated to the Nagaoka *daimios*, Etsu's sister's wedding, and the comforting *o-bon* festival for departed ancestors—which, when she was eleven, included her beloved dog Shiro and her father, who was only in his early thirties when he died.

Etsu found comfort in the Buddhist rites, including the "Enter into Peace" celebration of Buddha's death:

> I went to the temple with Toshi [a servant], carrying as a gift to the priest a lacquer box of little dumplings. They were made in the shapes of all the animals in the world, to represent the mourners at Buddha's death-bed, where all living creatures were present except the cat.[59]

After her father's death, her brother returned from America to take his place, and Etsu was betrothed to a man who had decided to make his life in America. The family council decided that, because of the highly unusual circumstances, Etsu should go to Tokyo for schooling, then join her husband-to-be in America.

Bechtel's book does not include the dramatic final chapters of *A Daughter of the Samurai*, which tell of Etsu's eight-day journey by *jinrikisha*, horseback, *kago*, and train to Tokyo; her four liberating years in a Tokyo missionary school; her journey to the United States, where she married Matsuo Sugimoto who had opened an import company and would die suddenly; and her return to Japan, a widow with two young daughters.

What happened to the Sugimoto family after their return to Japan is recalled by Sugimoto's American-born daughter, Chiyono Sugimoto Kiyooka,[60] in her memoir *But the Ships Are Sailing—Sailing* (1959). It reveals the loyalty of this prominent family to both Japan and the United States and tells of the family's survival after World War II.

Sugimoto wrote a number of other books, including *Daughter of the Narikin* (1932), *A Daughter of the Nohru* (1935), and *Grandmother O Kyo* (1940). Yet *A Daughter of the Samurai* remains her most important and influential work. As Junior Literary Guild editor-in-chief Helen Ferris wrote in 1930, that volume had "done more to further the friendship between Japan and the United States than any other single volume."[61] Despite this achievement, in 1950, the *Los Angeles Times* chose three stinging words to headline Sugimoto's brief obituary:

> Jap Author Dies.
>
> Tokyo, June 21.
>
> Mrs. Etsu Sugimoto, 76, author of "Daughter of the Samurai," died last night at her residence here. She was a lecturer on the cultural history of Japan at Columbia University from 1920 to 1927.[62]

The Story of Yoshitsune

Prince Bantam: Being the Adventures of Yoshitsune the Brave and His Faithful Henchman Great Benkei of the Western Pagoda by May McNeer and Lynd Ward[63] was perhaps Bechtel's most substantive book about Japan (fig. 7.12). After graduating from Columbia University in 1926, Ward, an artist and author, and his journalist wife, May McNeer, sailed for Germany, where Ward studied traditional printmaking for a year at the Leipzig Academy for Graphic Arts. In 1929, during the first week of the stock market crash, Ward published his stark *God's Man*, the first of the five woodcut novels that established his reputation.[64] In all, he illustrated more than one hundred children's books, which included the Newbery award-winning *The Cat Who Went to Heaven* (1930) written by Elizabeth Coatsworth.

Prince Bantam, the first children's book Ward and McNeer produced together, tells the story of Minamoto Yoshitsune, the great romantic Japanese hero, whose life story was first told in the thirteenth-century classic *Heike monogatari* (The Tale of the Heike). He lived during the Heian period (794–1185), the time in which Murasaki Shikibu's eleventh-century *Genji monogatari* (The Tale of Genji) was also set. After Yoshitsune's father, Lord Yoshitomo, was killed in the final

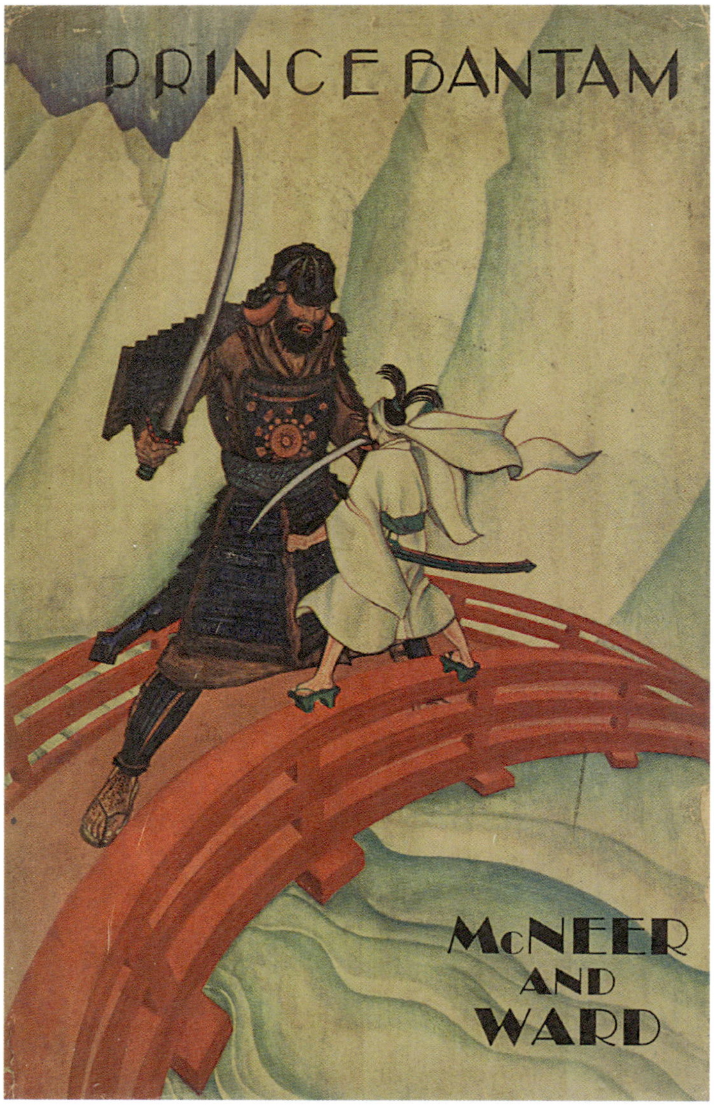

FIGURE 7.12
Prince Bantam: Being the Adventures of Yoshitsune the Brave and His Faithful Henchman Great Benkei of the Western Pagoda, written and illustrated by May McNeer and Lynd Ward. New York: Macmillan, 1929.

struggle between the military clans of the Taira (also called the Heike) and the Minamoto (or Genji), Yoshitsune, who had been brought up and guarded in a monastery, set out on a quest to gather the Minamotos once again and to avenge his father's death. With help from the supernatural King of the Tengus, the young prince studied the way of the sword, lyrically described by McNeer:

> With sudden whirls he practiced the Eight Side Sweep; with flourishes he used the Ten Side Cut, the Body Wheel, the Hanjou Turn, the play called the Wind so swift was it, the Flower Double, peculiarly graceful in its curve; the Roll, and the Blade Drop.[65]

Prince Bantam introduces readers to the lawless warrior-monk Benkei, whose deeds are told in detail, including one of the most famous—his theft of a great bell from the rival monastery of Miidera. With Benkei's help Yoshitsune overcomes grueling obstacles and escapes to northern Japan, where he finds refuge at the castle of one of his father's retainers. Here is how McNeer, evoking a Japanese setting worthy of an Akira Kurosawa film, describes the epic fight when the two heroes first meet:

> Night had darkened the mountains and the river; stars ventured out timidly from behind their daytime cloaks. Benkei tingled all over as he heard again the tones, thin and clear, of a flute. He hastened his steps and soon perceived the youth in white perched comfortably on the rail of the bridge. Benkei rushed at him with a growl as of ten thousand wolves issuing from his throat.
>
> The river flowed like a serpent under the moonlit bridge and the flute voice seemed to blend with that silver radiance. Benkei drew his sword and laid about him with blows that had so often annihilated fifty or a hundred men. The youth, however, laughed again that tantalizing laugh and leapt like a butterfly upon the railing of the bridge, where he stood in his wooden clogs and fought the giant priest.
>
> For hours they fought. Up and down the bridge, first from one side and then from the other; now from the height of the railing, now from the bridge itself, the priest was fiercely attacked. This youth managed his sword with such terrifying speed, and wheeled and advanced so rapidly, that Benkei, who had never been out of breath, now found himself panting wearily. For the first time in his many battles he felt a slight catch in his throat. Perhaps Tomi was right about this bantam fighter. Perhaps it was death he carried in his hand.
>
> "Kill me, master," cried the poor giant in gasps, a huge blur of black on the radiant bridge. "Kill me, but first tell me who is the youth who can conquer Benkei of the Western Pagoda?"
>
> "No, Benkei," said the youth, softly placing his hand on the big man's head, "I need you far too much to kill you. You will be my retainer; you will fight with me under the white banner against the Taira when the time comes. I am Yoshitsune, prince of the Minamotos."
>
> Benkei trembled and a great joy welled up within him. "Where my lord goes," he cried brokenly, "whether to victory or death, I shall follow him."[66]

In the catalog, Bechtel proudly printed excerpts from *Prince Bantam*'s fine reviews: "A tale that unfolds gracefully and beautifully 'Like a long, unwinding silk cocoon,'" wrote Josiah Titzell in *The Three Owls;* "Prince Bantam and his magnificent and excessive giant ally carry the reader straight to old Japan where legend and fact, beauty and humor blend in making this a book to read aloud and relish," stated the *New York Times*. A reviewer unidentified in the catalog called the book "a tale which moves swiftly and at the same time conveys the beauty of the ancient Oriental setting," while a reviewer for the Child Study Association wrote, "The volume itself is a triumph of book making, illustrations and print—the whole format enhances the tale with its rare harmony and artistic quality." May Lamberton Becker praised the "drawings in the Japanese manner."[67]

Ward's expressionistic wood engravings—reminiscent of the graphic style of Fritz Eichenberg, another illustrator of children's books with whom Ward had much in common (both studied in Germany and contributed to the revival of the woodcut tradition)—are underscored by the dramatic art deco typeface, the Chinese-art inspired endpapers, and the black-and-white vignettes and full-page illustrations. Ward wrote that his book was "the irresistible result of a tireless interest in the legends and folkways of Japan and friendship with many Japanese."[68] Choosing Japan's Chinese-inspired art, Ward's interpretation does not quite evoke the lyrical softness and understated emotion of the Heian period's setting.[69]

The Cat Who Went to Heaven

Finally, there was *The Cat Who Went to Heaven* by Bechtel's close friend Elizabeth Coatsworth (1930, fig. 7.13). Of all writers and illustrators of Bechtel's books about Japan, Coatsworth, a graduate of both Vassar and Columbia, was the most traveled. As she described in a memoir, the family might spend winters in California, or go to Paris, Egypt, Sicily or Spain or Morocco. Sometimes they might stay away for a whole year. At one point, they spent some "thirteen months traveling leisurely and according to [their] whims up and down the fabulous coasts of the Far East."[70]

Coatsworth's Far East experiences "colored [her whole] life," as she wrote in her autobiography.[71] She collected and distilled all these impressions and tidbits of information, which would linger "with a thousand other impressions, long in her mind."[72] A Japanese legend she heard in a Kyoto temple; the images of Buddhist temples of Borobodur in Java; a grand *stupa* (Buddhist structure); carvings of the animal rebirths of Buddha;[73] and a print, sent to her by artist Tom Handforth,[74] of a cat coming to mourn the death of the Buddha finally came together in her masterpiece *The Cat Who Went to Heaven* (fig. 7.14).[75] Coatsworth writes:

> Once upon a time, far away in Japan, a poor young artist sat alone in his little house, waiting for his dinner. His housekeeper had gone to market, and he sat

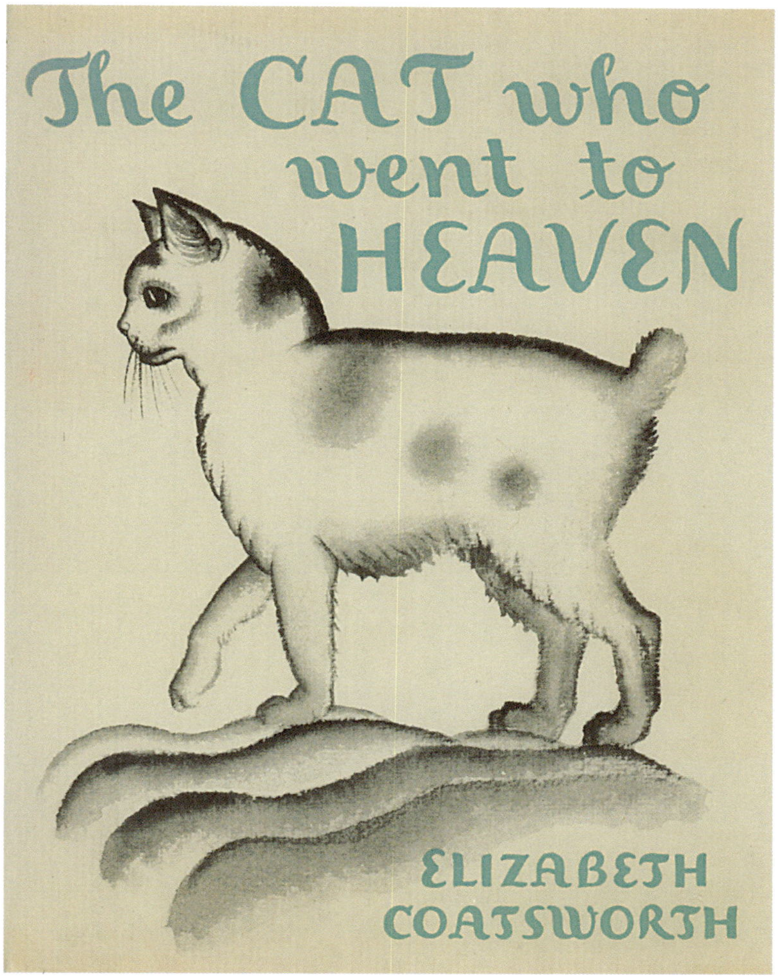

FIGURE 7.13
The Cat Who Went to Heaven, by Elizabeth Coatsworth, illustrated by Lynd Ward. New York: Macmillan, 1930.

sighing to think of all the things he wished she would bring home. He expected her to hurry in at any minute, bowing and opening her little basket to show him how wisely she had spent their few pennies. . . . He was very hungry!

But the housekeeper lingered by the door, and the basket stayed shut. "Come," he cried, "what is in that basket?"

The housekeeper trembled, and held the basket tight in two hands. "It has seemed to me, sir," she said, "that we are very lonely here." Her wrinkled face looked humble and obstinate. . . .

So the old woman put down the basket and opened the lid. Nothing happened for a moment. Then a round, pretty, white head came slowly above the bamboo, and two big yellow eyes looked about the room, and a little white paw appeared on the rim. Suddenly, without moving the basket at all, a little white cat jumped out on the mats, and stood there as a person might stand who hardly knew if she were welcome. Now that the cat was out of the basket, the artist saw that she had yellow and black spots on her sides, a little tail like a rabbit's, and that she did everything daintily.

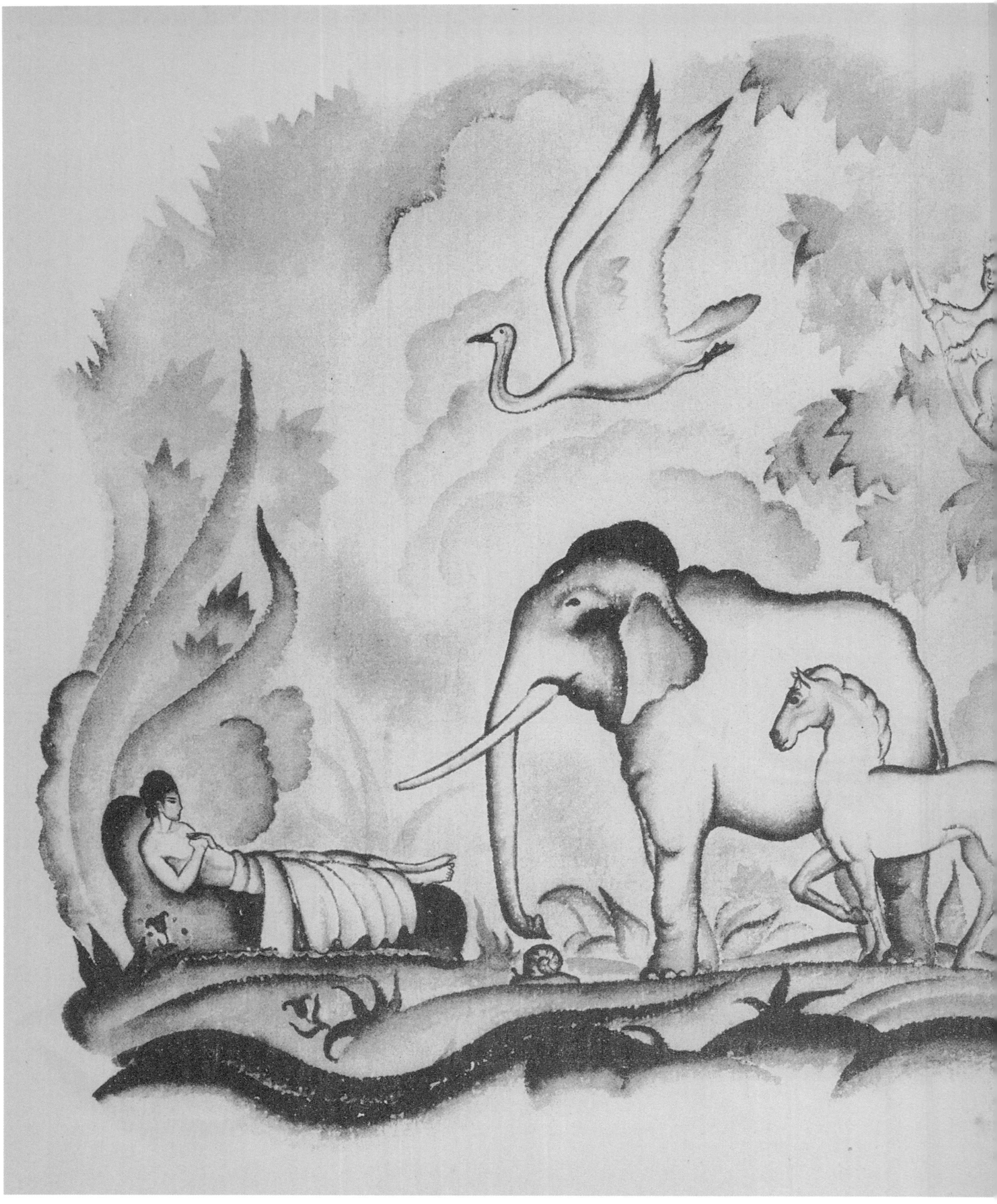

FIGURE 7.14
The Cat Who Went to Heaven, by Elizabeth Coatsworth, page 54.

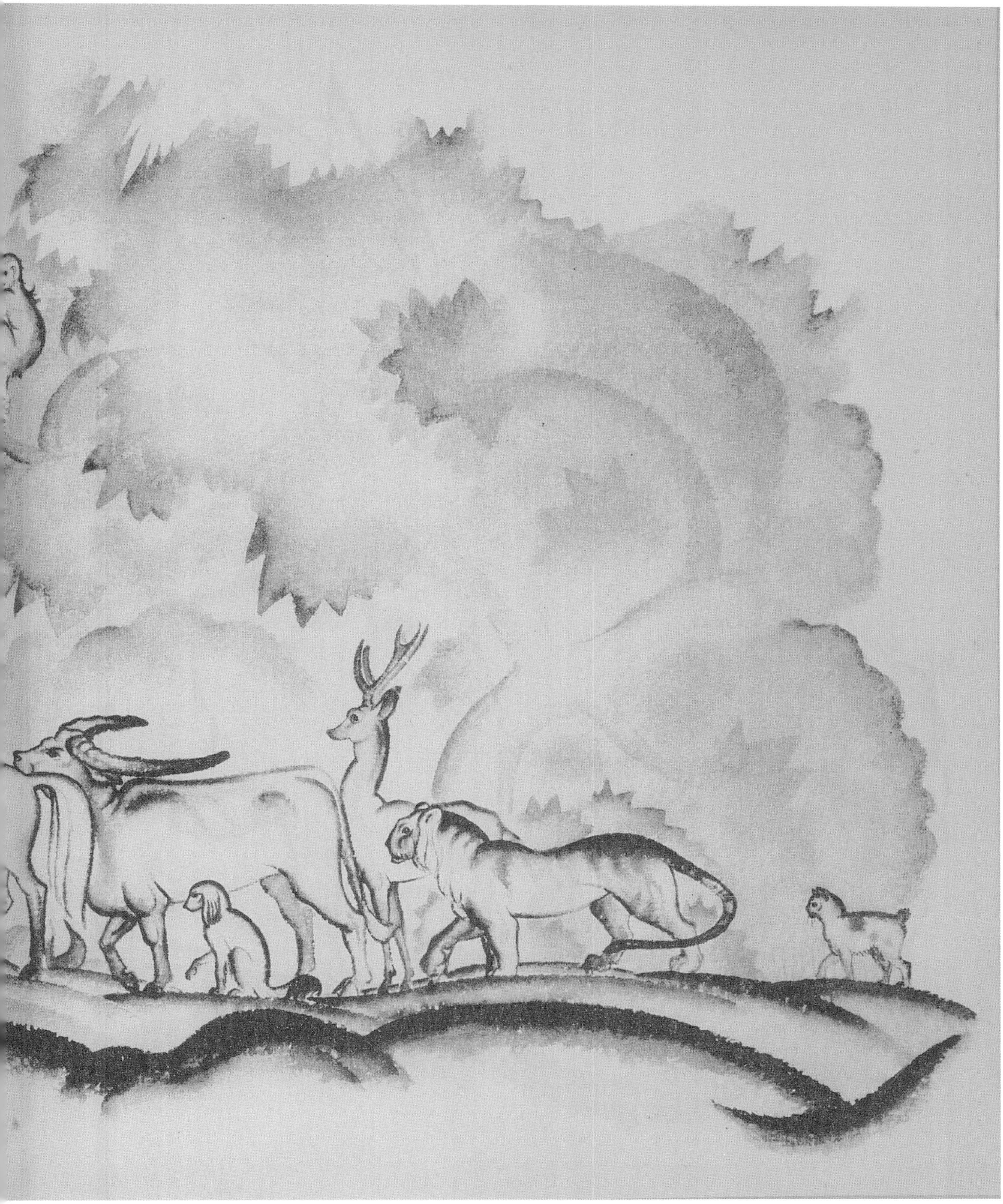

> "Oh, a three-colored cat," said the artist. "Why didn't you say so from the beginning. They are very lucky, I understand."
>
> As soon as the little cat heard him speak so kindly, she walked over to him and bowed her head as though she were saluting him, while the old woman clapped her hands in joy. The artist forgot that he was hungry. He had seen nothing so lovely as their cat for a long time.

They called her Good Fortune.[76]

And so, the artist continued painting pictures that no one wanted to buy, the housekeeper cooked their meager meals, and Good Fortune slept in the sun or looked up at the image of the Buddha in their room.

One day, the local priest came to visit. He asked the artist to make a painting of the death of Buddha for the village temple. For three days, the artist prepared himself for the grave task before him. He put on his best clothes, prayed at the household altar and reflected on the life of Prince Siddhartha, who became the Buddha. The cat sat beside him as if in prayer. The artist also recalled all the paintings he had ever seen of the Buddha's final parting from the Hindu gods of the heavens, his disciples, and the animals. None of the paintings included a cat:

> "Ah, the cat refused homage to Buddha," [the artist] remembered, "and so by her own independent act, only the cat has the doors of Paradise closed in her face."[77]

While Good Fortune was watching, the artist drew the image of the dying Buddha and the animals who came to bid him farewell. He saw Good Fortune's wish in her eyes and added an image of a cat to the animal gathering.

When he had finished the painting, Good Fortune looked at him with gratitude. Then she fell dead, "too happy to live another minute."[78]

The priest did not want to purchase the painting. But, lo, a miracle occurred. The artist sank down to his knees with a cry:

> "Oh, the Compassionate One!" For where the last animal had stood was now only white silk that seemed never to have felt the touch of ink; and the great Buddha, the Buddha whom he had painted reclining with hands folded upon his breast, had stretched out an arm in blessing, and under the holy hand knelt the figure of a tiny cat, with pretty white head bowed in happy adoration.[79]

Lynd Ward created some of his finest illustrations for *The Cat Who Went to Heaven*, depicting majestic animals—including Japan's indigenous, spotted, short-haired bobtail cat—with bold yet lyrical brush strokes, in Japanese ink style. While his images greatly enhanced the book, there is no doubt that the volume's enduring success (by 1958, when it was re-issued in a newly illustrated edition, it had already been reprinted twenty-four times) relied on the tender story of the cat, which, Bechtel acknowledged, was the book's main attraction for young readers.[80] On a deeper level, *The Cat Who Went to Heaven* was also one of the rare stories that introduced young American readers to the life of Siddhartha and the Buddhist legend of the cat that was redeemed.

* * *

Louise Seaman Bechtel entered the American children's book scene at a fortuitous time. The emphasis on library service for children, so passionately pursued by such early children's librarians as Caroline Hewins, was beginning to shift to the publishing of children's books. American children's literature was ready for a surge and for branching out. A new group of women, no less passionate, emerged to become children's book editors at a number of publishing houses. Bechtel had observed children in her previous job and seems to have had an intuitive understanding of what Johann Comenius had already advocated more than two hundred fifty years earlier. Children learn best when knowledge is presented in a playful manner. This would guide her bookmaking.

Self-assured in her taste and talent, she embraced innovative graphic styles, broadened subjects and themes, and created books especially geared to young children. She welcomed the talented artists who were fleeing political developments in Europe, and who were happy to accept work as children's book illustrators. They, in turn, would provide a fresh and international dimension to her list.

Relations between the United States and Japan were strained during the 1920s and 30s, and few children's books about Japan were published during that time. Yet Bechtel was curious about Japan, as she was about other countries. While her early books were conservative and traditional, she would eventually publish more expansive works—including *The Cat Who Went to Heaven*, a book that illustrates the imagination and sensitivities of America's first children's book editor.

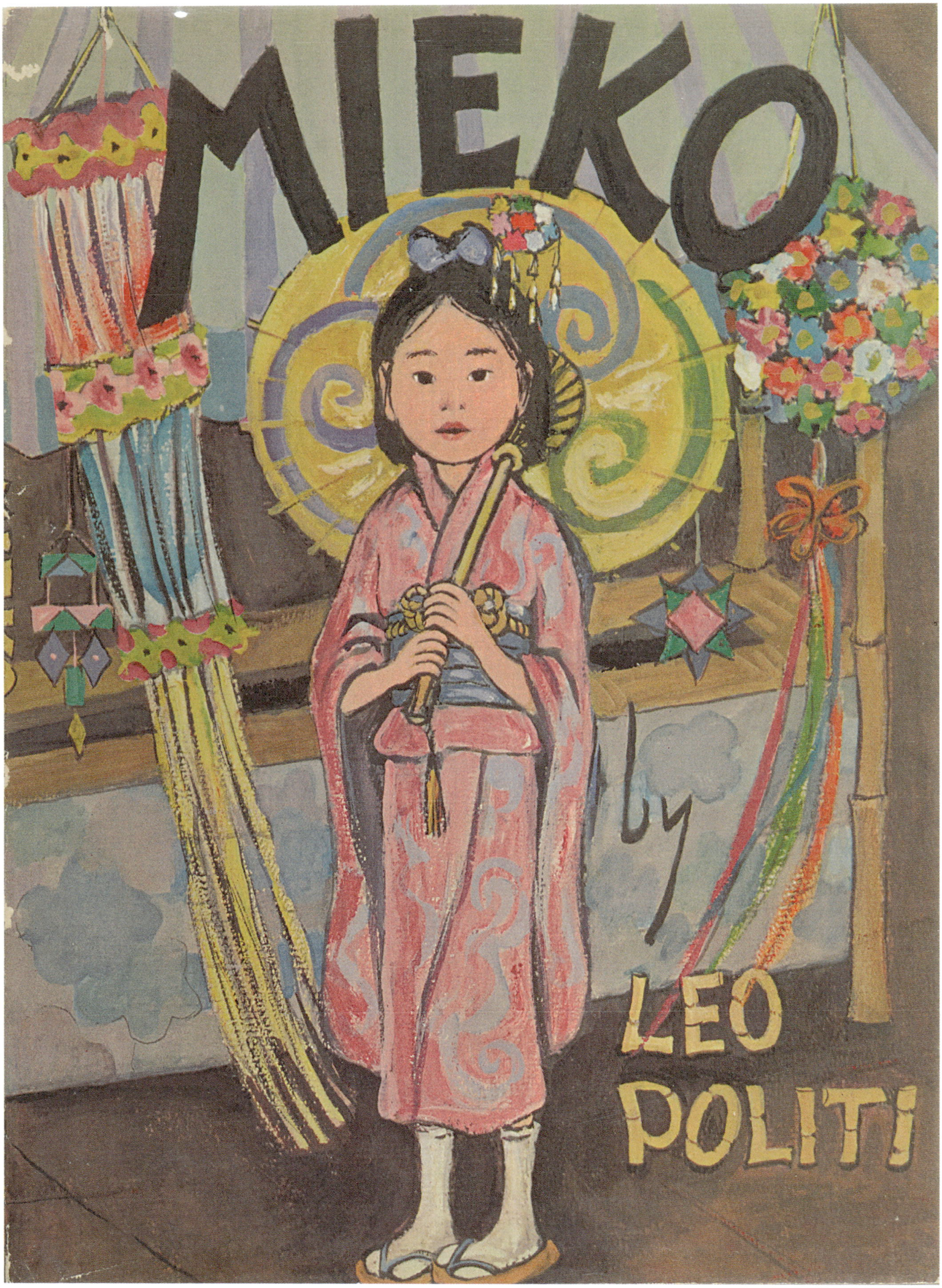
MIEKO
by
LEO
POLITI

8

The Post–World War II Years

On a January day in 1946, the future aide to General MacArthur, William J. Sebald, landed at Atsugi Airfield and described what he saw on his way to Tokyo:

> The once remote highway was alive with American army trucks, jeeps, and cars. Dust from the traffic swirled through the air and coated the thatched roofs. The Japanese people shocked me most. I was surprised by their smallness and lethargy, alongside the tall, well-fed, and vigorous Americans. They were, unmistakably, a beaten people, momentarily despairing and hopeless. Gone were the exuberance and animation of the Japanese crowd—clean and without smell, as Lafcadio Hearn once described it, in the distant past. Instead, on that ride to Yokohama, I saw the sad degeneration of humbled pride. Men and women, who once had preserved the appearance of neatness as a matter of honor, were slovenly, often dirty, mostly ill-dressed. The men no longer cared to hide their

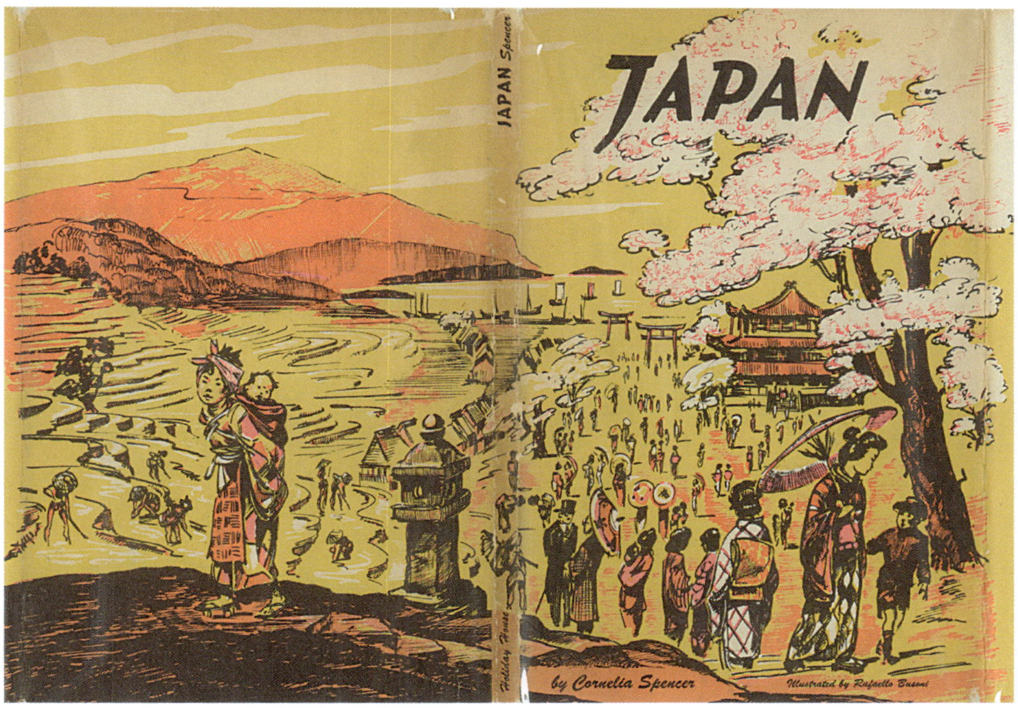

FIGURE 8.1 (OPPOSITE)
Mieko, written and illustrated by Leo Politi. San Carlos, CA: Golden Gate Junior Books, 1969.

FIGURE 8.2
Japan, by Cornelia Spencer, illustrated by Rafaello Busoni. New York: Holiday House, 1948.

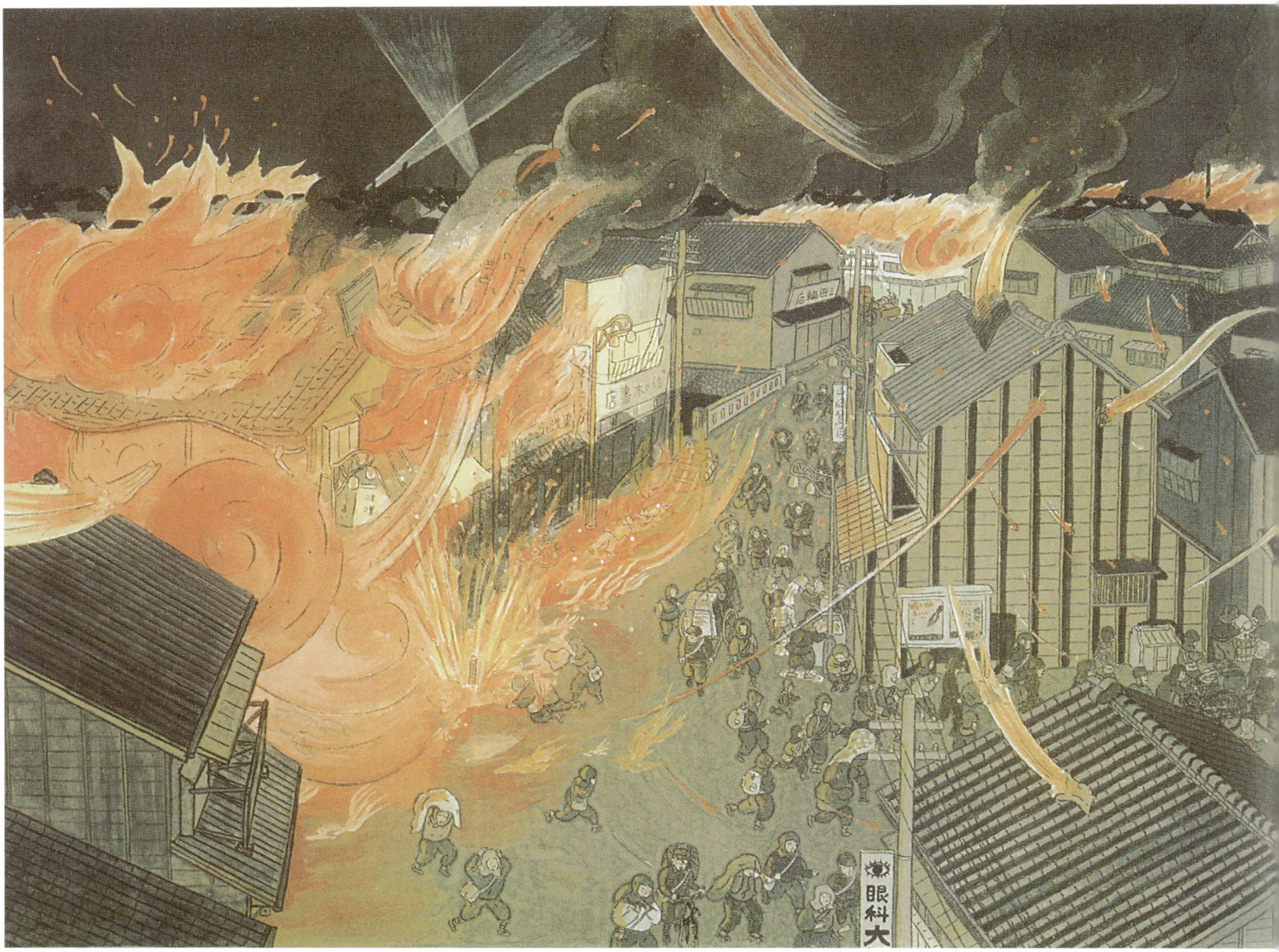

FIGURE 8.3
An Illustrated History of Japan, by Shigeo Nishimura. Rutland, VT: Tuttle, 1987, pages 56–57.

worry, their bewilderment, their depression. The women, less visibly concerned, were shapeless and characterless in their baggy wartime costumes, the practical but uninviting mompei, padded trousers. The fields were ragged, the picturesque thatched roofs, upon closer inspection, needed repairs, and the houses sagged. . . .

The road slipped into the plain containing Yokohama and Tokyo—and we entered the blackened domain of war. I remembered the 15-mile stretch between these two major cities as a tightly packed sweep of houses, factories, and public bathhouses, with scarcely a scrap of empty land. Now it was all a wilderness of rubble. The factories were marked by the locked hands of twisted steel girders. Tall, gaunt chimneys peered over emptiness. Of the wood and paper houses

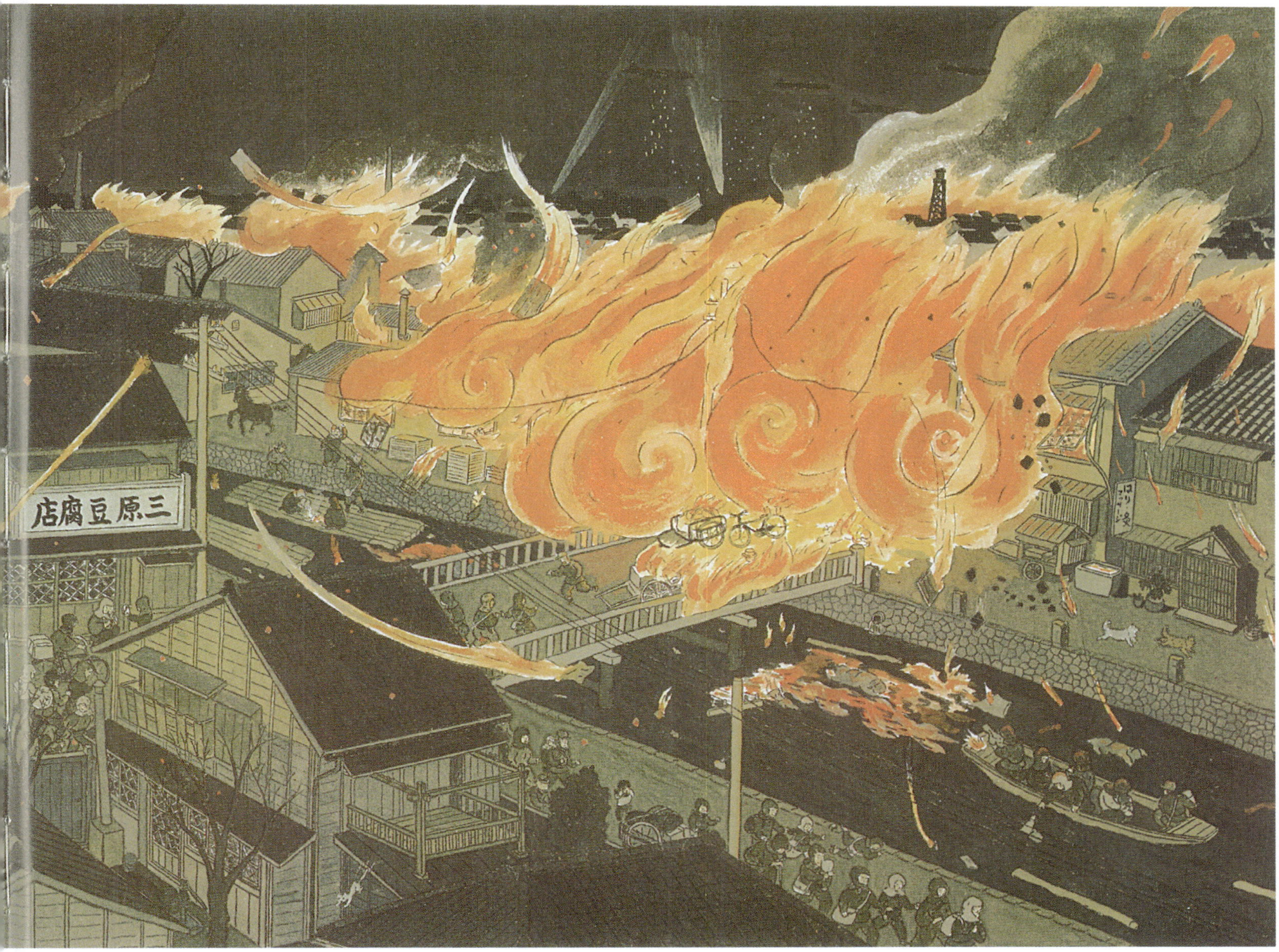

> which had distinguished this predominantly middle-class area, only powdered ash remained. For miles there was no sign of habitation and no sign of life. The fire bombs had scoured the land.[1]

While the meaning of firebombs was eventually shown to American children in books such as Shigeo Nishimura's *An Illustrated History of Japan* (1987, fig. 8.3)[2] and in the sorrowful, animated film *Grave of the Fireflies* (1988),[3] the early postwar children's books about Japan—picture books, books of information, and novels—revealed little of Japanese postwar reality. Yet, perhaps never before had authors of children's books written about Japan with such idealism.

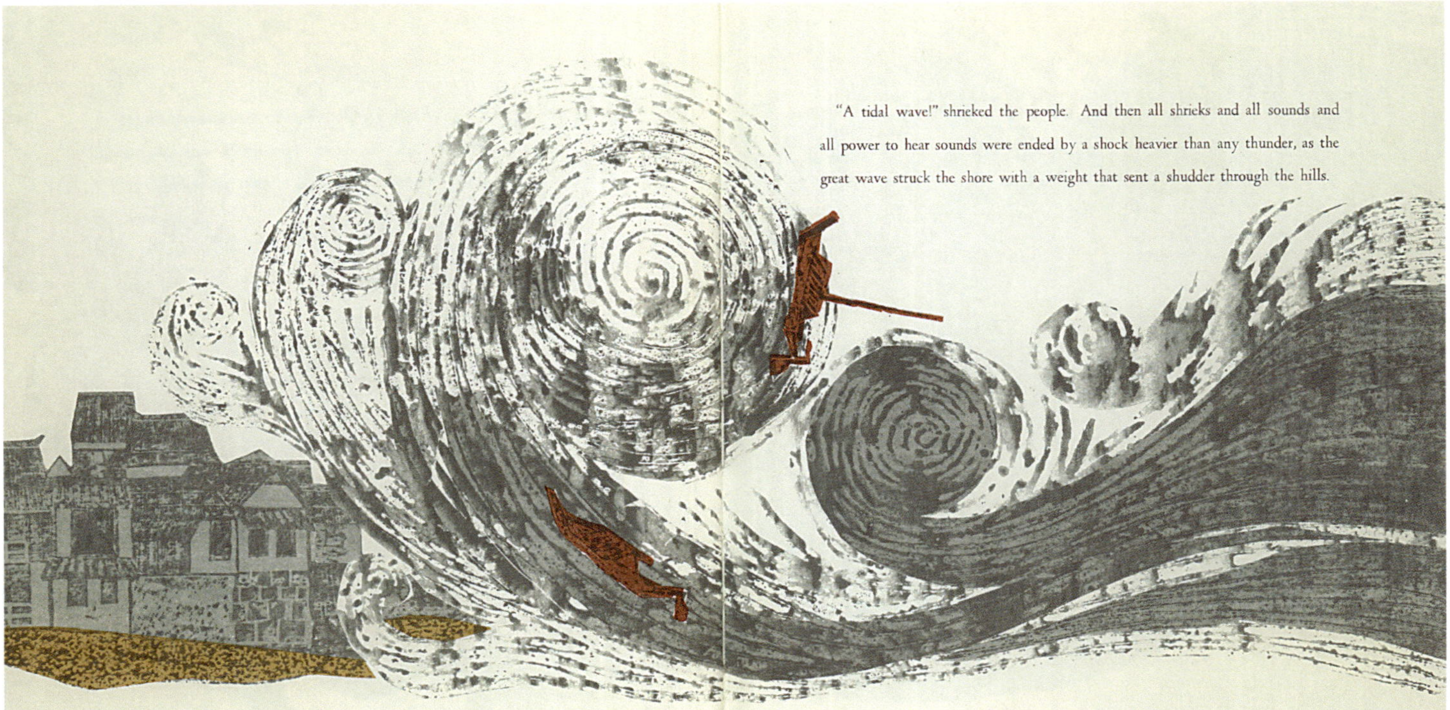

FIGURE 8.4
The Wave, adapted by Margaret Hodges, illustrated by Blair Lent. Boston: Houghton Mifflin, 1964, pages 34–35.

Picture Books about Japan

Innocent, cheerful, and inventive, the picture books of the early post–World War II years stressed Japan's beauty and its past. The early selection included Ryerson Johnson's *Gozo's Wonderful Kite* (1951), a small drama about a mysterious painting by the Japanese master Ogata Korin; *The Animal Frolic* (1954), based on the twelfth-century satirical animal scroll *Choju giga* by Toba Sōjō; Raymond Creekmore's *Fujio* (1951), about a young boy longing to climb Mount Fuji; and Thomas F. M. Adams's *The Adventures of Billie and Belinda in Tokyo* (1953), about two small parakeets, one of whom gets lost (the birds are staying at the Imperial Hotel with their sweet and wealthy owner, Mrs. Cecilia Murgatroyd). Another Adams book, *Adventures of Little Hound Dog and the Great Detective* (1953), takes the reader from the sushi-ya to the tempura-ya, from the unagi-ya to the soba noodle shop. In Eleanor B. Hicks's *Circus Day in Japan* (1953), Joji and his sister Koko get to ride an elephant, while Jeanette P. Brown's *Surprise for Robin* (1956), is the story of an American girl who speaks fluent Japanese and can bow just like her Japanese playmates. Astrid Lindgren's *Noriko-san, Girl of Japan* (1958), shows the idyllic world of a pretty Japanese girl and her equally pretty blond counterpart from Sweden.[4]

In 1952, the *New York Times* initiated its Choice of Best Illustrated Children's Books of the Year, an annual event that would elevate the status of American

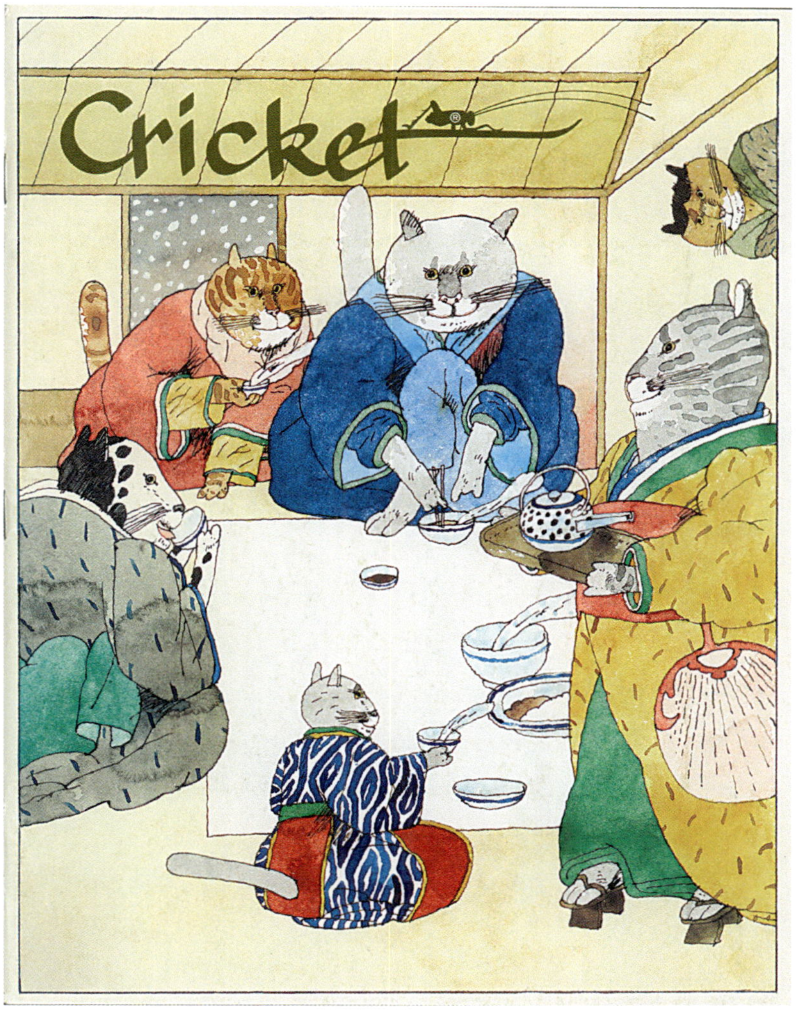

FIGURE 8.5
"Japanese Cats," by Friso Henstra. *Cricket* vol. 23, no. 5 (January 1996).

picture books considerably. Other developments reinforced this new standing. At Weston Woods Studios in Connecticut, Morton Schindel produced the groundbreaking film *The Lively Art of Picture Books* (1964) and began transforming picture books into "iconographic" filmstrips which were viewed by young children in public and school libraries all over America. In 1973 Marianne Carus established *Cricket*, an illustrated magazine that, in the words of *St. Nicholas* magazine editor Mary Mapes Dodge—whose work Carus had studied carefully—aimed not only to "inspire children with an appreciation of fine pictorial art," but to "introduce basic values of our own and . . . other cultures throughout the world."[5]

Illustrators responded to the challenge, creating picture books diverse in graphic styles, imaginative stories, and themes. Maurice Sendak's *Where the Wild Things Are* (1963), about Max who becomes king of the monster-things, and Eric Carle's *The Very Hungry Caterpillar* (1969), about a multi-legged creature that eats its way through the days of the week, became the most iconic.

Japan seems to have been a favorite subject during this picture book renaissance. Writers and illustrators, many of whom had by now visited Japan, participated in what felt like a celebration. The war did not seem part of the story. *A Thousand and One Buddhas* (1967) by Louise and Richard Floethe is the tranquil tale of the twelfth-century emperor Go-Shirakawa, who built the Sanjusangendo Temple in Kyoto. In *Noriko, Her Life in Japan* (1963), Dominique Darbois introduced, in black-and-white photographs, a serenely beautiful girl from Kyoto. Dressed in luxurious kimono, the young girl plays the traditional *shamisen* and *koto*; displays her exquisite set of emperor and empress dolls; learns how to make a perfect flower arrangement; and engages in other traditional activities of a privileged Japanese girlhood. Betty Jean Lifton's *Taka-chan and I: A Dog's Journey to Japan* (1967), interpreted with images by the renowned photographer Eikoh Hosoe, is the fanciful tale of a Weimaraner who digs a tunnel from Cape Cod to Japan. *A Child's Life in Japan* (1963, fig. 8.6), a set of twelve cards meant to be used in a small portable theater, included, on the New Year's card, a scene of little girls in colorful kimono playing the traditional battledore and shuttlecock in front of their fairy-tale thatch-roofed houses.[6]

There seemed no end to the picture book parade about Japan. Illustrations in *Magic Animals of Japan* by Davis Pratt and Elsa Kula (1967), an album of

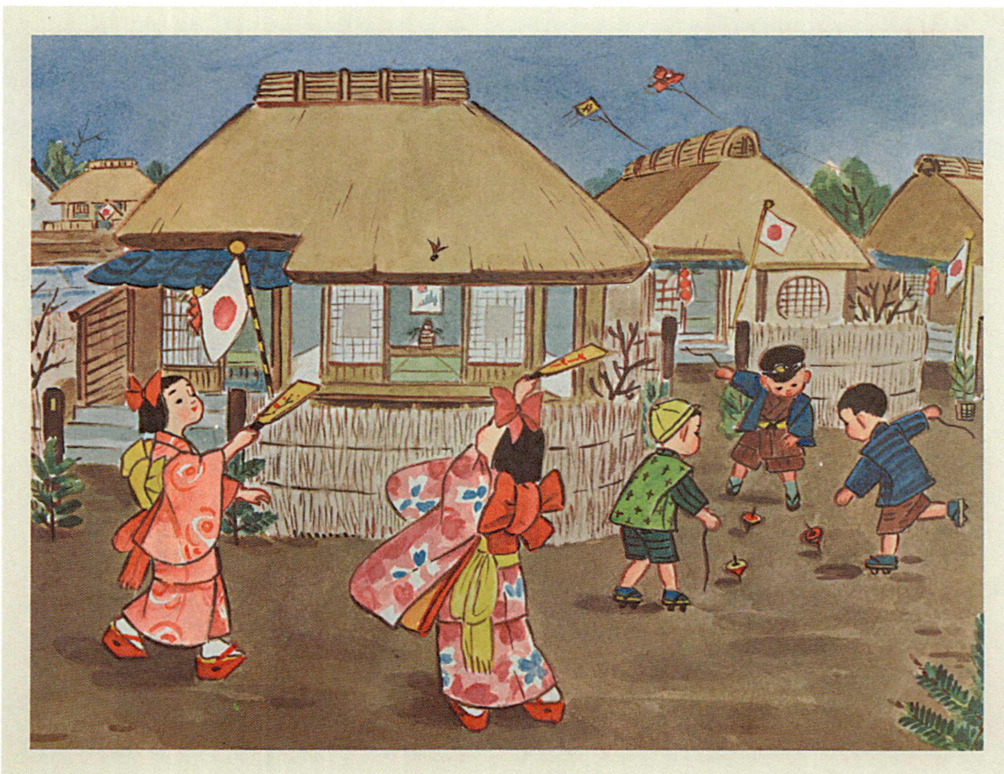

FIGURE 8.6
"New Year Sports," in *A Child's Life in Japan, People of Other Lands* [one of 12 prints]. Salt Lake City: Wheelwright Lithographing Co., 1963.

twelve animal legends, were a creative blend of individualistic designs and Japanese-style woodcuts. In *The Wave* (1964, fig. 8.4), Margaret Hodges retells the age-old legend—first introduced to Western readers in Lafcadio Hearn's *Gleanings in Buddha-Fields*—of the old man who saved local villagers from a tidal wave (see chapter 1). In *The Funny Little Woman* (1972), Arlene Mosel retells the story of the old woman who is captured by wicked *oni* goblins when she descends into their underground realm. Other stories from this time were Louis Slobodkin's *Yasu and the Strangers* (1965), the author's autobiographical reminiscence about a small boy who gets lost on a field trip to the Tōdai-ji temple in Nara. There was also Betty Jean Lifton's picture book, *Chirps from a Bamboo Cage* (1954), a satire about postwar Japanese husband-and-wife relationships, and Leo Politi's *Mieko* (1969, fig. 8.1), the tender story of a Japanese girl who dreams of becoming queen at the Japanese-American festival in Little Tokyo in Los Angeles.[7]

Religious presses as well published a number of picture books about Japan, among them the artful *Japan* (1946), part of the *Our World Travel Scenes*; *Japan* (1948), part of the *Cut 'n' Fold* series; *Japan, A Missionary Color Book for Children* (1948); and *A Coloring Book of Japan* (1971), which featured famous art images, including one of the legendary Prince Shotoku.

The array of books about Japan created for young Americans was further enhanced with books by Japan's own fine postwar picture bookmakers. Translated into English were *Onriku and the Carpenter* (1963), Tadashi Matsui's retelling of the tale of a carpenter who outsmarts an ogre, illustrated by Suekichi Akaba,[8] and *Issun Boshi, the Inchling: An Old Tale of Japan* (1967), retold by Momoko Ishii and illustrated by Fuku Akino. Other traditional tales included *The Crane Maiden* (1968), retold by Miyoko Matsutani and illustrated by Chihiro Iwasaki, about a mysterious maiden who is disguised as a crane; and *How the Withered Trees Blossomed* (1971), also retold by Miyoko Matsutani, with pictures by Yasuo Segawa, about a poor man and his wife who overcome their neighbor's cruelty.[9]

A New Magazine for Children

Silver Bells, the handsomely illustrated magazine for the youngest readers, was part of the postwar picture book parade (fig. 8.7). The American side of the story began with Charles E. Tuttle, who arrived in Japan in 1945 and was assigned to the staff of General Douglas MacArthur, the Supreme Commander for Allied

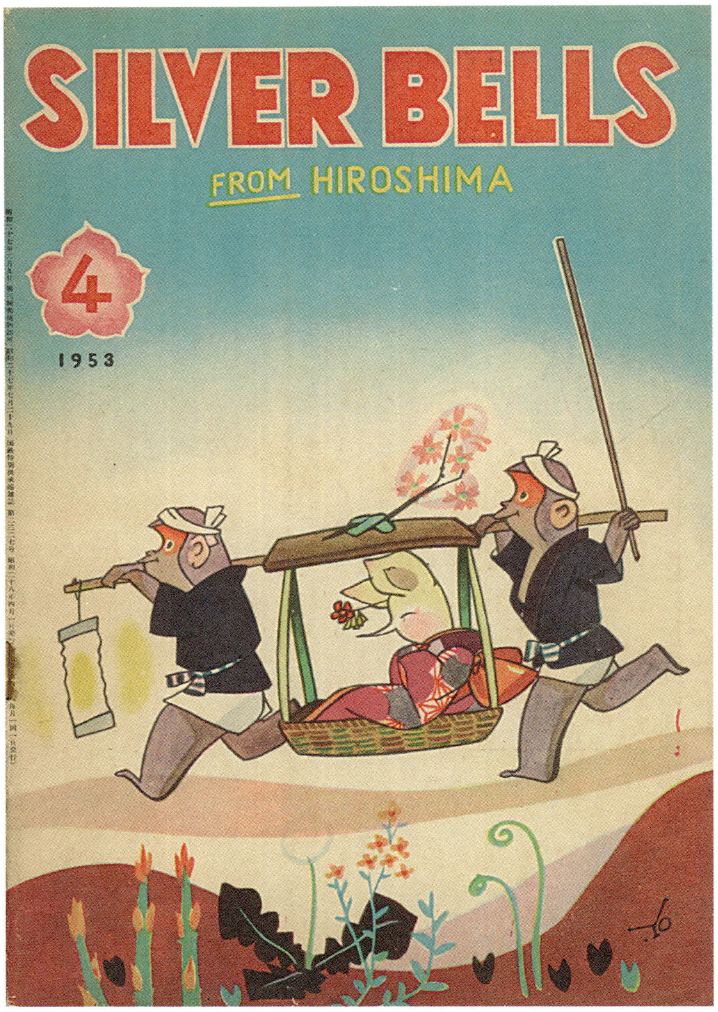

FIGURE 8.7
"Silver Bells from Hiroshima," by Yoshio Hayashi. *Silver Bells* vol. 2, no. 4 (April 1953).

Powers (SCAP). After his discharge from the Army, Tuttle decided not to return to his family's antiquarian book business in Rutland, Vermont. Instead, in 1948, among "the first to receive a business license from SCAP,"[10] he established a branch of the Tuttle Company in Tokyo and, the following year, opened his first book shop in the Takashimaya department store. He also established a publishing house. His impressive early publications included *The Best of Old Japan* (1951, fig. 8.8) by the photographer Francis Haar; *The Arts of Japan: An Illustrated History* (1957) and *The Folk Arts of Japan* (1958), both by Hugo Munsterberg; *The Hokusai Sketchbooks: Selections from the Manga* (1958); *Japanese Prints: From the Early Masters to the Modern* (1959) by James A. Michener; and *Modern Japanese Prints: An Art Reborn* (1959) by Oliver Statler. He also published such popular books as *Babysan: A Private Look at the American Occupation* (1953) by Bill Hume, as well as translations of Japanese novels, books on karate and flower arranging, and children's books.[11]

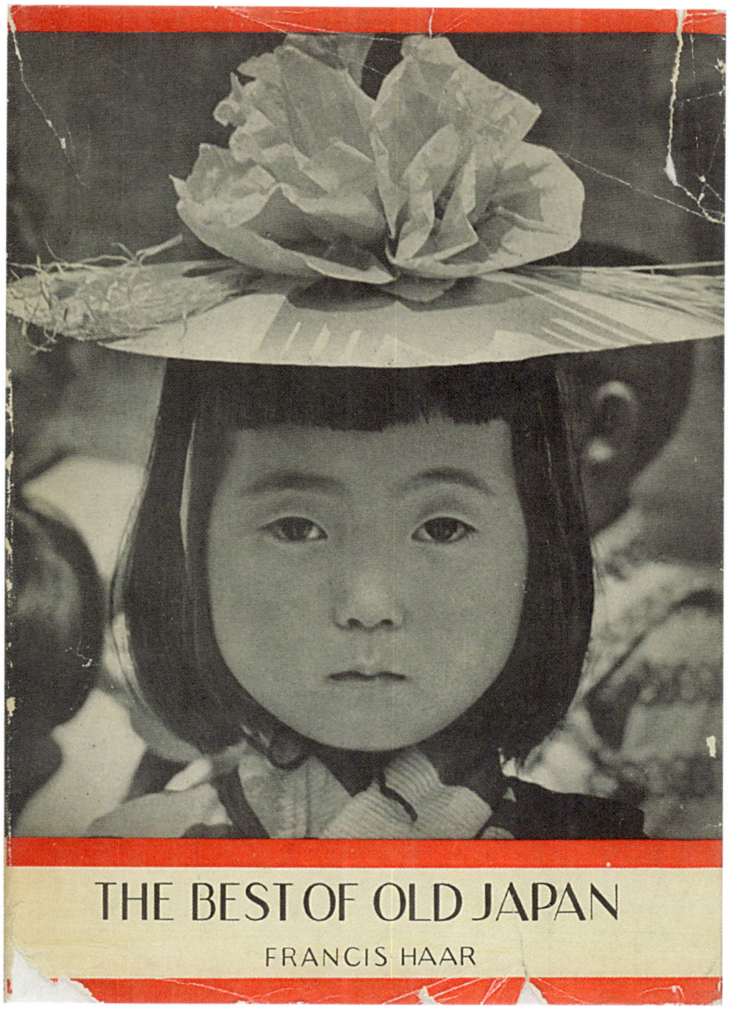

FIGURE 8.8
The Best of Old Japan, by Francis Haar. Rutland, VT: Charles E. Tuttle, 1951.

Tuttle's most intriguing publication was the children's magazine *Silver Bells*. This was an English-language edition of the Japanese children's magazine *Gin no suzu* (Silver Bells) created by Tomikazu Matsui, whose life would be dramatically changed by the bomb:

> In Hiroshima, a few minutes past eight on the morning of August 6, 1945, 37-year-old Tomikazu Matsui, owner of the largest printing company in town, was bicycling past a big wooden building on his way to his office. At that moment the bomb burst. The building collapsed, spilled into the street. Matsui was buried in the wreckage. His arm was broken and his head deeply gashed, but he managed to crawl from the wreckage.[12]

Returning to the area a few days later, Matsui came across a scene that caused him to take action. There in the rubble, surrounded by his pupils squatting on the ground, a teacher was writing his lesson on a broken piece of slate. Right then and there, Matsui decided that his company would no longer print such things as Greater East Asia Co-Prosperity Sphere bonds, as it did before the bomb, but that he would print books, especially books for children. He also began organizing bookmobiles, music festivals, and art competitions and—despite the SCAP-enforced censorship of "newspapers, radio scripts, films, plays, records, books, magazines, pamphlets, and even *kamishibai*"[13] (picture theatre for children)—Matsui launched *Gin no suzu* in 1946. It would be devoted to entertaining and educating Japan's children and teaching them about democracy and the world.

Matsui hired Florence Sakade to serve as the editor; her brother Rinkichi would join the company later.[14] Born in 1917, Florence Sakade had lived in Canada since the age of six, returned to Japan to complete her college education, and settled in Hiroshima after living in Manchuria and having been detained in Korea for a year. During one of her visits to the Civil and Education Section of General Headquarters in Tokyo, Sakade met Charles Tuttle, who would soon arrange shipments of educational materials from the United States for her.[15] In 1952, the year Tuttle married the beautiful Reiko Shiba, he began publishing an English edition of *Gin no suzu*, which, Sakade proudly noted, was the first Japanese children's magazine translated into English.[16] Tuttle was also assisted by some of his talented compatriots, including Meredith Weatherby, who would later found Weatherhill, producer of glorious books about Japan; and Donald Richie, who would live in Japan for more than sixty years, writing about its history and culture. Sakade, who became one of Tuttle's "most loyal employees,"[17] was not only responsible for the content of the magazine and "for much of Tuttle's early success,"[18] but, more importantly, it was she who articulated the magazine's idealistic spirit.[19] In an early issue of *Silver Bells* she wrote:

> The Japanese edition of the magazine has always included many stories with an American background—in the belief that a child who has been given a feeling of sympathy for the children of another country is on the way to becoming a true world citizen—[in this English-language edition] those stories have been chosen with Japanese backgrounds which will at the same time both give the American child a sense of identity with Japanese children and also explain some of the different customs.[20]

Silver Bells was illustrated by Japanese artists, some of whom were already well known before the war and had contributed to children's magazines like *Kodomo no kuni* and *Kinder Book*. Among them were Yoshio Hayashi, Yoshio Nakanashi, Noboru Murakami, and Yoshisuke Kurosaki.[21] While a *New York Times* review applauded *Silver Bells*'s illustrations as "extraordinarily varied," with the best of them "stem[ming] from the traditional style," the reviewer also noted that other illustrations were "gaudily occidentalized . . . in some cases [displaying] a distressing touch of Disney."[22]

Silver Bells featured Japanese folktales and Western nursery tales, serialized fiction, animal and nature stories, and articles about school activities, festivals, and the outdoors. There was a feature titled "Questions and Answers" that considered questions such as Why do Japanese wear facemasks? Are there any whales in Japan? and What is *kamishibai* (fig. 8.9)? The magazine also included poems and songs, crafts, picture dictionaries, coloring pages, and comic strips. The editor published photographs and pictures submitted by Japanese children and encouraged American readers to send their pictures as well.

The full-color fold-out pages, which, as Sakade noted, had been added to the English edition, were the most handsome. Conveying the beauty and richness

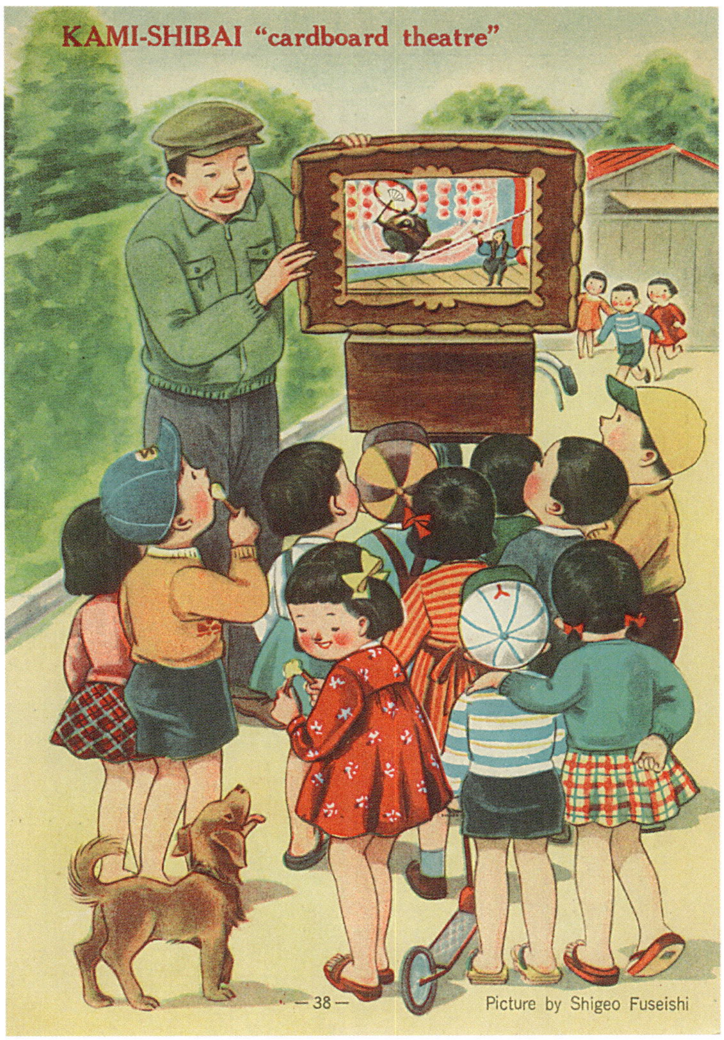

FIGURE 8.9
"A Kamishibai Performance," by Shigeo Fuseishi. *Silver Bells* vol. 2, no. 4 (April 1953): 5.

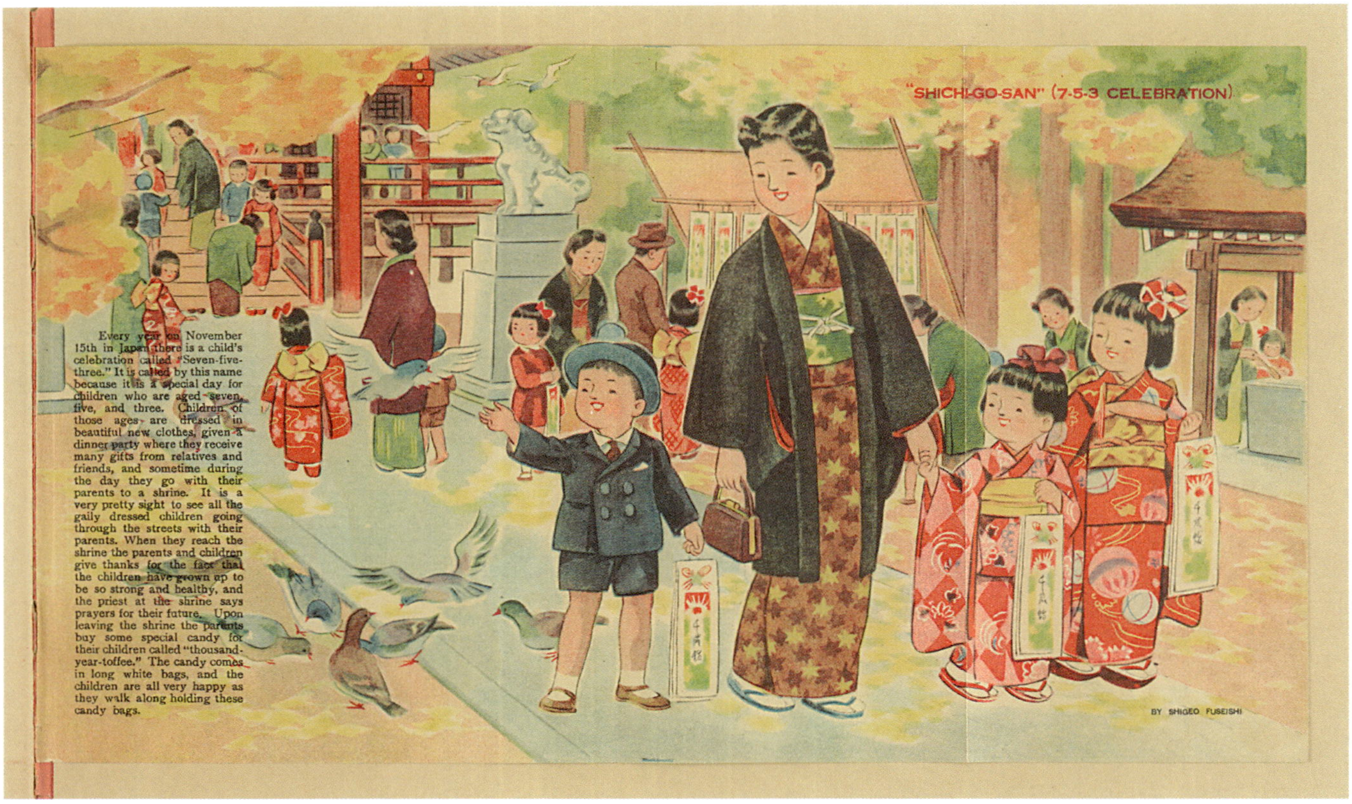

FIGURE 8.10
"*Shichi-go-san* (7-5-3 celebration)," by Shigeo Fuseishi. *Silver Bells* vol. 1, no. 11 (November 1952): 42.

of traditional Japanese home and child life—undisturbed by war and defeat—they included an idyllic scene with children and grandmother sitting around the *kotatsu* (table with a heating element); a springtime picnic; sidewalk shops on a summer evening; making *mochi* (rice cakes) for the New Year's celebration; and preparing for the doll's day festival. A particularly striking fold-out page depicted the celebration of *Shichi-go-san*, a festival for three- and seven-year-old girls and three- and five-year-old boys, showing an elegant mother in a lovely kimono and permed hair accompanying rosy-cheeked children to the shrine (fig. 8.10). Other fold-out pages portrayed an autumn festival with boys showing off their sumo wrestling skills; the *kamishibai* man; and yet another stylish mother sending her children off to school.[23]

Subscriptions to *Silver Bells* were sold in some ten countries, including the United States, Canada, the United Kingdom, and the Philippines. The magazine was not, however, sold in Japan, even though, according to Masami Tsugawa, a managing director at the time, "complimentary copies were sent to pro-Japanese people living in Japan."[24] Although *Silver Bells* ceased publication with the June 1955 issue ("undoubtedly," wrote Donald Richie, because "it had failed to show a profit"),[25] Tuttle continued publishing an array of children's books, among them the cheerful *Japanese Children's Stories from Silver Bells* (1952).[26]

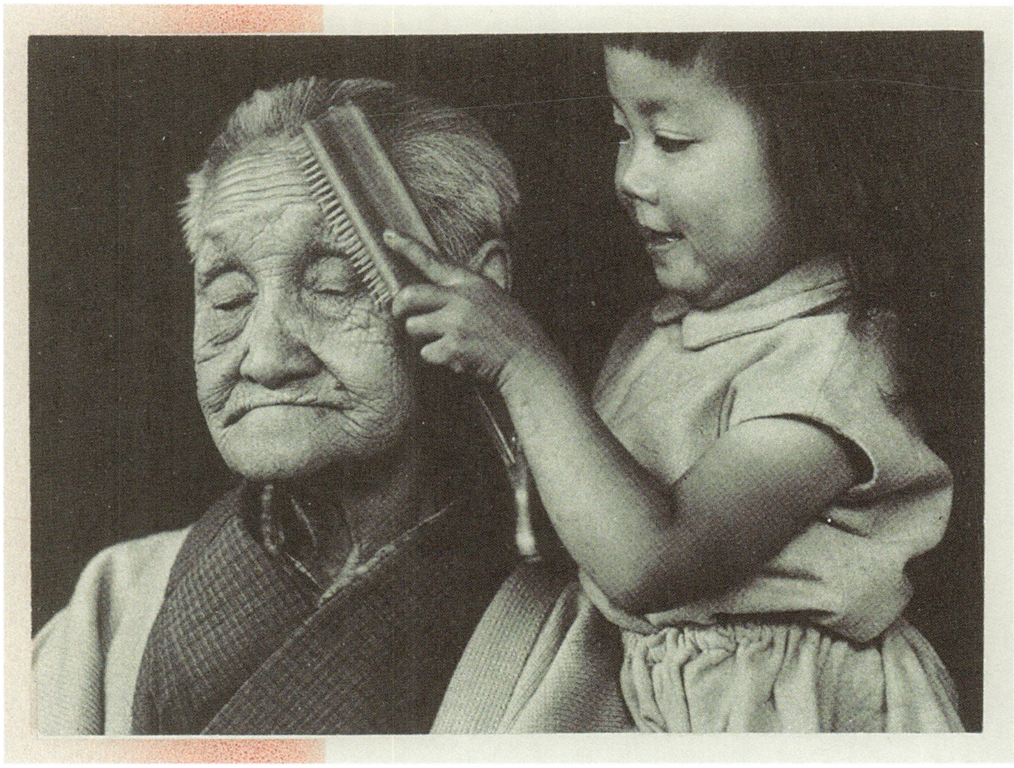

FIGURE 8.11
"I can make you pretty, grandma!" in *Children of the Sun*, by William and Patricia Clark, illustrated by Phyllis Brannen. Rutland, VT: Charles E. Tuttle, 1965, page 40.

Informational Books about Japan

Though picture books about Japan were the stars of the post–World War II period, they were complemented by a number of informational books. Thoughtful and earnest, they were remarkable as well, due in part to the authors' knowledge about Japan (a number of them had also written adult books about Japan) and their seemingly genuine sympathy for their subject. Interpreting Japanese life and history for young American readers, they seemed to look forward while avoiding the war and its devastation. The handsomely illustrated *Golden Encyclopedia* (1946), for example, introduces Japan with this paragraph—a year after the end of the war:

> Japan is . . . a country of Asia. On small islands off the coast of China the Japanese live very much like the Chinese in some ways, very unlike them in others. They belong to the yellow race, write somewhat like the Chinese, eat rice, wear silk, make 'china,' and paint on silk and paper. They sent students to other countries to study science and industry, and made remarkable progress in a short time. However, warlike leaders then led Japan into World War II. Defeated, the Japanese now work toward a new life of peaceful progress.[27]

The Golden Geography: A Child's Introduction to the World (1952, fig. 8.12) is profusely illustrated as well, including pictures of fishermen hauling in their nets,

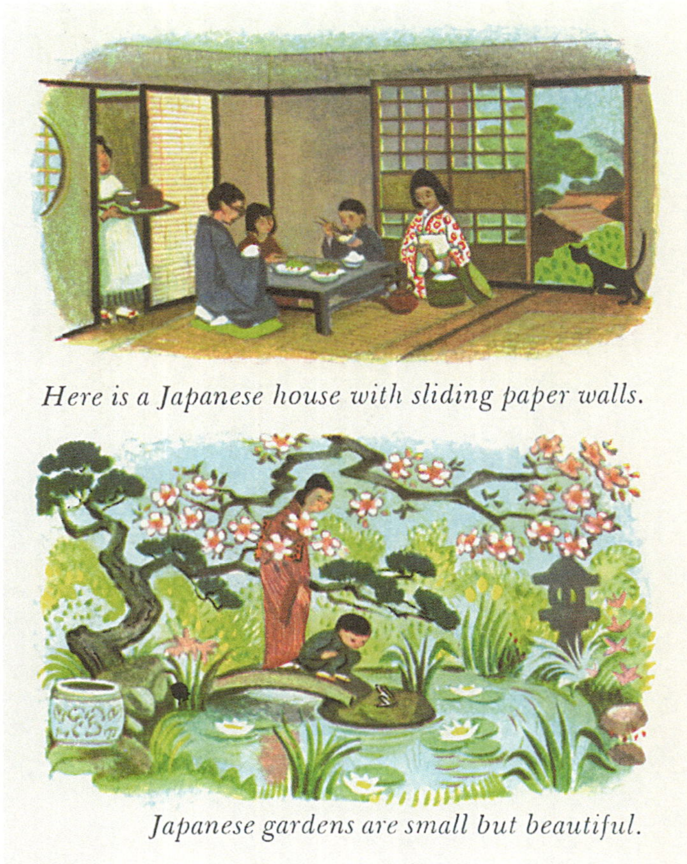

FIGURE 8.12
The Golden Geography: A Child's Introduction to the World, by Jane Werner Watson, illustrated by Cornelius DeWitt. New York: Simon and Schuster, 1952, page 29.

a family enjoying a meal served by a maid, and children in a Japanese garden.[28] Like the *Golden Encyclopedia*, it barely mentions the war. It also identifies the Japanese as part of the "yellow race, like the people of China," and notes that they "have built factories and schools and have sent some of their young people abroad to others countries to learn modern ways of living."[29]

American writers of these early postwar informational books displayed a remarkable sense of fairness and goodwill. John C. Caldwell, author of *Let's Visit Japan,* (1959) writes:

> Let's remember that at the end of the war, Japan was a ruined country. It has been an accomplishment to rebuild so fast. In less than fifteen years the country has completely recovered from the war.[30]

Sympathetic to Japan, the author continues:

> [Japan's] problem is now related to the problem of trade and the need to feed the growing population. We know that it was in part because Japan was so crowded that she went to war four times in less than fifty years. . . . But we must also realize that it was the ambition of some of the Japanese military leaders which led her into war and conquest.[31]

Lily Edelman's *Japan in Story and Pictures* (1953)—illustrated by black-and-white photographs, some by noted photographers—emphasized Japan's progress. There are cars and buses on the Ginza, stylish couples gliding along in a train, a grandmother hanging daikon radishes out to dry, and boys flying their kites. In one of the few allusions to the war the author writes:

> During the war, after their homes were bombed, many families were forced to live in lean-tos built out of sheets of rusty tin. To lighten their misery most people cleared the rubble to make room for a bit of a garden in back of their shanties.[32]

Helen Mears, author of *Year of the Wild Boar: An American Woman in Japan* (1942), who had lived in Japan in the mid-1930s, returned in 1946 as an adviser to the Occupation Command. Her children's book, *The First Book of Japan* (1953, fig. 8.13), reviewed as an "appealing informal study of Japan . . . whose two-color drawings complement the history, geography and customs discussed,"[33] tells the story of Ichiro and Toshiko Matsumoto and their traditional, upper-class family life undisturbed by war. Young Americans learn about the children's home and tiny garden, the way they dress, sleep, take a bath, eat, and play. Toshiko learns how to arrange flowers, while a maid helps their mother serve tea; both brother and sister learn the Japanese way of politeness:

> The Japanese are very polite and are sometimes surprised by our informal American manners. Their good manners are sensible, too. If you visit Toshiko

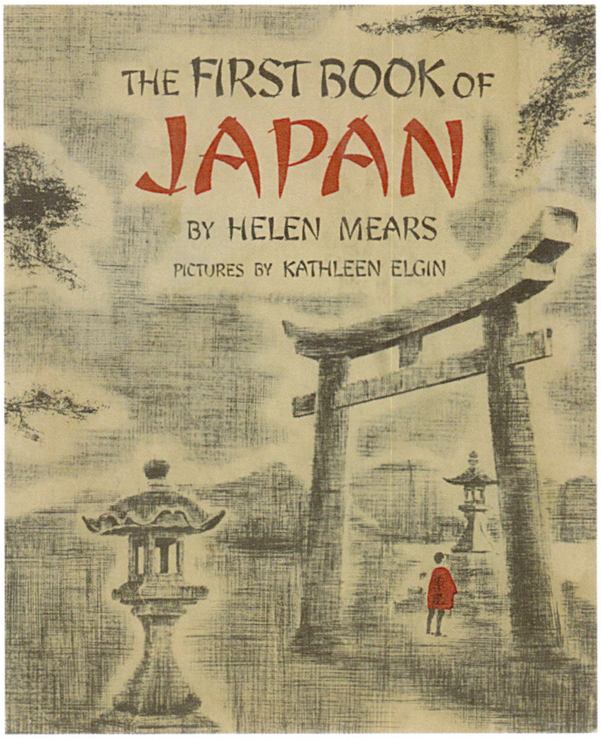

FIGURE 8.13
The First Book of Japan, by Helen Mears, illustrated by Kathleen Elgin. New York: Watts, 1953.

> for a few days you will see why. A whole family couldn't possibly live together happily in the Matsumoto's small house unless the members were polite to each other.[34]

After presenting numerous other subjects, including sports and theater, the Japanese writing system, religion, festivals, and holidays, Mears ends with an expansive view of modern Japan:

> Modern Japan developed as a result of reopening the doors to the West. During the second half of the nineteenth century the Japanese followed Western advice and guidance. They changed their government, their school system, their system of law, their army and other institutions, as well as many of their ways of life, to fit in with Western ideas. The Japanese learned about trains and electricity and machines and large factories. They learned about political parties and voting in elections. They learned how to build warships.
>
> So there grew up a new Japan, a modern nation, with a modern capital in Tokyo. In fifty years, the number of people living in Japan doubled. There were neither land nor resources enough to feed them or give them jobs. This modern Japan supported its people by trading with foreign countries. Like the Western nations before it, Japan began to spread out—into other Pacific islands, and into Korea, China, and Manchuria, in northern China.
>
> During its early years of spreading out, the Western nations sided with Japan. After 1931, however, when the Japanese began to control Manchuria, the Western nations were against Japan. This disagreement led to others. Finally it led to war between some of the Western powers and Japan—a part of World War II.
>
> With Japan's defeat in 1945, all of its lands outside the four home islands with the neighboring islets were taken away. Now Japan once again has the same area it had when Commodore Perry "opened the door." At that time, however, there were only 33 million Japanese living in the islands. Today there are 85 million.
>
> When Japan surrendered in 1945, the Western powers sent an Army of Occupation, commanded by Americans, which destroyed the military weapons of Japan, disbanded their armed forces, and helped the Japanese make many changes in their ways of living. The Occupation officially ended when the President of the United States signed the Treaty of Peace on April 28, 1952. By another treaty, Japan granted the United States the right to occupy military bases in and around the country and to keep troops there. . . .[35]
>
> But during the war most of their ships were sunk. Their cities and factories were badly damaged by bombs and fire. At the end of the war most of their industries had stopped working. The Japanese have found it hard to rebuild their cities and factories because even before they could begin they had to buy many materials from abroad.[36]

In *Year of the Wild Boar,* Mears wrote that "the lessons of Pearl Harbor would seem that today the world has grown so small that no nation, no matter how powerful or relatively isolated, can remain aloof from the world movements. In such a world it is not enough to hate aggressors; but it is necessary also to understand them."[37] She ends *The First Book of Japan* on the same high note:

> The Japanese cannot solve their problems alone. They must be able to trade freely about the world. They must be able to settle in countries with more space. These are difficult matters which all the nations of the world, working together, can help Japan to solve, just as she can help other nations, too.[38]

John C. Caldwell, in *Let's Visit Japan* (1959), presents another view of Japan's role in the war:

> For a time it appeared that Japan would be able to defeat the United States. Japanese war planes were faster than America's planes; her battleships were big and fast. The Japanese soldiers were fierce and often cruel fighters. Americans who were captured were brutally treated. Areas conquered by the Japanese were ruled harshly. Soon the Japanese were the most hated and feared people in the East.
>
> But the military leaders of Japan made a mistake. They did not understand the great industrial power of America. They thought Americans were soft and could not fight. They told their own people that Japan was protected by the Emperor and was invincible. . . .
>
> Although they were now losing the war, the Japanese still fought with unbelievable bravery. Japanese pilots known as *kamikaze,* or suicide fighters, gave their lives by plunging their planes into American ships. Even though their cities were in ruins, the Japanese people could not believe defeat was possible. . . .[39]
>
> It is unusual, after four years of war and six years of military occupation, for two enemy countries to be friends. In fact, the United States has become a sort of big brother to Japan. Our country is pledged to help defend Japan if it should ever be attacked by another country. . . .
>
> But we must also realize that it was the ambition of some of the Japanese military leaders which led her into war and conquest. And this brings us to another problem between Japan and the rest of the world. . . . The past cannot be completely forgotten. Some people ask, "Have the Japanese really changed?" or "Can we be sure that Japan will not again make war?" They are suspicious of the changes in Japan's government and in the thinking of her people. They wonder how deep and permanent will be the changes made during the American occupation.[40]

In his children's book *The Land and People of Japan* (1958), the noted writer Donald Richie explains modern Japan in yet another way:

> Everyone has heard something about Japan. It is a very special country with very special manners and customs. It is different from every other country in the world. There is only one Japan and it is unique.
>
> Since this is so, we often tend to emphasize the differences between our two countries. The Japanese do precisely the same thing. We think of them as being so different as to be ununderstandable [*sic*]. They think of themselves as being utterly different from other people of the world. Both we and they emphasize our differences rather than our similarities.
>
> And yet, we are actually quite similar, just as all peoples are really very much alike all over the world despite differences in manners and customs. We tend to think of the Japanese as a tiny, yellow people who live in houses made entirely of paper and spend all of their time arranging masses of flowers. The Japanese used to think of us as a gigantic people the color of chalk who all had red hair and enormous noses, and who lived entirely on raw beefsteak.
>
> They are wrong and we are wrong. Hence, my reason for writing this book is to try and show you what Japan is really like. It may be occasionally quaint and is rather often picturesque but, on the whole, it is a country filled with people who are very much like you and me.[41]

Like her sister, Pearl S. Buck, Grace Sydenstricker Yaukey, who wrote under the pen name Cornelia Spencer, was born in China. In her children's book *Japan* (1948, fig. 8.2)[42] she writes:

> The Japanese are a most careful people. One can see this in the strict plan of their society. Underlying their whole life is a fixed system of relationships between individuals, beginning with the Emperor and reaching to the lowliest worker. Every person has been expected to behave precisely in the way suitable to his social station or kind of work. To do otherwise would be a serious mistake, so carefully have patterns of behavior been laid down. If a Japanese can avoid an obligation he will, but if he cannot he meets it, even to giving his life.
>
> They are a painstaking, obedient people because from the earliest times they have had to be. Let us look at their homeland. Japan proper consists of four main islands, so mountainous that only about a fifth of the soil is good for farming. Hokkaido, the northern island, has bitter cold winters, and until recently was so barren, that few people could live there. The other three islands—big Honshu, and smaller Shikoku and Kyushu—are tormented by natural forces. Monsoon rainstorms flood the rivers. Typhoons harry the coast. Fifty of Japan's two hundred volcanoes are active. Earthquakes are frequent and are often followed by huge tidal waves. Thousands perish, and the survivors see about them the heartbreaking work of years destroyed.

> Confined to these perilous islands, the Japanese people have always felt insecure in a world of great continents. They have been made to feel they must follow rules carefully and work extra hard. Every disaster or invasion had made them more meticulous, repairing past losses and forestalling future ones.[43]

Spencer concludes:

> The First Great Change began when the Japanese people saw the glories of China and determined to match them. The Second Great Change occurred when the West pushed open the closed doors, so that the world's business rushed in upon Japan, and she became a competitor with the other nations in the struggle for world power—a struggle which led to world wars. The Third Great Change, now taking place, came through defeat in one of those wars. And once again a great difficulty confronted the Japanese people.
>
> "What is this thing called democracy?" they asked themselves. They watched to see how it would work. They saw their military leaders tried and doomed. They saw strange new textbooks in their schools. Everyone was asked to vote for local officeholders. The Americans brought new kinds of amusements. But what uncouth people these new teachers were! They did not know a bit about courtesy. They crowded the street cars, pushing their way in, while the Japanese still bowed decorously. . . . Always the group or class in which a person found himself would decide the kind of life he was to live. Now it did not matter about class; anyone could belong to any group he could manage to push into. And the Emperor—well, they still had their Emperor, but he seemed no longer a Son of the Gods, only a man holding his people together by a frail thread of tradition.
>
> The older Japanese sighed secretly, but the younger ones watched with wonder and a lightening of the heart. Could they, out of the ruins that were left them, build a new Japan? . . .
>
> They had less to work with now; so much had been destroyed in the War. But they still had these islands and their meticulous, nimble fingers.
>
> Who then can say what the Japanese may not yet achieve, once they are free and treated by other nations as a good neighbor? Perhaps the Third Great Change can bring the Japanese what they have been longing for all this time: to be secure, to be equal, to be honored as a people.[44]

Early Postwar Novels about Japan

Finally, there were the novels about Japan, adding their interpretations of Japan as it emerged from the war. The authors wrote their stories with emotion and sympathy, mentioning the war and its effects sparingly.

As the title indicates, *Toshio and Tama: Children of the New Japan* (1949, fig. 8.14) by Anne M. Halladay tries to emphasize the future, while glancing back at the war:

> During the war, while Father was still far away in the Philippine Islands, Toshio and Tamako had lived with Mother's elder brother. At first they had been in Tokyo. When the bombing had made it necessary to move many children away from the city, Uncle Yamato had brought Aunt Kata and Cousins Ritaro and Hana, with Toshio and Tama, to live here in the country, west of Tokyo. . . . Mother had not come to the country with Toshio and Tamako, though she visited them here at Uncle's house. For Mother had been a nurse in a Christian settlement in Tokyo most of the long time that Father was away from Japan. Mother had been brave. During the war she had stayed in Tokyo in spite of the bombing.[45]

Here and there, realistic descriptions of life after the war come to the surface. In her novel *Kenji* (1957), Gertrude Jenness Rinden tells the story of eleven-year-old Kenji and his five-year-old sister Michiko. They live with their mother, who can barely make ends meet and who decides on a desperate measure. She tells her children that little Michiko will be sent to live with Uncle Wajima, a rich silk merchant. While Michiko thinks she is going to be Uncle Wajima's "silkworm

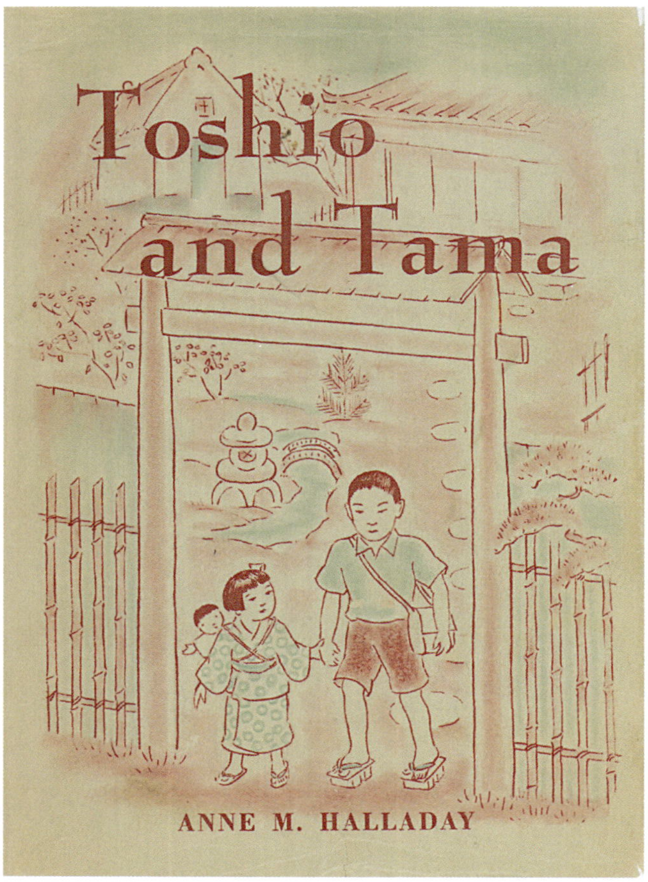

FIGURE 8.14
Toshio and Tama: Children of the New Japan, by Anne M. Halladay, illustrated by Henry Sugimoto. New York: Friendship Press, 1949.

princess," Kenji knows "that Wajima San is not a relative at all, but a man who needs child labor to make his precious silks."[46] Angry and heartbroken, Kenji is determined to bring Michiko home again.

Another incident that reveals the poverty of the villagers occurs when Kenji asks Mrs. Kimura, their landlady, if he could make a scarecrow for her field and if she would have some old clothes to dress the scarecrow. The old woman answers:

> "Where would we get old clothes these days? . . . We don't even have rags. . . . in the old days before the great war, we always had an old coat to put on our scarecrow." To Kenji and Michiko she did not need to dwell on the troubles that war had brought. It was in the great and terrible war that their father had become sick. Later, he had died, when Michiko was only a baby. Kenji hated the war that had made him lose his home and his father.[47]

But generally, signs of the war seem to have been covered up, overgrown with weeds like those discovered accidentally by the two boys Taro and Kenji in Albert J. Nevins's *The Adventures of Kenji of Japan* (1952, fig. 8.15):

> On the other side of the mountains, the land dropped steeply to meet the Japan Sea. The mountainside facing the sea was covered with concrete ruins. Once a bristling Japanese naval base and fortified area had stood there. During the great war with the Western Allies, repeated bombings had rendered the naval base useless. After the war the guns had been destroyed, and all the lumber and usable fixtures had been taken away to aid in rebuilding bombed cities. Finally the naval base lay in crumbling ruins, overgrown with vines and weeds, a sad and grim reminder of the folly of war. It was in those ruins that Taro and Kenji hoped to find a great many crickets.[48]

In *Toshio and Tama*, Halladay leaves the past behind and describes their father's homecoming:

> Would the streetcar never come?
>
> This was just one of many times that afternoon that [Toshio] had left his play with his cousins Ritaro and Hana and his sister Tamako to run to the gate. Today, any time now, Mother would be coming from Tokyo. And this time Father would come with her. Only the week before, Mother had received word that Father was coming home at last.
>
> Toshio had waited, oh, so long, for this coming. He did so want to have a real father again, to be part of a whole family! For Father was a soldier, and he was returning home. He had been away from Japan for nearly five long years. He had never seen four-your-old Tamako. She had been born after he had left Japan.
>
> Even to eight-year-old Toshio, Father was a sort of dream person. It was like remembering a shadow when he tried to picture him. Would Father remember

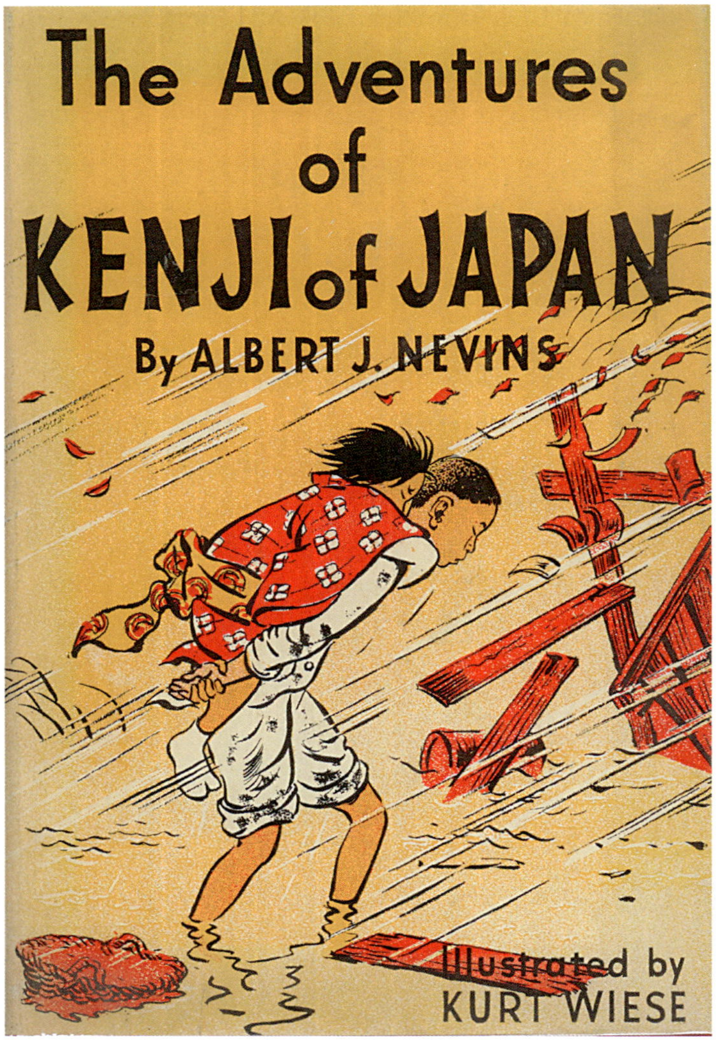

FIGURE 8.15
The Adventures of Kenji of Japan, by Albert J. Nevins, illustrated by Kurt Wiese. New York: Dodd, Mead, 1952.

> him? Would Father know him? Even though Toshio had waited and listened all the long afternoon, the clang of a bell and the rumble of wheels along a track down the road startled him. All in a minute his wondering stopped. For there was the streetcar, squeaking and swaying as it slowed down to a stop at the platform beside the road.
>
> Toshio's heart seemed to stand still for a moment. Then it pounded under his blue shirt. Yes, there was Mother, coming away from a group of people gathered under the trees along the track. And there was someone beside her—a man.
>
> "Otosan! Father!" Toshio could cry it out at last.[49]

Americans have a strong and positive presence in these stories. As Toshio's father settles back into the family, he learns about the Americans' arrival:

> Mother told how it had been on the day that the American soldiers had come to Tokyo, how fearful the Japanese people had been, and the questions they had asked one another. Would there be fighting? What would the Americans do to the Japanese people?

> "Many Japanese women hid with their children." Mother's eyes grew dark as she talked. "Early that morning we heard bands playing, and the Americans came marching in—lines and lines of them. The lines broke, and the soldiers took their places before the buildings that they were to guard. That was all. One soldier told me that they were wondering just as much as we were about what might happen.
>
> "Next morning Tokyo was about its business just as usual," Mother went on, "and it was not long before the Americans knew, too, that all was going to be peaceful. Toshio has become good friends with one of the soldiers stationed near the settlement. They play marbles together."[50]

Toshio had many other encounters with the Americans:

> Late that afternoon as Toshio was on his way to the bean-curd shop for Mother, a rumble far down the road to Tokyo made him stop. . . . The rumble grew louder . . . Far down the dusty highway two high, khaki-covered trucks came lumbering toward him—American Army trucks! . . . A sudden slamming of gates and the cry of children's voices let him know that he was not the only one in the village to hear the trucks. "Harro! Harro!" Already the children were calling their hellos, their 'l's sounding like 'r's because there is no 'l' in the Japanese language . . . The great trucks pulled up at the side of the road and stopped. The soldiers passed out candy and gum to the delighted children . . . "How do you like it in Yoshino? How goes school?" Joe San asked. "Fine," Toshio answered. He told Joe San what a time they were having at school with so few textbooks and no paper. "We have to share the pencils, and our teacher takes them up after school. She sharpens them herself so we will not waste them. My mother will come to Tokyo soon to see if she can get paper for us from the packages that come from America."[51]

Finally, new views of Japan and Japanese Americans began to emerge in American children's books published during the early postwar years. One of the new themes was celebrated during a luncheon at the Astor Hotel in New York City, where, on November 12, 1945, some 700 writers, editors, parents, librarians, and teachers gathered to celebrate Children's Book Week.[52] The novelist and social activist Dorothy Canfield Fisher presented the 1945 Child Study Association of America award to Florence Crannell Means for *The Moved-Outers* (1945, fig. 8.16).[53]

It was the first American children's book about the U.S. detention camps and tells the experiences of the Oharas, a Japanese American family living in a small California town. The story begins on a pre-Christmas Friday in 1941, when Sue comes home from school with her best friend Emily. Surrounded by the smell of "spice-sugar-coffee" and the Christmas packages ready to be mailed all around them, they dip into the cookie jar, sharing the crumbs with Skippy, the family's beloved fox terrier. A few days later, as Sue's father prepares to carve the Sunday chicken, there is an announcement on the radio: "Bulletin just in: Pearl Harbor bombed from the air. Extent of damage not yet known. U.S. fleet believed to be

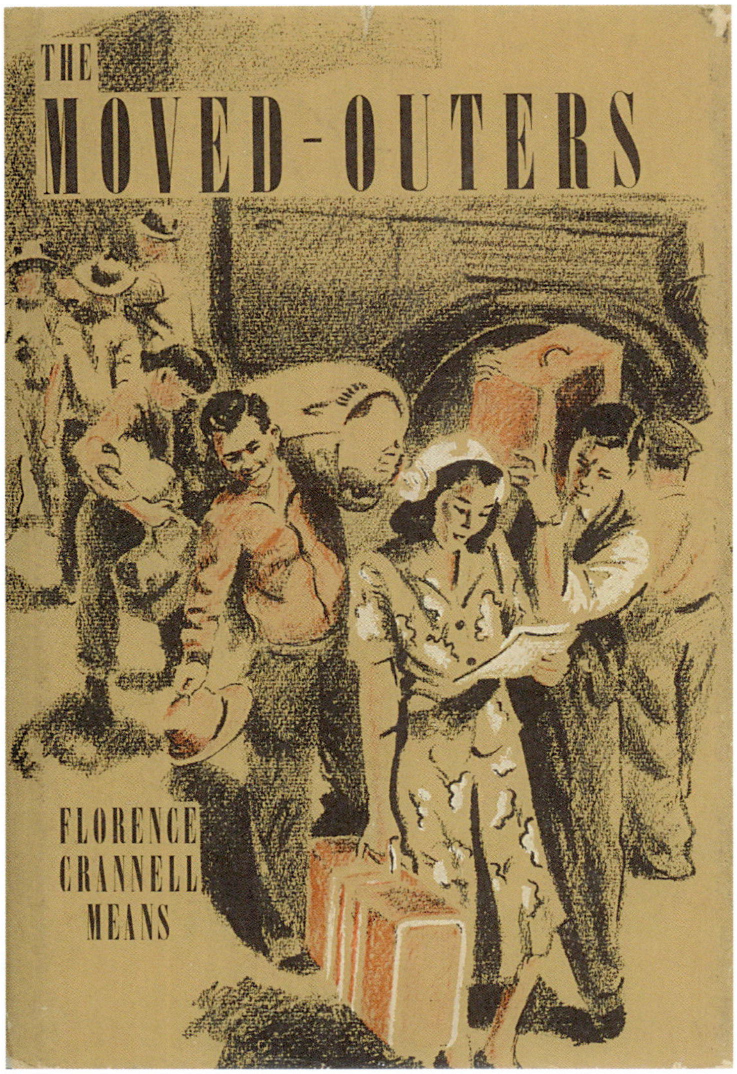

FIGURE 8.16
The Moved-Outers, by Florence Crannell Means, illustrated by Helen Blair. Boston: Houghton Mifflin, 1945.

destroyed."[54] Shortly afterwards, two FBI agents come to their house and search it. Later, they return and take Sue's father away. After that, the family's happy life begins to disappear.

Howard Pease, a Californian and a children's book writer, lamented the "disturbing fact" that there existed very few children's books "related to this modern world" which treated contemporary issues "without evasion."[55] Pease, who lauded *The Moved-Outers*, describes what happened to the Oharas:

> The story . . . follows Sue and her family to the Santa Anita concentration camp. Here they are assigned to one of the stalls in a stable. The camp itself is surrounded by barbed wires, soldiers tramp back and forth, and at night searchlights play in circles from watch towers. From Santa Anita the family is taken by guards to a train that has its windows broken by bullets from outside as it speeds eastward to another barbed-wire camp in the desolate wastes on the eastern slope of the Rocky Mountains. The story ends when Sue is finally released to enter the University of Colorado and Jiro is allowed to join the army and fight for his country, our country.[56]

Jiro is killed in action.

California children's librarian Clara Breed, whose aid to young detention-camp internees was the subject of the 2006 book *Dear Miss Breed: True Stories of the Japanese American Incarceration during World War II and a Librarian Who Made a Difference*, observed how remarkable it was that *The Moved-Outers* "[could] be published while the war in the Pacific [was] still going on and [that it] showed a certain amount of courage on the part of the publishers." She continued by noting that such a book belonged "to our picture of democracy in the United States, the democracy which is not finished but still in the making."[57]

Although *The Moved-Outers* was the only book out of the twenty-seven Newbery Medal winners and runners-up published until that time that addressed a contemporary issue, American children's books were beginning to embrace more realistic and socially relevant themes. *Desert Harvest: A Story of the Japanese in California* (1953, fig. 8.17) was such a book. Written by Vanya Oakes, a Far East newspaper journalist, *Desert Harvest* describes the lives of Japanese settlers who

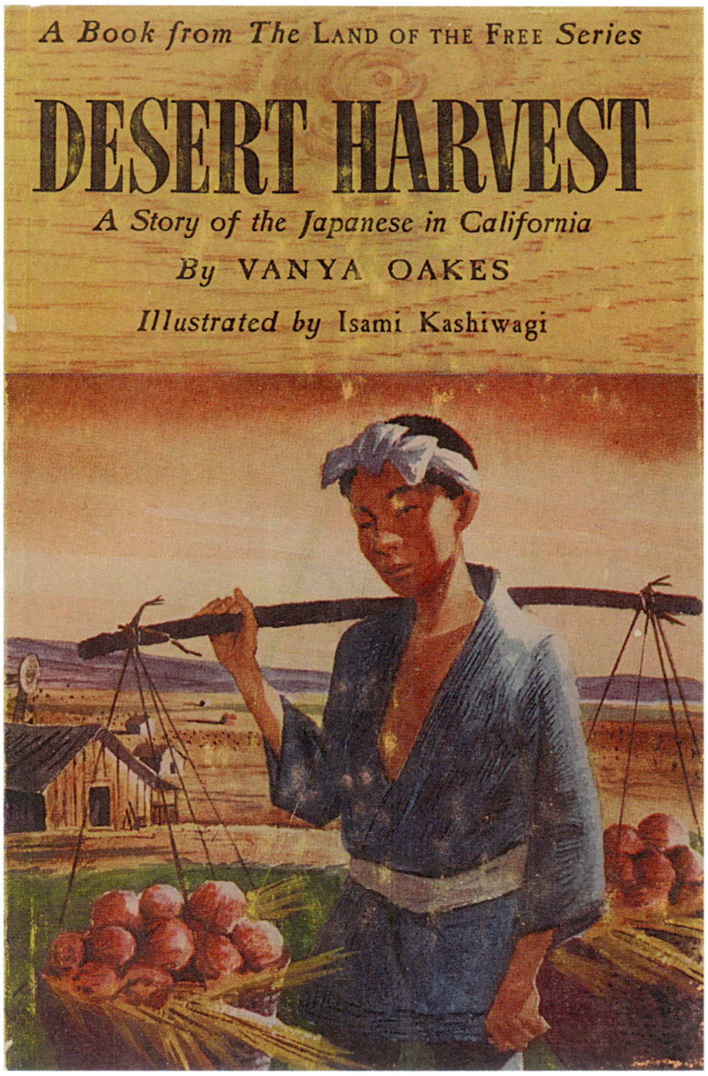

FIGURE 8.17
Desert Harvest: A Story of the Japanese in California, by Vanya Oakes, illustrated by Isami Kashiwagi. Philadelphia: Winston, 1953.

migrated to California's San Joaquin Valley in the early years of the twentieth century. She writes movingly of the immigrants' back-breaking labor and how they endured heat, drought, grasshoppers, torrential rains that washed away weeks of their labor, and mean-spirited American neighbors.

Sixteen-year-old Taro, who gives the story hope, gets into trouble the moment he arrives in California, when local farmhands Ed and Joe bully him:

> Fury boiled through him. Deliberately, his rice bowl had been broken; he had been laughed at, ridiculed. These two greatest of insults had been heaped upon him; his honor had been challenged.
>
> Like all Japanese boys he had learned something of jujutsu [*sic*] and instinctively he used it. He grabbed the man's two wrists, placed his right foot in the pit of his stomach, leaned backward and hurled the body over his head. The man hurtled through the air and landed with a thud in the dirt. There was a spasm of stunned silence. Then chaos. . . .[58]
>
> "Did I, as the others said, do wrong?" [Taro later asked his uncle.] Uncle Kato gripped together his gnarled, knotted fingers. "You did wrong, and you did not do wrong. . . ."
>
> "What you did would have certainly not been wrong in Japan," replied Uncle Kato, carefully choosing his words. "But here it is wrong to do anything which makes such trouble. . . ."
>
> "In the future, you are to stay away from the Americans," Uncle Kato instructed his nephew. "It is this way: We Japanese are not liked in this land. We are wanted, we are useful, but not liked. Therefore, it is better that we remain by ourselves."[59]

When the settlers deliver their first crop of strawberries to the depot, the station master reacts cynically:

> "So you've actually made something grow on that wasteland! Who would have thought of it." Taro did not understand all of his words, but enough to get the general idea. And he replied proudly, "We Japanese—we good farmers." "Maybe too good," muttered the stationmaster under his breath. Perhaps it was just his imagination, thought Taro, or perhaps he was not quite correct in his understanding of the words, but "too good" seemed to have an ominous undertone. . . .
>
> That Uncle Kato had also felt the antagonism was apparent from a remark he made as the train pulled out. "The Americans do not want us to succeed here. That is clear from their manner, from the expression on their faces. They will make trouble for us yet."[60]

And trouble they did make: they dynamited the irrigation dam the Japanese had built:

> When he reached the dam, the sight that met Taro's eyes hit him like a physical blow. A jumble of timbers, splintered and twisted, tossed into grotesque chaos. To one side, a mound of mud from the earth they had so carefully carried and packed firm. Just below this, a crater from which the earth had been wrenched by the force of the explosion. Rocks and ferns, slung together into a small island. Water spilling over everywhere, uselessly. Like a village after an earthquake, only in this case the earth had been made to groan and turn over by men—evil, cruel men.
>
> Taro sucked in his breath. "The devils!" Why had they done such a thing! It wasn't as if his countrymen were harming anyone, taking land others wanted. They were only trying to nurse the poorest of all the land in the valley back to life, land they had purchased with their hard-saved dollars. Beasts! Brutes! Barbarians! That's what they were, people like Ed and Joe. . . .[61]
>
> Why? Why did Ed and Joe, and some others too, dislike them so much? Was it because the color of their skin was different? . . . Their different customs and ways of doing things. . . . Most likely, Taro mused, Ed and Joe didn't dislike him or Moon Face [his friend] or any of the rest of the settlement personally; what they disliked were unfamiliar ways, strangers, foreigners. Perhaps Uncle Kato's feeling toward the Americans was much the same sort of thing. It was a fact to be faced, living in a country not yet his own. But there were plenty of Americans who did not feel that way; not only the kindly Wilsons, but look at the way Mr. Black had stood up for them that night in the store.[62]

And yes, there was hope that things would get better for the Yoshinos. One night when the family comes together to celebrate the ancient custom of viewing the full moon, Taro is at peace:

> [His] mind skipped across the ocean to the terraced rice fields clinging to the hillsides, to the thatched-roof villages he knew so well, nestled beneath the brow of the pine-crested mountain. It would be wonderful to see those familiar sights again one day . . . But he was content here, in this great sprawling valley—content and proud to be helping it to grow and flourish. . . . Yes, he was happy here . . . This, now was home.[63]

* * *

While American goodwill was helping to rebuild Japan—after the war had finally ended—her children's book writers began to create books about their former enemy with a new idealism and with remarkable sensitivity and fairness. In Japan, too, there was a new beginning. Dipping into their country's rich artistic heritage, children's book illustrators came forth with new picture books of great beauty and charm, sending them to America for translation.

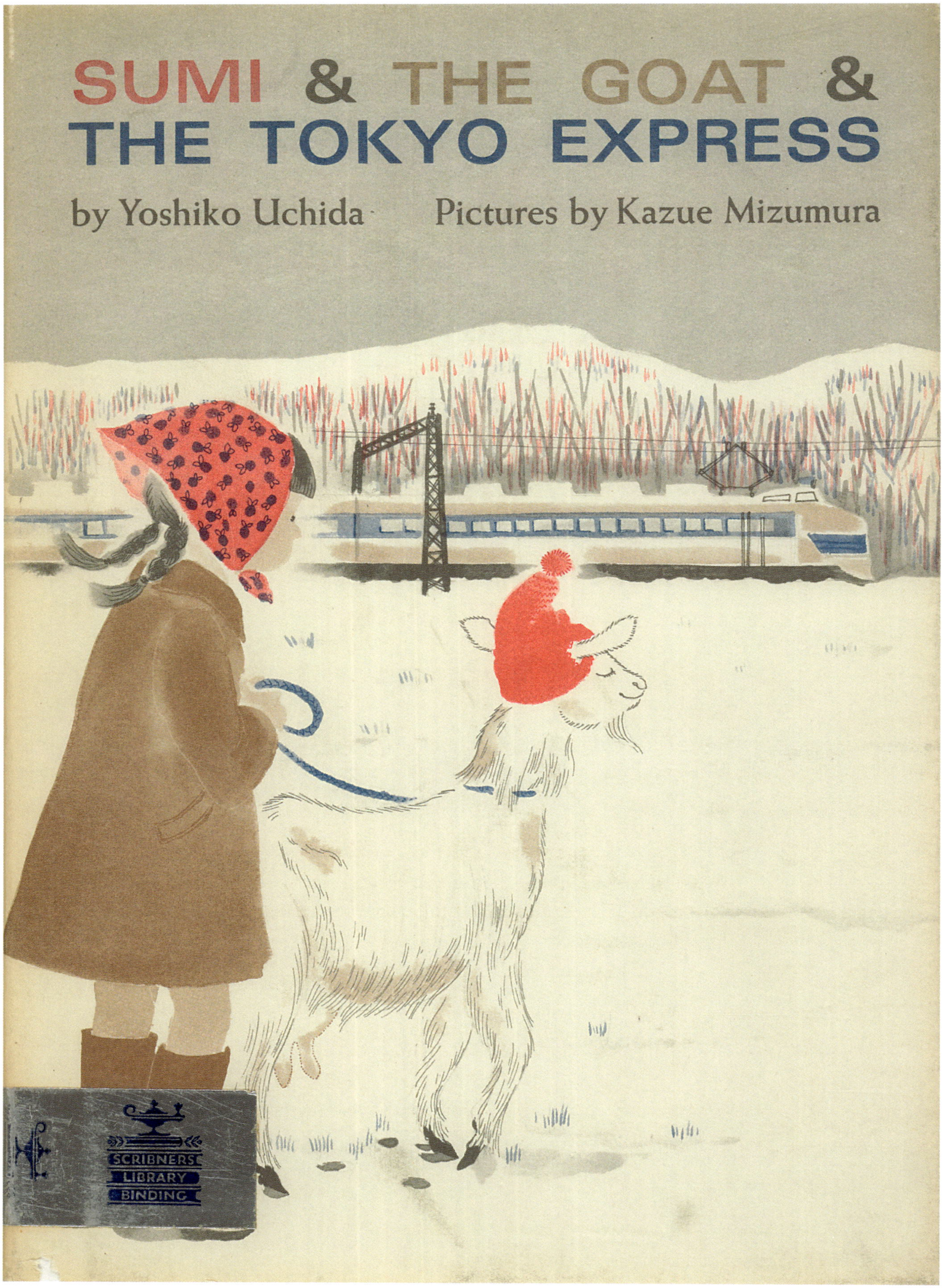
SUMI & THE GOAT & THE TOKYO EXPRESS
by Yoshiko Uchida
Pictures by Kazue Mizumura
SCRIBNERS LIBRARY BINDING

9

Three Japanese American Journeys

In the chronicle of American children's books about Japan, Allen Say's elegant 1993 autobiographical picture book, *Grandfather's Journey* (fig. 9.2), stands out. The three-generational saga received the Caldecott award, making Say the first Japanese American to achieve that honor.

At age twelve, Say apprenticed himself to cartoonist Noro Shinpei; at sixteen he went to America. A gifted writer and illustrator, he has devoted most of his books to his two countries. He describes the lives of the early Japanese immigrants in *Music for Alice* (2004) and life in post-war Japan in *The Bicycle Man* (1982) and *Kamishibai Man* (2005). He draws from his own life in *The Ink-Keeper's Apprentice* (1994), *Tea with Milk* (1999), and *Drawing from Memory* (2011). He has called *Grandfather's Journey* "a dream book, for life's journey is an endless dreaming of the places we have left behind and the places we have yet to reach."[1]

Say's "dream book" appeared at a time when American children's books increasingly absorbed and interpreted the reality of the world around them, including the harsh experiences endured by many Japanese Americans. It tells of his grandfather's sailing for America; returning to Japan to marry his childhood sweetheart; making a home in San Francisco; and returning, once again, to Japan, only to be caught up in the destruction of World War II. Say continued his grandfather's journeys between Japan and America, writing:

> After a time, I came to love the land my grandfather had loved . . .
>
> But I also miss the mountains and rivers of my childhood . . .
>
> So I return now and then, when I can not still
> the longing in my heart.
>
> The funny thing is, the moment I am in one country,
> I am homesick for the other.[2]

FIGURE 9.1 (OPPOSITE) *Sumi & the Goat & the Tokyo Express*, by Yoshiko Uchida, illustrated by Kazue Mizumura. New York: Charles Scribner's Sons, 1969.

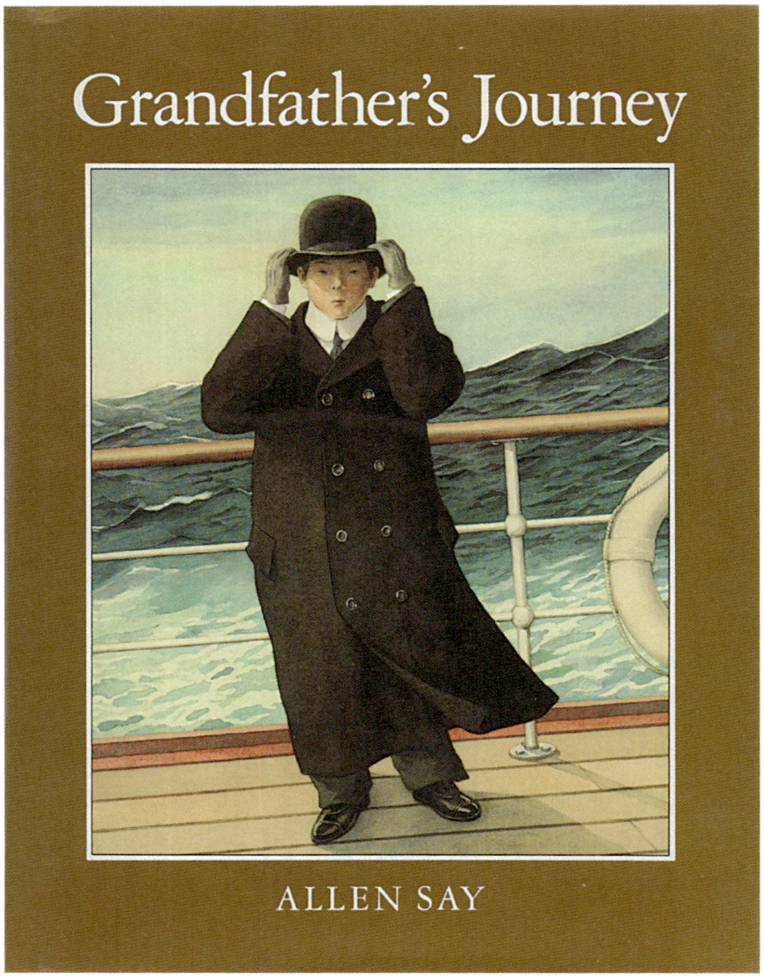

FIGURE 9.2
Grandfather's Journey, written and illustrated by Allen Say. Boston: Houghton Mifflin, 1993.

While Allen Say was bringing the immigrant and Japanese American experience to the front pages of American children's literature, books by earlier Japanese American children's book writers and illustrators were already becoming part of a bygone era. Taro Yashima, Yoshiko Uchida, and Kazue Mizumura were among those who produced books based on firsthand experience of the war and the camps. Deeply rooted in their own culture, they nevertheless tried to become part of America, creating poignant children's books that revealed their courageous lives.

Taro Yashima

The artist Jun Atsushi Iwamatsu, who later changed his name to Taro Yashima, was an idealist and a man of deep feelings who believed he could resist the brutality of Japan's militaristic government. For this he was imprisoned, beaten, and abused. He risked his life and lost a child and his country. Yet, this same Jun Atsushi Iwamatsu also believed that "Earth is beautiful! Living is wonderful!"[3] and once said to a friend, "Love is always the basis for real accomplishment."[4] He used his art—words and pictures—to express, subtly, the value and richness of life. As a reviewer of his children's books wrote in the 1960s, "Combining the bright light of the Impressionists with the subdued elegance of Japanese paintings, Taro Yashima produces an art which is distinctive and highly sensitive . . . he [fills his books with] a rare, poetic mood bound with a feeling of true, deep joy."[5]

Born in the town of Nejime, near the city of Kagoshima on the island of Kyushū, Iwamatsu transformed the scenes, feelings, and events of his childhood into the children's books he would later create. Yet he had to endure bitter times before he could recall that peaceful stage of his life in his autobiographical *The New Sun* (1943), which takes place early in the reign of Emperor Taishō (1912–1926):

> Tosa, a province in the southern part of the main Japanese island, was famous because the power that broke the feudal system in Japan had its beginning there.
>
> About eighty years ago a certain low-class samurai wandered onto the peninsula of this region.
>
> The samurai chose a plot of earth and built a little house with the help of the village people.
>
> Thirty years after the Meiji Revolution, his son built a new house which had painted on it a red cross, the symbol of the Doctor's profession he had chosen. This was my parents' home.[6]

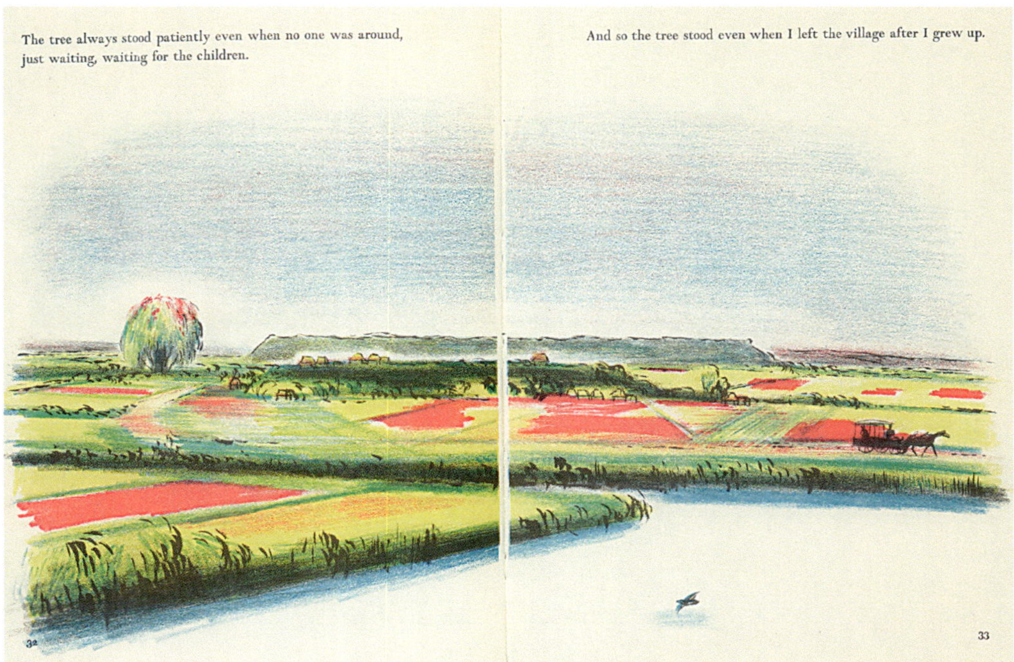

FIGURE 9.3
The Village Tree, written and illustrated by Taro Yashima. New York: Viking, 1953, page 32.

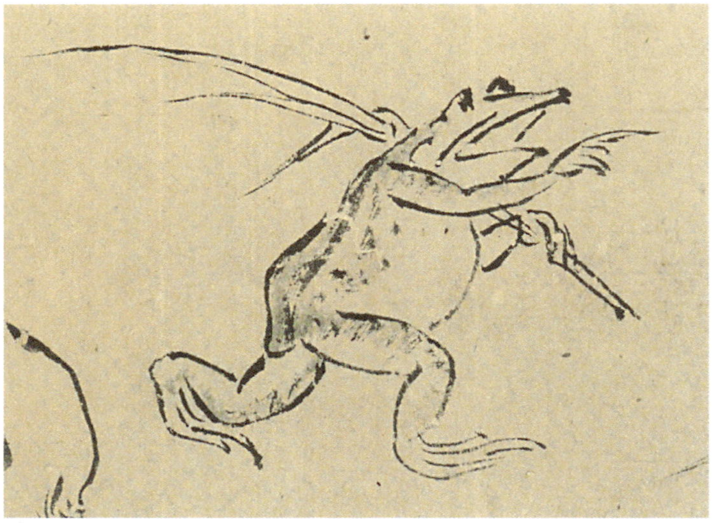

FIGURE 9.4
The Animal Frolic, by Toba Sōjō; text by Velma Varner. New York: G.P. Putnam's Sons, 1954.

It was here, in books from his father's shelves, where Iwamatsu learned about the Meiji and French revolutions, the rabbits drawn centuries earlier by Toba Sōjō (fig. 9.4),[7] and the humorous Yedo citizens of the artist Katsushika Hokusai.[8] He began to make pictures himself, roamed the hot summer countryside with its rice paddies and flowers, and played with abandon in the river with the farmers' children.

If his rural childhood was carefree and happy, the larger life around him was less so. Observing the villagers who lived in those thatch-roof *minka*—archetypes of Japanese architecture—but who were barely surviving, Iwamatsu would later write that "their lives were insulted lives."[9]

In 1921, at the age of thirteen, Iwamatsu entered *Kagoshima ni chu* (Kagoshima Second Junior High School), but in his fourth year contracted tuberculosis and had to stay home for many months. It was during this time that Goji Taniguchi, a student of the noted artists Seiki Kuroda, Fakeji Fujisima, and Eisaku Wada, became his tutor. By then, young Iwamatsu had abandoned his original ambition to become an admiral. He had discovered the French Impressionists and was now determined to become a painter. His father, who died in 1925, had given his blessing. In 1927, Iwamatsu was among those selected by the government to attend the Japanese Imperial Art School in Tokyo. He soon realized, however, that the study of traditional and academic art styles was not for him. Often skipping classes, he failed to pass two subjects: military drill and the drawing of perspective. When he complained about his failing grades, he got into a fight with one of the clerks and was expelled from school.

At about this time, he came under the influence of the Japanese political cartoonist Ippei Okamoto and sought out the art of Germany's George Grosz, the American William Gropper, and the Russian artists collectively known as

"Kukryniksy."[10] Iwamatsu's illustrations began to appear in such magazines as *Nappu, Senki, ProBijutsu,* and *Tokyo Pack.*[11]

In 1931, the year the Japanese army invaded Manchuria, Iwamatsu became editor of the monthly magazine *Bijutsu shinbun.* He also organized art exhibitions that traveled to villages and factories around the country and encouraged the workers and peasants to buy art reproductions. He paid no attention to the censorship rules that were increasingly enforced by the military government, nor did he fear its punishment. Once, when a whole village had refused an army drill, he drew a cartoon lampooning the militarists.[12] He continued making drawings critical of the government, including one captioned, "Stop the aggression in China!" He also taught oil painting and drawing at the Plastic Proletarian Art Institute. Future Japanese legends film director Akira Kurosawa and children's book illustrator Suekichi Akaba were among his students.

Iwamatsu and his wife[13] became members of the Japan Proletarian Artists' League, a group of left-leaning artists who published anti-militarism cartoons, posters, and articles. Gradually, however, Iwamatsu began to realize that they could not fight the Japanese police system and that his dream of engaging the proletariat in the fight against the government had been too optimistic. In Japan, as in Germany, art was being confiscated, publications were censored, and leaders of underground movements disappeared. The death of Takiji Kobayashi, a leading author of proletarian literature who succumbed to torture while under police arrest, was a major blow to the proletarian art movement. Iwamatsu drew Kobayashi's death mask.

In response to the growth of left-wing groups, the much-feared Tokko-ka (*Tokubetsu Koto Keisatsu*), the civilian counterpart of the Kempeitai (military police), increasingly targeted teachers, artists, writers, and anyone showing disrespect for the Emperor. Between 1933 and 1936 some 59,000 people were arrested for harboring "dangerous thoughts," and about 2,500 were imprisoned.[14] In the spring of 1933, while the Nazis were burning books and Franklin D. Roosevelt was beginning his first hundred days in office, Iwamatsu, his wife, and their young child moved to eastern Tokyo. They lived among factory workers and laborers who became the subjects for his art—which Iwamatsu believed remained "unbearably shallow."[15]

Between 1928 and 1933, Iwamatsu was arrested a number of times and spent a total of more than three years in prison, where he witnessed prisoners being beaten and brutally interrogated.[16] Realizing that his life would be more useful outside than inside a prison, he wrote a confession and was promptly released. For months he and his wife journeyed through Japan, sketching and painting and observing preparations for war. Government slogans such as "Kill the whites and smash democracy" were everywhere.[17] Soldiers were being sent to fight in Manchuria. Iwamatsu knew that he would soon become "a private under the Japanese Militarists."[18] He saw the "trains packed with soldiers . . . running toward the south day and night," while "the ashes in the little boxes were coming home much oftener."[19]

In 1939, Iwamatsu and his wife boarded a cargo ship for New York, traveling with tourist visas. In New York they joined other émigrés—architects, writers, film directors, composers, musicians, scientists—who had already arrived from Berlin, Vienna, Paris, and Moscow. Like many artists, the Iwamatsus found a haven at the Art Students League where they were students until 1942.[20] It was here where he finally met George Grosz, whose work the Nazis condemned as "*entartete Kunst*," (degenerate art), and who like him was now trying to find a new raison d'être for his art.[21]

Shortly after the Japanese attacked Pearl Harbor, on December 7, 1941, Iwamatsu enlisted in the U.S. Army and was attached to the newly created Office of War Information (OWI), a civilian agency charged with managing the flow of war-related information and propaganda. To protect his family in Japan, Iwamatsu took the new name Taro Yashima, which he translated as "healthy boy of peaceful Japan."[22]

Throughout the war, the OWI's Overseas Branch air-dropped nearly six billion propaganda leaflets over areas controlled by the major Axis nations, encouraging soldiers to surrender. Taro Yashima illustrated the propaganda booklet *Unga Naizo* (Mr. No Luck) that was "more widely distributed on the Pacific front than any other American propaganda material."[23] It tells the story of Unga Naizo, a young Japanese soldier who recites the *Gunjin Chokugo* (the oath of loyalty to the Emperor), goes to war, and dies with honor. His ashes come home in a wooden box.

In 1943, Yashima quit his job with the OWI (he had, once again, rebelled against his superiors) and published his memoir *The New Sun* (1943, fig. 9.5). Using minimal prose and stark sketches—some of them reminiscent of the work of George Grosz—Yashima told what he had experienced in Japan. The *New York Times* book reviewer wrote that Yashima's "narrative effect" was as "quick and violent as the quality of the drawings . . . [which were] often brash, harsh and sadistic, [like] ink . . . spilled and blotched over the page like blood."[24] Sales of the book were modest. A Henry Holt salesman reportedly said, "Nobody will buy a book from a Jap."[25]

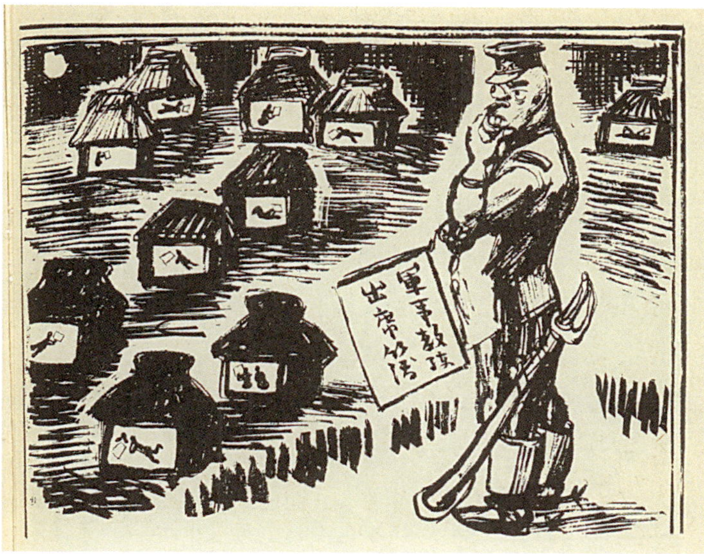

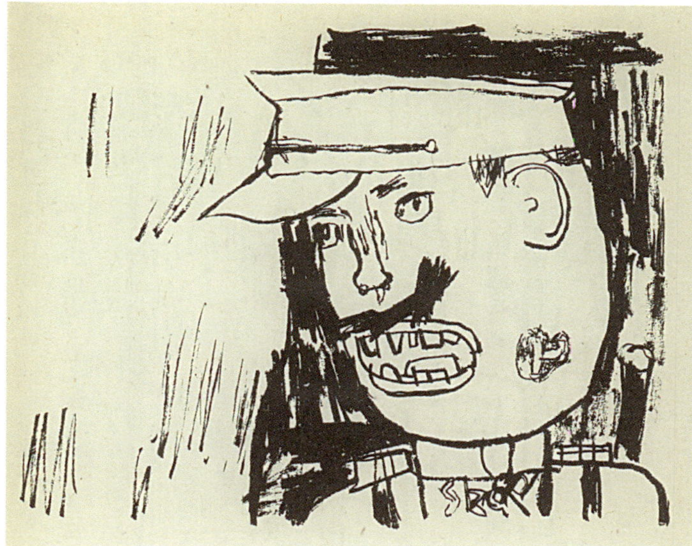

FIGURE 9.5 (LEFT)
The New Sun, written and illustrated by Taro Yashima. New York: H. Holt, 1943, page 169.

FIGURE 9.6 (RIGHT)
Horizon is Calling, written and illustrated by Taro Yashima. New York: H. Holt, 1947, page 231. Drawing by Yashima's son Makoto.

The following year, Yashima and his wife began to work for the Morale Operation of the Office of Strategic Services (OSS), precursor of the Central Intelligence Agency. After service in the China–Burma–India theater of operations, he was sent to Nagasaki, where the second atomic bomb had been dropped on August 9, 1945. As a member of a U.S. Army intelligence unit, he was there to interview survivors. There were dead bodies everywhere, he reported. "There wasn't enough wood [to cremate them]. Bodies were piled up, not burned yet."[26]

During this trip Yashima visited his native village in Kyushū and found the villagers friendly toward him despite rumors that he was a spy. An enemy of the prewar and wartime Japanese government, Yashima still saw himself as an ally to the Japanese people. Yet his role in the propaganda effort on behalf of his country's enemy would haunt him for a long time.[27]

When Yashima returned to the United States in 1946, he found that he and his wife had become illegal aliens. After many high-level discussions and questions about whether he had engaged in subversive activities, Congress passed a bill granting permanent residence to the Yashimas and their son Makoto, who was reunited with his parents the following year.[28] In 1947, Yashima published *Horizon is Calling* (fig. 9.6). A sequel to *The New Sun*, it records Yashima's life after his release from prison in 1935 and the work of the secret police, whom he called "inhuman creatures who did not care if the children of others were barbecued for the realizations of their own success."[29]

At about this time, Yashima met May Massee, the renowned American children's book editor, who took him under her wing. Massee went for the bold, the beautiful, and the foreign at a time when "many librarians and most booksellers resisted the appearance of 'foreign stories'" and when "young Americans had little in their reading to lead their imaginations and sympathies out to people in the world beyond their own dooryard."[30]

It was Yashima's deep love for a child—his fourth—that set him on a new path. His young daughter Momo's affection sustained him for nearly four years when he was "beaten flat by an ulcer." Yashima reflected, "I wanted to thank this little life and tell some nice stories to make this little girl happy."[31] He began with *The Village Tree* (1953), which a reviewer described as "A strikingly beautiful interpretation in poetic prose and picture of the author's childhood in Japan" that conveyed "an atmosphere of great peace and happiness."[32]

Plenty to Watch (1954, fig. 9.7) illustrated the crafts and trades Yashima had watched as a child, including those of the barrel maker, the candy man, and the *tatami* (floor mats) maker. His poignant, autobiographical *Crow Boy* (1955, fig. 9.8) tells about "Chibi" ("tiny boy"), who hid under the school and who "could not learn a thing." [33] Coaxed by the new teacher, Chibi participates in the annual talent show. He would "imitate the voices of crows," the teacher announced. Chibi sang a whole crow symphony, mimicking newly hatched crows, mother crows, or those who warned the villagers of danger. His schoolmates who had called him "stupid" and "slowpoke" cried in shame.[34] *Crow Boy* was perhaps the most "Japanese" picture book of its day. It was filled with Yashima's impressionistic, seemingly unfinished and abstract sketches of traditional Japan: Chibi in his dried zebra grass raincoat, the Japanese characters on the blackboard, and Chibi's own hauntingly illegible writing. It was named runner-up for the 1956 Caldecott award.

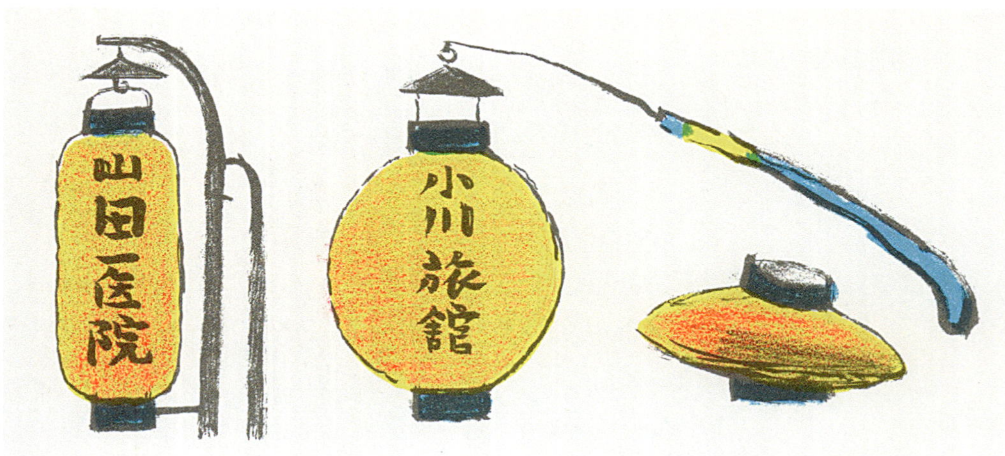

FIGURE 9.7
Plenty to Watch, written and illustrated by Mitsu and Taro Yashima. New York: Viking, 1954, page 17.

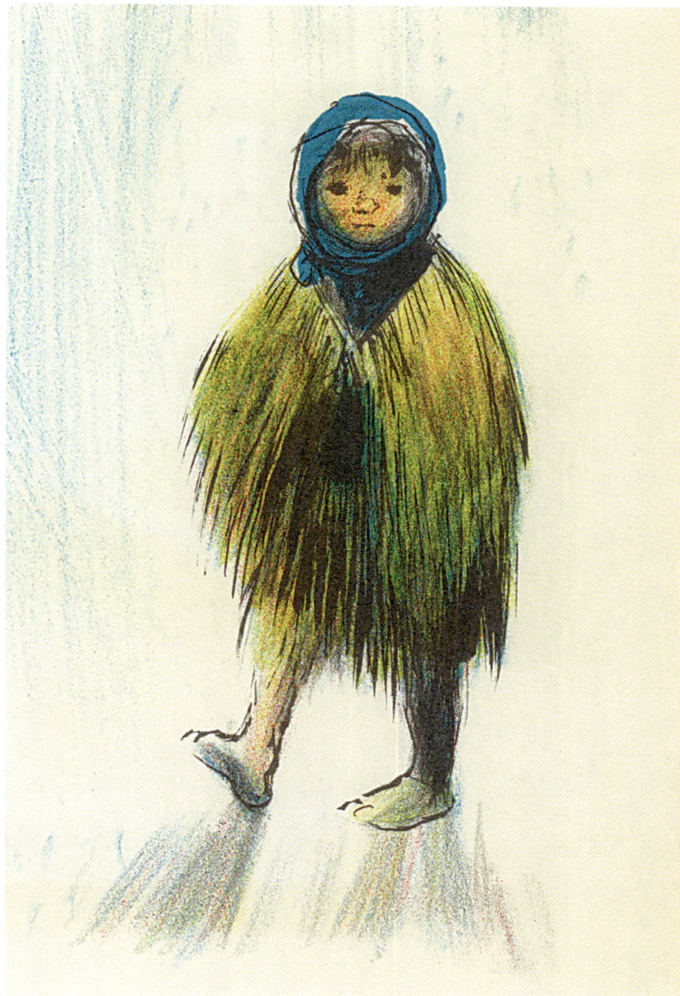

FIGURE 9.8
Crow Boy, written and illustrated by Taro Yashima. New York: Viking, 1955, page 17.

Yashima created *Umbrella* (1958, fig. 9.9) for Momo's eighth birthday. The tale conveys his "peach" girl's rejoicing in her brand new umbrella and boots (*momo* is the Japanese word for peach). Other books included *Momo's Kitten* (1961); *Youngest One* (1962), the story of a tiny, shy boy reminiscent of *Crow Boy*; *Soo Ling Finds a Way* (1965, fig. 9.10), about a young girl who saves grandfather Soo's Golden Lotus Hand Laundry; and *Seashore Story* (1967), a lyrical retelling of the ancient legend of Urashima Tarō, the fisherman who emerges as an old man from living under the sea.

In 1953, Yashima moved to Los Angeles where, in addition to painting, he taught at his newly opened school, the Yashima Art Institute; founded the Japanese American Artists Society; made more children's books; and painted a mural for the Bayshore Library in Long Beach. He gave lectures, appeared on panels, and contributed to his son Makoto's theater company, the East West Players—which staged a production of *Crow Boy*, for which Yashima created the set.[35] His art was exhibited at the Odakyu Department Store in Tokyo and in numerous

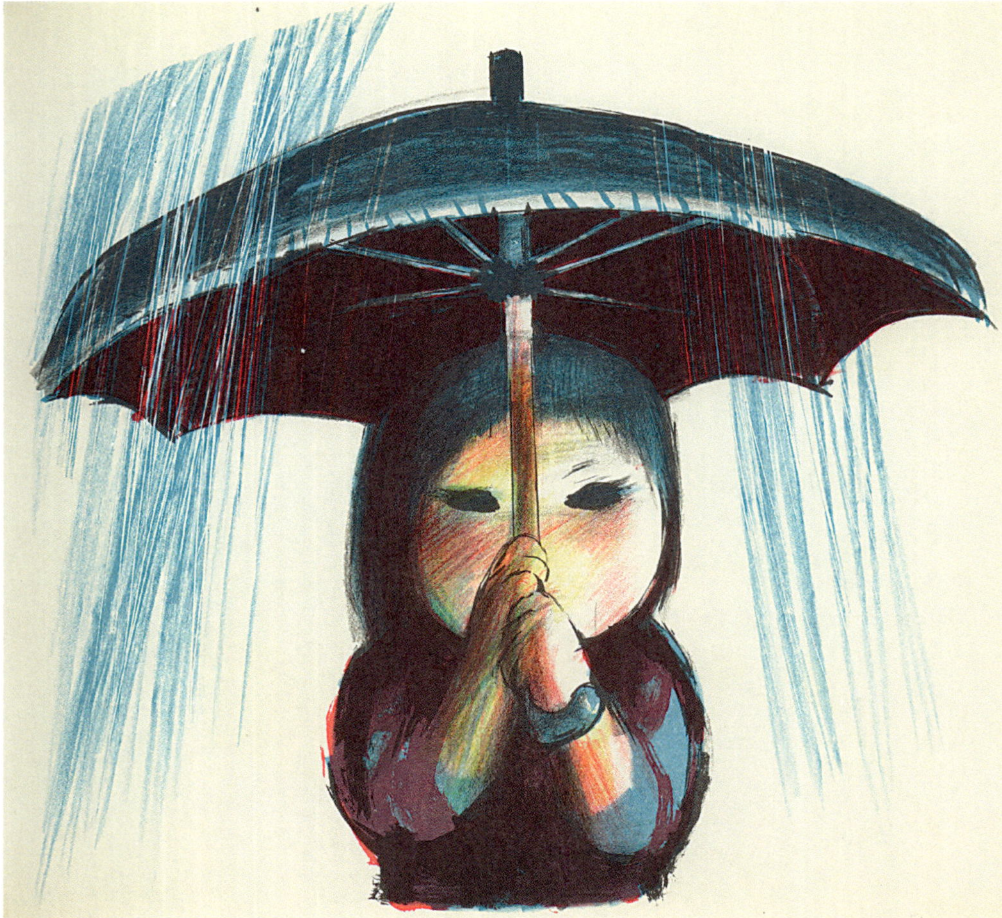

FIGURE 9.9
Umbrella, written and illustrated by Taro Yashima. New York: Viking, 1958, page 29.

shows in the Los Angeles area, among them a 1956 exhibition of paintings, drawings, and prints which, one reviewer noted, dealt "tenderly, yet authoritatively, with the human image."[36]

In 1960, when he was fifty-two, Yashima went back to his childhood village, where he stayed for a year to write and paint. On this journey—captured in the nostalgic film *Taro Yashima's Golden Village* [37]—he tried to see his childhood classmates once again. Using an old graduation photo, he looked at each boy's face and asked, "Who is alive and how [had] he lived and who is dead and how [had] he died?"[38] As the camera pans over the black-and-white photograph of the handsome, somber faces of the village boys in their home-spun kimono and Prussian-style school caps, Yashima identifies each boy, first by his father's profession, then by his face, then how he remembered him. There he is himself, in the left-hand corner of the photograph, "country doctor's third son who went to art school."[39] There is Akira, the town official's son, a great tennis player who played the bamboo flute and was killed in the war. Yashima visits Takeshi, the tailor; Suyekichi, the tallest boy in class, who was now blind; the carpenter who still uses the traditional tools of his trade.[40]

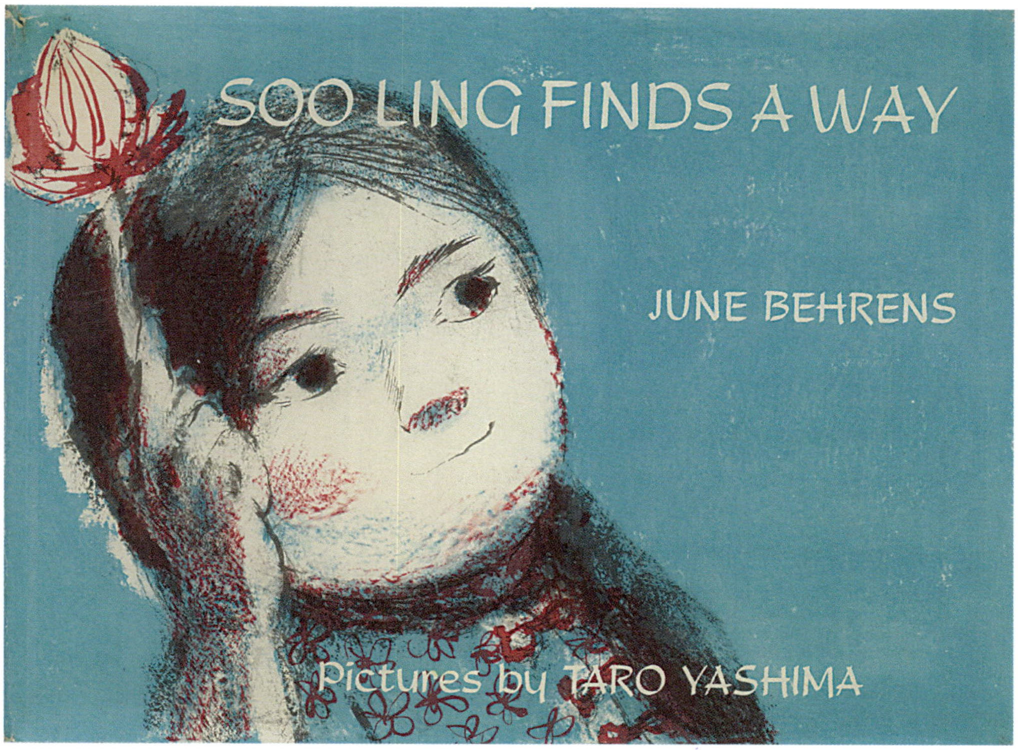

FIGURE 9.10
Soo Ling Finds a Way, by June Behrens, illustrated by Taro Yashima. San Carlos, CA: Golden Gate Junior Books, 1965.

The most poignant encounter is Yashima's visit to Tomizo's house. Says Yashima as he crosses the swinging cable bridge, "the more their lives are poor the further away are their houses from the lowlands."[41] Tomizo was Yashima's model for Chibi, the crow boy, and now lives in a run-down *minka*, with grass and weeds sprouting all over its thatch roof. Tomizo refuses to see Yashima, who turns away sadly, saying: "He did not know that I published *Crow Boy* and that I favored him as my childhood friend."[42]

As he walks back to the village, surrounded by rice fields and the mountains in the background, Yashima is at home again among his childhood friends, to whom he felt close all his life. Once again he could eat the food of home: *mikan*, *bontan*, *kaki*, and buckwheat soba.[43] Then there is a final farewell party. Despite the hardship and sacrifices this wartime generation endured, there is a solid and deep happiness in their weathered faces. Squatting on the *tatami* mats, they laugh as they feast and fill each other's cups from the small sake pitchers. An old, noble-faced woman plays the *shamisen*, and Taro Yashima beats the drum. At the end of his journey he said, with awkwardness in his adopted tongue, "I felt myself much taller, having a newly widened stability."[44]

Taro Yashima lived in America for more than fifty years. He never gave up his Japanese citizenship nor his dream of going home. It must have pleased him that, despite his long residence in the United States, the Japanese children's book community still thought of him as one of their own. His name appeared on the list of Japan's leading postwar artists in an exhibition organized in Tokyo during the 1986 Congress of the International Board on Books for Young People.[45] After his death in 1994 at age eighty-five, there were posthumous exhibitions of Yashima's art in Nejime, at the Chisana Ehon Museum in Nagano prefecture, the Iwasaki Chihiro Ehon Museum in Tokyo, the Reimai-kan Museum in Kagoshima, and the Japanese-American Cultural and Community Center in Los Angeles. Wrote his son Makoto:

> I began to understand, that, perhaps the major influence on my father's work was the era in which he lived. Without an understanding of that, one cannot evaluate the artist's struggle.[46]

Yoshiko Uchida

The life and work of Yoshiko Uchida were forged by the intertwining, sometimes strained, influences of Japan, the country of her parents, and America, the country of her birth. Uchida was a young woman when the United States entered World War II. Only later in life was she able to come to terms with the displacement she had to endure. In the epilogue of one of her last books, she wrote:

> I have written several short stories and books that tell of [the] wartime uprooting, and each time I find it hard to believe that such a thing actually took place in the United States of America. But it did.
>
> I find it painful to continue remembering and writing about it. But I must. Because I want each new generation of Americans to know what once happened in our democracy. I want them to love and cherish the freedom that can be snatched away so quickly, even by their own country.
>
> Most of all, I ask them to be vigilant, so that such a tragedy will never happen to any group of people in America ever again.[47]

Uchida's father, Dwight Takashi Uchida, arrived in California in 1906. He had hoped to go to Yale and become a doctor. Instead, he worked in several stores owned by a Japanese businessman before he got a job, in 1917, in the San Francisco branch of the Mitsui Company. He married Iku Umegaki, who had come from Japan in 1916. Both were graduates of Doshisha University in Kyoto, one of the leading Christian universities in Japan. Their daughters, Yoshiko and Keiko, grew up in Berkeley, California.[48] Their mother, a model housekeeper, loved books, wrote Japanese *tanka* poems, and read Japanese stories to them.

Both parents were active in their church,[49] taught Sunday school classes, and always helped those in need in any way they could.[50] Though she and her sister refused to learn Japanese because, they said, it made them feel like foreigners, Uchida wrote:

> Our lives—my sister's and mine—were quite thoroughly infused with the customs, traditions, and values of our Japanese parents, whose own lives had been structured by the samurai code of loyalty, honor, self-discipline, and filial piety. Their lives also reflected a blend of Buddhist philosophy dominated by Christian faith. So it was that we grew up with a strong dose of the Protestant ethic coupled with a feeling of respect for our teachers and superiors; a high regard for such qualities as frugality, hard work, patience, diligence, courtesy, and loyalty; a sense of responsibility and love, not only for our parents and family, but for our fellow man.[51]

Initially, life was sweet and privileged for young Yoshiko—filled with movies, concerts, and other entertainments, shopping, lunches with friends, piano lessons, and pleasant train rides on overnight sleepers to Los Angeles for New Year celebrations with her paternal grandmother and other relatives. Gradually, however, anti-Japanese sentiment, which had been stoked since the turn of the century, became more intense. Billboards appeared that read "Japs, don't let the sun shine on you here. Keep moving."[52] Yoshiko began to find that more and more doors to the world of her white friends and schoolmates were closing to her. During a vacation trip with her family, an incident reinforced her feeling that she was a stranger in her own country. While visiting friends in Cornwall, Connecticut, an elderly woman patted Yoshiko on the head, and said, "My, but you speak English so beautifully."[53] "She had meant to compliment me, I was so astonished, I didn't know what to say," Uchida later wrote. "I realized she had seen only my outer self—my Japanese face—and addressed me as a foreigner. I knew then that I would always be different, even though I wanted so badly to be like my white American friends."[54]

When she was about twelve, the family went to Japan:

> As I sat watching the fireflies darting about in the dark, I thought maybe I could get quite used to living in Japan. Here, at last, I looked like everyone else. Here, I blended in and wasn't always the one who was different.
>
> And yet, I was really a foreigner in Japan. I had felt like a complete idiot when an old woman asked me to read a bus sign for her, and I had to admit I couldn't read Japanese. Deep down inside, where I really dwelled, I was thoroughly American. I

> missed my own language . . . I longed for hot dogs and chocolate sodas and bathrooms with plumbing.
>
> But the sad truth was, in America, too, I was perceived as a foreigner.
>
> So what was I anyway, I wondered. I wasn't really totally American, and I wasn't totally Japanese. I was a mixture of the two, and I could never be anything else.[55]

"Imbued with the melting pot mentality," she wrote, "I saw integration into white American society as the only way to overcome the sense of rejection I had experienced in so many areas of my life."[56] Yet, through her junior high and high school years, she was increasingly excluded from her white classmates' social life—while also feeling alienated from her Japanese roots:

> Society caused us to feel ashamed of something that should have made us feel proud. Instead of directing anger at the society that excluded us . . .
>
> [M]any of us Nisei tried to reject our own Japaneseness and the Japanese ways of our parents. We were sometimes ashamed of the Issei in their shabby clothes, their rundown trucks and cars, their skin darkened from years of laboring in sun-parched fields, their inability to speak English, their habits, and the food they ate. . . .[57]
>
> Small wonder that many of us felt insecure and ambivalent and retreated into own special subculture . . . It was in such a climate . . . in December of 1941 that the Japanese bombs fell on Pearl Harbor.[58]

And still, Uchida wrote:

> None of us believed our government would imprison its own citizens, but on February 19, 1942, President Franklin D. Roosevelt issued Executive Order 9066 which would uproot 120,000 Japanese Americans and imprison us behind barbed wire, without trial or hearing, simply because we looked like the enemy. Two-thirds of us were American citizens, and I was one of them.[59]

On December 19, 1941, Yoshiko's father was arrested and sent to an army internment camp in Missoula, Montana. With only ten days' notice, the family had to dispose of the contents of their house and were then taken to Tanforan Racetrack in San Bruno, south of San Francisco, Barrack 16 (fig. 9.11). Their "barrack" was an old stable, their "apartment" "a small, dark horse stall, ten feet by twenty feet. I couldn't believe what I saw," Uchida wrote:

> Dust, dirt, and wood shavings littered the linoleum, and I could still smell the manure that lay beneath it. There were two tiny windows on either side of the

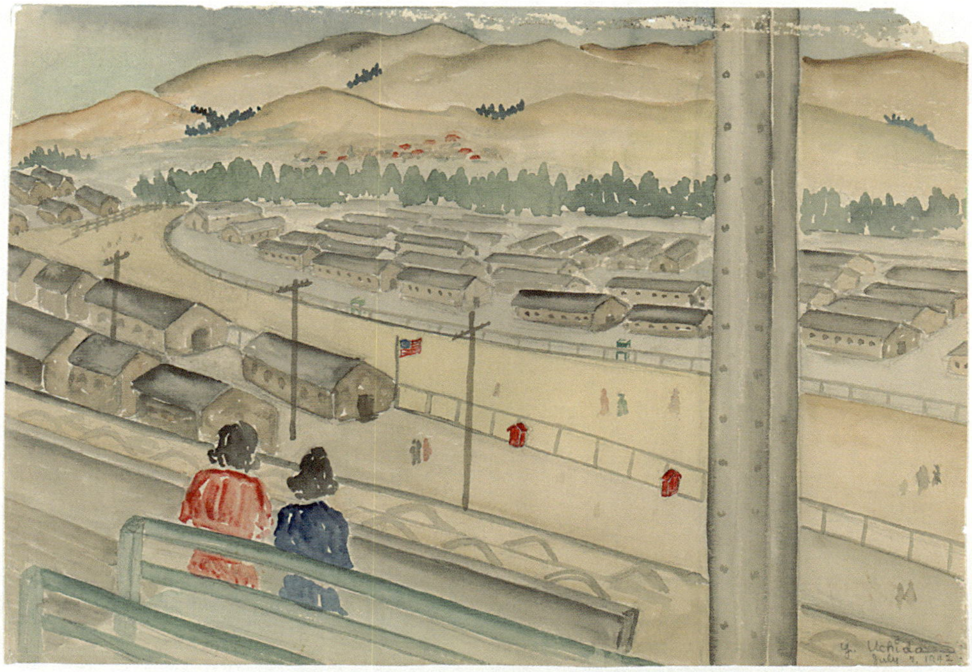

FIGURE 9.11
"View of Tanforan," watercolor by Yoshiko Uchida, July 7, 1942.

door (our only source of daylight), and the stall was divided into two sections by a Dutch door worn with teeth marks.

> On the walls I saw tiny corpses of spiders and bugs that had been permanently whitewashed to the boards by the army painters. A single light bulb dangled from the ceiling, and three folded army cots lay on the dirty floor. This was to be our "home" for the next five months.[60]

On September 16, 1942, after their father had been reunited with them, the government sent the family to the Central Utah Relocation Center (later renamed the Topaz Relocation Center, or simply Topaz, fig. 9.12). Uchida would write that she had "felt fairly hopeful, for we were passing small farms, cultivated fields and clusters of trees." As they neared the camp, however,

> there was an abrupt change . . . There were no trees or grass or growth of any kind, only clumps of dry skeletal greasewood. . . . As the bus drew up to one of the barracks, I was surprised to hear band music. Marching toward us down the dusty road was the drum and bugle corps of the young Boy Scouts who had come with the advance contingent, carrying signs that read, "Welcome to Topaz—Your Camp." It was a touching sight to see them standing in the burning sun, covered with dust, as they tried to ease the shock of our arrival at this desolate desert camp.[61]

The Uchidas were assigned to Apartment C, Barrack 2, Block 7:

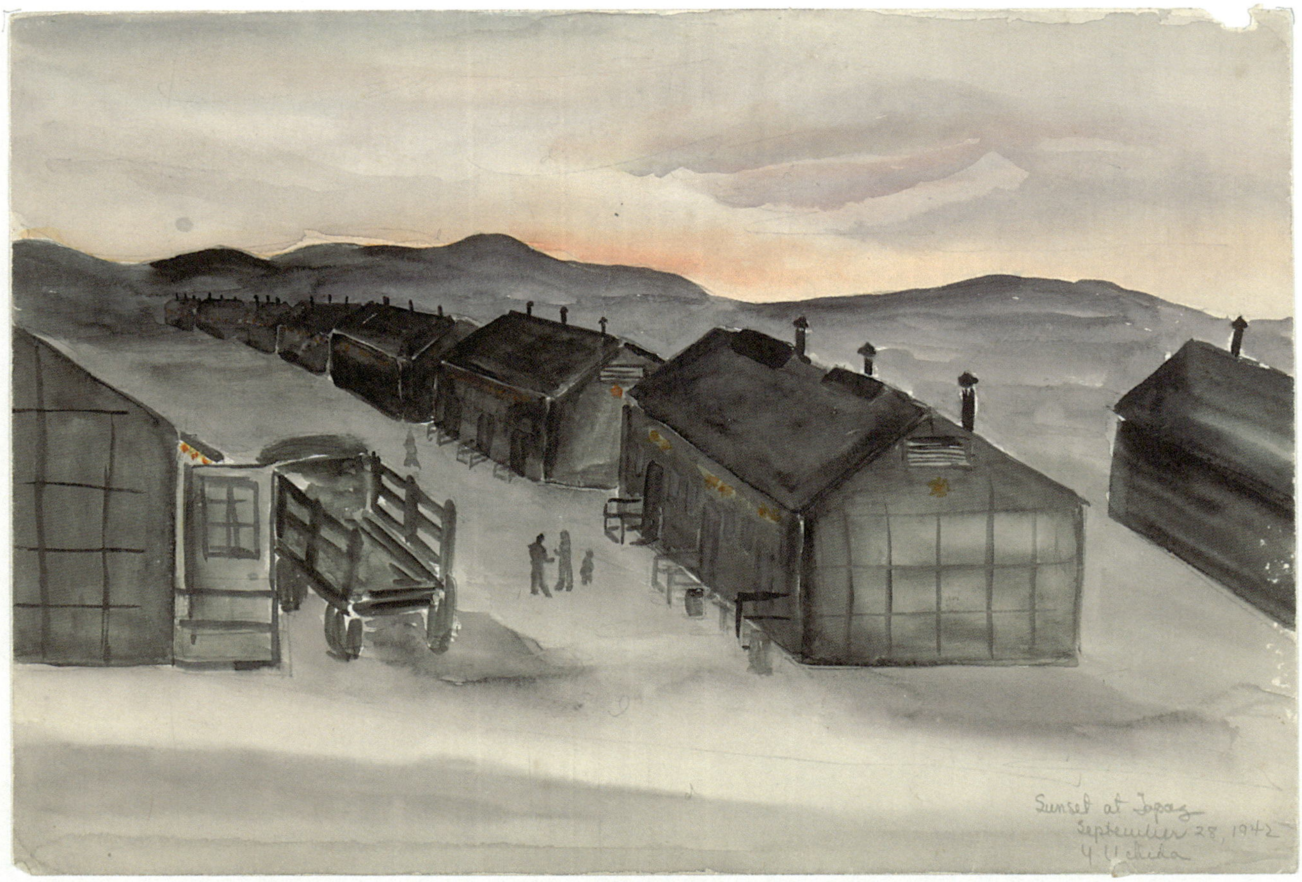

FIGURE 9.12
"Sunset at Topaz," watercolor by Yoshiko Uchida, September 28, 1942.

> When we stepped into our room it contained nothing but four army cots without mattresses. No inner sheetrock walls or ceilings had yet been installed, nor had the black pot-bellied stove that stood outside the door. Cracks were visible everywhere in the siding and around the windows, and although our friends had swept out our room before we arrived, the dust was already seeping into it again from all sides.[62]

Yoshiko's internment ended in May 1943, when she and her sister received government clearances to leave the camp.[63] She went to Northampton, Massachusetts, to attend Smith College, where she received, in 1944, her master's degree in education. "Some of our friends came with my mother and father to the gate to see us off," she later recalled, "but the joy of our impending freedom was greatly tempered by the pain of leaving them behind."[64]

Uchida taught first and second graders at the Frankford Friends School near Philadelphia, but after several attacks of mononucleosis she left for a secretarial job at the Institute of Pacific Relations in New York City. In June 1952, she received a check for $386.25 from the U.S. government as reimbursement for her material losses during the internment.

Uchida had been writing short stories since she was in sixth grade, and fondly remembered one of her early stories, "Jimmy Chipmunk and His Friends—a Short Story for Small Children."[65] Now she was writing again, receiving numerous rejection slips from such magazines as the *Atlantic Monthly* and the *New Yorker*. She did, however, receive encouraging words from one *New Yorker* editor who met with her and encouraged her to write about her "concentration camp experiences."[66]

In 1952, her life changed when she won a Ford Foundation Foreign Area Fellowship. While studying in Japan for two years, she slowly realized "that everything I admired and loved about Japan was a part of me. . . . My parents had been giving it to me, like a gift, every day of my life." When she was young, she had pushed her "Japaneseness" aside, she wrote. "Now at last, I appreciated it and was proud of it. I had finally come full circle. . . . Now it was time for me to pass on this sense of pride and self-esteem to the third generation Japanese Americans—the Sansei—and to give them the kinds of books I'd never had as a child."[67]

All of Uchida's children's books, many of which were translated into Japanese, were devoted to Japanese or Japanese American themes, including the history and traditions of Japan, the story of the detention camps, and her personal story. During her fellowship trip to Japan, she studied Japanese folk art and met the leaders of the Folk Art Movement, philosopher Soetsu Yanagi, and the potters Shoji Hamada and Kanjiro Kawai.[68] Uchida also collected folktales. In

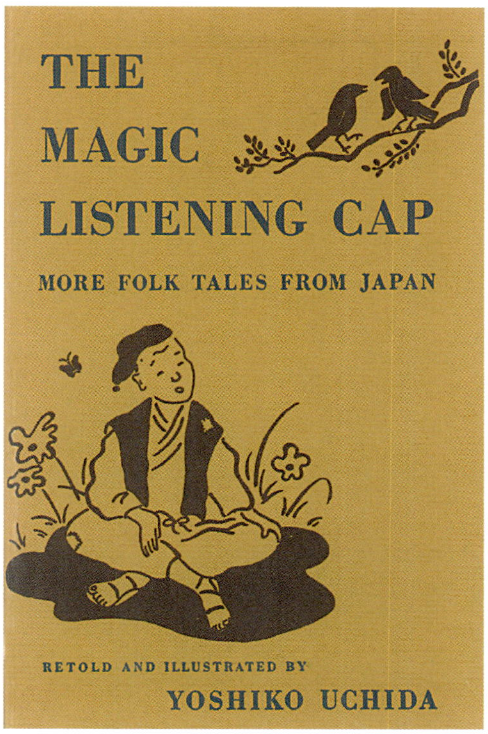

FIGURE 9.13
The Magic Listening Cap, retold and illustrated by Yoshiko Uchida. New York: Harcourt, Brace, 1955.

The Magic Listening Cap: More Folk Tales from Japan (1955, fig. 9.13), she included the story of the man whose magic cap allows him to understand the language of animals; the rice ball that rolls into the god's den; and the white stork that turns into a beautiful young maiden. She retold these stories, one reviewer noted, with the "same simplicity and directness"[69] as in her earlier collection, *The Dancing Kettle and Other Japanese Folk Tales* (1949).

During the 1960s Uchida wrote a number of books for young girls. Set in Japan, they feature strong female protagonists who are curious, independent, and full of ideas. *In-between Miya* (1967) tells about eleven-year-old Miya, who learns to appreciate life in her thatch-roofed farmhouse; a young girl's glass float brings luck to her father in *Keiko's Bubble* (1961). In *The Forever Christmas Tree* (1963) young Kaya brings Christmas to the villagers who had not known its meaning.

Uchida set her next stories—books for the youngest readers—in the Japanese American community. They included *The Birthday Visitor* (1975), a lighthearted story of young Emi's fear that Reverend Okura will spoil her birthday party; and *The Rooster Who Understood Japanese* (1976), about clever Miyo and Mrs. Kitamura's "friendly, intelligent, dignified" rooster.

Gradually Uchida began to tell stories that were closer to her own experience. All three books in her trilogy, *A Jar of Dreams* (1981), *The Best Bad Thing* (1983), and *The Happiest Ending* (1985), are set in Berkeley during the 1930s and tell the story of the Tsujimuras—Mama, Papa, big brother Cal, and younger brother Joji. The first-person narrator, twelve-year-old Rinko, whom Uchida endowed with many of her own personality traits—plus an extra dollop of "gumption"[70]—freely shares her opinions and loves to get into the thick of things: she calls a man a bully, dares the boys, and jumps on a freight train. As anti-Japanese sentiment builds, things get ugly. Someone slashes Papa's tires and later Maxie, Joji's dog, is shot dead.

After Mama opens a laundry in the basement, then gets a note that reads "GET OUT OF OUR TERRITORY JAP LAUNDRY, OR YOU'LL BE SORRY,"[71] Papa and Uncle Kanda go and face up to Mr. Starr, the owner of the big Starr Laundry. Rinko sneaks in when Mr. Starr says, "You people are all alike, undercutting us with your cheap labor and cheap prices. That's bad for all of us. Why don't you just go on back where you came from?" But her father stood up straight and replied in a voice "like taut steel wire cutting into Mr. Starr's soft white flesh," that the Japanese did work hard, that there was no law against working hard, and even though they charged less than Mr. Starr, they were no threat to him since the Starr company had "four trucks picking up laundry all over the city."[72]

Just then Joji pushed her and Rinko fell "and landed with a terrible racket right in front of everybody."[73] "'Get outta here, you damn no-good Jap kids,' [Mr. Starr] screamed . . . but Papa grabbed his arm before he could get near us. 'Don't you ever talk to my children like that again,' said Papa real slow, making every word count. 'And don't you or your men ever bother us again.'"[74]

In the end, Rinko and her family realized that it was Mama's sister, Aunt Waka, their quiet guest from Japan, who had told them to stand up for themselves and who had "stirred us up and changed us all so we'd never be quite the same again." "I was really beginning to feel better about myself," Rinko said, "even the part of me that was Japanese."[75]

It took many years, until after her mother's death in 1966, before Uchida was able to write her poignant, and perhaps finest book, *Journey to Topaz: A Story of the Japanese-American Evacuation* (1971, fig. 9.14), and its sequel *Journey Home* (1978). She later told the story in the picture book, *The Bracelet* (figs. 9.15–16).[76] "Although the characters are fictitious," she wrote in the prologue to *Journey*

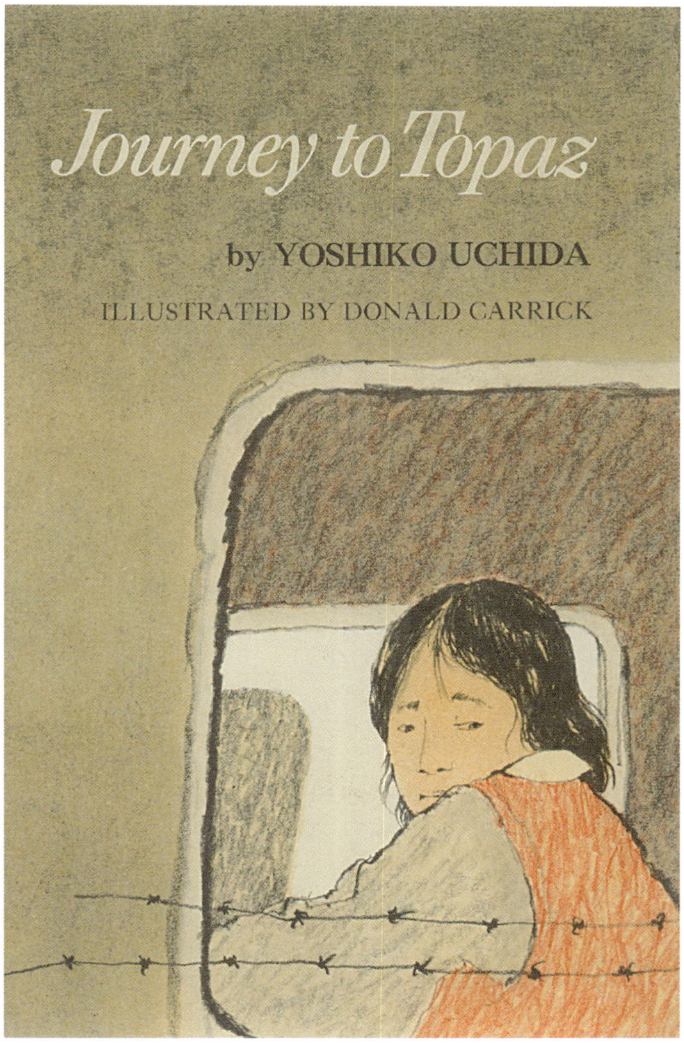

FIGURE 9.14
Journey to Topaz: A Story of the Japanese-American Evacuation, by Yoshiko Uchida, illustrated by Donald Carrick. New York: Scribner, 1971.

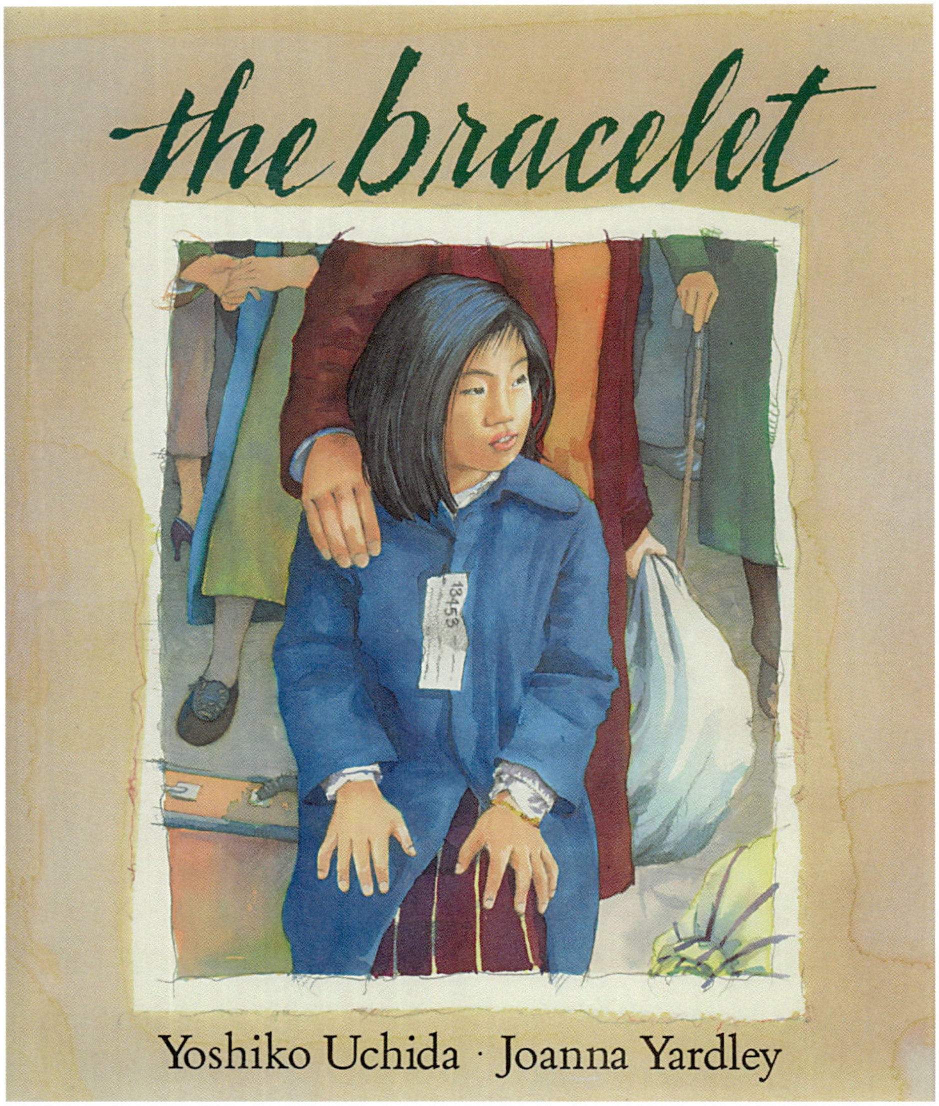

FIGURE 9.15
The Bracelet, by Yoshiko Uchida, illustrated by Joanna Yardley. New York: Philomel, 1993.

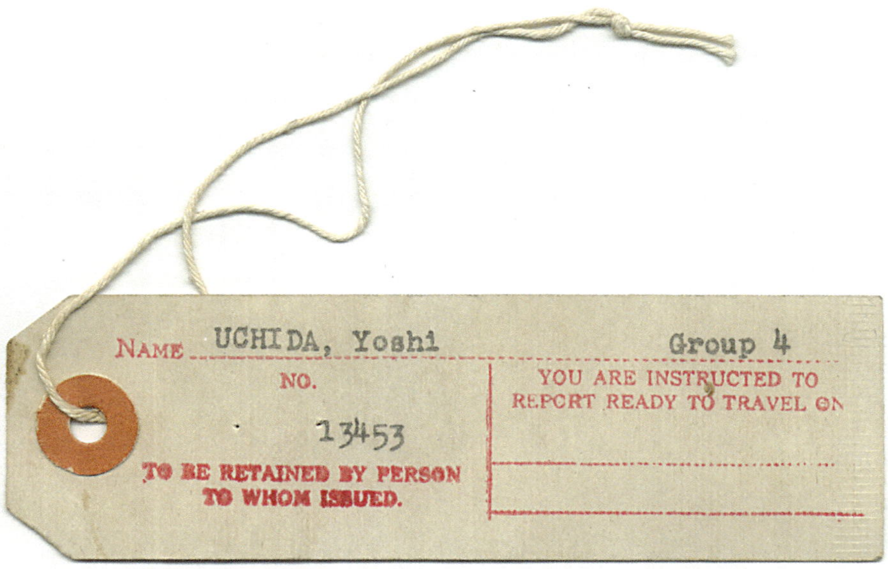

FIGURE 9.16
Nametag from Yoshiko Uchida scrapbook, 1942–45.

to Topaz, "the events are based on actual fact, and much that happened to the Sakane family also happened to my own."[77]

True to her Japanese upbringing, she told the story with restraint, simplicity, and without showing her anger. Eleven-year-old Yuki relates how FBI agents take her father away, how the family has to sell their possessions in a few days, and how they try to find a place to save diaries and other family mementos—including the scraps of paper on which her mother had written her Japanese poems. Uchida conveys the hurt caused by a headline in the April 21, 1942, Berkeley paper: JAPS GIVEN EVACUATION ORDERS HERE.[78]

In *Journey to Topaz*, Uchida describes Yuki's terror suffered through the Utah desert dust storm that would haunt her all of her life. In *Journey Home*, Yuki relives the storm in a nightmare:

> I CAN'T SEE, YUKI THOUGHT FRANTICALLY, I CAN'T BREATHE. The screaming desert wind flung its white powdery sand into her face, stifling her and wrapping her up in a smothering cocoon of sand so fine it was like dust. It blinded her and choked her and made her gag as she opened her mouth to cry out.
>
> The black tar-papered barracks on either side of the road had vanished behind the swirling dust, and Yuki was all alone in an eerie, unreal world where nothing existed except the shrieking wind and the great choking clouds of dust. Yuki stumbled on, doubled over, pushing hard against the wind, gasping as she felt the sting of sand and pebbles against her legs.
>
> Suppose she never got back to her barrack? Suppose the wind simply picked her up and flung her out beyond the barbed wire fence into the desert? Suppose no one ever found her dried, wind-blown body out there in the sagebrush?
>
> A cry of terror swelled up inside her. "Mama! Papa! Help me!"
>
> The sound of her own scream woke her up. Yuki's heart was pounding. Her damp fists were clenched tight. Her face was wet with tears.
>
> For several minutes she couldn't believe it was only a nightmare. It had all seemed so real, she could almost taste the flat, powdery dust in her mouth.[79]

After Yuki's father secures a "special clearance," the family leaves Topaz for Salt Lake City, where Yuki had to adjust to another new home, and to their new landlady, Mrs. Henley. Yuki felt she never quite trusted the Sakanes:

> Once she'd asked Yuki why they had been sent to the concentration camp in the first place.
>
> "Why would the President make all the Japanese leave the West Coast if you weren't dangerous?" she asked.

> "Papa says there were a lot of reasons," Yuki explained. "It was partly panic and partly because there've always been people in California who wanted to get rid of us."
>
> Mrs. Henley pursed her lips. "Well, it's possible you people might have tried to help Japan. After all, it *is* your country."
>
> "But it's *not* my country. The United States is," Yuki said impatiently.
>
> "But why would your own country put you behind barbed wire?"
>
> "They never should have."
>
> "Weren't there some Japanese who sent signals from their fishing boats?"
>
> "No! Those were lies."
>
> How could Mrs. Henley believe those stupid rumors? Yuki wished Ken were there to help explain everything to her. He'd know. She tried hard to think what Ken might say.
>
> "My brother Ken volunteered for the army from camp," she said, her voice rising, "'even if his country put him in a concentration camp."
>
> Mrs. Henley's eyebrows arched up in surprise. "He did?"
>
> "Sure. So did his friend Jim Hirai. They both went."[80]

The camps were often described euphemistically by government administrators and internees alike. "Evacuation" really meant forced removal, "assembly centers" were actually temporary concentration camps, "relocation centers" were permanent concentration camps. The term "protective custody" was also used. Only gradually did Uchida feel at ease with the more candid terms for the centers, even poking fun at them. In *Journey to Topaz*, when the family has been shown their new quarters, Yuki reads the instruction hand-out:

> "Listen," [Yuki] said, reading aloud, "You are now in Topaz, Utah. Here we say dining hall, not mess hall; Safety Council, not Internal Police; residents, not evacuees, and last but not least, mental climate, not morale." [81]

Yet there is also hope for Yuki and her family. After her brother Ken returns from the war—injured and grieving for his friend Jim—Mr. and Mrs. Olssen, their new neighbors, invite the family for Thanksgiving dinner. Ken asks about the family photo on the fireplace mantle. It is of the Olssens' son, Johnny. "'Our son was killed in Iwo Jima,' said Mr. Olssen in a low voice. "Mama gasped, 'Your only son was killed by the Japanese?'"[82]

Uchida's final books included her autobiography, *Desert Exile: The Uprooting of a Japanese American Family* (1982); her heavy-hearted adult novel *Picture Bride* (1987), the story of Hana Omiya, who sails to America in 1917, only to sacrifice her whole life for her husband and a daughter who elopes with a white boy; and *The Invisible Thread*, (1991) a young readers' version of *Desert Exile*. Concluding, Uchida wrote:

> I hope the young people who read [my books] will dare to have big dreams . . . I also hope they will learn to see Japanese Americans not in the stereotypical way, but as fellow human beings. For although it is important for each of us to cherish our own special heritage, I believe, above everything else, we must all celebrate our common humanity.[83]

Kazue Mizumura

Kazue Mizumura, a child of the Taishō era, displayed the independence and confidence for which that era became known. Tested by hardship and sorrow, Mizumura survived to become a teacher, painter, textile designer, jewelry maker, advertising artist, and, finally, an illustrator and writer of children's books.

Born in Kamakura, one of Japan's former capitals, Mizumura was the youngest of five children. Her grandfather, Seifu Takasaki, was a poet and scholar. Her father, Yumihiko Takasaki, a baron and member of the Upper House of the Diet, was among the Japanese officials who were posted to Dairen, Manchuria. It was there that Mizumura entered primary school in 1926. When the family returned to Japan in the early 1930s, she entered *Gakushuin*, the Peeresses' School, the elite institution established by Emperor Meiji for the children of the aristocracy, graduating in 1938. Many years later, her good friend and classmate Tsukiko Nakamura remembered how Mizumura made all her schoolmates "laugh in history class with her cartoon drawings" and recalled the "wonderful sketches" she made that were inspired by the popular artist Sentaro Iwata.[84] Mizumura, herself, noted that drawing was "the only thing I could do really well among all the things I had to learn during my school years. Thus it was natural for me to enter the Art Institute [in Tokyo], though I did not particularly want to be an artist."[85] It was at the Art Institute, which she entered in 1939, and from which she graduated in 1942, where her art-inspired path began.

Mizumura's father "doted on her," as a friend wrote, and though he strongly "objected to her first marriage" to a handsome young banker, he could not stop her. Mizumura gave birth to her daughter during World War II.[86] But her dream to be "just an ordinary happy wife and a mother" tragically ended after the war, when both her husband and daughter died.[87] Her life and her country in ruins, Mizumura began anew, as a friend reflected:

> Right after the war, it was very hard for Japanese women to be independent and to earn [their] own living. But [Kazue] made the most of her talent. She taught art, and got a job at the American P.X. in Tokyo, where she sold scarfs, pictures, [and] cards of her own designs which led her to the decision to study commercial art in the United States.[88]

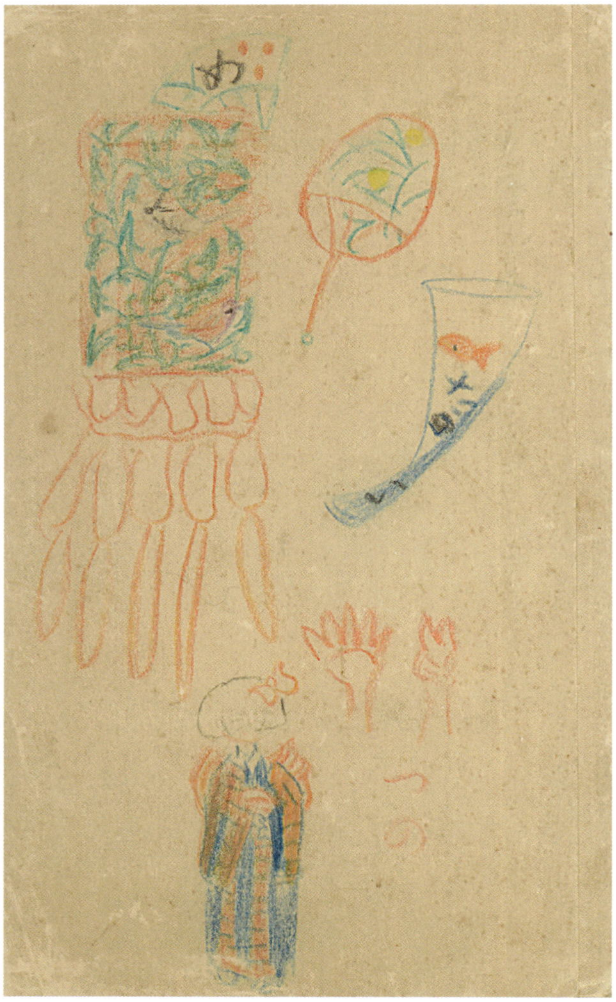

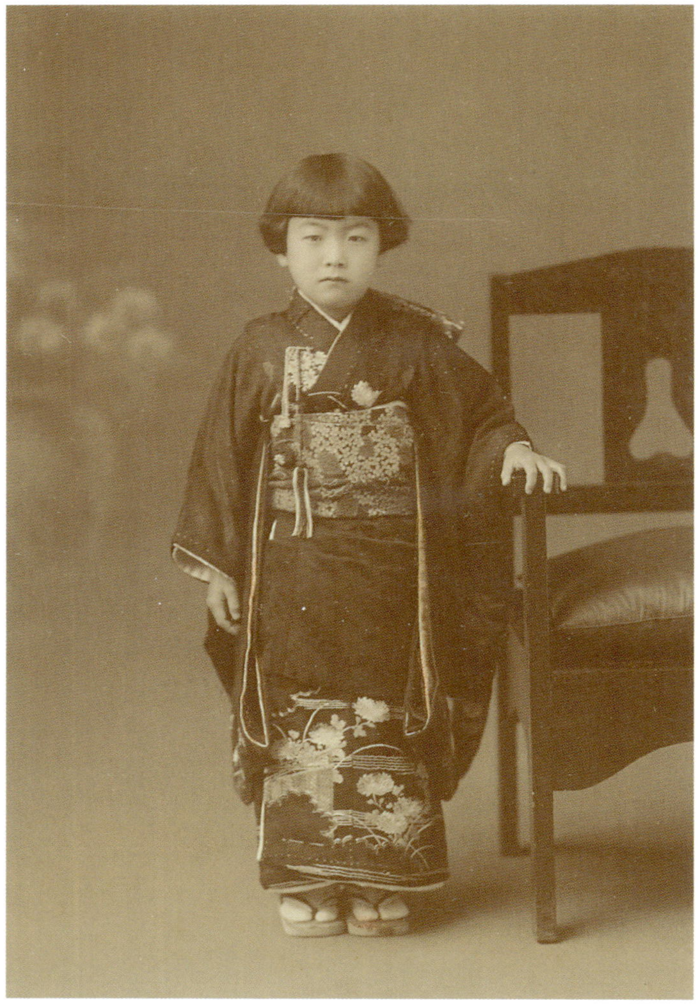

FIGURES 9.17 AND 9.18 Childhood drawing (left) by Kazue Mizumura (right), 1926.

Acting on that decision was not easy. To make ends meet, Mizumura wrote another friend, she had to work "at all manner of jobs, save those of ill repute."[89] Her friend later observed that "the energy and strength she showed during that time came not just from her character, but also from the moral education we received at school."[90] Mizumura taught calligraphy and *sumi-e* (traditional Japanese ink painting) to members of the American occupation forces. Some became lifelong friends.[91] One of them sponsored Mizumura's travel to America aboard a merchant vessel.[92] She arrived in New York in 1955, having won a two-year scholarship from Pratt Institute of Art in Brooklyn.[93]

After completing her studies, an American friend later reported, she "struggle[d] to make a living [with] textile design, upscale Japanese restaurant décor, jewelry, ceramics, and book illustration. To her dismay, the textile companies sometimes copied her designs in a back room and gave her neither credit nor payment."[94] She married the German writer and student of classical Japanese literature Claus Stamm.

Once again, she suffered heartbreaking sorrow when her second child died in infancy. Her marriage to Stamm ended in divorce. In 1963, with her friend Ruth Ueymura, Mizumura bought a house in Stamford, Connecticut. Here, from her picture window, she could watch Long Island Sound and observe the animals, birds, and plants she would feature in her children's books. Good fortune finally came Mizumura's way. It came about largely because of the Emperor's invitation to Elizabeth Gray Vining.

On October 1, 1946, Vining, a librarian, writer, and a Quaker, sailed to Japan to begin a four-year stay as tutor for then twelve-year-old Crown Prince Akihito. In her late forties, childless and widowed,[95] and on her first visit to Japan, Vining was chosen by the Emperor Hirohito himself from a list provided to him by the staff of General Douglas MacArthur. The Emperor was so pleased with the result that he was later overheard saying "If ever anything I did has been a success, it was asking Mrs. Vining to come here."[96]

"Teacher of Jap Prince finds Job Royal Plum,"[97] wrote the *Chicago Daily Tribune* irreverently, reflecting the tone of the time. "Tutor to Teach Jap Prince of American Ways of Peace," was the way the *Christian Science Monitor* announced Vining's teaching assignment, which would include "stories of Washington and Longfellow and of American thoughts and ideals."[98]

Vining lived in the Mejiro district of Tokyo, where she was able to observe the lives of ordinary Japanese who were trying to survive the postwar years. "For many months," she wrote, "I was not able to look at those wasted gardens and make-shift homes without seeing vividly in my mind the planes at night, the fire, the terror, the running people, the loss, and the sorrow."[99] She saw that "food was dreadfully scarce" and rice rations forced black market prices to skyrocket, making this Japanese staple exorbitantly expensive. One day she observed a woman picking up grains of rice from the gutter, "one by one, with a pair of tweezers."[100]

Vining was deeply moved by the absence of bitterness among the Japanese. "There was an acceptance of things as they were of which I think we as a people are incapable," she wrote. "People who had been burned out two or three times and who now were engaged in a desperate struggle to keep alive and to maintain standards, were able to put the past behind them and to go forward with patience and courage."[101]

Gradually, Vining fell in love with Japan and its people and came to understand and appreciate their culture and traditions. She distilled her love and admiration for Japan in her engaging children's book *The Cheerful Heart* (1959, fig. 9.19), which told the story of the Tamaki family—father, mother, grandfather, six-year old Ken, and eleven-year old Tomi. After almost three years living in the

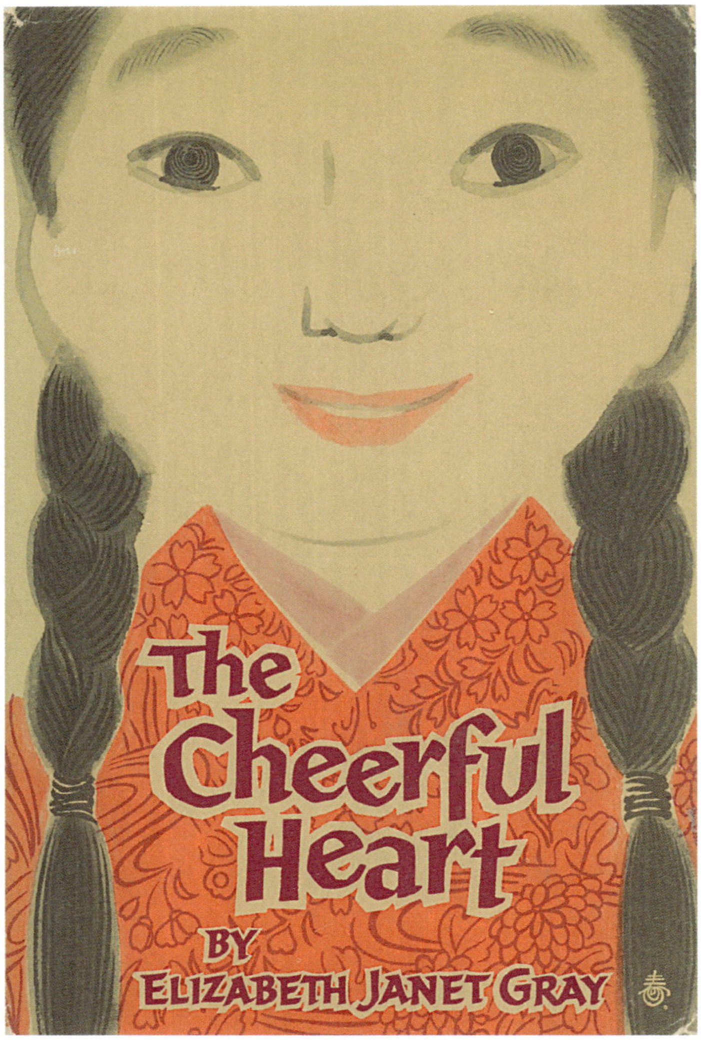

FIGURE 9.19
The Cheerful Heart, by Elizabeth Gray Vining, illustrated by Kazue Mizumura. New York: Viking Press, 1959.

country with Uncle Saburo, the Tamakis return to their old Mejiro neighborhood. They find their house destroyed; Mariko, their eldest daughter, dead, and Ichiro, their older son, still missing. As they slowly rebuild their lives, it is Tomi, the middle child, who cheers up the family with her exuberance and joy over her new bicycle, the puppy that wanders into their yard, the new house, and, finally, the family's own bath:

> There was great rejoicing, for the Japanese family feels about its bath the way a Western family feels about its open fireplace: it is the heart of the home. The bath means not only cleanliness to them, though that is very important, but it means warmth also and relaxation and family unity. In a strange, deep way it means belonging to Japan and not to some other country, however fine.[102]

Vining wanted a Japanese illustrator for her book, and Mizumura was chosen (Taro Yashima had been considered). To set the tone, Mizumura drew Tomi's face for the cover:

> [Tomi] was now, her grandfather said, all legs and pigtails. Her black braids hung down to her shoulder blades, and there was just a little wave in her hair, so that the short hairs curled up around her forehead and at the back of her neck where the straight pale part ended. She had a round little face with a neat nose and a mouth that naturally turned up at the corners. Her cheeks were pink, with dimples that came and went, but what people noticed especially about her was her eyes. They were wide apart and very clear and candid. They seemed to see everything, and when they saw something amusing they would shine as if there were a light behind them.[103]

The Cheerful Heart marked the beginning of Mizumura's children's book career.[104] Her illustrations for the book depict events in the story and other traditional Japanese scenes: the family moving into their new house carrying bundles and bags; shoes and clogs in the *genkan* (house entrance); the bathtub maker at work; children fashioning cucumbers and eggplants into horses for the *o-bon* festival; Tomi's deep bow as she offers her room to her Honorable Elder Brother, who comes home from Siberia.

After the success of *The Cheerful Heart*, other publishers called on Mizumura to provide illustrations. She found the work rewarding and restricting at the same time:

> My illustration assignments seemed to have been limited to books with Japanese themes. I believe that most publishers felt that since I was Japanese they could expect authenticity for the Japanese background from me. In doing the illustrations for the Japanese background stories, there was little I could do with my technique since the publishers expected authentic representational illustrations.[105]

Another young Japanese woman who had come to the United States on a scholarship, Masako Matsuno, wrote the text for Mizumura's first picture book. As an assignment for one of their classes at Columbia University, students were asked to write a story for children. To Matsuno's dismay, the teacher never mentioned her story during class. Afterwards, however, the teacher suggested that Matsuno publish the story.[106] In 1960, acclaimed children's book publisher Ann Beneduce published it as *A Pair of Red Clogs* (figs. 9.20–21). Enhanced by Mizumura's illustrations, the book was a great success. One reviewer wrote:

> The Japanese artist, now living in New York City, has pictured it with great liveliness and humor, showing wonderfully real views inside Mako's house, the shopping street where she selects her new clogs for school next day, and the playing of the weather-telling game with clogs—so disastrous for Mako.[107]

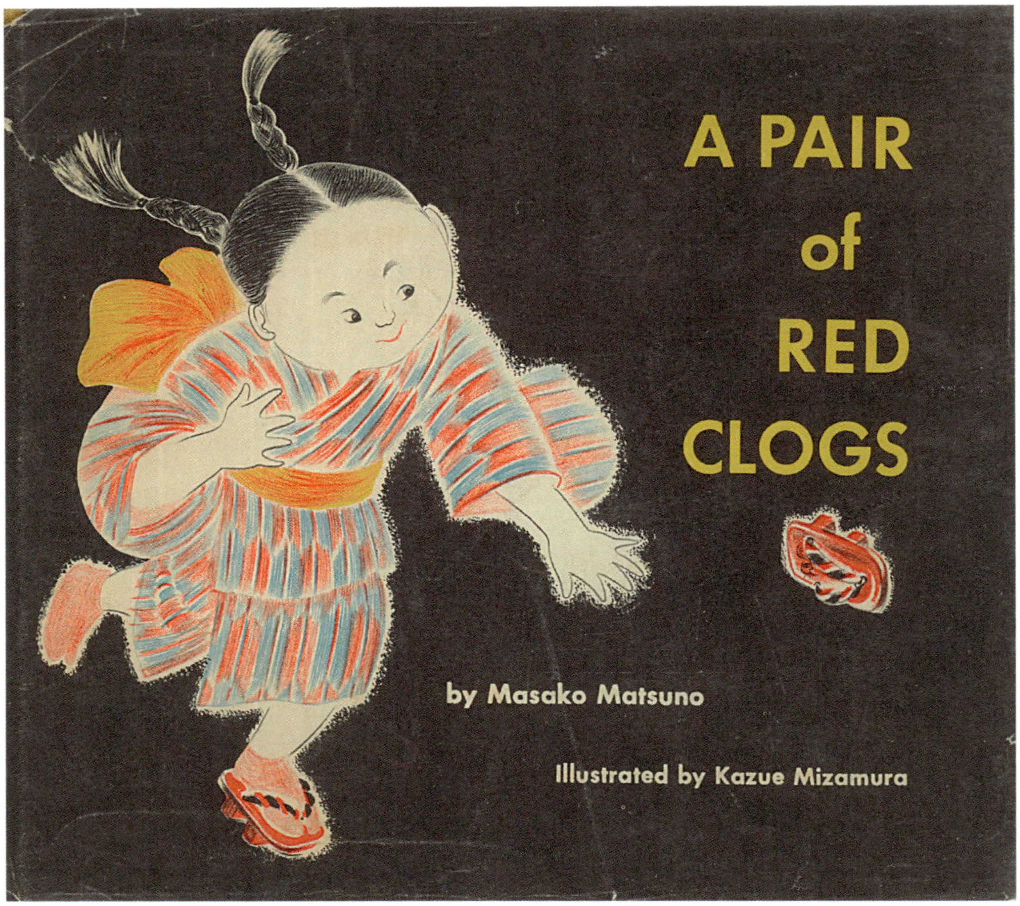

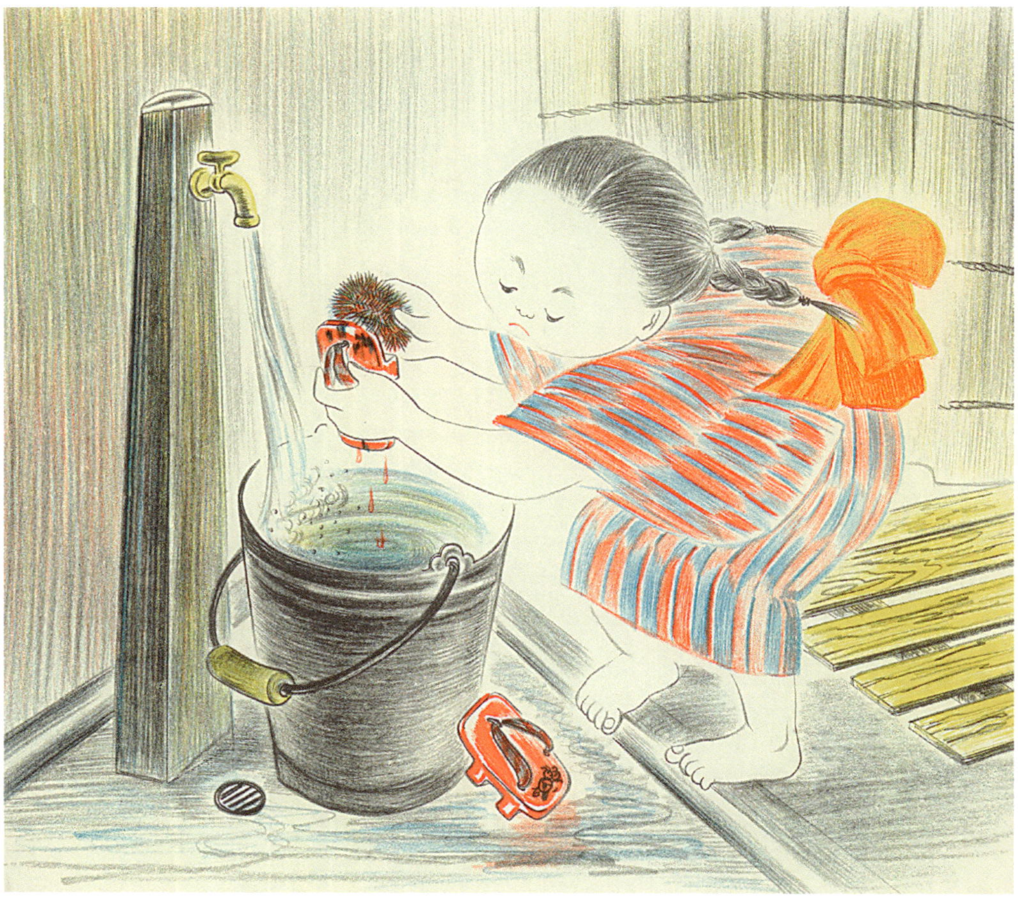

FIGURES 9.20 AND 9.21
A Pair of Red Clogs, by Masuko Matsuno, illustrated by Kazue Mizumura. Cleveland: World Publishing, 1960.

Mizumura continued to illustrate children's books with Japanese themes, including Claus Stamm's *Three Strong Women: A Tall Tale from Japan* (1962), in which Forever-Mountain, the famous wrestler, is done in by three unusual girls.

Mizumura went on to illustrate *Keiko's Bubble* (1961), a lyrical story of a poor Japanese fisherman's daughter; *Suzu and the Bride Doll* (1960), about oba-san's (grandma) surprise on Girl's Day; *Taro and the Tōfu* (1962), about a boy who is tempted to cheat the tofu maker; and *Chie and the Sports Day* (1965), about a young girl who wants to compete just like the boys.

Illustrating the sports day book, in which Chie finally gets a chance to team up with her brother Ichiro, Mizumura was "delighted to . . . show . . . contemporary Japanese children in modern dress, rather than in traditional costume," Ann Beneduce later wrote. "She felt it was important for American children to know what modern Japanese children were like, rather than getting the impression that they still wore kimonos [*sic*] and samurai outfits."[108]

Increasingly, Mizumura's work became recognized and her illustrations appeared in a number of books by noted children's book authors. She illustrated Yoshiko Uchida's *Sumi's Prize* (1964), the story of how Sumi almost wins first place in the kite flying contest, and *Sumi & the Goat & the Tokyo Express* (1969, fig. 9.1), in which Mr. Oda's pet goat Miki—wearing Sumi's red hat—stops the new bullet train. In these books Mizumura depicted traditional customs, many of which were beginning to disappear in Japan.

Gradually, Mizumura branched out into children's books set in other places.[109] Among fine writer-illustrator matches were *The Prince Who Gave up a Throne: A Story of the Buddha* (1966) by Nancy Serage, the tale of Siddhartha, the holy prince who leaves the splendor of his father's kingdom of Kapilavastu to seek the word of God; and *The Moon of the Winter Bird* (1969) by Jean Craighead George, in which Mizumura showed her talent for watercolors of small birds, Queen Anne's lace, wild thistles, and other delicate grasses native to America.

By the end of the 1960s, American post-war enthusiasm for things Japanese had waned. Mizumura, too, was ready to leave Japanese motifs behind. Her editor, Elizabeth Riley, agreed and encouraged her to write her own stories. "I do believe the mediums should differ according to the theme of the text," Mizumura later observed, "[and] by illustrating my own books, I hope that I can develop my technique and style without restraint."[110]

Under the direction of her new editor, Ann Beneduce, who, after Riley's retirement in 1969, became vice president and editor-in-chief of the children's book department at Crowell, Mizumura was very much encouraged to work without restraint. As she created more of her own stories, poetry, and books of nonfiction,

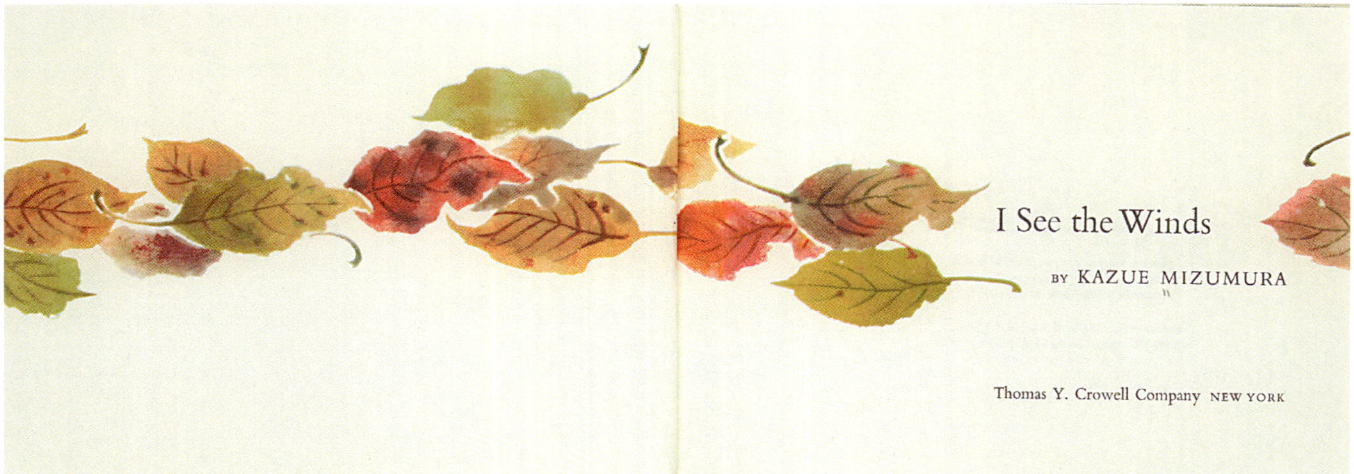

FIGURE 9.22
I See the Winds, by Kazue Mizumura. New York: Thomas Y. Crowell, 1966.

her artistic style broadened. An example is *The Emperor Penguins* (1969), one of the Let's-Read-and-Find-Out Science Books.[111] In all her books her love for the natural world was obvious as she drew, with ease, all kinds of creatures, including ants, jellyfish, pandas, and penguins.

Yet, looking back over her rich work, Mizumura's finest books were those that sprang from her Japanese heritage. Among them was the haiku-inspired *I See the Winds* (1966, fig. 9.22), which includes the following lines:

Once again
the wind rustled the young leaves
and the trees turned
to greet spring.
. . .
From a mountain of fallen leaves
totters a pheasant:
A windy night last night.[112]

Mizumura's own favorite book was the serene *Flower Moon Snow: A Book of Haiku* (1977, fig. 9.23),[113] a small album she illuminated with modest earth-toned woodcuts:

Is it waiting for me,
This one wildflower
In the empty lot?
. . .
White petals falling
In the moonlit mist;
The pear tree blossoms no more.
. . .

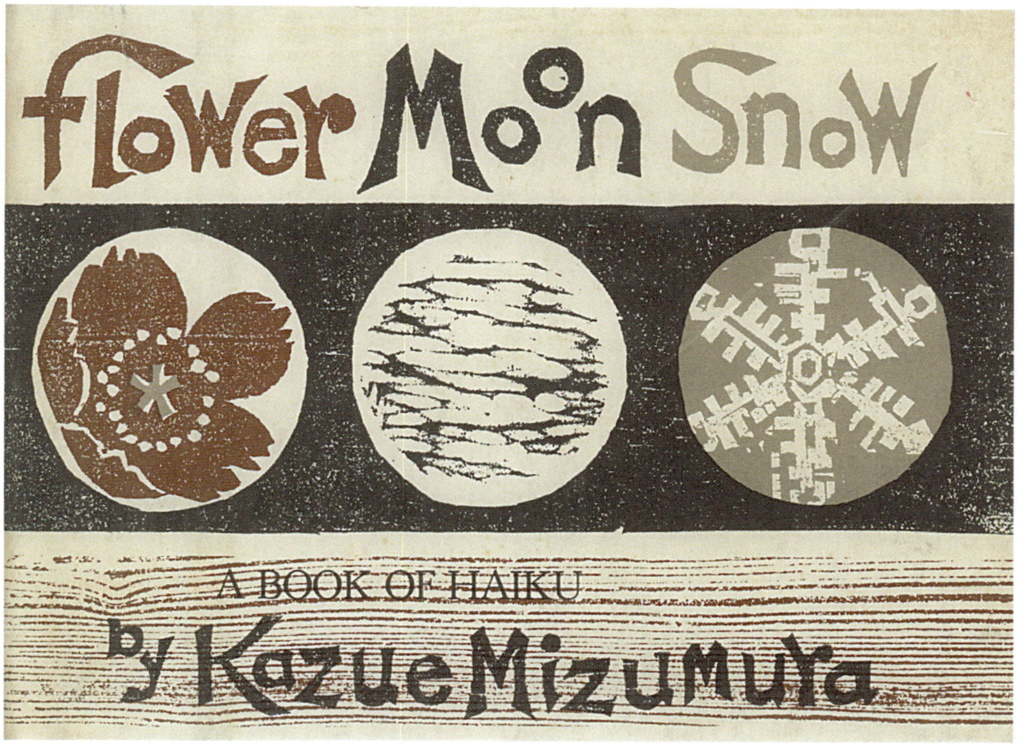

FIGURE 9.23
Flower Moon Snow: A Book of Haiku, by Kazue Mizumura, New York: Thomas Y. Crowell, 1977.

Clink!
An iced branch falls.
I see the shattered moonlight
Scatter at my feet
. . .
Snowflakes dancing, whirl and whirl
Then die at my door.[114]

Ann Beneduce wrote about Mizumura:

> A sensitive response to the beauty of nature was important to Kazue. She thought of it as part of her Japanese heritage . . . She gave a general impression of intelligence and quiet sophistication. She was well adapted to her two cultures, Japanese and American, and seemed comfortable living with a sort of dual personality.[115]

Mizumura kept her Japanese and American lives apart. A naturalized American citizen, she rarely spoke about her life in Japan, but, in her later years, often visited the country of her ancestors. She never lost her heavy Japanese accent, speaking with an immigrant's charming imperfections. Her friends remembered her resilience, her sense of humor, and her kindness.[116] They described her as a modest and private person[117] defined by her "simplicity and elegance: [in her] dress . . . art, [and] life."[118]

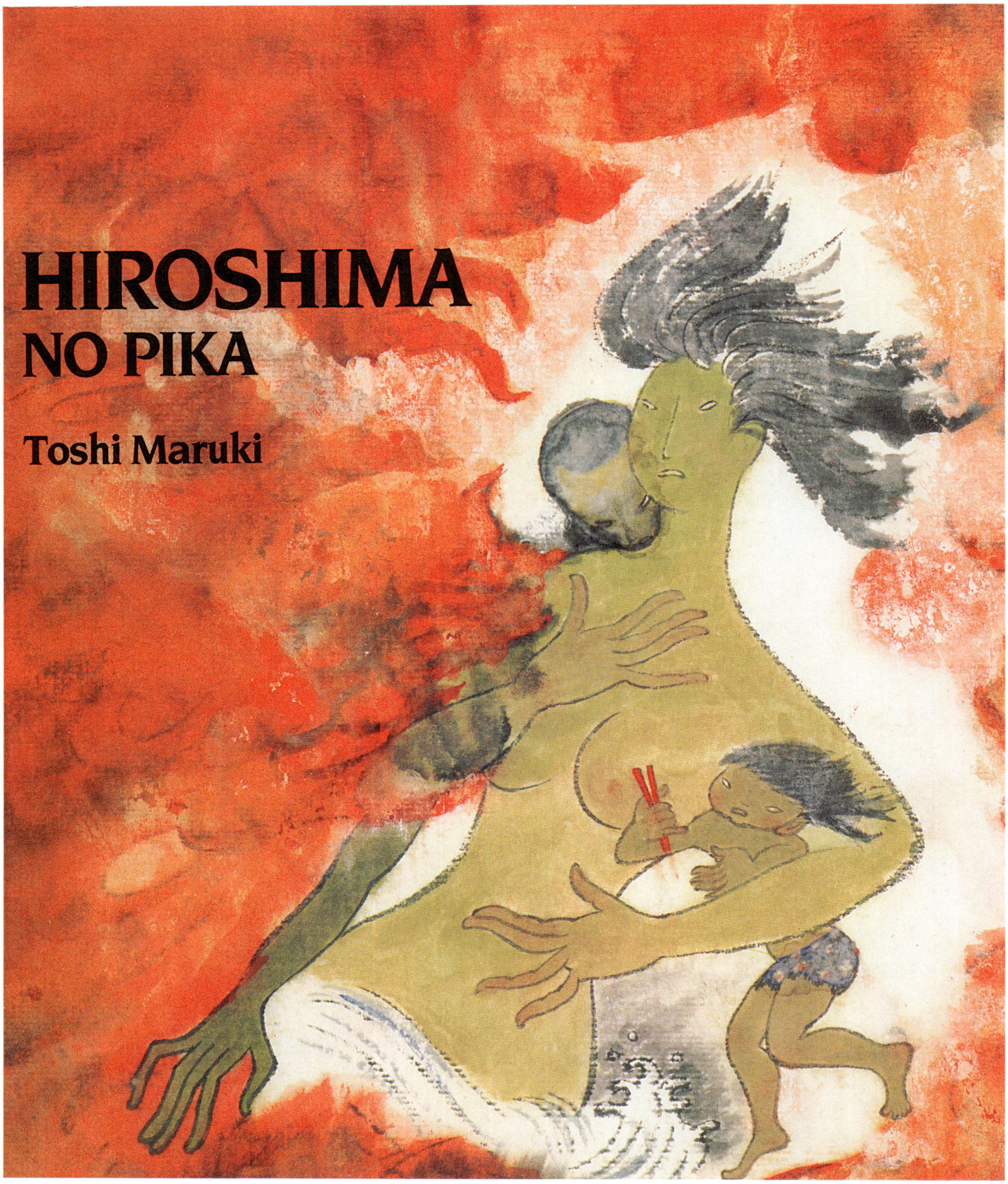
HIROSHIMA
NO PIKA
Toshi Maruki

10

Into the Twenty-First Century

In 1965, two years after Martin Luther King delivered his "I Have a Dream" speech on the steps of the Lincoln Memorial in Washington, DC, an article, called "The All-White World of Children's Books" made headlines in the children's book community. Its author, educator Nancy Larrick, reported that only a very small number of the approximately five thousand children's books published between 1962 and 1964 described the contemporary life of African Americans.[1] The same was undoubtedly true for children's books about Japan and the lives of Japanese American children. This, however, was going to change. Over the next decades, American children's books were to become more timely and relevant in their description of all strands of American life.

By 1979, when the Bologna Children's Book Fair celebrated the International Year of the Child, children's books about Japan were already presenting more information and writing on topics that a number of authors had found too painful to address earlier. The new children's books—many now written by Japanese Americans—revealed, for example, Japan's role as an aggressor nation in World War II and reported on the bombing of Hiroshima and Nagasaki and Japanese Americans' confinement to American internment camps.

Postwar Despair

Two autobiographical novels by Yoko Kawashima Watkins, *So Far from the Bamboo Grove* (1986, fig. 10.2) and its sequel *My Brother, My Sister, and I* (1994, fig. 10.3), stand out from the end of this period and are particularly haunting. Born in Japanese-occupied Harbin, Manchuria, in northeastern China, where her father was stationed as a Japanese government official, the author and her family moved to Nanam, North Korea, sometime in the early 1940s, while it was still under Japanese occupation. As the political situation in Korea became increasingly dangerous for the Japanese, and after having being warned and aided by a family friend, eleven-year-old Yoko, her sixteen-year-old sister Ko, and their mother abruptly fled

FIGURE 10.1 (OPPOSITE) *Hiroshima no Pika*, written and illustrated by Toshi Maruki. New York: Lothrop, Lee & Shepard, 1980.

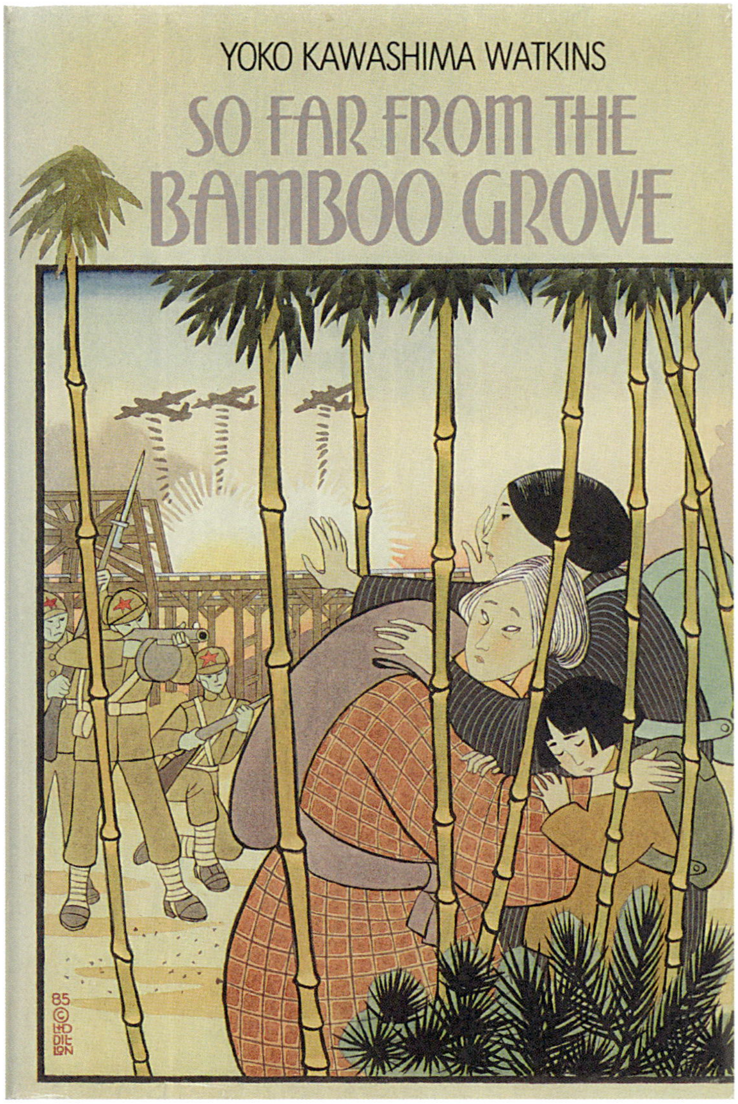

FIGURE 10.2
So Far from the Bamboo Grove, by Yoko Kawashima Watkins, cover by Leo and Diane Dillon. New York: Lothrop, Lee & Shepard, 1986.

from their home on July 29, 1945. Yoko's brother Hideyo, who was working in an ammunition factory, returned to the family's ransacked house not knowing where the rest of the family had gone. He fled as well. A Korean family took him in, after they found him nearly starved and frozen to death on their doorstep.[2]

Years later, while working as a translator at an American base, Yoko Kawashima met Donald Watkins, an American pilot, whom she married in 1953. Two years later she and her husband moved to the United States, where, in 1968, they were joined by her sister Ko (her brother remained in Japan). It would take her nearly twenty years before she was able to write the first of her novels about her family's horrendous wartime experiences.[3]

In *So Far from the Bamboo Grove*, Yoko, the storyteller in both volumes, describes in often graphic detail the family's gruesome experiences as they travel through Korea and on to Japan. On an overcrowded Korean train dead bodies are thrown out of the windows (and one young mother jumps out after her dead infant). As they walk to Seoul, the mother and her two daughters disguise themselves with bloodstained clothes, nearly starve, and witness brutality and death. After reaching Japan, where they desperately hope to be united with brother Hideyo, they struggle to survive, homeless, hungry, and exhausted. They find shelter in the Kyoto train station, where the girls remain while their mother travels to Aomori, in northern Japan. There she learns that her own and her husband's parents have been killed and their home destroyed. Despondent, she returns to Kyoto, where, on a bench in the train station, she slips away from life, even as Yoko assures her that Ko will be returning with some food any moment.

In *My Brother, My Sister, and I,* the sisters are reunited with their brother while their father remains a prisoner of war. Because of her makeshift clothes and unkempt look, Yoko is often bullied at school: one of the well-off girls hides an expensive watch, then accuses Yoko of stealing it. The family is accused of setting fire to the warehouse in which they live under the most primitive conditions. Yoko's sister Ko is seriously injured when she runs back into the burning building to save her mother's ashes and the family sword. Only after nine harrowing months in the hospital, as her brother and sister care for her and find ways to pay her medical expenses, is she finally able to walk again. The three siblings do whatever they can to earn money: Ko, whose right hand was injured in the fire, learns to use her left hand to sew children's clothes; Hideyo works as a night watchman; Yoko does all kinds of odd jobs, including helping a farmer harvest his daikon radishes. He lets her keep the green tops, which she brings home to add to their meager meals. There is rejoicing too. After earning some money by selling empty cans she has collected, Yoko splurges on a longed-for luxury: toothbrushes.

Kawashima Watkins closes this second volume with a poignant event. After six years in a Russian prison camp, their beloved father returns:

> The special Sunday arrived. Hideyo, Ko and I stood on the platform . . . Ko had wrapped Mother's urn in a thin bath towel. She held it close to her chest with both hands. Passersby, following Japanese tradition, bowed slightly to express their sympathy. . . .
>
> All the passengers were getting off. I searched for Father. I did not see him. Many travelers went by. Still no Father . . . "There he is!" Hideyo pointed . . . I still don't see Father. "He is coming. Go greet him, Little One!" . . . I saw a feeble old man. His shoulders were slumped, his hair thin and white. He carried a shabby burlap bag, and his head was bent to see where he was walking . . . I went very close to look at the old man. The old man lifted his head. He studied me for a couple of seconds. I stared at him, wondering, is this Father? "Ah, Little One! My! You have grown so much!" . . . I moved beside Father so that Ko could welcome him. She bowed deeply to him without words. Father saw what Ko was holding on her

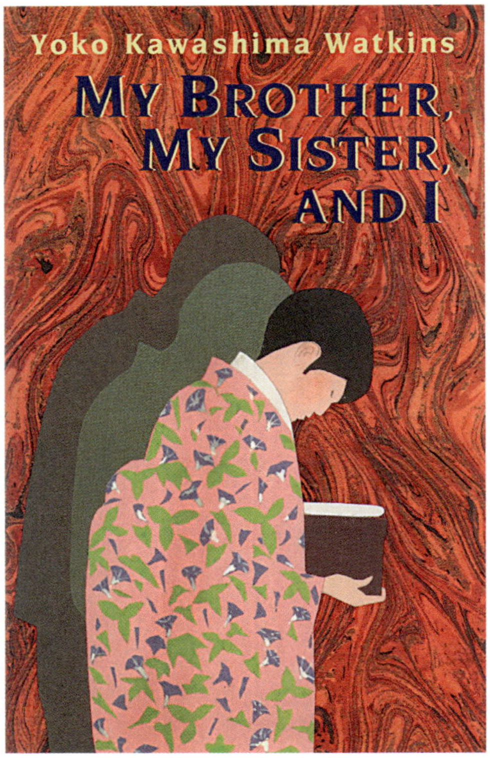

FIGURE 10.3
My Brother, My Sister, and I, by Yoko Kawashima Watkins, jacket illustration by Ed Young. New York: Bradbury, 1994.

> chest. "Is this Saki?" He asked. Saki was Mother's name. Ko began sniffling and barely whispered, "I am sorry, Father." . . . Father leaned on a crutch and extended his right hand to touch Mother's urn. He bit his lips. He tried hard not to cry and swallowed the bumps in his throat many times. Soon his eyes filled with tears. They streamed down his pale, wrinkled, tired face. . . . He then gave each of us a gentle stare, and smiled. My brother, my sister, and I were warmed by his gesture. His voice trembled, but he spoke slowly and clearly. "I must not cry over what I have lost. I must give thanks for what Mother has left me."
>
> He reached for my hand. "Now, Little One, show me the way to our home."
>
> I put my hand in that familiar palm. I clasped his hand and looked into his eyes. Then magic happened. The tired, worn old man faded. I saw Father—my strong, wise, kind father. Almost as quickly, six years of hardship and heartbreak disappeared in the air. At long, long last, Father was home.[4]

Books for young American readers did not only depict the suffering of the Japanese. In *In the Eye of War* (1990), Margaret and Raymond Chang tell the story of Shao-shao and his family, who live in Shanghai under Japanese occupation during 1944 and 1945. Ten-year-old Shao-shao enjoys school, cricket fights, and the family's celebrations, most especially the Chinese New Year. Yet life around him becomes increasingly difficult: there is less and less food, his school has no heat, and the streetcars stop running. Although, throughout the book, the political situation remains in the background, the "Japs" (as the Chinese call the occupation forces) appear from time to time. Gradually Shao-shao understands why his father is so strict and forbids him to make friends with Li-sha, the girl next door: Li-sha's family are Japanese sympathizers.[5]

The Year of Impossible Goodbyes (1991, fig. 10.4) by Sook Nyul Choi is a grim and heartbreaking autobiographical story of Koreans enduring Japanese occupation. Ten-year-old Sookan lives with her family in Kirimni, Pyongyang. Small for her age, she and her little brother, Inchun, are secretly taught Korean and Chinese by their grandfather and are not sent to the compulsory Japanese school her brothers and sister attend. In a shack the Japanese built in her yard Sookan's mother runs a small factory that makes socks for Japanese soldiers. Young "sock girls" work there long hours on the knitting machines.

Both the factory and Sookan's family are supervised by the sadistic Japanese captain Narita, who appears for frequent inspections with "his sword hanging from his small wiry frame" and treats them "with [apparent] disdain."[6] Narita does what he can to harass the family, taking away their possessions. One day, out of spite, he cuts down her grandfather's beloved pine tree.

When their grandfather feels his end coming near, he gathers the family around him. He asks Sookan's mother to bring out the box with the family's pictures. They reveal the family's story, which had been kept a secret. Sookan's mother explains the photo of grandfather as a young man. Under the special

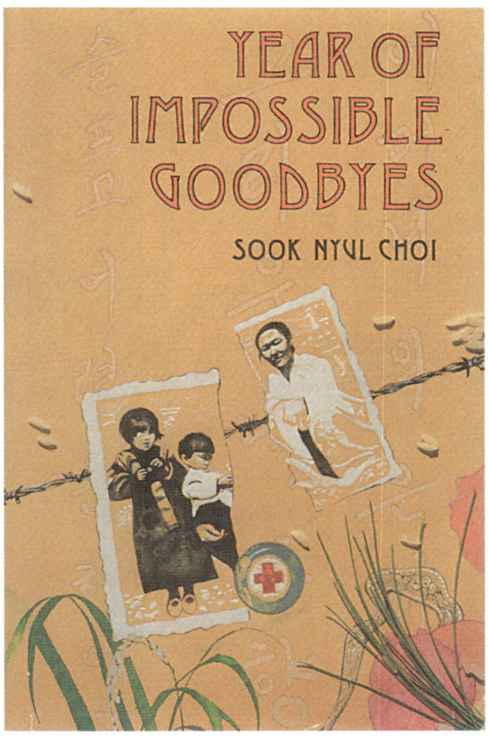

FIGURE 10.4
Year of Impossible Goodbyes, by Sook Nyul Choi, jacket by Maria Garafano. Boston: Houghton Mifflin, 1991.

hat he wore a topknot, a symbol of his culture and his status as an important scholar. The Japanese herded them all together in the town square and cut off their topknots. They forbade the Koreans to speak their language and tried to erase their culture.

Sookan's mother goes on to explain that the Japanese set fire to the village, shooting the people. Only she and grandfather survived. They escaped to Manchuria, where her mother met her future husband and where they began to publish a newspaper in *Hangul* (Korean script). But soon the Japanese found out about their underground activities. They set fire to the Koreans' houses, then shot people as they fled from the flames. Sookan's mother and her three sons and a daughter escaped to Pyongyang, but her father and grandfather stayed behind. Her father eventually rescued grandfather, who had been tortured by the Japanese.

As her grandfather becomes weaker, Sookan is asked to stay by his side. She rubs lemon oil on his forehead and feels privileged when he asks her to rub some of it on his feet, which seemed disturbingly strange to her:

> The tips of his toes were all wrinkled and looked like some little girl had practiced her sewing on them. He had no toenails. I knew he had no fingernails on his right hand, and I always thought he had hurt himself whittling. But no toenails! At first, I thought it strange, but then it occurred to me.
>
> Sadness washed over me like a big ocean tide. My fingers trembled as I went over each toe with lemon oil. My head started to throb as all the horrible stories I had heard of Japanese cruelty went rushing through my mind . . . "Grandfather, do they hurt?" "No, not anymore," Grandfather replied. . . . Grandfather died soon after we left him . . . three days after his beloved pine tree had been chopped down.[7]

Meanwhile, Captain Narita has a different kind of work in mind for the young "sock girls." One morning he comes with a truck to take the sock girls away. He yells:

> "You should all be very proud and honored that it is now your turn to serve Our Heavenly Emperor. You will give the soldiers the special spirit to fight harder against the White Devils . . . Our Heavenly Emperor will be happy that you volunteered to help the soldiers." . . . The two soldiers began to herd the girls toward the truck. Some screamed and fell to the muddy ground, but were jabbed with guns and forced onto the truck. "Please do not take them . . . some of them are not even fifteen," Mother implored.[8]

Then, finally, it is August 15, 1945. The war is over. Japan surrendered. Sookan's mother brings out the Korean flag. They dress in Korean silk *hanbok* that had been hidden in earthen jars. They are free, but their euphoria does not last. While many of the Japanese leave, the Koreans are anxiously waiting for their husbands, fathers, and brothers. Many do not return. Many return too ill to survive.

Mother takes off her Korean dress and puts on the grey workers' outfit when Russian soldiers arrive. The family hears that the country has been divided at the 38th parallel. The Russians have taken over the north, the Americans the south. Sookan, her mother, and little brother Inchun leave their home to go south. The guide who helps them escape turns out to be a double agent. The children are separated from their mother. They show heroic courage and endurance before they finally crawl under the barbed wire to freedom in South Korea, where they are eventually united with their mother.

Hiroshima: August 6, 1945

The day after the atomic bomb fell on Hiroshima, the artists Toshi and Iri Maruki went to the stricken city. Afterwards, they were determined to paint what they had seen. They began their sketches for *The Hiroshima Panels*—huge, grim paintings of horror—in 1947. The first panel was shown in 1950 at the Tokyo Metropolitan Art Museum while they completed the second and third panels. On August 6, 1950, the panels were published in a small book of drawings, *Pika-don* (flash-bang). However, at that time, "any visual record of nuclear destruction was . . . thoroughly suppressed" by Allied forces,[9] and the Marukis' book was almost immediately withdrawn from circulation. John Hersey's *Hiroshima*, in which he told the stories of six Hiroshima survivors, suffered nearly the same fate. The *New Yorker* devoted the entire issue of August 31, 1946, to the book, but it was withheld from publication in Japan until 1949.[10]

Toshi Maruki interpreted *The Hiroshima Panels* for young children in her picture book *Hiroshima no Pika* (The Flash of Hiroshima, 1980, fig. 10.1). In the documentary film *Hellfire: A Journey from Hiroshima* (1986), Maruki said that she had made the pictures attractive because she did not want to frighten children away from the story.[11] In 1982, nearly forty years after the bomb, Dorothy Briley, then editor-in-chief of Lothrop, Lee & Shepard Books, published a translation of *Hiroshima no Pika* in the United States. Admired for her risk-taking (apparently no other editor had dared to publish the book), Briley commented that the subject was long overdue for thoughtful discussion in the United States, especially how children would cope with learning about such a disaster.[12]

Hiroshima no Pika begins on an ordinary Hiroshima day. Seven-year-old Mii and her parents were having their breakfast of sweet potatoes:

Then it happened. A sudden, terrible light flashed all around. The light was bright orange—then white, like thousands of lightning bolts all striking at once. Violent shock waves followed, and buildings trembled and began to collapse.

Moments before the Flash, United States Air Force bomber *Enola Gay* had flown over the city and released a top-secret explosive. The explosive was an atomic bomb, which had been given the name "Little Boy" by the B-29's crew.

"Little Boy" fell on Hiroshima at 8:15 on the morning of August 6, 1945.

Mii was knocked unconscious by the force of the Flash, and when she woke up everything around her was still and dark. At first she couldn't move, and she heard crackling sounds that frightened her. Far off in the darkness she could see a red glow. Her mother's voice penetrated the dark, calling her.

Mii struggled out from under the heavy boards that had fallen on top of her. Her mother rushed to her and drew her close and hugged her. "We must hurry," she said. "The fire . . . your father is caught in the flames! . . ."

Mii watched as her mother examined her father. "He's hurt badly," she said. She untied the sash from her kimono and wrapped it around her husband's body as a bandage. Then she did something amazing. She lifted him onto her back and, taking Mii by the hand, started running. . . .

There were crowds of people fleeing the fire. Mii saw children with their clothes burned away, lips and eyelids swollen. They were like ghosts, wandering about, crying in weak voices. Some people, all their strength gone, fell face down on the ground, and others fell on top of them. There were heaps of people everywhere. . . .

Fire was moving toward them at a terrible speed. They ran among piles of cracked roof tiles, over fallen telephone poles and wires. Houses were burning on every side. . . .

At long last they reached the beach outside Hiroshima. They could see Miyajima island, wrapped in purple mist, across the water . . . Thinking that safety was not far away, Mii and her mother and her father fell asleep. . . .

That day, August 9, 1945, as Mii and her mother looked at the rubble that had been Hiroshima, an atomic bomb was dropped on Nagasaki. And there, as in Hiroshima, thousands of people died, and anyone who survived was left homeless. Among the victims, in addition to the Japanese, were people from many other countries, such as Korea, China, Russia, Indonesia, and the United States.[13]

Rarely had a picture book received such attention. More than fifteen reviews appeared in American children's literature journals, including *School Library Journal*, *Horn Book Magazine*, and the *Bulletin of the Center for Children's Books*; in specialized journals, such as *Interracial Books for Children*; and in national and

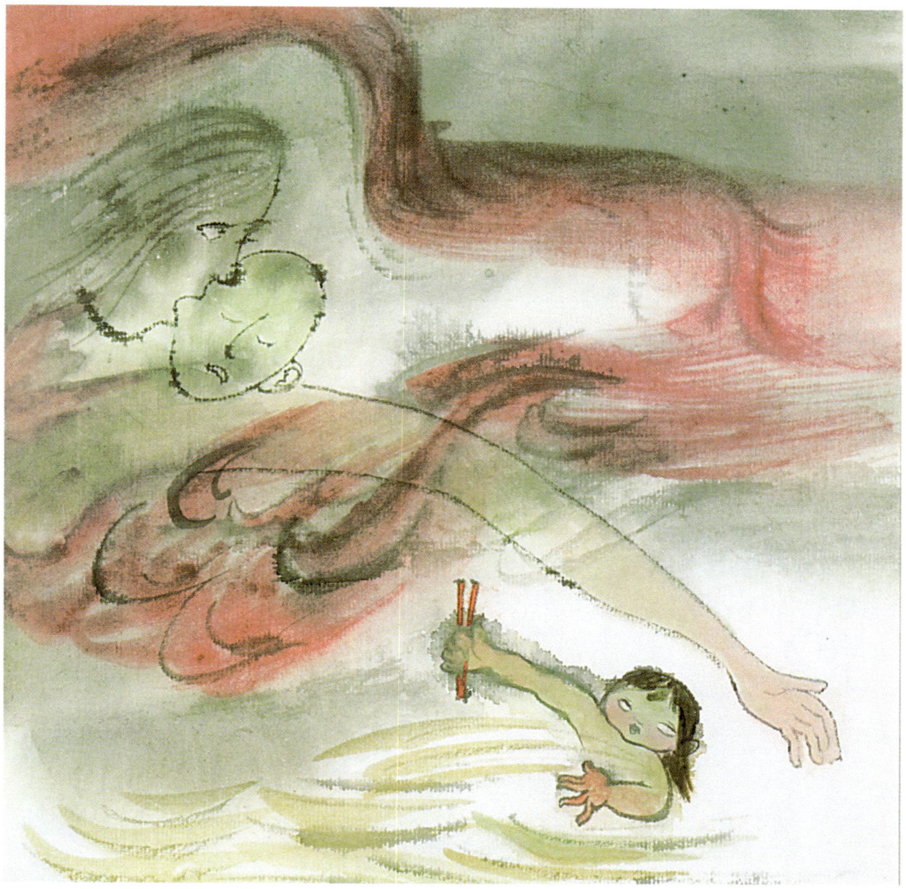

FIGURE 10.5
Hiroshima no Pika, by Toshi Maruki, page 14.

regional newspapers. Most were positive and sympathetic to the book. The *Los Angeles Times* cited the book for its "nobility" and its "fascinating, unsanitized blend of beauty and ugliness."[14] However, not all voices were positive. The *New York Times* reviewer asserted that,

> a young child will see in Mrs. Maruki's book only a nightmare of fire, nakedness and death . . . There is no lesson to be learned because no solution is suggested—there is only the nightmare . . . The author gives no answers . . . Children must learn on an ascending scale, according to their capability for understanding. They cannot swallow in one gulp such a graphic tract against nuclear warfare and be thereby prepared to stand against a recurrence.[15]

A teacher of children's literature wrote:

> *Hiroshima no Pika* . . . is so biased it should be worrying librarians far more than it does . . . Toshi Maruki's illustrations and text, moving as they are, have reduced a complicated subject to simplistic sensationalism . . . I feel that *Hiroshima no Pika* is no way to introduce this emotional subject to children. Wait until they are old enough to understand the event in its historical context. Then give them the facts,

complete with all the complicated contradictions with which history abounds, and say to them: "What do you think?" Whatever you do, don't give children *Hiroshima no Pika*. It is propaganda.[16]

Hiroko Nakamoto's *My Japan, 1930–1951* (1970), described Hiroshima as experienced by a young teenager whose life was destroyed in but a second.

Describing the day after the bombing, she wrote:

> Lying on the floor, a mosquito net over me, I could hardly believe that I was still alive. Pain covered my body. I could not move or talk. I felt as if I did not really exist. I did not even want a glass of water. If I had, my relatives would not have given one to me, as the word now was that water would poison burned people. Masako, my little stepsister Aiko, and her nurse, Baba, had been burned. I did not know how badly . . . As I lay on the floor, I heard the radio announcing that Hiroshima had been hit with a new type of bomb, used for the first time. . . .[17]

> On this day [August 15, 1945] our emperor's voice, for the first time in history, was heard on the radio. The war was ended. We had lost the war. Never before had Japan been defeated.

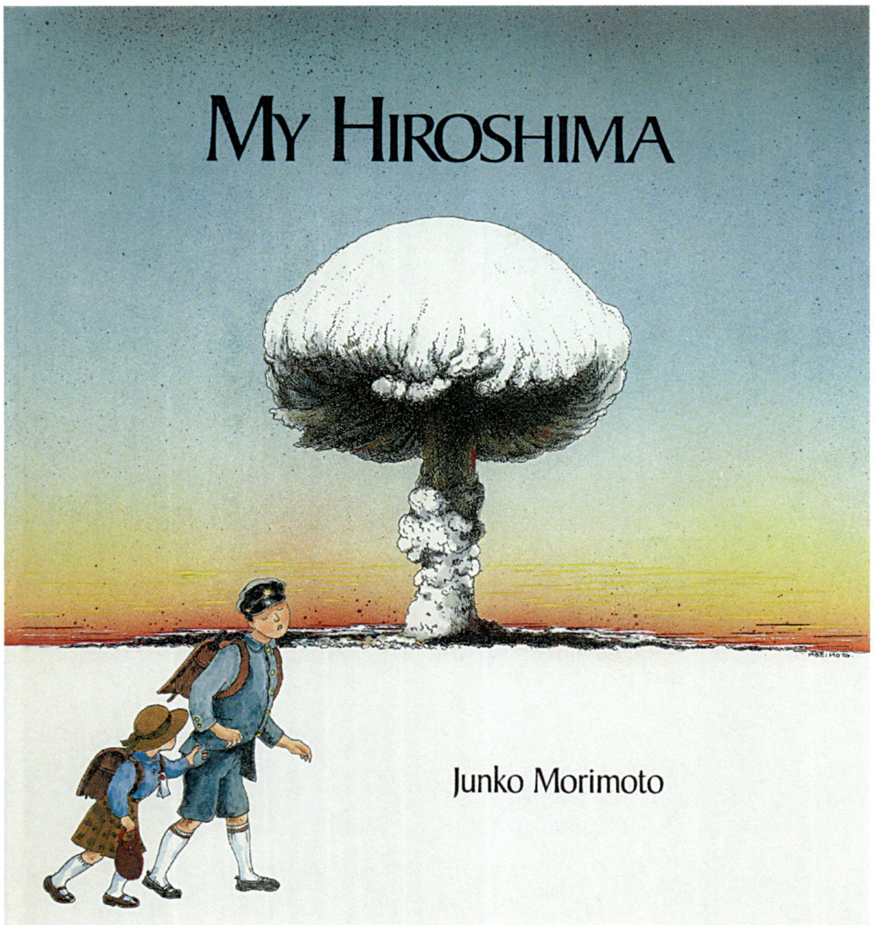

FIGURE 10.6
My Hiroshima, written and illustrated by Junko Morimoto. Sydney: Collins, 1987.

> Japan was the country of the gods. And always before, the gods had protected us. But this time, there was no miracle. It was a terrible shock to know we were a conquered nation.[18]

A few other children's books addressed the bombing of Hiroshima and Nagasaki. Two autobiographical works, *My Hiroshima* (1990, fig. 10.6) by Junko Morimoto and *Shin's Tricycle* (1995) by Tatsuharu Kodama, were translated from the Japanese. Betty Jean Lifton, a journalist and peace activist whose *Children of Vietnam* was nominated for the National Book Award in 1973 and who produced many children's books about Japan, wrote *Return to Hiroshima* (1970) about the city and its survivors. The book includes black-and-white illustrations by Toshi and Iri Maruki and photographs by the renowned photographer Eikoh Hosoe. *Sadako and the Thousand Paper Cranes* (1977) by Eleanor Coerr is based on the life of Sadako Sasaki, who was two years old when the bomb fell and seemed to have survived uninjured. But, like many others who survived the initial blast, she later developed leukemia. After a friend told her of the legend that those who folded one thousand origami cranes—symbols of long life—would recover from their illness, Sadako started folding cranes. She had only managed to fold

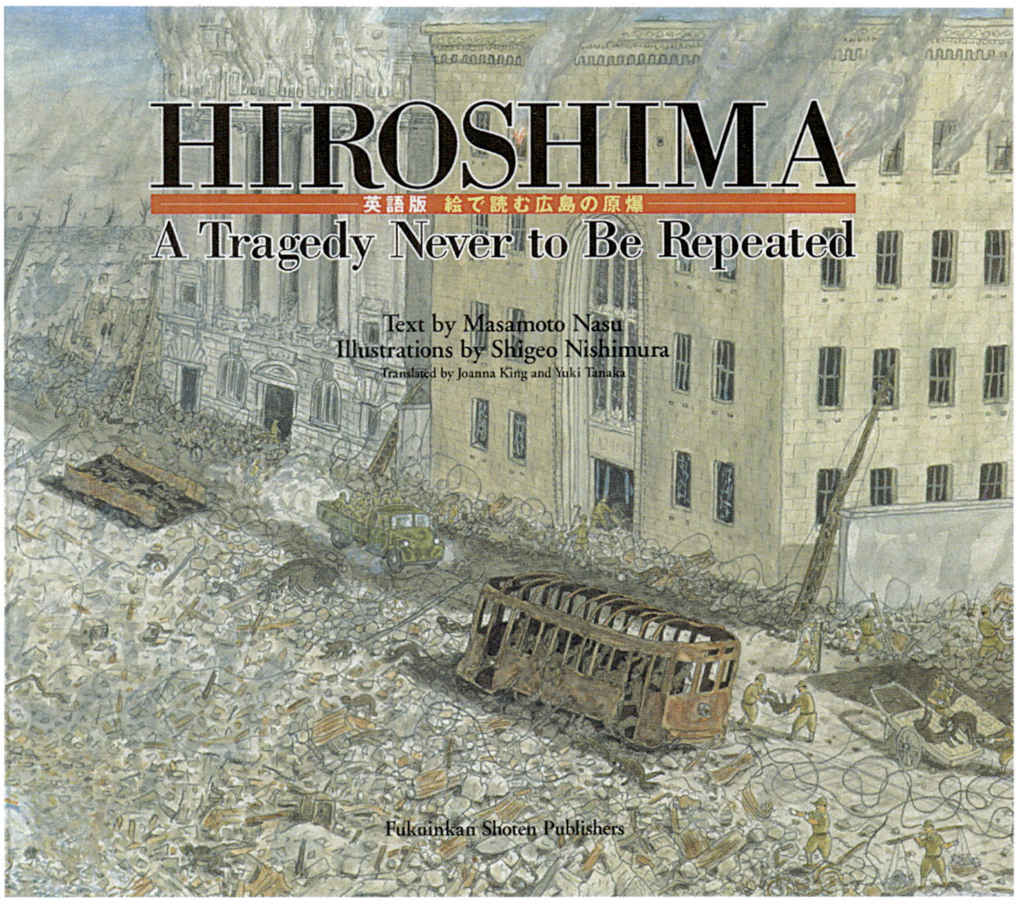

FIGURE 10.7
Hiroshima, A Tragedy Never to Be Repeated, by Masamoto Nasu, illustrated by Shigeo Nishimura. Tokyo: Fukuinkan Shoten Publishers, 1995. English text by Joanna King and Yuki Tanaka.

644 cranes when she died at age twelve. Her friends folded the rest and buried all one thousand cranes with her. They later raised funds for the Sadako statue which today stands on top of the Children's Peace Monument in Hiroshima's Peace Park.[19]

Hiroshima: A Tragedy Never to Be Repeated (1998, fig. 10.7) by Hiroshima survivor Masamoto Nasu is the English-language edition of *E-de yomu Hiroshima no nenbaku* (1995). This book, which includes scientific and historical information, is illustrated by the painter Shigeo Nishimura, who lived in Hiroshima for almost a year to interview survivors and gather information.[20]

Hiroshima: A Novella (1995) by the noted Chinese American writer Laurence Yep tells about the Hiroshima Maidens, twenty-five young women who received free medical help from American surgeons.[21] Prolific children's book author R. Conrad Stein, a former U.S. Marine, questioned the purpose of the bomb in his children's book *Hiroshima* (1982):

> By the summer of 1945, Japan was already a defeated nation. Most of the ships of her once-powerful navy had been sunk. She had no way to defend herself against the swarms of American bombers that pounded her cities every day. Her few planes were being saved to send against the expected American invasion fleet. Her army had almost no gasoline for its tanks and trucks. The Americans occupied Okinawa, only ninety miles from the shores of Japan. And it seemed that the Russians would soon join the war against Japan and attack the Japanese army stationed in Manchuria. So why use a weapon as terrible as the atomic bomb on an already defeated people? That question will be argued forever.[22]

New Perspectives in Books about Japan

Toward the end of the twentieth century, American children's book authors began to explore new subjects, perspectives, formats, and designs in their books about Japan. One album—Sheila Hamanaka's *In Search of the Spirit: The Living National Treasures of Japan* (1999)—looks back to traditional Japanese arts threatened by the wartime destruction and postwar modernization. The book highlights the work of six Japanese masters who have been designated cultural treasures: a textile dyer, a bamboo weaver, a *bunraku* puppet master, a sword maker, a Noh actor, and a potter.[23]

The husband-and-wife team Dorothy and Thomas Hoobler added to the new bounty of children's books with *Showa: The Age of Hirohito* (1990) and a series of historical mysteries, including *A Samurai Never Fears Death* (2007, fig. 10.8).[24] In *Japanese Portraits* (1994), they presented a new window on Japan, through which they highlight Japanese arts and letters and China's significant influence on

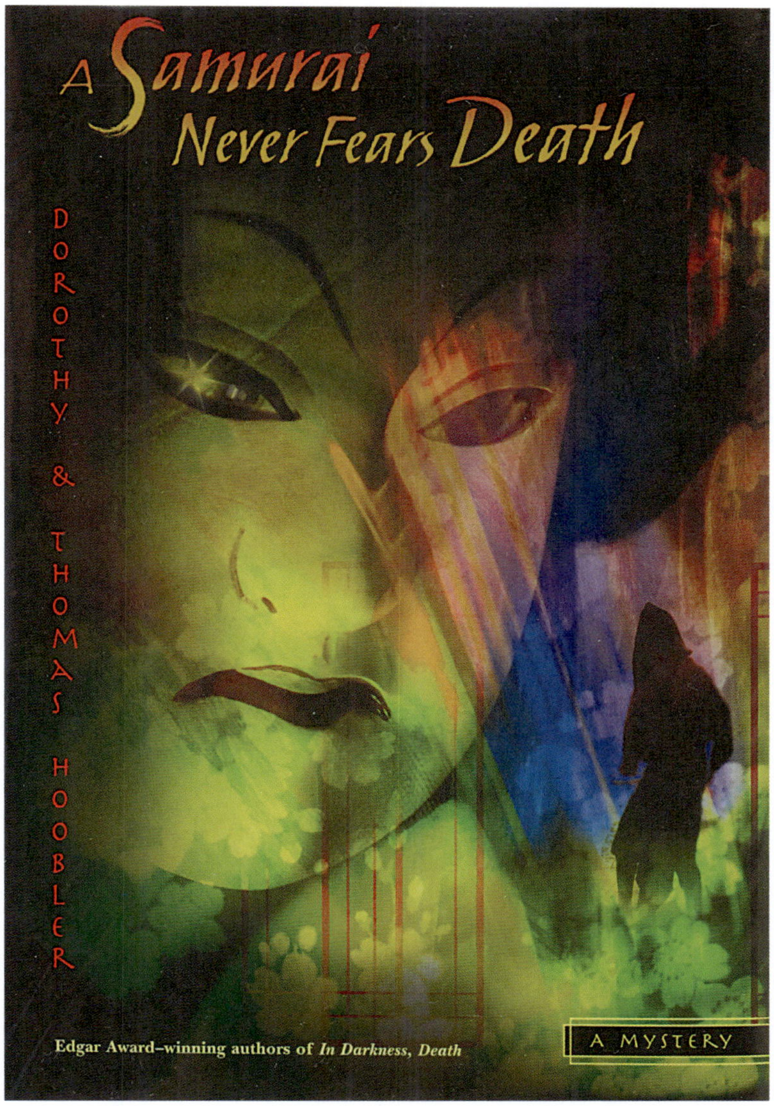

FIGURE 10.8
A Samurai Never Fears Death, by Dorothy and Thomas Hoobler, jacket by Cliff Nielsen. New York: Sleuth/ Philomel, 2007.

Japan. Some of the historical figures they included had rarely appeared in books for young American readers:

> Prince Shotoku [who lived in the sixth century] realized that Japan had even more to learn. He started sending Japanese educational missions to China to study the source of civilization. Shotoku's missions to China began an era of cultural borrowing by the Japanese. For the next two centuries, students and priests made the difficult and often dangerous journey.
>
> The Japanese proved to be adept learners. Many of the Chinese cultural customs became part of the Japanese heritage. Japan adopted Chinese writing, court ritual, and calendar. Devotion to Buddhism created a flowering of religious art modeled on Chinese styles. Not until the arrival of ships from the United States (more than 1,300 years later), would Japan be so open to outside influences.
>
> From this time, the Japanese adopted a new name for their nation. Formerly, they had called their land Yamato, but now they used Nihon or Nippon, a word that

combines the Chinese characters for "sun" and "source." Centuries later, when the Italian Marco Polo visited China, he heard the Chinese pronunciation of this name: "Jihpen." Polo's book about his travels brought the name Japan to the West.[25]

Japanese Portraits introduces two exceptional Japanese women who brought to life the elegant and intriguing setting of the Imperial court of the Heian period (794–1185): Lady Murasaki Shikibu, in her masterpiece and Japan's first novel, *The Tale of Genji*, and Sei Shōnagon, in *The Pillow Book* (fig. 10.9). The Hooblers write:

> Here the Japanese gained cultural assurance. The study missions to China stopped. Though the Japanese retained a high respect for Chinese culture, over time they began to develop one that was uniquely their own.
>
> An example was the creation of the *kana* in the ninth century. Kana is a simplified version of Chinese written characters. It is used like an alphabet, but instead of letters, there are 50 syllables corresponding to Japanese sounds. The kana became popular among women. But court officials and most males preferred Chinese. They called kana "women's writing." Yet Sei Shōnagon and Lady Murasaki, writing in kana, created works that are among the glories of Japanese literature.[26]

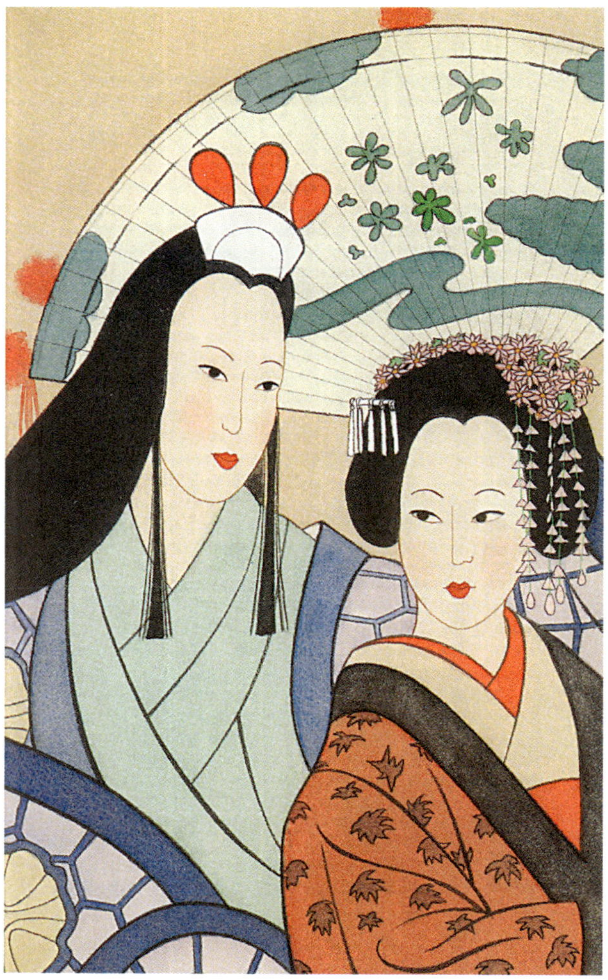

FIGURE 10.9
Lady Murasaki Shikibu and Sei Shōnagon in *Japanese Portraits*, by Dorothy and Thomas Hoobler, illustrated by Victoria Bruck. Austin, TX: Raintree Steck-Vaughn, 1994, page 13.

The Hooblers even ventured to explain "*aware*," a classic concept, which, most likely, had never been explored in a children's book about Japan:

> *The Tale of Genji* tells of the adventures and spiritual growth of Genji, "the Shining Prince." Genji represents all the ideals of Heian society. Physically beautiful, he is a fine poet, accomplished musician, and a gallant lover. He pursues beauty in all its forms. Most of all, Genji is touched by the most important Heian sentiment—*aware* (ah-wah-ray). *Aware* is the pathos or sorrow that one feels on beholding beautiful things—for one comes to realize that beauty cannot last. Indeed, it is precisely this short-lived character that makes things most beautiful. For example, the Japanese—even today—love to view the blooming of the cherry trees in spring. Though the blossoms cover the trees, they last for only a few days. The same is true of the autumn leaves and the harvest moon that shines on a single night each year. *Aware* combines a love of beauty with the strong Buddhist belief that all things are fleeting.[27]

In *The Japanese American Family Album* (1996, fig. 10.10), the Hooblers write about the lives of Japanese Americans, citing first-person accounts culled from oral histories and other sources. This volume is enriched by features that were

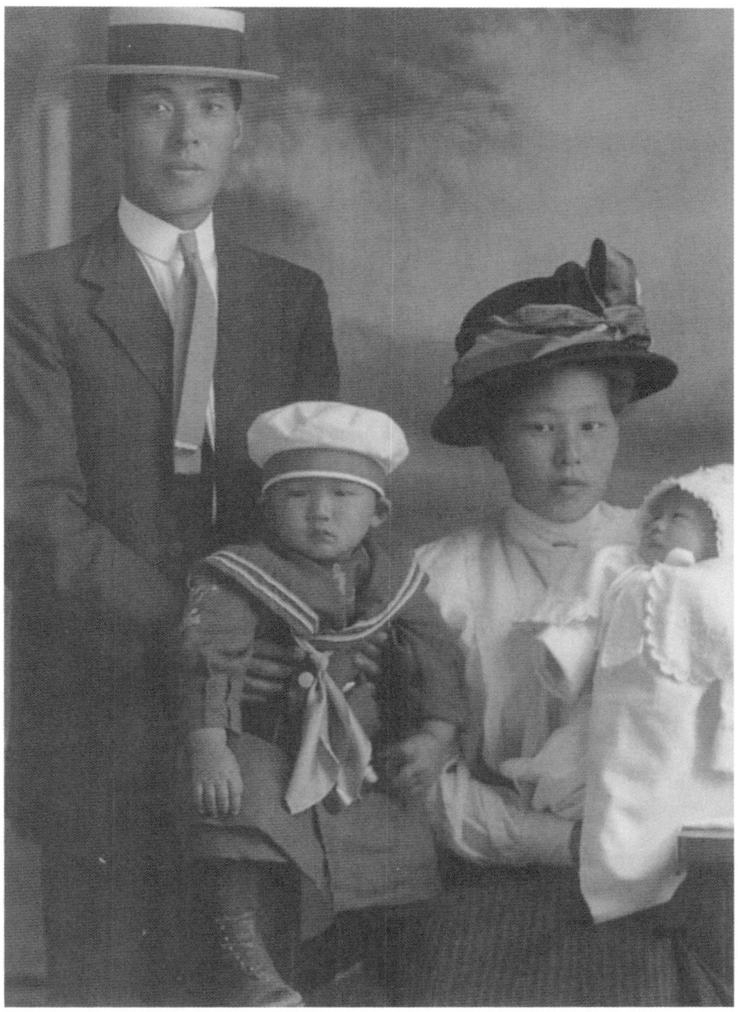

FIGURE 10.10
Photograph of S. Terakawa and his family, 1915, by Thomas J. Cronise. Reproduced in *The Japanese American Family Album*, by Dorothy and Thomas Hoobler. New York: Oxford University Press, 1996.

increasingly becoming part of American informational books for children (though taken for granted in books for adults). These included archival photographs; sidebars highlighting newspaper articles; book excerpts; biographical sketches of individuals such as the sculptor Isamu Noguchi, the Newbery-award-winning writer Cynthia Kadohata, and U.S. Senator Daniel K. Inouye; a timeline; text and picture credits; and a bibliography arranged by category.[28]

What could be achieved in these new children's books is shown with aplomb in Rhoda Blumberg's *Commodore Perry in the Land of the Shogun* (1985, fig. 10.11). There had been two earlier books for children about Perry, *Commodore Perry and the Opening of Japan* (by Ferdinand Kuhn, 1955), which featured black-and-white drawings, and *Commodore Perry in Japan* (1963, fig. 10.12) by Robert L. Reynolds, which was enhanced by handsome full-color illustrations.[29] However, these older books could not compete with Blumberg's tour de force, with its pleasing storytelling, inviting design, imaginative perspectives and observations and colorful details the dramatic event deserved:

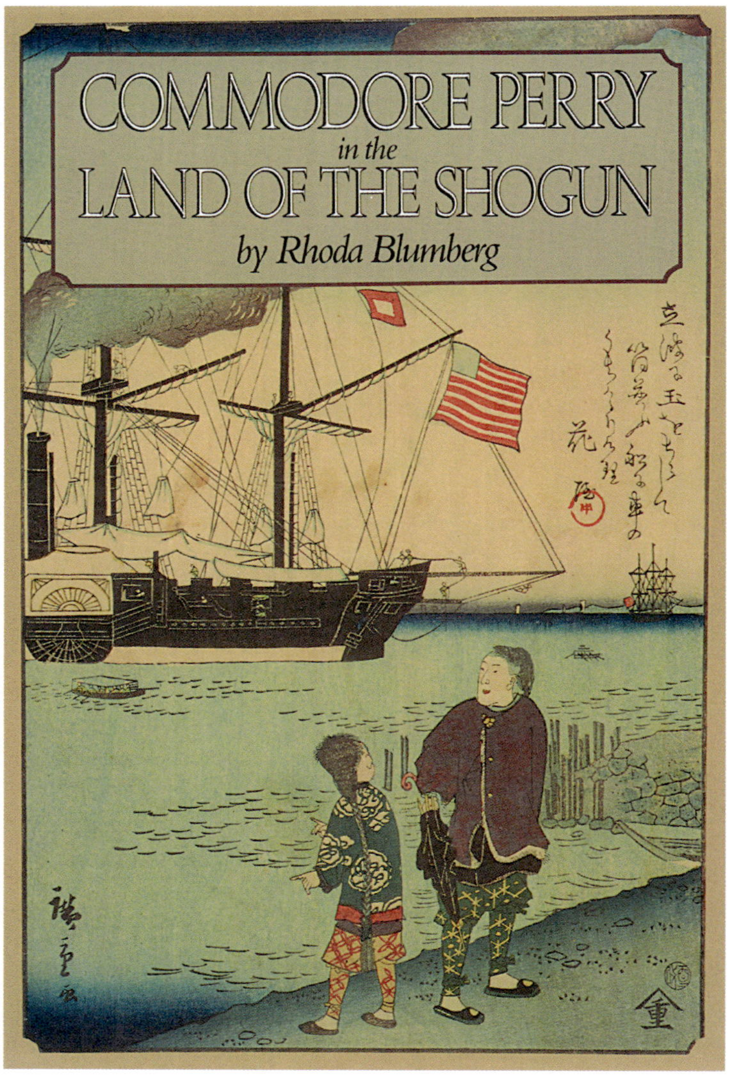

FIGURE 10.11
Commodore Perry in the Land of the Shogun, by Rhoda Blumberg. New York: Lothrop, Lee & Shepard, 1985.

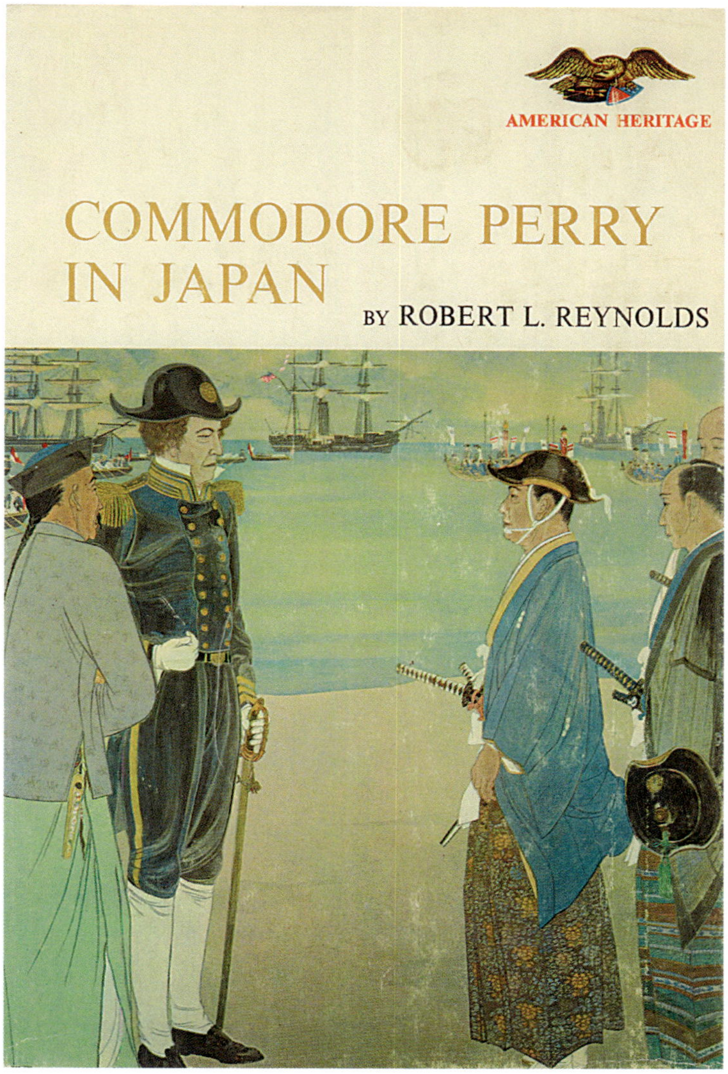

FIGURE 10.12
Commodore Perry in Japan, by Robert L. Reynolds. New York: American Heritage, distributed by Harper and Row, 1963.

If monsters had descended upon Japan the effect could not have been more terrifying. People in the fishing village of Shimoda were the first to spot four huge hulks, two streaming smoke, on the ocean's surface approaching the shore. "Giant dragons puffing smoke," cried some. "Alien ships of fire," cried others. Surely, something horrible was happening on this day, Friday, July 8, 1853.

Fishermen pulled in their nets, grabbed their oars, and rowed to shore frantically. They had been close up and knew that these floating mysteries were foreign ships. Black ships that belched black clouds! They had never seen anything like it. They didn't even know that steamboats existed, and they were appalled by the number and size of the guns.

Barbarians from out of the blue! Will they invade, kidnap, kill, then destroy everything? What will become of the sacred Land of the Rising Sun? . . .[30]

The Americans were enchanted by the kindness and friendliness of the Japanese. At one time they believed that they had sailed over the edge of world civilization and would encounter savages. Face to face, they were beginning to realize that these charming people were as courteous and hospitable as any they had

> ever met. They were yet to discover that Japan was a highly civilized, cultured nation. . . .[31]

> Perry arrived during the Tokugawa Period. Shoguns belonging to the Tokugawa family that ruled Japan after 1603 had deliberately preserved a medieval feudal society . . . How mistaken Commodore Perry was in his belief that Japan was uncivilized. Although technologically behind the West, no other country in the world was more civilized and artistic. Nor was any government anywhere more highly organized. However, the price paid for this productive peace was complete loss of freedom . . . Regulations listed 216 varieties of dress for everyone from the emperor down to the lowest class citizen. Even the shape, color, and size of stitches were specified.[32]

Several other books about Japan created for younger children emerge from this period. Ahead of its time was *Two Mrs. Gibsons* (1996, fig. 10.13) by Toyomi Igus, which describes the author's beloved African American grandmother and her Japanese mother:

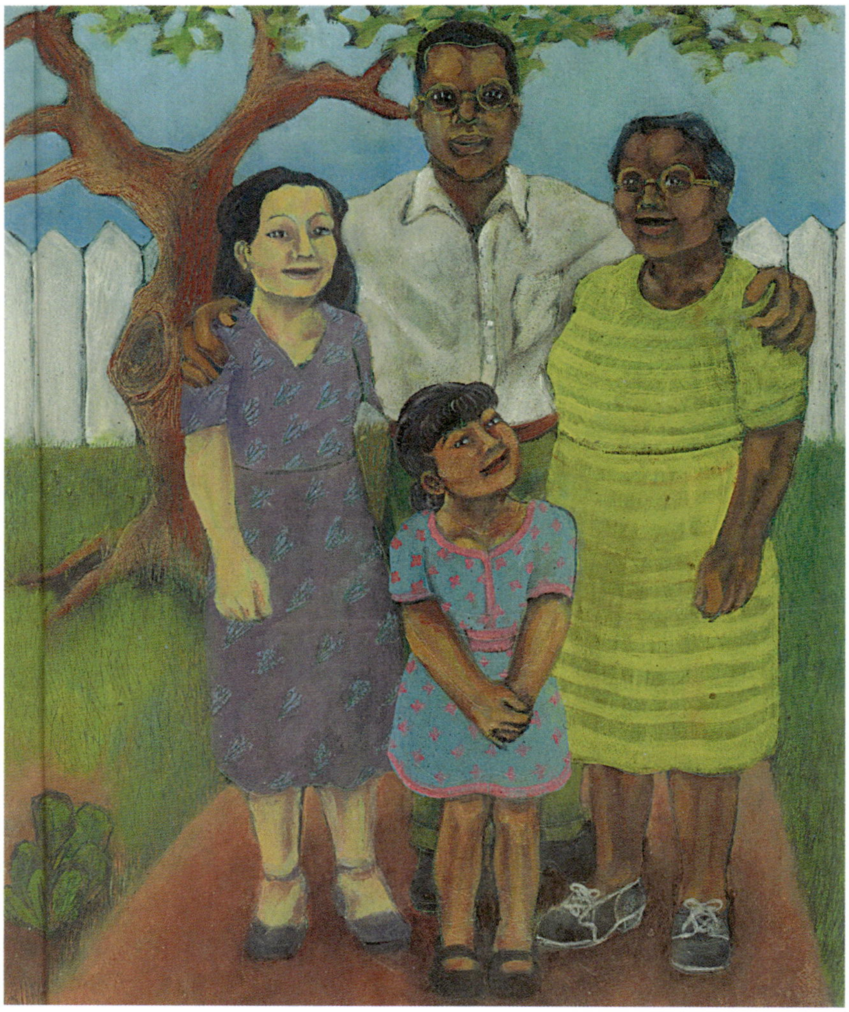

FIGURE 10.13
Two Mrs. Gibsons, by Toyomi Igus, illustrated by Daryl Wells. San Francisco: Children's Book Press, 1996.

> This Mrs. Gibson was tall. Her skin was the color of chocolate.
> She was born in America in a place called Tennessee.
>
> This Mrs. Gibson was small. Her skin was the color of vanilla. She was
> born in Japan in a place called Gifu. . . .
>
> This Mrs. Gibson was loud. She had a big laugh, and
> a big voice, which would get louder when she was angry
> or when she was singing. And she seemed to be singing all
> the time. "This little light of mine I'm gonna let it shine."
>
> This Mrs. Gibson was quiet. She would cover her mouth when she laughed, so you
> could never see her teeth. And when she was angry,
> she'd get even quieter.[33]

The autobiographical *Yoshiko and the Foreigner* (1996) by Mimi Otey Little deals with the issue of interracial and intercultural marriage as well. Yoshiko's father, who does not want her to marry an American soldier, warns that he is a gaijin, a foreigner, who "will not understand the ways of our people. Americans only laugh and scoff at our customs."[34] But the American surprises her father. He does not scoff at their Japanese customs, but learns to speak their language, then asks Yoshiko's father for her hand.

Another Looming Shadow: Executive Order 9066

Hiroshima, "a subject long overdue for serious discussion" in children's books,[35] as Dorothy Briley, the publisher of *Hiroshima No Pika* (1980) had written in 1983, never did get the attention for which she had hoped. Of the dozen or so children's books on the topic, most were translations from the Japanese, and few new books on the subject appeared after the 1980s and 1990s. However, the other shadow looming over Japanese American relations, the Japanese American detention camps, remained. While children's books on both topics were published in the early 1970s, the stories of the camps, most of them written by Japanese Americans, continued to appear into the twenty-first century.

Jeanne Wakatsuki Houston said that she "did not set out to write a best-seller" when asked about her memoir *Farewell to Manzanar* (1973), which by 2003 was in its sixty-third printing[36] and was made into a television film. After a long silence she finally found the courage to write her book. One day, when her nephew—who had been born in an internment camp—asked her about her experiences, she "became hysterical and started crying." "Nobody had ever asked me that question," she said.[37]

She told about what happened on Sunday, December 7, 1941, when her father and the other fishermen returned to Long Beach harbor after just venturing out. By then, everyone had heard the news of the Japanese attack on Pearl Harbor. Wakatsuki Houston was seven then and watched what happened next:

> That night Papa burned the flag he had brought with him from Hiroshima thirty-five years earlier. . . . He burned a lot of papers too, documents, anything that might suggest he still had some connection with Japan. These precautions didn't do him much good. He was not only an alien; he held a commercial fishing license, and in the early days of the war the FBI was picking up all such men, for fear they were somehow making contact with enemy ships off the coast. . . .[38]
>
> The next morning two FBI men in fedora hats and trench coats—like out of a thirties movie—knocked on [the] door, and when they left, Papa was between them. He didn't struggle. There was no point to it. He had become a man without a country. The land of his birth was at war with America; yet after thirty-five years here he was still prevented by law from becoming an American citizen. He was suddenly a man with no rights who looked exactly like the enemy.[39]

The family was given forty-eight hours to leave their home. Their possessions had to be reduced to almost nothing. With tears streaming down her cheeks, her mother, enraged and frustrated, took pieces of fine china out of their red velvet case and threw them at the feet of the second-hand dealers who had offered her fifteen dollars for the whole set. The American Friends Committee helped them find a small house in a minority ghetto filled with other evacuees. Later, they all assembled at the Buddhist temple in Los Angeles, received identification badges for their coats and bags, and were taken to Manzanar, more than 200 miles north of Los Angeles:

> We were taken to Block 16, a cluster of fifteen barracks that had just been finished a day or so earlier—although finished was hardly the word for it. The shacks were built of one thickness of pine planking covered with tarpaper. They sat on concrete footings, with about two feet of open space between the floorboards and the ground. Gaps showed between the planks, and as the weeks passed and the green wood dried out, the gaps widened. Knotholes gaped in the uncovered floor.[40] . . . We woke early, shivering and coated with dust that had blown up through the knotholes and in through the slits around the doorway. . . .
>
> Most of the families, like us, had moved out from Southern California with as much luggage as each person could carry. Some old men left Los Angeles wearing Hawaiian shirts and Panama hats and stepped off the bus at an altitude of 4000 feet, with nothing but sagebrush and tarpaper to stop the April winds pouring down off the back side of the Sierras. . . .[41]

[Papa] arrived at Manzanar on a Greyhound bus . . . [He] stepped out, wearing a fedora and a wilted white shirt. This was September 1942. He had been gone nine months. He had aged ten years. He looked over sixty, gaunt, wilted as his shirt, underweight, leaning on that cane. . . .[42]

Papa never said more than three or four sentences about his nine months at Fort Lincoln. . . . Not because of the physical hardship . . . It was the charge of disloyalty. For a man raised in Japan, there was no greater disgrace. And it was the humiliation. . . .[43]

Outside [Papa] had no job to go back to. A California law passed in 1943 made it illegal now for Issei [a first-generation Japanese immigrant] to hold commercial fishing licenses. . . .[44]

We were sitting on a bus-stop bench in Long Beach, when an old, embittered woman stopped and said, "Why don't all of you dirty Japs go back to Japan!" She spit at us and passed on. . . .[45]

Papa's life ended at Manzanar, though he lived for twelve more years after getting out.[46]

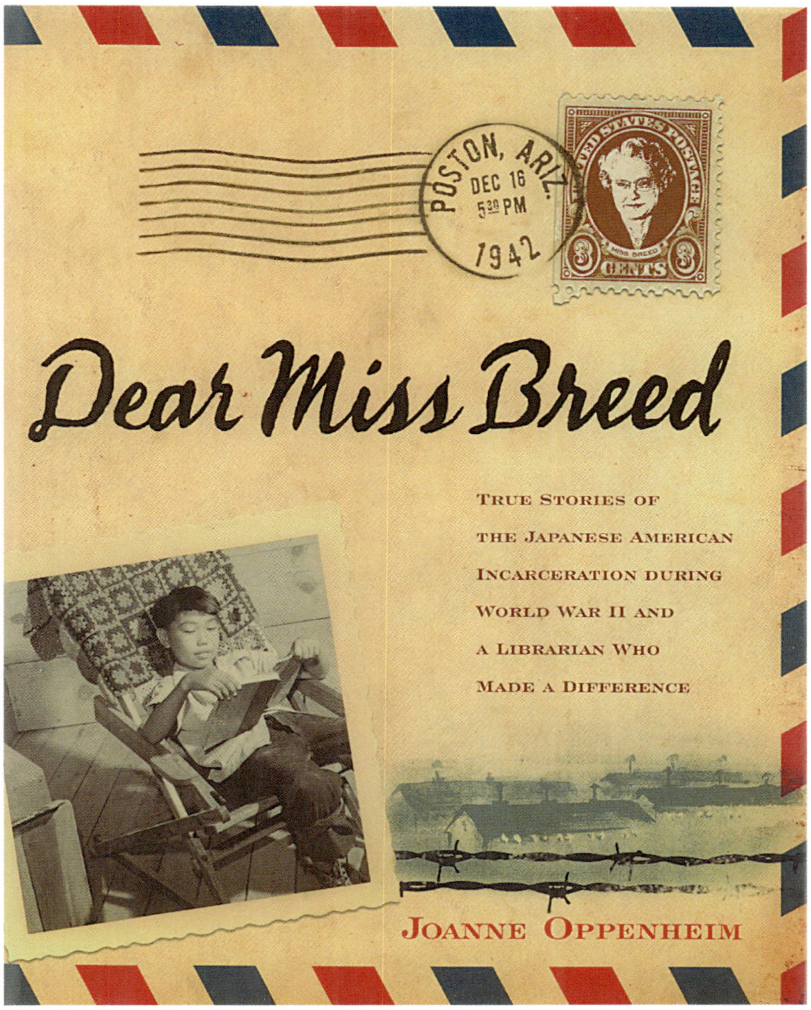

FIGURE 10.14
Dear Miss Breed: True Stories of the Japanese American Incarceration during World War II and a Librarian Who Made a Difference, by Joanne Oppenheim. New York: Scholastic, 2006.

The great variety of books about the camps that were published at the end of the twentieth century included Ken Mochizuki's *Baseball Saved Us* (1993), Eve Bunting's *So Far From the Sea* (1998), Rick Noguchi and Deneen Jenks's *Flowers from Mariko* (2001), and Amy Lee-Tai's *A Place Where Sunflowers Grow* (2006). Joanne Oppenheim's *Dear Miss Breed: True Stories of the Japanese American Incarceration during World War II and A Librarian Who Made a Difference* (2006, fig. 10.14) is based on some two hundred letters from students in the camps to the children's librarian at the San Diego Public Library.[47] Marlene Shigekawa, who was born in the Poston, Arizona, camp, the setting of her book *Blue Jay in the Desert* (1993), explained to young children in *Welcome Home Swallows* (2001, fig. 10.15) the bitter and divisive choice young camp inmates faced. Should they serve in the American military though they were incarcerated unlawfully?

Shigekawa tells the story of Junior, whose family comes back to Anaheim, California, after living for three years in the Poston, Arizona, internment camp. On the first day of school, the teacher introduces him to his "buddy" Peter, who is supposed to play with him during recess. One day, Junior invites Peter to his house and shows him some treasured possessions—including a picture of his uncle Willie in his U.S. Army uniform.

> "Is your Uncle Willie an American?" asked Peter.
>
> "Yes, he went away to Italy to fight in the war," explained Junior . . .
>
> Then Junior showed Peter a photograph of Uncle Min wearing a headband and a Japanese jacket called a "happi coat."
>
> "Did your Uncle Min go away to fight in the war too?" asked Peter.
>
> "No, he just went away. Nobody will tell me where he is," Junior explained. [He had been sent to the internment camp at Tule Lake, California.]
>
> "Is he a Jap?" blurted Peter.
>
> Startled, Junior said, "No, he isn't. And you shouldn't say that word!"
>
> "Why not," asked Peter.
>
> "Because it makes me feel bad."
>
> "But I didn't mean to make you feel bad," said Peter.
>
> "Then don't ever say that again."
>
> "Okay," replied Peter.
>
> They were quiet for a few minutes until Peter asked, "Are you an American like me?"
>
> "Yes, I'm an American," Junior answered. "I was born right here in Anaheim. My grandparents came from Japan a long time ago. . . ."[48]
>
> One day when his mother and his grandpa drove up to the school, Junior saw someone sitting in the back of the car. It was Uncle Willie! . . .

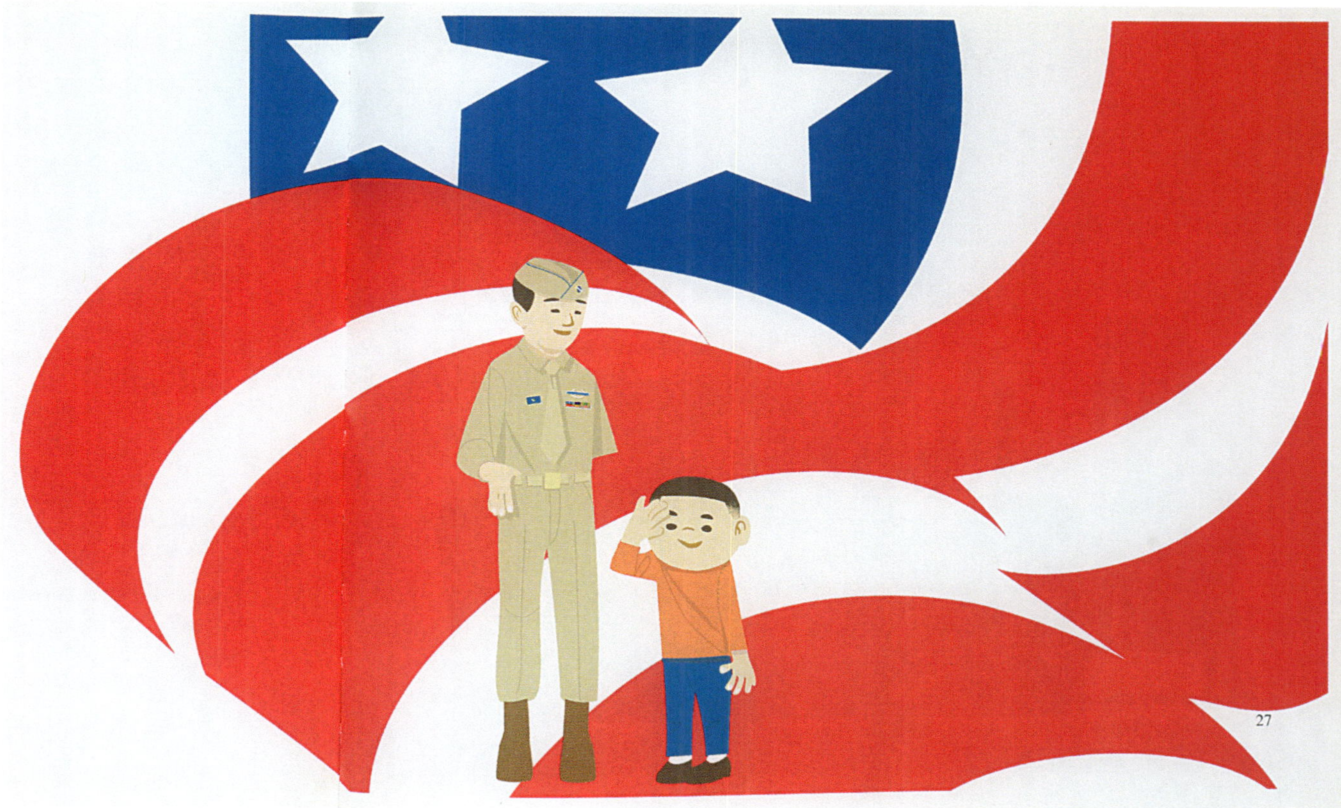

FIGURE 10.15
Welcome Home Swallows, by Marlene Shigekawa, illustrated by Isao Kikuchi. Torrence, CA: Heian International, 2001, page 27.

"You finally came back!" Junior shouted. Then he noticed that Uncle Willie had hugged him with only one arm. His left arm was missing.

"What happened to your arm?" Junior asked.

"I lost it in the war," Uncle Willie explained . . .

"Why did you go into the Army?" asked Junior. Uncle Willie paused and then said, "Because I wanted to show everyone that we are loyal Americans. We may look Japanese on the outside, but we're Americans in our hearts."[49]

The Journey: Japanese Americans, Racism, and Renewal

Finally, reaching the end of the century, there appeared a book, boldly illustrated, succinct and to-the-point, a "powerful, sometimes shocking account"—a cry. Based on a twenty-five foot long mural she had painted on canvases in her studio, the "passionate" book-album was created by Sheila Hamanaka, a third-generation Japanese American. Her uncle fought in World War II, while her parents, older brother, and sister were interned in the Jerome relocation center. Her grandfather died in the camp. In *The Journey: Japanese Americans, Racism, and Renewal* (1990, fig. 10.16), Hamanaka told the Japanese American story in chronologically arranged sidebars that follow her expressionistic, full-colored paintings.

Excerpts from her text reveal that here was a new kind of informational book for young American readers:

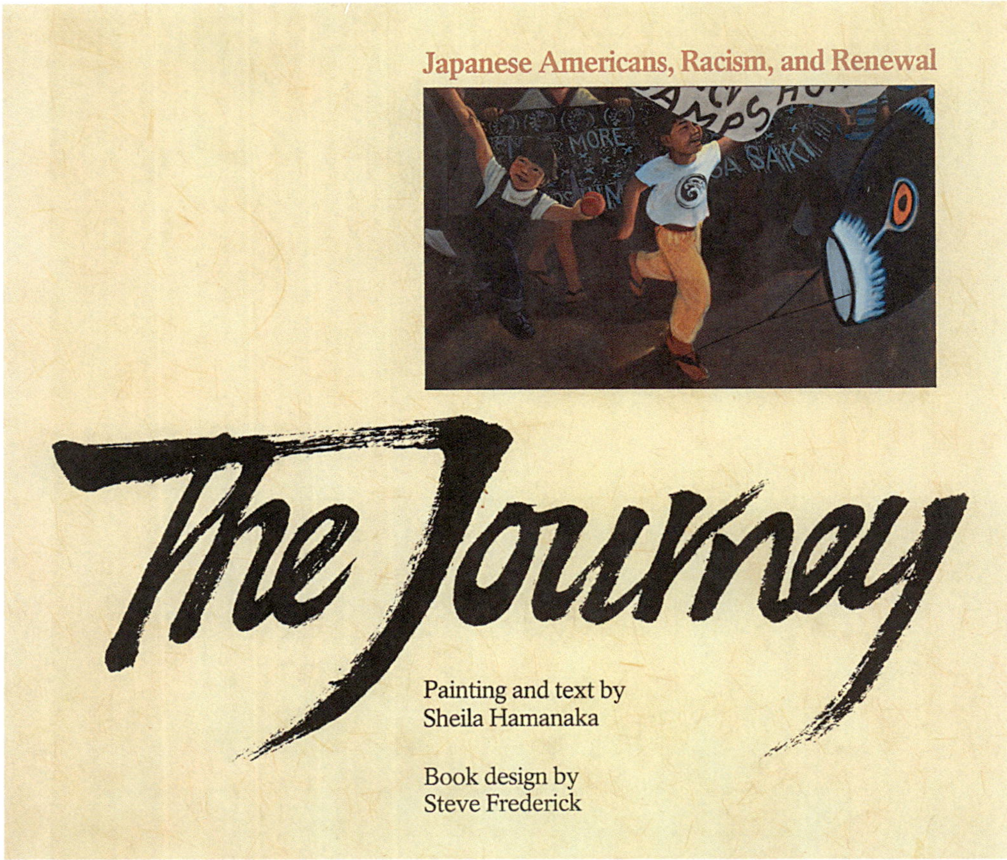

FIGURE 10.16
The Journey: Japanese Americans, Racism, and Renewal, written and illustrated by Sheila Hamanaka. New York: Orchard Books, 1990.

Japanese immigrants first sailed across the Pacific to Hawaii in the late 1800s. They were lured by the prospect of owning land and the promise of farm or factory work; but, like the Chinese before them, they met with prejudice. American farmers of European descent and the unions fought for the alien land laws (passed in California in 1913 and not repealed until 1952) which made it illegal for first-generation Japanese Americans to own a home, a farm, or a grocery store. They were prevented from becoming citizens. . . . In 1924, the U.S. Congress slammed shut "the golden door," and all immigration from Japan was halted. . . .

Excluded from trades and professions, Japanese worked as stoop laborers picking crops: as early as 1915, they were providing 75 percent of the fresh produce consumed in Los Angeles. . . .

December 7, 1941: The Japanese Imperial Navy bombed the U.S. Pacific Fleet at Pearl Harbor, a naval base in Hawaii. Within hours, FBI agents were knocking on doors, arresting many prominent members of Japanese American communities along the West Coast: ministers, business people, newspaper editors, farmers, fisherpeople, instructors of judo and flower arrangement. . . .

On December 8, the United States declared war on Japan. . . .

February 19, 1942: President Franklin D. Roosevelt, himself a believer in the racial inferiority of the Japanese, issued Executive Order 9066. All persons of Japanese ancestry living on the West Coast, including seventy thousand American-born citizens, were condemned to concentration camps without trial or hearing. . . .

Land that the Japanese had nurtured for years was gobbled up by greedy farmers. Desperate, people sold possessions for next to nothing . . . In the panic, precious books, mementos, and Japanese antiques were burned. A columnist for the *San Francisco Examiner* wrote: "Herd 'em up, pack 'em off, and give 'em the inside room in the badlands. Let 'em be hurt, hungry, and dead up against it . . . Personally, I hate the Japanese. And that goes for all of them. . . ."

Concentration camps were hastily erected on Indian reservations or swamp or desert wasteland. . . .

November 19, 1942: U.S. Military Police opened fire on Japanese American protestors at the Manzanar Relocation Center in California. Two dead. Eight wounded. . . .

As the war in Europe intensified, the U.S. Government began to conscript the Japanese it had earlier labeled "enemy aliens." In 1943, all prisoners in the camps over the age of seventeen were ordered to fill out Loyalty Questionnaires. Would you serve in combat wherever sent? they were asked. . . . Will you foreswear allegiance to the Japanese emperor, Hirohito? Prohibited by law from becoming U.S. citizens, the Issei feared they would be people without a country. . . .

In October 1944, the all-Nisei unit . . . suffered more than eight hundred casualties . . . a casualty rate five times greater than the average for other regimental combat teams and becoming the most highly decorated in U.S. military history. . . .

March 20, 1946: The last Japanese Americans left the concentration camps, each given twenty-five dollars and a ride home; but many of their homes had been burned by racists. Scores of camp survivors had contracted tuberculosis. Others suffered the effects of nervous breakdowns, or later died from aggravated heart conditions. Burdened by shame and grief, most walled off the past with silence. . . .

In 1988, after public hearings by the Commission of Wartime Relocation and Internment of Civilians, the government formally apologized to Japanese Americans: surviving victims of the camps were to be paid twenty thousand dollars each.[50]

The Turn of a New Century

It was time for the healing to begin. On November 9, 2000, on a small wedge of land near the U.S. Capitol in Washington, DC, a new memorial, years in the making, was formally dedicated. Surrounding a bronze sculpture of two cranes caught in barbed wire, a shallow, cascading water basin strewn with rocks, and a somber-toned bell, the retaining walls are engraved with the names of Japanese Americans who died in the war. Also engraved are the names of the ten camps:

Manzanar, Tule Lake, Poston, Gila, Minidoka, Heart Mountain, Granada, Topaz, Rohwer, and Jerome. Among the quotations carved into the granite of the National Japanese American Memorial to Patriotism During World War II are these eighteen words by Akemi Dawn Matsumoto Ehrlich:

> Japanese by blood
> Hearts and minds American
> With honor unbowed
> Bore the sting of injustice
> For future generations

An abundant assortment of new books about Japan arrived with the turn of the twenty-first century. Picture books, novels, nonfiction, and graphic novels, all handsomely illustrated, presented to young readers a variety of Japanese subjects. Noteworthy among them were the picture-book biographies—an emerging publishing trend in American children's literature—about noted Japanese. Examples include *Grass Sandals: The Travels of* [Matsuo] *Basho* (1997), the poet; [Katsushika] *Hokusai: The Man Who Painted a Mountain* (2001); [Soichiro] *Honda: The Boy Who Dreamed of Cars* (2008), and *The East-West House:* [Isamu] *Noguchi's Childhood in Japan* (2009), about the Japanese American artist and sculptor.[51]

Author Kimiko Kajikawa retold Japanese folktales, among them *Yoshi's Feast* (2000). Adapted from the story "Smells and Jingles," originally published in William Griffis's *Japanese Fairy World* (1880), it tells about Yoshi, the fan maker, and his neighbor's broiled eel.[52]

Other new books were Kajikawa's *Tsunami!* (2009, fig, 10.17),[53] dramatically illustrated in collage by Ed Young, which retells the story of the wise elder who saves the villagers from a deadly tsunami; *Hachiko: The True Story of a Loyal Dog* (2004) by Pamela S. Turner, one of several new books about this famous canine; the graphic novel *The Yellow Jar* (2002) by Patrick Atangan; and more retellings of old tales including *The Bee and the Dream* (1996) by Jan Freeman Long, *The Drums of Noto Hanto* (1999) by J. Alison James, *Tanuki's Gift* (2003) by Tim Myers, and *The Silver Charm* (2002), retold by Robert D. San Souci.[54]

New titles about the detention camps included *The Journal of Ben Uchida* (1999) by Barry Denenberg, *Remembering Manzanar* (2002) by Michael L. Cooper, and *Weedflower* (2006) by Cynthia Kadohata. Increasingly diverse themes were covered, such as the story of the shipwrecked Manjiro (who appeared in at least three books, including Rhoda Blumberg's *Shipwrecked!*, 2001), time travel, as in *Sam Samurai* (2001) by Jon Scieska, and the tea ceremony, in a book of the same title by Shozo Sato (2005).[55]

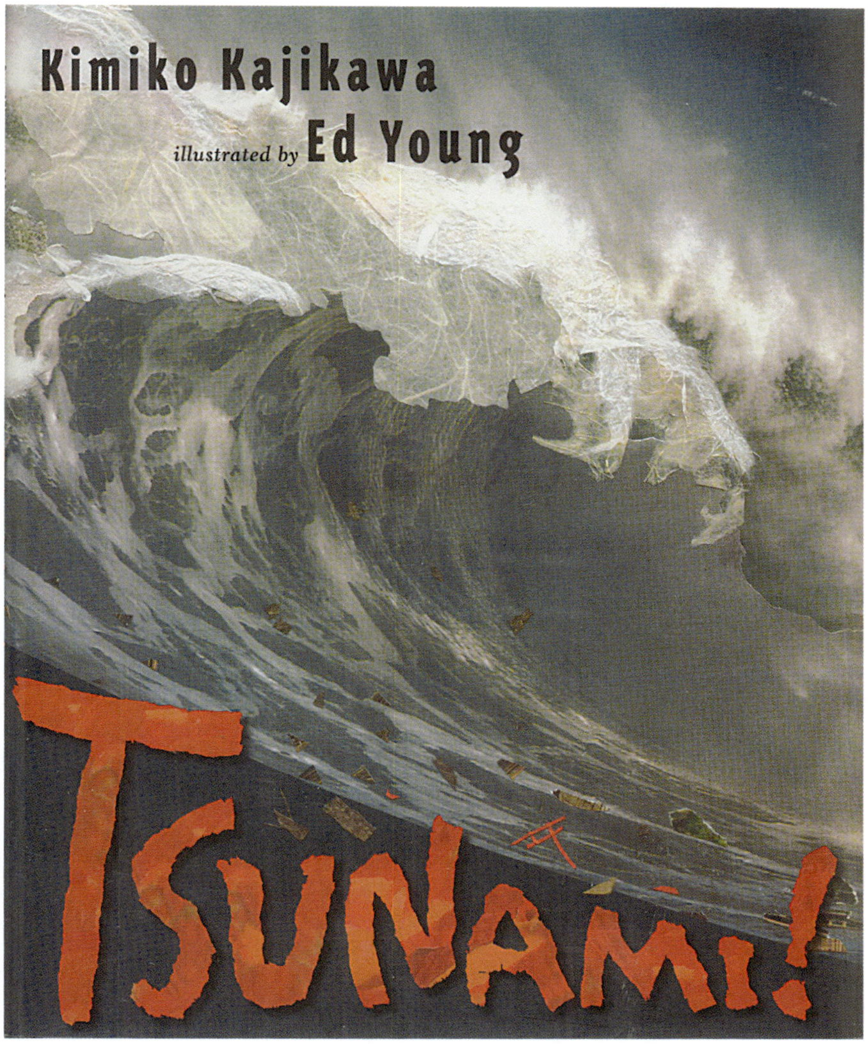

FIGURE 10.17
Tsunami! by Kimiko Kajikawa, illustrated by Ed Young. New York: Philomel Books, 2009.

Pearl Harbor was the subject of *A Boy at War* (2001), the first book in Harry Mazer's trilogy about Adam Pelko and his Japanese American friend Davi Mori. In *A Boy No More* (2004), Adam's friend and his family are sent to the Manzanar internment camp, while in *Heroes Don't Run* (2005), Adam enlists in the U.S. Navy and ends up in combat in Okinawa.[56]

Michael Morpurgo's intriguing *Kensuke's Kingdom* (1999) tells of a boy who finds himself on a deserted island with a mysterious Japanese man who had saved his life. The strongest titles from this time, however, were Graham Salisbury's *Under the Blood-Red Sun* (1994) and its sequel *House of Red Fish* (2006), both haunting stories of courage shown by thirteen-year-old Tomi Nakaji, whose father is sent to a camp after the attack on Pearl Harbor.[57]

* * *

American children's books about Japan had come a long way. "The world, you know, is round, and Asia is on the other side of it," America's Samuel Griswold

Goodrich had written in 1836.[58] By the end of his century, Japan had come much closer and was described, in one 1897 volume, as the "Island Paradise . . . the unique nation of the globe—the land of dream and enchantment . . . its people not of this world."[59] Yet American views of Japan soon began to change, and they continued to evolve in concert with Japanese-American relations. The decades between the two world wars produced few children's books about Japan, a lacuna that was remedied by the wealth of postwar publications of handsome and often idealistic books.

Increasingly, Japanese Americans came forward to tell their own dramatic experiences. Although images of the old Japan were still appearing, the stories of the early years of the twenty-first century were more likely to be about boys like Gregory, in Geneva Cobb Iijima's *The Way We Do It in Japan* (2002), whose father (who is Japanese) is transferred to Japan (his mother is from Kansas);[60] girls like Yoko in *Yoko's Paper Cranes* (2001), who lives in San Francisco and sends an origami birthday card to *obasan*, her grandmother in Japan;[61] or Hiromi, in

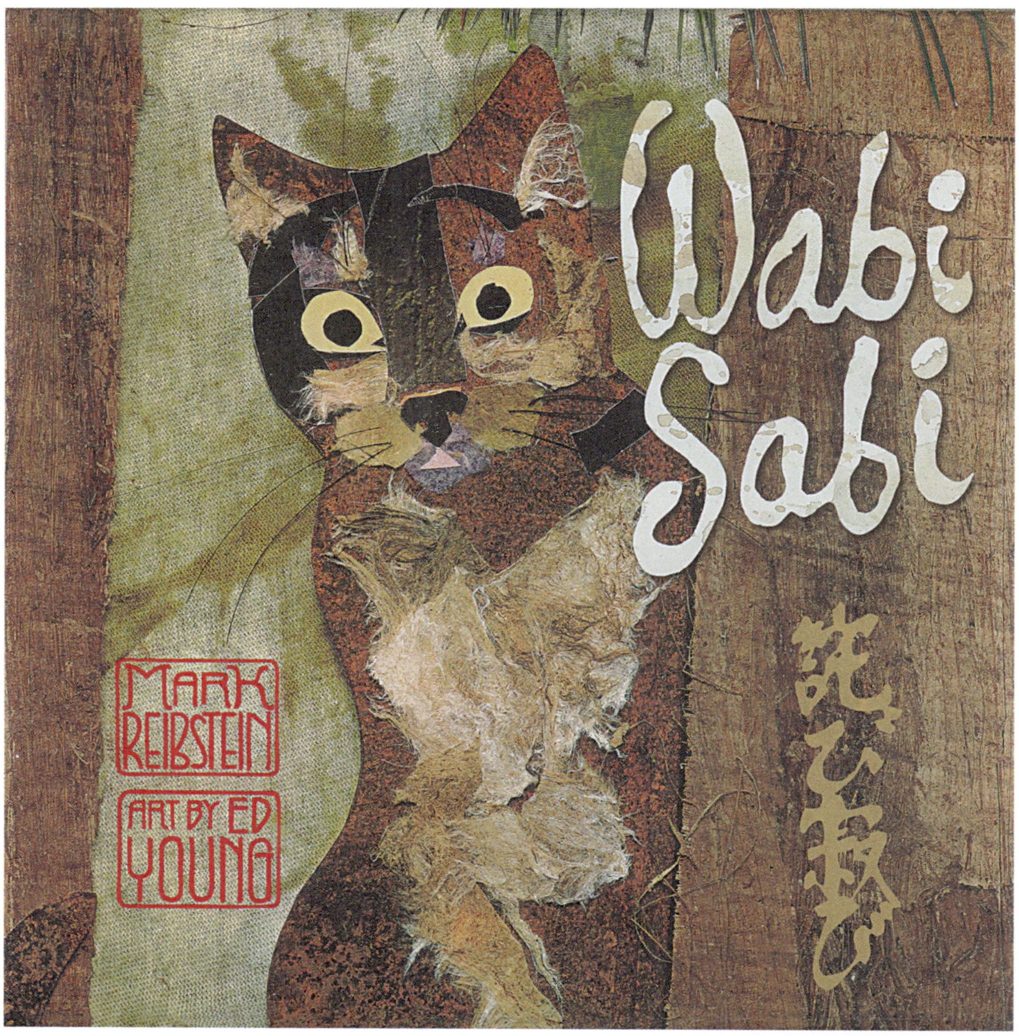

FIGURE 10.18
Wabi Sabi, by Mark Reibstein, illustrated by Ed Young. New York: Little, Brown, 2008.

Hiromi's Hands (2007), who, apprenticed to her Japanese father, becomes one of America's first female sushi chefs.[62]

It may seem that, over time, American children's books would have covered Japan, as one children's book title indicates, from *A to Zen*.[63] Yet some of Japan's most celebrated arts have rarely been noted. Little has been written about Nō, Kabuki, Bunraku, or even major historical events. Though newly chronicled in a magnificent album by Mitsumasa Anno[64] and in the elegantly droll picture book *Kaeru no Heike monogatari*,[65] in which the samurai are depicted as frogs in stylish Heian-period costumes, the grand epic *Heike monogatari* (The Tale of the Heike), about the twelfth-century fight between the Taira and Minamoto clans, remains nearly absent from American children's books. Though touched upon in some earlier titles, the age-old stories of the warrior-monk Benkei, the child hero Momotaro, and the sun goddess Amaterasu are little known in America.[66]

And yet, the search for Japan in American children's books continued into the twenty-first century. Two stories especially show the promise of a more deeply felt and nuanced understanding of "Japaneseness." While the novel *Eyes of the Emperor* (2005) lays bare the surreal cruelty provoked by hatred of the "Japs," the lyrical picture book *Wabi Sabi* (2008, fig. 10.18) tells young American readers about a feline who wanders into "the way of seeing the world that is at the heart of Japanese culture [and which] finds beauty and harmony in what is simple, imperfect, natural, modest, and mysterious."[67]

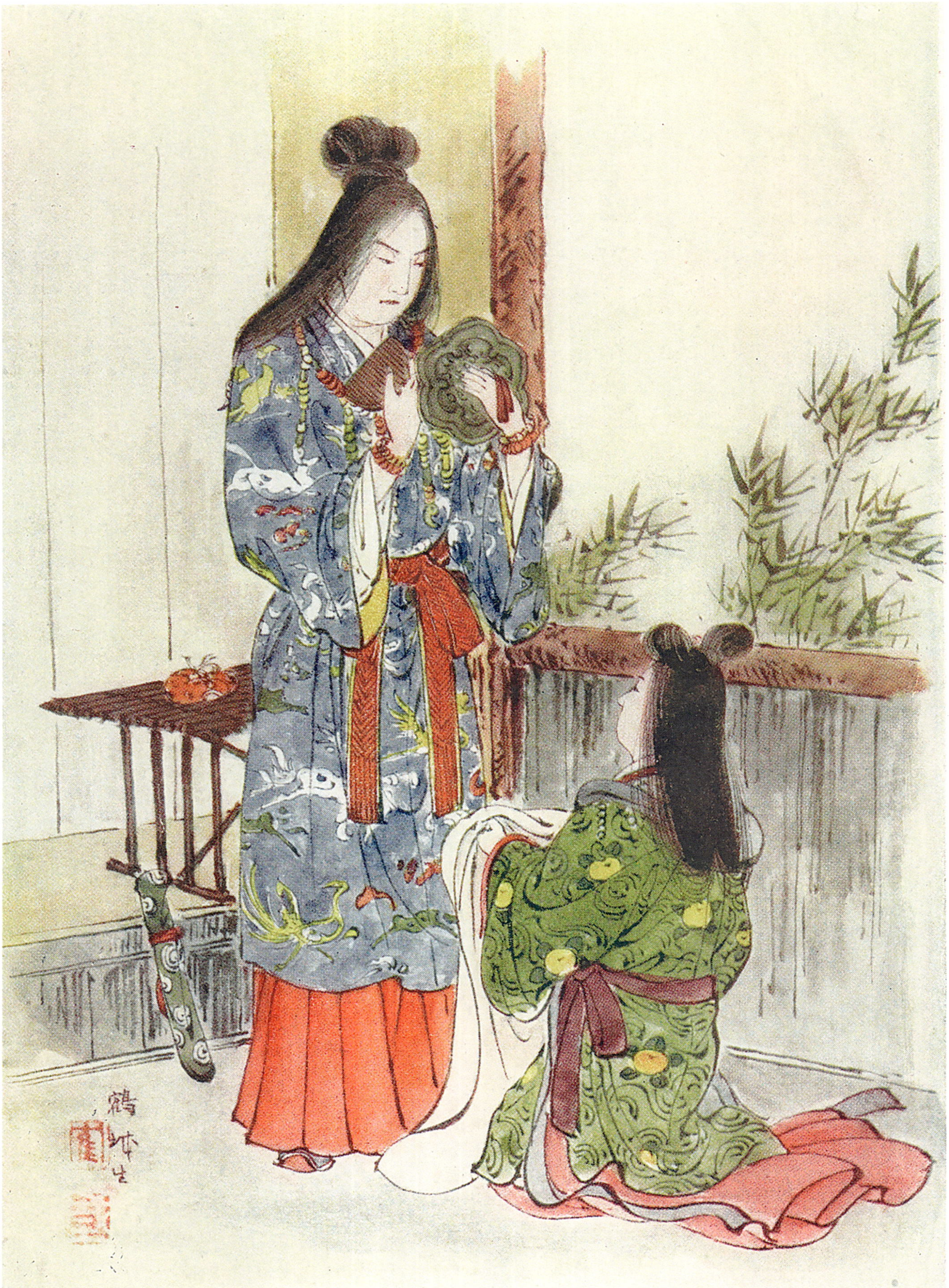

Appendix

The Gatekeepers

Leading American Children's Librarians and Their Influence on Children's Books about Japan

To celebrate the four hundredth anniversary of the discovery of America by Christopher Columbus in 1492, Chicago hosted, in 1893, the World's Columbian Exposition. The best architects were recruited to design a host of impressive buildings to house the wonders of technology, agriculture, the arts, and entertainment. Among the forty-two nations participating, Japan erected an elegant three-pavilion structure based on the eleventh-century Hōō-dō or Phoenix Hall of the Byōdō-in at Uji, near Kyoto. A small model library included in the United States pavilions was perhaps not as eye-popping as many of the exhibits, but it did highlight America's libraries, part of the country's great success story. The catalog[1] of the model library's collection of five thousand books included one children's book about Japan: *Adventures of Two Youths in a Journey to Japan and China* (1879, fig. A.2) by Thomas W. Knox.

Caroline M. Hewins was among the six committee members who had recommended books for the collection. Considered the godmother of America's

FIGURE A.1 (OPPOSITE)
"Prince Yamato Take bade his wife help him to attire himself like a woman," in *The Japanese Fairy Book*, rendered into English by Yei Theodora Ozaki, illustrated by Kakuzo Fujiyama. Tokyo: Fuzanbo, 1909.

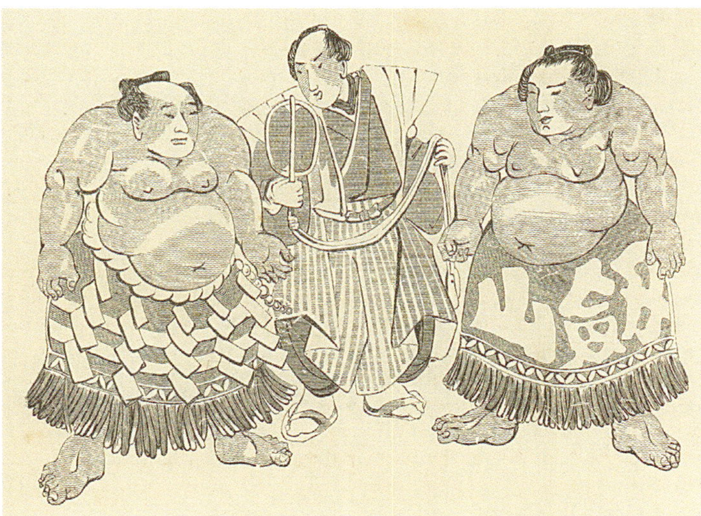

FIGURE A.2
"A Pair of Wrestlers and Their Manager," in *Adventures of Two Youths in a Journey to Japan and China*, by Thomas W. Knox. New York: Harper and Brothers, 1881, page 230.

children's libraries, Hewins was the quiet pioneer among a group of women who found their calling in leading America's youth to good books. Their work coalesced after they founded the Club of Children's Librarians at the 1899 Montreal Conference of the American Library Association. Anne Carroll Moore, who became, in 1906, head of the children's department at the New York Public Library, was elected chairwoman. Among the leaders of this group, which gradually embraced more members of America's leading libraries, were Alice M. Jordan (Boston Public Library), Frances Jenkins Olcott (Carnegie Library of Pittsburgh), Effie Power (Cleveland Public Library), and Clara Whitehill Hunt (Brooklyn Public Library). These women developed the nation's library work for children, and, to a large extent, determined what America's children were reading. Their book selections provide a window into twentieth-century American children's book publishing and the slow but steady growth of children's books about Japan.

Four women of the early children's book and library generations were particularly influential, given their strong personalities, unique professional positions, national and international networks, and their book lists, reviews, and publications. They were Caroline M. Hewins, the "first among equals";[2] Anne Carroll Moore, her forceful protégée; Bertha E. Mahony, editor of the first professional children's literature journal; and Virginia Haviland, who became the first children's book specialist of the Library of Congress. These women, and others in their network, played a decisive role in the selection of children's books—including those about Japan—that would become part of public and school library collections across the country.

Caroline M. Hewins

Born in 1846, Hewins was seven years old when Commodore Perry sailed for Japan; fifteen when the American Civil War broke out; and a young woman in 1865, when both *Alice in Wonderland* and *Hans Brinker, or The Silver Skates* were published. She began her library career in 1868, the year *Little Women* became a bestseller.

Hewins's early life had all the characteristics of a nineteenth-century upper-middle class girlhood. In a setting of gardens, afternoon teas, and rides through the country, she grew up surrounded by grandmothers and great-great grandmothers, aunts and uncles. She wrote that she knew few other children and books became her companions. As she would later describe in her unique autobiographical work, *A Mid-Century Child and Her Books* (1926), she read many of the classics, the Arabian Nights, German fairy tales, Shakespeare, and others. Among the early children's books were *The History of Goody Two Shoes* (1765), *The*

Swiss Family Robinson (1812), Washington Irving's *The Legend of Sleepy Hollow* (1820), Nathaniel Hawthorne's *Wonder-Book for Boys and Girls* (1852), and *Uncle Tom's Cabin* (1852). She also read the *London Art Journal*, *Parley's Magazine*, *Harper's Magazine*, the *Atlantic Monthly*, and the children's magazines *Our Young Folks* and *Riverside Magazine*.

With such a background, it is not surprising that, as an adult, Hewins gravitated to a career in books. In 1875, she became the librarian at the Young Men's Institute in Hartford, Connecticut. Shaping the children's book collection according to her own views was among her first priorities. With some exceptions for volumes that had become general favorites, she discarded books that she viewed as "vulgar and sensational," "cheap and slovenly in style," or "melodramatic in incident." Books in "endless series"[3] were also less than desirable.

By the turn of the century, Hewins had emerged as the national leader of the children's book and library field and had ushered in "the beginning of a new day in book selection for children."[4] Upon request by Frederick Leypoldt, editor of the newly established *Publishers' Weekly*, Hewins compiled *Books for the Young: A Guide for Parents and Children*.[5] Not only was this the first such list but, nearly two decades later, with many similar lists in circulation, one reviewer in a 1915 edition of *Library Journal* declared it still "easily the best of them all."[6]

Hewins's list, comprising selected volumes published since about 1850, emphasized the importance of books about English and American history, reflecting Hewins's belief that every American child should have a sound knowledge of the history of his "own country and its mother-land."[7] Other categories included "Home and School Life," "Travel and Adventure," and "Imaginary Voyages." The section titled "Stories of Various Countries" included subsections on Africa, North America, the West Indies, Australia, Europe, and Asia. Books on Japan listed in the Asia subsection included Matilda Chaplin Ayrton's *Child-Life in Japan and Japanese Child Stories* (1879); *Adventures of Two Youths in a Journey to Japan and China* by Thomas W. Knox (1879); and Edward Greey's first two volumes, *Young Americans in Japan* (1882) and *The Wonderful City of Tokio* (1883).

Books for the Young, which was re-issued a number of times under the new title *Books for Boys and Girls, A Selected List*, became a standard in the field. It influenced many other such lists, among them John Sargent's comprehensive *Reading for the Young* (1890)[8] —a much-cited publication at the time—which incorporated almost all of Hewins's *Books for the Young* in its 1890–1896 editions.[9]

Hewins's collection grew after 1893, when the Young Men's Institute became the Hartford Public Library. The rich children's book catalog of Hewins's "own library"[10] ranged from "Amusements" to "Zoölogy." Evidently, she had acquired

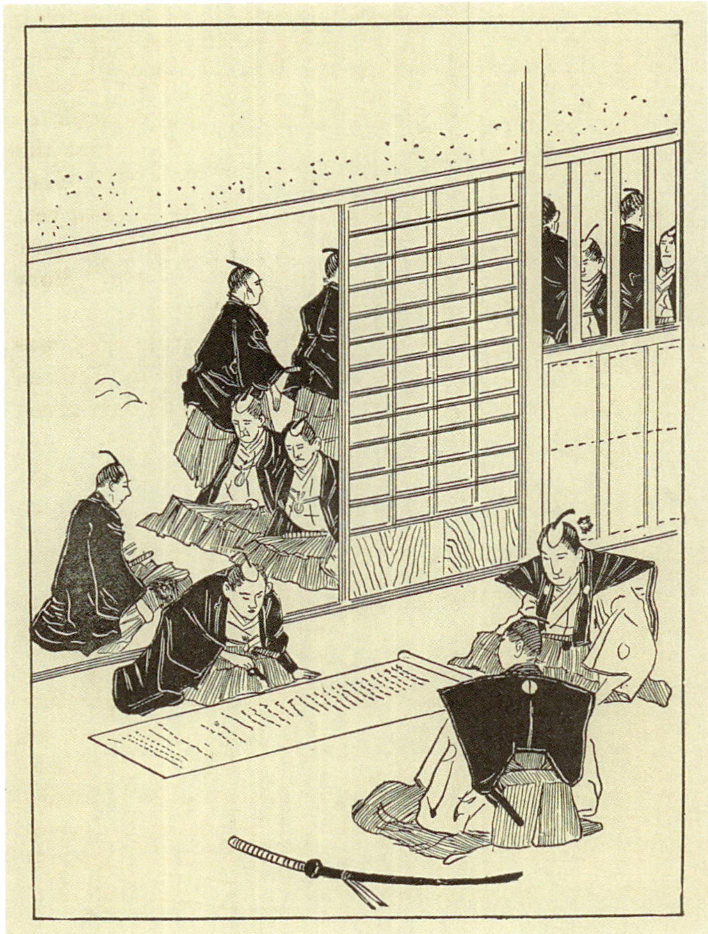

FIGURE A.3
"Given Our Signature that We are Not Christians," in *Honda the Samurai, A Story of Modern Japan*, by W. E. Griffis. Boston: Congregational Sunday-School and Publishing Society, 1890, page 194.

quite a few titles about Japan. In addition to the Greey and Knox titles, there were now also the William E. Griffis volumes *Japanese Fairy World* (1880) and *Honda the Samurai* (1890, fig. A.3) and Mae St. John Bramhall's *The Wee Ones of Japan* (1894). Also included were the adult titles *Unbeaten Tracks in Japan* (1880) by Isabella Bird, *Jinrikisha Days* (1891) by Eliza Scidmore, and *The Story of Japan* (1894) by David Murray. As her personal favorite, Hewins included *A Japanese Boy, By Himself* (1889) by Shiukichi Shigemi. (Curiously, by 1915, the Hewins list only included one title about Japan, *The Japanese Twins* [1912] by Lucy Fitch Perkins.)[11]

Hewins's influence reached beyond her own publications as she contributed her expertise to other works, including *Children's Catalog*, a standard bibliography first published in 1909 that has been used by librarians across the country for collection development and reference.

Bertha E. Mahony

As children's librarians became more influential, the field acquired an important newcomer. Born in 1882 in Rockport, Massachusetts, Bertha Mahony grew up in an Irish New England family, her life filled with music, storytelling, playing out-of-doors in the country, and summer picnics. Although she was able to read by age five, "Bertha's real possession by books began when she was ten" and fell in love with *Little Women.*[12] After graduating from high school, she entered the Training Class of the Public Schools of the City of Gloucester to become a teacher.

After a stint in a bookshop, she was hired, in 1906, as secretary for the Women's Educational and Industrial Union. An article in the *Atlantic Monthly*[13] about women as ideal bookshop proprietors gave Mahony the idea for her next step, which, as it turned out, was a step towards her life's mission. In 1916, she opened the Bookshop for Boys and Girls, a new department of the Women's Educational and Industrial Union, in an old house next door to the union's headquarters. Tutored by Alice M. Jordan of the Boston Library (who used Caroline Hewins's book lists in her teaching), Mahony sought the advice of some of the key players in the children's library community, including its leading supporter, Frederic Melcher, manager of the Stewart Bookstore in Indianapolis. Mahony also consulted May Massee, editor of the *American Library Association Booklist* in Chicago (who later became one of the country's leading children's book editors), Anne Carroll Moore at the New York Public Library, and Hewins in Hartford.

In her new shop, Mahony organized lectures, storytelling programs, Saturday morning book meetings, doll conventions, puppet parades, a bookmobile, and exhibitions of the work of major children's book illustrators. Increasingly, the bookshop became a Boston institution that would influence children's book publishing as well as library book purchases and children's reading throughout the country.[14]

In 1924, Mahony and Elinor Whitney, her assistant director, founded the *Horn Book Magazine*, the first children's literature journal in the United States. Like Mahony's bookshop, the new magazine was brimming with activity and excitement. It was filled with informal book notes, reviews of adult and children's books, and essays on children's book issues, authors, and illustrators. In 1934, both editors resigned from the bookshop to devote all their energy to the magazine, whose scope was increasingly broadened as Mahony went outside the traditional New England children's book circle to look for new ideas and new staff.[15] However, the old guard remained closely aligned with her. Both Louise Seaman Bechtel (see chapter 7) and Anne Carroll Moore became associate editors in the 1930s. Virginia Haviland would join them later.

In 1916, Mahony published *Books for Boys and Girls—A Suggestive Purchase List* prefaced by Caroline Hewins. Successive editions were published in 1917, 1919,

1922, and 1924. Mahony's *Realms of Gold in Children's Books,*[16] published in 1929 by May Massee (at that time the children's editor at Doubleday, Doran), had been planned as the fifth edition and supplement to the *Books for Boys and Girls* list. Instead, it grew into an 800-page volume, offering a wide-angle view of the state of American children's books of the 1920s. Filled with annotations, introductions, appreciations of artists, notes about artistic styles and techniques, and information on imported books, this massive work reveals Mahony's energy, diligence, and her belief in the transforming powers of children's books. "What we want in books for young people is what we want in books for ourselves—life in all its infinite variations and art in all its manifold forms," she wrote.[17] Mahony also believed that young readers were becoming "more and more discriminating and more unconsciously critical and [were] reading in a far wider range of subjects than ever before."[18]

Realms of Gold takes the reader from nursery stories through folk literature to nonfiction for the older child; it also includes school and adult books from the eighteenth century to the present. Surprisingly, this comprehensive volume lists very few books about Asia. There are three books about China, four about India, two about the Pacific Islands, and one about New Zealand. The only nonfiction title about Japan is *The Story of Japan* (1897) by Robert Van Bergen. Fiction about Japan included *The Japanese Twins* (1912), *A Daughter of the Samurai* (1925), *The Begging Deer and Other Stories of Japanese Children* (1928), *Wonder Tales of Old Japan* (1924), and Yei Theodora Ozaki's *The Japanese Fairy Book* (1903, fig. A.1), which was described as "a very attractive gift book with a delightfully smooth and flowing" style.

In 1936, Doubleday, Doran published Mahony's *Five Years of Children's Books: A Supplement to Realms of Gold* (fig. A.4). Compiled with the assistance of Elinor Whitney, this handsomely illustrated, 600-page volume documents the extraordinary richness and variety of children's books published between 1930 and 1935, at the height of the Great Depression. "We hope that our readers will be impressed, as we ourselves have been, with the large number of fine books written during this five-year period by people of genius who have thought their best, written their best and put life, breadth, and power into their books,"[19] Mahony wrote proudly in the introduction. Her subject categories barely managed to contain the enormous variety of topics and titles. Here was everything from legends, myths, and hero romances to history, geography and literature; from exploration and discovery to science, biography and books about children's literature. Children's books could truly be called "reservoirs of life," as Mahony noted.[20]

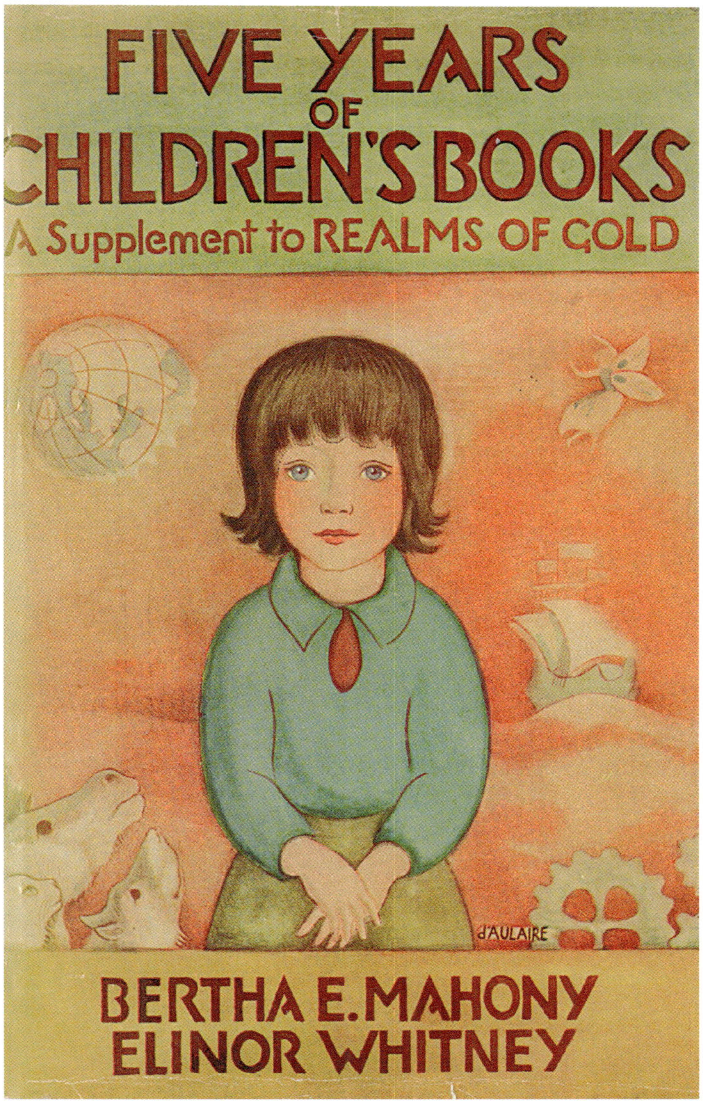

FIGURE A.4
Five Years of Children's Books, compiled by Bertha E. Mahony and Elinor Whitney, illustrated by Ingri and Edgar Parin D'Aulaire. Garden City, NY: Doubleday, Doran, 1936.

Five Years of Children's Books (to which both Anne Carroll Moore and Louise Seaman Bechtel contributed) is especially rich in its selection of books about other countries, including Albania, Brazil, Tibet, Sicily, Denmark, and Mexico. Asian countries are the least represented, perhaps a reflection of the National Origins Act of 1924, which barred all Asian immigrants to the United States. *Five Years* did list books about China, including Elizabeth Forman Lewis's *Young Fu of the Upper Yangtze* (1932), which was awarded the Newbery medal. Yet true representations of the Japanese were barely discernible in what Mahony described as the "rich multicolored strand" of American culture. By the time *Five Years* was published, Japan had become, to many in the United States, Asia's "evil empire," annexing Manchuria in 1932, withdrawing from the League of Nations in 1933, and preparing for war with China. The books representing Japan in *Realms of Gold* and *Five Years of Children's Books*, were safe and neutral, and were all about

Japan's past. They included *The Japanese Twins* (1912), Elizabeth Coatsworth's *Cricket and the Emperor's Son* (1932), and *A Daughter of the Samurai* (1934) by Etsu Sugimoto, which Mahony described as a book that would "widen horizons and quicken our understanding of people of other lands" and would be "an important book for some time to come."[21]

Other books about Japan listed in *Five Years* included Chiyono Sugimoto's *Chiyo's Return* (1935) and *Japanese Holiday Picture Tales* (1933), autobiographical reminiscences and Japanese tales by Etsu Sugimoto's daughter, which were pleasant historical narratives for young readers but minor works. This was also true of Lois Lignell's *Three Japanese Mice and Their Whiskers,* lyrically illustrated by Betz Pincehorn (1934). May McNeer and Lynd Ward's retelling of *Prince Bantam* (1929) was also a book of Japan's past. So was *The Cat Who Went to Heaven* (1930) by Elizabeth Coatsworth. All these titles portrayed Japan as a picturesque, sweet, well-ordered faraway land.

In 1931, Mahony issued a special children's book list. Tipped into the *Horn Book Magazine* and available as a separate brochure, "Boys and Girls Around the World: Points North, South, East and West"[22] featured approximately 150 books about other countries. The majority were devoted to Europe, dominated by Germany, France, and Holland. Of the fifteen books devoted to Asia, seven were about China, one about Tibet, and one about Siam. There were six books about Japan: Sakae Shioya's *When I Was a Boy in Japan* (1906), *The Japanese Twins* (1912), *The Begging Deer* (1928), Etsu Sugimoto's *A Daughter of the Samurai* (1925), her autobiographical *With Taro and Hana in Japan* (1926), and *Treasure Flower* (1916) by Ruth Gaines.

Realms of Gold and *Five Years* helped establish Mahony's personal connection with Japan.[23] Sometime in 1935 or 1936, Momoko Ishii—founder of *bunko,* Japan's children's home libraries, and a writer, translator, and editor, who has been called the "Anne Carroll Moore of Japan"[24]—found herself in front of the Kyobunkwan bookshop on the Ginza in Tokyo. There, in the shop window, were Mahony's two tomes. Ishii, who had never seen such volumes before, purchased them, subscribed to the *Horn Book Magazine,* and wrote Mahony a letter that included many questions. When, in 1954, Ishii received a grant from the Rockefeller Foundation to visit publishers and libraries in the United States, Mahony, then age 75, organized her itinerary, which featured all the important children's libraries and their leaders. During a second trip in 1961, Ishii visited her children's book friends in Los Angeles, Chicago, Pittsburgh, and New York, then stopped in Boston to see Mahony, who by that time had become a close friend. Awed by the pioneering leaders of the American children's library and

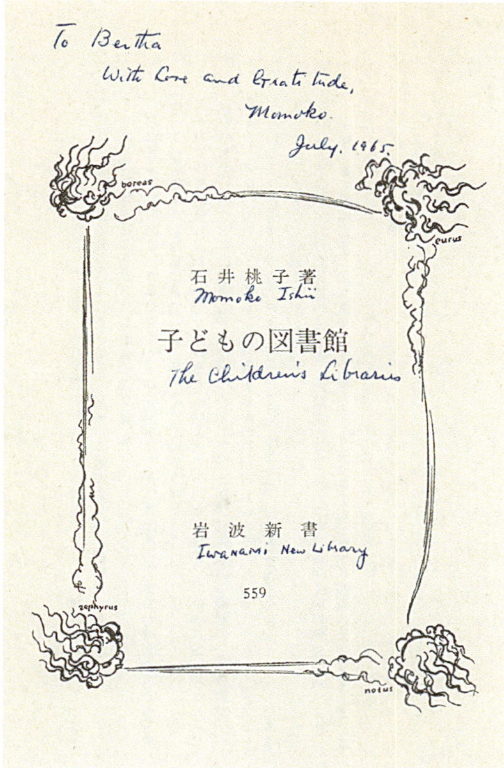

FIGURE A.5
Kodomo no toshokan [The Children's Libraries] by Momoko Ishii. Tokyo: Iwanami Shoten, 1965.

book community, Momoko Ishii took their ideas to Japan. She signed her book *Kodomo no toshokan* (Children's Libraries, 1965, fig. A.5) "To Bertha with Love and Gratitude."

Anne Carroll Moore, Gatekeeper at the New York Public Library

On the occasion of Anne Carroll Moore's silver anniversary at the New York Public Library, the English writer Eleanor Farjeon wrote: "In America, I suppose they take you as a real person; in England, you are a legend,"[25] to which she later added: "My beloved A. C. M. . . . you are not only the Mother of all American children but the Mother of all of us who write for them."[26]

Born in 1871 in Limerick, Maine, Moore was the youngest of ten children, and the only girl. She did not think of herself as a bookish child, yet she always liked to read and had the good fortune to have parents who saw to it that their children had an ample supply of books. Moore's dream was to become a lawyer like her father, but she knew that the legal profession was not open to women of her day. Instead, she entered the Pratt Institute Library School in Brooklyn, New York, in 1895 and graduated from the one-year course the following year. After serving ten years as head of the children's room of the Pratt Institute Free Library, she became, in 1906, the first supervisor of work with children at the New York

Public Library (NYPL).[27] Five years after Moore started working there, NYPL opened its iconic building on Fifth Avenue and 42nd Street. In the elegantly decorated Central Children's Room, filled with collections of rare and foreign-language children's books, Moore and her fine international staff welcomed distinguished visitors from all over the world. In this room the first Children's Book Week was celebrated in 1919 and children's books and their makers were discovered and promoted. In a note about the potentially positive effect of children's books upon international relations, Moore wrote:

> We have long contended that didacticism, condescension, and propaganda are the natural enemies of the reading habit in this country. Why are the library shelves containing books of science, travel, biography, especially collective biography, and European histories, so often called the deadest parts of a children's room? Not because the subjects in themselves are uninteresting. Not because children do not want to know what the world is like. Their interest is keen in knowing what the world is like . . . The answer to the question and the remedy for the condition lie with the authors, illustrators, and publishers, and we may add, that in the solution of this problem there may be found an open door to more intelligent and friendly international relations.[28]

In *A List of Books Recommended for a Children's Library,* which she had introduced in 1903, Moore recommended that many of the titles "be replaced by better books on the same subjects as soon as better books are published."[29] The list featured some five hundred titles organized into various categories, including "Easy Books for Little Children," "Legends and Fairy Tales," "Books about Nature," and "United States." Japan is represented in the "History and Travel" section by Matilda Chaplin Ayrton's *Child-Life in Japan* (1888), Charles Morris's *Historical Tales: Japan and China* (1898), F. P. Perry's *Tora's Happy Day* (1899), and Shiukichi Shigemi's *Japanese Boy* (1899).

Thirty years later, in 1933, Moore organized the first major retrospective children's book exhibition in the country, soliciting cooperation from the Pierpont Morgan Library, the Metropolitan Museum of Art, the American Antiquarian Society, and a number of private lenders. In the informative and witty exhibition catalog, *Children's Books of Yesterday* (1933), Moore wrote that the books had been chosen for their "originality, historical significance, for qualities of colorful illustration and ingenious design, [and] for their power of evoking memories of childhood and youth."[30]

The display of five hundred books, manuscripts, broadsides, and drawings dating from the late fifteenth century to the present was a beautiful tableau of Anglo-American children's literature and an affirmation of America's European

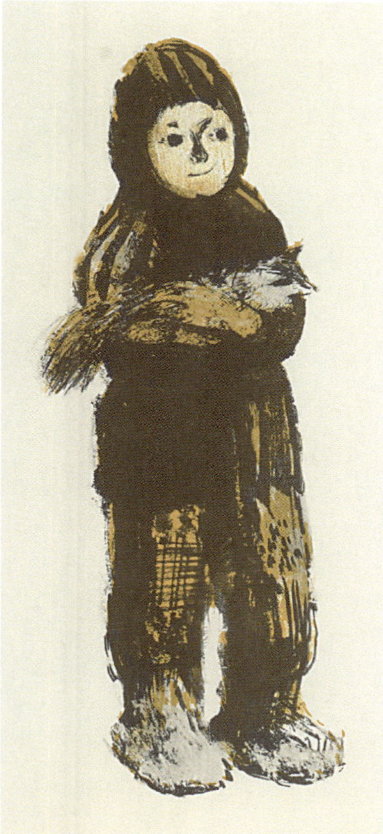

FIGURE A.6
The Golden Footprints, by Hatoju Muku, adapted and illustrated by Taro Yashima. Cleveland: World Publishing, 1960.

heritage. At this time England still dominated American children's literature (it was no coincidence that America's most prestigious children's book awards were named after British children's bookmen). The exhibition reflected this fact by including a number of British treasures, including such classic as *The Royal Primer* printed by John Newbery in 1762, William Roscoe's glorious *The Butterfly's Ball and the Grasshopper's Feast,* published in 1807 by John Harris, and *Alice in Wonderland* (1865) by Lewis Carroll.

German titles included editions of the first illustrated Aesop, printed in Ulm about 1476, and the first edition of Heinrich Hoffman's *Struwelpeter* (1844). Titles from France included a first edition of La Fontaine's *Fables* from 1668 and early editions of works by Charles Perrault, Madame La Comtesse d'Aulnoy, and Jules Verne. From Russia came Alexander Pushkin's *Tale of the Czar Saltan* with Ivan Bilibin's illustrations, and titles from Denmark included works by Hans Christian Andersen. American treasures included the Hiroglyphick Bible from 1788; *The New England Primer* of 1727; and Washington Irving's *Rip Van Winkle.* Among all this splendor and history Japan was represented by one title: Lafcadio Hearn's *Japanese Fairy Tales.*

In 1960, the New York Public Library presented another retrospective exhibition of children's books culled from its annual holiday book displays, which Anne Carroll Moore had initiated in 1910. Here, at last, was a step forward for books about Japan, which included *The Animal Frolic* by Toba Sōjō (1954), *Crow Boy* (1955) and *The Golden Footprints* (1960, fig. A.6) by Taro Yashima, *A Pair of Red Clogs* (1960) by Masako Matsuno, and *The Very Special Badgers* (1960) by Claus Stamm, illustrated by Kazue Mizumura.

A dozen years later, in 1972, during International Book Year, another noteworthy exhibition took place in the Central Children's Room of the New York Public Library. Co-sponsored in part by the Japanese Ministry of Foreign Affairs and the Japan Society of New York,[31] the display featured some 165 illustrated children's books from Japan.

Virginia Haviland

Little is known about the private Virginia Haviland, except that even in her youth she traveled abroad and met foreign visitors at her relatives' homes. This seems to have been the beginning of her life-long love for travel and exploration. Margaret Coughlan, reference librarian and her assistant at the Library of Congress, used to say that Haviland always kept a packed suitcase under her bed, ready to travel at a moment's notice.

Born in 1911 in Rochester, New York, Haviland moved with her family to Massachusetts. Cerebral and self-confident, Haviland received, in 1933, a B.A. in economics and mathematics from Cornell University. She did not, however, pursue these subjects in her career. Instead, following the advice of Alice M. Jordan, the highly respected children's library leader who was known for her nurturing of protégées, Haviland became a children's librarian at the Boston Public Library. Eventually she moved up to the positions of branch librarian and reader's advisor for children. Active in her children's library community, she participated in the activities of the Children's Services Division of the American Library Association, chaired the Newbery Caldecott Committee, taught at Simmons College of Library and Information Science, and engaged in numerous other book and library activities that made her a nationally known leader.[32]

In 1952, Frances Clarke Sayers, Anne Carroll Moore's successor and biographer, was asked to examine the children's book collections of the Library of Congress. Her report[33] became the blueprint for what initially called the Children's Book Section, later renamed the Children's Literature Center. Librarian of Congress Lewis Mumford called Haviland personally, asking her to become the head of the new section, which opened in March 1963.

In no time, Haviland filled the little "shoebox," as Margaret Coughlan fondly called the room originally reserved for the section, with a broad selection of reference books retrieved from the Library's vast general collection. She pushed the Library's administration into adopting the "Annotated Code" (an enhanced cataloging approach to children's books), acquired numerous rare and foreign language children's books, and organized exhibitions and lectures. She also compiled numerous bibliographies and other reference works, including *Children's Literature: A Guide to Reference Sources* (1966) and its two supplements; *Louisa May Alcott: An Annotated, Selected Bibliography* (1969); *Samuel Langhorne Clemens: A Centennial for Tom Sawyer* (1977); articles about children's books in the Library's *Quarterly Journal*;[34] the handsome list *Children's Reading in America 1776* (1976), and *The Openhearted Audience: Ten Authors Talk About Writing for Children* (1980).

Other publications include her sixteen-volume *Favorite Fairy Tales* series (begun in 1959), illustrated by noted artists such as Roger Duvoisin, Felix Hoffmann, Nonny Hogrogrian, and Margot Zemach; *Books in Search of Children: Speeches and Essays* by Louise Seaman Bechtel (1969), which she edited; *Subject Collections in Children's Literature* (1969), edited by Carolyn Field, herself a nationally recognized gatekeeper; *The Spirited Life: Bertha Mahony Miller and Children's Books* by Eulalie Steinmetz Ross (1973) for which she compiled the bibliography; and the small and handsome monograph *The Travelogue Storybook of the Nineteenth Century* (1950), which was based on her Caroline Hewins Lecture.

Although she was active in national American library work, Haviland's heart was in her international activities. As a cultural ambassador with the prestige of the Library of Congress behind her, she traveled all over the world. She was familiar not only with the leading children's book women in the United States but also with her counterparts in other countries. At a time when an increasing number of international children's book centers were being established and children's book events and literature—including reference books—about children's literature were proliferating,[35] Haviland was a board member of the International Board on Books for Young People, member and chair of its Hans Christian Andersen Award jury, and a member of the Section of Children's Librarians of the International Federation of Library Associations and Institutions. At home she worked as a member of the ALA International Relations Committee, edited *Children's Books of International Interest* (1972), and frequently consulted her friend James Fraser, an international children's book figure, who, in 1973, established *Phaedrus: A Newsletter of Children's Literature Research*, which later became *An International Journal of Children's Literature Research*, at the time the leading such periodical in the world.

In 1972, which had been designated UNESCO's International Book Year, Haviland organized *The Wide World of Children's Books: An Exhibition for International Book Year*. The exhibition featured eighty books from thirty-eight countries in their original languages, which Haviland selected from "the Library's rapidly growing collection of foreign children's books from its worldwide acquisition program"[36] (in which she was the moving force). She also produced a handsome, annotated exhibition catalog. Japan was represented by six books, all originally published in that country: Momoko Ishii's *Ariko no otsukai* (Ariko on an Errand, 1968); Miyoko Matsutani's *Yamanba no nishiki* (The Cloth of the Mountain Witch, 1969); Chiyoko Nakatani's *Mori no matsuri* (Festival of the Woods, 1971); Nankichi Niimi's *Gongitsune* (A Fox Named Gon, 1969); Yūzō Ōtsuka's *Suho no shiroi uma* (Suho and the White Horse, 1968); and Shigeo Watanabe's *Teramachi sanchōme juichibanchi* (A Family on Teramachi Street, 1969).

Of all of Haviland's publications, and perhaps of all her efforts to promote children's books, her most modest publication, at least in appearance, had the greatest impact. Soon after her arrival at the Library of Congress, Haviland began compiling *Children's Books*,[37] an annual, annotated list of the best children's books of the year. It became a Library of Congress perennial best-seller and was popular with parents, teachers, librarians, and school children all over the country.

Trying to define the characteristics of a fine children's book, Haviland wrote:

> I am searching for books that make a difference. This means that I welcome a book that is not just one more book, like many other books; this is the critic in me admiring originality and vitality of content and treatment. I want a book with freshness and integrity that while it entertains does something for the young reader.
>
> What do I mean—does something?
>
> I mean a book conceived with imagination which, through skilful storytelling or creative use of facts, stirs the child in some way. I mean a book that excites and satisfies curiosity, leads to a new interest, perhaps moves the child to new compassion, and leaves him convinced that he must read more. (He may become one of the 5% of adults who are known to read for enjoyment.)[38]

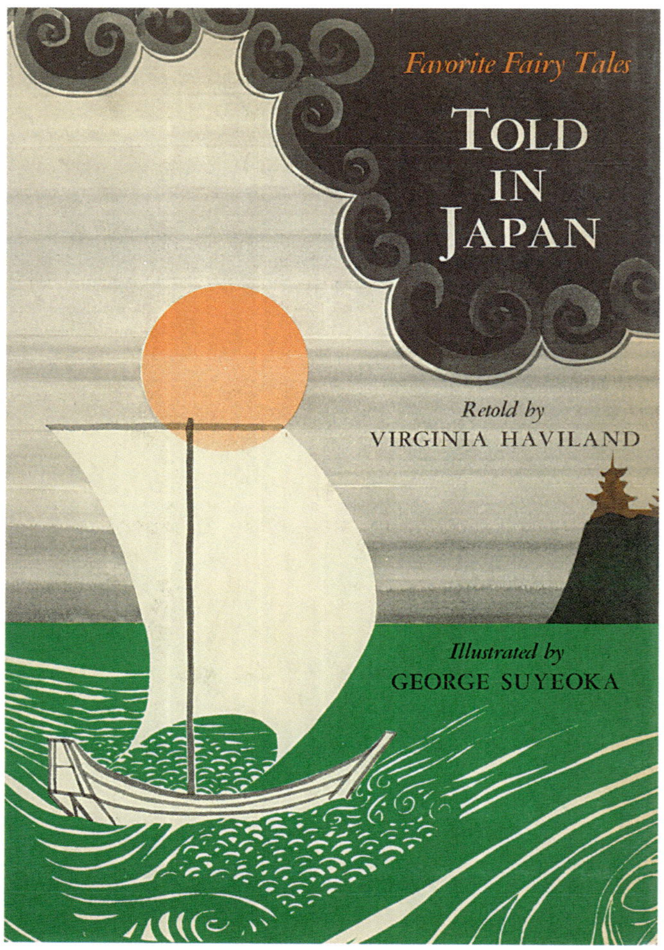

FIGURE A.7
Favorite Fairy Tales Told in Japan, retold by Virginia Haviland; illustrated by George Suyeoka. Boston: Little, Brown, 1967.

In 1980, Haviland published *The Best of Children's Books 1964–1978,* a compilation of the most noteworthy titles that were still in print. As she pointed out in her introduction, *The Best of Children's Books* showed the great increase of beginning-to-read books and nonfiction books that were designed for increasingly lower reading levels and that reflected contemporary American society ever more realistically.

The Best of Children's Books was divided into ten categories, including "Picture and Picture-Story Books," "History, People, and Places," and "Nature and Science." Reflecting the civil rights movement, the "Biography" section listed books about such influential figures as Malcolm X, Paul Robeson, Sojourner Truth, and Langston Hughes. There were titles about growing up in Nazi Germany and in Siberia; as a Hispanic, a Native American, a Puerto Rican, an Eskimo, or a Yahi Indian. Although there was no book about growing up Asian or as a Japanese American, Japan was represented by a number of titles, including Taro Yashima's *Seashore Story* (1967), Yoshiko Uchida's *Sumi's Prize* (1964), *The Wave* (1964) retold by Margaret Hodges, Haviland's own *Favorite Fairy Tales Told in Japan* (1967, fig. A.7), and *The Funny Little Woman* (1972) retold by Arlene Mosel. The poetry section included *Cricket Songs* (1964), a collection of haiku, translated by the poet Harry Behn, and *The Prancing Pony: Nursery Rhymes from Japan* (1968, fig. A.8), which had appeared on earlier lists. The list also included historical novels about Japan, including *The Sign of the Chrysanthemum* (1973); *The Master Puppeteer* (1976), a mystery set in the world of Japan's unique art of Bunraku that

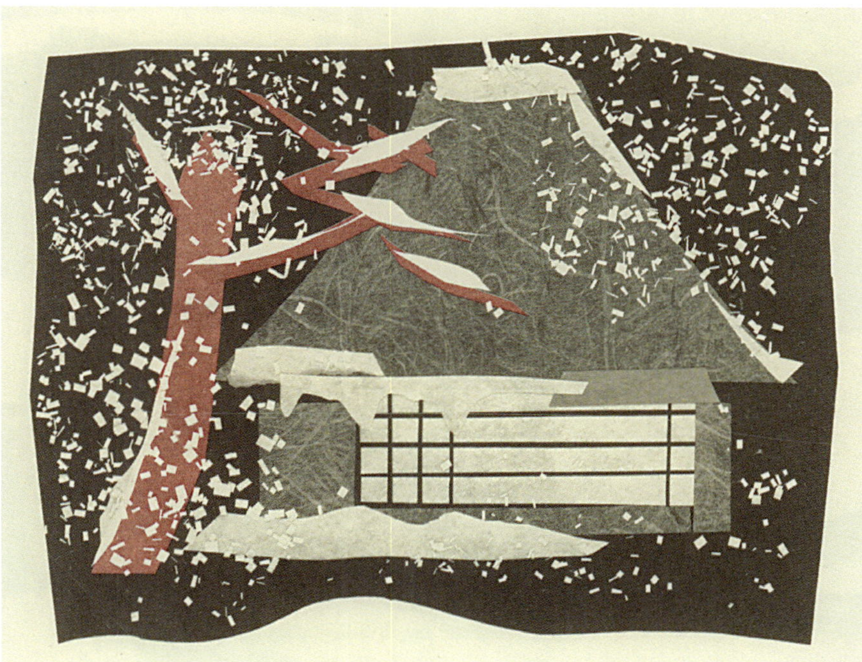

FIGURE A.8
The Prancing Pony: Nursery Rhymes from Japan, adapted by Charlotte B. DeForest, illustrated by Keiko Hida. New York: Walker/Weatherhill, 1967, page 26.

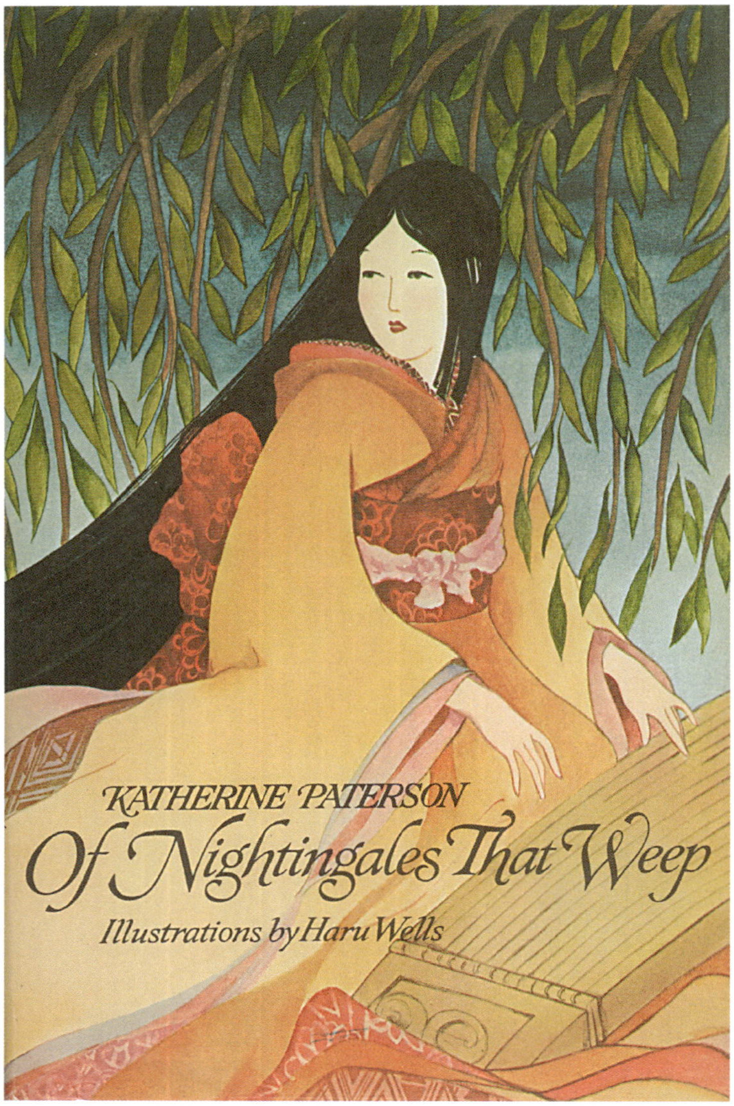

FIGURE A.9
Of Nightingales That Weep, by Katherine Paterson, illustrations by Haru Wells. New York: Crowell, 1974.

won the U.S. National Book Award for children's literature;[39] and *Of Nightingales That Weep* (1974, fig. A.9), a "dramatic story, rich in emotion and in historical detail" of twelfth-century court life.[40] All three of those titles were written with eloquence and feeling by Katherine Paterson, one of Haviland's many children's book friends, who had lived in Japan as a teacher and missionary and was on her way to becoming one of the world's most celebrated and beloved writers for young people.

At the end of the 1970s, which also marked the end of Haviland's career, the children's library and children's book worlds were changing.

The era of generous federal funding for libraries had ceased and library services to children had matured. So had children's book publishing. An era seemed to have come to an end.

* * *

On June 13, 1983, I succeeded Virginia Haviland as chief of the Children's Literature Center in the Library of Congress. Later that month, while attending my first ALA conference in my new position, I decided to introduce myself to one of the great children's book women who, among many other accomplishments, had played a major role in the creation of the center. Still formidable, Frances Clarke Sayers received me graciously in her fine house in Ojai, California. Standing by her grand piano, she said "Let me look you over." Which she did. Then, with a glass of champagne in her hand she declared: "Daahling, you will do just fine."

Meeting Sayers was among my reasons for beginning my series of children's book programs with a symposium the following year, reminiscing about and honoring all those who had been at the creative center of the remarkable growth of library services for children and the publishing of children's books throughout the twentieth century.[41] I invited the movers and shakers of America's children's book and library worlds to a festive day at the Library of Congress on November 15, 1984.[42]

Looking back at the gathering of the distinguished guests who came from as far away as England and Mexico, the celebration seemed a fitting salute to the commitment, the idealism, and the achievements of America's children's book and library community.

ACKNOWLEDGMENTS

It is with deep affection and gratitude that I dedicate this book to Hidekazu Sato, my dear friend who generously and over many years helped me experience and understand the art and culture and history of old Japan.[1] His thoughtful "tutorials" ranged from a soulful performance of Bunraku in Osaka; indigo dyers' and pottery workshops in Mashiko; the home of Chikuzan, the late shamisen player, in Aomori; the eleventh station of the Tōkaidō in the mountains of Hakone, and a magnificent samurai mansion in Shimabara.

To the end of my days will I remember our *shinkansen* excursions—enjoying our discussions about children's books and eating *eki-ben* along the way while observing bamboo forests, rice fields, and the old farmer's *minka,* so appealing to my Western eyes. Highlights of our many trips included the enactment of *yabusame,* the colorful horseback archery performed at the Tokugawa Ieyasu memorial site among Nikko's majestic cryptomeria trees or the exotic *kunchi* festival in Nagasaki, featuring floats shaped like riverboats on wheels, and the Chinese dragon dance featuring a giant, glistening dragon right out of a picture book. Thank you to Kimiko Abe, friend and fine interpreter who accompanied us on all our travels.

The seeds for this book were planted during the symposium, "Window on Japan: Japanese Children's Books and Television Today," held at the Library of Congress in 1987. I appreciate those who supported that program, among them Dr. Daniel J. Boorstin, Librarian of Congress, and his wife Ruth; children's book collector, philanthropist, and my friend and benefactor, Lloyd E. Cotsen, and his wife Margit; Setsutaro Kobayashi (Fuji Xerox); and Dr. J. Thomas Rimer, then chief of the Library of Congress's Asian Division. Years later, Dr. Rimer vetted the manuscript and wrote the elegant introduction to this book. Thank you also to Betsy Beinecke Shirley, long-time friend and supporter of the Children's Literature Center who, behind the scenes, as she preferred, arranged for my first presentation on the topic of Japan in American children's books.[2]

My appreciation further goes to the symposium participants who journeyed from Japan to Washington: Tayo Shima, spirited and charming mover and shaker, major contributor to the symposium and owner of Galérie Musée Imaginaire; Kyoko Matsuoka, writer, translator, and director of the Tokyo Children's Library; Akiko Kurita, director, Foreign Rights Centre; and Koichiro Noda.

Mr. Noda, a writer and television producer, moved the group especially when he introduced his "American family," a husband and wife who had come for the day from the Midwest to attend and whom he could finally thank in person for the food packages they had sent to his family after the war.

A special thank you to Mitsumasa Anno, one of Japan's most prominent children's book artists, who was introduced to the symposium audience by his American editor, Ann Beneduce. Mr. Anno's illustrations are featured in the symposium publications *Window on Japan* (1990) and *Japanese Children's Books at the Library of Congress* (1987).[3]

I can never adequately express my appreciation to many others who contributed to this book in all kinds of ways: Stephanie Abramson, Takako Akaboshi, Yoko Aso, James Boatman, Amie Cooper, Margaret Eberbach, Yasuko and Gizan Fuchimoto, Masato Fujimaki, Hisako Hashimoto, Mitsue Hashimura, Adair Heitmann, Haruko Ishikawa, Tomoko Kitagawa, Michiko Matsukata, Tsukiko Nakamura, Toshiko Nakai, Setsuko Ono, Emi Sato, Eijiro and Yoshiko Tanaka, Maniko Ueda, and Kazuto Yamaguchi.

Others who helped me experience Japan were the nō player Yasuyuki Konparu, who allowed me to try on his precious masks in his studio in Tenri; Michiko Matsui and her potter husband, Seizan, who invited me into their fine Japanese house with its kiln and garden and who taught me the art of Japanese flower arranging; Miyuki Kumasaka, who took me to the Katsura Imperial Villa; and Satoshi and Nobuko Kawabata, who hosted unforgettable days of gracious hospitality in Noto including visits to workshops of Noto's famous lacquer artisans.

Thank you also to Andrea Immel (Cotsen Children's Library, Princeton University), Takeshi Matsumoto (Chihiro Art Museum at Azumino and Tokyo), and Yuko Takesako (also of the Chihiro Art Museum) who, time and again, introduced me to the elegance of the arts and crafts of Japan; Yurika and Tadashi Yoshida (Japan Foreign Rights Centre) who took us to lovely out-of-the way places and festivals of old Japan; Tomoko Masaki, a leader of Japan's children's book community whose charming *bunko* children cooked *tako* balls for us; Tomoko Kameda (International Children's Library, National Diet Library of Japan); Hisayo Murakami (Gordon W. Prange Collection, University of Maryland); and Masao Tobari (Director, National Diet Library) and others of his kind staff who extended their gracious hospitality.

On many occasions, my friend Michiyo Fujita answered my questions and translated and interpreted numerous texts for me. Misako Ito, a dear friend, made many far-reaching introductions. Takako Yano, owner of the *Namban Bunkakan* in Osaka, opened her exquisite museum to me.

Among the memorable interviews that I was kindly granted were those with Kazue Mizumura's friends, Tsukiko Nakamura, Masako Matsuno, and Ruth Ueymura; Taro Yashima's daughter, Momo Yashima Brannen; and Charles E. Tuttle's wife, Reiko Shiba.

A special thank you to you, Michiko Sama, beloved Empress of Japan, for your warm friendship for all these many years and for granting me exquisite glimpses of your world.

My gratitude further goes to the elegant Ann Beneduce, icon of American children's book publishing. It was she who saw a book in my pile of notes and who became my first editor. Our years of working together will always belong to the fondest memories of this journey.

Thank you to Dr. Martin Collcutt for vetting the first and final drafts of the manuscript for historical accuracy.

Thank you to Becky Clark, director of the Library of Congress Publishing Office, who decided to take on this long book journey after reading just a few chapters of the manuscript. Thank you also to her superb editors Hannah Freece, Aimee Hess, and Margaret E. Wagner, and to Zachary Klitzman, editorial assistant.

I want to thank Mark Dimunation, chief of the Library's Rare Book and Special Collections Division, for his support. Thank you also to Domenico Sergi, who supervised the scanning of the many illustrations performed at the Library's Digital Imaging Center, and his colleagues, Jade Curtis and Ronnie Hawkins.

Thank you to the staff of Rutgers University Press, including Micah Kleit and Elisabeth Maselli, and to Fernanda Perrone at Rutgers Special Collections and University Archives. Thanks also to Marianna Vertullo, Integrated Books International, and Lisa Tremaine, who created the fine design for this book.

To those whose names I might have inadvertently left out, I apologize.

Finally, I would like to thank my husband, who accompanied me on this long and joyful journey.

Sybille A. Jagusch

NOTES

NOTE TO THE READER

1. In addition to the vast, comprehensive Library of Congress children's book collection—the nation's collection, really—I had access to the Library's unparalleled research collection. Examples include the diaries of the young William Speiden, excerpted in the text, and Clara Whitney, both held by the Manuscript Division; the geographical puzzle held by the Geography and Map Division; the Japanese scroll held by the Asian Division; cover images of *St. Nicholas* magazine, held by the Prints and Photograph Division; and crepe paper books in the Rare Book and Special Collections Division.

PROLOGUE

1. Johann Amos Comenius, *Orbis sensualium pictus.* Facsimile edition of the third London edition, 1672 (Sydney: Sydney University Press, 1967), 6–7.
2. Ibid., 187.
3. Madeleine Morton, preface, in Nicolas Lenglet du Fresnoy (1674–1755), *The Geography for Children, or A Short and Easy Method of Teaching or Learning Geography* (New York: Johnson Reprint Corporation, 1969), vii–ix.
4. Lenglet du Fresnoy, *The Geography for Children*, 1–3.
5. Ibid., 112.
6. Johann Bernhard Basedow (1724–1790), *Elementarwerk.* Herausgegeben von Theodor Fritsch (Hildesheim: Georg Olms Verlag, 1972), 147, 191.
7. There had been earlier booksellers who produced attractive books for children, including Thomas Boreman, publisher of the illustrated *Gigantick Histories*, a handsome, ten-volume miniature set bound, like many of Newbery's books, in decorative Dutch floral paper.
8. Charles Welsh, *A Bookseller of the Last Century: Being Some Account of the Life of John Newbery, and of the Books He Published, with a Notice of the Later Newberys* (Clifton, NJ: A. M. Kelley, 1972), vii.
9. *Geography Made Familiar and Easy to Young Gentlemen and Ladies* (London: printed for J. Newbery, 1748), 222–223.
10. *Atlas Minimus, or A New Set of Pocket Maps of the Several Empires, Kingdoms, and States of the Known World, with Historical Extracts Relative to Each Drawn and Engrav'd by J. Gibson* (London: J. Newbery, 1758), unpaginated.
11. *The Traveller, or An Entertaining Journey round the Habitable Globe: Being a Novel and Easy Method of Studying Geography. Illustrated with Forty-Two Plates, Consisting of Views of the Principal Capital Cities of the World, and the Costumes of its Various Inhabitants* (London: Printed for J. Harris, 1820), v–vi.
12. Ibid., 24, 87–88, 99, 103.
13. Ibid., 150.
14. Ibid., 147.
15. Jehoshaphat Aspin, *Cosmorama; A View of the Costumes and Peculiarities of All Nations* (London: J. Harris, 1827), 227–231. Aspin was known for his English edition of Abbé Gaultier's *A Complete Course of Geography, by Means of Instructive Games* (1795).
16. The series included *Scenes in Europe* (1818), *Scenes in Africa* (1820), *Scenes in America* (1821), and *Scenes in England* (1822).
17. Isaac Taylor (1759–1829), *Scenes in Asia: For the Amusement and Instruction of Little Tarry-at-Home Travellers* (London: Printed for Harris and Son, 1819), 2, 12, 15, 60, 66.
18. Ibid., 29–30.
19. Ibid., 31–32.
20. *The World in Miniature, or Panorama of the Costumes, Manners & Customs of all Nations* (London: Printed by T. Richardson, for John Bysh, 1825), 57–59.
21. Mary Anne Venning, *A Geographical Present: Being Descriptions of the Principal Countries of the World. With Representations of the Various Inhabitants in their Respective Costumes* (London: Printed for Darton, Harvey, and Darton, 1818), 83–84. Little is known of Mary Ann Venning's life.
22. Timon Screech, *Secret Memoirs of the Shoguns: Isaac Titsingh and Japan, 1779–1822* (London: Routledge, 2006), 70.
23. J. R. Abbey, *Travel in Aquatint and Lithography* (London: Privately printed at the Curwen Press, 1956), I:19.
24. Frederic Shoberl (1775–1853), *The World in Miniature: Japan* (London: R. Ackerman, 1823), v–vi.
25. Ibid., 17–19.
26. Ibid., 196–198.
27. *Das Nationen-Bilderbuch für die wissbegierige Jugend mit 23 gemalten Kupfern* (Reutlingen: Verlag von Fleischhauer & Spohn, 1835), 17–18. Text here translated by Sybille A. Jagusch.
28. For example, Isaiah Thomas, the noted printer who acquired John Newbery's children's books, adapted them for the American market (substituting Worcester for London, etc.), had new cuts made, printed them, and sold them to great success.
29. John A. Nietz, *Old Textbooks: Spelling, Grammar, Reading, Arithmetic, Geography, American History, Civil Government, Physiology, Penmanship, Art, Music, as Taught in the Common Schools from Colonial Days to 1900* (Pittsburgh: University of Pittsburgh Press, 1961), 200, 208.
30. Ruth S. Freeman, *Yesterday's School Books* (Watkins Glen, NY: Century House, 1960), 89.

31. Clifton Johnson, *Old-Time Schools and School-Books* (New York: Macmillan, 1917), 320.
32. Jedidiah Morse, *Geography Made Easy: Being an Abridgement of the American Universal Geography.* 10th ed. (Boston: J. T. Buckingham for Thomas & Andrews, 1806), 392.
33. Nathaniel Dwight (1770–1831), *A Short but Comprehensive System of the Geography of the World: By Way of Question and Answer, Principally Designed for Children and Common Schools* (Boston: Printed by Manning & Loring, for West & Greenleaf, 1801).
34. Ibid., 10.
35. Ibid., 110–111.
36. Elijah Parish, *A New System of Modern Geography, or A General Description of all the Considerable Countries in the World: Compiled from the Latest European and American Geographies, Voyages and Travels.* 2nd ed. (Newburyport, MA: E. Little, 1812), 302.
37. Ibid., 303–305.
38. Jesse Olney, *A Practical System of Modern Geography, or A View of the Present State of the World.* 4th ed. (Hartford: D. F. Robinson, 1830), 191.
39. Many of Goodrich's small and handsomely illustrated books were introduced by Peter Parley, a kindly, fatherly narrator who was shown in the frontispieces, surrounded by attentive children.
40. Helen S. Canfield, "Peter Parley," *Horn Book Magazine,* April 1970, 135.
41. In her memoir, *Daughter of the Samurai* (Doubleday, Doran, 1934), 127–129, Etsu Inagaki Sugimoto wrote about the happy "memory stones" of her childhood, which included her father's children's book gifts, with Peter Parley stories among them.
42. "Peter Parley's Universal History, on the Basis of Geography," *The Family Magazine, or Monthly Abstract of General Knowledge* 5 (May 1, 1838): 392.
43. Goodrich's books of geography and travel include *The Tales of Peter Parley about America* (1827), *The Tales of Peter Parley about Europe* (1828), *Peter Parley's Tales about the World* (1831), *The Child's Own Book of Geography* (1834), and *Peter Parley's Universal History on the Basis of Geography* (1837).
44. Samuel G. Goodrich, *The Tales of Peter Parley about Asia* (Philadelphia: Desilver, Thomas, 1836), 19–24.
45. Ibid., 73–78.
46. Samuel Griswold Goodrich, *Manners and Customs of the Principal Nations of the Globe* (Boston: Bradbury, Soden, 1845), 347–348.
47. Alice Hawthorne, *Stories of Asia* (Philadelphia: Charles H. Davis, 1855), 21.
48. Ibid., 62.
49. Ibid., 78.
50. Ibid., 113.
51. Ibid., 127–128.
52. "Japan," *Merry's Museum and Parley's Magazine,* January 1860, 11.

CHAPTER 1

1. Matthew Calbraith Perry, *Narrative of the Expedition of an American Squadron to the China Seas and Japan, Performed in the Years 1852, 1853, and 1854, under the Command of Commodore M.C. Perry, United States Navy, by Order of the Government of the United States.* (New York: Appleton, 1856); Douglas Moore Kenrick, *A Century of Western Studies of Japan; The First Hundred Years of the Asiatic Society of Japan 1872–1972* (Tokyo: The Asiatic Society of Japan, 1978), 13.
2. Excerpts from William Speiden, Jr., Manuscript Journal [March 9, 1852 to February 16, 1855]. William Speiden (1835–1920) Papers, Manuscript Division, Library of Congress.
3. Ruth Gaines (1877–1952), *Treasure Flower: A Child of Japan* (New York: E. P. Dutton, 1916), xvii–xviii.
4. Ibid., xi–xix.
5. Arthur May Knapp, *Feudal and Modern Japan* (Boston: Joseph Knight, 1897), I: 1.
6. Yuzo Ota, *Basil Hall Chamberlain: Portrait of a Japanologist* (Richmond, UK: Japan Library, 1998), 39.
7. A friend of Algernon Mitford, the scholar Ernest Satow, then the Legation's Secretary, wrote, "Those years from 1862 to 1869 were the most interesting portion of my life; then I lived, now I seem to vegetate." Bernard M. Allen. *The Rt. Hon. Sir Ernest Satow, G.C.M.G.: A Memoir* (London: Kegan, Paul, Trench, Trubner, 1933), 78.
8. Algernon Bertram Freeman Mitford, Lord Redesdale (1837–1916), *Memories.* (London: Hutchinson, 1915), I: Preface (unpaginated).
9. Like many of his contemporary Japan travelers, Mitford wrote heartily about the highlights of his career. His two-volume *Memories* (1915) went on for 800 pages and was followed by *Further Memories* (1917).
10. Algernon Bertram Freeman Mitford, Lord Redesdale, *Mitford's Japan: The Memoirs and Recollections, 1866–1906, of Algernon Bertram Mitford, the First Lord Redesdale,* ed. Hugh Cortazzi (London: Athlone Press, 1985), xviii.
11. Algernon Bertrand Freeman Mitford, *Tales of Old Japan* (London: Macmillan, 1871), 34.
12. Ibid., 248.
13. Ann King Herring, "Early Translations of Japanese Fairy-Tales and Children's Literature," *Phaedrus: An International Annual* (1988): 98.
14. Gardner Teall, "A Short List of Books on Things Japanese," *The Independent,* January 20, 1923, 66.
15. Marquise de Fontenoy, "A Peer who saw Hara-Kiri done," *Washington Post,* November 21, 1905, 6.
16. William Dinwiddie, "Miss Helen Hyde of Japan," *Harper's Bazaar,* January 1906, 13.
17. Ibid.
18. "Miss Helen Hyde shows Japanese Woodcut Prints," *Christian Science Monitor,* December 31, 1914, 4.
19. "A Painter of the Japanese," *New York Times,* April 15, 1906, 9.
20. "A Medley of Songs and Jingles," *The Dial* 31, no. 371 (December 1, 1901): 454.
21. Hyde's *Moon Babies,* a book about Chinese children with verses by G. Orr Clark, was published in 1900.
22. Dinwiddie, "Miss Helen Hyde of Japan," 13.
23. Hyde (1868–1919) left behind a 1901 watercolor dummy for *Songs of the Japanese Children.* The book dummy is held by the Jane Voorhees Zimmerli Art Museum, Rutgers, The State University of New Jersey, Ralph and Barbara Voorhees American Art Fund.
24. Mabel Hyde, *Jingles from Japan as Set Forth by the Ghinks* (San Francisco: A. M. Robertson, 1901), 10–41. Apparently, all remaining copies of the book were destroyed in the 1906 San Francisco earthquake. The book was published in a smaller format in 1907 by the Methodist Publishing House in Tokyo.
25. "San Francisco Girl Attains Eminence with Pictures of Japanese Life," *San Francisco Examiner,* August 24, 1910, 7.

26. Kiyoshi K. Kawakami, "Japanese Fairy-Tales," *New York Times,* January 14, 1911, BR 24.
27. Herring, "Early Translations of Japanese Fairy-Tales and Children's Literature," 98.
28. Lafcadio Hearn (1850–1904), "A Living God," *Gleanings in Buddha-Fields: Studies of Hand and Soul in the Far East* (New York: Benjamin Blom, 1971), 16–25. First published in Boston, 1897.
29. Ota, *Basil Hall Chamberlain,* 42.
30. Ibid., 45.
31. Ibid., 1.
32. Matilda Chaplin Ayrton (1846–1883), *Child-Life in Japan and Japanese Child Stories* (London: Griffith and Farrar, 1879), xiii–xiv.
33. Ibid., 4.
34. Belle M. Brain (1859–1933), *All about Japan: Stories of Sunrise Land Told for Little Folks* (New York: Young People's Missionary Movement, 1905), 151.
35. Ibid., 155.
36. Ibid., 156.
37. Ibid., 157.
38. Julia Carrothers (1845–1914), *The Sunrise Kingdom, or Life and Scenes in Japan and Woman's Work for Woman There* (Philadelphia: Presbyterian Board of Publication, 1879), 117–118.
39. Julia Carrothers, *Kesa and Saijiro, or Lights and Shades of Life in Japan* (New York: American Tract Society, 1879), 35–36.
40. Ibid., 240
41. Ibid., 293–295.
42. Ibid., 436.
43. Edward R. Beauchamp, *An American Teacher in Early Meiji Japan* (Honolulu: University Press of Hawaii, 1976), 7. In 1860, Griffis had watched the kimono-clad delegates of the first Japanese mission to America during their visit to his native Philadelphia.
44. Ibid., 22.
45. William Elliott Griffis (1843–1928), *Japan in History, Folk Lore and Art* (Boston: Houghton, Mifflin, 1892), 222.
46. Ibid.
47. Beauchamp, *An American Teacher in Early Meiji Japan,* 35.
48. Ibid., 38.
49. Ibid.
50. Ibid., 39–40.
51. Ibid., 4.
52. Ibid., 137. During the first year after his return to the United States in 1874, Griffis gave eighty-nine lectures.
53. Robert S. Schwantes, *Japanese and Americans: A Century of Cultural Relations* (New York: Harper & Brothers, 1955), 14.
54. D. E. Perushek, ed., *The Griffis Collection of Japanese Books: An Annotated Bibliography* (Ithaca, NY: China-Japan Program, Cornell University, 1982), 62.
55. Beauchamp, *An American Teacher in Early Meiji Japan,* 85.
56. William Elliott Griffis, *Honda the Samurai, A Story of Modern Japan* (Boston: Congregational Sunday-School and Publishing Society, 1890), 311.
57. Ibid., 358.
58. Ibid., 386.
59. Griffis, *Japan in History, Folk Lore and Art,* 224–227.
60. Herring, "Early Translations of Japanese Fairy-Tales and Children's Literature," 99.
61. William Elliot Griffis, *Japanese Fairy World: Stories from the Wonder-lore of Japan* (Schenectady, NY: James H. Barhyte, 1880), iii–iv.
62. Alexander Young, "Boston Letter," *The Critic* 14, no. 365 (December 27, 1890): 340.
63. Beauchamp, *An American Teacher in Early Meiji Japan,* 112.
64. Ibid., 140.
65. Ibid., 142.
66. Ibid., 58.
67. E. Warren Clark (1849–1907), *Katz Awa: "The Bismarck of Japan," or The Story of a Noble Life* (New York: B. F. Buck, 1904), 19.
68. E. Warren Clark, *Life and Adventure in Japan* (New York: American Tract Society, 1878), 41–42.
69. Ibid., 92.
70. Ibid., 94.
71. Ibid., 170–180.
72. Ibid., 246–247.

CHAPTER 2

1. "Illustrated Juveniles," *The Dial* 2, no. 20 (December 1881): 182.
2. There were as yet no separate children's book catalogs.
3. "Children's Books," *American Literary Gazette and Publishers' Circular* 3, no. 5 (July 1, 1864): 140.
4. E. A. O., "Boys and Girls," *Los Angeles Times,* November 20, 1892, 12.
5. Mary Mapes Dodge, *Hans Brinker, or The Silver Skates* (New York: Grosset & Dunlap, 1963), preface (unpaginated).
6. Virginia Haviland, *The Travelogue Storybook of the Nineteenth Century* (Boston: Horn Book, 1950), 19.
7. Hezekiah Butterworth (1839–1905), *Zigzag Journeys in Europe; Vacation Rambles in Historic Lands* (Boston: Estes and Lauriat, 1880), iv. The idea was based on *Voyages en Zigzag*—published in French by Henry Holt in 1901—by the Swiss artist and writer Rodolphe Töpffer (1799–1846).
8. Estes and Lauriat, publishers of the *Zigzag* books, also published the travelogues *The Knockabout Club* and *The Vassar Girls* (neither of which includes Japan), and the French travelogue, *Schoolboy Days in Japan* by André Laurie (1895).
9. Hezekiah Butterworth, *Zigzag Journeys around the World* (Boston: Estes and Lauriat, 1895), 109.
10. Ibid., 110.
11. Ibid.
12. B. B. Vallentine, "The Author of 'The Boy Travellers,'" *Harper's Young People* 12, no. 624 (October 13, 1891): 817.
13. Biographical information gleaned from Vallentine, "The Author of the Boy Travellers." It is interesting to note that, for his book *Adventures of Two Youths in a Journey to Siam and Java* (1881), Knox received the Order of the White Elephant from the King of Siam, who declared it the best book ever written about his country.
14. Thomas W. Knox (1835–1896), *Adventures of Two Youths in a Journey to Japan and China* (New York: Harper & Brothers, 1879), 9.
15. Ibid., 265.
16. Ibid., 160, 162.
17. Greey's antique shop at 20 East Seventeenth Street in New York was filled with his "Ancient and Modern Oriental Porcelain, Japanese Lacquers, Bronzes, Ivory Carvings, Kakemono, Screens, Curios, and Decorative Fabrics," part of which he had purchased from Captain Frank Brinkley, known for his multivolume work on Japan and China. See F[rank] Brinkley, *Description of "the Brinkley Collection" of Antique Japanese, Chinese and Korean Porcelain, Pottery and Faience* (New York: E. Greey, 1885). See also Edward Greey, *The Golden Lotus and Other Legends of Japan* (Boston: Lee and Shepard, 1883), endpages (unpaginated).
18. "A Fine Art Collection for Sale," *New York Times,* December 14, 1888, 8.

19. Edward Greey (1835–1888), "How the Japanese Amuse Themselves," *Frank Leslie's Popular Monthly* 9 (April 1880): 496.
20. Ibid., 33.
21. Edward Greey, "What the Japanese Eat," *Frank Leslie's Popular Monthly* 10, no. 2 (August 1880): 166.
22. Greey. *The Golden Lotus*, 89–93.
23. "Japanese Legends," *New York Times*, December 23, 1882, 7.
24. Edward Greey, *Young Americans in Japan; or, The Adventures of the Jewett Family and Their Friend Oto Nambo* (Boston: Lee & Shepard, 1882); Edward Greey, *The Wonderful City of Tokio; or, Further Adventures of the Jewett Family and Their Friend Oto Nambo* (Boston: Lee & Shepard, 1883); Edward Greey, *The Bear-Worshippers of Yezo and the Island of Karafuto (Saghalin)* (Boston: Lee & Shepard, 1884).
25. Greey, *Young Americans in Japan*, [vii].
26. Ibid., [viii].
27. Ibid., 1.
28. Ibid., 3–4.
29. Ibid., 5.
30. Ibid., 12.
31. Ibid., 5.
32. Ibid., 14.
33. "A Book about Japan," *New York Times*, November 7, 1883, 3.
34. Greey, *Young Americans in Japan*, 47.
35. Ibid., 80.
36. Ibid., 196.
37. Greey, *The Wonderful City of Tokio*, 41.
38. Saghalin (i.e., Sakhalin) was later exchanged with Russia for the Kurile Islands.
39. Greey, *Young Americans in Japan*, 151.
40. Greey, *The Bear-Worshippers*, vi.
41. Ibid., 244.
42. Ibid., 56.
43. Ibid., 252–253.
44. "The Bear Worshippers," *The Critic*, issue 92 (November 24, 1883): 473.
45. Shiukichi Shigemi, *A Japanese Boy, By Himself* (New Haven, CT: E. B. Sheldon, 1889), 128.
46. Ibid., 45.
47. Deidre Johnson, *Stratemeyer Pseudonyms and Series Books: An Annotated Checklist of Stratemeyer and Stratemeyer Syndicate Publications* (Westport, CT: Greenwood Press, 1982), xiii.
48. Mary-Agnes Taylor, "Edward Stratemeyer," in Glenn E. Estes, ed., *American Writers for Children before 1900* (Detroit: Gale Research Company, 1985), 356.
49. "Stories," *Congregationalist* 83, no. 39 (September 29, 1898): 419.
50. "Books for Young People," *Outlook* 60, no. 6 (October 8, 1898): 398.
51. Edward Stratemeyer (1862–1930), *Under Togo for Japan; or, Three Young Americans on Land and Sea* (Boston: Lothrop, Lee & Shepard, 1906), v.
52. Taylor, "Edward Stratemeyer," 359. Taylor also notes that a 1926 survey found that 98 percent of the audience listed a Stratemeyer title among their favorite books, 355.
53. Edward Stratemeyer, *On to Peking, or Old Glory in China* (Boston: Lee and Shephard, 1905), 5.
54. Edward Stratemeyer, *Under the Mikado's Flag; or; Young Soldiers of Fortune* (Boston: Lee and Shephard), vi.
55. Edward Stratemeyer, *At the Fall of Port Arthur; or, A Young American in the Japanese Navy* (Boston: Lee and Shephard, 1905), 89.
56. Ibid., 144.
57. "Other Recent Publications," *The Watchman* 88, no. 16 (April 19, 1906): 19.
58. "Comment on Current Books," *Outlook* (March 31, 1906): 764.
59. "For Young Folks," *Congregationalist and Christian World* 91, no. 20 (May 19, 1906): 720.
60. Stratemeyer, *Under Togo for Japan*, 8.
61. Ibid., 131.
62. Willis Boyd Allen (1855–1938), *The North Pacific: A Story of the Russo-Japanese War* (New York: Dutton, 1905), 6.
63. Ibid., 77, 254–255.
64. Ibid., 2–3
65. Ibid., 203–204.
66. Ibid., 252–253.
67. A pseudonym derived from the names of the two collaborators, George Herbert Ely and James L'Estrange.
68. "A Russo-Japanese War Story," *New York Times*, April 29, 1905, BR 276.
69. Herbert Strang, *The Story of the Russo-Japanese War* (New York: G.P. Putnam's Sons, 1905), 164.
70. Ibid., viii.
71. Ibid., 37–38.
72. Kirk Munroe appears as one of the twenty most circulated authors of the Muncie (Indiana) Public Library circulation records from November 5, 1891, to December 1, 1902. "What Middletown Read," Center for Middletown Studies, Ball State University Libraries, accessed December 16, 2011, www.bsu.edu/libraries/wmr/.
73. Kirk Munroe (1850–1930), *For the Mikado, or A Japanese Middy in Action* (New York: Harper & Brothers, 1905), 15–16.
74. Kirk Munroe, *A Son of Satsuma, or With Perry in Japan* (New York: Charles Scribner's Sons, 1901), 118.
75. Ibid., 120.
76. Ibid., 226–227.
77. Lucian L. Knight, ed., "In the Literary World," *Atlanta Constitution*, January 19, 1902, A8.
78. "Children's Books," *New York Times*, October 28, 1905, 20.
79. Haskell was also the author of the popular Russian-inspired Katrinka books. One paper was very enthusiastic about another Haskell tale, *Billy's Princess* (1907). See "'Billy's Princess,' a delightful Juvenile Book," *Boston Daily Globe*, November 17, 1907, SM 11.
80. "News of Boston's Book Activities," *New York Times*, May 23, 1908, BR 297.
81. Helen Eggleston Haskell (1871–1963), *O-Heart-San: The Story of a Japanese Girl* (Boston: L.C. Page, 1908), 1–3.
82. Ibid., 64.
83. Ibid., 75.
84. Macaulay's niece, Alice Hegan Rice, author of the best-selling *Mrs. Wiggs of the Cabbage Patch* (1901), edited Macaulay's letters from Japan and suggested the pen name Frances Little to the future writer.
85. Frances Little (1863–1941), *Little Sister Snow* (New York: Century, 1909), 52–55.
86. Ibid., 112–113.
87. Ibid., 118–119.
88. Ruth Gaines (1877–1952), *Treasure Flower: A Child of Japan* (New York: E. P. Dutton, 1916), 31–33.
89. Ibid., 46.
90. Ibid., 51–52.

CHAPTER 3

1. Edward Seidensticker, *Low City, High City: Tokyo from Edo to the Earthquake* (Cambridge, MA: Harvard University Press, 1991), 52–61.
2. Frederic A. Sharf, "Takejiro Hasegawa [1853–1938]: Meiji Japan's Preeminent Publisher of Wood-Block-Illustrated Crepe-Paper Books," *Peabody Essex Museum Collections* (October 1994): 9.
3. Ibid., 8.
4. Ibid., title page.

5. T. Philip Terry, *Terry's Guide to the Japanese Empire* (Boston: Houghton Mifflin, 1928), 124.
6. George Caiger, *Tell Me about Tokyo* (Tokyo: Hokuseido Press, 1939), 65.
7. Paul Waley, *Tokyo: City of Stories* (New York: Weatherhill, 1991), 102–105.
8. T. Philip Terry, *Terry's Guide to the Japanese Empire Including Korea and Formosa* (Boston: Houghton Mifflin, 1930), 232.
9. William E. Griffis, *The Tokio Guide by a Resident* (Yokohama: F. R. Wetmore, 1874), 9.
10. Ibid., 10.
11. Seidensticker, 8.
12. Ibid.
13. Mary Crawford Fraser (1851–1922), *A Diplomat's Wife in Japan: Sketches at the Turn of the Century*, ed. Hugh Cortazzi (New York: Weatherhill, 1983), 48.
14. William Elliot Griffis, *The Mikado's Empire* (New York: Harper & Brothers, 1876), 550.
15. Griffis, *The Tokio Guide by a Resident,* 6.
16. Barbara Rose, *Tsuda Umeko and Women's Education in Japan* (New Haven, CT: Yale University Press, 1992), 61. The schools that had opened included St. Margaret's, the Rikkyo Shigaku (St. Paul's school) and the Tsukiji Kaigan Jogakkō, a girls' school.
17. Gertrude D. LaCroix, *Tokyo Decades: The Story of the Tokyo Union Church from 1872* (Tokyo: Tokyo Union Church, 1962), 10–11.
18. Julia Carrothers, *The Sunrise Kingdom, or Life and Scenes in Japan and Woman's Work for Woman There* (Philadelphia: Presbyterian Board of Publication, 1879), 394.
19. LaCroix, *Tokyo Decades,* 9.
20. *Terry's Guide to the Japanese Empire*, 140.
21. Jun'ichiro Tanizaki, *Childhood Years: A Memoir*, trans. Paul McCarthy (Tokyo: Kodansha International, 1989), 123.
22. Waley, *Tokyo: City of Stories*, 106.
23. George C. Baxley, "The Tokyo Tsukiji Type Foundry," *Baxley Stamps*, accessed November 13, 2009, http://www.baxleystamps.com/litho/tsukiji_type.shtml.
24. Douglas Moore Kenrick, *A Century of Western Studies of Japan* (Tokyo: Asiatic Society of Japan, 1978), 346–347.
25. Otto Schmiedel, *Die Deutschen in Japan* (Leipzig: Verlag von K.F. Koehler, 1920), 185. Chamberlain seems to have been the society's most active member; he was also an honorary member of the society's German counterpart, the Deutsche Gesellschaft für Natur- und Völkerkunde Ostasiens, which celebrated some of its special occasions in Tsukiji.
26. Ibid., 106.
27. Belle M. Brain, *All about Japan: Stories of Sunrise Land Told for Little Folks* (New York: Young People's Missionary Movement, 1905), 186–189.
28. Sakae Shioya (1873–1961), *When I Was a Boy in Japan* (Boston: Lothrop, Lee & Shepard, 1906), 59–61.
29. Mrs. W. H. Smith, *The Children's Japan,* 2nd ed. (Tokyo: Hasegawa, 1895), introduction (unpaginated). Illustrated by Shōsō Mishima (1856–1928).
30. Chiyomaro Aoki, "Chirimen-e to Chirimen-bon," *Hyakumanto*, vol. 35 (Tokyo: Paper Museum, February 1973), 25.
31. Yasuo Kume, *Washi-tasai na yo to bi* (Tokyo: Tamagawa University Press), 63.
32. Ibid., 207.
33. Johann Justus Rein (1835–1918), *Japan nach Reisen und Studien im Auftrage der Königlich Preussischen Regierung*, vol. 2 (Leipzig: Verlag von Wilhelm Engelman, 1886), 486–490. (Rein uses the German term "Putzleder.")
34. Sharf, "Takejiro Hasegawa," 18.
35. Smith, *The Children's Japan*, Introduction (unpaginated). *The Children's Japan* was so popular that Hasegawa issued two editions.
36. Ibid., 1.
37. Ibid., 5.
38. Mary G. Kimura, *A Day with Mitsu* (Tokyo: T. Hasegawa, 1894), 1–4.
39. Mae St. John Bramhall, "Christmas-Day in a Japanese Go-Down," *Godey's Magazine* 131, no. 786 (December 189): 641.
40. Ibid., 641.
41. Ibid., 647.
42. Mae St. John Bramhall, *The Wee Ones of Japan* (New York: Harper & Brothers, 1894), 1–2.
43. Bramhall, "Christmas Day in a Japanese Go-Down," 641.
44. Bramhall, *Wee Ones of Japan*, 137.
45. Ibid., 2–3.
46. Bramhall also published poems in *The Ladies' Home Journal, St. Nicholas*, and other magazines.
47. Mae St. John Bramhall, *Japanese Jingles* (Tokyo: T. Hasegawa, 1891), unpaginated. Illustrated by Kason Suzuki (1860–1912).
48. Carrothers, *The Sunrise Kingdom*, 120.
49. Ibid., 127.
50. Thanks to Dr. Rimer for the additional information about the artists in this paragraph. Eitaku Kobayashi (1843–1890); Kason Suzuki (1860–1912); Yōsai Kikuchi (1781–1878); Shōsō Mishima (1856–1928); Yoshimune Arai (1873–1945); Gyokushō Kawabata (1842–1913).
51. David Thompson (1835–1915), trans., *Momotaro; or, Little Peachling.* 2nd ed. (Tokyo: Kobunsha, ca. 1889), unpaginated.
52. David Thompson, trans., *Nedzumi no yome-iri* [*The Mouse's Wedding*] (Tokyo: Kobunsha, [1885]).
53. F. Hadland Davis, *Myths & Legends of Japan* (London: George G. Harrap, 1912).
54. Sally Fisher, *The Tale of the Shining Princess.* Adapted from a translation by Donald Keene. (New York: The Metropolitan Museum of Art and Viking, 1981).
55. Basil Hall Chamberlain (1850–1935), *The Language, Mythology, and Geographical Nomenclature of Japan Viewed in the Light of Aino Studies* (Tokyo: Imperial University, 1887), 4.
56. Chamberlain preferred the rendering of Ainu—the term the Ainu use to call themselves—as Aino.
57. Basil Hall Chamberlain, *Aino Folk-Tales* (London: Folk-Lore Society, 1888), v–7. The English missionary John Batchelor lived among the Ainu of northern Japan and wrote extensively about their lives and lore.
58. Basil Hall Chamberlain, *The Hunter in Fairy-Land* (Tokyo: Kobunsha and Boston: Ticknor, 1887), unpaginated.
59. Ibid.
60. William W. Fitzhugh and Chisato O. Dubreuil, eds., *Ainu: Spirit of a Northern People* (Washington, DC: Arctic Studies Center, National Museum of Natural History, Smithsonian Institution, in association with the University of Washington Press, 1999), 282.
61. Elizabeth Bisland, ed., *The Japanese Letters of Lafcadio Hearn* (Wilmington, DE: Scholarly Resources, 1973), 277.
62. Kazuo Koizumi, comp., *More Letters from Basil Hall Chamberlain to Lafcadio Hearn and Letters from M. Toyama, Y. Tsubouchi and Others* (Tokyo: Hokuseido Press, 1937), 34. Hearn lived in Matsue from 1890 to 1891. It is located in Chugokū on Honshu, one of Japan's main islands.

63. Sharf, "Takejiro Hasegawa," 45.
64. Koizumi, *More Letters from Basil Hall Chamberlain to Lafcadio Hearn,* 137.
65. Lafcadio Hearn, *The Old Woman Who Lost Her Dumpling* (Tokyo: T. Hasegawa, 1902), 1.
66. Tanio Nakamura, *Sesshu Toyo,* with English text by Elise Grilli (Rutland, VT: Charles E. Tuttle, 1957), unpaginated. In 1431, at the age of eleven, Tōyō—the name Sesshū had at the time—entered the Hōfuku-ji temple and later served at the Sōkoku-ji, a Zen temple in Kyoto, an important artists' center of its day.
67. Lafcadio Hearn, trans., *The Boy Who Drew Cats* (Washington, DC: Library of Congress, 1987), 1–18.

CHAPTER 4

1. Alice M. Jordan, *From Rollo to Tom Sawyer* (Boston: Horn Book, 1948), 131.
2. Other distinguished writers and illustrators whose work appeared in *St. Nicholas* included Frances Hodgson Burnett, L. Frank Baum, Palmer Cox, Charles Lutwidge Dodgson (Lewis Carroll), Rudyard Kipling, Henry Wadsworth Longfellow, Howard Pyle, Robert Louis Stevenson, Arthur Rackham, and Jessie Willcox Smith.
3. Richard L. Darling, "Foreword," *A St. Nicholas Anthology: The Early Years,* ed. Burton C. Frye (New York: Meredith Press, 1969), unpaginated.
4. May Lamberton Becker, "Introduction," *The St. Nicholas Anthology,* ed. Henry Steele Commager (New York: Greenwich House, 1983), xvii.
5. Earnest Elmo Calkins, "When St. Nicholas Was Very Young. Our Very First Reader Tells What He Read and How He Enjoyed It!" *St. Nicholas* 58, no. 8 (June 1931): 566.
6. Frank Luther Mott, "Scribner's Monthly – The Century Magazine," *A History of American Magazines, 1865–1885* (Cambridge, MA: Harvard University Press, 1938), 459–460.
7. Mary Mapes Dodge (1831–1905), "Children's Magazines," *Scribner's Monthly,* July 1873, 352, 354.
8. Title changes: *St. Nicholas: Scribner's Illustrated Magazine for Girls and Boys* (1873–1881); *St. Nicholas: An Illustrated Magazine for Young Folks* (1881–1930); *St. Nicholas For Boys and Girls* (1930–1940; 1943).
9. "Fifty Years of St. Nicholas," *St. Nicholas* 51, no. 1 (November 1923): 16.
10. R. Gordon Kelly, ed., *Children's Periodicals of the United States* (Westport, CT: Greenwood Press, 1984), 378.
11. William Elliot Griffis, "Blossom Boy of Tokio," *St. Nicholas* 6, no. 9 (July 1879): 589.
12. William Elliot Griffis, "The Golden Fish of Owari Castle," *St. Nicholas* 4, no. 5 (March 1877): 324.
13. Eliza Ruhamah Scidmore (1856–1928), *Jinrikisha Days in Japan* (New York: Harper & Brothers, 1891), 1.
14. Mary Fenollosa (1865–1954), *Blossoms from a Japanese Garden: A Book of Child-Verses* (London: William Heinemann, 1913), 45.
15. Mary Fenollosa, "The Fifth of May in Japan," *St. Nicholas* 28, no. 7 (May 1901): 632.
16. Ichy Zo Hattori, "Japanese Games, By a Japanese Boy," *St. Nicholas* 1, no. 3 (January 1874): 167.
17. "The Peach-Boy: A Japanese Story," trans. Isaac Yaunkahama, *St. Nicholas* 1, no. 7 (May 1874): 386–388.
18. M. C. Griffis, "Little Kiné," *St. Nicholas* 12, no. 5 (March 1885): 331.
19. Arthur Shumway, "Seeing the Real Mikado," *St. Nicholas* 16, no. 4 (February 1889): 268.
20. Aldis Dunbar, "O Santa San," *St. Nicholas* 31, no. 3 (January 1904): 216.
21. Ida C. Hodnett, "Great Japan: The Sunrise Kingdom," *St. Nicholas* 16, no. 1 (November 1888): 31.
22. H. Irving Hancock, "Japanese Athletics for American Boys," *St. Nicholas* 31, no. 3 (January 1904): 237.
23. A. N. Benjamin, "Japanese Yoshien," *St. Nicholas* 28, no. 1 (November 1900): 59.
24. Bertha Runkle, "Child Life in China and Japan," *St. Nicholas* 32, no. 3 (January 1905): 229.
25. Theodore Wores, "Glimpses of Child Life in Japan," *St. Nicholas* 28, no. 9 (July 1901): 810.
26. Griffis, "Blossom Boy of Tokio," 596.
27. C. A. W. "Jiro—A Japanese Boy," *St. Nicholas* 9, no. 11 (September 1882): 850.
28. William Elliot Griffis, "The Feast of Dolls," *St. Nicholas* 2, no. 5 (March 1875): 317–318.
29. Anna A. Rogers, "Saigo's Picnic," *St. Nicholas* 26, no. 7 (May 1899): 534.
30. Ibid., 534.
31. Ibid., 534–535.
32. Ibid., 537.
33. Ibid., 537.
34. Ibid., 538.
35. Ibid., 539.
36. Ibid., 541.
37. Jack London (1876–1916), "In Yeddo Bay," *St. Nicholas* 30, no. 4 (February 1903): 293–295.
38. Ibid., 296.
39. Isabel Eccleston MacKay, "The Jingle of the Little Jap," *St. Nicholas* 30, no. 8 (June 1907): 716.
40. Hodnett, "Great Japan: The Sunrise Kingdom," 30.
41. Teiichi Yamagata, "A Japanese 'Middy.' Recollections of Service in the Mikado's Navy," *St. Nicholas* 31, no. 6 (April 1904): 514–517.
42. Examples of articles and illustrations include "Herbert C. Hoover: A Citizen of the World" (May 1917), the poem, "Young Patriots," and the column, "Christmas mail for our soldiers in France" (December 1917). There were photos of "an ocean liner armed to resist enemy submarines" (May 1917), and of a captured submarine on exhibit in Central Park in New York (December 1917). Throughout 1918, cover designs featured patriotic themes. For example, the January cover showed a little girl, accompanied by her dog, holding up her cup adorned with a red cross; the July cover showed a victory garden; and the October cover featured Uncle Sam offering U.S. Liberty Bonds to two youngsters.
43. Charles Edward Morris, "From the Cradle of True Politeness," *St. Nicholas* 45, no. 11 (September 1918): 1030.
44. Ibid., 1031.
45. Ibid.
46. Ibid.
47. "Watch Tower," *St. Nicholas* 42, no. 11 (September 1915): 963–964.
48. Fairmont Snyder, "Little People of Japan," *St. Nicholas* 50, no. 9 (July 1923): 990–991; Edward N. Teall, "The Watch Tower: Crown Prince Hirohito," *St. Nicholas* 49,

no. 2 (December 1921): 200–201; Edward N. Teall, "The Watch Tower: A Little Hero of Japan," *St. Nicholas* 53, no. 1 (November 1925): 98.

49. S. E. Forman, "The Watch Tower: Our Friends the Japanese," *St. Nicholas* 44, no. 11 (September 1917): 1125–1126.
50. Edward N. Teall, "The Watch Tower: Through the Watch Tower Telescope," *St. Nicholas* 51, no. 5 (March 1924): 549.
51. Edward N. Teall, "The Watch Tower: A Test of Friendship," *St. Nicholas* 51, no. 8 (June 1924): 883–884.
52. Edward N. Teall, "The Watch Tower: Our Friendship for Japan," *St. Nicholas* 51, no. 10 (August 1924): 1108.
53. Edward N. Teall, "The Watch Tower: Those 'Yankees of the East,'" *St. Nicholas* 54, no. 4 (February 1927): 316.
54. Kenneth Miller Gould, "The Watch Tower: The Cockpit of Asia," *St. Nicholas* 59, no. 2 (November 1931): 31.
55. Kenneth Miller Gould, "The Watch Tower: War in the Far East," *St. Nicholas* 59, no. 6 (April 1932): 324.
56. Kenneth Miller Gould, "The Watch Tower: League Forces Manchurian Settlement," *St. Nicholas* 59, no. 2 (December 1931): 87.
57. Kenneth Miller Gould, "The Watch Tower: The Manchurian War," *St. Nicholas* 59, no. 3 (January 1932): 150.
58. Phyllis Ayer Sowers, "Suki-san's Guest," *St. Nicholas* 62, no. 6 (April 1935): 53.

CHAPTER 5

1. Hezekiah Butterworth, *Zigzag Journeys around the World* (Boston: Estes and Lauriat, 1895), preface, unpaginated.
2. William Dalton, *The English Boy in Japan; or, The Perils and Adventures of Mark Raffles among Princes, Priests, and People of That Singular Empire* (London: T. Nelson and Sons, 1858), preface, unpaginated [5].
3. Edward Greey, *Young Americans in Japan; or, the Adventures of the Jewett Family and their Friend Oto Nambo* (Boston: Lee and Shepard, 1884), viii.
4. William Elliot Griffis, *Japan in History, Folk Lore and Art*, rev. ed. (Boston: Houghton, Mifflin, 1892), vii–viii.
5. The American Board is most probably the American Board of Commissioners for Foreign Missions, established in 1810.
6. D. C. Angus, *Japan: The Eastern Wonderland* (London: Cassell, Petter, Galpin, ca. 1885), v–vii.
7. Edward Reed (1830–1906), a naval architect and a member of Parliament, used many sources he diligently listed in the preface to his two-volume work, *Japan: Its History, Traditions, and Religions* (London: J. Murray, 1880).
8. Annie R. Butler, *Stories about Japan* (London: Religious Tract Society, 1888), 5–6. The first Japanese translation of *Pilgrim's Progress* was serialized in the magazine *Shichiichi zappo* from April 1876 to August 1877. The translation was published in book form in 1879. This information was kindly provided by the staff of the National Diet Library, Tokyo, August 18, 2017.
9. Thomas W. Knox, *The Travels of Marco Polo for Boys and Girls with Explanatory Notes and Comments* (New York: G.P. Putnam's Sons, 1885), iii–iv.
10. Paul Graf Teleki, *Atlas zur Geschichte der Kartographie der Japanischen Inseln.* Vertrieb der deutschen Ausgabe (Leipzig: Karl W. Hiesemann, 1909), 4.
11. Knox, *Travels of Marco Polo*, 411–412.
12. Ibid., 422–423.
13. Belle M. Brain, *All about Japan: Stories of Sunrise Land Told for Little Folks* (New York: Young People's Missionary Movement, 1905), 88–90.
14. Butler, *Stories about Japan*, 32–34.
15. Brain, *All about Japan*, 123–125.
16. Dalton, *The English Boy in Japan*, preface, unpaginated [5].
17. Ibid., 143.
18. Ibid., 12–15.
19. *Kaempfer's Japan: Tokugawa Culture Observed by Engelbert Kaempfer*, ed. and trans. Beatrice M. Bodart-Bailey (Honolulu: University of Hawaii Press, 1999), 3.
20. Otto Schmiedel, *Die Deutschen in Japan* (Leipzig: Verlag von K.F. Koehler, 1920), 24.
21. *Kaempfer's Japan*, 21.
22. Karl Meier-Lemgo, *Engelbert Kaempfer (1651–1716) erforscht das seltsame Asien* (Hamburg: Cram, De Gruyter, 1960), 13.
23. Meier-Lemgo, *Engelbert Kaempfer*, 13.
24. *Kaempfer's Japan*, 213.
25. Paul Graf Teleki, *Atlas zur Geschichte der Kartographie der Japanischen Inseln* (Tokyo: Yushodo Booksellers Ltd., 1966), 154. Reprint of the 1909 Budapest edition.
26. *Kaempfer's Japan*, 245.
27. Ibid., 356.
28. Ibid., 361–365.
29. Brain, *All about Japan*, 125–126.
30. Fukui Hidetoschi, Miyasaka Masahide, and Tokunaga Hanna, *Siebold's Japan* (Nagasaki: Siebold Memorial Museum, 2001), 30.
31. Robert Van Bergen, *The Story of Japan* (New York: American Book Company, 1897), 114.
32. Ibid., 112–113.
33. Ibid., 110–111.
34. Charles [Carl] Peter Thunberg (1743–1828), *Travels in Japan and Other Countries* (Philadelphia: J. & J. Crukshank, 1801), 55–56.
35. Alice Hawthorne, *Stories of Asia* (Philadelphia: Charles H. Davis. 1855), 127.
36. M. Léon Pagès, *Bibliographie Japonais ou catalogue des ouvrages relatifs au Japon qui ont été publiés depuis le XVe siècle jusqu'a nos jours* (Paris: Benjamin Duprat, Librairie de L'Institut Impérial de France, 1859).
37. Basil Hall Chamberlain, *Things Japanese: Being Notes on Various Subjects Connected with Japan for the Use of Travellers and Others* (London: Kegan Paul, Trench, Trübner, 1890), 47–48.
38. William Elliot Griffis, "How To See Japan without Crossing the Pacific," *Christian Union*, May 14, 1891, 633.
39. Rein was a member of the 1860 Prussian Japan expedition led by Count Fritz zu Eulenburg.
40. Chamberlain, *Things Japanese*, 48.
41. Butler, *Stories about Japan*, 3.
42. Isabella L. Bird (1831–1904), *Unbeaten Tracks in Japan: An Account of Travels on Horseback in the Interior, Including Visits to the Aborigines of Yezo and the Shrines of Nikko and Ise* (New York: G. P. Putnam's Sons, 1880), I: 82.
43. Ibid., I: 83.
44. Ibid., II: 50, 76.
45. Butler, *Stories about Japan*, 61–63.
46. Robert A. Rosenstone, *Mirror in the Shrine: American Encounters with Meiji Japan* (Cambridge, MA: Harvard University Press, 1988), x.
47. William Elliot Griffis, *The Mikado's Empire* (New York: Harper & Brothers, 1876), 7.

48. Edward R. Beauchamp, *An American Teacher in Early Meiji Japan* (Honolulu: University Press of Hawaii, 1976), 50.
49. Griffis, *The Mikado's Empire,* 414.
50. In *Japan: Its History, Traditions, and Religions, With the Narrative of a Visit in 1879* (London: John Murray, 1880), vi, Reed complained that Griffis did not acknowledge his sources.
51. Chamberlain, *Things Japanese,* 49.
52. Griffis, *The Mikado's Empire,* 526.
53. Ibid., 533–535.
54. Ibid., 536.
55. Ibid., 545.
56. Joseph Rogala, comp., *A Collector's Guide to Books on Japan in English* (Richmond, England: Japan Library, 2001), 89.
57. Richard Hildreth (1807–1865), *Japan as It Was and Is* (Boston: Phillips, Sampson, 1855), 389.
58. Ibid., iii.
59. Aimé Humbert (1819–1900), *Japan and the Japanese,* trans. Mrs. Cashel Hoey and ed. H. W. Bates (New York: D. Appleton, 1874), v–vi.
60. Ibid., 26.
61. "The Capital of the Tycoon," *Littell's Living Age* 76, no. 981 (March 21, 1863): 553.
62. Chamberlain, *Things Japanese,* 2.
63. Ibid., 354.
64. Butler, *Stories about Japan,* 49–50.
65. Setsuko Ono, "A Western Image of Japan: What Did the West See through the Eyes of Loti and Hearn?" (Ph.D. diss., Genève: Université de Genève, 1972), 253. The author notes that Loti's *Madame Chrysanthème* was one of the two works that had tempted Hearn to go to Japan.
66. W. L. Schwartz, *The Imaginative Interpretation of the Far East in Modern French Literature, 1800–1925* (Paris: Librairie Ancienne Honoré Champion, 1927), 128; cited in Ono, "A Western Image of Japan," 7.
67. Loti's other books about Japan included *Japoneries d'automne* (1889) and *La troisième jeunesse de Madame Prune* (1905).
68. Leslie Blanch, *Pierre Loti: Travels with the Legendary Romantic* (London: Tauris Parke Paperbacks, 2004), 30.
69. Ibid., 203.
70. "Pierre Loti's New Novel, 'Madame Chrysanthème,'" *The Critic: A Weekly Review of Literature and the Arts,* issue 220 (March 17, 1888): 125.
71. Chamberlain, *Things Japanese,* 52.
72. Pierre Loti, *Madame Chrysanthème,* trans. Laura Ensor (Paris: Edouard Guillaume et Cie, 1889), 7–8.
73. Ibid., 56.
74. Ibid., 241.
75. Ibid., 71–72.
76. Ibid., 82.
77. Ibid., 323.
78. Jennie Correll and her husband, Dr. Irvin H. Correll of the American Methodist Mission, stayed in Nagasaki from 1895 to 1897. Dr. Correll was headmaster of the Chinzei Gakkan school for boys. See Jan van Rij, *Madame Butterfly: Japonisme, Puccini, & the Search for the Real Cho-Cho-San* (Berkeley, CA: Stone Bridge Press, 2001), 58.
79. John Luther Long, "Madame Butterfly," *Madame Butterfly, Purple Eyes, Etc.*, The American Short Story Series, vol. 25 (New York: Garrett Press, 1968), 80–81. Reprinted from the 1898 edition.
80. Long's story and Loti's book (which five years after its original publication was already in its twenty-fifth edition) had wide influence. David Belasco made *Madame Butterfly* into a play, which premiered on March 5, 1900, at the Herald Square Theatre in New York and was an instant success. In 1904, Giacomo Puccini premiered *Madama Butterfly,* which went on to become among the most often performed operas in the United States. "Ten Most Frequently Produced Operas [in North America]," *Notes,* National Opera Teacher and Educator Source, accessed January 29, 2018, https://www.operaamerica.org/Applications/Notes/topTen.aspx.
81. Frances Little, *Little Sister Snow* (New York: Century, 1909), 52.
82. Ibid., 67.
83. Ibid., 71–72.
84. Ibid., 73–74.
85. Ibid., 132–134.
86. Ibid., 141.

CHAPTER 6

1. Annie [*sic*] Carroll Moore (1871–1961), *Roads to Childhood: Views and Reviews of Children's Books* (New York: George H. Doran, 1920), 84–85.
2. Ibid., 53.
3. Etta Blaisdell McDonald (1872–1963) and Julia Dalrymple (1863–1947), *Ume San in Japan* (Boston: Little, Brown, 1909).
4. Amelia Howard Botsford (1856–1933), *Child Life in All Nations; or, The Earlingtons' Trip around the World* (Philadelphia: American Book and Bible House, 1901), 96.
5. Ibid., 88.
6. Ibid., 98.
7. Mary Hazelton Wade (1860–1936), *Our Little Japanese Cousin* (Boston: L. C. Page, 1901), 9–10.
8. Ibid., 63–65.
9. McDonald and Darlrymple, *Ume San in Japan*, preface (unpaginated).
10. Mary Hazelton Wade, *Dolls of Many Lands* (Boston: W. A. Wilde Company, 1913), 12.
11. Lindley Smyth, *True Stories about Children of All Nations* (Philadelphia: World Bible House, 1906), 215–217.
12. Frank G. Carpenter (1855–1924), *Around the World with the Children: An Introduction to Geography* (New York: American Book Company, 1917), 46.
13. Lenore E. Mulets, (1877–1921) [Mary Muller, pseud.], *Little People of Japan: A Story of Japanese Child-Life* (Chicago: A. Flanagan, 1925), 17.
14. Ibid., 81.
15. Lois Hawks Swinehart (1869–1971), *Jane in the Orient* (New York: Fleming H. Revell, 1924), 18.
16. Ibid., 25.
17. Ibid., 20.
18. Bertha Upton (1849–1912), *The Golliwogg's Bicycle Club* (London: Longmans, Green, 1896).
19. "Children's Picture Books," *The Literary World; A Monthly Review of Current Literature* 32, no. 12 (December 1, 1901): 220; Henry Mayer (1868–1954), *The Adventures of a Japanese Doll* (New York: E. P. Dutton, 1901).
20. Grace Bartruse, *The Children in Japan* (London: George G. Harrap, 1911), unpaginated.
21. Ibid.
22. Helen L. Campbell, *Story of Little Metzu: The Japanese Boy* (Philadelphia: David McKay, 1914), 6–49.
23. Gustine G. Weaver (1873–1942), *The House That a Jap Built* (Chicago: Reilly & Britton, 1909), preface (unpaginated).
24. Alice Calhoun Haines (1874–1965), *Little Japs at Home* (New York: Frederick A. Stokes, 1905).
25. Helen Marion Burnside (1841–1923), *Only a Jap Dollee* (London: Tuck & Sons, 1900).

26. G. E. Farrow (1862–1919), *Ten Little Jappy Chaps* (Chicago: M. A. Donohue, n.d.), 1–3, 34–36. The *Stump Books* were also unique because of their unusual trim size: two inches high and six inches across.
27. Clara Bell Thurston, *The Jingle of a Jap* (Boston: H. M. Caldwell, 1906), unpaginated. This story is reminiscent of an earlier Japanese American doll friendship in *A Cup of Tea: Pictures from Doll Life* (1892) by Elizabeth S. Tucker.
28. Stanley J. Kunitz and Howard Haycraft, eds., *The Junior Book of Authors* (New York: H. W. Wilson, 1934), 242.
29. Lucy Fitch Perkins also wrote the *American Twins* series, which included *The Colonial Twins of Virginia* (1924), *The American Twins of the Revolution* (1926), and *The Pickaninny Twins* (1931).
30. Lucy Fitch Perkins (1865–1937), *The Japanese Twins* (Boston: Houghton Mifflin, 1912), 3–5.
31. Ibid., 37–39.
32. Ibid., 123.
33. Ibid., 118.
34. Conversations with the author, between 1990 and 2000.
35. A member of the English Literature Department at Wellesley College, and an editorial staff member at the *Atlantic Monthly*, Converse worked as a missionary in Japan; taught school there, and wrote *Kin Chan and the Crab* (New York: Friendship Press, 1927), the story of a young Japanese girl.
36. Florence Converse, "A Letter to One Who Reads This Book," in Ruth Gaines, *Treasure Flower: A Child of Japan* (New York: E. P. Dutton, 1916), xi–xii.
37. Ibid., xxii–xxviii.
38. Dorothy Loring Taylor, *Olive Beaupré Miller and the Bookhouse for Children* (Chicago: Chicago Review Press, 1986), 7.
39. Ibid., 15.
40. Ibid., 17.
41. Olive Beaupré Miller (1883–1968), "My Bookhouse is Your Child's Foundation in Culture and Character," in *The Right Path Through Storyland* (Chicago: The Book House for Children, 1921), miscellaneous printed matter, unpaginated.
42. Miller, *The Right Path Through Storyland*, 6.
43. "Briefer Mention: My Book House," *The Dial*, November, 1921, 612.
44. Miller, *The Right Path Through Storyland*, miscellaneous printed matter, unpaginated.
45. Taylor, *Olive Beaupré Miller and the Bookhouse for Children*, 55.
46. Ibid., 43.
47. Ibid., 105–106.
48. Olive Beaupré Miller, ed., *Little Pictures of Japan* (Chicago: The Book House for Children, 1925), 163.
49. Ibid., 124.
50. Ibid., 141.
51. Ibid., 179.
52. Ibid., 95.
53. Ibid., 182–184.
54. "Artists Localize our Silk Designs," *New York Times*, November 1, 1925, XX16.
55. Adah F. Whitcomb, "Travel for Tots," *Chicago Daily Tribune*, November 14, 1925, 10.
56. "A Children's Treasure," *Los Angeles Times*, February 4, 1934, A6. *My Travelship*, including *Little Pictures of Japan*, is still one of the most popular children's books about Japan. It is always available on eBay and on many book dealers' lists.
57. Taylor, *Olive Beaupré Miller and the Bookhouse for Children*, 58.
58. Donald Culross Peattie, *A Child's Story of the World, From the Earliest Days to Our Own Time* (New York: Junior Literary Guild and Simon and Schuster, 1937).
59. Jane Werner Watson, *The Golden History of the World: A Child's Introduction to Ancient and Modern Times* (New York: Simon and Schuster, 1955).
60. Taylor, *Olive Beaupré Miller and the Bookhouse for Children*, 106, 108.
61. Esther Brann, *'Round the World with Esther Brann* (New York: Macmillan, 1935), unpaginated.
62. Esther Wood (1906–?), *Great Sweeping Day* (New York: Longmans, Green, 1936), 15.
63. Edith May Kovar [Mary Windsor, pseud.], *Little Friends from Many Lands* (Racine, WI: Whitman, 1935), unpaginated.
64. Eva D. Edwards, *Haruko, Child of Japan* (San Francisco: Harr Wagner, 1934), 58–61.
65. Stella Burke May (1877–1961), *Children of Japan* (Chicago: Rand McNally, 1936), 1.
66. Elinor Hedrick and Kathryne Van Noy, *Kites and Kimonos* (New York: Macmillan, 1936), 6–7, 94.
67. Holling C. Holling (1900–1973), *The Twins Who Flew around the World* (New York: Platt and Munk, 1931), 20–21.
68. Peggie Porcher, *The Magic City of Children* (New York: Lynn, 1936).
69. Maud (1890–1971) and Miska Petersham (1888–1960), *The Story of Silk* (Chicago: John C. Winston, 1939).
70. Enid La Monte Meadowcroft (1898–1966), *Aren't We Lucky!* (New York: Thomas Y. Crowell, 1939), 22, 25, 27.
71. Ibid., 36.
72. Ibid., 31, 33–34.
73. Ibid., 37–38.
74. Margaret McConnell, *Bobo the Barrage Balloon* (New York: Lothrop, Lee & Shepard, 1943), 38.
75. Arensa Sondergaard (1900–1984), *My First Geography of the Pacific* (Boston: Little, Brown, 1944), 21–22.
76. "Folk Rhymes for Children," *New York Times*, November 5, 1944, SM27.
77. Ibid.

CHAPTER 7

1. George P. Brett, "The Macmillan Children's Book Department," *Horn Book Magazine* 4, no. 3 (August 1928): 25. Macmillan Company was founded in Britain in 1843. The New York office opened in 1869 under George E. Brett, who was the company president from 1896 to 1931. In 1891, the New York office existed in an independent partnership. In 1896, the Macmillan Company of New York was incorporated and became a separate business. See Elizabeth James, ed., *Macmillan: A Publishing Tradition* (Houndmills, Basingstoke, Hampshire: Palgrave Macmillan, 2002), 48.
2. By 1926, a number of other houses had created children's departments, including Doubleday, Stokes, Harcourt, Dutton, and Harper. See John Tebbel, "For Children, with Love and Profit: Two Decades of Book Publishing for Children," in Sybille A. Jagusch, ed., *Stepping Away from Tradition: Children's Books of the Twenties and Thirties* (Washington, DC: Library of Congress, 1988), 20.
3. Brett, "The Macmillan's Children's Book Department," 25.
4. Bertha E. Mahony (1882–1869), "The First Children's Department in Book Publishing," *Horn Book Magazine* 4, no. 3 (August 1928): 24.
5. Margaret Pinckney King, "The Person Makes the Publisher—Louise Seaman," *Horn Book Magazine* 4, no 3, (August 1928): 29. After Seaman's 1929 marriage to Edwin DeTurck Bechtel, Seaman was known as Louise Seaman Bechtel.

6. *Books in Search of Children: Speeches and Essays by Louise Seaman Bechtel* (New York: Macmillan, 1969), 43.
7. Anne Carroll Moore, *My Roads to Childhood* (New York: Doubleday, Doran, 1939), 333.
8. Anne MacLeod, "Literacy and Social Aspects of Children's Books of the Twenties and Thirties," in Jagusch, *Stepping Away from Tradition*, 52.
9. Louise Seaman Bechtel (1894–1985), *Books on the Ladder of Time* (New York: Macmillan, 1969), 23.
10. Brett "The Macmillan Children's Book Department," 26.
11. Ibid., 26–27.
12. Ibid., 25.
13. Louise Seaman Bechtel, "Long, Long Ago by Louis Seaman Bechtel," *The Macmillan Children's Book Department* Newsletter 3, no. 2 (June 1969): 2.
14. Bechtel, *Books on the Ladder of Time*, 14.
15. *Macmillan Books for Boys and Girls* (New York: Macmillan, 1930), 61.
16. *Books in Search of Children,* 245.
17. *Macmillan Books for Boys and Girls,* 62.
18. Regarding Mahony's lament about the dearth of American picture books, see Mahony, "The First Children's Department in Book Publishing," 4: "Our pitiful small list of picture books remained the same year after year with no addition to the masters' group occupied by [the British Walter] Crane, [Randolph] Caldecott, Kate Greenaway and Leslie Brooke. We examined wistfully the beautiful German, Swedish, Bohemian and French picture books, wondering why we could not make beautiful books like these in America."
19. Elsa Eisgruber (1887–1968), *Spin, Top, Spin* (New York: Macmillan, 1929); Tom Seidmann-Freud (1892–1929), *Peregrin and the Goldfish* (New York: Macmillan, 1929); Elizabeth Coatsworth (1893–1986), *The Sun's Diary* (New York: Macmillan, 1929); Boris Artzybasheff (1899–1965), *The Fairy Shoemaker and Other Fairy Poems* (New York, Macmillan, 1928).
20. Brett, "The Macmillan Children's Book Department," 27; Albert Bigelow Paine (1861–1937), *A Girl in White Armor: The True Story of Joan of Arc* (New York: Macmillan, 1927); Ida M. Tarbell (1857–1944), *The Boy Scouts' Life of Lincoln* (New York: Macmillan, 1921).
21. In 1932, Bechtel published *Cricket and the Emperor's Son* by Elizabeth Coatsworth, about a young Japanese boy who saves the life of an Imperial prince by reading to him from his magic scroll.
22. Even his own country's *Oxford Companion to the Literature of Wales* provides but a small and vague paragraph about Finnemore. Meic Stephens, comp. and ed., *The Oxford Companion to the Literature of Wales* (Oxford: Oxford University Press, 1986), 5: 200. The entry includes another possible death date for Finnemore—1928. Other information about the author is sketchy: he is believed to have been a native of East Anglia, was appointed, in 1891, head teacher at the Tanygarreg School in Mynydd Bach, and at a later date became a farmer near the village of Llanilar.
23. Ibid., 200.
24. John Finnemore (1863–1915?), *Peeps at Many Lands: Japan* (London: Adam and Charles Black, 1907), 23.
25. Ibid., 2–3.
26. Ella du Cane (1874–1943) also produced *The Flowers and Gardens of Japan* (London: A. and C. Black, 1908).
27. Finnemore, *Japan* (1907), 20.
28. Ibid., 8.
29. Ibid., 61–62. Bechtel re-issued *Japan* in 1921, combining it with *China*, written by Lena E. Johnston.
30. John Finnemore, *Peeps at Many Lands: Japan* (London: Adam and Charles Black, 1911), 45–49.
31. Ibid., 91.
32. Ibid., 93.
33. James (1882–1965) wrote other Japan-inspired books, including *The Three Dwarf Trees* (1936), a play about Lord Sano of the Taira clan; and her autobiographical works, *Japan: Recollections and Impressions* (1936) and *John and Mary's Aunt* (1950).
34. Grace James, *Japan: Recollections and Impressions* (London: George Allen & Unwin, 1936), 26.
35. Grace James, *Green Willow and Other Japanese Fairy Tales* (London: Macmillan, 1910), xvii.
36. Ibid., 37–38.
37. Selections from *Green Willow* written in a simpler style were published in Grace James's children's book *John and Mary's Japanese Fairy Tales* (London: Frederick Muller Ltd., 1957), a volume in her series about John and Mary.
38. Edith Eliza Ames Norton (1864–1929) [Karlene Kent, pseud.], *Little Black Eyes: The Story of a Little Girl in Japan* (New York: Macmillan, 1927).
39. Ibid., 24–25.
40. Ibid., 16–17.
41. Ibid., 61.
42. Ibid., 67–73.
43. Ibid., 71.
44. Dorothy Rowe, *The Begging Deer and Other Stories of Japanese Children* (New York: Macmillan, 1928).
45. *Macmillan Books for Boys and Girls*, 28.
46. Rowe, *The Begging Deer*, x.
47. Ibid., 29.
48. "The Bird Who Said Baga," in Rowe, *The Begging Deer*, 107–109.
49. Berta (1890–1976) and Elmer Hader (1889–1973), *The Picture Book of Travel: The Story of Transportation* (New York: Macmillan, 1928).
50. *Macmillan Books for Boys and Girls*, 17. Benday is a type of shading.
51. Helen Ferris, ed., *When I Was a Girl: The Stories of Five Famous Women as Told by Themselves* (New York: Macmillan, 1930).
52. Widely read in the United States and Japan, *A Daughter of the Samurai* was already in its fourteenth edition by 1931.
53. Helen Ferris, one of Bechtel's Vassar friends, introduced Sugimoto's story with appreciation and most likely unintended condescension. She described the author, who was then on the faculty of "one of the greatest universities in the world" and had written her book in English, as "a gently hovering butterfly or a gay flower nodding in the breeze" who was overwhelmed by the "enormous size of things [in America], the wide streets, the tall buildings, the great trees," which "became characteristic to her of the Americans whom she had met, with [their] large person, generous purse, broad mind, strong heart and free soul." See *When I Was a Girl*, 224–225.
54. Etsu Inagaki Sugimoto (1874–1950), *A Daughter of the Samurai* (Garden City, NY: Doubleday, Doran, 1934), 308.
55. Ibid., 4–5.
56. Ibid., 5.
57. Ibid., 15.
58. Ibid., 22–23.
59. Ibid., 45.
60. Chiyono Sugimoto married Eiichi Kiyooka, grandson of Fukuzawa Yukichi, the noted scholar and progressive leader of the Meiji era.
61. Ferris, *When I Was a Girl*, 224.

62. "Jap Author Dies," *Los Angeles Times,* June 22, 1950, 1.
63. May McNeer (1902–1994) and Lynd Ward (1905–1985), *Prince Bantam: Being the Adventures of Yoshitsune the Brave and His Faithful Henchman Great Benkei of the Western Pagoda* (New York: Macmillan, 1929).
64. Ward's acclaimed wordless children's book, *The Silver Pony,* was not published until 1973. Ward also illustrated Esther Forbes's *Johnny Tremain* (1943), and he received the Caldecott award for *The Biggest Bear* (1953), which he both wrote and illustrated.
65. McNeer and Ward, *Prince Bantam,* 14–15.
66. Ibid., 69–71.
67. *Macmillan Books for Boys and Girls,* 41.
68. McNeer and Ward, *Prince Bantam,* jacket.
69. *Ushiwaka Maru,* a contemporary Japanese retelling of the Yoshitsune story, has a very different style. Mikio Chiba, *Ushiwaka-Maru,* illustrated by Shiun Kondo (Tokyo: Kodansha, 2002).
70. Elizabeth Coatsworth, *Personal Geography: Almost an Autobiography* (Brattleboro, VT: Stephen Green Press, 1976), 29.
71. Ibid., 39.
72. Louise Seaman Bechtel, "From Java to Maine with Elizabeth Coatsworth," in Bertha Mahony Miller, ed., *Newbery Medal Books: 1922–1955* (Boston: Horn Book, 1955), 94.
73. Ibid.
74. Thomas Handforth illustrated several of Coatsworth's books and traveled extensively to Africa, India, China, and Japan.
75. Elizabeth Coatsworth, *The Cat Who Went to Heaven,* (New York: Macmillan, 1930).
76. Ibid., 1–5.
77. Ibid., 18.
78. Ibid.
79. Ibid., 56.
80. Bechtel, "From Java to Maine with Elizabeth Coatsworth," 96.

CHAPTER 8

1. William J. Sebald with Russell Brines, *With MacArthur in Japan: A Personal History of the Occupation* (New York: W.W. Norton, 1965), 38–41.
2. Translated from the Japanese; written and illustrated by Shigeo Nishimura.
3. The film was based on the autobiographical novel by Akiyuki Nosaka.
4. Ryerson Johnson (1901–1995), *Gozo's Wonderful Kite* (New York: Crowell, 1951); Toba Sōjō, *The Animal Frolic* (New York: G. P. Putnam's Sons, 1954); Raymond Creekmore (1905–1984), *Fujio* (New York: Macmillan, 1951); Thomas F. M. Adams, *The Adventures of Billie and Belinda in Tokyo* (Tokyo: S. Okuyama, 1953); Thomas F. M. Adams, *Adventures of Little Hound Dog and the Great Detective* (1953); Eleanor B. Hicks, *Circus Day in Japan* (Rutland, VT: Charles E. Tuttle, 1953); Jeanette P. Brown, *Surprise for Robin* (New York: Friendship Press, 1956); Astrid Lindgren (1907–2002), *Noriko-san, Girl of Japan* (New York: Macmillan, 1958).
5. Marianne Carus, ed., *Celebrate Cricket: 30 Years of Stories and Art* (Chicago: Cricket Books, 2003), 3–4.
6. Louise (1913–1988) and Richard Floethe (1901–1988), *A Thousand and One Buddhas* (New York: Farrar, Straus & Giroux, 1967); Dominique Darbois (1925–2014), *Noriko, Her Life in Japan* (London: Chatto & Windus, 1963); Betty Jean Lifton (1926–2010), with photographs by Eikoh Hosoe (b. 1933), *Taka-chan and I: A Dog's Journey to Japan* (New York: Norton, 1967).
7. Davis Pratt and Elsa Kula, *Magic Animals of Japan* (Berkeley, CA: Parnassus Press, 1967); Margaret Hodges (1911–2005), *The Wave* (Boston: Houghton Mifflin, 1964); Arlene Mosel (1921–1996), *The Funny Little Woman* (New York: E. P. Dutton, 1972); Louis Slobodkin (1903–1975), *Yasu and the Strangers* (New York: Macmillan, 1965); Betty Jean Lifton, *Chirps from a Bamboo Cage* (Tokyo: Tokyo News Services, 1954); Leo Politi (1908–1996) *Mieko* (San Carlos, CA: Golden Gate Junior Books, 1969).
8. Suekichi Akaba would be the first Japanese person to receive the prestigious Hans Christian Andersen Award for illustration.
9. Tadashi Matsui (b. 1926), illustrated by Suekichi Akaba (1910–1990), *Onriku and the Carpenter* (Englewood Cliffs, NJ: Prentice-Hall, 1963); Momoko Ishii (1907–2008), illustrated by Fuku Akino (1908–2001), *Issun Boshi, the Inchling: An Old Tale of Japan* (New York: Walker, 1967); Miyoko Matsutani (1926–2015), illustrated by Chihiro Iwasaki (1918–1974), *The Crane Maiden* (New York: Parents' Magazine Press, 1968); Miyoko Matsutani, with pictures by Yasuo Segawa (1932–2010), *How the Withered Trees Blossomed* (Philadelphia: Lippincott, 1971).
10. Joyce Moore, "The Hustling Antiquarian: A History of the Charles E. Tuttle Publishing Company" (master's thesis, Graduate School of the Texas Woman's University, School of Library Science, 1971), 11.
11. Francis Haar (1908–1997), *The Best of Old Japan* (Rutland, VT: Charles E. Tuttle, 1951); James A. Michener (1907–1997), *Japanese Prints: From the Early Masters to the Modern* (Rutland, VT: Charles E. Tuttle, 1959); Oliver Statler (1915–2002), *Modern Japanese Prints: An Art Reborn* (Rutland, VT: Charles E. Tuttle, 1959); Bill Hume (1916–2009) *Babysan: A Private Look at the American Occupation* (Rutland, VT: Charles E. Tuttle, 1953).
12. "Magic in Hiroshima," *Time* 55, no. 2 (January 9, 1950): 44.
13. Raymond Lamont-Brown, *Kempeitai; Japan's Dreaded Military Police* (Stroud, UK: Sutton, 1998), 143.
14. Rinkichi Sakade (1925–2015), letter to the author, January 7, 2005.
15. Stephen Comee and Nina Raj "SWET Interview: Florence Sakade" in *SWET-newsletter* no. 78 (December 1997): 8.
16. "Dear Friends," *Silver Bells from Hiroshima* 1, no. 2 (February 1952): 33.
17. Mrs. Reiko Shiba Tuttle, interview with the author, Rutland, Vermont, October 28, 2004.
18. Donald Richie (1924–2013), letter to the author, November 26, 2004.
19. Ibid.
20. *Silver Bells* 1, no. 10 (October 1952): back cover.
21. Yoshio Hayashi (1905–2010); Yoshisuke Kurosaki (1905–1984).
22. E. L. B., "Tales of Japan," *New York Times,* January 4, 1953, BR20.
23. Toshio Suzuki, "Japanese Home," *Silver Bells,* 1, no. 2 (February 1952): 32; Toshio Suzuki, "Flower Viewing," *Silver Bells* 1, no.4 (April 1952): 42; Kanichi Kaji, "Sidewalk Shops," *Silver Bells* 1, no. 8 (August 1952): 43; Teiji Kawame, "Making 'mochi' (rice-cakes)," *Silver Bells* 1, no. 12 (December 1952): 3–4; "Doll Festival," *Silver Bells* 2, no. 3 (March 1953): 3–4; Shigeo Fuseishi, "Shichi-go-san (7-5-3 Celebration)," *Silver Bells* 1, no. 11 (November 1952): 43; "August Festival," *Silver Bells* 2, no. 9 (August 1953): 6–7; "Kami-Shibai 'Cardboard theatre,'" *Silver Bells* 2, no. 4

(April 1953): 38; "School Flower Viewing," *Silver Bells* 3, no. 5 (May 1954): 2–3.

24. Seiko Mira, letter to the author, August 10, 2004.
25. Donald Richie, letter to the author, November 26, 2004.
26. His list included such folktales as *Little One-Inch and Other Japanese Favorite Stories* (1958); craft books like *American Japanese Riding, Coloring and Talking Book* (1952) and *Origami Storybook, Japanese Paper Folding Play* (1960); and children's stories such as *The Dragon's Tears* (1964), a paper theater play, and *Kobo and the Wishing Pictures* (1964), a story about *ema* (tablets) on which worshippers write their wishes.
27. Dorothy A. Bennett, *The Golden Encyclopedia* (New York: Simon and Schuster, 1946), 18.
28. Jane Werner Watson, *The Golden Geography: A Child's Introduction to the World* (New York: Simon and Schuster, 1952), 53.
29. Ibid., 53.
30. John C. Caldwell, *Let's Visit Japan* (New York: John Day, 1959), 85.
31. Ibid., 92.
32. Lily Edelman (1915–1981), *Japan in Stories and Pictures* (New York: Harcourt, Brace, 1953), 47.
33. Virginia Haviland, "About Japan," *Horn Book Magazine,* August 1953, 286.
34. Helen Mears (1900–1989), *The First Book of Japan* (New York: Franklin Watts, 1953), 11–12.
35. Ibid., 37–38.
36. Ibid., 67–68.
37. Helen Mears, *Year of the Wild Boar: An American Woman in Japan* (New York: J. B. Lippincott, 1942), 9.
38. Mears, *The First Book of Japan,* 68.
39. Caldwell, *Let's Visit Japan,* 41–43.
40. Ibid., 9–10, 92. Reviewers were divided on *Let's Visit Japan.* In her review of the book in *Library Journal* (December 15, 1959, 3923), Jane Marquis lauded it as "another valuable [title in the] 'Let's Visit' series in which the importance of Japan as a nation and the influence of the United States upon Japan's progress in western ways are paramount." The Virginia Kirkus Bookshop Service review (March 15, 1959, 226) objected to the book's "chauvinistic" tone and its apparent attempt to "boost American relations."
41. Donald Richie, *The Land and People of Japan* (New York: Macmillan, 1958), 5.
42. *Understanding the Japanese,* her compact history written for adults, was published a year later.
43. Grace Sydenstricker Yaukey (1899–1994) [Cornelia Spencer, pseud.], *Japan* (New York: Holiday House, 1948), 3.
44. Ibid., 22–24.
45. Anne M. Halladay, *Toshio and Tama: Children of the New Japan* (New York: Friendship Press, 1949), 11, 12.
46. Gertrude Jenness Rinden, *Kenji* (New York: Friendship Press, 1957), 9.
47. Ibid., 4–5.
48. Albert J. Nevins (1915–1997), *The Adventures of Kenji of Japan* (New York, Dodd, Mead, 1952), 3.
49. Halladay, *Toshio and Tama,* 7–9.
50. Ibid., 15–16.
51. Ibid., 77–78.
52. Established in 1919.
53. "Child Book Award Presented for '45," *New York Times,* November 13, 1945, 18. Lee Kingman, children's book editor at Houghton Mifflin, accepted the award on behalf of the author.
54. Florence Crannell Means (1891–1980), *The Moved-Outers* (Boston: Houghton Mifflin, 1945), 12.
55. Howard Pease, "Without Evasion: Some Reflections after Reading Mrs. Means' 'The Moved-Outers,'" *Horn Book Magazine,* January–February 1945, 9.
56. Ibid., 10.
57. Clara Breed, "Books that Build Better Racial Attitudes," *Horn Book Magazine,* January–February, 1945, 61.
58. Vanya (Virginia Armstrong) Oakes (1909–1983), *Desert Harvest: A Story of the Japanese in California* (Philadelphia: Winston, 1953), 5.
59. Ibid., 16.
60. Ibid., 167–168.
61. Ibid., 223.
62. Ibid., 216–217.
63. Ibid., 233–234.

CHAPTER 9

1. *Allen Say's Journey: The Art and Words of a Children's Book Author, July 28, 2000–February 11, 2001.* Los Angeles: Japanese American National Museum, 2000. Exhibition brochure.
2. Allen Say (b. 1937), *Grandfather's Journey* (Boston: Houghton Mifflin, 1993), 31.
3. Taro Yashima (1908–1994), "On Making a Book for a Child," in Frances Lander Spain, *The Contents of the Basket and Other Papers on Children's Books and Reading* (New York: New York Public Library, 1960), 49.
4. Glenn L. Johnson, "Golden Village," *Horn Book Magazine,* April 1967, 183.
5. Evelyn Taylor, "Artists in the Gladys English Collection of Original Illustrations for Children's Books," in *Illustrations for Children: The Gladys English Collection* (Los Angeles: California Library Association, 1963), 42.
6. Taro Yashima, *The New Sun* (New York: Henry Holt, 1943), 95–98. Note Tosa is part of Shikoku Island, south of the main island of Japan.
7. A picture scroll featuring anthropomorphized rabbits and monkeys accredited to the monk Toba Sōjō (1053–1140). The wordless scroll became the basis for the American picture book *The Animal Frolic,* with text by Velma Varner (New York: G. P. Putnam's Sons, 1954).
8. Katsushika Hokusai (1760?–1849), was the creator of *The Wave,* among other paintings and prints.
9. Taro Yashima, *Horizon is Calling* (New York: Henry Holt, 1947), 19–21.
10. This collective pseudonym is derived from the names of the Russian political caricaturists Mikhail Kupriyanov, Porfiry Krylov, and Nikolay Sokolov.
11. *Yashima Taro no Sekai.* [The World of Taro Yashima] (Tokyo: Chihiro Art Museum, 1996), unpaginated.
12. Yashima, *The New Sun,* 169.
13. Iwamatsu's wife, Tomoe Sasago, a fine artist in her own right (and a graduate of Kobe Women's College and Bunka Gakuin in Tokyo, where she became acquainted with the teachings of Karl Marx and Friedrich Engels) began using the pseudonym Mitsuko Arai.
14. Raymond Lamont-Brown, *Kempeitai: Japan's Dreaded Military Police* (Phoenix Mill: Sutton Publishing, 1998), 16.
15. Yashima, "On Making a Book for a Child," 48.
16. Naoko Shibusawa, "'The Artist Belongs to the People': The Odyssey of Taro Yashima," *Journal of Asian American Studies* 8, no. 3 (October 2005): 263. See also Yashima, *The New Sun,* 37–38.
17. Yashima, *Horizon is Calling,* 59.
18. Ibid., 62.
19. Ibid., 117.
20. Ibid., 162.

21. No records at the Art Students League could be located regarding Yashima's registration, classes, or other activities.
22. David Holley, "Japanese Artist Who Aided U.S. in War Finds Acceptance," *Los Angeles Times*, August 2, 1982, C1. Yashima refers to Japan's eight major islands born from the union of two gods, according to Japan's ancient creation myth. Taro or Kintaro refers to the legendary boy hero who, brought up by wild animals, grew so strong that he could overcome the mighty *oni*, monsters of Japanese folklore. Iwamatsu's wife now called herself Mitsu Yashima.
23. Ibid.
24. Christopher Lazare, "Japanese Liberal," *New York Times*, November 21, 1943, BR6.
25. Shibusawa, "The Artist Belongs to the People," 257.
26. Holley, "Japanese Artist," C1.
27. In an article he wrote for a popular Japanese magazine (translated as "As a vanguard for Japan's surrender," in *Bungei Shunju*, December 1962, 214–222), Yashima described his feeling of shame and his overwhelming sense of sorrow over the fate of Japanese soldiers. Years later, he defended himself on several occasions, saying, "No one says I'm against my country now," and, "at the time it was easy to say I was one who was against his own country . . . that's the most terrible thing, because my feeling (was), I'm doing (it) because I love my country."
28. "Votes Bill Aiding Author: House Acts to Grant Residence to Japanese Who Aided U.S.," *New York Times*, June 16, 1948, 27. Regarding the Yashimas' long separation from their son, see Mitsu Yashima, "Letter to Mako to meet again," *Common Ground*, Spring 1949, 41–46.
29. Yashima, *Horizon is Calling*, 140.
30. Elizabeth Gray Vining, "May Massee: Who Was She?" in George V. Hodowanec, ed., *The May Massee Collection: Creative Publishing for Children, 1923–1963, A Checklist* (Emporia, KS: Emporia State University, 1979), viii.

    However, not all "dooryards" were closed. After the purchase of a children's book collection from the German collector Dr. Albert Weiske, the Brooklyn Museum announced, in 1926, its exhibition of children's books by well-known artists from many European countries including France, Germany, Russia, and Scandinavia. See "Art for Children as Shown by Modern European Picture Books," Brooklyn Museum Archives. Records of the Department of Public Information. Press Releases, 1916–1930, April 27, 1926.
31. Yashima, "On Making a Book for a Child," 48. Yashima's first son, Chihiro Isa, was born to Masako Nishina in 1929.
32. Virginia Haviland, "Taro Yashima," *Horn Book Magazine*, December, 1953, 454–455.
33. Taro Yashima, *Crow Boy* (New York: Viking, 1955) 6.
34. Ibid., 14.
35. Yashima's son and daughter both acted in film, television, and on stage. Makoto Iwamatsu, often billed simply as "Mako," was nominated for an Academy Award for his performance in *The Sand Pebbles* (1966).
36. "Five in Lively Exhibit," *Los Angeles Times*, January 10, 1960, E.
37. *Taro Yashima's Golden Village*. Written and narrated by Taro Yashima. Produced by Glenn Johnson. Distributed by World University Media USA, 2000, DVD.
38. *Taro Yashima's Golden Village.*
39. Ibid.
40. Johnson, "Golden Village," 187.
41. *Taro Yashima's Golden Village.*
42. Ibid.
43. Johnson, "Golden Village," 186.
44. *Taro Yashima's Golden Village.*
45. *Japanese Children's Picture Books and Original Illustrations in Celebration of World Congress on Children's Books, 20th IBBY Congress, Tokyo, August 1986* (Tokyo: Japanese Board on Books for Young People and the Asahi Shimbun, 1986), 39.
46. Mako Iwamatsu, untitled article in *Taro Yashima: A Tribute, An Exhibition in Los Angeles, June 29–July 25, 1996,* (Los Angeles: Japanese American Cultural and Community Center, Doizaki Gallery, 1996), 11. Exhibition catalog.
47. Yoshiko Uchida (1921–1992), *The Invisible Thread: An Autobiography* (Englewood Cliffs, NJ: Julian Messner, 1991), 133.
48. Ibid., 2.
49. Uchida wrote about the church in *The History of Sycamore Church* (El Cerrito, CA: Sycamore Congregational Church, 1974).
50. When the Uchida family lived in the camp in Topaz, Yoshiko's parents always looked out for their fellow internees. When they received a box of Christmas greens from their friends in Connecticut, her mother immediately shared them with her friends. See Uchida, *Invisible Thread*, 106.
51. Yoshiko Uchida, *Desert Exile: The Uprooting of a Japanese American Family* (Seattle: University of Washington Press, 1982), 36.
52. Ibid., 4.
53. Ibid., 20.
54. Uchida, *Invisible Thread*, 15.
55. Ibid., 52.
56. Uchida, *Desert Exile*, 40
57. Ibid., 42. Nisei refers to first generation Japanese Americans; Issei to Japanese immigrants.
58. Ibid., 45.
59. Yoshiko Uchida, "Yoshiko Uchida (1921–)," in Adele Sarkissian, ed., *Something about the Author: Autobiography Series* (Detroit, MI: Gale Research Company, 1986), I: 271.
60. Uchida, *Invisible Thread*, 75.
61. Uchida, *Desert Exile*, 105–106.
62. Ibid., 106–109.
63. Uchida's sister became a nursery school teacher at Mount Holyoke College's Department of Education. Her parents left Topaz for Salt Lake City, Utah, in August, 1943.
64. Uchida. *Desert Exile*, 144.
65. Uchida, *Invisible Thread*, 31–32.
66. Uchida, "Yoshiko Uchida," 273.
67. Uchida, *Invisible Thread*, 131.
68. Uchida, "Yoshiko Uchida." Uchida translated some of Kawai's poetry and wrote about it in her chapbook, *We Do Not Work Alone: The Thoughts of Kanjiro Kawai* (Kyoto: Folk Art Society, 1953).
69. J. D. L., "Review," *Horn Book Magazine*, April 31, 1955, 112.
70. Uchida, *Invisible Thread*, 132.
71. Yoshiko Uchida, *A Jar of Dreams* (New York: Atheneum, 1981), 61–62.
72. Ibid., 90.
73. Ibid., 91.
74. Ibid., 89–92.
75. Ibid., 130.
76. Yoshiko Uchida, *The Bracelet* (New York: Philomel, 1993).
77. Yoshiko Uchida, *Journey to Topaz* (New York: Charles Scribner's Sons, 1971), vii.
78. Ibid., 39.
79. Yoshiko Uchida, *Journey Home* (New York: Atheneum, 1978), 3–4.
80. Uchida, *Journey Home*, 15–16.

81. In her later books Uchida freely used the term "concentration camp" (one chapter in *Journey to Topaz* is called "Concentration Camp Christmas"). She justified the term by maintaining that the relocation centers should be called concentration camps not to invoke the Nazi camps but as a place in which "prisoners of war, political prisoners, foreign nationals, refugees, and the like, are confined." Uchida, *Journey to Topaz*, 99.
82. Ibid., 122.
83. Uchida, *Invisible Thread*, 132.
84. Tsukiko Nakamura, "About Takabo," an article in the Peeresses' School Alumni Magazine, 2000. Translated by Eiko Fukuda Gustavson, July 2, 2008. Sentaro Iwata (1901–1974) was known for his images of *bijin*, beautiful women.
85. Kazue Mizumura (1920–1996), "Biographical Sketch," Kazue Mizumura Papers. Author's collection. Undated. The full name of the Art Institute is Tokyo Joshi Bijutsu Kaikan (Kenkyusho) [Tokyo Women's Art Club (Institute)].
86. Tsukiko Nakamura, letter to the author, July 2, 2008.
87. Mizumura, "Biographical Sketch."
88. Yoko Fukuda, letter to the author, May 12, 2008.
89. Tsukiko Nakamura, letter to the author, July 2, 2008.
90. Ibid.
91. James Boatman, telephone interview with the author, June 22, 2008
92. Yoko Fukuda, letter to the author, May 12, 2008.
93. Tsukiko Nakamura, letter to the author, July 2, 2008.
94. Margaret Eberbach, letter to the author, May 5, 2008.
95. Elizabeth Gray Vining, *Being Seventy: The Measure of a Year* (New York: Viking, 1978), 40. Vining's husband had been killed in an automobile accident four years into their marriage.
96. Elizabeth Gray Vining, *Windows for the Crown Prince* (Philadelphia: Lippincott, 1952), 85.
97. Rita Fitzpatrick, "Teacher of Jap Prince finds Job Royal Plum," *Chicago Daily Tribune*, October 26, 1947, 18.
98. "Tutor to Teach Jap Prince of American Ways of Peace," *Christian Science Monitor*, August 27, 1946, 4.
99. Vining, *Windows for the Crown Prince*, 23–24.
100. Ibid., 99.
101. Ibid., 150.
102. Elizabeth Gray Vining, *The Cheerful Heart* (New York: Viking, 1959), 62.
103. Ibid., 15.
104. Mizumura did create one other children's book when she was younger. "During the war years, when there were no books to be bought," she wrote, "I made by hand a picture book for my daughter. And that was the only book she ever had for the three years of her life. It was my first children's book, and of course, I did not realize at that time, that it was the beginning of a career for me." Mizumura, "Biographical Sketch."
105. Doris De Montreville and Donna Hill, *Third Book of Junior Authors* (New York: H. W. Wilson, 1972), 199.
106. Masako Matsuno, interview with the author, Osaka, July 8, 2006.
107. Virginia Haviland, "A Pair of Red Clogs," *Horn Book Magazine*, October 1960, 398–399.
108. Ann Beneduce, letter to the author, March 22, 2008.
109. These include books by Eleanor Coerr, Joanna Cole, Norma Farber, Roma Gans, Laurence Pringle, and Charlotte Zolotow.
110. De Montreville and Hill, *Third Book of Junior Authors*, 199.
111. The Let's-Read-and-Find-Out Science Books were part of a trend in the 1970s to publish appealing, entertaining, and even whimsical books for beginning readers that presented an imaginative approach to nonfiction.
112. Kazue Mizumura, *I See the Winds* (New York: Thomas Y. Crowell, 1966), unpaginated.
113. About *Flower Moon Snow*, Ann Beneduce wrote: "I felt strongly that it was part of my responsibility to offer to really gifted artists the opportunity to create works about which they felt passionately, to publish these in the best possible form and to bring them to a wide audience of young people. Nothing I could have commissioned, for example, could have produced such a book as *Flower Moon Snow*, a work of art spontaneously created by Kazue and offered to me for publication." Letter to the author, June 5, 2008.
114. Kazue Mizumura, *Flower Moon Snow: A Book of Haiku* (New York: Thomas Y. Crowell, 1977), unpaginated.
115. Ann Beneduce, letter to the author, March 22, 2008.
116. Yoko Fukuda, letter to the author, May 12, 2008.
117. Adair Heitmann, telephone interview with the author, May 4, 2008.
118. Margaret Eberbach, letter to the author, May 5, 2008.

CHAPTER 10

1. Nancy Larrick, "The All-White World of Children's Books," *Saturday Review*, September 11, 1965, 63–65; 84–85.
2. Alan Hedblad, ed., *Something about the Author* (Detroit: Gale, 1997), 93: 211.
3. Yoko Kawashima Watkins (b. 1933), *My Brother, My Sister, and I* (New York: Bradbury, 1994), 264.
4. Ibid., 259–264.
5. Margaret Scrogin (b. 1941) and Raymond Chang (b. 1939), *In the Eye of War* (New York: Margaret K. McElderry Books, 1990).
6. Sook Nyul Choi (b. 1937), *Year of Impossible Goodbyes* (Boston: Houghton Mifflin, 1991), 6.
7. Ibid., 43–44.
8. Ibid., 59.
9. John W. Dower, *Embracing Defeat: Japan in the Wake of World War II* (New York: W. W. Norton/The New Press, 1999), 414.
10. Ibid. See also Toshi Maruki (1912–2000), *The Hiroshima Panels: Joined Works of Iri and Toshi Maruki* (Tokyo: Komine Shoten, 2000), 188–202, and "Imagination Without Borders: Maruki Toshi and Iri Collection," Northwestern University, accessed March 2018, http://imaginationwithoutborders.northwestern.edu/collections/muruki-toshi-and-iri-collection.
11. *Hellfire—A Journey from Hiroshima*, a film by John Junkerman and John W. Dower; directed by Michael Camerin and James MacDonald. Produced and written by John Junkerman. First Run Features, 1986.
12. Correspondence, Dorothy Briley to Toshi Maruki, November 18, 1983. Author research file.
13. Toshi Maruki, *Hiroshima no Pika* (New York: Lothrop, Lee & Shepard, 1980), [7–28].
14. Dan Dailey, comp., "The Unthinkable for Kids," *Los Angeles Times*, August 9, 1998, 8.
15. Natalie Babbit, "Hiroshima no Pika," *New York Times*, October 10, 1982, BR24.

16. Jo Carr, "Picture Book Propaganda," *School Library Journal* 29, no. 10 (August 1983): 4.
17. Hiroko Nakamoto (b. 1930), *My Japan, 1930–1951* (New York: McGraw-Hill, 1970), 68–69.
18. Ibid., 72.
19. Junko Morimoto (1932–2017), *My Hiroshima* (New York: Viking, 1990); Tatsuharu Kodama, *Shin's Tricycle* (New York: Walker, 1995); Betty Jean Lifton, *Return to Hiroshima* (New York: Atheneum, 1970); Eleanor Coerr (1922–2010), *Sadako and the Thousand Paper Cranes* (New York: Putnam, 1977).
20. Masamoto Nasu (b. 1942), *Hiroshima: A Tragedy Never To Be Repeated* (Tokyo: Fukuinkan Shoten, 1998).
21. Laurence Yep (b. 1948), *Hiroshima: A Novella* (New York: Scholastic, 1995).
22. R. Conrad Stein, *Hiroshima* (Chicago: Children's Press, 1982), 32–34.
23. Sheila Hamanaka, *In Search of the Spirit: The Living National Treasures of Japan* (New York: Morrow Junior Books, 1999).
24. Dorothy (b. 1941) and Thomas Hoobler, *Showa: The Age of Hirohito* (New York: Walker, 1990) and *A Samurai Never Fears Death* (New York: Sleuth/Philomel, 2007).
25. Dorothy and Thomas Hoobler, *Japanese Portraits* (Austin, TX: Raintree Steck-Vaughn Publishers, 1994), 10.
26. Ibid., 14.
27. Ibid., 19–20.
28. Dorothy and Thomas Hoobler, *The Japanese American Family Album* (New York: Oxford University Press, 1996).
29. Ferdinand Kuhn, *Commodore Perry and the Opening of Japan* (New York: Random House, 1955); Robert L. Reynolds, *Commodore Perry in Japan* (New York: American Heritage, 1963).
30. Rhoda Blumberg, *Commodore Perry in the Land of the Shogun* (New York: Lothrop, Lee & Shepard, 1985), 13.
31. Ibid., 28–29.
32. Ibid., 44–45.
33. Toyomi Igus, *Two Mrs. Gibsons* (San Francisco: Children's Book Press, 1996), unpaginated.
34. Mimi Otey Little, *Yoshiko and the Foreigner* (New York: Farrar, Straus and Giroux, 1996), unpaginated.
35. Correspondence, Briley to Maruki, November 18, 1983.
36. Annie Nakao, "Farewell to Manzanar Author Returns to Internment Days in First Novel," *San Francisco Chronicle*, December 14, 2003, E1.
37. Ibid.
38. Jeanne Wakatsuki Houston (b. 1934) and James D. Houston (1933–2009), *Farewell to Manzanar* (Boston: Houghton Mifflin, 1973), 3–6.
39. Ibid., 7.
40. Ibid., 18.
41. Ibid., 25.
42. Ibid., 38–39.
43. Ibid., 62.
44. Ibid., 116.
45. Ibid., 162.
46. Ibid., 169.
47. Ken Mochizuki (b. 1954), *Baseball Saved Us* (New York: Lee & Low Books, 1993); Eve Bunting (b. 1928), *So Far From the Sea* (New York: Clarion Books, 1998); Amy Lee-Tai, *A Place Where Sunflowers Grow* (New York: Childrens Book Press, 2006); Joanne Oppenheim (b. 1934), *Dear Miss Breed: True Stories of the Japanese American Incarceration during World War II and a Librarian Who Made a Difference* (New York: Scholastic, 2006).
48. Marlene Shigekawa, *Welcome Home Swallows* (Torrance, CA: Heian International, 2001), 20–21.
49. Ibid., 24–25.
50. Sheila Hamanaka, *The Journey: Japanese Americans, Racism, and Renewal* (New York: Orchard Books, 1990), 5–34.
51. Dawnine Spivak, *Grass Sandals: The Travels of Basho* (New York: Athenaeum Books for Young Readers, 1997); Deborah Kogan Ray (b. 1940), *Hokusai: The Man Who Painted a Mountain* (New York: Farrar, Straus and Giroux, 2001); Mark Weston (b. 1953), *Honda: The Boy Who Dreamed of Cars* (New York: Lee & Low Books, 2008); Christy Hale, *The East-West House: Noguchi's Childhood in Japan* (New York: Lee & Low Books, 2009).
52. Kimiko Kajikawa, *Yoshi's Feast* (New York: DK Ink, 2000).
53. Based on Lafcadio Hearn's "A Living God," in *Gleanings in Buddha Fields* (1897). Kimiko Kajikawa, *Tsunami!* (New York: Philomel Books, 2009).
54. Pamela S. Turner, *Hachiko: The True Story of a Loyal Dog* (Boston: Houghton Mifflin, 2004); Patrick Atangan, *The Yellow Jar: Two Tales from Japanese Tradition* (New York: NBM, 2002); Jan Freeman Long, *The Bee and the Dream: A Japanese Tale* (New York: Dutton Children's Books, 1996); J. Alison James, *The Drums of Noto Hanto* (New York: DK Publishing, 1999); Tim Myers, *Tanuki's Gift: A Japanese Tale* (New York: Marshall Cavendish, 2003); Robert D. San Souci, *The Silver Charm: A Folktale from Japan* (New York: Doubleday Books for Young Readers, 2002).
55. Barry Denenberg, *The Journal of Ben Uchida* (New York: Scholastic, 1999); Michael L. Cooper, *Remembering Manzanar: Life in a Japanese Relocation Camp* (New York: Clarion Books, 2002); Cynthia Kadohata, *Weedflower* (New York: Athenaeum Books for Young Readers, 2006); Rhoda Blumberg, *Shipwrecked! The True Adventures of a Japanese Boy* (New York: HarperCollins, 2001); Jon Scieszka, *Sam Samurai* (New York: Viking, 2001); Shozo Sato (b. 1933), *Tea Ceremony* (Boston: Tuttle, 2005).
56. Harry Mazer (1925–2016), *A Boy At War* (New York: Simon & Schuster, 2001); Harry Mazer, *A Boy No More* (New York: Simon & Schuster, 2004); Harry Mazer, *Heroes Don't Run* (New York: Simon & Schuster, 2005).
57. Michael Morpurgo (b. 1943), *Kensuke's Kingdom* (London: Egmont, 1999); Graham Salisbury (b. 1944), *Under the Blood-Red Sun* (New York: Delacorte, 1994); Graham Salisbury, *House of the Red Fish* (New York: Wendy Lamb Books, 2006).
58. Samuel G. Goodrich, *The Tales of Peter Parley about Asia,* (Philadelphia: Desilver, Thomas, 1836), 17.
59. Arthur May Knapp, *Feudal and Modern Japan,* (Boston: Joseph Knight, 1897), I:1.
60. Geneva Cobb Iijima, *The Way We Do It in Japan* (Morton Grove, IL: A. Whitman, 2002).
61. Rosemary Wells (b. 1943), *Yoko's Paper Cranes* (New York: Hyperion Books for Children, 2001).
62. Lynne Barasch (b. 1939), *Hiromi's Hands* (New York: Lee & Low Books, 2007).
63. Ruth Wells, *A to Zen: A Book about Japanese Culture* (Saxonville, MA: Picture Book Studio, 1992).
64. Mitsumasa Anno (b. 1926), *Ehon Heike monogatari* (Tokyo: Kodansha, 1996).
65. Kazunari Hino, *Kaeru no Heike monogatari* (Tokyo: Fukuinkan Shoten, 2002).
66. The illustrator Remy Charlip (1929–2012) died before he could realize his dream of creating a picture book about Amaterasu.
67. Graham Salisbury, *Eyes of the Emperor* (New York: Wendy Lamb Books,

2005); Mark Reibstein, *Wabi Sabi* (New York, Boston: Little, Brown, 2008), unpaginated.

APPENDIX

1. U.S. Bureau of Education, *Catalog of A. L. A. Library: Selected by the American Library Association* (Washington, DC: Government Printing Office, 1893).
2. Sybille A. Jagusch, "First Among Equals: Caroline M. Hewins and Anne C. Moore, Foundations of Library Work with Children." Ph.D. diss, University of Maryland, 1990.
3. Caroline M. Hewins (1846–1926), comp., *Books for Boys and Girls: A Selected List*, 3rd ed. (Chicago: American Library Association, 1915), 10.
4. Jennie Lindquist, *Caroline M. Hewins, Her Book* (Boston: Horn Book, 1954), 82.
5. Caroline M. Hewins, *Books for the Young: A Guide for Parents and Children* (New York: F. Leypoldt, 1882).
6. J. I. Wright, review of *Books for Boys and Girls, A Selected List,* by Caroline M. Hewins, *Library Journal,* March 15, 1915, 194.
7. Hewins, *Books for the Young,* 5.
8. John F. Sargent, comp., *Reading for the Young* (Boston: ALA Publishing Section, Library Bureau, 1890–1896).
9. Jagusch, "First Among Equals," 124.
10. Caroline Hewins, *Boys and Girls Books in the Hartford Public Library*, 2nd ed. (Hartford, CT: Hartford Public Library, 1995).
11. Hewins, *Books for Boys and Girls*, 3rd ed., 1915.
12. Eulalie Steinmetz Ross, *The Spirited Life: Bertha Mahony Miller and Children's Books.* Selected bibliography compiled by Virginia Haviland (Boston: Horn Book, 1973), 13.
13. Earl Barnes, "A New Profession for Women," *Atlantic Monthly*, August 1915, 234.
14. Bertha E. Mahony and Elinor Whitney, comps., *Five Years of Children's Books* (Garden City, NY: Doubleday, Doran, 1936), vii.
15. Among the newcomers were Siri Andrews, from the School of Librarianship of the University of Washington in Seattle, Washington; Gladys English, Director of Children's Work at the Los Angeles Public Library; Leone Garvey from Berkeley, California, and Della McGregor, Supervisor of Children's Work at the St. Paul Public Library, in St. Paul, Minnesota.
16. Bertha E. Mahony and Elinor Whitney, *Realms of Gold in Children's Books* (Garden City, NY: Doubleday, Doran, 1929).
17. Ibid., 725.
18. Ibid., 727.
19. Mahony and Whitney, *Five Years of Children's Books,* 1.
20. Ibid., 3. Mahony wrote that this achievement was due in part to the people of many countries who had brought "their heritage of Old World traditions and cultures, experience of other ways, wide knowledge and abilities [which had] gone into the making of the rich, multicolored strand . . . the atmosphere and life of America" (2).
21. Bertha E. Mahony, "Adventures Among New Books," *Horn Book Magazine,* November 1926, 22.
22. "Boys and Girls around the World: Points North, South, East and West," *Horn Book Magazine,* November 1931, 361.
23. The following information was gleaned from a translation by Kimiko Abe of Momoko Ishii's *Jido Bungaku no Tabi* (Tokyo: Iwanami Shoten, 1981).
24. Akiko Kurita, "Postwar Children's Book Publishing: Its Turning Points," in Sybille A. Jagusch, ed., *Window on Japan: Japanese Children's Books and Television Today* (Washington, DC: Library of Congress, 1990), 23.
25. Letter from Eleanor Farjeon to Anne Carroll Moore, October 9, 1931. Arendts Collection, New York Public Library.
26. Letter from Eleanor Farjeon to Anne Carroll Moore, September 23, 1960. Arendts Collection, New York Public Library.
27. She held this position, the most important in the United States, until her retirement in 1941, when she accepted a teaching appointment at the Graduate School of Librarianship at the University of California, Berkeley.
28. Annie [sic] Carroll Moore, *Roads to Childhood: Views and Reviews of Children's Books,* (New York: George H. Doran, 1920), 82–84.
29. Annie [sic] Carroll Moore, *A List of Books Recommended for a Children's Library,* compiled for the Iowa Library Commission (Des Moines: Iowa Printing Company, 1903), 3.
30. Anne Carroll Moore, *Children's Books of Yesterday: An Exhibition from Many Countries* (New York: New York Public Library, 1933), 5.
31. Tamiyo Togasaki, *Japanese Children's Books on Exhibition in the Central Children's Room* (New York: New York Public Library, 1972).
32. That year Haviland became the children's librarian at the Library's Philipps Brooks Branch where she worked until 1948, when she was promoted to branch librarian; then, in 1952, she was promoted to the position of Reader's Advisor in the Open Shelf Department. (In 1951, Haviland began reviewing for the *Horn Book Magazine* for which she served as associate editor from 1952 until 1963, and remained a reviewer until her retirement from the Library of Congress in 1981).
33. Frances Clarke Sayers, *Children's Books in the Library of Congress: A Report Based on a Study Made at the Request of the Librarian of Congress and a Joint Committee of the American Association of University Women and the Association for Childhood Education International, April 1–June 30, 1952* (Washington, DC: Library of Congress, 1952).
34. Virginia Haviland (1911–1988), *Serving Those Who Serve Children: A National Reference Library of Children's Books.* Reprinted from the *Quarterly Journal of the Library of Congress* (Washington, DC: Library of Congress, 1966).
35. One of the new resources was *Children's Books in Print* (1969), an annual bibliography published by the Bowker Company. A title, author, and illustrator index to 35,000 children's books available in the United States that year, it was based on entries from publishers' current and backlist catalogs. The following year, Bowker added the *Subject Guide to Children's Books in Print* (1970).
36. Virginia Haviland, *The Wide World of Children's Books: An Exhibition for International Book Year* (Washington, DC: The Library of Congress, 1972), iii.
37. Virginia Haviland and Lois Watt, comps., *Children's Books 1964: A List of 200 Books for Preschool Through Junior High School Age* (Washington, DC: Library of Congress, 1965).
38. Virginia Haviland. "One Critic's Philosophy of Reviewing." Draft statement prepared for her panel presentation at the

Association for Childhood Education International—Children's Book Council program: "The Many Ways of Looking at Children's Books," ACEI Conference, Washington, DC, April 15, 1974. Children's Literature Center, Library of Congress. Emphasis in original.

39. Virginia Haviland, "The Master Puppeteer," *Horn Book Magazine,* April 1976, 157–158; "The Sign of the Chrysanthemum," *Horn Book Magazine,* October 1973, 468.

40. Beryl Robinson, "Of Nightingales That Weep," *Horn Book Magazine,* February 1975, 53.

41. The proceedings were published in Sybille A. Jagusch, ed., *Stepping Away from Tradition: Children's Books of the Twenties and Thirties* (Washington, DC: Library of Congress, 1988). An appendix lists the symposium attendees' names.

42. Aside from the speakers John Tebbel, Abe Lerner, Anne MacLeod, and Mildred Batchelder, the guest list included many distinguished names. Among those representing the leading libraries were Helen Canfield (Hartford, CT), Carolyn W. Field (Philadelphia), Amy Kellman (Pittsburgh), Angeline Moscatt (New York), Barbara Moody (Baltimore), Margaret Maloney and Judith St. John (current and past directors of the Osborne Collection, Toronto Public Library).

Children's book editors included Grace Hogarth, Margaret K. McElderry, Mary Silva Cosgrave, Susan Hirschmann, Jean Karl, Barbara Lucas, and Charlotte Zolotow. Anita Silvey and Ethel and Paul Heins were current and past editors of the *Horn Book Magazine.*

Among the writers, critics, and educators were Michael Patrick Hearn, James H. Fraser, Selma Lanes, Nancy Larrick, and Selma K. Richardson. Others were John Donovan, executive director, Children's Book Council, Barbara Atkinson, Reading is Fundamental, and Ann Weeks, Association for Library Service for Children, American Library Association. The reticent children's book illustrator Robert McCloskey traveled all the way from his island in Maine.

ACKNOWLEDGMENTS

1. Mr. Sato is founder of Koguma Publishing and a much honored member of Japan's children's book and library community.

2. The lecture "Japan in American Children's Books from Commodore Perry to Today" was delivered on March 28, 2002, at the Beinecke Rare Book & Manuscript Library, Yale University.

3. The publication was designed by John Michael of Acorn Press who produced many of the Center's exquisite program keepsakes.

SELECTED BIBLIOGRAPHY AND FURTHER READING

WORKS FOR ADULTS

Alcock, Rutherford. *Capital of the Tycoon: A Narrative of a Three Years' Residence in Japan.* London: Longman, Green, Longman, Roberts & Green, 1863.

Allen, Bernard M. *The Rt. Hon. Sir Ernest Satow, G.C.M.G., A Memoir.* London: Kegan, Paul, Trench, Trubner, 1933.

American Library Association. *Notable Children's Books, 1940–1970.* Chicago: American Library Association, 1977.

Avery, Gillian. *Behold the Child: American Children and Their Books.* Baltimore: Johns Hopkins University Press, 1995.

Bacon, Alice. *Japanese Girls and Women.* Boston: Houghton Mifflin, 1891.

Baelz, Toku, ed. *Awakening Japan: The Diary of a German Doctor: Erwin Baelz.* Translated by Eden and Cedar Paul. New York: Viking, 1932.

Barr, Pat. *The Coming of the Barbarians: The Opening of Japan to the West, 1853–1870.* New York: E. P. Dutton, 1967.

———. *The Deer Cry Pavilion: A Story of Westerners in Japan, 1868–1905.* New York: Harcourt, Brace & World, 1969.

Bingham, Jane and Grayce Scholt. *Fifteen Centuries of Children's Literature: An Annotated Chronology of British and American Works in Historical Context.* Westport, CT: Greenwood Press, 1980.

Blomhoff, Jan Cock. *The Court Journey to the Shōgun of Japan: From a Private Account by Jan Cock Blomhoff.* Edited by F. R. Effert. Leiden: Hotei Publishing, 2000.

Bramhall, Mae St. John. *The Wee Ones of Japan.* New York: Harper & Brothers, 1894.

Caiger, George. *Tell Me about Tokyo.* Tokyo: Hokuseido Press, 1939.

Carrothers, Julia. *The Sunrise Kingdom, or Life and Scenes in Japan and Woman's Work for Woman There.* Philadelphia: Presbyterian Board of Publication, 1879.

Carus, Marianne, ed. *Celebrate Cricket: 30 Years of Stories and Art.* Chicago: Cricket Books, 2003.

Children's Catalog. A Guide to the Best Reading for Young People Based on Twenty-four Selected Library Lists, first published in 1909 by H. W. Wilson.

Children's Books in the Rare Book Division in the Library of Congress. Totowa, NJ: Rowman and Littlefield, 1975.

Children's Books Suggested as Holiday Gifts. New York: New York Public Library, 1938.

Clark, E. Warren. *Life and Adventure in Japan.* New York: American Tract Society, 1878.

Cooper, Michael, ed. *The Southern Barbarians: The First Europeans in Japan.* Tokyo: Kodansha International in cooperation with Sophia University, 1971.

Cortazzi, Hugh. *Isles of Gold: Antique Maps of Japan.* New York: Weatherhill, 1983.

Darton, F. J. Harvey. *Children's Books in England: Five Centuries of Social Life.* Cambridge: Cambridge University Press, 1932.

De Bodt, Saskia. *Kinderen van Holland: Het beeld van Nederland in Amerikaanse Kinderboeken.* Harderwijk: D'Jonge Hond, Koninklijke Bibliotheek, 2009.

Dower, John W. *Embracing Defeat: Japan in the Wake of World War II.* New York: W. W. Norton/The New Press, 1999.

Freeman, Ruth S. *Yesterday's School Books.* Watkins Glen, NY: Century House, 1960.

Fukuzawa, Yukichi. *The Autobiography of Yukichi Fukuzawa.* Tokyo: Hokuseido Press, 1948.

Goodrich, Samuel Griswold. *Recollections of a Lifetime, or, Men and Things I Have Seen; In a Series of Familiar Letters to a Friend, Historical, Biographical, Anecdotal, and Descriptive.* Detroit: Gale Research Company, 1967. First published 1856.

Gordon, Rev. Marquis Lafayette. *An American Missionary in Japan.* Boston: Houghton Mifflin, 1892.

Gribbin, Jill. *Japanese Antique Dolls.* New York: Weatherhill, 1984.

Griffis, William E. *Hepburn of Japan and his Wife and Helpmates.* Philadelphia: Westminster Press, 1913.

———. *The Mikado's Empire.* New York: Harper & Brothers, 1876.

Haar, Francis. *The Best of Old Japan.* Rutland, VT: Charles E. Tuttle, 1951.

Haviland, Virginia. *Children's Literature: A Guide to Reference Sources.* Washington, DC: Library of Congress, 1966.

———. *The Travelogue Storybook of the Nineteenth Century.* Boston: Horn Book, 1950.

———. *Yankee Doodle's Literary Sampler of Prose, Poetry, & Pictures; Being an Anthology of Diverse Works Published for the Edification and/or Entertainment of Young Readers in America before 1900.* New York: Thomas Y. Crowell, 1974.

Hersey, John. *Hiroshima.* New York: Alfred A. Knopf, 1946.

Hewins, Caroline M. *Books for Boys and Girls: A Selected List.* 2nd ed., rev. Boston: ALA Publishing Board, 1904.

———. *Books for the Young: A Guide for Parents and Children.* New York: F. Leypoldt, 1882.

———. *A Mid-Century Child and Her Books.* New York: Macmillan, 1926.

Hodowanec, George V., ed. *The May Massee Collection: Creative Publishing for Children, 1923–1963, A Checklist.* Emporia, KS: Emporia State University, 1979.

Humbert, Aimé. *Japan and the Japanese.* Translated by Mrs. Chashel Hoey and edited by H. W. Bates. New York: D. Appleton, 1874.

Hürliman, Bettina. *Three Centuries of Children's Books in Europe.* Cleveland: World Publishing Company, 1968.

Jagusch, Sybille A. "First Among Equals: Caroline M. Hewins and Anne C. Moore, Foundations of Library Work with Children." PhD diss., University of Maryland, 1990.

———, ed. *Japanese Children's Books at the Library of Congress: A Bibliography of Books from the Post-War Years, 1946–1985.* Compiled by Tayo Shima. Washington, DC: Library of Congress, 1987.

———, ed. *Stepping Away from Tradition: Children's Books of the Twenties and Thirties.* Washington, DC: Library of Congress, 1988.

———, ed. *Window on Japan: Japanese Children's Books and Television Today.* Washington, DC: Library of Congress, 1990.

Jordan, Alice M. *From Rollo to Tom Sawyer.* Boston: Horn Book, 1948.

Japanese Board on Books for Young People. *Japanese Children's Picture Books and Original Illustrations in Celebration of World Congress on Children's Books. 20th IBBY Congress –Tokyo, August 1986.* Tokyo: Japanese Board on Books for Young People and the Asahi Shimbun, 1986.

Johnson, Clifton. *Old-Time Schools and School-Books.* New York: Macmillan, 1917.

Kaempfer, Engelbert. *Geschichte und Beschreibung von Japan. Aus den Originalhandschriften des Verfassers hrsg. von Christian Wilhelm Dohm. Erster Band [and] zweiter und lezter Band. Mit Kupfern und Charten.* [Two vols.] Lemgo: Im Verlage der Meyerschen Buchhandlung, 1777, 1779.

———. *The History of Japan, Together with a Description of the Kingdom of Siam, 1690–92.* Translated by J. G. Scheuchzer. Three vols. Glasgow: James MacLehose and Sons, 1906.

———. *Kaempfer's Japan: Tokugawa Culture Observed.* Edited, translated, and annotated by Beatrice M. Bodart-Bailey. Honolulu: University of Hawaii Press, 1999.

Keene, Donald. *Bunraku: The Art of the Japanese Puppet Theatre.* Tokyo: Kodansha International, 1965.

———. *The Japanese Discovery of Europe: Honda Toshiaki and Other Discoverers, 1720–1798.* London: Routlege and Kegan Paul, 1952.

———. *Nō: The Classical Theatre of Japan.* Tokyo: Kodansha International, 1966.

Keene, Donald, Anne Nishimura Morse, Frederic A. Sharf, and Louise E. Virgin. *Japan at the Dawn of the Modern Age: Woodblock Prints from the Meiji Era, 1868–1912.* Boston: Museum of Fine Arts, Boston, 2001.

Kelly, R. Gordon, ed. *Children's Periodicals of the United States.* Westport, CT: Greenwood Press, 1984.

Kenrick, Douglas Moore. *A Century of Western Studies of Japan: The First Hundred Years of the Asiatic Society of Japan, 1872–1972.* Tokyo: Asiatic Society of Japan, 1978.

Kiefer, Monica. *American Children through Their Books, 1700–1835.* Philadelphia: University of Pennsylvania Press, 1948.

Koizumi, Kazuo, compiler. *More Letters from Basil Hall Chamberlain to Lafcadio Hearn and Letters from M. Toyama, Y. Tsubouchi and Others.* Tokyo: Hokuseido Press, 1937.

Kunitake, Kume, compiler. *The Iwakura Embassy, 1871–73.* Edited by Graham Healey and Chushichi Tsuzuki. Vol. 1, *The United States of America.* Translated by Martin Collcutt. Chiba, Japan: Japan Documents, 2002.

Lancaster, Clay. *The Japanese Influence in America.* New York: Walton H. Rawls, 1963.

Lanman, Charles. *The Japanese in America.* New York: University Publishing Company, 1872.

———. *Leaders of the Meiji Restoration in America.* Tokyo: Hokuseido Press, 1931.

———. *Leading Men of Japan.* Boston: D. Lothrop, 1883.

Lindquist, Jennie. *Caroline M. Hewins, Her Book.* Boston: Horn Book, 1954.

Loti, Pierre. *Madame Chrysanthème.* Translated by Laura Ensor. Paris: Edouard Guillaume et Cie, 1889.

Mahony, Bertha E. and Elinor Whitney. *Realms of Gold in Children's Books.* Garden City, NY: Doubleday, Doran, 1929.

———, compilers. *Five Years of Children's Books.* Garden City, NY: Doubleday, Doran, 1936.

Makino, Yasuko. *Japan through Children's Literature: An Annotated Bibliography.* Westport, CT: Greenwood Press, 1985.

Maruki, Toshi. *The Hiroshima Panels: Joint Works of Iri and Toshi Maruki.* Tokyo: Komine Shoten, 2000.

Mears, Helen. *Year of the Wild Boar: An American Woman in Japan.* New York: J. B. Lippincott, 1942.

Meech-Pekarik, Julia. *The World of the Meiji Print: Impressions of a New Civilization.* New York: Weatherhill, 1987.

Meier-Lemgo, Karl. *Engelbert Kaempfer (1651–1716) erforscht das seltsame Asien.* Hamburg: Cram, De Gruyter, 1960.

Milton, Giles. *Samurai William: The Englishman Who Opened Japan.* New York: Farrar, Straus and Giroux, 2002.

Mitford, Algernon Bertram Freeman, Lord Redesdale. *Mitford's Japan: The Memoirs and Recollections, 1866–1906, of Algernon Bertram Mitford, the first Lord Redesdale.* Edited by Hugh Cortazzi. London: Athlone Press, 1985.

———. *Tales of Old Japan.* London: Macmillan, 1871.

Moon, Marjorie. *John Harris's Books for Youth, 1801–1843.* Kent: Dawson Publishing, 1992.

Moore, Anne Carroll. *Children's Books of Yesterday: An Exhibition from Many Countries.* New York: New York Public Library, 1933.

Murasaki, Shikibu. *The Tale of Genji.* Translated by Arthur Waley. London: George Allen & Unwin, 1929.

Nietz, John A. *Old Textbooks: Spelling, Grammar, Reading, Arithmetic, Geography, American History, Civil Government, Physiology, Penmanship, Art, Music, as Taught in the Common Schools from Colonial Days to 1900.* Pittsburgh: University of Pittsburgh Press, 1961.

Okada, John. *No-No Boy.* Rutland, VT: Charles E. Tuttle, 1957.

Ono, Setsuko. "A Western Image of Japan: What did the West see through the Eyes of Loti and Hearn?" PhD diss., Université de Genève, 1972.

Ota, Yuzo. *Basil Hall Chamberlain: Portrait of a Japanologist.* Richmond, UK: Japan Library, 1998.

Perry, Matthew Calbraith. *Narrative of the Expedition of an American Squadron to the China Seas and Japan, Performed in the Years 1852, 1853, and 1854, under the Command of Commodore M. C. Perry, United States Navy, by Order of the Government of the United States.* New York: Appleton, 1856.

Pierpont Morgan Library. *Early Children's Books and Their Illustration.* Boston: D. R. Godine, 1975.

Potter, Marion E., compiler. *Children's Catalog: A Guide to the Best Reading for Young People Based on Twenty-Four Selected Library Lists.* Minneapolis: H. W. Wilson, 1909.

Rein, Johann Justus. *Japan nach Reisen und Studien, im Auftrage der Königlich Preussischen Regierung.* Leipzig: Wilhelm Engelmann, 1881–1886.

Rogala, Joseph, compiler. *A Collector's Guide to Books on Japan in English.* Richmond, UK: Japan Library, 2001.

Roselle, Daniel. *Samuel Griswold Goodrich, Creator of Peter Parley: A Study of his Life and Work.* Albany: State University of New York Press, 1968.

Ross, Eulalie Steinmetz. *The Spirited Life: Bertha Mahony Miller and Children's Books.* Bibliography compiled by Virginia Haviland. Boston: Horn Book, 1973.

Sayers, Frances Clarke. *Anne Carroll Moore: A Biography.* New York: Atheneum, 1972.

———. *Children's Books in the Library of Congress: A Report Based on a Study Made at the Request of the Librarian of Congress and a Joint Committee of the American Association of University Women and the Association for Childhood Education International, April 1–June 30, 1952.* Washington, DC: Library of Congress, 1952.

Scidmore, Eliza Ruhamah. *Jinrikisha Days in Japan.* New York: Harper & Brothers, 1891.

Schmiedel, Otto. *Die Deutschen in Japan.* Leipzig: Verlag von K. F. Koehler, 1920.

Sears, Minnie Earl, compiler. *Children's Catalog.* 3rd ed., revised and enlarged. New York: H. W. Wilson, 1926.

Sebald, William Joseph. *With MacArthur in Japan: A Personal History of the Occupation.* With Russell Brines. New York: W. W. Norton, 1965.

Sharf, Frederic. *Takejiro Hasegawa: Meiji Japan's Preeminent Publisher of Wood-Block-Illustrated Crepe-Paper Books.* Peabody Essex Museum Collections, vol. 130, no. 4 Salem, MA: Peabody Essex Museum, 1994.

St. John, Judith. *The Osborne Collection of Early Children's Books.* Two vols. Toronto: Toronto Public Library, 1958.

Statler, Oliver. *The Black Ship Scroll.* Rutland, VT: Charles E. Tuttle, 1963.

———. *Japanese Inn.* New York: Random House, 1961.

Sugimoto, Etsu Inagaki. *A Daughter of the Samurai.* Garden City, NY: Doubleday, Doran, 1934.

Tanizaki, Jun'ichiro. *Childhood Years: A Memoir.* Translated by Paul McCarthy. Tokyo: Kodansha International, 1988.

Taylor, Dorothy Loring. *Olive Beaupré Miller and the Bookhouse for Children.* Chicago: Chicago Review Press, 1986.

Teleki, Paul Graf. *Atlas zur Geschichte der Kartographie der Japanischen Inseln.* Leipzig: Karl W. Hiesemann, 1909.

Togasaki, Tamiyo. *Japanese Children's Books on Exhibition in the Central Children's Room.* New York: New York Public Library, 1972.

van Rij, Jan. *Madame Butterfly: Japonisme, Puccini, & the Search for the Real Cho-Cho-San.* Berkeley, CA: Stone Bridge Press, 2001.

Vining, Elizabeth Gray. *Return to Japan.* New York: J. B. Lippincott, 1960.

———. *Windows for the Crown Prince.* Philadelphia: Lippincott, 1952.

Welch, d'Alté A. *A Bibliography of American Children's Books Printed Prior to 1821.* Worcester, MA: American Antiquarian Society, 1972.

Yashima, Taro. *Horizon is Calling.* New York: Henry Holt, 1947.

———. *The New Sun.* New York: Henry Holt, 1943.

Yoshikawa, Eiji. *The Heike Story.* New York: Alfred A. Knopf, 1956.

MANUSCRIPTS

Kazue Mizumura Papers. Author's collection.

Kirk Munroe Papers, 1850–1930. Manuscript Division, Library of Congress, Washington, DC.

William Speiden Papers. Manuscript Division, Library of Congress, Washington, DC.

Yoshiko Uchida Papers. Bancroft Library, University of California, Berkeley.

Clara W. Whitney Papers, 1872–1975. Manuscript Division, Library of Congress, Washington, DC.

WORKS FOR CHILDREN

Adams, Thomas F. M. *The Adventures of Billie and Belinda in Tokyo.* Tokyo: S. Okuyama, 1953.

Allen, Willis Boyd. *The North Pacific: A Story of the Russo Japanese War.* New York: Dutton, 1905.

American Japanese Riding, Coloring and Talking Book. Tokyo: Charles E. Tuttle, 1952.

Anno, Mitsumasa. *Ehon Heike monogatari.* Tokyo: Kodansha, 1996.

Atlas Minimus, or A New Set of Pocket Maps of the Several Empires, Kingdoms, and States of the Known World, with Historical Extracts relative to each Drawn and Engrav'd by J. Gibson. London: J. Newbery, 1758.

Ayrton, Matilda Chaplin. *Child-Life in Japan and Japanese Child Stories.* London: Griffith and Farrar, 1879.

Baruch, Dorothy Walter. *Kobo and the Wishing Pictures.* Rutland, VT: Charles E. Tuttle, 1964.

Blumberg, Rhoda. *Commodore Perry in the Land of the Shogun.* New York: Lothrop, Lee & Shepard, 1985.

———. *Shipwrecked! The True Adventures of a Japanese Boy.* New York: HarperCollins, 2001.

Brain, Belle M. *All about Japan: Stories of Sunrise Land Told for Little Folks.* New York: Young People's Missionary Movement, 1905.

Burke, Stella. *Children of Japan.* Chicago: Rand McNally, 1936.

Butterworth, Hezekiah. *Zigzag Journeys around the World.* Boston: Estes and Lauriat, 1895.

Caldwell, John C. *Let's Visit Japan.* New York: John Day, 1959.

Choi, Sook Nyul. *Year of Impossible Goodbyes.* Boston: Houghton Mifflin, 1991.

Coatsworth, Elizabeth. *The Cat Who Went to Heaven.* New York: Macmillan, 1930.

Coerr, Eleanor. *Sadako and the Thousand Paper Cranes.* New York: Putnam, 1977.

Comenius, Johann Amos. *Orbis sensualium pictus . . . Comenius's Visible World, or A Picture and Nomenclature of all the Chief Things Suitable to Children's Capacities . . .* Translated by Charles Hoole. London: Printed for J. Kirton, 1664.

The Costume, Manners, and Peculiarities of Different Inhabitants of the Globe Calculated to Instruct and Amuse the Little Folks of all Countries. London: Printed for J. Harris, 1822.

Cook, Canfield. *Wings over Japan.* New York: Grosset & Dunlap, 1944.

Dalton, William. *The English Boy in Japan; or, The Perils and Adventures of Mark Raffles among Princes, Priests, and People, of That Singular Empire.* London: T. Nelson and Sons, 1858.

Dodge, Mary Mapes. *Hans Brinker, or The Silver Skates.* New York: Grosset & Dunlap, 1963. First published 1865.

Dwight, Nathaniel. *A Short but Comprehensive System of the Geography of the World: By Way of Question and Answer, Principally Designed for Children and Common Schools.* Boston: Printed by Manning & Loring, for West & Greenleaf, 1801.

Edelman, Lily. *Japan in Stories and Pictures.* New York: Harcourt, Brace, 1953.

Edwards, Eva D. *Haruko, Child of Japan.* San Francisco: Harr Wagner, 1934.

Fenollosa, Mary. *Blossoms from a Japanese Garden.* London: William Heinemann, 1913.

Finnemore, John. *Peeps at Many Lands: Japan.* London: A. and C. Black, 1907.

Floethe, Louise and Richard. *A Thousand and One Buddhas.* New York: Farrar, Straus & Giroux, 1967.

Gaines, Ruth. *Treasure Flower: A Child of Japan.* New York: E. P. Dutton, 1916.

Geography Made Familiar and Easy to Young Gentlemen and Ladies. London: printed for J. Newbery, 1748.

Goodrich, Samuel G. *The Tales of Peter Parley about Asia.* Philadelphia: Desilver, Thomas, 1836.

Greey, Edward. *The Bear-Worshippers of Yezo and the Island of Karafuto (Saghalin).* Boston: Lee and Shepard, 1884.

———. *The Wonderful City of Tokio; or, Further Adventures of the Jewett Family and Their Friend Oto Nambo.* Boston: Lee and Shepard, 1883.

———. *Young Americans in Japan; or, The Adventures of the Jewett Family and Their Friend Oto Nambo*. Boston: Lee and Shepard, 1882.

Griffis, William Elliot. *Japanese Fairy World: Stories from the Wonder-lore of Japan*. Schenectady, NY: James H. Barhyte, 1880.

Haines, Alice Calhoun. *Japanese Child Life*. New York: Frederick A. Stokes, 1905.

———. *Little Japs at Home*. New York: Frederick A. Stokes, 1905.

Halladay, Anne M. *Toshio and Tama: Children of the New Japan*. New York: Friendship Press, 1949.

Hamanaka, Sheila. *In Search of the Spirit: The Living National Treasures of Japan*. New York: Morrow Junior Books, 1999.

———. *The Journey: Japanese Americans, Racism, and Renewal*. New York: Orchard Books, 1990.

Hearn, Lafcadio. *The Boy Who Drew Cats*. Washington, DC: Library of Congress, 1987. First published 1898.

Hedrick, Elinor and Kathryne Van Noy. *Kites and Kimonos*. New York: Macmillan, 1936.

Hicks, Eleanor B. *Circus Day in Japan*. Rutland, VT: Charles E. Tuttle, 1953.

Hodges, Margaret. *The Wave*. Boston: Houghton Mifflin, 1964.

Hoobler, Dorothy and Thomas. *The Japanese American Family Album*. New York: Oxford University Press, 1996.

———. *A Samurai Never Fears Death*. New York: Sleuth/Philomel, 2007.

Houston, Jeanne Wakatsuki and James D. *Farewell to Manzanar*. Boston: Houghton Mifflin, 1973.

Hungerford, Edward. *Forbidden Island*. Chicago: Wilcox & Follett, 1950.

Hyde, Mabel. *Jingles from Japan as Set Forth by the Ghinks*. San Francisco: A. M. Robertson, 1901.

Igus, Toyomi. *The Two Mrs. Gibsons*. San Francisco: Children's Book Press, 1996.

James, Grace. *Green Willow and Other Japanese Fairy Tales*. London: Macmillan, 1910.

Kajikawa, Kimiko. *Tsunami!* New York: Philomel, 2009.

Knox, Thomas W. *Adventures of Two Youths in a Journey to Japan and China*. New York: Harper & Brothers, 1879.

Levine, Israel E. *Behind the Silken Curtain: The Story of Townsend Harris*. New York: Julian Messner, 1961.

Lifton, Betty Jean. *Chirps from a Bamboo Cage*. Tokyo: Tokyo News Services, 1954.

———. *Return to Hiroshima*. New York: Atheneum, 1970.

Little, Frances. *Little Sister Snow*. New York: Century, 1909.

Maruki, Toshi. *Hiroshima no Pika*. New York: Lothrop, Lee & Shepard, 1980.

Matsui, Tadashi. *Onriku and the Carpenter*. Englewood Cliffs, NJ: Prentice-Hall, 1963.

Matsuno Masako. *A Pair of Red Clogs*. Cleveland: World Publishing Company, 1960.

Matsutani, Miyoko. *The Crane Maiden*. New York: Parents' Magazine Press, 1968.

Mayer, Henry. *The Adventures of a Japanese Doll*. New York: E. P. Dutton, 1901.

McConnell, Margaret. *Bobo the Barrage Balloon*. New York: Lothrop, Lee & Shepard, 1943.

McNeer, Mary and Lynd Ward. *Prince Bantam: Being the Adventures of Yoshitsune the Brave and His Faithful Henchman Great Benkei of the Western Pagoda*. New York: Macmillan, 1929.

Meadowcroft, Enid La Monte. *Aren't We Lucky!* New York: Thomas Y. Crowell, 1939.

Means, Florence Crannell. *The Moved-Outers*. Boston: Houghton Mifflin, 1945.

Mears, Helen. *The First Book of Japan*. New York: Franklin Watts, 1953.

Miller, Olive Beaupré. *Little Pictures of Japan*. Chicago: Book House for Children, 1925.

Mochizuki, Ken. *Baseball Saved Us*. New York: Lee & Low Books, 1993.

Morimoto, Junko. *My Hiroshima*. New York: Viking, 1990.

Morpurgo, Michael. *Kensuke's Kingdom*. London: Egmont, 1999.

Morse, Jedidiah. *Geography Made Easy: Being an Abridgement of the American Universal Geography*. 10th ed. Boston: J. T. Buckingham for Thomas & Andrews, 1806.

Say, Allen. *The Bicycle Man*. Boston: Houghton Mifflin, 1982.

———. *Drawing from Memory*. New York: Scholastic Press, 2011.

———. *Grandfather's Journey*. Boston: Houghton Mifflin, 1993.

———. *Music for Alice*. Boston: Houghton Mifflin, 2004.

Scrogin, Margaret and Raymond Chang. *In the Eye of War*. New York: Margaret K. McElderry Books, 1990.

Shioya, Sakae. *When I Was a Boy in Japan*. Boston: Lothrop, Lee & Shepard, 1906.

Shigemi, Shiukichi. *A Japanese Boy, By Himself*. New Haven, CT: E. B. Sheldon, 1889.

Slobodkin, Louis. *Yasu and the Strangers*. New York, Macmillan, 1965.

Smyth, Lindley. *True Stories about Children of All Nations*. Philadelphia: World Bible House, 1906.

Sōjō, Toba. *The Animal Frolic*. Text by Velma Varner. New York: G. P. Putnam's Sons, 1954.

Spivak, Dawnine. *Grass Sandals: The Travels of Basho*. New York: Athenaeum Books for Young Readers, 1997.

Stokes, Katherine. *The Motor Maids in Japan*. Chicago: M. A. Donohue, 1913.

Taylor, Isaac. *Scenes in Asia: For the Amusement and Instruction of Little Tarry-at-Home Travellers*. London, Printed for Harris and Son, 1819.

Uchida, Yoshiko. *The Bracelet*. New York: Philomel Books, 1993.

———. *Desert Exile: The Uprooting of a Japanese American Family*. Seattle: University of Washington Press, 1982.

———. *The Full Circle*. New York: Friendship Press, 1957.

———. *The Invisible Thread: An Autobiography*. Englewood Cliffs, NJ: Julian Messner, 1991.

———. *A Jar of Dreams*. New York: Atheneum, 1981.

———. *Journey Home*. New York: Margaret K. McElderry Books, an imprint of Simon & Schuster, 1978.

———. *Journey to Topaz: A Story of the Japanese-American Evacuation*. New York: Charles Scribner's Sons, 1971.

Venning, Mary Anne. *A Geographical Present: Being Descriptions of the Principal Countries of the World*. London: Printed for Darton, Harvey, and Darton, 1818.

Van Loon, Hendrik. *Around the World with the Alphabet and Hendrik Willem van Loon: To Teach Little Children Their Letters and at the Same Time Give Their Papas and Mamas Something to Think about*. New York: Simon and Schuster, 1935.

Vining, Elizabeth Gray. *The Cheerful Heart*. New York: Viking, 1959.

Weaver, Gustine. *The House That a Jap Built*. Chicago: Reilly & Britton, 1909.

Yashima, Taro. *Crow Boy*. New York: Viking, 1955.

———. *The Seashore Story*. New York: Viking Books for Young Readers, 1967.

———. *The Village Tree*. New York: Viking, 1953.

———. *Umbrella*. New York: Viking, 1959.

Yashima, Mitsu and Taro Yashima. *Plenty to Watch*. New York: Viking, 1954.

Yaukey, Grace Sydenstricker [Cornelia Spencer, pseud.] *Japan*. New York: Holiday House, 1948.

ILLUSTRATION AND TEXT EXCERPT CREDITS

All of the reproduced text and images in this volume come from books in the Library of Congress's collections unless otherwise noted. Some images were made from books in the author's personal collection; if that book also exists in the Library's collections, the Library's call number has been given.

ILLUSTRATION CREDITS

Cover

Jagusch Collection, PZ7. B28568 Ch 1953. Courtesy of John Pogany.

Note to the Reader

N.1: General Collection, Z1037.8. J3 L53 1987.
N.2: General Collection, Z1037.8. J3 W56 1990.

Prologue

P.1: Rare Book and Special Collections Division, LT101. C5 1664.
P.2: Geography and Map Division, G7401. A9 1772. A8.
P.3: Geography and Map Division, G1015. G5 1758.
P.4: Jagusch Collection.
P.5: Jagusch Collection.
P.6: Jagusch Collection, G125. V46 1829.
P.7: Jagusch Collection.
P.8: Jagusch Collection.
P.9: Jagusch Collection.
P.10: Jagusch Collection.
P.11: Rare Book and Special Collections Division, G133. S14 1830z.
P.12: General Collection, DS809. M28 1841a.

Chapter 1

1.1: Prints and Photographs Division, LC-DIG-ds-13956.
1.2: Prints and Photographs Division, LC-DIG-pga-10330.
1.3: MSS 83045: Box 1, William Speiden Journals, Naval Historical Foundation Collection, Manuscript Division.
1.4: Asian Division, DS881.8. K56 1854.
1.5 and 1.6: General Collection, GR340. R3 1871.
1.7: Jagusch Collection, PS3513. I555 J5 1901.
1.8–1.10: General Collection, DS825. A95.
1.11: Jagusch Collection, DS809. C31.
1.12: General Collection, PE1130. J3 G87.
1.13: Jagusch Collection, PZ8. G875 F.
1.14: General Collection, PZ8. G875 Jap.

Chapter 2

2.1: General Collection, PZ7. D664 Han 1918.
2.2: Jagusch Collection, G570. B85.
2.3: Jagusch Collection, G570. K74 1880.
2.4: Rare Book and Special Collections Division, G570. K74 1880.
2.5: Jagusch Collection.
2.6 and 2.7: Jagusch Collection, DS809. G82.
2.8: Rare Book and Special Collections Division, DS809. G817.
2.9 and 2.10: General Collection, DS809. G815.
2.11 and 2.12: Jagusch Collection, DS832. G81.
2.13: Jagusch Collection, PZ7. S91 Unto.
2.14: Jagusch Collection, PZ7. M926 Fo.
2.15: Jagusch Collection, PZ7. M926 So.
2.16: General Collection, PZ7. H273 O.
2.17: General Collection, PZ3. M12 Li.
2.18: General Collection, PZ9. G127 T.

Chapter 3

3.1: General Collection, DS897. T6 C3.
3.2: Jagusch Collection, DS825. S5.
3.3: General Collection, DS809. R349.
3.4: Jagusch Collection, DS821. S6426 1892, Oliver Wendell Holmes Collection.

3.5: Rare Book and Special Collections Division, PZ8. K5275 D39 1894.
3.6: Jagusch Collection, DS825. B8.
3.7: Rare Book and Special Collections Division, PZ8. J272 no. 2.
3.8: Rare Book and Special Collections Division, PZ8. J27 no. 6b.
3.9: Special Collections and University Archives, Rutgers University Libraries.
3.10: Rare Book and Special Collections Division, PZ8. C3383 H868 1887.
3.11: Rare Book and Special Collections Division, PZ8. J272 no. 10, Holmes Collection.
3.12: Rare Book and Special Collections Division, PZ8. J272 2nd ser., no. 1.
3.13: Rare Book and Special Collections Division, PZ8. J272 no. 23.

Chapter 4

4.2: Prints and Photographs Division, LC-DIG-ppmsca-43376.
4.6: Jagusch Collection, PZ8.3.F366 Bl 1913, Joseph and Elizabeth Robins Pennell Collection.
All other illustrations in this chapter: General Collection, AP201. S3.

Chapter 5

5.1: Jagusch Collection, DS809. A75.
5.2: Jagusch Collection, DS835. S64.
5.3: Jagusch Collection, G570. R3.
5.4: General Collection, BV2615. C6.
5.5: Jagusch Collection, G370. P69.
5.6–5.8: General Collection, DS835. K2.
5.9: Jagusch Collection.
5.10: General Collection, DS835. G85.
5.11: Jagusch Collection, DS809. H91.
5.12: Jagusch Collection, DS809. Q3.
5.13: General Collection, DS809. A35.
5.14: General Collection, PZ3. V658 J.

Chapter 6

6.1: Jagusch Collection.
6.2: Jagusch Collection.
6.3: Jagusch Collection, PZ9. W119 Oja.
6.4: Jagusch Collection.
6.5 and 6.6: Rare Book and Special Collections Division, PZ8.3. U72 Gj 1896.
6.7: Jagusch Collection.
6.8: Jagusch Collection, PZ7. B28568 Ch 1953. Courtesy of John Pogany.
6.9: Jagusch Collection, PZ7. C153 Sm.
6.10: Jagusch Collection.
6.11: Jagusch Collection.
6.12: Rare Book and Special Collections Division, PZ8.3. T43 J.
6.13 and 6.14: Jagusch Collection, PZ7. P43 J.
6.15: General Collection, PL884. M5.
6.16: General Collection, D21. M6 1929.
6.17: General Collection, PZ7. B7375 Ro.
6.18 and 6.19: General Collection, PE1119. H44.
6.20: General Collection, PZ7. P799 Mag.
6.21: General Collection, PZ10. P442 Strs. Courtesy of Mary Petersham Reinhard.
6.22: General Collection, PZ7. M135 Bo.
6.23: General Collection, GC771. S6.

Chapter 7

7.1–7.3: General Collection, DS810. F4 1907.
7.4: General Collection, DS835. F7. Courtesy of Bloomsbury UK.
7.5 and 7.6: General Collection, DS835. F7.
7.7: Jagusch Collection.
7.8: Jagusch Collection.
7.9: Jagusch Collection, PZ9. R79 Be.
7.10: General Collection, PZ9. H117 Pi.
7.11: Jagusch Collection.
7.12: Jagusch Collection, PZ8.1. M233 Pr.
7.13 and 7.14: Jagusch Collection, PZ10.3. C629 Cat. From *The Cat Who Went to Heaven* by Elizabeth Coatsworth with illustrations by Lynd Ward. Text copyright 1930 by Simon & Schuster, Inc; copyright renewed 1958 by Elizabeth Coatsworth Beston. Illustrations copyright 1958 by Simon & Schuster, Inc. Reprinted with the permission of Simon & Schuster Books for Young Readers, an imprint of Simon & Schuster Children's Publishing Division. All rights reserved.

Chapter 8

8.1: Jagusch Collection, PZ7.P753 Mg. Courtesy of Paul Leo Politi, Suzanne Politi Bischof, and the Leo Politi Family.
8.2: Jagusch Collection.
8.3: Jagusch Collection. Courtesy of Fukuinkan Shoten Publishers.
8.4: General Collection, PZ8.1. H69 Wav. Illustration by Blair Lent from *The Wave* by Margaret Hodges. Illustrations copyright © 1964, renewed 1992 by Blair Lent. Reprinted

by permission of Houghton Mifflin Harcourt Publishing Company. All rights reserved.

8.5: Jagusch Collection, AP201. C8. Courtesy of Tessa van Lankeren.

8.6: Jagusch Collection.

8.7: Jagusch Collection.

8.8: Jagusch Collection, DS811. H2.

8.9 and 8.10: Jagusch Collection.

8.11: General Collection, PZ9. C3743 Ch.

8.12: General Collection, G133. W4.

8.13: Jagusch Collection, DS806. M394.

8.14: Jagusch Collection, PZ7. H154 To.

8.15: Jagusch Collection, PZ7. N4657 Ac.

8.16: Jagusch Collection, PZ3. M46354 Mo. This permission is dedicated to the memory of Joan Crosbie Planek, daughter of Helen Blair Crosbie.

8.17: Jagusch Collection, PZ7. O104 De. Courtesy of Earl Kashiwagi, trustee for Isami Kashiwagi.

Chapter 9

9.1: Jagusch Collection, PZ7. U25 Ss. From *Sumi & the Goat & the Tokyo Express* by Yoshiko Uchida. Copyright © 1969 by Yoshiko Uchida. Reprinted with the permission of Atheneum Books for Young Readers, an imprint of Simon & Schuster Children's Publishing Division. All rights reserved.

9.2: Rare Book and Special Collections Division, PZ7. S2744 Gr 1993. Cover from *Grandfather's Journey* by Allen Say. Copyright © 1993 by Allen Say. Reprinted by permission of Houghton Mifflin Harcourt Publishing Company. All rights reserved.

9.3: Rare Book and Special Collections Division, PZ7. Y212 Vi. Courtesy of Momo Yashima Brannen.

9.4: General Collection, ND1059.6. C46 C46132.

9.5: General Collection, NC1709. Y3 A23. Interior illustration courtesy of Momo Yashima Brannen.

9.6: General Collection, NC1709. Y3 A2. Courtesy of Momo Yashima Brannen.

9.7: Rare Book and Special Collections Division, PZ9. Y27 Pl. Courtesy of Momo Yashima Brannen.

9.8: General Collection, PZ7. Y212 Cr. Courtesy of Momo Yashima Brannen. Illustration from *Crow Boy* by Taro Yashima, copyright © 1955 by Mitsu Yashima and Taro Yashima, renewed 1983 by Taro Yashima. Used by permission of Viking Children's Books, an imprint of Penguin Young Readers Group, a division of Penguin Random House LLC. All rights reserved.

9.9: Rare Book and Special Collections, PZ7. Y212 Um. Courtesy of Momo Yashima Brannen. Illustration from *Umbrella* by Taro Yashima, copyright © 1958 by Taro Yashima, renewed © 1986 by Taro Yashima. Used by permission of Viking Children's Books, an imprint of Penguin Young Readers Group, a division of Penguin Random House LLC. All rights reserved.

9.10: Jagusch Collection, PZ7. B388234 So. Courtesy of Momo Yashima Brannen.

9.11 and 9.12: Courtesy of the Bancroft Library, University of California, Berkeley, BANC MSS 86/97 c.

9.13: Jagusch Collection, PZ8.1. U35 Mag. *The Magic Listening Cap*, PS3541.C3 M35 1955, © The Regents of the University of California, The Bancroft Library, University of California, Berkeley.

9.14: Jagusch Collection, PZ7. U25 Jo. From *Journey to Topaz* by Yoshiko Uchida. Copyright © 1971 by Yoshiko Uchida. Reprinted with the permission of Atheneum Books for Young Readers, an imprint of Simon & Schuster Children's Publishing Division. All rights reserved.

9.15: Jagusch Collection, PZ7. U25 Br 1993. Courtesy of Joanna Yardley.

9.16: Bancroft Library, University of California, Berkeley, BANC MSS 86/97 c.

9.17: Jagusch Collection. Courtesy of the estate of Kazue Mizumura.

9.18: Jagusch Collection. Courtesy of the estate of Kazue Mizumura.

9.19: Jagusch Collection, PZ7. V746 Ch. Courtesy of the estate of Kazue Mizumura.

9.20 and 9.21: Jagusch Collection, PZ7. M43155 Pai. Courtesy of the estate of Kazue Mizumura. Illustrations by Kazue Mizumura, copyright © 1960, renewed 1988 by Kazue Mizumura; from *A Pair of Red Clogs* by Masako Matsuno. Used by permission of Philomel, an imprint of Penguin Young Readers Group, a division of Penguin Random House LLC. All rights reserved.

9.22: General Collection, PZ8.3. M7 I. Courtesy of the estate of Kazue Mizumura.

9.23: Jagusch Collection, PZ8.3. M7 Fl. Courtesy of the estate of Kazue Mizumura.

Chapter 10

10.1: Jagusch Collection, D767.25.H6 M2913 1980. Cover from *Hiroshima No Pika* by Toshi Maruki. Illustrated by: Toshi Maruki. Used by permission of HarperCollins Publishers.

10.2: Rare Book and Special Collections Division, PZ7. W3235 So 1986. From *So Far from the Bamboo Grove* by Yoko Kawashima Watkins. Used by permission of HarperCollins Publishers.

10.3: Jagusch Collection, PZ7. W3235 My 1994. From *My Brother, My Sister, and I* by Yoko Kawashima Watkins. Copyright © 1994 by Yoko Kawashima Watkins. Reprinted with the permission of Simon & Schuster Books for Young Readers, an imprint of Simon & Schuster Children's Publishing Division. All rights reserved.

10.4: Jagusch Collection, PZ7. C44626 Ye 1991. Cover from *Year of Impossible Goodbyes* by Sook Nyul Choi. Copyright © 1991 by Sook Nyul Choi. Cover illustrations copyright © 1991 by Mary Garafano. Reprinted by permission of Houghton Mifflin Harcourt Publishing Company. All rights reserved.

10.5: Jagusch Collection, D767.25.H6 M2913 1980. Interior art selection from *Hiroshima No Pika* by Toshi Maruki. Illustrated by: Toshi Maruki. Used by permission of HarperCollins Publishers.

10.6: Jagusch Collection, DS897.H5 M6713 1987. Cover image reprinted with permission from *My Hiroshima* by Junko Morimoto, Hachette Australia, 2014.

10.7: Jagusch Collection. Courtesy of Fukuinkan Shoten.

10.8: Jagusch Collection, PZ7. H76227 Sam 2007. Courtesy of Shannon Associates on behalf of Cliff Nielsen.

10.9: General Collection, DS834. H66 1994. Courtesy of Victoria Bruck Vebell.

10.10: General Collection, E184.J3 H584 1996.

10.11: Jagusch Collection, DS881.8. B53 1985. Cover from *Commodore Perry in the Land of the Shogun* by Rhoda Blumberg. Copyright © 1985 by Rhoda Blumberg. Used by permission of HarperCollins Publishers.

10.12: Jagusch Collection, DS881.8. R4. Courtesy of American Heritage Publishing.

10.13: General Collection, PZ7. I26 Tw 1996. Image from *Two Mrs. Gibsons*. Illustration Copyright © 1996 by Daryl Wells. Permission arranged with Children's Book Press, an imprint of Lee & Low Books, Inc., New York, NY 10016. All rights not specifically granted herein are reserved.

10.14: Jagusch Collection, D769.8.A6 O67 2006. Courtesy of Scholastic Library Publishing, Inc.

10.15: Jagusch Collection. Courtesy of Marlene Shigekawa.

10.16: Jagusch Collection, E184.J3 H35 1990. Courtesy of Sheila Hamanaka.

10.17: Jagusch Collection, PZ8.1. K1274 Ts 2009. Illustrations copyright © 2009 Ed Young. Reprinted with permission of McIntosh & Otis, Inc.

10.18: Jagusch Collection, PZ7.R262 Wa 2008. Cover of *Wabi Sabi* by Mark Reibstein, copyright © 2008. Reprinted by permission of Little, Brown Books for Young Readers, an imprint of Hachette Book Group, Inc.

Appendix

A.1: Jagusch Collection, 4GR 34.

A.2: Rare Book and Special Collections Division, G570. K74 1880.

A.3: General Collection, PZ3.G8759 H.

A.4: Jagusch Collection, Z1037. M637. Courtesy of Nils Daulaire and Per Ola Parin d'Aulaire.

A.5: Jagusch Collection. Reproduced by permission of Tokyo Children's Library and Iwanami Shoten, Publishers.

A.6: Jagusch Collection, PZ7. K948 Go. Courtesy of Momo Yashima Brannen.

A.7: Jagusch Collection, PZ8.H295 Favl 1967. Cover of *Favorite Fairy Tales Told in Japan* by Virginia Haviland, copyright © 1976. Reprinted by permission of Little, Brown Books for Young Readers, an imprint of Hachette Book Group, Inc.

A.8: General Collection, PN6110.C4 D37.

A.9: Jagusch Collection, PZ7. P273 Of. Courtesy of Haru Miyashiki, and Miyashiki Family.

TEXT CREDITS

Chapter 7

The Cat Who Went to Heaven by Elizabeth Coatsworth, pages 1–5, 18, 56. Text copyright 1930 by Simon & Schuster, Inc; copyright renewed 1958 by Elizabeth Coatsworth Beston. Reprinted with the permission of Simon & Schuster Books for Young Readers, an imprint of Simon & Schuster Children's Publishing Division. All rights reserved.

Chapter 8

Let's Visit Japan by John C. Caldwell, pages 85, 92, courtesy of John Caldwell's loving daughter, Betsie Richards.

The Moved-Outers by Florence Crannell Means, page 12, published with consent given by the family of Florence Crannell Means.

Chapter 9

Grandfather's Journey by Allen Say, page 31, copyright © 1993 by Allen Say. Reprinted by permission of Houghton Mifflin Harcourt Publishing Company. All rights reserved.

The New Sun by Taro Yashima, pages 95–98, courtesy of Momo Yashima Brannen.

The Invisible Thread by Yoshiko Uchida, pages 2, 15, 31–32, 52, 75, 131–133, copyright © 1991 by Yoshiko Uchida. Reprinted with the permission of Simon & Schuster Books for Young

Readers, an imprint of Simon & Schuster Children's Publishing Division. All rights reserved.

Desert Exile: The Uprooting of a Japanese American Family by Yoshiko Uchida, pages 4, 20, 36, 40, 42, 45, 105–06, 144, © 1982. Reprinted with permission of the University of Washington Press.

A Jar of Dreams by Yoshiko Uchida, pages 61–62, 89–92, 130, copyright © 1981 by Yoshiko Uchida. Reprinted with the permission of Margaret K. McElderry Books, an imprint of Simon & Schuster Children's Publishing Division. All rights reserved.

Journey Home by Yoshiko Uchida, pages 3–4, 15–16. F869.B5.91. J3 U3, © The Regents of the University of California, The Bancroft Library, University of California, Berkeley.

Journey to Topaz: A Story of the Japanese American Evacuation by Yoshiko Uchida, pages vii, 39, 99, 122, PS3541.C3 J6 1971, © The Regents of the University of California, The Bancroft Library, University of California, Berkeley.

Kazue Mizumura "Biographical Sketch," courtesy of the estate of Kazue Mizumura.

Margaret Eberbach, letter to the author, May 5, 2008, courtesy of Jessica C. Love, DVM.

Ann Beneduce letters to the author, March 22, 2008 and June 5, 2008, courtesy of Ann Beneduce.

I See the Winds by Kazue Mizumura, courtesy of the estate of Kazue Mizumura.

Flower Moon Snow: A Book of Haiku by Kazue Mizumura, courtesy of the estate of Kazue Mizumura.

Chapter 10

My Brother, My Sister, and I by Yoko Kawashima Watkins, pages 259–64, copyright © 1994 by Yoko Kawashima Watkins. Reprinted with the permission of Simon & Schuster Books for Young Readers, an imprint of Simon & Schuster Children's Publishing Division. All rights reserved.

Year of Impossible Goodbyes by Sook Nyul Choi, pages 6, 43–44, 59, copyright © 1991 by Sook Nyul Choi. Reprinted by permission of Houghton Mifflin Harcourt Publishing Company. All rights reserved.

Hiroshima no Pika by Toshi Maruki, pages 7–28, used by permission of HarperCollins Publishers.

My Japan, 1930 to 1951 by Hiroko Nakamoto, pages 68–69, 72, courtesy of Hiroko Nakamoto.

Hiroshima by R. Conrad Stein, pages 32–34, reprinted by permission of Children's Press, an imprint of Scholastic Library Publishing, Inc. All rights reserved.

Japanese Portraits by Dorothy and Thomas Hoobler, pages 10, 14, 19–20, courtesy of Dorothy and Thomas Hoobler.

Commodore Perry in the Land of the Shogun by Rhoda Blumberg, pages 13, 28–29, 44–45, copyright © 1985 by Rhoda Blumberg. Used by permission of HarperCollins Publishers.

Two Mrs. Gibsons by Toyomi Igus, copyright © 1996 by Toyomi Igus. Permission arranged with Children's Book Press, an imprint of Lee & Low Books, Inc., New York, NY 10016. All rights not specifically granted herein are reserved.

Farewell to Manzanar by Jeanne W. Houston and James D. Houston, pages 3–6, 7, 18, 25, 38–39, 62, 116, 162, 169, copyright © 1973 by James D. Houston, renewed 2001 by Jeanne Wakatsuki Houston and James D. Houston. Reprinted by permission of Houghton Mifflin Harcourt Publishing Company. All rights reserved.

Welcome Home Swallows by Marlene Shigekawa, pages 20–21, 24–25, courtesy of Marlene Shigekawa.

The Journey: Japanese Americans, Racism, and Renewal by Sheila Hamanaka, pages 5–34, courtesy of Sheila Hamanaka.

INDEX

Page numbers in *italics* refer to illustrations.

ABOUT THE AUTHOR

Dr. Sybille A. Jagusch, chief of the Children's Literature Center in the Library of Congress since 1983, is widely recognized for her expertise in the field of national and international children's literature. She has organized numerous symposia, lectures, and exhibitions and has edited, among other publications, *Window on Japan: Japanese Children's Books and Television Today* (1990); *Japanese Children's Books at the Library of Congress: A Bibliography of Books from the Postwar Years, 1946–1985* (1987), compiled by Tayo Shima; and *Stepping Away from Tradition: Children's Books of the Twenties and Thirties* (1988).